The Sydney Morning Herald
good food guide 2006

MATTHEW EVANS AND SIMON THOMSEN

WITH REGIONAL EDITOR JAMES MAYSON

PENGUIN BOOKS

PENGUIN BOOKS

Published by the Penguin Group
Penguin Group (Australia)
250 Camberwell Road, Camberwell, Victoria 3124, Australia
(a division of Pearson Australia Group Pty Ltd)
Penguin Group (USA) Inc.
375 Hudson Street, New York, New York 10014, USA
Penguin Group (Canada)
90 Eglinton Avenue East, Suite 700, Toronto ON M4P 2Y3, Canada
(a division of Pearson Penguin Canada Inc.)
Penguin Books Ltd
80 Strand, London WC2R 0RL, England
Penguin Ireland
25 St Stephen's Green, Dublin 2, Ireland
(a division of Penguin Books Ltd)
Penguin Books India Pvt Ltd
11 Community Centre, Panchsheel Park, New Delhi – 110 017, India
Penguin Group (NZ)
Cnr Airborne and Rosedale Roads, Albany, Auckland, New Zealand
(a division of Pearson New Zealand Ltd)
Penguin Books (South Africa) (Pty) Ltd
24 Sturdee Avenue, Rosebank, Johannesburg 2196, South Africa

Penguin Books Ltd, Registered Offices: 80 Strand, London WC2R 0RL, England

First published by Penguin Group (Australia), a division of Pearson Australia Group Pty Ltd, 2005

10 9 8 7 6 5 4 3 2 1

Text copyright © John Fairfax Publications Pty Ltd 2005
Illustrations copyright © John Fairfax Publications Pty Ltd 2005 unless otherwise attributed below

The moral right of the authors has been asserted

All rights reserved. Without limiting the rights under copyright reserved above, no part of this publication may be reproduced, stored in or introduced into a retrieval system, or transmitted, in any form or by any means (electronic, mechanical, photocopying, recording or otherwise), without the prior written permission of both the copyright owner and the above publisher of this book.

Cover design by Jay Ryves © Penguin Group (Australia)
Text design by Ann Loveday, *The Sydney Morning Herald*, and Jay Ryves, Penguin Group (Australia)
Internal photographs courtesy of John Fairfax Publications Pty Ltd, except pages 80, 170 and 174–5 by Simon Thomsen
Cover photograph by Jennifer Soo of smoked salmon consommé, created by Tim Pak Poy and prepared by Chui Lee Luk, at Claude's, served in porcelain beakers hand-thrown by Anders Ousback, April 2005
Maps by Country Cartographics
Hat design by David Band
Typeset in Helvetica by J&M Typesetting, Melbourne, Victoria
Printed and bound in Australia by McPherson's Printing Group, Maryborough, Victoria
Advertising Sales (02) 9282 1365

www.penguin.com.au

The editors would like to thank the following tasty people: our crispy and committed reviewing team (see Meet the Reviewers, page x); Angie Schiavone and Tania Edwards, for keeping their heads when all about were losing theirs; the 26th floor cheer squad, especially Tom Burton and Sue Ritchie, plus *Herald* editor Robert Whitehead and editor-in-chief Mark Scott; photographers Steve Baccon, Janie Barrett, Natalie Boog, Angela Brkic, Marco Del Grande, Eddie Jim, Quentin Jones, Louise Kennerley, Lucinda Marland, Fiona Morris, Marina Oliphant, Robert Rough and Jennifer Soo for their images; Tracy O'Brien for picture research; Ann Loveday, our favourite type; Mark Polden and Richard Coleman for their legal genius; Jennifer Soo and Jay Ryves for another great cover; the encouraging and gently cajoling Susan McLeish and her Penguin team; our friends and family, especially Megan, Sally and the child-friendly tester, Archie; and extra servings of gratitude to Anouska Jones for fixing up the ungood stuff what we have writed.

CONTENTS

Introduction	iv
Meet the Editors	v
About the Book	vi
The Scores	vii
Awards	viii
Meet the Reviewers	x
Stop Press	xii
City	**1**
BYO	41
Fish & Chips	81
Penny Pinching	121
Cafes	153
Bars	159
Provedores	164
Regional	**174**
Blue Mountains	176
Canberra & Snow Regions	184
Hunter Valley	199
Central Coast & Newcastle	208
South Coast	218
Southern Highlands	229
North Coast	236
The West	248
Interstate	262
Index	271
Maps	285

Introduction

Australians are great consumers. We love a good meal. A nice bottle of wine too, thanks. But, as we write, it seems we have another big mouth to feed and it's affecting our restaurants. Oil prices are climbing and, when push comes to shove, we'll make sure our car has a full belly at the expense of going out for a meal. It signals a tough time ahead for the industry, but the good news is that restaurateurs are adept at meeting the challenge. While some meals have never been more expensive – welcome to $30-plus entrées and $70 mains – there are plenty of good-value restaurants still offering excellent food for less than the cost of a full tank.

It's been a year of contrasts: some chefs toying with (sometimes too) bold combinations – cured ocean trout with parmesan ice-cream – but it's been balanced by a welcome resurgence in comfort food, led by that retro classic corned beef.

And, while the past 12 months have been notably quiet on Big Openings, there's been a gentle rise in standards. Some excellent newcomers have made enjoyable debuts, including Bistro 163, The Bellevue, Sugaroom, Pilu at Freshwater, Bistro Moore and Alchemy 731.

Uncertainty has also incited caution at some of our finest. There's less risk-taking on the plate, a dulling of some excitement, but typically greater consistency, so your money is wisely invested. Strong, technique-focussed, classically influenced cooking is on the rise. A slew of young chefs with a Brit bent are doing smart versions of 'Franglish' fare. Meanwhile, others are doling out dishes we haven't seen for some time – think steak diane, chicken pie, and beef cheeks – with modern flair.

For the first time in its 21-year history, this year the *Guide* is fully booked with a record number of entries. The 2006 edition is overflowing with 400 scored restaurant reviews. Add cafes, bars, provedores, wineries and interstate recommendations and you'll find more than 800 places listed. 2006 sets another benchmark with the first female stand-alone three-hat chef, Chui Lee Luk at Claude's.

But we do have some concerns. For starters, too many sweet tooths in the kitchen. And while we agree that fat adds flavour, we don't want everything drowned in way too much burnt-sage butter. Truffle oil has become a culinary lantana, invading dishes everywhere; to anyone who loves truffles, it's like being a chocoholic and being offered carob.

Wagyu beef is on almost every menu, often leading us to ponder its provenance. On the fusion front, we've found that molecular gastronomy is a volatile experiment that can be prone to bubble over if your name isn't Ferran Adria. And we are rapidly tiring of more weird-sounding combinations than you can poke a sugar stick at.

That said, there's much to enjoy, from old faves like pork belly and duck confit to tomato tarte Tatin. Pre-desserts are becoming more commonplace, and there's a revival of the twice-baked soufflé. For dessert, soft-centred chocolate pud and pannacotta are being usurped by chocolate sorbet, millefeuille in a thousand forms, and that enduring classic tarte Tatin. We also spied bombe Alaska, sometimes set on fire at the table in a suitably retro flourish.

Taking a lead from London and New York, restaurant design is at the forefront – sometimes at the expense of good produce. And while it's nice to enjoy a meal with position, position, position, such real estate comes at a price, making diners pay more for the view than what's on the plate, that's while the drought continues to bite, pushing produce prices (cloudless) sky-high. It's a testament to chefs that dining remains affordable in so many places.

New regional editor James Mayson has scoured the state adding even more depth to the restaurants, cafes and provedores featured in our eight regions. And while two-hat regional restaurants are as scarce as rain, it's pleasing to see the Collits Inn, in the western foothills of the Blue Mountains, joining this elite group.

Right across Australia we've done our best to seek out the passionate and enthusiastic farmers, producers and chefs who make this nation such a great place for eating. We hope you find somewhere for every occasion. They're worth every cent of petrol to visit.

Bon appetit. Enjoy.

Matthew Evans and Simon Thomsen

Meet the Editors

Matthew Evans, co-editor
Matthew is the chief restaurant reviewer for *The Sydney Morning Herald*, writing reviews that appear in each Tuesday's 'Good Living' section. A former chef by trade and a recipe writer, he has been co-editor of the *Good Food Guide* for five years. He writes regularly for *Good Weekend* magazine and *the(sydney)magazine,* and is the author of three books on food. Matthew is also a great fan of the only food restaurants can't serve: the home-cooked meal.

Simon Thomsen, co-editor
Simon divides his time between Sydney and Lismore, northern New South Wales, where he owns and edits a weekly newspaper. He was a chef and waiter but now writes about food for numerous publications. His newborn son, Archie, loves going out to dinner and can't wait to eat solids. Simon is known as the World's Most Sustainable Fisherman because, despite his best efforts, he takes nothing from the sea. He has reviewed for the *Guide* for nine years and was the regional editor for four.

James Mayson, regional editor
As the peripatetic regional editor, James has been everywhere, man, from Dubbo to Bello, Wagga to Wingham. He's also visited some 40 countries to author the book *Street Food from Around the World*. He cooked in restaurants and cafes for several years but now writes about food for 'Good Living' and *Gourmet Traveller* and has been a *Good Food Guide* reviewer for six years.

About the Book

How we review
Each and every scored restaurant in the Good Food Guide is visited unannounced in the previous year by one of our team of experienced reviewers (see 'Meet the Reviewers' on page x). We pay for our meal in full and sample at least two courses, usually three. Every three-hat candidate has been visited numerous times by various reviewers over the year; likewise many of the two-hatters. We visit many more restaurants than will fit into this book to give you a guide to the best we can find. If we wouldn't feel comfortable recommending a restaurant to a friend, we don't include it.

As usual, we've updated our cafe section, giving you widespread cafe options from all points of the compass as well as the CBD. We've kept the bar section large and lively, like Sydney's bar scene itself, and for those who have private cellars we've listed our 10 favourite BYOs in a city that's always asking us where people can take their own wine.

Feedback
We welcome your recommendations and comments. Contact us at goodfoodguide@smh.com.au or write to *The Sydney Morning Herald Good Food Guide*, GPO Box 506, Sydney, 2000.

Bill
We want you to be in no doubt about how much eating out will cost, so we've listed the range of prices for entrée (E), main (M) and dessert (D). Remember, though, that this is only an indication, typically based on prices at dinner, and we don't include share plates, oysters by the dozen or cheese platters, as they tend to skew the results. Prices rise (and sometimes fall) but all are provided by the restaurant and confirmed by the *Guide* before going to press.

Wine
Wine is a very important part of the dining experience, so we've given you a user-friendly description for each restaurant as well as the cost of BYO. Corkage is either per person (e.g. $2 pp) or per bottle. Most of the restaurants in this guide are BYO for bottled wine only – no beer, spirits or casks. A wine glass indicates a particularly good wine list.

Wheelchair access
Using information supplied to us by the restaurants, we list wheelchair access only if restaurants also provide accessible toilet facilities. Many restaurants have a side or back access for patrons in wheelchairs, so always ring ahead.

Bookings
Bookings are recommended for all restaurants that take them. We have mentioned bookings only if the restaurant regards them as essential or if they are not accepted at all.

And...
Because we want to provide as much information as we can in a limited space, this is to let you know something incidental, interesting and hopefully useful, but not necessarily essential.

Smoking
Smoking is banned inside Australian restaurants and cafes. You can usually smoke outside and at some bars directly adjoining restaurants. If in doubt, ring and check.

Accuracy
We don't check the information in the guide once – we check it at least four times, from the address to the phone number to the spelling of the chef's name. First, the restaurant fills out a questionnaire, then our team of reviewers gathers the information and, later, as close to publication as possible, phone checks are

made for every entry. However, even our best efforts can occasionally come unstuck if a restaurant closes suddenly or changes its pricing or chef. This is, unfortunately, beyond our control.

The Scores

Apart from our chef's-hat ratings, we score restaurants out of 20 to give you a more useful sense of their merits. The score comprises 10 points for food, 5 for service and 3 for ambience, with an extra 2 points possible for a sprinkling of magic, whether it be the great location, the stunning service or food that is sublime beyond belief. Places we score less than 11/20 are not included.

11		Some rewards from a visit
12		Likeable
13		Some respectable highlights
14		A solid, enjoyable experience (a chef's hat is possible)
15	♟	Reliably good
16	♟♟	A bit of that WOW factor
17	♟♟	Amazingly good
18	♟♟♟	World class
19	♟♟♟	Truly spectacular
20	♟♟♟	Are we in heaven?

Awards

Along with our chef's-hat awards, we also have other awards to recognise greatness in various fields. Some are self-explanatory, the others are listed below.

Restaurant of the Year – a place that has shown remarkable energy and consistency and sets a standard others should aspire to.

Chef of the Year – an award solely for a supremely talented individual behind the stove, someone we believe to be on the ascendancy.

Editors' Picks – these are the restaurants we love to go to when we're not clasping a notebook and we're spending our own money.

Professional Excellence Award – for long-term contribution to the restaurant industry.

Silver Service Award – for defining, redefining or showing the ultimate level of service.

The Josephine Pignolet Young Chef Award – chosen by chefs, the ultimate accolade for a passionate, talented young cook.

Symbols

★	Award-winning restaurant
♀	Unusually good wine list
AE	American Express
BC	Bankcard
DC	Diners Club
MC	MasterCard
V	Visa
Eftpos	Electronic funds transfer (this does not imply you can withdraw extra cash)

Awards

(see page vii for explanations)

Restaurant of the Year
est.

Chef of the Year
Mark Best from Marque

Best New Restaurant
Pilu at Freshwater

Best Regional Restaurant
Collits Inn (Hartley Vale)

Editors' Picks

Favourite Bistro	Tabou
Favourite Mediterranean	Perama
Favourite Asian	Spice I Am
Favourite Seafood	Pier
Favourite Yum Cha	Marigold Citymark
Favourite Bar	Bridge Bar
Favourite Cafe	Bertoni Casalinga

The *Sydney Morning Herald* award for Professional Excellence
Michael Manners from Selkirks in Orange, for redefining cooking in regional New South Wales and for four decades of inspiration.

The *Sydney Morning Herald* Silver Service Award
Maurice Terzini of Icebergs for bringing the sexy, Italian–Melbourne style to Sydney and for his attention to detail.

The *Good Food Guide* Sommelier Award
Christopher Morrison from Guillaume at Bennelong, for passion, personality and enthusiasm backed up with impeccable knowledge of wine.

The Josephine Pignolet Best Young Chef Award
Daniel Puskas from The Boathouse on Blackwattle Bay. The young chef receives a substantial sum of money donated by Sydney chefs and suppliers, a set of Füritechnics knives and an international return-flight with Qantas.

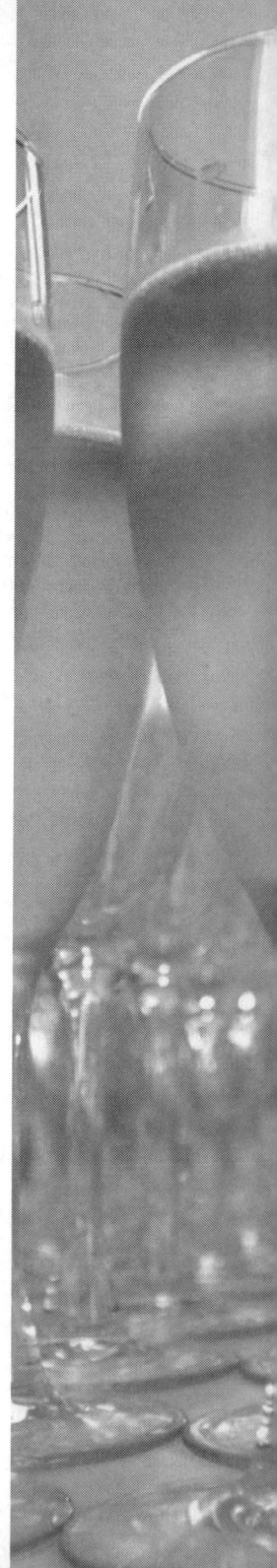

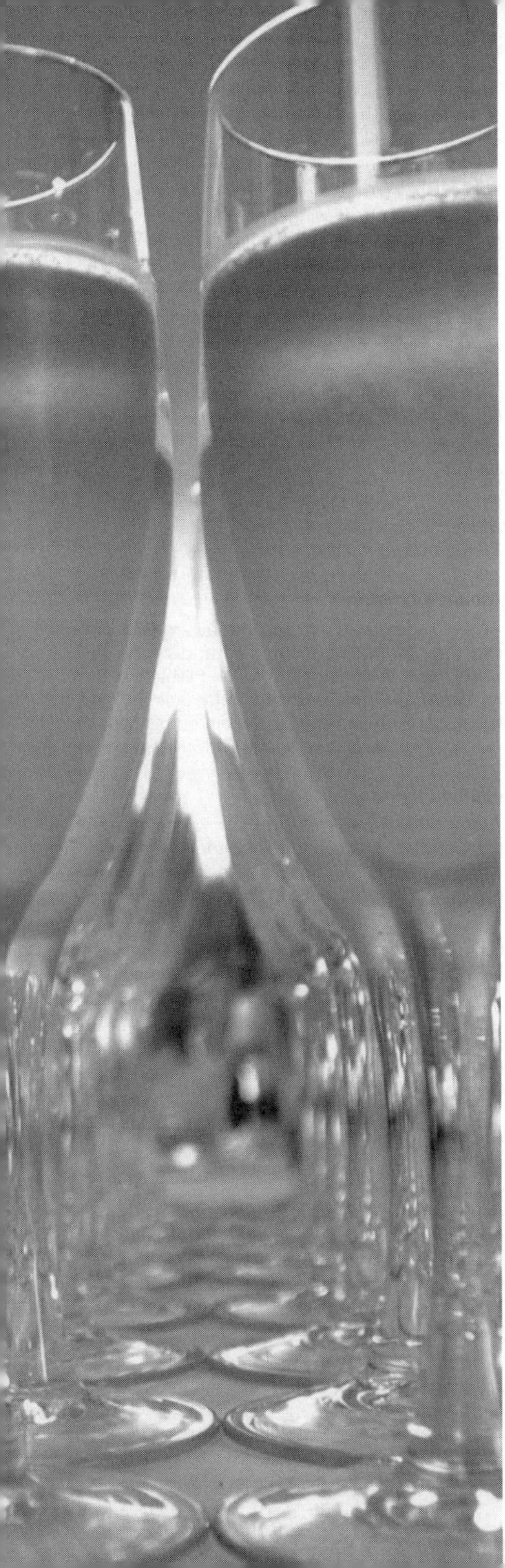

City

Claude's, est., Guillaume at Bennelong, Marque, Quay, Tetsuya's

Aria, Bilson's, Bistro Moncur, Buon Ricordo, Icebergs Dining Room & Bar, Longrain, Lucio's, Omega, Pello, Pier, Pilu at Freshwater, Restaurant Balzac, Rockpool, Sean's Panaroma, Yoshii

The Bathers' Pavilion Restaurant, Bistro LuLu, Bistro Moore, Catalina Rose Bay, Fish Face, Flying Fish, Forty One, Galileo, Golden Century, Grand National, Hugo's, Il Piave, Lotus, Manta, Milsons, Otto, Perama, Post Seafood Brasserie, Restaurant Atelier, Ristorante Riva, Sea Treasure, sushi e, Three Weeds, The Wharf, Ying's

Regional

Collits Inn (Hartley Vale), Fins (Byron Bay), Selkirks (Orange), Vulcans (Blue Mountains), Waters Edge (Canberra)

Ashcrofts (Blackheath), Artespresso (Canberra), Boomerang (Byron Bay), Caveau (Wollongong), The Chairman & Yip (Canberra), Courgette (Canberra), Darley's (Katoomba), dish (Byron Bay), Lochiel House (Kurrajong Heights), Lolli Redini (Orange), Lorenzo's Diner (Wollongong), Lynwood Cafe (Collector), Neila (Cowra), No. 2 Oak Street (Bellingen), The Old George & Dragon (East Maitland), Ottoman Cuisine (Canberra), Solitary (Leura), Tonic (Millthorpe), Zest (Nelson Bay)

Meet the Reviewers

Caroline Baum

Caroline researched Time Life's *The Good Cook* series of books. She has been a judge of the Food Media Awards and writes for *Australian Gourmet Traveller*, *The Qantas Magazine* and *Good Weekend*. She also presents *Talking Books* on Foxtel.

Scott Bolles

Scott is the omniscient chronicler of the New South Wales food scene, revealing all in the 'Good Living' Short Black column for more than six years. He also reviews for The *Sun Herald*'s 'Eat Streets' and has written about food for more than a decade.

Anthony Dennis

Anthony has reviewed for the *Guide* for several years, and is editor of the new magazine *Travel + Leisure Australia*, published by John Fairfax. A former editor of 'Spectrum' as well as a news and feature writer at the *Herald*, he has written extensively about food and restaurants.

Bruce Elder

Bruce was regional editor of the *Guide* for three years. His quest took him to almost every town and village in New South Wales and his skills with the pen earned him the Pascall Prize for Critical Writing.

Hugh Fitzhardinge

A passionate foodie, Hugh has written about food for numerous titles, including *Delicious*, and has been part of the reviewing team for three years. He usually makes money in advertising, only to hand most of it over to the restaurant industry.

Molly Foskett

Molly has been part of the reviewing team for the last five years, traversing the South Coast for its finest fare, as well as prowling the urban jungle. By day, she pursues her marketing career.

Helen Greenwood

Helen is a former 'Good Living' editor and co-editor of the *Guide*. These days, she spends her time in food shops and restaurants writing Off the Shelf for 'Good Living' and reviewing eateries for 'Spectrum'. She also co-authored *The Food Shoppers' Guide to Sydney*.

Guy Griffin

Guy joined the reviewing team in 1995. His motto is 'Ever seen a hearse with luggage racks?' He is a restaurant columnist for *the(sydney)magazine* and a senior writer for *Australian Gourmet Traveller*. He also writes for other local and international food and wine publications.

Huon Hooke

Huon has written about wine for Fairfax newspapers every week for 23 years and for *The Sydney Morning Herald* for most of that time. He also writes for *The Age*, *Uncorked* magazine, *Gourmet Traveller Wine*, *Decanter* and *Good Weekend*, as well as co-authoring the annual *Penguin Good Australian Wine Guide*.

Amanda Hooton

As a food reviewer in Scotland, award-wining journalist Amanda once had a haggis explode in her face. A staff writer for *Good Weekend* for six years, she now leads a quieter culinary life, indulging her interest in food with occasional reviews for *The Sun Herald*'s 'Eat Streets'.

Jessica Hough

Jessica is the editor of the *Illawarra Mercury*'s food section 'Taste' and joined the *Guide* team this year, using her local knowledge to help find the best places to dine on the South Coast.

Lisa Hudson

Lisa is editor of *The Sydney Morning Herald*'s glossy monthly *the(sydney)magazine* and Group Editor of Fairfax General Magazines. She is a former editor of 'Good Living' and the *Good Food Guide*, has co-authored a cookbook, and tests and writes recipes in her spare time.

Catriona Jackson

Catriona joined the team this year with a 20-year background in writing about food. She has been co-editor of *The Canberra Times Good Food Guide*, that paper's restaurant reviewer and Food and Wine editor, and has written for *Vogue Entertaining + Travel* and others.

Belinda Jeffery

Belinda lives on the beautiful north coast. She is an award-winning TV food presenter, restaurant-cook-turned-reviewer and cooking teacher. She has written three cookbooks and has recently released a series of cooking DVDs.

Dugald Jellie
Dugald grows vegies by his back door and makes mayo to his grandmum's recipe. He has edited *The Age Cheap Eats* guide, and contributed to 'Good Living'. He regularly glances over his shoulder when walking home from a review.

Catherine Keenan
Catherine is a *Herald* writer with a strong interest in food. She writes for 'Good Living', and regularly reviews for 'Eat Streets' in *The Sun Herald*. She has been on the reviewing team for four years.

Les Luxford
Former *Guide* editor Terry Durack called him the man who would eat anything. Les spent his culinary youth in the starred restaurants of France and Italy but now seeks out simple, honest food. His day job as a commercial film director takes him throughout Asia, where he loves exploring the rustic regional food of China.

Bonnie Malkin
Bonnie has been drinking since she arrived from London in 2001. After time at *Australian Bartender Magazine*, she joined *The Herald* in 2003. She keeps a drink in her hand as bar reviewer at *the(sydney)magazine* and moonlights as Urban Affairs and Property reporter for the *Herald*.

Lyndey Milan
An energetic, multi-award-winning communicator, author, teacher and presenter on all things gastronomic, Lyndey is Food Director of *The Australian Women's Weekly* and co-host of *Fresh* on the Nine network. With a strong following for her four popular cookbooks and radio broadcasts on 2GB, she has reviewed for the *Guide* since 1987.

Roberta Muir
Roberta manages the Sydney Seafood School, holds a Master of Arts Degree in Gastronomy and writes freelance food, wine and travel articles. Her passion for food and wine, together with her curiosity about foreign cultures and languages, has led her on adventures around the globe.

Lynne Mullins
Lynne writes the weekly Produce page for 'Good Living' and is an award-winning food writer, restaurant critic, broadcaster, teacher and author. She has travelled extensively to master her culinary skills.

Philip Putnam
Philip has been a reviewer for eight years. A lifetime in advertising not only is an excuse to travel and eat out a lot but also feeds his curiosity about the whole wide, wild and wonderful world of food. He can often be found scribbling notes in restaurant toilets.

Alan Saunders
Alan is the author of *A is for Apple* and an ABC Radio National presenter specialising in food, wine, architecture and philosophy. A winner of the Pascall Prize for Critical Writing, he has written several books and is a columnist for *delicious* magazine.

John Saxby
John is the editor of the *Herald*'s award winning 'Good Living' food and fashion section. He has previously contributed reviews for 'Eat Streets' in *The Sun-Herald* and Good Living's 'Eat Up' column.

Rosemary Stanton
Rosemary is an expert in the nutritional qualities and flavours of good food. Based in the Southern Highlands, she is the author of 31 books, writes for many magazines, lobbies for better food information, and lectures to doctors, medical students and the general public.

Sally Webb
Sally has been writing about food and travel for more than a decade and is the co-author of a series of Lonely Planet travel guides. She has worked for *Vogue Entertaining + Travel* and is now deputy editor of *Travel + Leisure Australia*. When not eating out, she can often be found baking and braising.

Stop Press

Changes due as we go to press.

Assiette
48 Albion Street, Surry Hills
Tel 9212 7979
Former Cruise chef Warren Turnbull is taking over the old Bécasse site in Surry Hills in mid-July 2005. With prices set at around $18 for entrees and $28 for mains, expect more of Turnbull's formerly hatted take on mod-Euro cooking.

Bécasse
204 Clarence Street, Sydney
Tel 9283 3440
Last year's two-hat restaurant is moving to a bigger, earthy coloured city space and will open lunches. Prices will rise slightly, entrees now starting at about $22, mains at about $32 and the Brit/French flavours will continue.

Bistrode
478 Bourke Street, Surry Hills
Tel 9380 7333
Former two-hat chef Jeremy Strode is opening a bistro (hence the name) in the former Dragonfly site in mid-September 2005. His French/British and Australian experience will show in the flavours, but mains will cost under $30.

360 Bar and Restaurant
Centrepoint Tower, 100 Market Street, Sydney
Tel 8223 3800
The Truffle Group's sky-high Centrepoint has snared former two-hat chef Darren Vaughan and a Michael McCann refit. Entrees such as pressed rabbit and foie gras with Madeira dressing are priced at $19; mains are $33 and desserts are $14.

Courtney's Brasserie
70 Phillip Street, Parramatta
Tel 9635 3288
Parramatta's loveable 21-year-old is moving to smaller premises, in a brick cottage dating from the 1840s. Paul Kuiper remains in the kitchen but the wine list will be less ambitious.

Cruise
Level 3, Overseas Passenger Terminal, West Circular Quay
Tel 9251 1188
As Warren Turnbull heads off to open Assiette, Cruise is moving upstairs and ex Nove chef Ed Halmagyi has stepped in. Halmagyi has written books on Italian food, and worked at Sydney's MG Garage and Rockpool, plus Britain's Le Gavroche. The new space will be smaller, more comfortable and offer a broader European menu with Italian/French bias.

Glass
488 George Street, Sydney
Tel 9265 6068
Former hatted Salt chef Luke Mangan is due to open at the relaunched Hilton Hotel before the *Guide* hits the streets. Expect an up-market brasserie menu in a smart space.

Kirketon Hotel
229 Darlinghurst Road, Darlinghurst
Tel 8354 5400
James Ingram (ex International) is renovating and enclosing the former Salt space at the Kirketon Hotel for an oyster bar and restaurant (plus a big bar in the former Fix space out the back). He's promising carpet, timber panelling and leather booths, along with classical French food from Jocelyn Rivière who had a hat at The International. It's slated for an early November opening with a name to be confirmed after we go to press.

Restaurant II
8 Bolton Street, Newcastle
Tel 4929 1233
Peter Bryant, who ran the one-hat Scott Street restaurant in Newcastle, is back cooking contemporary food at the former Two Chefs on Bolton site. Bryant is serving roast duckling with caramelised endive, and calamari with Sichuan pepper, for dinner Tues–Sat from 6pm and lunch on Fridays.

city + suburbs

Abhi's

163 Concord Road, North Strathfield
Tel 9743 3061   Map 6

Indian

Score 13/20

How can you go wrong when your entrée looks like dessert? Palak patta chaat: lentil-battered spinach leaves coated in three sauces – date and tamarind, chilli, and mint – looks more like a sundae than a starter. It's devoured just as greedily. Masala dosa, a rolled South Indian pancake, could pass as a pud, too, although the spiced potato and onion filling and accompanying sambar and coconut chutney plant it firmly in savoury territory in this long, comfortable sliver of a shopfront, overseen by a benevolent deity. Textbook naan and roti and a comforting paneer counter the more robust flavours of split and fried baby eggplants in a paste of cashew, peanut, sesame and coconut. Alas tandoor-roasted lamb cutlets marinated in yoghurt, sandalwood powder, ginger and saffron seemed dry and an occasionally stretched floor team might have delivered the odd hiccup. But many other dishes and a constant stream of locals exiting with takeaway confirm that Abhi's has every reason to celebrate its fifteen years.

Hours Lunch Sun–Fri noon–3pm; Dinner daily 6–10pm
Bill E $9.80–$16.90 **M** $15.80–$21.80 **D** $9.80
Cards AE BC DC MC V
Wine Well-priced, interesting mix, including the odd French; 13 by the glass; BYO (corkage $2 pp)
Chefs Ranjan Choudhury & Kumar Mahadevan
Owners Kumar & Suba Mahadevan
Seats 180; private room; wheelchair access
www.abhisindian.com.au
And...an outdoor seating area and cocktail lounge upstairs are planned

Agni

540–542 King Georges Road, Beverly Hills
Tel 9580 2190   Map 6

Indian

Score 13/20

It would be very easy to overlook this drab shopfront, with plastic chairs and tables, and dull-coloured carpet that looks as though it's been around since Gandhi's time. But it would be a mistake because this small and friendly place offers warm service and truly interesting halal food, like the Agni crab nariyal – lettuce cups of sweet, soothing crabmeat mixed with rich coconut cream, mustard seeds and fresh curry leaves. Even seemingly clichéd Indian dishes, such as fish tikka, are given new life in this rich, moist and potent version; and the Andhra chicken korma has the subtlety and delicacy of fine incense. The saag gosht – chunky lamb in an aromatic spinach sauce – is marvellously appealing and harmonious, and even dry dishes like the vegetable achaari stand out. Portions are large, but if you have room left try the irresistible rose-scented egg custard – a sort of subcontinental crème brûlée.

Hours Dinner daily from 5.30pm
Bill E $6.20–$13.90 **M** $14.90–$19.90 **D** $6.50–$7.50
Cards BC DC MC V Eftpos
Wine BYO (corkage $1.50 pp)
Chef Krishna Bhagwat
Owners Krishna & Rashmi Bhagwat
Seats 80
And...banquet menus $28.90–$34.90 pp

city + suburbs A

Aki's

Shop 1, The Wharf,
6 Cowper Wharf Road, Woolloomooloo
Tel 9332 4600   Map 2

Indian

Score 14/20

In late 2003, Kumar Mahadevan established this sexy sister to the teenaged Abhi's in North Strathfield. It's a plush space with black carpet and a dark, smooth, modernist interior, plus posh lampshades and candlelight adding to the mood. Service is attentive and jovial, catering for business people and hotel guests staying in the adjacent W Hotel. The Indian twist of a tamarind and ginger dipping sauce is perfectly suited to delicately fried and suitably spicy salt-and-pepper squid. Black mustard seeds atop appam bread (imagine a Tamil pappadam and naan hybrid) heightens the spicing of shelled blue swimmer crab with coconut and ginger. However, some mains felt less accomplished, like a slightly bland duck curry, and almond- and cheese-stuffed veal rolls that lacked both finesse and spice. Things pick up though for succulent butter chicken lifted by a superb blend of tomatoes and cream. Sublime desserts include Indian crème caramel served with rose petal ice-cream.

Hours Lunch Sun–Fri noon–3pm; Dinner daily 6–10.30pm
Bill E $11.80–$21.80 **M** $18.80–$32.50 **D** $12.80–$13.80
Cards AE BC MC V
Wine Formidable Australian list; 16 by the glass
Chefs Vikram Arumugam & Kumar Mahadevan
Owners Kumar & Suba Mahadevan
Seats 145; outdoor seats
www.akisindian.com.au
And...dine outside to watch the passing parade of promenaders

Alchemy 731

731 Military Road, Mosman
Tel 9968 3731   Map 7

Modern European

Score 14/20

The energy is palpable: from the two chefs running the kitchen to their co-owner on the floor there's a sense of enthusiasm about this newcomer that we only hope translates into even more quality given time. The two-level diner is a little functional but pleasant, with tables dressed in paper-covered linen and picture windows for staring out at Military Road. Alchemy boasts an impressively crafted menu for these prices. There's everything from rillettes to three things from a lamb and red mullet with an eggplant raviolo. Along with Sydney's best blushing-pink duck liver parfait, there could be a charlotte of goat's cheese and zucchini: the delicate acidity of the chèvre as bright as the waiters' smiles. A long strip of pork belly is darkly caramelised, presented on last year's favourite plate (aka the rectangular white). But the only thing you'll notice after delighting in the apple and walnut frangipane tart topped with meringue is that the plate's left bare way too quickly.

Hours Lunch Thurs–Sat noon–2.30pm; Dinner Tues–Sat from 6pm
Bill E $18 **M** $28 **D** $14; 6-course dégustation $75 pp; 10% surcharge on public holidays
Cards AE BC MC V
Wine Concise but clever; 9 by the glass; BYO Tues–Thurs only (corkage $10 per bottle)
Chefs Derek Baker & Keith Cawthorne
Owners Derek Baker, Keith Cawthorne & Bronwyn Kabboord
Seats 50; private rooms
And...it's a work in progress with subtle changes planned even as we go to press

city + suburbs

Alhambra

Shop 1, 54 West Esplanade, Manly
Tel 9976 2975   Map 7

Moroccan/Spanish

Score 12/20

OK, so it's not quite old Castile – your closest landmark is the Manly ferry terminal – but with enough sangria you can believe anything. The walls are red, the tables wooden and the esplanade traffic loud, especially if you're sitting outside. But the staff are friendly, if no more Spanish than gelato, which is on the menu. Tapas include succulent prawns sizzling in garlic, subtle broad bean and eggplant dips, and robust calamari sometimes on the wrong side of chewy. Mains range from solid to sublime, although the lamb M'choui – marinated fillets on couscous – seemed disappointingly meagre. A fabulous chicken and preserved lemon tagine made amends, the generous chunks infused with lemon, tomato, saffron and olive, and bolstered by potato. Moroccan chef Aziz Bakalla is a couscous expert, steaming it three times, then adding fresh herbs, almonds and raisins. His delicious desserts include cream custard with pistachios and brown sugar, and gelato with fresh raspberries and a sprig of mint. Italiano? Français? Español? Why worry!

Hours Lunch Mon–Sat noon–3pm, Sun all day; Dinner daily 6–10.30pm
Bill E $10–$16 **M** $19–$25 **D** $12–$14; 10% surcharge on public holidays
Cards AE BC DC MC V
Wine Small but reasonably priced, several Spanish; 4 by the glass; BYO (corkage $3 pp)
Chef/owner Aziz Bakalla
Seats 120; wheelchair access; outdoor seats
www.alhambra.citysearch.com.au
And...flamenco guitarist on Thursday; dancers on Friday and Saturday

Alio

5 Baptist Street, Redfern (East)
Tel 8394 9368   Map 3B

Italian

Score 14/20

Just across from Crown Street's popular food strip, Alio sits among a mixed bag of houses, offices, pubs and retailers in what is generally regarded as Surry Hills. The well-spaced, contemporary interior is warmed by vibrant tomato and chocolate tones, geometric designs and friendly service. There are crisp white-clad tables while a great-looking slatted banquette stretches the length of the restaurant (and it's surprisingly comfortable!). Mod Italian best describes seasoned chef Ashley Hughes's inspiring menu. He delivers stunning simplicity, clearly revealed in the humble salad of buffalo mozzarella, roma tomatoes and basil, dressed with a 25-year-old balsamic. Hand-rolled pasta and risotto made to order (so be prepared to wait at least 20 minutes) show similar care. Squid ink fettuccine delicately tossed with cuttlefish, ginger and a hint of chilli expands in flavour. Creative mains, such as grilled salmon with a dash of anchovy and rosemary sauce, combine perfectly with zucchini flowers filled with blue swimmer crab. Desserts shine, especially a soft chocolate pudding and roasted coconut ice-cream.

Hours Dinner Mon–Sat from 6pm
Bill E $16–$18 **M** $26–$35 **D** $11–$13
Cards AE BC DC MC V Eftpos
Wine Well-considered local and Italian selection; 16 by the glass; BYO Mon–Thurs (corkage $7 per bottle)
Chef Ashley Hughes
Owners Tracey & Ashley Hughes
Seats 115; private room; wheelchair access
www.alio.com.au
And...don't miss the house-made parmesan grissini and herb focaccia

Italian Bluebottles hit Bondi

Italian mineral water. Bottled at the source in the Little Dolomite Mountains.

SANTA VITTORIA®

ACQUA MINERALE

AVAILABLE AT LEADING RESTAURANTS, CAFÉS AND COLES

SPOIL
Someone you like

Somewhere you'll love

Right now, there's a special place to spoil that certain someone. Lunch al fresco with a view of the water, a torte and café au lait in a leafy courtyard, or just a quiet stroll by the harbour. A special place for your special someone.

And it's all at The Rocks, right now.

www.therocks.com

city + suburbs A

All India Restaurant

2a Rowntree Street (cnr Darling Street),
Balmain
Tel 9555 8844 Map 5B

Indian

Score 12/20

This is a calm retreat from the frenzy of dining in nearby Darling Street. The large, handsome room has mood lighting, carpet to soak up the noise and a colour scheme that echoes India's spicy food colours: mustard, eggplant and saffron. The food tries for something more than the usual, ranging across the subcontinent from Goan or Bengal fish curries to Persian beef with apricots and Mysore lamb chops. Savour the tangy flavours of tamarind and tomato in a chicken rogani or go mellow with the warm clove-tinted creaminess of the southern Indian duck 'quilon' with cinnamon and curry. The spicing is skilful and you have a choice of heat levels because they vary from dish to dish; the kitchen is happy to adjust them in either direction. Excellent breads include the peshwari naan, which has a layer of sugared coconut and sultanas inside. It's a great dipping vehicle for the curries. Desserts are not a strong suit, but the service is so relaxed you leave with a smile on your face.

Hours Dinner daily 5.30–10.30pm
Bill E $11.50–$14.50 **M** $14.90–$18.90
D $5.50–$6.50
Cards AE BC DC MC V Eftpos;
bookings essential
Wine Serviceable; 6 by the glass, but beer is ideal; most people seem to BYO (corkage $2 pp)
Chef Mourty Murga
Owner Bijou Christy
Seats 135; wheelchair access; outdoor seats
www.all-india.com.au
And...you get free parking and can book online

The Alley @ Cronulla

Shop 5, Beach Park Arcade, Cronulla
Tel 9523 1530 Map 8

Contemporary

Score 14/20

You'll find this cheerfully unpretentious room, with its tables spilling out onto the footpath, along a laneway near a park. An appetising venison sausage with an intense wild berry jam signals Alley's intentions early – stacks of food, both in presentation and amount. Three juicy scallops perch atop crisp polenta fritters, enjoying the lovely sour tang of tamarind. Thyme and parmesan make their presence felt in a mound of risotto draped with ample john dory fillets. Two slow-cooked duck thighs almost lose their way in a Thai red curry. And even if service does get charmingly absentminded, it doesn't hurt to have a break before tucking in to a solid, citrus-laced bavarois crowned with a cloud of vanilla cream. We love restaurants run by couples who invariably display a genuine pride and will to please, and Alley is no exception. If you believe in confident cooking that doesn't overreach in honest, straightforward food with generous flavours, then Alley is right up your ah, alley.

Hours Lunch Wed–Fri noon–3pm (summer only);
Dinner Tues–Sat 6pm–late
Bill E $14–$17 **M** $20–$31 **D** $11;
2/3-course set menu $31.50/$40
Cards AE BC MC V Eftpos
Wine Very short, just adequate; 3 by the glass;
BYO (corkage $3.50 per bottle)
Chef Dean Castle
Owners Dean & Shona Castle
Seats 42; outdoor seats
And...read more reviews on the back of the ladies' loo door

city + suburbs

Altitude

Level 36, Shangri-La Hotel,
176 Cumberland Street, The Rocks
Tel 9250 6123   Map 1

Contemporary

Score 13/20

There's a lot to like about the Shangri-La's lofty diner perched 36 floors up atop The Rocks, overlooking that Bridge, that Harbour and that Opera House. A lush fit-out has transformed the former Japanese restaurant into a modern gem with comfy padded chairs and deep carpet. The food has been memorable, but sometimes for the wrong reasons, as it swung from sumptuous to strangely fused. On a good day, you could be swooning over smoked tomato risotto with a splendid olive oil-poached marron. You may be treated to a just-made spinach and oyster soup or delight in Queensland sea scallops on a paste of sweet corn and topped with crisped pancetta. At other times you may wonder about overwhelming truffle oil on everything, watermelon with otherwise superb suckling pig, or vanilla with seafood. The service also has its good days and lifts beyond the usual hotel mood to personable and mutedly passionate.

Hours Lunch Fri noon–2.30pm;
Dinner Mon–Sat 6–10.30pm
Bill E $25–$28 **M** $35–$40 **D** $18;
dégustation menu $120
Cards AE BC DC MC V
Wine Large, wide-ranging list, hotel prices; 14 by the glass
Chef George Jardine
Owner Shangri-La Hotels
Seats 95; private room; wheelchair access
www.altitudesydney.com
And…if you have deep pockets the hotel has valet parking

Amici

465 Miller Street, Cammeray
Tel 9922 2222   Map 5A

Italian/Pizza

Score 13/20

Oh mamma mia. How long has the North Shore waited for this kind of Italian? The sort where good-looking, long-suffering waiters treat regulars like, well, *amici* (friends) and the pizze are so reminiscent of the old country that you can taste Napoli in the darkly spotted crust? With its white tiles the size of flagstones and wood-fired oven up the back, Amici is the kind of pizzeria with chairs that make your bum sore only two *stagioni* into a *quattro*. Yes, the noise levels really strain the friendship and yes, the kids will love it as much as you do. But braised octopus with green olives and rocket is as tender as a saint. The pinkest lamb loins come with a whole forest floor of sautéed mushrooms, laid on cavolo nero, black truffle paste adding its own layer of flavour. Affogato is finished with excellent coffee and Frangelico, while the crème brûlée, on fresh pear and scented with anise, cardamom and cinnamon, will keep you coming back.

Hours Dinner Mon–Sat 6pm–late
Bill E $14.50–$16.50 **M** $17.50–$30.50
D $8.50–$12.50; 10% surcharge on public holidays
Cards AE MC V Eftpos
Wine Tiny list, but thoughtful; only two Italians; 6 by the glass; BYO (corkage $3 pp)
Chefs Lucio De Falco & El Mostafa Solaihan
Owners Jac Soghomonian, Antonio Castelnuovo & Marco Pietrobon
Seats 85; private room; wheelchair access; outdoor seats
And…they cook the food of a different region every second month

city + suburbs   A

An Restaurant

27 Greenfield Parade, Bankstown
Tel 9796 7826   Map 6

Vietnamese
Score 12/20

Hopefully, they serve pho noodle soup in whatever heaven you aspire to. They certainly do in Bankstown at this newly refurbished, modernist dining hall with colourful (plastic) floral arrangements and enough tables to resemble an up-scale Asian food court. Pho (pronounced like 'far', hence the whimsical motto by the electric front door: 'So pho so good') is a restorative, glistening broth with all manner of chicken and/or beef cuts. The big bowls of lily-white rice noodles are scented with star anise, crunchy with beanshoots, fragrant with Vietnamese mint, tangy with lime juice and hot with extra chilli. We chose option 10 (rare beef and beef tendon, tripe and brisket), then with chopsticks in right hand, spoon in left, and head down over the bowl, it's slurp, slurp, slurp. It's not fine dining but it is good food – fresh and healthy and flavoursome, fast food for the soul. Bring the extended family, don't dress in white linen, and enjoy the simple pleasures of one of Sydney's best pho.

Hours Daily 7am–9pm
Bill M $9.70–$11.50 **D** $4; $1.10 pp surcharge on public holidays
Cards None; no bookings
Wine No alcohol
Chef Xuan Doan Phan
Owner Anbito Pty Ltd
Seats 350; wheelchair access
www.anrestaurant.com
And...they have Paddle Pops and other ice-creams, which is kool for kids

Aqua Dining

Cnr Paul & Northcliff streets, Milsons Point
Tel 9964 9998   Map 5A

Contemporary   ♀
Score 14/20

This is one spectacular view: the mammoth Harbour Bridge pylon looms above, boats and ferries trundle by, the Opera House and city lights glisten beyond, and the ferris wheel of Luna Park twirls to the west. Below, the aqua glows from the pool where, during our visit, a swimming meet provided entertainment. Past a nice little bar, the finger-shaped restaurant is an elegant space of banquettes and cloth'd tables. A complimentary appetiser of celeriac soup gets the tastebuds going. A tumble of baby spinach with pine nuts, pancetta, egg and olives is lifted by a memorable red wine and pesto dressing; and glassy scallops have a heavenly companion in light, frothy horseradish sauce. But john dory with wood mushrooms, chive spaetzle and pea purée was not a marriage made in heaven, and salmon on a bed of mashed potato with yabby and bacon seemed overpowered by a syrupy dark shiraz jus. Yet outside on the balcony on a balmy Sydney night, you could forgive almost anything.

Hours Lunch daily noon–2.30pm; Dinner daily 6.30–10pm
Bill E $22–$29; **M** $35–$48; **D** $18–19 (lunch is cheaper)
Cards AE BC DC MC V
Wine Long and well chosen but pricey; 13 by the glass
Chef Jeff Turnbull
Owner Bill Drakopoulos
Seats 120; outdoor seats
www.aquadining.com.au
And...try a sherry aperitif from the impressive list

good food guide   7

city + suburbs

Arabella

Shop 12, 489–491 King Street, Newtown
Tel 9550 1119   Map 8

Lebanese

Score 12/20

This sleek, discreet restaurant, bathed in muted chocolate browns and warm greys, has a classy fit-out, with banquettes, arabesque alcoves in the walls holding Middle Eastern paraphernalia and a gleaming open kitchen. It's all juxtaposed with giant plasma screens sporting cavorting arabesque pop idols. If you dare to visit on Friday or Saturday nights, then take the ceiling disco lights as a warning of what's coming. You can order a banquet – ideal for big families or table-dancing parties – or choose from a simple menu that keeps things pared back. Bowls of hummus and baba ghanoush arrive with wells of olive oil. Lebanese sausages are pan-fried in fresh tomato. Tender vine leaves are folded around rice, tomato, mint, shallot and parsley, then simmered in an oil and lemon sauce. Three chargrilled skewers of impossibly tender chicken breast are marinated in garlic, lemon and tomato paste, while chunky chips accompany enormous BBQ king prawns. And with a cushion room, what more could you want?

Hours Lunch Fri–Sun from noon; Dinner daily 5–11pm
Bill E $6–$12 **M** $15–$20 **D** $5–$8
Cards AE BC DC MC V Eftpos
Wine Five cheap 'n' cheerful choices; BYO (corkage $2 pp)
Chef Daniel Diab
Owner Mohamad Zouhour
Seats 120; wheelchair access; outdoor seats
www.arabella.com.au
And...belly dancing on Friday and Saturday nights

Arena

212 Bent Street, Fox Studios, Moore Park
Tel 9361 3930   Map 4B

Contemporary

Score 12/20

This is certainly the most up-market restaurant in Fox Studios, one of the few that's a destination in its own right rather than somewhere to eat after a movie. There is a dim and sexy bar on one side and this soft-edged, very large bistro on the other. Service can be a little erratic – you're either swamped by waiters or left entirely alone – while the food is more dependable, if not always memorable. A starter of guinea fowl and foie gras mousseline had a slightly grainy texture and a too-subtle flavour that didn't quite stand up to the wood mushroom and lentil sauce. A tomato tart with fetta and basil oil was much more robust, though we hoped for better-quality raw tomatoes. Seared tuna with peperonata is much smarter, and the veal medallions on rice with mushrooms and porcini sauce are perhaps the best dish of the night: adeptly cooked, rich and balanced. That Aussie classic, peach Melba, brings down the curtain.

Hours Tues–Sun noon–10pm
Bill E $16–$19 **M** $25–$29 **D** $10–$16
Cards AE BC DC MC V
Wine An encyclopaedic list in price ranges that defy imagination; 27 by the glass; BYO (corkage $15 per bottle)
Chef Graeme Jones
Owner Paul Dawson
Seats 400; private rooms; wheelchair access; outdoor seats
www.arenabistro.com.au
And...during footy season it's $25 for a main and house wine or beer, before 1pm or between 5 and 7pm

city + suburbs   A

Aria

1 Macquarie Street, East Circular Quay, Sydney
Tel 9252 2555   Map 1

Contemporary

Score 16/20

This elegant dining room offers front-row seats of the Bridge, the Harbour and the Opera House in all their glory. While opera lovers scurry to make opening curtain, a serene atmosphere pervades the plush Aria, where an expectation of a Big Night Out is matched by service that anticipates and meets your every whim (though we do find there are two levels: one for reviewers, one for everybody else). An exquisite complimentary kingfish carpaccio is a taste of things to come from the ubiquitous Matt Moran, whose classical approach nonetheless shows imaginative flair. A salad of baby squid and rocket is teamed perfectly with quail egg and a warm cod brandade. Crisp-skinned barramundi sits atop chat potatoes along with the vibrant colours and flavours of baby beetroot and tarragon salsa. An aged beef fillet with potato mash and bourguignonne sauce is a hearty French classic. Fig with goat's curd sorbet, meringue and caramel sauce is a sassy balance of sweet and tart. Aria gives you so many reasons to sing.

Hours Lunch Mon–Fri noon–2.30pm; Pre-theatre Mon–Sun 5.30–7pm; Dinner Mon–Sat 7–11.30pm, Sun 6–11.30pm
Bill E $30–$39 **M** $42–$49 **D** $20–$24; Pre-theatre & supper 1/2/3 courses $36/$58/$72; 10% surcharge on Sundays & public holidays
Cards AE BC DC MC V
Wine Awesome list, one of the best in town; 16 by the glass
Chef Matthew Moran
Owners Matthew Moran & Peter Sullivan
Seats 220; private rooms; wheelchair access
www.ariarestaurant.com
And...there is pre- and post-theatre dining

The Art Gallery Restaurant

Art Gallery of NSW, 1 Art Gallery Road, Domain, Sydney
Tel 9225 1819   Map 2

Contemporary

Score 14/20

With a billion-dollar view to the east across the naval fleet and Woolloomooloo Bay, this elegant white room with its red rug and parquetry floor is modern Sydney with a difference – totally European inspiration, with nary a sweet chilli sauce or wasabi dip to be seen. The menu is short and sophisticated, and there are some wonderfully contrasting flavours that almost qualify as artworks in their own right. Seared pork fillet is cooked with chorizo, pearl barley and shallots; a special of veal loin – two satisfyingly thick slices – comes with taleggio and potato galette and a flavoursome reduction. Barramundi is served with a daring red wine sauce. Even the salad shows class, using a finely balanced dressing. Oddly, some of the simpler entrées don't work so well. Fish cakes, big enough for a main, with a delightfully crisp exterior, were a tad dry and the flavours seemed bland. You can finish with roasted peach, moscato and raspberry tart or there's a good cheese platter.

Hours Brunch Sat–Sun 10–11.30am; Lunch daily noon–3pm
Bill E $16–$19 **M** $20–$30 **D** $14–$16; 10% surcharge on Sundays & public holidays
Cards AE BC DC MC V
Wine Small but interesting list, 9 by the glass
Chef John McFadden
Owner Brien Trippas
Seats 120; private rooms; wheelchair access
www.trippaswhite.com.au
And...the art exhibitions, of course

city + suburbs

Arte e Cucina

2 Short Street, Double Bay
Tel 9328 0880   Map 4A

Italian

Score 13/20

Sister restaurant to Paddington institution Lucio's, Arte e Cucina is a well-seasoned campaigner for contemporary Italian food. Enter the cosy, softly lit bar, with its inviting lounges, via a back lane. The restaurant opens out into a long conservatory-style room – all glass on one side and the opposing wall dedicated to Lucio Galletto's other passion: modern Australian art. Among these hard surfaces, and with so much art as a conversation point, noise levels can crescendo. The menu offers uncluttered, unadulterated flavours, beautifully cooked and presented. Linguini with octopus, cuttlefish and red and green chillies is a cephalopod lover's delight. Marinated lamb fillet with celeriac, apple and walnuts is a playful mesh of texture and flavours. Kingfish with eggplant and pea purée could have enjoyed a little more gusto. Service is efficient and knowledgeable, if sometimes aloof – perhaps this younger sibling could do with her father's firm hand and diplomatic charm. To finish, a sublime pear zuccotto reclaims the legacy.

Hours Lunch Mon–Sat noon–3.30pm; Dinner Mon–Sat 5.30–11pm

Bill E $16–$20 **M** $25–$32 **D** $14; set menus 2–3 courses $27.50, $47.50 or $62.50

Cards AE BC DC MC V

Wine Extensive list of local and imported (mainly Italian) varieties; 18 by the glass

Chef Timothy Fisher

Owners Lucio Galletto & Timothy Fisher

Seats 120; private room; outdoor seats

www.artecucina.com.au

And... Lucio intends to close Arte e Cucina around Christmas 2005.

Arun Thai

28 Macleay Street, Potts Point
Tel 9326 9132   Map 2

Thai

Score 14/20

A mini water bridge symbolically separates busy Macleay Street from the tranquillity of an 18th-century-Thailand interior of panelled walls, carvings and paintings. And while the damask-covered tables, comfortable upholstered chairs, hand-painted plates, and service under seasoned professional Kham Signavong may also be old world in the best sense, the menu at this 17-year-old stayer is not; and thankfully, there's ne'er a carved vegetable in sight. Betel leaves stacked with peanut, lime, ginger, dried shrimps, chilli and toasted coconut are a textural, exciting mouthful; grilled chicken is coated with a rich, luscious peanut sauce. Signature dishes deserve their reputation, like mildly spiced red duck curry; and volcano chicken, marinated and roasted, stuffed with sticky rice, nuts and shiitake mushrooms, wrapped in foil to resemble a hen, and served with a fabulous house-made chilli sauce. Salads include soft white scallops with fragrant greens and herbs and crisp fried shallots. There's plenty to please the vegetarian and, to finish, sticky rice encased in egg custard tastes much better than it looks.

Hours Lunch Thurs–Sun noon–3pm; Dinner daily 6–10.30pm

Bill E $12–$15 **M** $17–$26.50 **D** $10–$12; $2.50 pp surcharge on public holidays

Cards AE BC DC MC V Eftpos

Wine Extensive list with both museum and European stocks; 21 by the glass

Chefs Chaiwat and Supot

Owners Tess & Kham Signavong

Seats 250; private rooms

www.arunthai.com.au

And... enjoy the front bar section for drinks and Thai 'tapas', or a main

city + suburbs   A

Astral

80 Pyrmont Street, Pyrmont
Tel 9657 8767/1800 700 700   Map 5B

Modern French

Score 14/20

Astral certainly is reaching sky high. It's 17 floors up in the casino hotel, with glorious 270-degree city views observed from super-comfy, high-backed chairs. The champagne list is designed to claw back as much of your high-roller winnings as it can. Smart punters put their money on Yorkshire boy Sean Connolly's menu, which runs from barramundi with ham hock and vegetable bouillon, to a duck pie floater with an extravagant foie gras flourish. Sure, prices are on the high side, too, but Astral's kitchen demonstrates technique that rises above so many other hotel dining rooms. That pie floater arrives on crushed fresh peas with a deep caramel-coloured shiraz jus. Kingfish ceviche is served with avocado and the finest sesame wafers. We experienced the occasional slip in service, something Connolly – who now manages the whole restaurant, not just the kitchen – is keen to fix. It's of little consequence with an excellent cheese board that leaves everyone feeling a winner.

Hours Breakfast daily 6–10am; Dinner Tues–Thurs 6–10pm, Fri–Sat 6–10.30pm
Bill 2 courses $70 pp, 3 courses $85 pp
Cards AE BC DC MC V Eftpos; bookings essential
Wine Big on champers, big on price, good depth; 23 by the glass
Chef Sean Connolly
Owner Star City
Seats 90; wheelchair access
www.starcity.com.au
And...they're having a million-dollar refit as we go to press

Avalon Chinese

First Floor, Barefoot Boulevard,
6/74 Old Barrenjoey Road, Avalon
Tel 9918 6319   Map 7

Chinese (Cantonese)

Score 13/20

All over the world tonight people will say, 'Let's go down the local Chinese.' We hope their welcome is as warm and the service as helpful and enthusiastic as at the Avalon Chinese. The wallpaper is all-too-familiar red and gold flock, the carpet and white metal-backed chairs clean and new at (perhaps too) close together white-cloth'd tables. Chilled water and face towels quickly appear. Families chatter and choose a long list of standards: sizzling, deep-fried and steamed; or more interesting specials, all in generous serves. Fish is their forte. Four fat, soft-shell Vietnamese crabs are fried crisp. 'Pink' flounder is filleted, the flesh sautéed with a sweet chilli sauce and green capsicum, while the bones are deep-fried. Neatly tied yam noodle bundles are smothered in mushrooms, asparagus and snowpeas. Ma po tofu (grandmother's bean curd) delivers good chunks of tofu in a characteristic red chilli sauce with minced pork. There's nothing to frighten the timid, but if you do fancy some wobbly bits, there's always coconut or mango pudding.

Hours Lunch Mon–Sat 11.30am–3pm; Dinner daily 5–10pm
Bill E $4.50–$12.80 **M** $9.80–$20 **D** $3–$4.80; $1.80 pp surcharge on public holidays
Cards AE BC DC MC V
Wine Short and obvious, several by the glass; good Asian beers; BYO (corkage $5 per bottle)
Chef Leon Yu
Owner Simon Wong
Seats 100
And...there's a car park around the corner

city + suburbs

Azteca's

140 Avoca Street, Randwick
Tel 9398 1020   Map 9

Mexican

Score 12/20

The state of Mexican food in Australia is an outrage. We've reduced one of the world's great cuisines to little more than a swampy mess of tacos smothered in melted cheddar. In a situation like this, Azteca's gets marks just for trying and, happily, it gets more marks for achievement even if service waivers and the décor does resort to sombrero-and-poncho predictability. You can tell how serious they are just by the menudo, an unctuously soupy tripe stew, which you won't encounter at your local Tex-Mex joint and you're sternly told that ceviche (fish 'cooked' simply in the heat of an acidic marinade) is available only in daylight-saving months. Things are not perfect: that glorious classic, chicken in mole poblano (a sauce exquisitely marrying chocolate and chilli), was just a little too light on the chilli, though they'll bring you more if you ask for it. But this is a friendly place, serious about a serious cuisine, and that makes it worth a visit.

Hours Dinner Tues–Thurs & Sun 6–9.30pm, Fri–Sat 6–10.30pm
Bill E $5.20–$9.90 **M** $12.20–$19.90 **D** $5–$5.50
Cards BC MC V
Wine A functional, basic, Australian list; 6 by the glass; BYO (corkage $2 pp)
Chef Anne Leeson
Owners José Cruz & Anne Leeson
Seats 64
And...they sell imported Mexican treats, so stock up on chilli sauce

Azuma

Level 1, Chifley Plaza, 2 Chifley Square, Sydney
Tel 9222 9960   Map 1

Japanese

Score 13/20

Kimitaka Azuma may well be one of Sydney's most misunderstood chefs. And that's not just because he speaks scarcely a word of English (despite several years in Australia). Azuma, who leaves the PR (and the local lingo) to his more than capable maître d' wife, Yuki, is among our most creative Japanese cooks. You wouldn't ask for spag bol in a great Italian restaurant, so eschew the familiar at this elegant CBD diner in favour of dishes with the chef's distinctive stamp, like his 'amuse bouche' – a delightful and inventive platter of sushi-like morsels. Perfectly pink grilled duck breast (plus a dash of rock salt) with rocket and mushroom salad is a salubrious triumph of tenderness. We did find some combinations a little weird; the wagyu beef didn't really need salmon roe (erroneously called caviar), and deep-fried prawns with a nanban sauce were lacklustre. Azuma Unique Sushi is served with salt and lemon and lime juice or mirin and soy. To wash it all down try the trio of regional sakes from different brewers across Japan, served in glasses delivered on a ceramic tray.

Hours Lunch Mon–Fri noon–2.30pm; Dinner Mon–Sat 6–10pm
Bill A la Carte $3–$39; hotpot $58–$66; **D** $10–$28; dégustation menu $110 pp
Cards AE BC DC MC V
Wine Extensive selection; 8 by the glass plus a good range of sake and shochu (Japanese distilled spirit); BYO (corkage $5.50 pp)
Chef Kimitaka Azuma
Owners Kimitaka & Yuki Azuma
Seats 90; private rooms; wheelchair access
www.azuma.com.au
And...get your Chifley Plaza car park ticket validated for free parking for Azuma guests

city + suburbs B

Bambini Trust

Ground floor, 185 Elizabeth Street, Sydney
Tel 9283 7098   Map 1

European

Score 14/20

This slice of Europe, or Melbourne perhaps, is a grown-up, stylish room with a menu to match and prices that won't set off alarm bells in Accounts. Low lighting, a coffered ceiling and wood-panelled walls dressed with mirrors and art make a favourable first impression. Warm sourdough rolls and a complimentary shot of bright-green pea and sage soup from the open kitchen back it up. Antipasto and pasta feature heavily amidst the vegetarian-friendly entrées. Seared scallops appeal the most, arriving on a silky cauliflower purée crowned with a single zucchini flower and garlicky salsa verde. Service is assured, but the roasted spatchcock with baby beetroot and goat's curd ravioli fell short of expectations. Cracked-pepper spaghettini with Yamba prawns, chilli and garlic hits its mark; and grain-fed aged sirloin with morel mushroom butter is noted for a return visit. Desserts such as buttermilk pannacotta, baked Valrhona chocolate tart and a cheese plate provide further incentive to linger. A proposed renovation promises a new bar and an extra 20 seats.

Hours Mon–Fri: Breakfast 7–11am, Lunch noon–3pm; Afternoon tea 3–5pm; Dinner 5–10pm
Bill E $16–$24 **M** $30–$35 **D** $12
Cards AE BC DC MC V; bookings essential
Wine Very pleasant, concise list; 20 by the glass
Chef Wayne Rowe
Owners Michael & Angela Potts
Seats 55; private room; wheelchair access; outdoor seats
www.bambinitrust.com.au
And…if under-dressed, pick up a bespoke tie from the arcade next door

Banana Blossom

318a Military Road, Cremorne
Tel 9908 1588   Map 5A

Modern Asian

Score 12/20

Ben Thomas (a former Sailor's Thai sous chef) has opened this long, narrow restaurant in one of the most challenging dining suburbs north of the Bridge. A heavy antique wooden bench with candles and a Buddha divides the simple cream room of paper-over-linen table tops. Further on, the gilt- and mirror-backed bar faces an open kitchen. Chatty locals can raise the noise levels, although soundproofing plans are afoot. Friendly service wasn't quite polished in those early days. A short menu begins with a superb, slightly chewy turmeric wafer filled with salty chicken, sweet lychees and a good spike of chilli. The cooking styles vary thoughtfully in search of a balanced meal, yet a southern-style yellow curry of chicken dumplings, while hot and slightly sweet, felt a bit one-dimensional. More pleasingly, grilled, sweet soy-marinated beef is well seared, medium–rare and tender. Pomelo and crabmeat salad with mint, kaffir lime leaf and eschalots tastes fresh and offers the promise that Thomas will truly blossom.

Hours Dinner Mon–Sat 6–10pm
Bill E $3–$16 **M** $24–$29 **D** $8
Cards AE BC MC V Eftpos
Wine Reasonable selection, nothing over $40 (except champagne); 10 by the glass; BYO (corkage $6 per bottle)
Chef Ben Thomas
Owners Ben & Natchanan Thomas
Seats 116
www.bananablossom.com.au
And…you can often score a parking spot quite close by on Military Road

B city + suburbs

Barolo

Upstairs, 32 Frederick Street, Oatley
Tel 9580 9122   Map 8

Italian

Score 13/20

When will a politician finally promise that, by some date, no Australian suburb shall exist without a decent local restaurant? Meantime, give thanks and your vote to Barolo. Like the acclaimed Italian wine it's named after, this is a pleasant restaurant, serving very pleasant Italian fare with – yep, you guessed it – pleasant, friendly service. Sure the building is 1980s blonde-brick less than pleasant, but the sizeable chocolate-brown dining room is smarter than many an Italian competitor. The no-nonsense dishes feature meat that's hard to pass up, especially because the pork comes directly from chef Fran Abdallaoui's family's farm in the Hunter and the rest from their other business, Bresnahan's Fine Food at Mortdale. Penne with Italian sausage and tomato has a hint of chilli that won't scare timid palates. A scallopine mushroom is similarly smart without being too sassy, and of course there are mussels in white wine, tomato and fresh chilli. A right neighbourly policy means prices are all under $25 and you're onto a winner.

Hours Dinner Tues–Sat from 6.30pm
Bill E $13–$16 **M** $18–$24.50 **D** $8–$12
Cards AE BC MC V
Wine Standard selection; 5 by the glass; BYO wine (corkage $3.50 per bottle)
Chefs Angela Bresnahan & Fran Abdallaoui
Owners Fran & Jamal Abdallaoui
Seats 95; outdoor seats
And…don't fancy the wine list? Ask for the owner's private selection

The Bathers' Pavilion Cafe

4 The Esplanade, Balmoral
Tel 9969 5050   Map 7

Mediterranean

Score 13/20

The palatial grandeur of Balmoral's old change shed is matched by stunning views up Middle Harbour and out through Sydney Heads. Inside, it's all louvres and windows that open on pleasant days, and tightly packed tables where waiters might bump your chair just once too often. There's also a menu of more-than-usual cafe sophistication. The offerings might range from pasta, perhaps casarecce with a slow-cooked beef and pork ragù, to wood-fired pizza, fougasse (a bread) in the style of Arles, and Meredith goat's cheese tart cut like a slice of quiche. Smoked and cured salmon terrine took liberties with the definition: smoked salmon was rolled around a very 1970s mousse and cubes of cured salmon were dotted through very modern micro-cress. The lemon delicious is rightly named and a mango tart with coconut ice-cream simply superb. At any other location these prices may feel opportunistic, but it seems just a little mean-spirited to complain when it's obviously all about this location and that stunning view.

Hours Daily 7am–midnight
Bill E $14.50–$22.50 **M** $19.50–$30.50 **D** $14.50
Cards AE BC DC MC V; no bookings
Wine Concise, interesting list; cocktails and breakfast juices, too; 8 by the glass
Chefs Serge Dansereau & Phillip Sajowitz
Owner Serge Dansereau
Seats 80; wheelchair access
www.batherspavilion.com.au
And…no bookings can mean big waits on Sundays, but other times are usually just fine

city + suburbs B

The Bathers' Pavilion Restaurant

4 The Esplanade, Balmoral
Tel 9969 5050   Map 7

Mediterranean

Score 15/20

A glass of crisp white in hand, you gaze out through the Heads. A ferry floats past, the seagull convention perches atop the shark net and waves lap gently. Sigh. As dusk falls you might forget momentarily that you're here for Serge Dansereau's equally seductive food. His genius is letting quality produce shine. Expect quality and precision – albeit at enthusiastic prices – from this indefatigable North Shore institution. Each dish is a work of art, from suitably rare and tender spring lamb with delicate, minted vegetables, fondant potato, red pepper and garlic jam to a crowd-pleasing barramundi with pancetta, shimeji mushrooms, cauliflower and horseradish purée. A sweet and sour casserole of king prawns, yabbies, squid and mussels is a triumph of minimalism and restraint. Perhaps it's because the room is shared with the equally enjoyable cafe, but things seem a little more formal and earnest than such relaxed surrounds imply. Regardless, Bathers' remains one of Sydney's seriously good dining destinations.

Hours Lunch daily noon–2.30pm; Dinner daily 6.30–10pm
Bill Set menu 2–3 courses $90–$110 pp (less for weekday lunch); dégustation menu $135 pp
Cards AE BC DC MC V
Wine Outstanding, international range; 18 by the glass; BYO Monday night only (corkage $10 pp)
Chefs Serge Dansereau & Simon Bestley
Owner Serge Dansereau
Seats 78; private rooms; wheelchair access
www.batherspavilion.com.au
And...check out the new Bathers' Pavilion kiosk

The Bayswater Brasserie

32 Bayswater Road, Kings Cross
Tel 9357 2177   Map 2

Contemporary

Score 14/20

While other restaurants come and go, the Bayz is a true stayer. It's been a fixture of the Sydney dining scene since 1982 – a place for power lunches and fashionable dinners – and the buzzy atmosphere has never waned. What makes it such a classic? You could start with an ever-changing selection of five to eight types of oysters, shucked to order. Then there's the simple perfection of the much-loved steak with porcini butter and chips, and the seasonal specials from the sure hands of Robert Hodgson. Beaufort cheese and sage soufflé, swimming in a lake of velvety sauce, is a serious start, while gazpacho with prawns is its opposite: refined, light and refreshing. Lamb rump is artfully arranged on a bed of creamed leeks and discs of beetroot, tasting as tempting as it looks. The white-tiled floor, the wooden chairs, and the white cloth'd-and-papered tables all lend the Bayz an air of timeless ease. Hope it still needs us, and still feeds us, when we're 64.

Hours Lunch Fri noon–3pm; Dinner Mon–Sat 6pm–late, Sun 5–10pm
Bill E $15.50–$18 **M** $22–$31 **D** $13.50; set menus 3/4 course $65/$70 pp
Cards AE BC DC MC V
Wine Succinct, well-chosen list, plus excellent cocktails; 17 by the glass
Chef Robert Hodgson
Owners Nigel Lacy & Robert Smallbone
Seats 185; private rooms; outdoor seats
www.bayswaterbrasserie.com.au
And...there is a great bar out the back for pre- or post-dinner cocktails

B city + suburbs

Beach Road

1 Beach Road, Palm Beach
Tel 9974 1159 Map 7

French/Mediterranean

Score 12/20

Proof that the peninsula's tip is a playground for the rich can be found at this landmark beach house. Lobster is a regular feature on a seafood-inclined, Med- and Asian-influenced menu where even the mash is studded with the posh crustacean. Yet swanky ingredients are no guarantee of success. A brioche lobster 'burger' with smoked chilli rouille and large cos lettuce leaves lacked panache and the luxe feel we'd hoped for. Thankfully, excellent pastry complements a richly pleasurable duck confit pie with a watercress and pomegranate salad. But spatchcock mignons with celeriac and beetroot pappardelle didn't quite live up to the promised succulence. Beef fillet with béarnaise, plus garlic and tarragon flan, is simply satisfying. It's easy to enjoy such a relaxed and airy setting amidst the casual, aquatic décor, even if the service can sometimes be too relaxed. Yet basking in the sun on the front verandah over a slow weekend brunch of eggs Benedict would make anyone feel not only rich but also famous.

Hours Wed–Fri noon–late; Sat–Sun 11am–late
Bill E $16–$18 **M** $30–$36 **D** $15–$18; $4 pp surcharge on Sundays & public holidays; 2-course lunch with glass of wine $38
Cards AE BC DC MC V Eftpos
Wine Modest mix of familiar brands at eager mark-ups; 12 by the glass; BYO Mon–Thurs (corkage $5 pp)
Chef Tom Rutherford
Owners Tom & Edwina Rutherford
Seats 90; wheelchair access; outdoor seats
www.beachroad.net.au
And...brunch and live jazz in the afternoon on weekends

bel mondo

Gloucester Walk, The Rocks
Tel 9241 3700 Map 1

Contemporary

Score 12/20

The industrial warehouse look is the same: long, open kitchen, ancient floorboards and postcard view of the Bridge. But the new, vibrant organza curtains, plush velvet Queen of Hearts' chairs and bright, high-backed Mad Hatter's chairs at the entrance create an almost nightclub atmosphere not seen during bel mondo's earlier incarnation. And unless you don't mind paying for the million-dollar view, you might struggle to find good value on the dinner menu. Caprese salad is pleasant, but the small bocconcini lacked the longed-for lactic sweetness of good buffalo-milk mozzarella. Fresh squid ink pasta, cooked al dente, with large, sweet prawns, suffered from an unnecessarily creamy sauce. There are plenty of finer moments: the richness of duck confit is lifted by the bitterness of caramelised witlof; rabbit pie has fine, crisp, buttery pastry and a chunky filling of rabbit and eschalots. Service is friendly and efficient, the tables are comfortable and well spaced, and there's plenty of care and attention shown to small details such as good, warm bread rolls.

Hours Lunch Wed–Fri noon–3pm; Dinner Wed–Mon 5.30–10pm; Sun noon–8pm
Bill E $16–$26 **M** $34–$42 **D** $13–$17; Lunch 1/2/3 courses $29/$39/$49 pp; 10% surcharge on public holidays
Cards AE BC DC MC V
Wine Reasonable range of varieties and regions, almost nothing under $40; 19 by the glass
Chef Wayne Morris
Owners Michael & Inka Lloyd
Seats 140; private rooms; outdoor seats
www.belmondo.com.au
And...great value, three-course à la carte lunch for $49; two courses for $39

city + suburbs B

Bella Mia

11 Hill Street, Roseville
Tel 9412 3999   Map 7

Italian

Score 13/20

In a previous incarnation as La Belle Helene, this converted Federation-era house was a well-loved North Shore local. Times change, but with Giovanni and Rita Caraboutli now installed as owners, the good ol' days seem set to return. Under Rita's eagle eye, there's a warm welcome and the service is personable and attentive. The landscaped front offers outdoor dining. Inside there are appealing nooks and crannies for canoodling couples, as well as space for larger celebratory crowds. The firmly Italian menu might feature a daily special of juicy ripe figs with prosciutto. Alas, flavoursome spaghetti was spoilt by the somewhat gritty clams. A lemony sauce cuts the richness of lamb brains. Deboned quails are fragrant with garlic, rosemary and thyme, stacked on a bed of English spinach. Kingfish speaks for itself, perfectly grilled with simple steamed vegies. Crème brûlée is a silky finale – and then there's good coffee to keep a grappa or two company.

Hours Dinner Mon–Sat from 6pm
Bill E $13.50–$18.50 **M** $24.50–$34.50 **D** $10
Cards AE BC MC V
Wine Extensive with some old faithfuls; 9 by the glass; BYO (corkage $3 pp)
Chef Ermanno Izzo
Owners Rita & Giovanni Caraboutli
Seats 50; private room; outdoor seats
And...there is a good selection of spirits and digestivi

Bellevue Hotel Dining Room

159 Hargrave Street, Paddington
Tel 9363 2293   Map 4B

Contemporary

Score 14/20

We didn't arrive by Tardis, but it feels like you've stepped through a time warp at this Paddo pub. Sure, it's been given a little bit of a dust-off thanks to Bistro Moncur owners Damien Pignolet and Ron White, but it's not schmoozy or swanky, just a little less dingy. You can still bag a snag in the back dining room, thanks to former Moncur sous chef Tahlia Gilbert. The menu reads like it was written in the 1970s – comfortingly retro yet with some of today's sensibilities. Steak diane is better than you might remember it, heady with garlic and spiced with worcestershire. Three fat beef bangers from Vic's Meats, sweet with onion gravy, are dotted with peas and very cosily bedded down on good mash. The plain square dining room is ringed with smart botanical prints. The waiters are chirpy and the beer is well pulled. Excellent figs with savoiardi and mascarpone are one of the few clues that Billy McMahon is no longer PM.

Hours Lunch daily 12.30–3pm; Dinner Mon–Sat 6.30–10pm
Bill E $14–$19.50 **M** $16.50–$32 **D** $13.50
Cards AE BC DC MC V
Wine Concise, yet appealing, low-price list; 19 by the glass
Chefs Damien Pignolet & Tahlia Gilbert
Owners Damien Pignolet & Ron White
Seats 60; private rooms
And...you can place your bets at the in-house TAB during the day

city + suburbs

Beppi's

Cnr Yurong & Stanley streets, East Sydney
Tel 9360 4558   Map 2

Northern Italian
Score 12/20

Beppi's is like a favourite old jumper. Sure, there are frayed edges, and others only see the holes, but you love its reassuring familiarity nonetheless. In 2006, Beppi Polese celebrates a remarkable 50 years of Italian hospitality in Sydney. The children who once crossed the tiled floor, and thrilled at being seated in a grotto in the wine cellar, are now bringing their own kids. Somehow, Beppi's can be simultaneously wonderful and frustrating. The well-seasoned black-tied waiters might be your best friend or in a hurry to be elsewhere. Your order might be there within minutes or the wrong thing might turn up. A traditional menu might showcase fresh figs and prosciutto, while carpaccio with rocket and parmesan never goes out of style. Nevertheless, an indifferent risotto let down its porcini mushrooms, while pan-fried guinea fowl with olives and herbs was drier than expected. Barramundi with capers and lemon, however, has eloquent simplicity and the wine list encourages 50 more years of visits to savour its endless pleasures.

Hours Lunch Mon–Fri noon–3pm; Dinner Mon–Sat 6–11pm; closed public holidays
Bill E $16–28 **M** $24–42 **D** $16–18
Cards AE BC DC MC V
Wine Marvellous range and vintages of Aussie and Italian marques; 8 by the glass
Chef Djamel Douadi
Owners Beppi, Norma & Marc Polese
Seats 130; private rooms
www.beppis.com.au
And...if you want a vertical tasting of classic Aussie wines, here's your restaurant

Berowra Waters Inn

Near Public Ferry Terminal, Berowra Waters
Tel 9456 1027   Map 7

Contemporary
Score 14/20

Okay, so you may have heard of this place. Been here, perhaps, in the 1980s when they were really pushing the boat out with the food? Well, it's not quite reliving those glory days, but it's still a magical place to come and dine and 'Mick' Micklewright's food is more accessible and cheaper than it was back then. The gorgeous, Glen Murcutt-designed, louvre-fronted river house is still just as inaccessible. There's no road in, so you'll need to book and arrive by boat, or give a time and they'll pick you up at their private wharf. Location is a big part of the charm, but so is an exquisite entrée of seared, still-glassy scallops with warmed black pud and satiny cauliflower purée. Venison is dutifully pink, a blue cheese mousse marries with fresh pear, and there could be fresh girolle mushrooms gracing a piece of expertly seared Moondarah wagyu beef fillet. Staff treat the venue with so much love it's like they own it, and with the delightful Fiona Jones on the floor, at least one of them does.

Hours Lunch Thurs–Sun noon–3pm; Dinner Thurs–Sat from 6pm
Bill E $25 **M** $35 **D** $18; $6 pp surcharge on Sundays & public holidays
Cards AE BC DC MC V; bookings essential
Chef Mick Micklewright
Owners Jeremy Laws & Fiona Jones
Wine Strong, well-priced list with few marques; 8 by the glass
www.berowrawatersinn.com
And...so you're looking for an idyllic wedding venue, are you?

city + suburbs (B)

Billingsgate Fish Bistro

38–40 St Pauls Street, Randwick
Tel 9398 1011   Map 9

Seafood

Score 14/20

The original seafood market in London has been around for 300 years. This Aussie namesake has yet to notch up two, but it's a suburban seafood stunner that continues to work wonders. The simple space – white walls, dark wooden floors, big glass windows – is crowded with diners, cheerfully sitting cheek by jowl and shouting to be heard as they chow down on some of the best, and best value, seafood in town. Start with the delicate salmon carpaccio with blue swimmer crab, the classic salt-and-pepper squid or the steamed scallop and prawn wontons. Follow with a deep fillet of herb-crusted mahi mahi, or snapper with steamed greens and ginger, Thai basil and jasmine rice. The fish is perfectly cooked, flaking onto the fork; the service friendly rather than perfect; and there are generous touches, like free bread with homemade taramasalata. The pavlova with strawberries, or chocolate truffle with mascarpone, ensures that any wavering converts are enslaved forever: Billingsgate's boat has emphatically come in.

Hours Dinner Tues–Sat (plus 3rd Sunday of every month) 5.30–10.30pm
Bill E $11–$16 **M** $18–$22 **D** $11
Cards AE BC MC V Eftpos
Wine One-pager, with emphasis on value whites; 10 by the glass; BYO Tues–Thurs (corkage $6 per bottle)
Chef Matthew Kemp
Owners Matthew Kemp & Lela Radojkovic
Seats 45
And…they do a great post-movie, two-course special from 9pm every night

bills

433 Liverpool Street, Darlinghurst
Tel 9360 9631   Map 2

Contemporary

Score 13/20

Devotees travel across town (and even the world!) to this inauspicious Darlo corner for the legendary breakfasts of creamy scrambled eggs and ricotta hotcakes with honeycomb butter. The clean modern décor is inviting – all bright-eyed, vibrant and blonde. Service is proficient with an enthusiasm that suggests happy and committed staff. In a city devoid of eye contact, there's delight in the vast communal table, often decorated with a huge platter of yet-to-be scrambled eggs or dazzling lemons, which brings everyone together over good coffee. A vast blackboard menu tempts you to linger longer for the celebrated lunchtime steak sarnie adorned with watercress, tomato, caramelised onion and garlic crème, now also offered simply as a salad, sans carbs. Dinner might feature luscious Hervey Bay scallops with garlic, parsley and breadcrumbs and the freshest, flavour-infused spring pea, fetta and mint salad. Then there's superb crisp-skinned salmon with radish, green bean, asparagus and anchovy vinaigrette. Buttermilk pudding, crème caramel-style, served with crushed raspberries and almond biscotti is undeniably bills.

Hours Mon–Sat 7.30am–3pm & 6–10pm; Sun 8.30am–3pm
Bill E $5–$19 **M** $22–$29 **D** $6.50–$12; 10% surcharge on weekends & public holidays
Cards AE BC MC V Eftpos
Wine BYO (corkage $6 per bottle at night, $3 per bottle at day)
Chef Daniel Mosedale
Owner Bill Granger
Seats 46
www.bills.com.au
And…keep the neighbourhood happy at night by leaving quietly

city + suburbs

bills surry hills

359 Crown Street, Surry Hills
Tel 9360 4762   Map 3B

Contemporary   Score 13/20

The décor is harder edged than its older Darlinghurst sister, but this bills is often as hard to get into. Under a wall covered by a blackboard menu, food followers with spray-on tans, mobile-phone necklaces, backpacks and well-behaved kids tuck into the signature creamy scrambled eggs and popular ricotta hotcakes for breakfast and brunch. Or they go for lunch favourites such as chicken club roll and the justly renowned wagyu beef burger. The cafe feel shifts into bistro mode for dinner, although it repeats some lunch offerings, such as penne with vongole, and treviso salad with gorgonzola piccante. Then there's an old-fashioned chicken kiev; the latest fashion-roasted lamb rump, on a mod-East mix of eggplant, artichoke, tomato and za'atar; and always-in-fashion grilled T-bone with anchovy butter. Service begins with a flourish of good intentions but can sometimes wither to inattentiveness. The coffee, however, is worth waiting for; the desserts – like chocolate pudding with sauce and cream, or meringue with rosewater, raspberries and yoghurt cream – are seductive; and no-one hurries you from your seat.

Hours Daily 7am–10pm
Bill E $5–$18 **M** $16–$27.50 **D** $4.50–$14; 10% surcharge on weekends & public holidays
Cards AE BC MC V Eftpos; no bookings
Wine A small, enticing list laced with a couple of glamour imports; 14 by the glass
Chef Neville Salmon
Owner Bill Granger
Seats 69; wheelchair access; outdoor seats
www.bills.com.au
And...don't be surprised if an English tourist cracks it for a chat

Billy Kwong

3/355 Crown Street, Surry Hills
Tel 9332 3300   Map 3B

Modern Chinese   Score 14/20

By 6pm the first of two or maybe three squishy sittings in this smart teahouse gets underway. All of the small room's crazy-legged stools support a smug bum and the woks in the tiny open kitchen are already breathing, sizzling and hissing. Hopefuls leave their mobile numbers at the door and are sent off to wait (perhaps at a nearby pub) for that all-important call. Kylie Kwong's crossover style of modern Chinese cooking uses the best organic and biodynamic produce and is rightly praised for its creativity. We really admire the carefully calibrated balance of sweet, bitter, cool and hot flavours. The signature crisp-skinned duck with fresh blood orange sauce focuses on bold flavours in gorgeous harmony. Whole fresh snapper dressed with soy sauce, sesame oil, ginger and shallots relies on Kwong's delicate master stock for its dazzling flavours. A salad of black fungus, tofu, pickled carrot and Asian herbs is as cooling as a mountain pool. Go the banquet option for the complete Kylie tour.

Hours Dinner Sun–Thurs 6–10pm, Fri–Sat 6–11pm
Bill E $15–$29 **M** $18–$39 **D** $7; banquet $75 pp; $2.20 pp surcharge on weekends, 10% on public holidays
Cards AE BC MC V; no bookings
Wine Smart, interesting list hand-picked by the owner; 9 by the glass; BYO (corkage $7 per bottle)
Chefs Kylie Kwong & Hamish Ingham
Owner Kylie Kwong
Seats 48
And...forget parking unless it's a Sunday night

eat & drink

From stylish cocktails and supper to five star dining

Make it a night to remember at Sydney Opera House

sydneyoperahouse.com (612) 9250 7111

SYDNEY OPERA HOUSE

Red or white?

Or...

JAMES SQUIRE AMBER ALE

A unique blend of three malts and three Tasmanian hops plus an original 125 year-old ale yeast creates an easy drinking, deep copper-coloured ale with a mild citrus finish. **Try it with a steak or rack of lamb with mint sauce.**

or...

JAMES SQUIRE PILSENER

Brewed using only pale and Munich malts, imported Saaz hops and a special yeast, James Squire Pilsener has a remarkably creamy head, spicy bitterness and a sparkling golden brilliance. **Ideal with Thai stir-fries, spicy pizzas and seafood.**

or...

JAMES SQUIRE PORTER

Brewed with roasted barley and wheat, then fermented with a lager yeast with long cellaring, James Squire Porter displays hints of bitter malt chocolate and a pillowy head. **Delicious with roast beef, Yorkshire pudding, and even better with mud cake.**

or...

JAMES SQUIRE INDIA PALE ALE

Brewed with all pale and Munich malts, James Squire India Pale Ale is rich and robust with the earthy floral dry hop character of Fuggles hops. Made for tasting with respect. **Complements rich duck dishes and spicy Indian cuisine.**

James Squire

AUSTRALIA'S FIRST NAME IN BEER.

Malt Shovel Brewery 99 Pyrmont Bridge Road Camperdown Sydney NSW 2050 T: 02-9519 3579 F: 02-9516 2504 www.maltshovel.com.au

city + suburbs   B

Bilson's

The Foyer, Radisson Plaza Hotel,
27 O'Connell Street, Sydney
Tel 8214 0496   Map 1

Contemporary/French   👑👑🍷

Score 17/20

Hotel fine dining seemed to vanish a few years back when the bean counters couldn't find a spot on the balance sheet for panache, finesse and the occasional dash of exuberance. But tucked at the back of the Radisson, unabashed Francophile Tony Bilson carries an elegant torch for the Michelin-starred experience, from padded, damask-clad tables to a well-honed French-accented floor and Bilson's intriguing art collection. His classicist inclinations deliver a simple pursuit of beauty – with a flash of decadence. Three decades are distilled into blissful dishes, such as slinky fettuccine and oysters with a whiff of chervil; an exquisitely scented salad of black figs, Périgord truffle and walnut oil; and emerald-green broad beans sparkling beside a lush lobster boudin. We could be naughty and call scallops and cepes with a foie gras mousse tart the world's most regal surf 'n' turf, but what superlative suits wild South Australian pigeon salmis on a crouton and the small epiphanies of sommelier Miles Brown's thoughtful wine pairings?

Hours Lunch Mon–Fri noon–2.30pm; Dinner Mon–Sat 6–10pm
Bill E $25 **M** $40 **D** $25; express menu, 2 courses $55
Cards AE BC DC MC V
Wine Quirky and fascinating, littered with wonderful French lesser lights; 10 by the glass
Chef Manu Feildel
Owner Tony Bilson
Seats 80; private room; wheelchair access
www.bilsons.com.au
And...have the seven-course dégustation ($120), with matching wines ($200), at least once in life

Bistro 163

163 King Street, Sydney
Tel 9231 0013   Map 1

Contemporary

Score 14/20

Fans of Sydney dining in the 1990s (and more recently Republic Tower residents) will be familiar with 163's chef Paul Merrony. At this tiny but smart bistro, almost at cellar height in King Street, the mood – and the food – feels right. It's little more than a rectangle of black carpet, with cute French prints on the walls and a waiter flying fast and solo. Merrony's menu showcases all that's right with bistro food. Corned beef brisket is pan-fried crisp then married with big starchy butter beans and seeded mustard dressing. There could be shanks or fish and chips or the best prawn omelette with tomato and bisque-flavoured sauce that you've ever tasted. Occasionally dishes move out of Europe, such as the excellent version of Sichuan's bang bang chicken, dressed with peanut and sesame, on chunks of cucumber. Back in the Old Dart, the Eton mess – a pav lover's concoction of crumbled meringue, chopped strawberries and cream – is a perfect partner to a whole poached peach.

Hours Lunch Mon–Fri 11.30am–2.30pm; Dinner Tues–Fri 6–9.30pm
Bill E $10.50–$16 **M** $23.50–$28 **D** $8–$10
Cards AE BC MC V
Wine Food- (and price-) friendly one-pager with a couple of internationals; 4 by the glass; BYO (corkage $5 per bottle)
Chef Paul Merrony
Owner Tracey Petersen
Seats 35; outdoor seats
www.m-dash.com.au/bistro
And...try using it for a pre-theatre dish or two

city + suburbs

Bistro CBD

Level 1, 52 King Street (cnr York Street), Sydney
Tel 8297 7010 Map 1

French Bistro

Score 14/20

Good old pubs are offering some of the best dining in the city, and Bistro CBD is no exception. Make your way through the noisy bar downstairs and up a circular staircase to an elegant off-white dining room with polished boards and huge arched windows. Colourful modern art and an open kitchen form the backdrop to a lunchtime crowd – mostly PC pushers in their suits – loving the perfectly tender fillet steak with bordelaise sauce and frites; peppered tuna with green beans, watercress and aïoli; or sophisticated salads, like fig, blue cheese and witlof with hazelnut dressing; and prawn, fennel and pistachio nuts crowned with a soft-poached egg. Baby-faced chef James Privett has a CV that belies his years, and the influence of his experience at Bistro Moncur is obvious. With professional floor staff under the watchful eye of Nigel Butement, CBD shows a lot of flair, from the freshly shucked oysters to the petits four. Little wonder the business lunch is far from dead.

Hours Lunch Mon–Fri noon–3pm; Dinner Mon–Fri from 6pm
Bill E $16–$22 **M** $30–$36 **D** $14
Cards AE BC DC MC V
Wine As good as you would expect, thanks to one of our best sommeliers, Stuart Halliday; 15 by the glass
Chef James Privett
Owners The Hemmes family
Seats 80
www.bistrocbd.com
And...it's just as nice at night

Bistro Fax

Cnr Pitt & O'Connell streets, Sydney
Tel 8214 0400 Map 1

Contemporary

Score 14/20

There's a modernist aesthetic to this old dame – the tight-corner, late 1920s, once-upon-a-time downtown 'prestige' office of John Fairfax & Sons (hence the name). It's long since been the Radisson Hotel's contemporary dining room, with new exec chef Jeremy Clark (ex-Sheraton, Bathers' Pavilion, W, et al.) continuing his five-star cookery of classic French bistro fare that has bespoke suits, travelling salesmen and glamour girls suitably impressed. All key performance indicators measure up: the King Island sirloin, chargrilled tenderly pink, on traditional béarnaise sauce; a Kangaroo Island chicken breast wrapped in pancetta; deliciously crisp pork belly atop a clove-spiced apple purée accompanied by colcannon (mash and cabbage); a white asparagus salad with beets, goat's cheese and hazelnut dressing. It's all fine food, beautifully presented in a tiered space with a high ceiling and soft lighting. There's a buzz of expectation that is not disappointed thanks to impeccable service and, to end things on a truly high note, a dark chocolate truffle and caramel parfait.

Hours Breakfast Mon–Fri 6.30–10.30am, Sat–Sun 7–11am; daily noon–10.30pm
Bill E $16–$19 **M** $24–$29 **D** $14.50; 15% surcharge on public holidays
Cards AE BC DC MC V Eftpos
Wine Circumspect and compact list of mostly SA labels (only 2 NSW); 11 by the glass
Chef Jeremy Clark
Owner Radisson Plaza Hotel Sydney
Seats 100; wheelchair access
www.bistrofax.com.au
And...freshly shucked Clare de Lune oysters are a treat

city + suburbs B

Bistro LuLu

257 Oxford Street, Paddington
Tel 9380 6888   Map 4B

French Bistro

Score 15/20

There is something very accomplished about the LuLu experience. It's a dimly lit, sexy sort of bistro, and while the waiters whiz by with lightning efficiency, they are never too busy to give you a cheeky smile. The short menu is full of long-time favourites, done with a beguiling mix of confidence and elegance. The steak, for instance, comes cut into neat pieces, drizzled with a silky béarnaise or café de Paris butter or sauce champignon, and paired with perfect frites. There is skill, but less spark, in venison carpaccio with a goat's cheese pannacotta. A tart of caramelised fig, gorgonzola polenta and basil is a subtle, creeping sort of dish, the flavours slowly and tantalisingly revealing themselves. Soufflés change daily: the strawberry and coconut version is pitch perfect though slightly overwhelmed by the accompanying chocolate ice-cream. Many restaurants aspire to LuLu's modern take on the classics, but few do it as well as this.

Hours Lunch Fri–Sat noon–3pm; Dinner daily from 6pm
Bill E $17.50–$22.50 **M** $29.50–$31.50 **D** $16.50; 10% surcharge on public holidays
Cards AE BC DC MC V
Wine Long, wide-ranging, exciting list; 13 by the glass; BYO Sundays & Mondays only (corkage $10 per bottle)
Chef Mark Philpott
Owners Lucy Allon & Luke Mangan
Seats 80; outdoor seats
www.bistrolulu.com.au
And…a tasting menu is available for $80 pp; $110 with matching wine

Bistro Moncur

The Woollahra Hotel, 116 Queen Street, Woollahra
Tel 9363 2519   Map 4B

French

Score 16/20

Moncur is remarkable. How else can you describe a restaurant that just gets better, setting new standards every year? Start with some of the best and friendliest floor staff with an in-depth knowledge of their food and put them amidst the polished timbers and playful and distinctive wall-length Michael Fitzjames mural. Add time-honoured classics such as Pignolet's marinated salmon, French onion soup, pure pork sausages or grilled sirloin Café de Paris, and we'll return over and over again. The menu changes every few months to surprise regulars. Blue swimmer crab omelette is a perfect summer entrée, full of briny charm. Tuna carpaccio has a rich olive oil dressing balanced with capers and grapefruit. Prawn boudin – like a quenelle in a skin – holds an extraordinary concentration of flavour. The prime fillet is best with the bistro's fine, crisp French fries. Our only quibble is that all this perfection comes at a price, and costs are now more restaurant than bistro. Yet what price a sublime chocolate cake or fine cheese platter?

Hours Lunch Tues–Sun noon–3pm; Dinner Mon–Sat 6–10.30pm, Sun 6–9pm
Bill E $16.50–$21.50 **M** $26–$39.90 **D** $14.50–$15.70
Cards AE BC DC MC V; no bookings
Wine Clever, inspirational list, including lesser-seen labels; 21 by the glass
Chefs Damien Pignolet & Scott Mason
Owners Damien Pignolet & Ron White
Seats 108; private room; outdoor seats
www.bistromoncur.com.au
And…relax in the pub bar next door while waiting for a table

B city + suburbs

Bistro Moore

Olympic Hotel, 308 Moore Park Road, Paddington
Tel 9361 6315   Map 4B

Modern Italian

Score 15/20

The square dining room with the occasional piece of art, a black banquette along the wall and a pull-down screen where they used to show black-and-white films isn't the first place you'd expect to find Italian flair. Nor would you normally go looking in an oft-boisterous pub opposite the SCG. But find it you do, thanks to chef Giovanni Spinazzola's passion and talent on the pans. Feather-light gnocchi are doused in slow-cooked rabbit ragù with broad beans and black olives. Long-stemmed artichokes are draped with prosciutto, needing little more than olive oil, balsamic and more of those squeaky double-peeled broad beans. Zampone, the all-too-rarely spied pig's trotter, is stuffed with chicken and porcini and comes deftly rich but not fatty, with the sticky lentils underneath acting as the perfect counterpoint. And how can you argue with such cheerful waiters, offering clove and chestnut pannacotta with pear, or a decadent semifreddo of nougat, drizzled with honey and snappy crushed pistachios?

Hours Dinner Tues–Sat 6–10pm
Bill E $15–$16 **M** $20–$28 **D** $10
Cards AE BC DC MC V
Wine A well-priced, well-chosen list that is very food friendly; 11 by the glass
Chef Giovanni Spinazzola
Owner Paul William Duggan
Seats 80; private room
www.olympichotel.com.au

And…don't come on nights when there's a game on at the SCG, unless you like jostling with crowds on the way to and from the restaurant

Bistro Stock

3 Beattie Street, Balmain
Tel 9810 7707   Map 5B

Modern Mediterranean

Score 14/20

More than a year on, Bistro Stock has evolved for the better. Regulars return for serious cooking in this otherwise typical bistro tucked away behind busy Darling Street. It has the look: wooden floors, tables and chairs, paper-on-cloth, blackboard specials and a wine list with personality. It has the sound, especially in the noisy back room, though the front is quieter. It has the feel, with confident, black-clad waiters. But the food really sets it apart: such as a large, perfectly cooked oxtail and scallop raviolo with oyster mushrooms and crisp leeks, in a well-developed jus. Pavé of veal fillet is prettily pink in a stack with baby eggplant, tahini, shelled chickpeas and parsley. A delightful salad of baby spinach, roasted pine nut, pumpkin and yoghurt cheese faltered only because the lemon and oregano dressing lacked punch. Sydney's favourite, slow-cooked pork belly, is contrasted with swede purée, spinach, and a currant and red pepper relish. A beautifully caramelised tarte Tatin beside silky vanilla bean ice-cream shows why the Sydney bistro love affair continues.

Hours Dinner Tues–Sat 6.30pm–late
Bill E $16–$18 **M** $26–$28 **D** $12
Cards AE BC MC V
Wine Small but interesting list; 12 by the glass; BYO (corkage $6 per bottle)
Chefs Christopher Stockdale & Oliver Roberts
Owners Christopher Stockdale & Rodney Burrell
Seats 110; private rooms; wheelchair access; outdoor seats

And…there's a good weekend brunch menu

city + suburbs Ⓑ

Bit Brasserie

12 Waters Lane, Neutral Bay
Tel 9953 9999   Map 5A

European

Score 13/20

Take a stool at the bar and consider the impressive European beer list, hand-picked by Bit's friendly (and very European) owner, Lothar Winkler. It's a good way to build up your appetite because the dishes are nothing if not generous in this friendly alehouse-cum-brasserie. A mainly local crowd piles into the relaxed split-level room for a drink at high stools by the windows, or settles into a full meal at wooden tables spilling out onto an undercover courtyard. Divert your gaze from the luminous supermarket sign opposite to the blackboard specials where generous, hearty food is the order of the day. There's good respect for fresh produce, such as Hanging Rock rainbow trout, baked whole to moist perfection; or confit duck, both crisp (skin) and tender (flesh), as it should be. Specials might include battered zucchini flowers with tomato purée, but generous serves of schnitzel, venison and spicy sausages are always popular. The house-made apple strudel is wrapped in perfect pastry, as only the Europeans know how.

Hours Daily noon–late
Bill E $6–$18 **M** $18–$29 **D** $9.50–$10.50
Cards AE BC DC MC V Eftpos
Wine It's really all about the beer, but there's a short list of respectable Australian labels; 16 by the glass; BYO (corkage $6 per bottle)
Chef Lothar Winkler
Owners Lothar & Carolyn Winkler
Seats 170; private room; wheelchair access; outdoor seats
www.bitbrasserie.com.au
And...pop in for brunch on weekends

Blue Orange

49 Hall Street, Bondi Beach
Tel 9300 9885   Map 9

Contemporary

Score 14/20

Cafe by day, sexy low-lit restaurant by night, Blue Orange succeeds where so many Bondi tragics fail. From its mannerly, often French-accented waiters to the timber-lined, low-ceiling room, which has an exotic Finnish sauna kind of feel, it's all good. Shane Lurie's food ranges the globe, cherry-picking ideas and mixing 'n' matching at will. His za'atar-dusted bread with labna (yoghurt cheese) is perfect for the first cocktail. A spicy prawn laksa may be offered as a free appetiser, as you perch precariously on low bench seats. An unfortunate corn profiterole with excellent chorizo wasn't his finest moment. But all is quickly forgiven after slow-braised oxtail, stripped from the bone and formed into a pillow using cabbage as the cover, with parsnip purée and aromatic dusky red chunks of quince making perfect bedfellows. The signature lamb shoulder with eggplant is superb, and the spire of chocolate marquis in spun sugar is the kind of thing that gives chocolate a devilishly bad name.

Hours Breakfast & Lunch Wed–Sun 7am–5pm; Dinner Tues–Sat from 6.30pm
Bill E $9.50–$15.50 **M** $21.50–$30.50 **D** $11.50–$12.50
Cards AE BC MC V Eftpos
Wine Food-friendly one-pager with emphasis on quality at good prices; 8 by the glass; BYO (corkage $3.50 pp)
Chef Shane Lurie
Owners Shane Lurie & Tasia Doukakis
Seats 60; outdoor seats
www.blueorangerestaurant.com.au
And...free two-hour parking on the same drag, just a few minutes' walk up the hill

B city + suburbs

The Boathouse on Blackwattle Bay
End of Ferry Road, Glebe
Tel 9518 9011   Map 5B

Seafood   ♀
                  Score 14/20

To lose one chef is unfortunate, to lose two, well... For the third *Guide* in a row, changes have been in the air at this flagship seafood diner. The fantastic waterside location – all city views and rowboats – remains as beautiful as ever, and the waiters are a mix of stern and aft...oops, we mean caring. The wine list is still as good as it is pricey, and the excellence of the bread and coffee remains thanks to part-owner Tony Papas' other businesses as roaster and baker. But a chef change, mid-2005, has Keith Higginson (ex Tilbury) steering the ship. The menu continues to offer a huge range of oysters (we think Clair de Lune are the cat's pyjamas). There could also be barbecue bonito on seaweed egg custard with shiso essence, grilled Tassie scallops with a herbaceous sauce vièrge, or olive-roasted bass grouper with a mussel and vongole emulsion. Perhaps all the focus on the kitchen has left the floor to drift. On an early visit after Higginson hit the pans, we found the wine service wanting, timing awry and the usual food knowledge lacking. But the pedigree is there, and we hope these are isolated incidents for this iconic restaurant.

Hours Lunch Tues–Sun noon–3pm;
Dinner Tues–Sun 6.30–10pm
Bill E $21–$26 **M** $37–$43 **D** $16–$19
Cards AE BC DC MC V; bookings essential
Wine Classical, solid list of mostly Aussie boutique labels; 18 by the glass
Chef Keith Higginson
Owners Tony Papas & Robert Smallbone
Seats 100; wheelchair access
www.boathouse.net.au
And...plans are in place for a water taxi stop nearby; call and check

Bond Cafe
Colonial Centre, 111 Phillip Street, Sydney
Tel 9223 9332   Map 1

Italian
                  Score 12/20

From just after midday, a locust plague of suits descends to swap gossip and seal deals in under an hour. They might sit outside in the covered atrium or plonk in the modern cafe space between the long white counter and rouge-coloured wall. Service can be snappy, but sometimes you need to let them know if you're clock watching. Most go for the much-loved steak sarnie with caramelised onion, mustard mayo and fries. It's their loss, because chef Heydeon Young has flair and a love of fresh herbs to invigorate familiar cafe fare. It could be shellfish broth studded with tomato concasse and fragrant with mint, basil and coriander. Tartufo is a pie-sized raviolo filled with spinach, ricotta and runny egg yolk, though the promised truffle flavour appears more as if the egg waved as the truffle passed by, rather than the two spending the night together. Lamb shanks, cut osso buco-style, are succulently satisfying on herbed risotto. And banana pancakes are a good start to the day. Now get back to work.

Hours Mon–Fri 6am–3pm
Bill E $9.90–$16.90 **M** $19.90–$24.50
D $3–$6.90
Cards AE BC MC V Eftpos
Wine Good, diverse mix of interesting names at reasonable prices; 13 by the glass
Chef Heydeon Young
Owner Carmela Musumeci
Seats 140; wheelchair access; outdoor seats
www.bondcafe.com.au
And...a bar licence is in the offing

city + suburbs B

Botanic Gardens Restaurant

Royal Botanic Gardens, Mrs Macquarie's Road, Sydney
Tel 9241 2419   Map 2

Contemporary

Score 14/20

You couldn't choose a better spot: a pavilion loud with the noise of bird life, looking out onto thick greenery and trees with bats hanging from their higher boughs and flapping in the breeze. This is a bright, welcoming and fragrant space: in summer, you're smelling the gardens; in winter, the room is full of the sweet aroma of an open wood fire. It's as Sydney a place as you could imagine. Look down at your plate and what you see is pretty Sydney, too: a bit Mediterranean, a bit French, a bit Asian. The grilled blue-eye is given an Asian twist with bok choi, oyster mushrooms and coconut sauce; the poached corn-fed chicken with chicken bouillon is made Italian with salsa verde. And if none of the food quite takes thrilling flight – as if it's just dangled before you like the bats on the trees, though much more appealingly – the whole enchilada remains an essential delight of life.

Hours Lunch daily noon–3pm; Brunch Sat–Sun from 9.30am
Bill E $15–$18 **M** $24–$29 **D** $13–$15; 10% surcharge on Sundays & public holidays
Cards AE BC DC MC V
Wine A short but user-friendly list; 11 by the glass
Chef Mark Vlcek
Owner Brien Trippas
Seats 130; private rooms; wheelchair access; outdoor seats
www.trippaswhite.com.au
And…try the toasted brioche and eggs Benedict for a weekend brunch

Brass Razoo

533 Willoughby Road, Willoughby
Tel 9958 5734   Map 7

Contemporary

Score 14/20

The shopfront is unassuming; the interior welcoming, restrained and elegant. This is the very model of that special species of suburban restaurant, where a husband-and-wife team cares for front and back of house, and consistent standards are rewarded by loyal followers and an invariably full house – with which they cope admirably. The menu is well balanced and lifted by clever touches. Baba ghanoush is an unexpectedly apt partner for nori rolls of minced prawns, and sweet Chinese sausage enhances a chicken and sweet corn soup with kernels crunchily intact. Caramel chilli sauce lifts the red-braised pork hock with Asian greens, while tea-smoked salmon wrapped in pancetta is cushioned by a potato pikelet with a stab of wasabi. Ice-cream means five dreamily smooth scoops of the day: say strawberry with balsamic, coffee, passionfruit, pistachio, and honeycomb. If the food sometimes calls for a little more oomph, this will surely come. With 10 years' dedication behind them, we'll be looking for Brass Razoo in the 2016 *Guide*.

Hours Dinner Tues–Sat 6.30–10pm
Bill E $16.50 **M** $26 **D** $10
Cards AE BC DC MC V
Wine The cannily chosen wine list continues to impress as it grows; 9 by the glass; BYO (corkage $5 per bottle)
Chef Anthony Fischbeck
Owners Anthony Fischbeck & Sharnette Jol
Seats 45
And…do not go past the pie of the day

city + suburbs

Brown Sugar Nights

106 Curlewis Street, Bondi
Tel 9130 1566 Map 9

Contemporary

Score 13/20

The team behind Brown Sugar, one of Bondi's better cafes, has now opened one of the suburb's better restaurants. The back-lit coloured jam jars and kitchen skills will be familiar to the coffee crowd, but Nights takes things up a notch, adding wine to the noisy, neighbourly appeal that's also prominent at its elder North Bondi sibling. The menu is varied – five entrées, seven mains and three desserts seasonally driven and very well priced. Entrées might include duck pâté and pear salsa; figs with prosciutto and salsa verde; and salmon carpaccio. Then there's the pure comfort food: duck confit with caramelised figs and thyme roesti; a generous fish pie with fennel and truffle oil; and chargrilled beef fillet with mash. We'd happily order them again and again. Figs reappear in an excellent tart with mascarpone, the only disappointment being that we'd actually ordered the chocolate mousse. Hopefully there'll be more than one on the floor to cope with the heat next time things are pumping.

Hours Dinner summer Mon–Sat 6–10pm, winter Tues–Sat 6–10pm
Bill E $10–$15 **M** $20–$30 **D** $10–$11
Cards BC MC V Eftpos
Wine Well-priced, interesting list; 6 by the glass; BYO (corkage $6 per bottle)
Chefs James Clarke & Nickolai Alexeeff
Owners James & Toni Clarke
Seats 45; outdoor seats
And... dine early or late to avoid noise

Bukhara

Upstairs, 55 Bay Street, Double Bay
Tel 9363 5510 Map 4A

Mauritian/Indian

Score 13/20

A large, bright space one flight above street level where cane chairs and slate flooring provide a Caribbean touch but where India dominates the menu. There's spirited debate at one table about where Mauritius is, exactly, but it takes a birthday celebration elsewhere to bring to life a quiet night midweek. In the 16 years since Bukhara opened, Indian has become commonplace around town, but the menu's Mauritian touches remain a worthy point of difference. Entrées such as black-pepper calamari cooked in the tandoor, steamed crab and duck farata – well-spiced and shredded roast duck meat wrapped in a paratha – reveal the cuisine's French, Creole and Indian influences. The spicing elsewhere is Indian but the intensity milder, as in the spicy Creole prawn cameron curry, perfect for mopping up with naan; and Mauritian lamb, a dry curry of young lamb, peas, potatoes and cauliflower. Prices are reasonable for the neighbourhood and the service is friendly.

Hours Dinner daily 5.30–10.30pm
Bill E $6.90–$11.90 **M** $14.90–$21.90 **D** $6–$9
Cards AE BC DC MC V Eftpos
Wine Reasonable, mid-range list; 10 by the glass; BYO (corkage $3 pp)
Chef/owner Vijay Baboo
Seats 80
And... India's own Kingfisher lager on the wine list

28 good food guide

city + suburbs B

Buon Ricordo

108 Boundary Street, Paddington
Tel 9360 6729   Map 2

Italian

Score 16/20

If it wasn't for landlord troubles about 20 years back, Armando Percuoco would be well into his third decade at the same restaurant. No matter, because Buon Ricordo feels like it's been in Boundary Street since the fall of Rome, with its classic rendered façade, faded tapestry at the entry, and timeless padded chairs. The menu, however, isn't set in *pietra*. The signature favourites – figs with gorgonzola sauce, the truffled egg fettuccine – are joined by more recent, and arguably better, additions. It could be an amazing stuffed penne mound, filled with quail eggs, meatballs and peas. It could be triangular fresh pasta with an intense and delectable veal ragù. Or it could even be new head chef Massimo Bianchi's semolina gnocchi. Percuoco's hospitality remains as boisterous and seductive as the legend that surrounds it. The prices are still stratospheric and the wine list has never looked more seductive. The food is richer than it needs to be, but if you've space (and you should always have space) the mille mele is a seriously wonderful apple pud.

Hours Lunch Fri–Sat noon–3pm; Dinner Tues–Sat 6.30–11pm
Bill E $19–$29.50 **M** $36.50–$47.50 **D** $17.50; dégustation menu $110 pp
Cards AE BC DC MC V
Wine Stunning list, heavy Italian emphasis, plenty of local legends, all at legendary prices; 15 by the glass
Chefs Armando Percuoco & Massimo Bianchi
Owners Armando Percuoco & Gemma Cunningham
Seats 100; private room
www.buonricordo.com.au
And...expect to see the occasional Roman dish from recent addition Massimo Bianchi

buzo

3 Jersey Road, Woollahra
Tel 9328 1600   Map 4B

Italian

Score 14/20

It's been an almost seamless move from the bottom of Jersey Road to the top, near Oxford Street, for this modern Italian trattoria. It's a much smarter space, with gorgeous timber steps leading from the ground-floor dining room to a smaller space above. The colour scheme is all soft browns, greys and greens; the walls are lined with wine racks and the tables topped with white paper. Grilled figs with buffalo mozzarella show textbook use of excellent produce. Valpolicella risotto is a *cucina povera* variation on fair Verona's amarone version, the red wine sending the rice deep purple – although Buzo's rice remained overtly crunchy. While we don't miss the gingham from the old Buzo, sometimes we do pine for a little more of the '*vecchio paese*' in the dishes. We'd rather not endure mushroom lasagne 'truffled' with truffle oil instead of Umbria's finest, but excellent raspberries with meringue show a sensibility that has us yearning for more.

Hours Dinner Mon–Sat 6pm–late
Bill E $14.50–$15.50 **M** $21.50–$27 **D** $8.50–$13.50
Cards AE BC DC MC V
Wine Modern, boutique-laden list with a tilt to Italy and Italian styles; 13 by the glass
Chefs James Hird & Todd Garratt
Owners Traci Trinder, James Hird & Todd Garratt
Seats 70
www.buzorestaurant.com
And...book early as it's just as busy since the move

city + suburbs

Cafe Mint

579 Crown Street, Surry Hills
Tel 9319 0848   Map 3B

North African

Score 14/20

Potato and roast garlic ravioli never tasted so good – or so Middle Eastern. Topped with spicy lamb mince, sweet red onions, black pepper and pine nuts, the richness of the dish is cut by the cleansing acidity of mint yoghurt. Hugh Foster cooks with his heart and a sensitivity to North African culture, so flavours and combinations ring true. Mechoui plate is an appealing selection of smoky chicken, lamb kofta and merguez sausages (made with a spice mix by Vic's Meats) with bread and tzatziki, though the fattoush was lacklustre, with disappointing tomatoes and undefined dressing. Saffron shows clever restraint in ice-cream dotted with nougat and pistachios, finished with walnut filo wafers and tufts of pashmak (Persian fairy floss). While the staff may not be as informed, they are friendly – and the whole experience is customer-focussed. Eat breakfast (try the sweet couscous) any time of day, or pop in for a frappe at the communal table in the long, wood-panelled space beneath a photographic mural of Middle Eastern dining.

Hours Mon–Sat 7am–5pm; Dinner Tues–Wed until 9.30pm, Thurs–Fri until 10.30pm
Bill E $6.50–$11.50 **M** $14.50–$21.90 **D** $5.50–$8.50; 10% surcharge on public holidays
Cards None; no bookings
Wine BYO (corkage $2 pp)
Chefs Hugh Foster & Peter Xuereb
Owner Hugh Foster
Seats 40; outdoor seats
www.cafemint.com.au
And...the mezze plate is perennially popular

Café Sel et Poivre

263 Victoria Street, Darlinghurst
Tel 9361 6530   Map 2

French

Score 13/20

Café Sel et Poivre is everything a first-time traveller might hope Paris to be: friendlier and much more easygoing than you've been led to believe. This sunny, street-side bistro oozes bonhomie, chiefly from the exuberant maître d' and co-owner Daniel Perchey, who somehow seems to get younger (and for that matter cheekier) with every visit. This immensely popular Darlo bistro is still attracting newcomers but these days it enjoys a faithful following of fans for its consistency, value and generally efficient, if occasionally erratic, service. Open from breakfast to dinner, the joint really comes alive at night, serving competent, though not outstanding, Gallic favourites, such as veal casserole à la provençale with spring vegetables and mashed potato, and, yes, gratinated snails with parsley and garlic butter. There's also (somewhat less successful) fish of the day and a few un-French pasta dishes. If you hanker for a classic, cooked-to-order pepper steak with requisite frites (and, aside from the odd vegan, who doesn't?) Sel et Poivre delivers one of Sydney's most reliable.

Hours Breakfast daily 7am–3pm; Lunch daily 11am–3pm; Dinner daily 6pm–late
Bill E $8.90–$15.90 **M** $15.50–$29.50 **D** $12.90; 10% surcharge on public holidays
Cards AE BC DC MC V
Wine Standard list of locals (plus a few Gallic imports); 16 by the glass
Chef Olivier Mauchien
Owners Daniel Perchey & Olivier Mauchien
Seats 70; outdoor seats
www.selp.citysearch.com.au
And...match wits between courses with wisecracking French owner, Daniel

city + suburbs

Cafe Sopra

7 Danks Street, Waterloo
Tel 9699 3174   Map 9

Italian

Score 14/20

This upstairs eatery in a trendy precinct continues to go beyond the call of duty, providing enchanting food at great prices while remaining resolutely relaxed. The big warehouse space above Fratelli Fresh is casually whitewashed, features high Gothic windows and still believes that tables should be generously spaced so you can speak with, rather than shout at, your companions. Chef Andy Bunn has lost none of his skill in doing simple things beautifully. Roast chicken with lemon and broccolini is just that: both bird and brassica are fresh, moist and tender. Seafood casarecce sings of the sea, and juicy prawns are mouth-wateringly complemented by avocado salsa and a tart tomato dressing. Fittingly, the most basic dish on the menu – frittata with goat's curd and fresh sage – is perhaps the best: perfect, velvety eggs and creamy curd, cooked to order. Thankfully you'll have room around the table to loosen a few buttons and try dessert: perhaps gelato – made on the premises – or the fantastic steamed cheesecake with cinnamon and peach.

Hours Tues–Fri 10am–3pm; Sat 8am–3pm
Bill E $12.50–$14.50 **M** $16–$18 **D** $1.50–$9
Cards AE BC MC V Eftpos; no bookings
Wine BYO (no corkage); look out for the upcoming wine list
Chef Andy Bunn
Owner Fratelli Fresh
Seats 50
And... you can get takeaway, or buy the ingredients for almost everything you've eaten upstairs, downstairs

Cafe Sydney

Level 5, Customs House, 31 Alfred Street, Circular Quay
Tel 9251 8683   Map 1

Contemporary

Score 12/20

Walk in to this top-floor restaurant in beautiful, historic Customs House perched opposite Circular Quay, and you know you're in one of the best cities in the world. While the interior is grand, eating on the verandah is iconic Sydney: Opera House, Bridge and large vessels. The only disappointment is that the food struggles to live up to the view. A mound of well-cooked baby octopus was lost amidst an overpowering salad of avocado with tahini dressing. Delicate barramundi with baba ghanoush was let down by the taste of burnt molasses. Spaghettini with truffled cream, however, satisfies: the creaminess offset by plump peas and asparagus. And also on the money is summer pudding with yoghurt and honey ice-cream, and the passionfruit crème brûlée with poached pear. Staff continue to look after your every need as city office workers and tourists put on their sunnies to reflect the glare of this beautiful view.

Hours Mon–Fri noon–11pm; Sat 5–11pm; Sun noon–4pm
Bill E $19.50–$26 **M** $26–$39 **D** $16
Cards AE BC DC MC V
Wine Solid Aussie list; 24 by the glass
Chefs Nino Borgo & Dudley Wood
Owner Customs House Cafe Pty Ltd
Seats 200; private room; wheelchair access; outdoor seats
www.cafesydney.com
And... there's a great bar for pre- or post-dinner drinks

city + suburbs

Catalina Rose Bay

1 Sunderland Avenue, Lyne Park, Rose Bay
Tel 9371 0555   Map 9

Contemporary

Score 15/20

In a city blessed with more than its fair share of iconic dining locations, Catalina is one of the best and not afraid to flaunt it. The gentle arc of the modern, uncluttered room offers sweeping views of the glistening harbour as the seaplanes and yachts glide by and a proud pelican patrols the balcony awaiting the post-lunch fish scraps. With so much sunshine, it's a shame the only clouds come with occasionally saturnine service. While there's plenty for the piscatorially inclined, such as Sydney rock oysters shucked to order, chef Paul McMahon is generous to fans of darker proteins, including lush, pie-sized braised duck ravioli topped with a nameko mushroom ragù and the decadent flourish of porcini butter. Poached lobster salad with fresh figs, peas and spiced miso is a colourful interplay of fresh and fragrant sweetness, while grilled john dory delights in a Mediterranean mix of roasted tomato, artichoke and tarragon. With excellent cheeses to accompany another bottle from a sterling list, kick back, relax, and drink in that view.

Hours Lunch daily noon–5pm; Dinner Mon–Sat 5pm–late

Bill E $25–$29 **M** $33–$40 **D** $16–$18; 10% surcharge on Sundays & public holidays

Cards AE BC DC MC V

Wine Brilliant and endlessly interesting mix of local and European; 23 by the glass

Chef Paul McMahon

Owners Michael & Judy McMahon

Seats 150; outdoor seats

www.catalinarosebay.com.au

And…brilliant sushi and sashimi from Yoshinori Fuchigami available Wed–Sun

Certo Ristorante

340 Kent Street, Sydney
Tel 9290 1145   Map 1

Italian

Score 13/20

If you've ever wondered what the words antipasto, insalata mista and carpaccio look like written in Japanese, this is the place to find out. In a handsome wood-lined dining room overlooking Kent Street the friendly staff are Japanese and 70 per cent of the clientele is too. The Japanese adore Italian cuisine – as any visit to Tokyo will attest – so the chef puts a broad smile on every face with a simple, appetising linguine vongole made from Tassie clams and garnished with salty, mysterious bottarga. Perfectly pink agnello arrosto (roast lamb cutlets) are flavoured with white wine, roasted garlic cloves, smoky pine nuts and seasonal vegies. How on earth does a Japanese chef make us nostalgic for the old boot? Finish with the popular tiramisu or maybe zuppa di fragole con spumante (marinated strawberries and strawberry purée topped with Asti spumante) and find your disbelief suspended permanently. You haven't seen the world until you've watched a Japanese businessman eat spaghetti carbonara with a spoon.

Hours Lunch Mon–Fri noon–2.30pm; Dinner Mon–Sat 6–9.30pm

Bill E $7.50–$22 **M** $26–$30 **D** $9–$18; dégustation menu 4/6/8 courses $44/$66/$88

Cards AE BC DC MC V Eftpos

Wine Extensive, well-priced list including French and Italians; 8 by the glass; BYO (corkage $10 per bottle)

Chef Tatsuya Yakabe

Owner Ritsuko Yumikake

Seats 90; private room

www.certo.com.au

And…on a sunny day ask staff to open the big front windows onto Kent Street

city + suburbs (c)

The Chelsea Tea House

2/48 Old Barrenjoey Road, Avalon
Tel 9918 6794   Map 7

Contemporary

Score 13/20

A lustrous rainbow lorikeet pinches a sachet of sugar. Phew! It keeps off the king prawns and clams tangled in a bowl of fettuccine. This tea house, a relaxed little front garden courtyard with crazy paving and twisted bougainvillea, serves an all-day menu many notches above usual cafe fare. It could be crumbed and beautifully browned pilchard fillets, deliciously crisp and perched on leaves with radish, shaved fennel and orange. The esteemed Lucienne Francisco could be serving rocket with chorizo and poached egg for brunch to locals chatting about travel plans, the children or buying off the plan. There's an intimate room for nighttime dining on weekends when the place really shows what it can do. Most come earlier, in summer dresses or wet cossies, for coffee in dappled sunshine and service that's unfussed ('guys', 'no drama', 'cool'). There's the odd miscue – a lifeless egg and potato hash with gruyère cheese, perhaps – but all's forgotten and forgiven when sweets are served. Very Pearl Bay and *Home & Away*. BYO sunnies.

Hours Daily 8.30am–4pm; Fri–Sat 6.30–9pm
Bill E $12–$16 **M** $20–$28 **D** $7–$9 (lunch is cheaper)
Cards None; bookings essential
Wine BYO (corkage $5 per table)
Chef/owner Lucienne Francisco
Seats 30; outdoor seats
And... teas sold by the bag include Formosa oolong, Darjeeling organic, jasmine, sencha or plain old Earl Grey

Chequers

Shop 200–220, Mandarin Centre,
65 Albert Avenue, Chatswood
Tel 9904 8388   Map 7

Chinese (Cantonese)

Score 14/20

Chatswood is an increasingly safe bet for reliably smart Chinese, but shopping centres aren't usually synonymous with good food. It takes Chequers to put the two together successfully. Cloth serviettes, fresh flowers, attentive and helpful service, a relaxed atmosphere and decent wine by the glass lift everything well above the average suburban standard. The fish tanks at the entrance and along the back wall, plus a supplementary menu of live seafood, signal they're serious. Small live prawns, simply steamed, are sweet and springy with a soy dipping sauce. Scallops in a meaty but not too spicy XO sauce are rich, oily and more-ish. Non-aquatic dishes are just as appealing: five spice-baked chicken has crisply glazed skin and succulent flesh. Even the ubiquitous salt-and-pepper tofu is a winner – just one of the many lessons in the clarity of flavour and contrast of textures that makes Chequers so popular from yum cha until well after sundown.

Hours Lunch Mon–Fri 11am–3pm, Sat–Sun & public holidays 10am–3pm; Dinner Mon–Sat 5.30–11pm, Sun & public holidays 5.30–10pm
Bill E $5.80–$30 **M** $16.80–$25 **D** $5–$20; more for seafood; $2.50 per adult, $1 per child surcharge on public holidays
Cards AE BC DC MC V
Wine Limited list with some good wines at good prices; 10 by the glass including a couple of decent options; BYO (corkage $4 pp)
Chef Sum Chow
Owners Tong Lau & Winkie Chan
Seats 300; private rooms; wheelchair access
And... they have a short menu of specials

city + suburbs

CherriJam

16–18 Cross Street, Double Bay
Tel 9363 0555 Map 4A

Contemporary

Score 13/20

What at first appears to be a very dark, London-style bar – standard lamps, glistening chandeliers, expansive booths that gaze across the room beyond the bar and a clever wine list – turns out to double as a diner of some note. The seemingly private upstairs space, off an average street in ultra-staid Double Bay, plays host to plenty of lithe young things in slinky togs and their sculpted suitors. They purse and preen and order the $50 a head 'graze', and get a sample of things to share. Or they order larger versions of the same dishes from the menu, perhaps quail sausage with fresh fig and walnuts. Or crisped pork belly paired with crab. The roasted barramundi with eggplant caviar is lifted by a salty and lightly bitter tapenade. While the flash-fried squid with aïoli could have retained less aroma of the deep-fryer, the essential simplicity of iceberg salad – dressed appropriately skimpily with little more than eschalot vinegar – is very fine indeed.

Hours Dinner Wed–Sun 6–11pm; Supper 11pm–2am
Bill E $16–$24 **M** $26–$33 **D** $12; 10% surcharge on public holidays
Cards AE BC DC MC V Eftpos
Wine Good-quality brands, well selected, almost all (22) by the glass
Chef Karl Friederich
Owners Mark Knight, Mez Sheahan & Martin Graham
Seats 64; private room
www.cherrijam.com.au
And... you don't need to be young to dine here, but it certainly doesn't hurt

Chez Pascal

250 Rocky Point Road, Ramsgate
Tel 9529 5444 Map 8

French Provincial

Score 12/20

Forget that nouvelle cuisine ever existed – this is pure, old-fashioned French cooking. It's Larousse not Bocuse here, with all the heavy flour, butter and cream-based sauces that messieurs Bocuse, Troisgros and Guérard vowed to eliminate back in the 1970s. A special of seafood au gratin has flavoursome and fresh-peeled bug meat, prawns and scallops swimming in a cheesy baked béchamel. The rib of beef is a perfectly trimmed piece of prime meat, cooked rare and drowning in a rich brown sauce with three vegies incongruously sharing the same fate. The signature dish of slow-cooked beef cheeks is huge, with two whole cheeks atop a good potato mash, all on a bed of sticky brown gravy. These cheeks are correctly gelatinous, rich in flavour and exceptional value at $16.50. The cooking may be yesterday, but the quality of the produce is first rate, and when owner/chef Philippe bellows at the top of his lungs from the open kitchen, 'Is everybody 'appy?' everyone shouts back 'Oui!'

Hours Dinner Tues–Sat 7–9.30pm
Bill E $6.50–$21 **M** $16–$26.50 **D** $9.50–$12.50
Cards BC DC MC V Eftpos
Wine BYO (corkage $1.50 pp)
Chef Philippe Lebreux
Owners Philippe, Yolande & Pascal Lebreux
Seats 44
And... no children on weekends

city + suburbs

China Doll

4/6 Cowper Wharf Road, Woolloomooloo
Tel 9380 6744   Map 2

Modern Asian

Score 13/20

From the old XO came the new China Doll with several familiar floor staff, chefs and dishes (Malaysian-style son-in-law eggs, pipis in XO sauce). A table on the wharf is very Sydney and very pleasant in all but the most inclement weather, and the open, modern Halliday design – dominated by a large, etched-glass wall in blue willow china pattern – suits the bright young things who come to see and be seen. Although the menu is divided into entrées, mains and sides, this is food best shared. Produce is fresh and top quality and presentation is smart. Simple classics such as salt-and-pepper tofu, prawn wontons and chilli salt squid are all above average. Crisp pork belly with blood lime, caramel and chilli is a textured delight, crisp crackling encasing melt-in-the-mouth meat; while white-cut chicken coleslaw is cool and fresh but a little sweet. In fact, sweet remains the dominant taste among the savoury dishes. If you still need more sweetening, sago pudding and passionfruit is a refreshing and memorable dessert.

Hours Lunch Mon–Sat noon–3pm, Sun noon–4pm; Dinner Mon–Sat 6–10.30pm, Sun 6–10pm
Bill E $14–$22 **M** $25–$38 **D** $10–$12; 10% surcharge on Sundays & public holidays
Cards AE BC DC MC V
Wine Good range of appropriate wines (local and imports), little under $40; 19 by the glass
Chef Tané Malcolm
Owner W-Retail Pty Ltd
Seats 140; private room; outdoor seats
www.chinadoll.com.au
And...an interesting cocktail list – try the honey and salt margarita

Chinta Ria...Temple of Love

Level 2, The Roof Terrace, Cockle Bay Wharf, Darling Park, 201 Sussex Street, Sydney
Tel 9264 3211   Map 1

Modern Malaysian

Score 12/20

A giant, beaming Buddha squats over a bowl of floating frangipanis and several sticks of fragrant incense, staring blissfully out over Darling Harbour. This is the centrepiece of Chinta Ria's pagoda, nowadays looking a little spent although a fitting image to greet the tourist hordes and city slickers. The food is labelled 'hawker-style' – perhaps a starting point rather than a destination – and the groovy beats 'DJ jazz'. Both elements help name many a dish on a menu that includes plenty of deep-fried entrées such as Ella's Wrap: stuffed prawns in crispy spring roll wraps; or lohbak: minced chicken in beancurd skin. King Toh beef was full of flavour, if overly sweet and, like the roti, a little oily. Scallops tossed with curry powder, butter and asparagus are better – naturally moist and bouncy fresh. Service can feel detached, but then again with so much activity – this is one busy hawker's nest – it is best to be like the beaming big guy and just sit back, chill out and spread the love.

Hours Lunch daily noon–2.30pm; Dinner Mon–Sat 6–11pm, Sun 6–10.30pm
Bill E $6.80–$9 **M** $12.50–$26 **D** $7.50; 10% surcharge on public holidays
Cards AE BC DC MC V; bookings lunch only
Wine Lucky dip of all sorts; 24 by the glass; BYO (corkage $6 per bottle)
Chef Donny Pang
Owner Simon Goh
Seats 160; wheelchair access; outdoor seats
www.chintaria.com
And...reserve an outdoor table at lunch

city + suburbs

Clareville Kiosk

27 Delecta Avenue, Clareville
Tel 9918 2727   Map 7

Contemporary
                                Score 14/20

It's easy to overlook this stayer, tucked in an unlikely corner of the Northern Beaches. Despite the fact that there are no water views, there's a sense of Pittwater in the air at this 70-year-old weatherboard cottage. Don't be fooled by the name; this is no longer a pie and a Magnum kind of kiosk, rather a casual restaurant of quite some note. Steven Proctor's reliably deft modern food is served in a room dressed with floral pictures and tables dressed with white linen. Similarly dressed diners tuck into appetisers of diced raw tuna served in Chinese spoons, or slices of the same yellow fin bordered by Sichuan pepper with celeriac remoulade and a whisper of horseradish. Chunks of duck confit are brightened with pickled cucumber in curious and unnecessary open ravioli. Blushing pink venison is dewily moist, teaming effortlessly with the racy natural acidity of beetroot, while a wedge of white chocolate ice threaded with buttery sweet caramelised macadamias is a thrilling finish.

Hours Lunch Sun noon–3pm; Dinner Wed–Sun 6–10.30pm

Bill E $17.50–$22.50 **M** $27.50–$36.50 **D** $14

Cards AE BC DC MC V

Wine A tiny but well picked list with just about everything under $40; 2 by the glass; BYO (corkage $10 per bottle)

Chef Steven Proctor

Owner Tanya Deer

Seats 40

www.clarevillekiosk.com

And...sit by the open windows on balmy nights

Claude's

10 Oxford Street, Woollahra
Tel 9331 2325   Map 4B

Modern French
                                Score 18/20

Other restaurants sway with fickle fashions, but not Claude's. Change is rare here, so when long-time chef Tim Pak Poy left the kitchen in 2004 to make way for his Malaysian–Chinese sous chef, Chui Lee Luk, devotees of fine dining nervously waited to see what would alter at the altar. The answer is: not much. The small room remains timelessly serene with well-spaced tables and Limoges dinnerware on the walls. The food remains French with modern accents, a showcase for virtuoso technique and complex flavours – sauces, in particular, really highlight Luk's superlative talent. Asia meets France, but neither is trying to outdo the other; rather there's a harmony lesser chefs only dream about. Stand-outs are the sumptuous seared wagyu fillet, inspired by the medicinal dishes Luk watched people eating on a trip to China, and the Aylesbury duck with a sauce from the press. Desserts are sensational, especially the mango soufflé, a lesson in airy perfection, served with mango and Drambuie cream – some things are best left unchanged (such as the smoked salmon consommé featured on our cover). Claude's remains one of the most polished dining experiences in town.

Hours Dinner Tues–Sat from 7.30pm

Bill 3-course dinner $135 pp; tasting menu $165 pp

Cards AE BC DC MC V; bookings essential

Wine Short but seriously good list of moderately priced French and Australian wines; up to 10 by the glass; BYO (corkage $15 per bottle)

Chef/owner Chui Lee Luk

Seats 44; private room; wheelchair access

www.claudes.org

And...service is unobtrusive and near faultless

For those who love design (and perfect results).

You're looking at the 800 Class by Breville. Each design is made from tough, 21st Century materials including commercial grade stainless steel. Each is made to do the job in a clean, simple and effective manner, with the power to perform, and do it with minimum effort. *The 800 Class Espresso* can deliver the perfect crema, with an intelligent system of pre brew, and auto purge. *The 800 Class Citrus Press* is so

M&P B3645 GFG L

versatile it can squeeze juice from a tiny green lime to a giant pink grapefruit. *The 800 Class Professional Grill* converts from a contact grill to an open barbeque. *The 800 Class Commercial Juicer* is the one that can take whole apples. Best of all, each of the Breville 800 Class range looks at home in the classiest of kitchens.

www.breville.com.au

M&P B3645 GFG R

city + suburbs

The Clock Hotel

470 Crown Street, Surry Hills
Tel 9331 5333   Map 3B

Modern Mediterranean

Score 14/20

Tick-tock, tick-tock. At 6.50pm in Surry Hills the clocks downstairs say it's 10.56 in Damascus, 8.52 in Reykjavik, 6.20 in Limerick. Seems nobody's keeping the time – they're all out considerably. Thankfully the upstairs dining room of this popular pub is in sync, under the sure hand of journeyman chef Trevor Schneider (most recently ex-bills) who in the past year has fine-tuned his seasonal menus, each set to a rhythm of prime cuts and choice ingredients. The mostly 30-something crowd – arriving post meridian in dressy shirts and frocks, dabbed in perfume – sipping cocktails are happy scoffing lightly crumbed buffalo mozzarella fritters with thickly sliced tomato and basil. The simple cooking, like the buzz, is smart but casual. Compliments to the chef for the grilled steak cuts, the baked hapuka fillet with velvety potato and chive mash, the roasted duck with braised mushrooms, the bug risotto, the good-sized servings, the warmed plates, the contentment, the pub food a good many rungs above grub. Artwork is appealing, and service runs like, well...clockwork.

Hours Lunch Mon–Fri noon–3pm; Dinner Mon–Fri 6–10pm; Sat–Sun all day from noon
Bill E $13.50–$16.50 **M** $24.50–$27.50 **D** $5.50–$9.50
Cards AE BC DC MC V; bookings essential
Wine Varied list of mostly Oz boutique labels (e.g. Ten Minutes by Tractor); 17 by the glass
Chef Trevor Schneider
Owner Solotel Pty Ltd
Seats 80; outdoor seats
www.clockhotel.com.au
And... there are $7 cocktails 6–7pm nightly at the Balcony Bar

Coast

The Roof Terrace, Cockle Bay Wharf,
201 Sussex Street, Sydney
Tel 9267 6700   Map 1

Contemporary

Unscored

We've always been a fan of Coast, with its effortless grace at making business diners, abandoned lovers and stray tourists feel at home. Looking out over Cockle Bay, the mood is all restrained panache, conservative elegance and ever-reliable food. There's a satisfactory hum even when the place is only partly full and it's a great date restaurant; the welcome smile on arrival is one of the warmest in town. As you gaze out of the gloriously large wall of timber-framed windows that angle away at the top, waiters glide like swans between banquettes. This year, we found standards pleasantly high, though the years had started to show in the décor. As we go to press, however, plans are afoot for a spruce-up, including the menu. Steve Manfredi, chef at the owners' now-hatted other restaurant, Manta, is due to add his modern Italian flourish to the kitchen after the *Guide* hits the presses. We're happy, so long as we can continue to finish a meal with that excellent and elegantly thin pear tart.

Hours Lunch Mon–Fri noon–2.30pm; Dinner Mon–Sat 6–10.30pm
Bill E $18–$26 **M** $29–$38 **D** $15; 10% surcharge on Sundays & public holidays
Cards AE BC DC MC V
Wine Long, lovely list with great pinots, at reasonable mark-ups; 12 by the glass
Chefs Steve Manfredi & Hamish Pollitt
Owners Tim Connell & Michael McCann
Seats 260; private room; wheelchair access; outdoor seats
www.coastrestaurant.com.au
And... Manta's Steve Manfredi is revamping the menu as we go to press

good food guide   37

city + suburbs

Cochin

61 Fitzroy Street, Surry Hills
Tel 9358 5388   Map 3B

French–Vietnamese
Score 14/20

You get a feeling about the contemporary nature of the food at Cochin as you enter via the side glass door; the traditional imposing central doors are purely ornamental. This is the French-influenced cuisine of Vietnam's south-western city of Cochin: five-spice duck à l'orange; wagyu beef with an intense dark, red wine reduction; a cylinder of sourdough bread pudding, but with Connor Phung's personal twist. Everything is carefully composed and prettily presented, from four neat rectangular pillars of minced squid, spiked with pepper and topped with curls of galangal, to the mixed platter of desserts. Flavours are as precise as the white-painted, high-ceiling room; service is brisk and friendly. Two long rows of tables are separated by well-upholstered benches and chairs. Portions can be petite, though a large translucent orange dome of melting pumpkin is huge, sitting in a beguiling, long-simmered vegetable broth. When finally you lift the filter off your glass of fragrant Vietnamese coffee, do remember to stir in the layer of condensed milk.

Hours Dinner daily 6.30–10pm
Bill E $14–$18 **M** $22–$34 **D** $14; Tasting menu $52–$62 pp
Cards BC MC V
Wine BYO (corkage $3 pp)
Chef Connor Phung
Owners Connor Phung & Ian Brice
Seats 50; wheelchair access; outdoor seats
And...attractive courtyard dining

Cottage Point Inn

2 Anderson Place, Cottage Point
Tel 9456 1011   Map 7

Contemporary   ♆
Score 14/20

It's an expedition well worth embarking on: allow 50 minutes by car from the CBD, or opt for a seaplane, water taxi or ferry, or moor your own yacht. However you land, this water's-edge setting is a tranquil haven that retains the charm of its origins as Cottage Point Boatshed, with a canoe suspended from the ceiling inside, and outside a deck that offers the ultimate Sunday lunch setting. Seafood dominates the menu with some bold unions such as seared rainbow trout on a celeriac, orange and herb salad, with a walnut dressing and sharp salsa of lime, avocado and chilli. Pan-fried Western Australian sardine fillets are sublime, sitting pretty on preserved lemon and currant couscous, with spicy tomato chutney, roti and tzatziki. But the pork seemed to crash the party in a confit of pork belly and duck leg with pear chutney, green peppercorn jus and mint oil, although the flavoursome duck is superb. Layered pineapple, mango and white chocolate parfait matches the perfect vista.

Hours Lunch daily noon–3pm; Dinner Fri–Sat 6.30–9pm, daylight saving Fri–Sun 6.30–9pm
Bill E $16.50–$23 **M** $27–$34.50 **D** $16.50–$21.50; dégustation menu $125 pp; $6.50 pp surcharge on weekends & public holidays
Cards AE BC DC MC V
Wine An impressive and comprehensive range; 9 by the glass
Chef Kevin Kendall
Owners Amanda Cameron & Dan McKinnon
Seats 70; outdoor seats
www.bestrestaurants.com.au/cottagepoint
And...allow time to visit surrounding national parks while you're there

city + suburbs

Credo

504 Miller Street, Cammeray
Tel 9922 6662   Map 5A

Italian

Score 14/20

The first sign was that the place was full to bursting midweek, the second sign was the complimentary taster of exceptionally good cauliflower and leek purée. And by the end of dinner we were left in no doubt as to why this relative newcomer in quiet Cammeray is as popular as a water view in its roadside North Shore location. It's good. Very good, in fact, starting with crisp battered zucchini flowers plump with pumpkin and ricotta stuffing, and the sweetest prawns served with house-made goat's cheese tortellini. Duck is fall-off-the-bone tender and subtly flavoured with star anise, cinnamon and herbs; a staple of tender beef fillet with snap-fresh green beans, mash and red wine jus is slickly executed. A knockout wine list, including nearly 20 pinot noirs and 15 bubblies, beautifully complements former Banc chef Will Smirnios's menu. With its modern interior – cafe-style upstairs, intimate restaurant downstairs – slick service and wallet-friendly prices, we hope there are more Credos on the North Shore very soon.

Hours Tues–Sun 8am–late
Bill E $14–$20 **M** $22–$29 **D** $13; 7.5% surcharge on Sundays, 10% on public holidays
Cards AE BC DC MC V Eftpos
Wine Long, thoughtful, high-quality list, mainly Oz/NZ; plenty of interesting lesser-known drops; over 25 by the glass
Chef William Smirnios
Owners Stella & Michael Tregurtha
Seats 119; private room; wheelchair access; outdoor seats
www.credocafe.com.au
And...drop in for breakfast or a nightcap at the bar

Cucina 105

105 Moore Street, Liverpool
Tel 9602 1300   Map 6

Italian

Score 12/20

What a joy it is to find such a smart, modern restaurant in too-often-neglected Liverpool. With its polished-concrete floors, louvred windows, plus slatted timber screening a delicate rock garden, it really has the goods in the looks department. On one side, the roof opens up on good days, while the friendly, mostly pizza- and pasta-focused menu is written on the opposite wall. Despite our experience of a spiky-haired waiter who seemed short-sighted, and another smelling too strongly of cigarette smoke, there's still plenty to recommend. An oh-so-nearly al dente penne with a lively puttanesca sauce is perfect for the price. The pizze are excellent, thin and minimalist, and an Italian sausage and cherry tomato calzone is passable. Sadly, the antipasto platter disappointed, slightly chewy eggplant and watery roasted capsicum only just lifted by the addition of sweet milky bocconcini. Lamb cutlets on roasted pumpkin mash seem a long way from the Italian homeland, but are perfect for an Aussie suburb.

Hours Lunch Mon–Fri noon–3pm; Dinner Sun–Thurs 5.30–10pm, Fri–Sat 5.30–11pm
Bill E $11–$15 **M** $21–$26 **D** $7–$10
Cards AE BC MC V Eftpos
Wine Price-focussed list with a handful of Italians; 8 by the glass
Chef Maurizio Cefuentus
Owners Frank & Pasquale Angilletta
Seats 100; private rooms; wheelchair access; outdoor seats
And...separate children's menu available

good food guide   39

VINTAGE
1996
RÉSERVE

DE RÉSERVE
MPAGNE

BYO

The Chelsea Tea House
2/48 Old Barrenjoey Road, Avalon
Tel 9918 6794
Mostly it's a simple outdoor cafe that grows up into a (mostly) outdoor bistro complete with lap rugs at night. Lucienne Francisco's food is all calm elegance, just gagging for a glass of something to wash it down.

Claude's
10 Oxford Street, Woollahra
Tel 9331 2325
Is there a more egalitarian tradition than taking a bottle (or three) to this serene institution? Chui Lee Luk's sublime food demands the best, so lash out to savour the luxury. That Claude's also has a brilliant wine list means the best of both worlds.

Il Tratto Ra Ro Pizzeria
108–110 Majors Bay Road, Concord
Tel 8765 8866
Like a good bottle of red, Il Trat's a spot to kick back, take a satisfying swig and enjoy the moment over easy-going Italian dishes. Everyone's having a good time and, washing it down with a favourite drop. You will too.

La Goulue
17 Alexander Street, Crows Nest
Tel 9439 1640
The Glutton is still here, doing magical French-inclined fare and letting you bring your own wine. The food favours hearty, so bring lusty, buxom wines and try not to do your own version of Moulin Rouge-style high-kick dancing.

La Locanda
65B Macpherson Street, Bronte
Tel 9389 3666
This cosy little mod-Italian joint is the perfect place to park your Vespa and your posterior. Bring something white and savoury to match the eggplant parmigiana or a lively little trebbiano blend to bring out the best in Andrea Vagge's excellent pasta.

Macleay Street Bistro
73A Macleay Street, Potts Point
Tel 9358 4891
Punters pile in for reliable, comforting fare in this cosy space. Because Macleay Street keeps everyone happy, it's no wonder the expensive apartments nearby don't need kitchens.

Manna
Cnr West & Station streets, Petersham
Tel 9568 4644
One of our favourite suburban haunts. Manna has a really good wine list, but allows you to bring your own if you insist. From pie nights to Sunday roast and far more sophisticated everyday fare, it's wine-friendly food lovingly served by people you'd be happy to call friends.

Perama
88 Audley Street, Petersham
Tel 9569 7534
Amazing Greek food that goes way, way beyond moussaka is rare enough in this town. That this place lets you bring your own wine (as well as having a decent list including Greek wines of its own) is just the icing sugar on the kourambiethes.

Relish at Balmain Bug
55 Darling Street, Balmain East
Tel 9810 5510
The 150-year-old Bug's a legend and the Garske family makes everyone feel at home with a well-priced Europe-via-Asia menu. Nick across the road to 60 Darling Street for a suitable drop.

Strangers with Candy
96 Kepos Street, East Redfern
Tel 9698 6000
The colours are bold and the name is cheeky, the service chirpy and the food striking. So take something perky or quirky to quaff, chill out in the courtyard or cosy up at the front, and let the pleasures wash all over you.

city + suburbs

Danks Street Depot

1/2 Danks Street, Waterloo
Tel 9698 2201   Map 9

Contemporary
                                    Score 14/20

When they first opened their cafe in a dodgy part of town and surrounded by factories, Jared Ingersoll and Melanie Starr probably had no idea what they'd started. Now Danks Street has other cafes and an amazing provedore – and the Depot has bloomed too, with a grown-up wine list and doubling in size just to keep up. Thankfully, the honest, flavour-packed food that we loved from Ingersoll remains. It could be (sadly, slightly past al dente) bigoli with sweet, succulent rabbit. Calf's liver arrives with a sticky jus and a fabulous fat slice of chargrilled speck, while shaved braised octopus is perfect with equally fine slivers of fennel. Strawberry breast is aptly named: caramel poached berries are clouded in a gentle mound of nude-pink goat's cheese cream mixture, topped by a glistening and succulent strawberry nipple. The warehouse space still has sky-high ceilings, though now the entry has a long wall feature that looks like a Maori tattoo. And you can drink it all in with a thoughtful wine list.

Hours Breakfast & Lunch Mon–Fri 7.30am–4pm, Sat 8am–4pm; Dinner Tues–Sat 6–10pm; bar menu 4pm–midnight
Bill E $10–$18 **M** $10–$30 **D** $2.50–$10.50
Cards BC MC V Eftpos
Wine Smart, well-priced boutique-driven list; 10 by the glass; BYO lunch only (corkage $3 pp)
Chefs Jared Ingersoll & Penny Williams
Owners Jared Ingersoll & Melanie Starr
Seats 100; wheelchair access; outdoor seats
www.2danksstreet.com.au

And...it's much easier to find a place to park at dinner

Darbar

134a Glebe Point Road, Glebe
Tel 9660 5666   Map 5B

Indian
                                    Score 13/20

Many Indian restaurants on this popular strip are cheap, noisy and fun, but Darbar offers a more refined dining experience and the best Indian in the neighbourhood. The sandstone building has a cathedral-like feel, with arched doorways, a sometimes hushed atmosphere, and service that can be tentative but is always endearing. The menu is extensive and piques your interest, though some dishes pack more punch than others. The lamb vindaloo, for instance, was relatively light on the chilli but more robust than the Madras fish curry (a trifle on the bland side). Much better are the light, crisp dosa or the excellent Darbar chaat, with crisp spinach, potato, chickpeas and swirls of tamarind sauce. There are some fun touches at this restaurant, from the glass-covered hole in the floor with a jeroboam of wine underneath to the pictures of freedom fighters on the wall. It's slightly eccentric, memorable and no more expensive than the rowdy places nearby.

Hours Lunch Tues–Sun noon–2.30pm; Dinner Mon–Fri 5–10.30pm, Sat–Sun 5–11pm
Bill E $8.90–$18.90 **M** $13.90–$17.90 **D** $5.90
Cards AE BC DC MC V
Wine Small, workmanlike list with few surprises; 6 by the glass; BYO (corkage $3 pp)
Chef Bekha Maharjan
Owner Bobba Prakash
Seats 250; private room; wheelchair access
www.darbar.com.au

And...if you're looking for it, remember this is the old Darling Mills

city + suburbs   D

Darcy's

92 Hargrave Street, Paddington
Tel 9363 3706   Map 4B

Italian (Northern)

Score 13/20

Darcy's feels like the best kind of private club: dark wood, blindingly white tablecloths, and the reassuring sense that nothing will ever change. The staff, august masters of their trade led by owner Attilio Marinangeli, are solicitous without being stifling. They decant the wine, divine the need for finger bowls, and make you feel witty when ordering – a generous ability that more fashionable restaurant staff often fail to understand. The food, like most of the patrons, is comfortable and substantial. Carpaccio of beef is served with piquant parmesan; saffron and prawn risotto is bright yellow, well-textured and tastes emphatically of the sea. Veal medallions are tender and the lamb rack is perfectly pink, if a little salty. Vegetables – the same choices distributed to everyone, like boarding school – may arrive slightly overdone (also like boarding school), but pannacotta with orange, firmer and more upright than some pretenders to the name, is all grown up. Loved by its patrons, Darcy's remains a beacon of tradition in our increasingly modern world.

Hours Lunch Mon–Fri noon–3pm; Dinner Mon–Sat 6.30–10.30pm
Bill E $15–$28.50 **M** $30–$49 **D** $10–$11
Cards AE BC DC MC V
Wine Expensive and comprehensive, several Italian; 8 by the glass
Chef Roberto Simeoni
Owner Attilio Marinangeli
Seats 80; private rooms
And…ask about the private cellar

DISH

352 Barrenjoey Road, Newport
Tel 9999 2398   Map 7

Contemporary

Unscored

Consider arriving early, kicking off your shoes and strolling along Newport beach first. But don't think this sexy, glamorous interior – all white and chocolate brown with big bright canvases on the walls, white-cloth'd tables and subtle lighting – is a place for shorts and thongs. There's a cute, well-stocked bar, a banquette lining one wall and foldaway doors that open onto the street, allowing friendly waiters to greet you on the pavement. The food, too, has always been way beyond beach-casual, designed and executed with flair. As we go to press, however, George Francisco is departing for Jonah's, and Paul Greening is taking over the kitchen. After stints at MG Garage and Pier in Sydney, and La Tante Claire in the UK, Greening hopes to bring more precision to his menu of ocean trout ceviche with pink grapefruit foam, roasted blue-eye with a mussel and fennel salad, and a rolled ham hock terrine. Sadly, however, as this change is too late for the 2006 *Guide*, we must leave DISH unscored.

Hours Dinner summer daily, winter Mon–Sat, 6.30–10pm
Bill E $18–$20 **M** $28–$31 **D** $14; 10% surcharge on Sundays & public holidays
Cards AE BC MC V
Wine Well-chosen list including some worthy lesser-known labels; 20 by the glass; BYO except Fri–Sat night (corkage $5 pp)
Chef Paul Greening
Owners Tony Deger, Thomas Olsen & George Francisco
Seats 90; wheelchair access; outdoor seats
And…there's a good bar menu

Divino

70 Stanley Street, East Sydney
Tel 9360 9911   Map 2

Italian

Score 12/20

The inner west may be the heart of Italian dining, but the original Little Italy still remains, along with the romance of this up-market cafe facing onto busy Stanley Street. Even if the service sometimes slows, from your bentwood chair at a white-linen table you can listen to the 1940s music and be amused by the passing array of Marcello Mastriano look-alikes, gym junkies and trendoids. The menu is cafe happy, with plenty of old faves and daily specials, although the results can be mixed. Mussels in a spicy tomato broth were workmanlike. Lightly fried squid with rocket is a deliciously simple combo. Perfectly cooked homemade spinach and ricotta ravioli have pomodoro sauce zing, but a mushroom and chicken risotto was disappointingly gluggy. A slab of juicy porterhouse beef with rosemary potatoes and field mushrooms certainly hits the spot. Fluffy, moist tiramisu with hints of alcohol would bring a smile to the face of an old nonna.

Hours Lunch Mon–Fri noon–3pm; Dinner Mon–Sat 6–10.30pm
Cards AE BC DC D MC V Eftpos
Bill E $9–$16 M $18–$26 D $9–$12
Wine Small Australian and Italian selection; 12 by the glass; BYO (corkage $2.50 pp)
Chefs Felix Rutz & Ryan Haigh
Owners Felix Rutz & Ryan Haigh
Seats 92; private rooms; outdoor seats
And...there's a lovely enclosed courtyard out the back

Dome

First Floor, ArtHouse Hotel, 275 Pitt Street, Sydney
Tel 9284 1230   Map 1

Contemporary

Score 13/20

Walking up the stairs, past the bar, to this first-floor restaurant you're confronted by a fusion of styles. From old-world art deco to sleek city nightclub minimalism to a fresco dome that dominates the ceiling of the large, distinguished dining room that once housed an art school. Somehow though, it all seems to work. Service is efficient and agreeable from black-clad waiters who wield good wine lists and a menu with Italian influences. A buzz infects the room as businessmen, tourists and ladies lunch while Ella Fitzgerald croons. Handmade corzetti pasta with fresh grilled prawns is a knockout when perfectly teamed with asparagus and lifted by fresh chilli bite. Pan-fried Atlantic salmon fillet is delicately cooked, with skordalia, rocket and capers lifting the flavour. A delicious beef fillet, topped with old-style béarnaise, is good, honest fare, and sautéed potatoes and mushrooms are perfect for mopping up the juices. For dessert, coffee crème brûlée rises above the everyday and the macchiato is hot and strong.

Hours Lunch Mon–Fri noon–3pm; Dinner Tues–Sat 6–10pm
Bill E $19–$20 M $28–$32 D $13
Cards AE BC DC MC V
Wine Solid Australian list; 22 by the glass
Chefs Tim Michaels, Franca Manfredi & Frank Manfredi
Owner Liz Willis-Smith
Seats 120; wheelchair access
And...at lunch try Franca Manfredi and her son's delicious pasta

DOV

252 Forbes Street, Darlinghurst
Tel 9360 9594   Map 2

Contemporary

Score 13/20

This cafe-inclined diner on the corner of an 1850s terrace, opposite the old Darlo gaol, is the kind of place you need close by for nights when you want to find solace in good-value comfort food. It's also a top spot to sit street-side and watch the passing parade. Inside, the Spartan beauty balances historic sandstone sensibilities with a few modern flourishes. In the mornings, fuel up on eggs Benedict on brioche, ricotta pancakes and sultana couscous; or swing by for a takeaway Grinders coffee. Lunch is sarnie and salad territory, then it switches to unfussed bistro at day's end. Not everything's on song, but there's plenty to raise a smile. A warm gruyère custard and Turkish toast is richly pleasurable, but corn and shallot cakes were gluggy beneath smoked salmon and herbed mascarpone. Steak and Guinness pie is big, bold and beaut; gently spiced lamb on kumera mash with aïoli salves any workday woes. A self-saucing Frangelico and choccie pud, or a scoop of Nice Cream ice-cream, sends you home contented.

Hours Mon 7am–4pm, Tues 7am–5pm, Wed–Sat 7am–10pm, Sun 9am–3pm
Bill E $8.50–$15 **M** $15.50–$22 **D** $6–$10; 10% surcharge on Sundays & public holidays
Cards AE BC MC V Eftpos
Wine 4 whites, 4 reds; no vintages, but at suburban prices; 2 by the glass; BYO (corkage $3 per bottle)
Chef Jason Powell
Owner Mathew Onions
Seats 50; outdoor seats
And...dine for $25 for two courses before 6.30pm

city + suburbs

Dragon Star Seafood

Level 3, Market City, 9 Hay Street, Haymarket
Tel 9211 8988 Map 3A

Chinese (Cantonese)

Score 13/20

There are three ways to approach dining at this functionally designed Haymarket giant. You join the throng early on weekend mornings for the regular yum cha frenzy. But sometimes you must wait a looong time to be seated. Or you can take the slightly more sedate option of yum cha during the week. Either way you'll enjoy classic Cantonese gow gee filled with fresh prawns; addictive crisp-skin pork; cold and crunchy jellyfish; excellent braised or steamed tripe in a clinging red sauce; tender squid, deep-fried and served with fresh chilli; perhaps a noble saltwater fish, such as coral trout, from the tanks, simply steamed and dressed in light soy, ginger and shallots. Staff are helpful when you're unsure if it's animal, mineral or vegetable on the trolley. The third way to enjoy Dragon Star is to visit at night for fascinating provincial specialities, including bone marrow with '3 Precious' (mushrooms, prawns, snowpeas); superb tofu filled with minced prawn; and classic Hakka-style steamed pork belly with mui choi (preserved mustard leaves).

Hours Lunch Mon–Fri 10am–3pm, Sat–Sun 9am–4pm; Dinner daily 5.30–10.30pm
Bill E $6–$20 **M** $15–$50 **D** $5–$11; $2 pp surcharge on public holidays
Cards BC MC V Eftpos
Wine Commercial list; house wine only by the glass; BYO (corkage $10 per bottle)
Chef Mr Lee
Owner Eddie Ng
Seats 600; private rooms; wheelchair access
And... talk to the fish in the tanks on your way out

East Chinese

Shop 8, 1 Macquarie Street, Circular Quay
Tel 9252 6868 Map 1

Chinese

Score 13/20

No, this isn't the food of Eastern China, rather the dishes China has brought to East Asia, from Mongolian lamb to laksa. In a long menu you'll find Cantonese, Shanghainese, Sichuan, Hakka, Pekingese, and Chiu Chow favourites in generous portions. Even Chinese fish cakes – bouncy, finely minced mousse fried in a patty – have a Thai affinity. Soft-shell crab comes in a succulent chewy, deep-fried pile. And where minced pork is normally an accent to snake beans with chilli, it has equal billing here. The more interesting dishes are the most rewarding. Plump king prawns glisten in a hotpot amidst a handful of basil leaves, the '3A' sauce tempered by a rich splash of black vinegar. The restaurant's clean design makes the most of the setting beneath the colonnades of East Circular Quay, with tables inside the glass walls, outside and almost harbourside. While the ubiquitous desserts include deep-fried ice-cream, we're not sure the Chinese would claim a selection of gelati as their idea originally.

Hours Lunch Mon–Thurs noon–3pm, Fri–Sat noon–5pm; Dinner Sun–Thurs 5–10.30pm, Fri–Sat 5–11.30pm
Bill E $8.80–$27.80 **M** $19.80–$36.80 **D** $8.50; 10% surcharge on public holidays
Cards AE BC DC MC V
Wine Long list (includes Grange and Hill of Grace) and interesting (Farr by Farr Saignee); 20 by the glass
Chef Tony Ma
Owner Lee Ly
Seats 208; outdoor seats
And... try the signature dish: Mandarin duck in chef's special sauce

city + suburbs   E

Eat City

Level 1, 349 Kent Street (cnr King Street), Sydney
Tel 9262 5900   Map 1

Contemporary

Score 13/20

Square plate? Tick. Wood-fired oven? Tick. Share plates, good flavours, interesting wines? Tick away, because Eat City is an upstairs corner-pub dining room of and for our times. It's all ball light fittings, gorgeous parquetry floors and timber bistro chairs facing the corner banquettes. Don't be frightened by the claims that Jeff Schroeter has cooked for Madonna – this is real food, where flavours are bold, ingredients first rate and the results mouth-watering. Garlic bread comes from the aforementioned oven. The tasting menu features tempura-battered prawns, a lively tuna Niçoise and plenty of meaty options. Organic chicken liver pâté is dense, dark and intense, lightened by the presence of pear and mizuna. Duck may come à l'orange or with roasted beetroot and we've enjoyed some perfectly roasted kangaroo, too, sport. Moreton Bay bug tail is served in the shell with carrot sticks, while the mustard-smeared wagyu is superb. We found the dessert trolley overladen with gelatine and dull-flavoured desserts, so stick to the savoury courses and you can't go wrong.

Hours Lunch Mon–Fri noon–4pm; Dinner Wed–Fri 6–11pm
Bill E/M $8–$20 **D** $8; set menu 3 dishes $44 per couple
Cards AE BC DC MC V Eftpos
Wine Really likeable one-pager with a few surprises; 9 by the glass
Chef Jeff Schroeter
Owners Andrew Williams & Jeff Schroeter
Seats 120; private room
www.eatcity.com.au
And...the pub is due for a make-over, but the restaurant already looks the goods

Ecco

Drummoyne Sailing Club, 2 St Georges Crescent, Drummoyne
Tel 9719 9394   Map 8

Italian

Score 13/20

This beautiful, modern glass-wrapped room and all-weather deck offers soothing views across the upper Harbour as thrilling as the wonderfully evocative, modern Italian menu. Friendly service is not always grounded in knowledge, though the welcome is always warm and you don't want for much in the way of attention. Start with good crusty crostini, with interesting mixes of smoked salmon, mushroom, prosciutto and parmesan. Lightly floured, crisp-fried calamari in a classic Amalfi Coast style is full of natural flavour. House-made tagliolini with scampi, vongole and peas has clean and clear flavours that demonstrate remarkable subtlety. Alas our gnocchi was rather gluggy and the meat and tomato ragù lacked personality, while some mains tried too hard, adding unnecessary flavours – like the beef fillet's gorgonzola sauce, and dried figs with pork. There's no doubt the quality shines in every dish, though simpler dishes work best, such as the john dory with salad. And there's nothing finer than the pannacotta and poached pear.

Hours Lunch Tues–Fri & Sun noon–3pm; Dinner Tues–Sat 6–10pm
Bill E $18–$23.50 **M** $28–$34.50 **D** $12–$14
Cards AE BC DC MC V Eftpos
Wine Good medium-size list with a few Italians; 10 by the glass
Chef Vince Mazzotta
Owners Claudio & Carmel Carnevale
Seats 180; private rooms; wheelchair access; outdoor seats
www.ecco.com.au
And...watch the sailing club in action below

city + suburbs

Elio

159 Norton Street, Leichhardt
Tel 9560 9129 Map 5B

Italian

Score 14/20

In a street where there's no shortage of *cucina* of the boot, Elio has always been ahead of the pack. Renovations after the *Guide* went to press promise a less noisy, more comfortable, plush and sophisticated room downstairs, with a new marble bar, timber floors and softer colourings. The make-over will suit the elegance in Robyn Touchard's vibrant pan-Italian menu. Beef carpaccio is lifted by salmoriglio (an olive oil, lemon juice, garlic and oregano dressing) and wild rocket. Braised beef cheeks adorning perfectly al dente casarecce pasta has a lush earthiness. Whole snapper, baked al cartoccio (in paper), is redolent with the scent of roasted fennel and cherry tomatoes with potato. A wonderful inch-thick pork cutlet is cleverly hollowed out and stuffed with the bullish flavours of sausage and mustard fruits. The house-made gelati are tempting, especially the coffee version beside a decadent chocolate and hazelnut praline crostata. With Elio himself suggesting clever tipples from a ripper list, it's hard to say no when he suggests a grappa too.

Hours Dinner daily from 6pm
Bill E $13.50–$15.50 **M** $19.50–$29.90 **D** $7–$11; 10% surcharge on public holidays
Cards AE BC DC MC V
Wine Smart Oz, New Zealand & Italian, plus great reserve list; 7 by the glass; BYO (corkage $5.50 per bottle)
Chef Robyn Touchard
Owners Elio & Daniel Cordaro
Seats 100; private rooms; wheelchair access; outdoor seats
www.elio.com.au
And...there are great cheeses too

Emma's on Liberty

59 Liberty Street, Enmore
Tel 9550 3458 Map 8

Lebanese

Score 13/20

This very popular dining room on busy Liberty Street has its customers pegged. At each sitting, they pack them in like dolmades: along the shared central table or at the smaller ones squeezed down the sides. So be warned: it's noisy, and your neighbours will be very close by. But if you don't mind that, there are some fantastic dishes to sample, such as the succulent, chilli-tinged arak prawns, or the super smoky and smooth baba ghanoush. There aren't too many surprises on the menu, but Emma and Anthony Sofy make classics come alive, such as the vine leaves with a tangy yoghurt sauce, a vibrant tabbouleh and the savoury tenderness of the lamb sis kebab. The room is mercifully free of the usual clichéd Lebanese trappings of belly dancers and hookah pipes. This is a place to come for a well-priced and well-executed meal and some fun times with friends – or the new friends you'll make at the next table.

Hours Dinner Tues–Sat 6pm–late
Bill E $6–$10 **M** $12–$14 **D** $2.50–$6.50; banquet $29 pp
Cards None; bookings essential
Wine BYO (corkage $1.50 pp)
Chefs/owners Anthony & Emma Sofy
Seats 60
And...they really don't take any cards and bookings really are essential

Emperor's Garden BBQ

213 Thomas Street, Haymarket
Tel 9281 9899   Map 3A
Also **Emperor's Garden Seafood**
Level 1, 100 Hay Street (cnr Dixon Street), Haymarket
Tel 9211 2135   Map 3A

Chinese (Cantonese)

Score 12/20

Eating at the Emperor's is about as far from glamorous as Sydney is from Hong Kong. This is fluoro lighting, Laminex table, thick glass tumbler and paper napkin territory, ideal for a big group chow-down, with efficient (albeit finesse-free) service. It's the food that makes this a Chinatown favourite, specifically the robust noodle soups and succulent barbecued meats. Siu gau is a stand-out: a delicate broth full of delicious seafood dumplings. The barbecue fare – including delectable crisp-skinned suckling pig, golden roasted duck and occasionally pigeon and quail – does a massive takeaway trade from the window open to the street. Inside, share a platter of meats or indulge in a menu of Greatest Hits (sadly salt-and-pepper squid and whitebait was disappointing: heavy on batter and light on seafood) and cleansing side dishes such as wok-tossed greens or spinach sautéed with chilli and beancurd. The Hay Street sister version is good for banquets, but beware the live seafood prices.

Hours Daily 9.30am–11pm
Bill E $3–$11 **M** $9–$39 **D** $2.50–$6; $2 pp surcharge on public holidays
Cards AE BC DC MC V
Wine Very limited selection; BYO (corkage $2 pp)
Chef Pang Lam
Owner Stanley Yee
Seats 120
And…portions are huge, so order the small mixed barbecue platter if there are only a few of you

encasa

423 Pitt Street, Sydney
Tel 9211 4257   Map 3A

Spanish

Score 13/20

Take your cue from the winsome Spanish maiden on the poster by the door. You're here not for the pizze and pasta for passing backpackers but for the Spanish side of the menu. The floor is red wood, the walls crème caramel and the chairs iron-backed, with ample space for groups around the corner of the L-shaped room. Linger over tapas, as it takes 45 minutes to prepare your paella. Grilled octopus has good char and bite; garlic prawns keep their bounce. Mushrooms are earthy, chorizo is pleasantly pungent and chewy. Marinated sardine fillets are reminiscent of the boquerones (anchovies) in a Madrid bar. The paella arrives with a rampart of mussel shells and central pile of pipis. Trawl for fish, chicken, calamari and prawns among the firm, chalky rice, rich with sauce – though you may look in vain for a typically crisped bottom. Squid-ink rice has the refreshing tang of a rock pool. And to finish there's banana pudding or a fig crème brûlée that rises above many of its peers.

Hours Lunch Tues–Fri noon–2.30pm; Dinner Mon–Sat 5.30pm–late
Bill E $6.50–$12 **M** $9–$25 **D** $5–$9
Cards AE BC MC V Eftpos
Wine Friendly locals mingle with usual Spanish suspects Caceres and Torres; 8 by the glass; BYO (corkage $1.50 pp plus $2 per bottle)
Chefs Heike Huebner & Alfonso Ojeda Navarro
Owner Heike Huebner
Seats 100
www.encasarestaurant.com
And…order extra bread to mop up the chilli and garlic oil after those prawns

city + suburbs

Epoque

429 Miller Street, Cammeray
Tel 9954 3811 Map 5A
Also **Heritage**
135 Harrington Street, The Rocks
Tel 9241 1775 Map 1

Belgian

Score 12/20

The answer to what to eat with beer used to be a kebab, especially after six schooners. Thankfully, Epoque promises life beyond lager and, even better, the in-crowd's flitted to the Next Big Thing, so getting a table's much easier. The chatter-filled bar buzzes as you settle at timber pews amidst dark wood panelling and pigeon-racing trophies. You don't need to be Hercule Poirot to know the main course is really beer, with mainly comforting, blokey food to soak it up. Efficient, chirpy service knows the right hop for your order. Many tuck in to the mussels, served ten ways – perhaps 'Tintin un Congo' (coconut, lemongrass and chilli). Mushroom and asparagus monk's tart – 'a Middle Ages recipe' – was flayed by flabby pastry. Pickled herring, potato, apple and lettuce salad has perfectly salty acidity for a refreshing Lucifer blonde beer (8 per cent). A kilo of crisp-skinned pork knuckle on stoemp (Belgian bubble and squeak) is no oil painting, but it's succulent and satisfyingly primeval.

Hours Mon–Thurs & Sun noon–10pm; Fri-Sat noon–10.30pm
Bill E $8.50–$16.80 **M** $17.50–$25.50 **D** $9.80; $3 pp surcharge on Sundays
Cards AE BC DC MC V
Wine Surprisingly interesting small Oz list; 22 by the glass; 35 Belgian beers
Chef Ben Cochrane
Owner Olivier Massart
Seats 120
www.belgian-beer-cafe.com.au
And...you can buy the beers for home at North Shore Liquor Cellars, a few doors away

Essence

11 Lime Street, King Street Wharf, Sydney
Tel 9290 3500 Map 1

Contemporary

Score 13/20

The most striking thing about this smart, contemporary dining space is its incredible setting, looking out over the water to the casino. Although located in one of Sydney's busiest restaurant strips, it remains serene, especially at night. Tables are dressed in white linen and there are padded cream chairs and soothing earthy tones, while downstairs a plush lounge bar offers bistro fare. This is Paul Sarlas's (Milsons & Jaspers) most recent food foray and, with Jaspers stalwart Carl Ellis heading the kitchen, it comes with a good pedigree. After a confused start, things are looking up, though service still needs to lift to match the calibre of the surrounds. The highlight of the entrée sampler plate is grilled bug tails atop a chilli rice cake with baby coriander and coconut bean salad. Buttermilk-steamed duck leg, with pink roast breast and ginger–orange–caramel flavours, on scorched greens, is good. Hickory-smoked barramundi is delicately balanced with creamy garlic potato purée, silverbeet and white truffle dressing. Desserts like iced cherry marshmallow cone – solid cherry–marshmallow ice-cream inside a white chocolate cone – are rich and enticing.

Hours Lunch daily noon–3pm; Dinner daily 6–10.30pm
Bill E $19–$26 **M** $28–$36 **D** $16–$18;
Cards AE BC DC MC V
Wine Extensive, intelligent list; 14 by the glass
Chef Carl Ellis
Owners Paul Sarlas & Richard Nicholl
Seats 200; private rooms; wheelchair access; outdoor seats
www.essencerestaurant.com.au
And...enjoy luscious cocktails downstairs

city + suburbs

est. ★

Level 1, 252 George Street, Sydney
Tel 9240 3010   Map 1

Contemporary

Score 18/20

Restaurant of the Year

A corps of waiters brings entrées in one swift choreographed movement. A couple ooh and aah over upstanding, outstanding soufflés, reluctant to disturb the trembling, sugar-dusted towers. Sommelier Stuart Halliday quietly notes a host's wine budget and picks just the right drop. A burst of laughter dissolves among the tall pillars in this grand old room, with its comfortable chairs and banquettes in muted tones. Peter Doyle's food shows innate confidence and control. Taking seasonal produce he coaxes out every iota of pure, clean, bright flavour. Tastes magically meld in a salad of sand crab, avocado, witlof, pink grapefruit and coriander, with cucumber jelly. Melting lamb rib-eye is accompanied by a fragrant tomato fondue and herb-scented polenta panisse. Southern rock lobster is gently bathed in an ethereal sauce, with black fungi, snowpeas and basil. The mash is sublime. Passionfruit sorbet is a distilled essence of the fruit. est. is a superlative dining experience, conducted with all-encompassing grace and humour.

Hours Lunch Mon–Fri noon–3pm; Dinner Mon–Sat 6–10pm
Bill E $25–$32 **M** $39–$42 **D** $19; dégustation menu $125 pp
Cards AE BC DC MC V
Wine Encyclopaedic and impeccable, with good half-bottles; 23 by the glass
Chef Peter Doyle
Owner The Hemmes family
Seats 90; private room; wheelchair access
www.merivale.com
And...very different bars, above and below, for pre- and post-dinner drinks

Fare Nosh

117 Smith Street, Summer Hill
Tel 9716 6300   Map 8

Contemporary

Score 13/20

Grab a bottle and call in to this friendly local, tucked away in a peaceful, village-like area (and yippee, plenty of parking!) – especially since it's affordable enough for regular visits. Andrew Hickey delivers some of the city's best and most professional service throughout this long narrow room of timber tables and dark floorboards. A generous seafood antipasto includes a shot glass of silky seafood gazpacho; scallop drizzled with salsa verde atop a plump corn cake; whitebait and prawns with chilli jam. It can also deliver less successful offerings, like a doughy, undercooked salmon spring roll; and a light, crisp-battered zucchini flower with an undistinguished seafood filling. Bocconcini-stuffed veal backstrap was cooked beyond the promised medium–rare, on a wet, rather than creamy, mushroom risotto. There's no doubt the green curry paste crust on swordfish packs a punch, especially with a palm sugar caramelised pear, bok choi and a pear and chilli reduction. The climax is great coffee and sensational pear and almond tart with a terrific, golden shortcrust base plus classic frangipane filling.

Hours Dinner Tues–Sat 6–10pm
Bill E $13.50–$16 **M** $19.50–$26 **D** $9.50
Cards AE BC MC V
Wine BYO (corkage $2.50 pp)
Chef/owner Peter Meijer
Seats 33; wheelchair access
And...ask about the nightly specials and 'Noshian favourites'

city + suburbs

Fifi's

158 Enmore Road, Enmore
Tel 9550 4665   Map 8

Lebanese

Score 13/20

Fifi Fudda and her sons prove that there's more to Sydney's Lebanese food than scatter cushions and belly dancers since the start of the new millennium. The restaurant is a simple and restrained affair, with little decoration, so as not to distract from the very good things on your plate. Of late, the dishes have become more complex, but Fifi's kitchen still delivers a-cut-above-the-cliché favourites for very few dollars, with sons Garry and Mohammed El Hassan on the floor. You might start with crisp and deep brown felafel that are plump and pea-green inside. Squashed onto pita bread with the terrific baba ghanoush – some of the best in town – they are delicious. Alas lamb kebabs did an already maligned dish no favours, since the flavours underwhelmed in contrast to everything else. Silky and rich fish, baked in tahini, with brown rice and caramelised onions is a stand-out. And, if you insist, they'll even order in a belly dancer for you.

Hours Dinner Tues–Sun 5.30pm–late
Bill E $9.50–$10.90 **M** $10.50–$25 **D** $4.50
Cards AE BC DC MC V Eftpos
Wine Very limited but reasonably priced list, plus cocktails; 4 by the glass; BYO (corkage $2 pp)
Chef Fifi Fudda
Owners Fifi Fudda, Garry El Hassan & Mohammed El Hassan
Seats 62; outdoor seats
And…the banquet selections are good value at $28 for three courses; $37 for five

Fiorenzoni

Shop 1, 809 Pacific Highway (cnr Victoria Avenue), Chatswood
Tel 9419 6411   Map 7

Modern Italian

Score 13/20

Next time you're in Chatswood, try swapping chow for ciao. In a Marco Polo move, Italy now has a toehold in this suburban stronghold of Chinese cuisine. Fiorenzoni is light and bright, with a tiled floor and sling-back leather chairs, and adorned with photos of Italy. Service is brisk and friendly, specials rattled off with brio. Generous antipasto platters to share are a cheerful jumble of Italian cheeses, grilled peppers and eggplant, zucchini, sun-dried tomatoes and good salumi, including finely sliced bresaola (cured beef). An intriguing and intelligent menu can deliver some surprising flavours. Lamb fillets are marinated in orange juice; juicy king-sized prawns have the zing of ginger; a fine julienne of fennel, along with juniper berries, is strewn across two chicken breasts, with a side of borlotti beans in a tangy tomato salsa. Perhaps the mains could occasionally use a more extravagant hand with the herbs, but when it comes to desserts, there's certainly no lack of Belgian chocolate to pour over a coffee pannacotta.

Hours Lunch Mon–Fri noon–3pm; Dinner Tues–Sat 6–9.30pm
Bill E $10.90–$15.90 **M** $22.90–$32.90 **D** $12.90–$14.90
Cards AE BC DC MC V Eftpos
Wine A good selection, fairly priced, with prosecco and moscato; 12 by the glass; BYO (corkage $2.50 pp)
Chef/owner Mario Nogarotto
Seats 55; wheelchair access; outdoor seats
And…several amari (bitter herbal liqueurs) to aid the digestion

GPO Building
No. 1 Martin Place

experience the best in fine food, drinks & entertainment at no. 1 martin place

Restaurants	Casual Dining	Bars	Cafés
Prime Restaurant	GPO Wood Fired Pizza	1874	Sports Café
Post Seafood Brasserie	GPO Oyster Bar	Senate Bar	Express Café
Intermezzo Ristorante	GPO Table	Sports Bar	
Sosumi Sushi Train	GPO Cheese & Cellar	Post Cocktail Bar	

city + suburbs

Firefly Winebar

Pier 7, 17 Hickson Road, Walsh Bay
Tel 9241 2031   Map 1

Tapas
Score 12/20

Sydney could do with more of this kind of wine bar/restaurant: small, right by the water, and almost entirely outside (though it is covered). It's a very casual, intimate place, with groovy tunes playing discreetly in the background: perfect for enjoying a glass of wine and watching the sun play off the harbour, or for tucking in to something more substantial. They offer tapas-sized dishes that range from Spanish-inspired meatballs and olives to bruschetta, Asian-accented salads and mod-Oz specials. Perhaps such diversity means quality can vary too. Blissfully tender lamb skewers are packed with flavour but sesame oil-heavy dressing smothered a shredded chicken and watercress salad. Meatballs with pine nuts and a chunky tomato sauce are more assured; and the ricotta, rocket and chickpea salad is well balanced, interesting and very tempting. Choose carefully and you'll leave happy, especially after working your way through the cocktail list.

Hours Mon–Sat noon–10pm, Sun 3pm–sunset
Bill Tapas $8–$16, more for seafood; **D** $8; 10% surcharge on public holidays
Cards AE BC MC V Eftpos
Wine Comprehensive and interesting list; 27 by the glass
Chef James Gates
Owner Daniel Sofo
Seats 45; outdoor seats
www.fireflybar.net
And...service is brisk if you're heading to the theatre afterwards

Fish Face

132 Darlinghurst Road, Darlinghurst
Tel 9332 4803   Map 2

Seafood
Score 14/20

They don't waste an inch of this small, narrow space with a stainless-steel sushi counter at one end of the open kitchen and desserts displayed tantalisingly at the other. Diners perch on bar stools around small round tables – the hubbub would make conversation impossible at anything larger. As the menu says, it's all about fish: how it's caught, killed, stored and cooked. Stephen Hodges, previously of Pier, passionately sources the best fish from around Australia, storing it in a specially designed refrigerator. Excellent sushi and sashimi come with freshly grated horseradish and pickled ginger. Specials, such as a salad of lightly salted and par-cooked blue-eye – a sort of bacalao – with a just-poached egg and tangle of wild rocket, supplement the short menu. Beer-battered flathead and hand-cut chips served in a paper cone are hard to resist, though the blue-eye with potato scales, a contrast of succulence and crispness enhanced with cubes of earthy beetroot, is truly memorable. To finish, macadamia and date tart shows not everything good comes from the ocean.

Hours Dinner Mon–Sat 6–10pm
Bill E $14.50–$16.50 **M** $24.50–$29.50 **D** $12.50
Cards AE BC MC V; bookings for 6–7pm only
Wine BYO (corkage $4.50 per bottle)
Chefs Stephen Hodges & Taka Mori
Owner city-biz Pty Ltd
Seats 32; outdoor seats
www.fishface.com.au
And...probably the best takeaway fish 'n' chips in town (ask for double helpings of the tartare sauce)

city + suburbs

Flavour of India Edgecliff

120–128 New South Head Road, Edgecliff
Tel 9326 2659/9328 6186   Map 4A

Indian

Score 13/20

Sydney, thankfully, is a city of dependably good (no more, no less) Indian restaurants. And this Flavour of India (there's another, unrelated, FoI in Glebe), halfway between Rushcutters and Double Bay, is no exception, serving the usual South Indian favourites in a spacious room with a dark-timbered ceiling and Goan-cum-Balinese décor, plus attentive, near-effusive, service from the friendly floor staff. The generous servings of curries, ranging from creamy beef Kerala to a dryer Goan prawn curry, are just one of the elements that give this long-standing establishment an edge. The highlight is rissole-like, spicy pan-fried fish cakes with a hint of chilli, ginger, garlic and turmeric. If you like what they're serving in the restaurant, they also do home delivery for nights when you don't feel like leaving your palace.

Hours Lunch Friday noon–3pm; Dinner daily 6–11pm

Bill E $6.50–$12.90 **M** $14.50–$22 **D** $8.50–$9.90

Cards AE BC DC MC V

Wine Small to medium list of Australasians; 11 by the glass; BYO (corkage $5 per bottle)

Chefs Hayat Mahammed & Privin Singh Bisht

Owner Lola Crossingham

Seats 100

And...complimentary sorbet-cum-ice-cream palate cleanser between courses

Flavours of Peking

7/100 Edinburgh Road, Castlecrag
Tel 9958 3288   Map 7

Northern Chinese

Score 13/20

The long row of highchairs that greets you in reception will delight young parents and family groups – this is a child-friendly dining gem. Local Chinese families are regulars and know just what to order, so observe or seek the amicable advice on the floor. Despite the shopping centre surrounds and pleasant but rather bland décor, the quality northern Chinese delicacies are outstanding. You will need a black belt in chopsticks to chase the mermaid's tresses (crisp, finely shredded seaweed) around the bowl. Peking pastries, pancakes, dumplings and handmade noodles are highly recommended, as is the vast array of duck, beef, chicken or fresh seafood choices. Shallot pancakes are a scrumptious blend of sweet and savoury, and a simple dish of chicken and vegetable Peking noodles delivers a feast of flavours. Peking duck is obviously the house hero with a theatrical ceremony of two or three courses, ensuring that you savour every delectable morsel. And there are plenty of familiar dishes such as crisp salt-and-pepper king prawns at this popular Castlecrag local.

Hours Lunch daily noon–3pm; Dinner Sun–Thurs 5.30–10.30pm, Fri–Sat 5.30–11.30pm

Bill E $6.80–$16.80 **M** $15.50–$25.80 **D** $5.80–$9.80; seafood at market price; $2.50 pp surcharge on public holidays

Cards AE BC DC MC V; bookings essential

Wine Well-priced, reliable labels; BYO (corkage $2.50 pp)

Chef/owner Chen Zhi Feng

Seats 170; private room

And...perfect for that overdue family get-together

city + suburbs

Flying Fish

19–21 Pirrama Road, Jones Bay Wharf, Pyrmont
Tel 9518 6677   Map 5B

Seafood

Score 15/20

It's the sexiest of waterfront spaces, in a restored wharf facing the business end of the harbour. The free-flowing, two-floor room pays tribute to the building's heavy-timbered, maritime origins, adding a splash of 21st century wit, while the spectacular lights shine like your own private galaxy. We don't know whether flying fish can have an Icarus moment but, after such a vibrant start, it seems that the soaring delight in Peter Kuruvita's dreamy food is now a lot closer to earth. The cleverness remains, like seared rare tuna finding harmony with ruby grapefruit and sweet crackling pork, but other flavours felt a little flat and the farmed barramundi had a slightly mushy texture; and we could also do with a little less sweetness, especially in the salad dressing. No such complaints about the spice-redolent Sri Lankan snapper curry with all the trimmings (and instructions on the order in which to eat them). Finish on a high, tucking into vanilla bavarois with poached strawberries.

Hours Lunch Tues–Fri & Sun noon–2.30pm; Dinner Tues–Sat 6.30–10.30pm
Bill E $27–$29 **M** $39–$49 **D** $17; seafood degustation, $125 pp; 8% surcharge on public holidays
Cards AE BC DC MC V; bookings essential
Wine Smart, trim, international list at accessible prices
Chefs Peter Kuruvita & Kim Kenig
Owners Con Dedes & Peter Kuruvita
Seats 199; private rooms; wheelchair access
www.flyingfish.com.au
And...enjoy a drink on the very comfy deck bar outside

Fook Yuen

Level 1, 7 Help Street, Chatswood
Tel 9413 2688   Map 7

Chinese (Cantonese)

Score 13/20

Walk up the stairs from the concrete jungle of downtown Chatswood to this huge room, which can pack in more than 300 punters. The place bustles as waiters hand you a ticket to hold onto until your number's up for yum cha. It's full of upper-North Shore Chinese feasting on traditional morsels, including fresh, delicious prawn and scallop dumplings, other succulent steamed dim sum, deep-fried squid and the ubiquitous pork buns and custard tarts. The popularity keeps the yum cha coming fresh and piping hot. At night, ignore a menu filled with mainly standard Chinese fare, from Sichuan chicken to steamed pork ribs. What you want are the interesting specials, written in Chinese just to add to the challenge, so ask, because the managers will translate. Of course, the real highlight is the live seafood – crab, abalone, scallops, parrotfish – in the tanks that line the walls, and needing little more than ginger and shallots to highlight their decadent freshness. But be prepared to spend up big to have a really good time.

Hours Lunch Mon–Fri 10.30am–3pm, Sat–Sun 10am–3pm; Dinner daily 5.30–11pm
Bill E $5.40–$12 **M** $15–$30 **D** $5–$6.50; seafood at market prices; $2 pp surcharge on public holidays
Cards AE BC DC MC V
Wine Small, standard list; only house wine by the glass
Chef KC Leung
Owner ALLFX Pty Ltd
Seats 320; private rooms
And...yum cha is very busy on weekends

city + suburbs

Forty One

Level 42, The Chifley Tower, 2 Chifley Square, Sydney
Tel 9221 2500   Map 1

French

Score 15/20

Having your ears pop as you're whisked up 42 floors creates a degree of expectation. The views east from the city are certainly eye-popping too. This plush room and all its elegant accoutrements – from the Christofle cutlery to Riedel glasses and Alessi pepper grinders – are up to the task, even if the service can range from deferential to occasionally forgetful. After some aberrations last year, it's pleasing to see finesse and delicacy return to Dietmar Sawyer's thoughtful blending of French technique with Asian flourishes. Luxury doesn't come cheaply, so a six-course 'gourmand' dégustation seems like value, priced at little more than three courses. A careful arrangement of ocean trout and vinaigrette-dressed leeks with angassi oyster has just a hint of ginger and lemon zest. An evocative Indian-spiced foam, with carrot and blood orange purée, is a clever companion for yabby tails and scallops. Venison on a blackcurrant vinegar jus is made merrier by a foie gras-stuffed fig. And caramelised quince millefeuille with yoghurt and almond cream tastes as sublime as it looks.

Hours Lunch Tues–Fri noon–2.30pm; Dinner Mon–Sat from 6pm
Bill E $25 **M** $39 **D** $20; dinner set price $125 pp; dégustation menu $140 pp
Cards AE BC DC MC V; bookings essential
Wine Simply stunning, comprehensive new and old world list, sometimes at prices that are also stunning; 8 by the glass
Chef/owner Dietmar Sawyer
Seats 120; private rooms; wheelchair access
www.forty-one.com.au
And... don't leave without going to the loo

Fratelli Paradiso

12–16 Challis Avenue, Potts Point
Tel 9357 1744   Map 2

Italian

Score 14/20

Perhaps you've never been here but does that wallpaper – huge, richly lip-sticked, mouth full of spaghetti – look strangely familiar? You've probably seen it in many a photo spread with a supermodel perched in front of it. So, yes, this is a groovy spot but it's friendly too: large sliding doors inviting you in, a daily blackboard menu written in Italian italics and a little pasticceria right next door. This is a very local restaurant with a smart floor team who know their locals and tend all with grace and charm. You can see why so many keep coming back. Does anybody else turn out lightly floured calamari so delicately cooked on a bed of rocket? How often do you come across spaghetti alla carbonara – a classic so classic that it's almost a cliché – done as well as it is here? And how many places can do risotto that so closely measures up to perfection: that creamy liquidity, a nutty heart in every grain of rice? It's a class act, with style but no attitude. And the Vittoria coffee is very good.

Hours Mon–Fri 7am–11pm; Sat–Sun 7am–5pm
Bill E $15–$18 **M** $18–$29 **D** $8–$12; 10% surcharge on public holidays
Cards AE BC DC MC V; no bookings
Wine A manageable list from Europe and the Antipodes, but, naturally, with an Italian accent; 20 by the glass
Chef Andrea Mantese
Owners Giovanni & Enrico Paradiso & Marco Ambrosino
Seats 58; private room; wheelchair access; outdoor seats
And... they're also loved for their breakfasts

city + suburbs   F

Frattini

122 Marion Street, Leichhardt
Tel 9569 2997   Map 5B

Italian (Southern)

Score 12/20

Every day is a good day at Frattini. There's always something a little celebratory about the meal, from waiters who move with the speed of Ferrari drivers to the comfortable rooms on the prominent corner site and the feel-good food. So lean forward to talk over the white paper-topped, white cloth'd tables (or you may have to lip read your companion's conversation over the noise), then tuck into chicken soup, laced with lots of parsley and good, tiny, bready dumplings. Find refreshing simplicity in mushrooms that are simply fried – no more, no less – served on shredded lettuce with lemon for squeezing. This is comfort food for the soul. Sure, we think they could provide a pepper grinder for every table, and the butter in individually wrapped pats seems very down market. And okay, nonna's fettuccini wouldn't be drowning in tomato sauce. But these are small prices to pay for the kind of invigorating food you could eat every day of your life. And celebrate.

Hours Lunch Mon–Fri noon–3pm; Dinner Mon–Thurs 6–9.30pm, Fri–Sat 6–10pm
Bill E $12.90–$15.90 **M** $18.90–$20.90 **D** $9.50
Cards AE BC DC MC V; bookings essential
Wine BYO (no corkage)
Chef Cettina Caroleo
Owner Tony Sama
Seats 120
And...lunchtime is quick, efficient and you're more likely to get in at short notice

Fresh Ketch

77A Parriwi Road, The Spit, Mosman
Tel 9969 5665   Map 7

Seafood

Score 13/20

It's top-deck dining, upstairs in a large light room, the décor superior Scandinavian cruising yacht with lots of blond wood, railings and detailed fittings. Sit back and let your view cruise Middle Harbour as a splendid hunk of warm sourdough arrives. The regulars are obviously very comfortable with the surroundings and familiar flavours. If there are inconsistencies – gnarly gnocchi lets down a duet with pumpkin tortellini in brown butter with shaved fontina cheese; salad dressing a tad sharp; a tart cries for more rhubarb – they are redeemed by the mains. Slow-cooked Thirlmere duck is moist, the skin sweetly caramelised, with walnuts adding a festive crunch. A generous wild barramundi fillet is cushioned by snowpeas; simple, whole baby snapper is deliciously charred; and tempura batter on delicate whiting fillets is wafer-crisp. Poached pear comes with caramelised rice pudding, and chocoholics are never left wanting. With friendly, brisk service from a well-drilled crew, Fresh Ketch sails serenely on.

Hours Lunch Mon–Sat noon–3pm; Dinner Mon–Sat 6–10pm; Sun noon–9pm
Bill E $18–$22 **M** $27–$33 **D** $13; 10% surcharge on public holidays, $1 pp on Saturdays, $2 pp on Sundays
Cards AE BC DC MC V
Wine Extensive, well-priced, sympathetic to the cuisine; 10 by the glass; BYO (corkage $5 pp)
Chef Benjamin Comins
Owner George Seferian
Seats 130; outdoor seats
www.freshketch.com.au
And...car parks on both sides of the road

city + suburbs

Friendship Oriental Seafood

477 King Georges Road, Beverly Hills
Tel 9586 3288   Map 6

Chinese (Cantonese)

Score 13/20

There's an ice-cream freezer by the front door but there are live seafood tanks too. And while the mildly garish décor is typical of its genre (and thumbs down to the TVs), admiring the BBQ ducks and chickens hanging in the glass-walled kitchen is compensation enough (but thumbs down also to shark-fin soup). On a strip where there's no shortage of dining choices, Friendship Oriental is deservedly packed with large families laughing and chattering. Put the English menu of Cantonese staples aside, and ask a floor team with eager smiles what's on offer from the colourful paper strips of Chinese calligraphy stuck on the wall. Baby abalone steamed with ginger, shallot and sesame oil is surprisingly soft and luxurious. The two-course Peking duck has the theatre of the whole bird's lacquered skin carved at the table for decadent pancakes, followed by chunky meat in sang choi bau. A giant salt-and-pepper king crab is succulent and spicy with chilli and fried eschalots. It's an indulgence everyone should try at least once.

Hours Dinner daily 5pm–2am
Bill E $3.80–$13.80 **M** $14.80–$34.80
D $3.50–$4.80; $2.80 per adult, $1.40 per child surcharge on public holidays
Cards AE BC MC V Eftpos
Wine Basic, short, functional; 2 by the glass; BYO (corkage $2 pp)
Chef Zhi Qiang Zhong
Owners Warren Ng & Albert Lai
Seats 250; wheelchair access
And...it's fresh fruit for dessert; and that ice-cream for kids

Fu Manchu

249 Victoria Street, Darlinghurst
Tel 9360 9424   Map 2

Asian

Score 12/20

While many will lament the loss of its Bondi sibling, this small stalwart dumpling and noodle house woks on to packed crowds every night. It's a long, narrow casual room adorned with Chinese lanterns over stainless-steel communal tables with red-vinyl stools, plus tables of two down the back. You score a tumbler for wine and a container of red chopsticks, and you get your own water. Service delivers just enough to keep things ticking along. The 40-odd mostly northern Chinese dishes range from soups to noodles and rice, never stinting on spicing and flavour. Most patrons come to pick over the dumplings – more-ish potstickers stuffed with pork and cabbage – or ginger-fragrant steamed chicken buns. But fried blue swimmer crab parcels were disappointingly light-on with filling; and Beijing chilli noodles topped with minced pork, beansprouts and cucumber matchsticks were no great leap forward. They use free-range chicken (yay!) – perfect in a rich nonya potato and coconut curry; and deep-fried whole snapper with sweet and sour sauce rises above its cliché.

Hours Dinner daily 5.30–10.30pm
Bill E $5.50–$18.50 **M** $11–$25 **D** $5; $1.50 pp surcharge on weekends & public holidays
Cards None
Wine BYO (corkage $1.50 pp)
Chef Sun Jian Xin
Owner Annie Lee
Seats 35; private rooms
www.fumanchu.com.au
And...there are two banquet rooms upstairs for large groups (you need to book)

city + suburbs (G)

Fuel Bistro

476–488 Crown Street, Sydney
Tel 9383 9388 Map 3B

Contemporary
                            Score 14/20

Don't be deceived by the quiet start that Fuel makes in the early evening. A fuel injection kicks in past 7pm and suddenly it accelerates. Whether you think of this as a restaurant or a Peugeot and Volvo showroom, there's a high chance you'll be lured into a seat by Damian Head's disarmingly simple menu. He's equally at home working with Mediterranean or Asian flavours. The cool, spicy thrill of seared tuna with green pawpaw, chilli, lime and cashew is matched by a beautifully nimble pecorino, grape tomato and fennel salad with braised borlotti beans. Our fillet of lamb was dryish in a North African-style dish with fetta, currant and almond couscous, but the flavours were arrestingly good. The textural contrasts in a perfectly cooked crisp-skin snapper fillet with warm kipflers, aïoli, cress and pine nuts are a knockout. Finish on a very coconutty peach crumble tartlet with a graceful Muscat de Beaumes de Venise. You'll find service is a cushioned ride with floor veteran Mandy Saddington at the wheel.

Hours Brunch Sat–Sun 9am–3pm; Lunch Mon–Fri noon–3pm; Dinner Tues–Sat from 6pm
Bill E $14–$18 **M** $18–$30 **D** $10–$14; pre-theatre menu, 2/3 course $29/$37; 10% surcharge on public holidays
Cards AE BC DC MC V
Wine Could do with more personality & a few good-value Europeans; 15 by the glass; BYO Dinner Tues–Fri only (corkage $4 pp)
Chef Damian Heads
Owner Greg Duncan
Seats 60; wheelchair access; outdoor seats
www.fuelbistro.com.au
And...perve at the Peugeots and dream of French country back roads

Galileo

The Observatory Hotel, 89–113 Kent Street, Millers Point
Tel 9256 2215 Map 1

French–Japanese
                            Score 15/20

We have nothing but praise for The Observatory for maintaining its grand dining room with aircraft carrier-sized tables, lovely antique sketches and wonderful clubby feel. 1920s glamour meets 2006 head-on as chef Haru Inukai seamlessly blends his Japanese heritage with French training. It could be simply stunning garfish with a dice of Mediterranean vegetables and smudges of excellent tapenade on the regulation square plates. His oysters are always sensational, perhaps paired with plum wine jelly. We were amazed at the salt-crusted Kangaroo Island chicken, cut open at the table, and though the meat had lost some of its lustre, the flavours went on and on like a politician at election time. Not everything works so well: a pre-dessert of sweetcorn ice-cream with croutons was about as interesting as fat-free yoghurt. Thankfully, service seems more switched on than ever, adding an entrancing, friendly quality to what could be a too stuffy, but deliriously old-fashioned, dining room.

Hours Breakfast daily 6.30–10.30am; Dinner daily 6.30–10pm
Bill D 2/3 courses $75/$90; dégustation menu $90 pp
Cards AE DC MC V
Wine A cracker of a list, with great focus on top-end Aussies; 16 by the glass
Chef Haru Inukai
Owner The Orient Express Group
Seats 65; private rooms; wheelchair access
www.observatoryhotel.com.au
And...ask for the dégustation, or the children's, menu depending on your time of life

city + suburbs

Garfish Crows Nest

6/29 Holtermann Street, Crows Nest
Tel 9966 0445   Map 5A
Also **Garfish Kirribilli**
2/21 Broughton Street, Kirribilli
Tel 9922 4322   Map 5A

Seafood

Score 13/20

Here's the plan: pick a fish from the daily blackboard, perhaps South Australian jewfish or local skate, they'll suggest the best way to cook it (ignore them at your peril), then choose the garnish: from tomato relish and mash to a saffron, fennel and mussel broth. After things were somewhat askew when the Crows Nest sibling opened last year, we're pleased the Garfish duo are back on sea shanty. They care about the seafood and it shows. The slickly modern room is airy, spilling out onto the footpath, and the 95 per cent seafood menu ranges from freshly shucked oysters to the ubiquitous (but beautifully done) salt-and-pepper squid. A lush smoked kingfish and celeriac tart is studded with the buttery crunch of pine nuts, then offset by the salty tang of capers and sweetly piquant roasted capsicum. Whole fried barra didn't leave quite enough juicy flesh inside, but everyone loves the beer-battered flathead. To end, try the affogato.

Hours Mon–Fri 7.30am–10pm; Sat 8am–10pm; Sun 9am–9pm
Bill E $15–$17 **M** $19.50–$32 **D** $9–$12; 5% surcharge on Sundays, 10% on public holidays
Cards AE BC DC MC V; no bookings, except Mon–Fri lunch & Mon–Sun dinner 6–6.30pm
Wine Short, smart list with good fishy reds; 12 by the glass; BYO (corkage $3.30 pp)
Chefs Stewart Wallace, Michael Nash & Christine Ware
Owners Mark Dickey & Mark Scanlan
Seats 84 (50 Kirribilli); outdoor seats
www.garfish.com.au
And...there's a bar with simple dishes and oysters 3–9pm at Crows Nest

Golden Century

393–399 Sussex Street, Sydney
Tel: 9212 3901   Map 3A

Chinese (Cantonese)

Score 14/20

It pays to be in the know (or known) here – then you might not have to queue when you have a booking and the service may be warmer rather than brusque and efficient. The vast menu comes in varied forms: from the big laminated number to the specials with a range of interchangeable sauces. You could dine quite inexpensively or indulge in the excellent live seafood from the huge tanks at the front. Selections are bagged, priced and presented, so there are no surprises. The freshness and flavours are fantastic. Plump pipis with XO sauce don't come better than this; nor does crab, perhaps broken up and deep-fried with a light coat of salt, pepper and chilli to offer just enough contrast to the sweet flesh. Suckling pig is crisp-skinned and moist-fleshed, on crunchy jellyfish and surprisingly sweet beans. Tender Sichuan beef contrasts with crisp zucchini slices; and spinach with garlic is a soft and aromatic classic. Two decades later, this vast bustling room remains one of the city's finest and most rewarding Cantonese.

Hours Daily noon–4am
Bill E $6–$18 **M** $11.80–$29.80 **D** $2.50–$6; seafood at market prices; $2 pp surcharge on public holidays
Cards AE BC DC MC V Eftpos
Wine Big-brand wine list; 12 by the glass; a good choice of Chinese specialities; BYO (corkage $5 pp)
Chef Lee Ho
Owners Eric Wong & Kevin Kam
Seats 600; private rooms
And...dine with Sydney's chefs late at night – maybe on congee

city + suburbs

Golden Kingdom

147 Anzac Parade, Kensington
Tel 9662 1616   Map 9

Chinese

Score 13/20

If restaurant aesthetics are the breath of life to you, don't go to Golden Kingdom. Tangled between the entrance and toilets of a serviced apartment building, this suburban stalwart has grey chairs, lemon tablecloths, and mysteriously placed lavatories. Thankfully, the food is far better than the décor. The dumplings especially are things of beauty: shirred and pintucked outside, filled with delicate minced vegetables, pork or seafood inside. The house special, fresh seafood, is a generous combination of chilli-and-garlic-touched scallops, prawns, squid and fish. Other dishes are solid: crisp-skinned duck with pancakes finds a good balance between richness and excess, though it lacks the spring onion zing of true Peking duck; sang choi bau is nutty and nicely textured, if just a little too authentically oily. The staff are cheerful and efficient, the clientele diverse and loyal. And as a good neighbourhood Chinese, Golden Kingdom is right in the running. Who cares about design awards anyway?

Hours Lunch daily noon–3pm;
Dinner daily 5–11pm
Bill E $5.50–$20 **M** $11.80–$25.80 **D** $4.50–$8; live seafood at market prices; $2 pp surcharge on public holidays
Cards AE BC DC MC V
Wine Small list; 5 by the glass; BYO ($5 corkage per bottle)
Chef Kwok Wah Yeung
Owner Queenie Wong
Seats 200; private rooms
And... bus stop and car park nearby

Grand National

161 Underwood Street, Paddington
Tel 9363 4557   Map 4B

Contemporary

Score 15/20

After a period of variable standards, the Grand Nash is back, with another chef of notable talents at the helm. Sure, the kitchen is still open to the room, the staff still friendly and the pub so far away up one end as to be hardly noticeable to the casual diner. But since Ian Oakes took up the reins, the place has been going from strength to strength in the food stakes. His leek and parmesan tart has the finest base, with good pancetta and a fried quail's egg for comfort. The rabbit rillettes are unctuous and rich, house-pickled cherries the perfect garnish. Oakes coaxes the best out of Aylesbury duckling, matching its richness with the mouth-watering bitterness of witlof; while the slow-roasted salmon with cauliflower purée and cider butter is divine. Dessert is no let down, even if it sounds like you've eaten it all before. Chocolate hazelnut tart is delightfully complex, and the ubiquitous vanilla pannacotta is given a little jazz up with amaretto sabayon.

Hours Lunch Fri–Sun noon–3pm;
Dinner Tues–Sat 6–10.30pm, Sun 6–9pm
Bill E $14.50–$18.50 **M** $24.50–$29.50
D $14.50–$15.50
Cards AE BC DC MC V
Wine Nicely structured, food-friendly list, some bargains; 8 by the glass
Chef Ian Oakes
Owner Alexander Avramides
Seats 65
And... there's a refurb planned for after the *Guide* hits the streets

good food guide   61

city + suburbs

Grappa

Shop 1, 267–277 Norton Street, Leichhardt
Tel 9560 6090   Map 5B

Italian

Score 14/20

Who would have thought that, at the unfashionable end of Norton Street, in a car park next to a bottleshop and adjacent to a freeway, you'd find this sexy-like-Sophia-Loren space? Walking through the doors of this huge, long white room with large open bar and an exposed wood-fired pizza oven, you feel like an extra in that ode to Italian food, *Big Night Out*. Yes it's loud. Service is swift, friendly, professional and gracious. A large, varied menu includes a generous serving of delicately fried whitebait fritters with a more-ish aïoli and zesty rocket. A large bowl of freshly steamed mussels is enhanced by pungent chilli in a beautiful tomato sauce broth best mopped up with fresh bread. The signature veal cutlet is succulent in a marinade of lemon and sage with a salsa accompaniment. Alas a half-roasted duck with roasted tamarillo and brandy sauce fell a bit flat. It's a small quibble when the coffee is spot-on and a tiramisu with an assortment of mixed berries is something special.

Hours Lunch Tues–Fri noon–3pm, Sun noon–3pm; Dinner daily 6–10pm
Bill E $16.50–$30 **M** $17–$48 **D** $13–$19.50; pizze $13.50–$22; dégustation menu $75 pp
Cards AE BC DC MC V Eftpos
Wine Comprehensive and classy Italian/Oz list; 23 by the glass; BYO (corkage $4.50 pp)
Chef John O'Riordan
Owners Charlie Colosi, Tony Colosi & John O'Riordan
Seats 150; wheelchair access; outdoor seats
www.grappa.com.au
And...amazing wood-fired pizza

Green Bamboo

159 Tower Street, Panania
Tel 9773 0262   Map 6

Vietnamese

Score 12/20

What a joy to wander into a room that feels as if it's one big party and you're the guest of honour. The staff here make everybody feel that it's their special night. On a menu that tries too hard to please everybody, you may struggle to find true Vietnamese flavours, but persist. There are hidden delights such as rice paper rolls with pork and prawn, tiny little spring rolls (including a vegetarian version), and a duck salad fragrant with coriander and mint and plenty of noodles. We found the roasted chilli sauce on the barramundi fillet complex and interesting, if a tad oily. You can mix and match: beef, chicken, lamb or duck, with chilli and basil, perhaps, or ginger and shallots. While the crisp pancake lives up to its name, too many dishes stray into the rest of Asia. No matter, as the hubbub ricochets off the tiled floor and hard walls, the mood is upbeat, the flavours are worthwhile and the cheerio so infectious that you almost want to make another booking before you leave.

Hours Dinner daily 5–10pm
Bill E $6–$15 **M** $9–$18 **D** $6
Cards AE BC DC MC V Eftpos
Wine Short but spice-friendly; BYO (corkage $2 pp)
Chefs Thens Tran & Sonny Bui
Owners Yen Dinh
Seats 110; wheelchair access; outdoor seats
And...takeaway is available at 10% off restaurant prices

city + suburbs

Guillaume at Bennelong

Sydney Opera House, Bennelong Point
Tel 9241 1999   Map 1

Contemporary/French   Score 18/20

Sydney has much to boast of: most notably the spectacular Opera House and, with Guillaume Brahimi on the dining stage, this equally inspiring restaurant tucked under the southern sail. It more than lives up to its iconic status, presenting pure pleasure on a plate and highly skilled service, all under the breathtaking Utzon architecture that soars above. Aside from the city and Harbour views, you get to savour exquisite French-influenced dishes such as succulent Western Australian crabmeat seated on a bed of avocado and coriander, circled by a vibrant red capsicum coulis and lightly covered by a fan of finely sliced cucumber. Tender grain-fed beef tenderloin is partnered superbly with a tombe of field mushrooms, baby spinach and a delicate shallot confit and merlot sauce. Roast barramundi is divinely accompanied by a sublime blend of eggplant caviar, olives, capers, spring onion and capsicum. And just when it seems heady enough, along comes a pyramid of nougat glace on hazelnut, almond and strawberry coulis, lightly embraced by a swirl of Turkish fairy floss.

Hours Lunch Thurs–Fri noon–3pm; Dinner Mon–Sat from 8pm; pre-theatre Mon–Sat 5.30–7.45pm
Bill E $26–$35 **M** $39 **D** $20; pre-theatre menu, 2–3 courses $58–$68 pp
Cards AE BC DC MC V; bookings essential
Wine Dazzling, exhaustive, global list of gems; 17 by the glass
Chef/owner Guillaume Brahimi
Seats 110; private rooms
www.guillaumeatbennelong.com.au
And...tapas at the bar, pre- or post-theatre, or à la carte – indulge at least once in your lifetime

harbourkitchen&bar

7 Hickson Road, The Rocks
Tel 9256 1661   Map 1

Contemporary   Score 13/20

Bar and restaurant wend their way around the foreshore so closely that the tide slurps beneath as you sip a cocktail. With foldaway windows stowed in this quietly modern room, it's a delightful setting for a front-stalls view of the Opera House and to dive into Danny Drinkwater's perhaps overly imaginative menu. A goodly hunk of pork hock terrine wrapped in silverbeet with a pile of lentils was let down by an assertively vinegared salad. Succulent chargrilled sardine fillets arrive in a shoal with a grainy brandade and cress and radish salad. Pink slow-roasted lamb rump enjoys its old sparring partners of oregano and garlic. Salt-baked salmon with speck-flecked white bean purée emerges from under its crust succulent and briny, robust and generous in both size and flavours. A luscious chocolate and orange pavé will have you rolling in the aisles. Service, while solicitous, can be inconsistent. But with this view and wine list to hand, why care if you have to linger longer?

Hours Breakfast daily 6.30–10.30am; Lunch daily noon–2.30pm; Dinner Mon–Thurs & Sun 6–10pm, Fri–Sat 6–10.30pm
Bill E $23–$28 **M** $36–$41 **D** $17;
10% surcharge on Sundays & public holidays
Cards AE BC DC MC V
Wine A fine, interesting list; 16 by the glass
Chef Danny Drinkwater
Owner Park Hyatt Sydney
Seats 118; private rooms; wheelchair access
www.harbourkitchen.com.au
And...bounce on the fun rocking chairs in the bar

good food guide   63

city + suburbs

Hickson Road Bistro

20 Hickson Road, Walsh Bay
Tel 9250 1990   Map 1

Contemporary

Score 13/20

Most people dine here before catching a show at the adjoining Sydney Theatre, but this comfortable bistro is worth a visit in its own right. It's airy and open, with doors that fold right back, tables on the footpath and white paper over the white tablecloths. The menu is short but punchy, and entrées are heavy on the seafood. A salad of blue swimmer crab, avocado and pink grapefruit is delightfully light, marrying flavours with real zing and crispness. Duck confit with figs is the polar opposite in style – rich and sweet – but just as successful. Waiters do their darnedest to get the punters in and out but never seem harried. They deliver beef as tender as mercy itself, pure comfort when paired with the potato fondant, and oyster and shiitake mushrooms. The strawberry and raspberry sablé (a shortbread-style biscuit) with lime-leaf ice-cream, beautifully whipped together by a boysenberry-based sauce, will make you want to stand up and applaud a fine ending.

Hours Lunch on Sydney Theatre matinee days; Dinner Tues–Wed 6–10pm, Thurs–Sat 6–11pm
Bill E $19 **M** $26–$30 **D** $12; 10% surcharge on Sundays & public holidays
Cards AE BC DC MC V; bookings essential
Wine Not overly long, but decent; 20 by the glass
Chef Simon Collier
Owners Charles Wilkins & Richard Brown
Seats 140; wheelchair access; outdoor seats
www.culinaryedge.com.au
And... if you're coming for the show, you can pre-order dessert for interval; and be careful of the parking after 10pm

Hilltop Phoenix

Shop U7, The Piazza, Castle Towers Shopping Centre, Castle Hill
Tel 1300 883 892/8850 1133   Map 6

Chinese (Cantonese)

Score 13/20

It's not quite a hilltop, but the upper level of the piazza at Castle Towers certainly feels like the highest point for miles. Fight your way through the movie-goers below to Hilltop Phoenix's spacious interior, where the newly redone décor is clean and modern – lots of glass and white linen – but the dishes are wonderfully old fashioned and filling. The Peking duck is very good, carefully constructed by the friendly, competent staff, and the Mongolian lamb pancakes are well poised just this side of richness. The Sichuan beancurd is hearty western peasant food, as is the minced pork and eggplant hotpot, though meat lovers might hope for more pork. Even lesser-known dishes are good. Broad beans with preserved Chinese olives (actually a type of plum) combines fried beans, garlic and surprisingly tender olive leaves: salty, spicy, and lip smacking. All this while strategically placed flat-screen televisions show Jackie Chan rising cheerfully from the ashes of various high-speed car chases: a phoenix indeed.

Hours Lunch daily 11am–3pm; Dinner daily 5.30–10.30pm
Bill E $3.80–$20.80 **M** $14.80–$24.80 **D** $3–$6.80; live seafood at market prices; 10% surcharge on public holidays
Cards AE BC MC V Eftpos
Wine Reasonable Australian list; 4 by the glass; BYO (corkage $2.50 pp)
Chef Sun Hua
Owners Alice & Edmund Lee & Anita Fung
Seats 350; private rooms; wheelchair access; outdoor seats
www.phoenixrestaurants.com.au
And... they'll pack up any leftovers for you to take home

city + suburbs

Hugo's

70 Campbell Parade, Bondi Beach
Tel 9300 0900   Map 9

Contemporary/Seafood
Score 15/20

Attentive service from casual young waiters, paper-over-linen tablecloths, low lights and smart but laid-back regulars pressed side by side at small tables set the tone in this cosy space. It's been synonymous with 'cool' in the Sydney dining scene for almost 10 years. Peter Evans's seafood-oriented menu of six entrées, six mains and a few specials skips from Europe to Asia to North Africa in its influence, but flavours in each dish stay fresh and true to their origins. Goat's cheese tortellini with sage and brown butter are small, rich, melting nuggets. Lobster 'martini' is a modern take on the old prawn cocktail with sweet chunks of lobster meat folded through slivers of young coconut, mango and lime; while pan-roasted corn-fed chicken breast is enlivened by spiced couscous, apricots and pomegranate. It's hard to go past the mouth-puckering lemon tart for dessert, unless you throw caution to the wind and share a tasting plate of four miniature sweets.

Hours Breakfast & Lunch Sat–Sun 9am–4pm; Dinner daily 6–11pm (Mon–Sat in winter)
Bill E $25–$28 **M** $34–$38 **D** $16; 10% surcharge on Sundays & 15% on public holidays
Cards AE BC DC MC V
Wine Interesting collection, featuring some lesser-known wines from known wineries; 14 by the glass
Chefs Peter Evans & John Pye
Owners David Corsi, David & Peter Evans
Seats 60; outdoor seats
www.hugos.com.au
And…efficient heaters make kerb-side dining a year-round option

Hugo's Lounge

Level 1, 33 Bayswater Road, Kings Cross
Tel 9357 4411   Map 2

Contemporary
Score 13/20

You could be forgiven for thinking the food isn't really the focus. Many of the thin beautiful customers nestled into booths seem to idly push it around their plates, straining in the dark to check out the other beautiful people doing the same. Hugo's Lounge is better known as an up-market bar than a restaurant, so it's no wonder the chefs can sometimes slip from their game. Otherwise-sprightly salt-and-pepper soft-shell crab with green mango, chilli, peanuts, and young coconut caramel was unbalanced by an overly bitter aftertaste. The grain-fed beef fillet with onion and thyme roesti, poached bone marrow and red wine butter is more controlled, as is the blue-eye with wild mushrooms, globe artichokes and its own cooking liquor. A passionfruit soufflé with a shot glass of buttermilk bavarois hits the heights we expect, almost living up to the standards of the other Hugo's, on Bondi Beach. Wonder how many of the thin blondes order it?

Hours Dinner Wed–Sat 7–11pm
Bill E $18–$26 **M** $32–$38 **D** $16
Cards AE BC DC MC V (ATM)
Wine Decent list; 10 by the glass; the cocktail list is fab
Chefs Peter Evans & John Lanzafàme
Owners David & Peter Evans, David Corsi & Daniel Vaughan
Seats 120; private room; wheelchair access
www.hugos.com.au
And…there are half-price meals during the week if you become a member

city + suburbs

Icebergs Dining Room & Bar

1 Notts Avenue, Bondi Beach
Tel 9365 9000   Map 9

Mediterranean

Score 17/20

The sting of salt may have taken its toll on everything from the hinges to the drawer runners, but Icebergs still has that glamour-puss air and nonchalant, you-want-me look. Thanks to Maurice Terzini's eye, the details are everything. Short banquettes are dotted with silk cushions in blues and greens that mirror Bondi beach and the congregation of surfers hustling for waves outside. Diners ooze in from the bar, all taut and terrific, jousting lazily with waiters and forking up incredible al dente pasta with pork and sage. Robert Marchetti's food keeps the mod-Med sex appeal we love without getting uptight. Scallops recline in the shell under radish and watercress; fish may be baked in cartoccio – in a bag with oil and lemon. Desserts, such as the marvel of grappa-marinated raspberries and mascarpone tart, cry out to be eaten. There'll always be someone who thinks the food should be trickier, the waiters more obsequious and the mood more subdued. Hopefully they're dining somewhere else.

Hours Lunch Tues–Sun noon–3pm; Dinner Tues–Sun 6.30–10pm
Bill E $16–$24 **M** $29–$44 **D** $9–$17.50; 10% surcharge on Sundays & public holidays
Cards AE BC DC MC V Eftpos
Wine Marvellous, well-sourced list; good Italians; 17 by the glass
Chef Robert Marchetti
Owners Mario Venneri & Maurice Terzini
Seats 105; private room; wheelchair access
www.idrb.com
And...there's a new private room planned for late 2005

Il Baretto

496 Bourke Street, Surry Hills
Tel 9361 6163   Map 3B

Italian

Score 12/20

Il Baretto used to set the standard for excellent pasta, but is it a case of too many chefs spoiling the consistency? This chic BYO corner bistro still delivers competent food but some of the old magic has gone. The famous pappardelle with duck ragù is a generous serve flavour-packed with perfect pasta, although the sauce was too thin to merge with the pappardelle on one visit. And gnocchi napoli laboured under a heavy tomato sauce and equally heavy gnocchi. There are brighter moments, like a squeaky-fresh salmon carpaccio dressed with virgin olive oil and balsamic; a wild rocket salad is peppery with a well-balanced dressing; and vermicelli with vongole is textbook perfect, thanks to plenty of juicy bivalves shedding their sea juices to scent the pasta. This is still a fun place to be, especially for your wallet. It's immensely popular with locals dropping in for a quick pasta or families having an easy night out.

Hours Breakfast & lunch Tues–Sat 8am–3pm; Dinner Mon–Sat 6pm–10pm
Bill E $6–$15 **M** $10–$19.50 **D** $6.50
Cards None; no bookings
Wine BYO (corkage $1 pp)
Chef Domenico Santopadre
Owner Gabriella Fedeli
Seats 50; wheelchair access; outdoor seats
And...good pub across the road for your BYO

city + suburbs

Il Perugino

171 Avenue Road, Mosman
Tel 9969 9756   Map 7

Italian

Score 13/20

Warm neutral tones, white linen and a few bright Italian ceramics set the scene. Closely packed tables of locals drinking good wine over animated conversation create the ambience. Decision-making is easier with a recited menu – you can't ponder options for long when they're not written down, so whatever you remember is what caught your fancy. Attentive, friendly waiters weave between tables, filling glasses, delivering and whisking away plates. Generous serves of well-cooked dried pasta are lightly sauced: delicate spaghetti with broccoli, ricotta and pine nuts; hearty penne with salsicce. Quality produce shines in simple classics: carpaccio with generous shaves of parmesan and salty anchovies; an insalata caprese with Italian buffalo mozzarella. Small lamb cutlets, pink and moist, are served with an apple jam and large, doughy pan-fried gnocchi. Pearly garfish fillets are lighter, cooked simply with olive oil and lemon juice, topped with a bright pink thatch of pickled onion. Seasonal fruits feature in desserts, such as fig and rhubarb torta or the legendary peach and almond crostata.

Hours Lunch Wed–Fri noon–2.30pm; Dinner Mon–Sat 6–10pm
Bill E $16.90–$19 **M** $19–$27 **D** $12
Cards BC DC MC V
Wine BYO (no corkage)
Chef Lesley Mencio
Owners Maurizio & Lesley Mencio and family
Seats 90; private rooms
And... Maurizio is everywhere, greeting and farewelling regulars and first-timers alike

Il Piave

639 Darling Street, Rozelle
Tel 9810 6204   Map 5B

Northern Italian

Score 14/20

This family-run ristorante offers true Italian hospitality, from the complimentary bread and olives that arrive when you do to generous serves and the care that's taken in explaining dishes and looking after special requests. The simple white dining area, with paper-over-linen cloths, good linen napkins and quality tableware, wanders over several small rooms in an old terrace house, including an enclosed courtyard perfect for groups. Antipasto is ideal for sharing, with tastes of a number of entrées (figs and prosciutto, insalata caprese, prawn-stuffed zucchini flowers) plus whatever else the kitchen's come up with on the day. Pastas, especially the gnocchi, are exceptional and made in-house each day. Rabbit is braised with fresh tomato and a profusion of very savoury mushrooms, then served on an unusually smooth polenta cake. Desserts are also made in-house daily; the tiramisu is a creamy, coffee, cakey, more-ish delight, and the thin tower of nougat semifreddo is coated in a crisp chocolate shell.

Hours Dinner Tues–Sat 6.30–10pm; Sun from noon
Bill E $17.90–$18.90 **M** $25.90–$33.90 **D** $12.90–$14.90
Cards AE BC DC MC V Eftpos; bookings essential
Wine Appropriate list with a sprinkling of Italians; 11 by the glass; BYO Tues–Thurs & Sun (corkage $4.50 pp)
Chefs Vanessa Martin & Joshua Macri
Owners Vanessa & Robert Martin
Seats 60
And... pay attention to the specials – they are often real gems

city + suburbs

Il Tratto Ra Ro Pizzeria

108–110 Majors Bay Road, Concord
Tel 8765 8866   Map 6

Italian (Central)

Score 13/20

Remember when restaurants used to be fun? Well, this is the place to come for a great time, good food and excellent service of the kind that Sydney rarely dishes up. Housed in a smartly renovated shopfront, this family-run pizzeria has an extensive list of wonderful offerings. The pizze arrive fired up with fresh ingredients on a chiffon-thin base that is crunchy and chewy at the same time. Calamari are tender and lightly fried; the pizza bianca is justifiably a favourite. The kitchen pays attention to the seasons, like all good Italian cooking, so that what is best at the market will hit the specials board that day. Always count on pasta such as spinach and ricotta ravioli; risotto like the one with chicken, asparagus and mushroom; grilled fish like barramundi; and a hearty dish like meatballs or veal cutlets in port wine sauce. The desserts are the usual tiramisu, cheesecake and mudcake, but they also offer good gelati and a splendid affogato (ice-cream 'drowned' with coffee).

Hours Lunch Tues–Fri & Sun noon–3pm; Dinner daily 6–10.30pm
Bill E $15–$18 **M** $19–$28 **D** $9; pizze $10–$19.50
Cards AE BC DC MC V Eftpos
Wine BYO (corkage $3 per bottle)
Chef Rita Viscontini
Owners Roberto & Rita Viscontini
Seats 120; private rooms; outdoor seats
And...outside is as popular as the air-conditioned inside

Indigo

304 Pacific Highway, Lindfield
Tel 9416 1229   Map 7

Indian (Regional)

Score 13/20

Indigo is not your average suburban Indian. The room is simply decorated in a soothing, modern style and the menu is pure and simple. Dahi papdi, a Delhi street dish of crushed, crisp puri dressed with a mix of yoghurt, chutneys and spicy potato, is a good way to start. Calamari with ginger and basil is quickly tossed in the *kadai* (pan), showing the simplicity of modern Indian cooking. Tamarind and poppyseed glazed prawns come on a bed of kitchri (described as Indian risotto – we'd call it kedgeree), the succulent fresh prawns with a spicy coating. Shamee kebabs are smoke-roasted in the tandoor for a suitably rich flavour with aggressive spicing. Lamb shanks are served whole, with a traditional rogan josh sauce enriched with the lamb juices to create a subtle and satisfying blend of flavours. We did find seemingly unsophisticated spicing in some dishes, but the breads are very good, especially the paratha, with a crisp skin hiding layers of hot, flavoursome just-cooked dough.

Hours Dinner daily 5.30pm–late
Bill E $9.95–$13 **M** $11.95–$22 **D** $8.50
Cards AE BC DC MC V Eftpos
Wine Respectable but not very developed list; 5 by the glass; BYO (corkage $2.50 pp)
Chef/owner Sandeep Chatterjee
Seats 50
And...there's free parking in the council car park behind

city + suburbs

Industrie – South of France

107 Pitt Street (cnr Hunter Street), Sydney
Tel 9221 8001   Map 1

Southern French

Score 12/20

Pardon? QUOI?! It's 7.30pm and this smart, sleek industrial-tinged room is pumping to a jazzy dance beat. The balcony bar overlooking the bistro is a dull roar of post-work gossip; so to shout sweet nothings in the ear of a beloved, curl up on the long, cushion-strewn banquette. Industrie is part cafe, part cocktail lounge, part nightclub and part bistro. If you can handle the din, the food is just as invigorating: from a bar menu of baguettes and assiettes to light and breezy all-day dishes that are mostly French brasserie with the occasional Italian influence. Soothing cod brandade, sprinkled with crisp eschalots, drifts in a shallow sweetcorn broth with fragrant basil oil. Dill-cured salmon curls underneath a crab salad. A lush, wet, seafood and tomato risotto is satisfying. But smoked bacon dominated a stuffed chicken leg on mash with madeira jus; and, despite Gallic charm, the floor can be askew, looking busy, just – sadly – not with you. It's hip, happening and groovy, but to hear yourself eat visit by daylight when the room is (naturally) more businesslike.

Hours Mon–Fri 7.30am–midnight, Sat 6pm–midnight
Bill E $13–$28 **M** $22–$45 **D** $12–$23
Cards AE BC DC MC V Eftpos
Wine Well-priced, interesting, exclusively French list; 22 by the glass
Chef Tauheed Khan
Owners Craig & Monique Anderson
Seats 150; private room; wheelchair access; outdoor seats
www.industriebar.com.au
And…sommelier Andrew Stewart gives French wine appreciation classes every Wednesday night

Infusion@333

Mezzanine level, 333 George Street, Sydney
Tel 9290 3333   Map 1

Modern Asian

Score 14/20

This calm space, located upstairs from an up-market pub and bar where bachelor stockbrokers come to play, looks down on a little urban square and those who've (heh heh) packed their lunch. Zen world music is mixed with a modern interior of glass and chrome complete with slick table settings. Service is attentive and caring, as bizoids grab chopsticks and share their food from a small but well thought-out menu. Homemade prawn and pork dumplings are plump and hearty with soy, chilli and hoisin dipping sauces. Ultra-fresh slivers of salmon are delicious in a honey marinade, and the moistness counterbalances a crisp noodle salad perfectly. A soy-poached Kangaroo Island chicken is juicy and tender and lifted by spicy Sichuan pepper and Chinese cabbage. A green curry of prawns and scallop didn't reach the same heights as the previous dishes, although the addition of apple eggplant is an authentic touch. Linger well past lunch over a wicked caipiroska in the lounge next door.

Hours Lunch Mon–Fri noon–3pm
Bill E $16–$18 **M** $28 **D** $12–$20
Cards AE BC DC MC V Eftpos
Wine Premium Australian list with more than a little interest in boutiques; 10 by the glass
Chef Darrien Potaka
Owner John Ryan
Seats 90; wheelchair access
www.bar333.com.au
And…there's delicious Osaki beer on tap

city + suburbs

Jaspers

54 Alexandra Street, Hunters Hill
Tel 9879 3200   Map 7

Contemporary

Score 14/20

It's genteel in this leafy neck of the woods and Jaspers sits comfortably in its well-dressed sandstone cottage. Warm chocolate tones fashion the plush interior of intimate dining rooms where locals graze contentedly at candle-lit, double-damask-cloth'd tables. The peaceful ambience encourages gentle conversation and the service matches the mood. Prodigal chef Carl Ellis (also at Essence) has returned to lead the kitchen and his elegant style and emphasis on game, bold flavours and good produce are typified by the entrée sampler: a beautifully balanced trio of creamy goat's curd pannacotta with a grilled fig, radicchio, walnuts and crisp pancetta salad; gently smoked venison carpaccio with a dab of cranberry dressing and parmesan wafer; and a delicate salad of blue swimmer crab, avocado, tomato and baby herbs. Equally adept are mains like glazed muscovy duck breast resting atop crushed potatoes with wholegrain mustard; and South Australian marron. A simple platter of house-churned ice-creams, sorbets and fresh fruit provides a cleansing finish.

Hours Lunch Tues–Fri & Sun noon–3pm; Dinner Mon–Sat 6–10pm
Bill E $21–$24 **M** $32–$38 **D** $14–$16
Cards AE BC DC MC V
Wine Well-chosen, interesting list; 13 by the glass; BYO (corkage $7 pp)
Chefs Carl Ellis & Peter Barter
Owners Paul Sarlas & Richard Nicholl
Seats 78; private rooms
www.jaspersrestaurant.com.au
And...this is a stellar suburban that locals cherish

jimmy liks

188 Victoria Street, Potts Point
Tel 8354 1400   Map 2

South-East Asian

Score 14/20

Another Asian restaurant with a long, shared, narrow table? Well, to be absolutely truthful, this is two long, narrow rooms; one with a great bar and the other with a series of tables as long and narrow as the clientele. While waiting you can mooch in the bar, perv on the very happening fellow customers, down a few saketinis (vodka, sake and gin shaken with pickled ginger), then stagger in to dinner. Begin with a few little one-mouthful starters such as betel leaves (chicken or a delicious smoked eel). The menu contentedly wanders South-East Asia, taking in Vietnam (salt-and-pepper squid with Vietnamese dipping sauce), Thailand (red curry of tofu) and sometimes several places at once (Vietnamese braised wagyu beef with Thai basil and Vietnamese mint and lime dressing). It's very satisfying up-market Asian, though slightly marred by that strange love of sweetness to which flesh is heir.

Hours Dinner daily 6–11pm
Bill E $3.50–$16 **M** $24–$29 **D** $12–$13; 10% surcharge on Sundays & public holidays
Cards AE BC MC V Eftpos
Wine Trim, international list, well matched to the food; 23 by the glass
Chefs Adam Woodfield & Fiona Hatchett
Owner Joe Elcham
Seats 100; outdoor seats
And...excellent bar food to soak up some of those cocktails

city + suburbs K

Jonah's

69 Bynya Road, Palm Beach
Tel 9974 5599   Map 7

Contemporary
                                    🍷
                          Unscored

Jonah's long ago eclipsed its beginnings as a simple roadhouse, and since the end of World War II has been luring the rich and fashionable to this most opulent corner of the northern beaches. The view is drop-dead spectacular, a 180-degree panorama of beautiful Whale Beach. But even at night there is much to admire, from the well-spaced tables to the impeccable service and, most importantly, smart and snappy contemporary Oz food with a tinge of classical French. Seafood dominates and we don't expect this to change under new chef George Francisco, previously hatted at Newport's DISH. But his new dishes might also include cumin-infused lamb and duck sausage with labna tortellini and pickled beetroot, and a nine-course dégustation menu, including one for vegetarians. The view, the food and the genteel hush make eating at Jonah's an indulgence for all the senses. But with so many changes, including plans for a new round of renovations, for now we must leave Jonah's unscored.

Hours Breakfast Sat–Sun 8.30–9.45am; Lunch daily noon–2.30pm; Dinner Wed–Sun 6.30–9pm
Bill E $22–$24 **M** $36–38 **D** $19; $6 pp surcharge on Sundays & public holidays
Cards AE BC DC MC V Eftpos; bookings essential for breakfast
Wine Long and interesting list; 23 by the glass
Chef George Francisco
Owner Jonah Pty Ltd
Seats 100; private room; wheelchair access
www.jonahs.com.au
And...tables are allocated as people arrive: make an early booking if you want a window seat

Kam Fook
Bondi Junction

Shop 6010–6011, Level 6, Westfield Shopping Centre, Bondi Junction
Tel 9386 9889   Map 9

Chinese (Cantonese)
                                    Score 14/20

Kam Fook is just the tonic for consumer fatigue. When feet ache from doing the rounds of this whopping shopping centre, punters swap the shopping trolley for the less taxing pursuit of the yum cha cart. While it's fast and furious on the floor, a basket of steaming hot dumplings is tailored with the sort of precision you'd find at the neighbouring boutiques. Kam Fook offers some great window shopping on wheels: if the beef balls with water chestnuts make an appearance, flag the trolley down. The restaurant is a more subdued experience at night when à la carte kicks in and destination diners mingle with the cinema crowd. The menu is more erratic, dishes both hitting and missing the mark. Peking duck and sang choi bau are reliable, yet a spicy salt prawn dish was short-changed on flavour. The warm, modern décor and comfortable chairs are also worth a mention, because once you're back in the thick of the retail action, you'll crave them as much as the food.

Hours Lunch daily 10am–3pm; Dinner daily 5.30–10.30pm
Bill E $5.30–$15 **M** $15–$25 **D** $5.30–$6
Cards AE BC DC MC V Eftpos
Wine Above par for Chinese; 10 by the glass; strong selection of sparkling wine and cognac; Chinese wine and sake; BYO (corkage $10 per bottle)
Chefs Lam Ping & Shane Lai
Owner Edward Ng
Seats 250; wheelchair access
And...two hours' free parking in the building

city + suburbs

Kam Fook Chatswood

Shop 600, Level 6, Westfield Shoppingtown,
Help Street, Chatswood
Tel 9413 9388   Map 7

Chinese (Cantonese)

Score 13/20

Yes, you're in the middle of a shopping centre, but that can have its advantages: a vast space with towering ceilings and a wall of windows letting in daylight give Kam Fook the edge over its glummer Chinese rivals. Burgundy carpet, gold columns and subtle downlighting add to the ambience, offering a welcome retreat from the retail rush. But don't wait until you need to do some shopping: Kam Fook's food is well worth the journey. Yum cha is one of the reasons hordes of people flock here: steaming dumplings of garlic chives; sweet prawns and glassy scallops; superior rice noodles with a texture like silk but a gentle bite; and specials such as chicken and rice steamed in lotus leaves. At night, the menu is long and varied. Live fish features, along with regional specialities and the usual Chinese favourites. We'd be happy there day or night, and we love the helpful staff – smiling most impressively, even during the yum cha rush.

Hours Lunch Mon–Fri 10am–3.30pm, Sat–Sun 9.30am–3.30pm; Dinner daily 5.30–11pm
Bill E $6–$19 **M** $15–$29 **D** $4.50–$9; $2 pp surcharge on public holidays
Cards AE BC DC MV V Eftpos
Wine A standard list with no surprises and few by the glass; BYO (corkage $3 pp)
Chef Lam Ping
Owner Rosetta Lee
And...there's parking in the building

Kensington Peking

172 Anzac Parade, Kensington
Tel 9313 7100   Map 9

Chinese (Northern)

Score 13/20

Dinky chandeliers, black lacquered chairs, an over-lit room and a whiteboard with specials and fish of the day – proof that you can't judge a restaurant by its décor. Handmade noodles, dumplings done most ways, and eight different noodle soups proclaim the hearty, home-style nature of the food. Chicken (drunken, princess or beggar's) is a favourite, while students share salted fish tofu with diced chicken hotpot and regulars go straight to the specials card (highlights off the main menu). Salt-baked chicken is unbelievably moist and gentle, Shanghai noodles are delicate and subtly sauced, but the pork dumplings proved to be gluey on the night. Shredded chicken with aromatic soybean sauce was perky, but not enough to offset some bland pancakes. Crab with egg white is a winning dish: ocean sweet, light and flavoursome with the surprise richness of egg yolk. Many rave about the mermaid's tresses and we are staggered by the size of the portions.

Hours Lunch Thurs–Tues 11am–3pm; Dinner Sun–Tues & Thurs 5–10.30pm, Fri–Sat 5–11pm
Bill E $4–$13 **M** $9–$29 **D** $7–$12
Cards BC MC V Eftpos
Wine BYO (corkage $2 pp)
Chef/owner Peter Lo
Seats 80; wheelchair access
And...24 hours' notice for the beggar's chicken

city + suburbs   K

King 143

Level 1, 143 King Street, Sydney
Tel 9231 0143   Map 1

French
                                    Score 13/20

At first glance you've stepped back into a Dickensian room, with lovely old windows and bookish alcoves, comfortable and soothing in its warm forest tones. Then you notice the 1970s light fittings, the mezzanine floor and some contemporary touches. Toshi Ishihara cooks modern French, but his antecedents are evident. A tomato concasse stuffed with shredded lamb shoulder is joined by steamed oysters with bacon and sherry vinegar; the contrary tastes work well. Ditto for well-trimmed wedges of pork belly topped with scallops. Beef fillet is presented in its salt crust before plating, although sadly, ours was a whisker more than the requested rare. A delicate dice of stewed vegetables highlights the nuances in a fillet of barramundi with a herb crust. Of course there's crème brûlée, with soft nubbins of pear. Toshi's charming wife Yoshiko can get you out fast at lunchtime, but why not join the legal eagles moving from the Loire to McLaren Vale and back, until you exclaim 'Good gracious, are we the last here?'

Hours Lunch Mon–Fri noon–2.30pm; Dinner Tues–Sat 6–9.30pm
Bill E $12–$20 **M** $23–$29 **D** $9.80; 4 courses $55 pp
Cards AE BC DC MC V
Wine Interesting, local and French; 12 by the glass (including 4 dessert)
Chef Toshi Ishihara
Owners Toshi & Yoshiko Ishihara
Seats 45; private room
And… by city standards, wine prices are a steal

Kingsleys Steak & Crabhouse

The Wharf, 6 Cowper Wharf Road, Woolloomooloo
Tel 1300 546 475   Map 2

Steakhouse/Seafood
                                    Score 12/20

The name sums things up nicely, but really it's all about the beef: dry-aged at least 30 days; grain-fed for 70 to 150 days (or grass-fed); fillet, rib-eye, rump or T-bone; from 160 grams to a kilo (gulp!). Kingsley's is a protein paradise: just add chips or baked potato, and a big red or a beer. More delicate souls are tempted by the beer-battered barra, or a salt 'n' pepper muddie. If you're silly enough to try the tomato and fetta salad special, perhaps bland under-ripe fruit are carnivore karma. Desserts can also be lacklustre, but the beef shines – richly flavoured, perfectly cooked and rested, and tender – and the steak tartare is an evocative classic, so keep it simple for a good time, helped by an eager and joyful floor. Sitting in padded timber chairs at bare timber tables or tucked into a booth (the décor is sports-bar blokey), soaking up the water views to the city or eyeing off the posh aquatic parade, it ain't half bad.

Hours Daily noon–10pm
Bill E $14.90–$21.90 **M** $15.90–$58.90 **D** $8.90–$22
Cards AE BC DC MC V Eftpos
Wine Thorough list of Aussie signature brands and marques; 14 by the glass; BYO (corkage $25 per bottle)
Chef Lars Svensson
Owners Kingsley Smith & John Jeffresom
Seats 220; private room; wheelchair access; outdoor seats
www.steak.com.au
And… there are lunchtime discounts on selected wines

good food guide   73

city + suburbs

Kuali

1st Floor, Lane Cove Arcade, 115 Longueville Road, Lane Cove
Tel 9418 6878   Map 7

Malaysian

Score 13/20

Named for the Malaysian equivalent of the wok, Kuali is tucked away above an arcade off the main drag. Surprisingly large, including a glassed-in smokers' room, it's dominated by large photo-murals while tablecloths are topped with butcher's paper. Service is friendly, if a little unsure with wine service. Pan-fried parsnip cake is seductive with crisp beansprouts and garlic chives. Even though drowned by chilli sauce, a special of scallops on the shell was delicious; and spinach-like kangkong is brightened with shrimp paste while roti chanai is suitably flaky. Hainanese chicken rice may be served with roast chicken rather than the usual poached, but the traditional chicken broth comes with the typical rice, sauce and condiments. Whole baby barramundi is deep-fried, de-boned at the table and served in a curry sauce packed with seasonal vegetables. Soft, round pearls of sago gula melaka are refreshing post-curry thanks to palm sugar and sweet coconut cream – like dipping one's toes in the ocean on a hot Malaysian day.

Hours Dinner Tues–Sun 5.30–10pm
Bill E $4.50–$10 **M** $10–$29.50 **D** $6.50–$8.80; $2 pp surcharge on public holidays
Cards AE BC MC V Eftpos
Wine Reasonable if commercial list, chosen for food style; little by the glass; BYO (corkage $2 pp or $10 per bottle)
Chef/owner John Poh
Seats 120
www.kuali.com.au
And... Queensland mud crab with Poh's curry sauce is legendary

La Goulue

17 Alexander Street, Crows Nest
Tel 9439 1640   Map 5A

Modern French

Score 14/20

'La Goulue' (the glutton), was a dancer at the Moulin Rouge who had a voracious appetite for food, wine and men. The restaurant that bears her nickname is BYO and the men in attendance all appear to be taken, but this lower north-side stayer would at least satisfy her hunger for the meals she might have devoured at a Parisian bistro. Smartly attired waiters in black vests stroll polished floorboards with a professionalism that is never stuffy, while chef Wayne Smith provides a menu driven equally by local produce and traditional French technique. Starters might include scallops with ginger butter, octopus carpaccio, or roasted salmon and scampi with a white miso sauce. Mains are similarly assured and include roasted white rabbit with truffled cannellini beans, stuffed pig's trotter, and a seared kangaroo loin with beetroot, all accompanied by silver-served green beans and mash. It would not be excessive to finish with champagne-poached peach with lemon verbena mousse, or parfait of liquorice with slow-roasted blood plums and plum sorbet.

Hours Dinner Tues–Sat 6pm–late
Bill E $16.50–$18.50 **M** $26–$29 **D** $12–$13; dégustation menu $80 pp
Cards AE BC DC MC V
Wine BYO (corkage $2.50 pp)
Chef Wayne Smith
Owners Wayne Smith & Emmanuelle Delaunay
Seats 100; private rooms
And...private dining room upstairs

city + suburbs L

La Grande Bouffe

2/758 Darling Street, Rozelle
Tel 9818 4333   Map 5B

French
Score 14/20

La Grande Bouffe is the local French restaurant we all need; and if you don't live nearby, the generous servings of classic country cooking at great prices are worth travelling for. Heavy wooden tables, chairs and floorboards offer little to dampen the sounds of passing traffic and chatting diners, making it buzzy at best and noisy at worst. Once the food arrives, all is forgiven. It's bright and breezy by day, with a lighter menu offering dishes such as a creamy, cooling cucumber soup topped with slippery ribbons of crunchy cucumber. There are baguettes, salads and good French omelettes. Chef Colin Fassnidge's time with Raymond Blanc in the UK and Liam Tomlin at Banc in Sydney shows in his skill with offal and interpretations of classic dishes such as French onion soup and cassoulet. The suspicion that a French restaurant has no business serving risotto, however, proved well founded. Service can be a bit casual at lunch, but at dinner owner David Poirier turns on his Gallic charm.

Hours Daily 7am–3.30pm; Dinner Tues–Sat 6.30pm–late
Bill E $15–$18 **M** $24–$26 **D** $4.50–$7
Cards AE BC DC MC V Eftpos; bookings essential
Wine Very well priced; 9 by the glass, all French; BYO Tues–Thurs (corkage $8 per bottle)
Chef Colin Fassnidge
Owners David & Meredith Poirier
Seats 50; wheelchair access; outdoor seats
And… they roast their own coffee and serve great breakfasts until midday

La Grillade

Cnr Alexander & Albany Streets, Crows Nest
Tel 9439 3707   Map 5A

French/Steakhouse   ♇
Score 13/20

The name (The Grill) clearly heralds the intent of this North Shore institution. They take steak seriously, with half a dozen choices, from hereford to angus, wagyu and wagyu-cross. This charmingly old-school restaurant of double-cloth'd tables, dark heavy timbers and polished service is a honey pot for meat-seeking businesspeople who also love a good Burgundy from the cracker wine list. Peter and Bev Hammerschmidt have played affable hosts for more than 20 years, with solid soul food and the occasional French cliché – snails with garlic butter – to please all-comers. They might enjoy grilled quail with a salad of roasted chestnuts, eschalots, pancetta and fragrant herbs. However, while French onion soup with a gruyère crouton was pleasant, it lacked the piquancy and oomph we'd hoped for and, on one visit, the steak, while perfectly cooked, seemed light on flavour. Thankfully, the lush Thirlmere spatchcock with Jerusalem artichokes, celeriac, Swiss browns and a thyme jus is truly scrumptious and the Grand Marnier soufflé will keep everyone coming back for more.

Hours Lunch Mon–Fri noon–4pm; Dinner Mon–Sat 6–10.30pm
Bill E $15–$25 **M** $28–$45 **D** $15–$16
Cards AE BC DC MC V
Wine A breathtaking choice of 500-plus wines at reasonable prices; 13 by the glass
Chef Roger Barstow
Owners Peter & Bev Hammerschmidt
Seats 140; private rooms; outdoor seats
www.lagrillade.com.au
And… you can also drop by for a drink in the outdoor bar area

city + suburbs

La Locanda

65B Macpherson Street, Bronte
Tel 9389 3666   Map 9

Italian

Score 14/20

'The Inn', as this place literally translates, has a black-and-white renaissance feature wall, tightly packed timber tables and mod-Italian fare from Andrea Vagge (ex Otto). Perch yourself on a hard bistro chair and get into squid filled with ricotta, scented with mint and sage – the squid, like the one you love, showing a perfect balance of resilience and tenderness. Or find a little space on the banquette lining the narrow rectangular room to indulge in a fine and fabulous eggplant parmigiana, with its glossy caramelised topping of mozzarella. Vagge is a dab hand at risotto, but the finest touch in the room could well be that of co-owner Fiona Bloomer who works the room with unbridled enthusiasm. If you have room for something sexy, wait until you try the sensual roasted peach halves with a cloud of mascarpone. Or for those who prefer a little more bitterness in their life, the chocolate mousse is spiced with 70 per cent Callebaut, sparring with the cut and thrust of amaretti biscuits.

Hours Dinner Tues–Sun 6–9.30pm
Bill E $13 **M** $20–25 **D** $11
Cards MC V Eftpos
Wine A snappy but well-picked list; 7 by the glass; BYO Tues–Thurs & Sun (corkage $3 pp)
Chef Andrea Vagge
Owners Fiona Bloomer & Andrea Vagge
Seats 50; wheelchair access; outdoor seats
And...parking is easy and the street-side tables are perfect for perving

La Perla

255 Victoria Road, Gladesville
Tel 9816 1161   Map 7

Southern Italian/Seafood

Score 13/20

Giorgio Colosi is one of Sydney's pioneer Italian restaurateurs – one of many (think Swordfish, Grappa) who had their start in this Calabrian-inspired semi-open kitchen overlooking a large modern room, simply decorated. That southern favourite, fritelle di nannata (small whitebait pan-fried as fritters) are full of flavoursome crunch. Deep-fried harbour prawns are simple and satisfying. Antipasto di mare is more Aussie than necessary to include oysters and smoked salmon. You're better off with the swordfish carpaccio simply served on rocket with virgin olive oil. A prime piece of red emperor relaxing on caponata (stewed eggplant and capsicum) is rich and satisfying. Risotto pescatore (with prawns, vongole, calamari and mussels) has a well-balanced ocean flavour with correctly nutty textured rice and just the right amount of juice. Desserts include a fine pannacotta with strawberry coulis and a good choice of gelato. Best avoid non-Italian sounding dishes (such as Swedish prawns with chilli, garlic and paprika) and rejoice in simple, genuine southern flavours.

Hours Lunch Tues–Fri noon–3pm;
Dinner Tues–Sun 6–10pm
Bill E $14–$25 **M** $21–$40 **D** $8–$14
Cards AE BC DC MC V
Wine Smallish well-considered list with some interesting Italians; 14 by the glass
Chef/owner Giorgio Colosi
Seats 130; private room; wheelchair access
www.laperla.com.au
And...check out the long list of seafood specials

city + suburbs L

Les Trois Freres

16 The Princess Highway, Sylvania
Tel 9544 7609   Map 8

Contemporary

Score 13/20

The sign outside still says 'Trois Freres' and the bill says 'three brothers', but it's all Tod Laurence now, and the décor has changed. The room now boasts warm beige and chocolate walls and smart lights. A large timber-framed mirror balances an equally large blackboard of specials, such as seared scallops with basil and tomato gratin. The food is still a cut above most suburban offerings. Toasted Turkish bread has a deep and intensely green chive glaze for dipping. Spiced duck pancakes are not that spicy, but the meat falls apart and the pancake is gentle. Pumpkin and ricotta-filled zucchini flowers are sensational with a remoulade that has a secret extra ingredient, basil. Veal medallions arrive juicy and sweet and taste oh-so-Greek with fetta and sage and caper butter. The duck confit may be given edginess from figs laced with balsamic. Desserts could be more inventive to match the other courses, but it would be mean-spirited to complain about a white chocolate brûlée or the 'Original 3 Brothers Sticky Toffee Date Pudding'.

Hours Dinner Tues–Sat from 6.30pm
Bill E $15.50–$20 **M** $26–$30 **D** $14
Cards AE BC DC MC V
Wine BYO (corkage $2 pp)
Chef/owner Tod Laurence
Seats 50
And...you can take home the chive glaze and the caesar and vinaigrette dressings

liquidity

1 James Craig Road, Rozelle Bay
Tel 9810 3433   Map 5B

Contemporary

Score 13/20

Supercruisers dominate the maritime view, but Rozelle Bay's comparatively modest dragon boats are more likely to make an impact on your order. There's nothing like watching other people sweat to steer you away from 800 grams of Darling Downs wagyu T-bone – that and the $48 price tag. Liquidity makes a big deal of its hand-selected prime beef, befitting chef Nathan Tillott's previous stint at Prime and 300 grams of rump, served with roasted eschalots and baby spinach showcases his talent. But lighter (and cheaper) options, perhaps better suited to the restaurant's waterside locale, abound. Dill-flecked, gin-cured yellow fin tuna reclines in a pool of chilled dashi broth. Perfectly seared estuary scallops arrive topped with poached black figs. The only slip-up was an unheralded substitution of peas for broad beans in an otherwise comforting slow-roasted organic chicken. Service is steady but can lose its grip on busy nights. The dessert tasting plate, featuring mini-donuts in lemon sugar, is one of the best we've had.

Hours Tues–Sat noon–10pm; Sun noon–9.30pm
Bill E $17–$22 **M** $25–$48 **D** $10–$16
Cards AE BC DC MC V Eftpos
Wine Wide-ranging at waterfront prices; 16 by the glass
Chef Nathan Tillott
Owners Rob Rubis & Chris James
Seats 260; private room; wheelchair access; outdoor seats
And...quiet nights earlier in the week can be a bit funereal

city + suburbs

Local

211 Glenmore Road, Paddington
Tel 9332 1577   Map 4B

Mediterranean

Score 14/20

So you want a cocktail bar down the road, do you? Somewhere not too smart, where normal people will fit in but the drinks are luscious? Some very good bistro food, perhaps, delivered by a waiting team that punches well above its weight? And a leafy courtyard out the back to park the pram once the baby comes? Well, have we got the local for you! Ex Hugo's boy Tristian Hope has stripped the short-lived Booker's, brightened and lightened the space with modern neutral tones and installed a menu that runs from smoked salmon on rye for brekkie to oysters with champagne-and-vanilla jelly at night. His paella has prawns, mussels and the less traditional (but we like it) chorizo. The richness of duck confit is cut with earthy lentils and a slightly too sweet caramelised pear. Scallops with pancetta and skordalia are given the pepperiness of rocket. And the strawberry tart with scorched almonds and balsamic syrup is enough to make you want to move in to the neighbourhood.

Hours Breakfast Sat–Sun 9am–3.30pm; Lunch Fri–Sun noon–3.30pm; Dinner Mon–Sat 6–10.30pm
Bill E $13–$17 **M** $16–$29 **D** $12–$15; 10% surcharge on public holidays
Cards AE BC MC V
Wine Benchmark modern bistro list; 15 by the glass; good cocktails
Chef Tristian Hope
Owner S.H.516 Group
Seats 90; outdoor seats
www.localwinebarandrestaurant.com.au
And…Karl Edmonds on the floor adds that extra flourish

Loco

9/81–91 Military Road, Neutral Bay
Tel 9953 9387   Map 5A

Contemporary

Score 13/20

As clean and bright as a glorious Sydney day, Loco keeps that summer feeling with its pristine interior: vibrant turquoise touches, surfboards ready to tuck under the arm and bright Aboriginal art. There's also the relaxed, personable service from owner Charles Schmidt as he cruises the tables in this oasis just off busy Military Road. While mud crab remains a stand-out, there are plenty more pleasures to choose from. But don't look for Peking in the duck pancakes with plum sauce, shallots and chilli: it's a large, soft pancake wrapped around shredded, but skinless, meat. Chargrilled calamari arrived a touch too chewy with a Moroccan salsa dominated by smoked paprika. A well-executed crisp roasted salmon fillet with asparagus, fennel tops and crab beurre blanc is rich but clean – so too a creamy blue cheese caramelised onion tart beneath beautifully rested slices of venison. Sorbets win in the dessert stakes, perhaps strawberry beside a strawberry-and-mascarpone millefeuille – all crisp leaves, creamy filling and fresh fruit.

Hours Lunch Tues–Fri noon–3pm; Dinner Mon–Sat 6pm–late
Bill E $15–$18 **M** $24–$32 **D** $10–12
Cards AE BC DC MC V Eftpos
Wine Reasonably priced, diverse list with small museum stock; 8 by the glass; BYO (corkage $3.50 pp)
Chef David Allan
Owner Charles Schmidt
Seats 60; wheelchair access; outdoor seats
www.loco.net.au
And…regular mud crab nights still pack 'em in

city + suburbs L

Logues

21 Elizabeth Bay Road, Elizabeth Bay
Tel 9358 2600   Map 2

Italian

Score 13/20

For more than a decade, caterer Simmone Logue has been putting food on the tables of Sydney's swankier homes. Now she wants everyone to come to her place – the old Sebel Townhouse – for dinner, and a relaxed and comfortable Italianesque bistro menu. Wander past the display cabinets brimming with an honour guard of sweet temptations and settle on the banquette in a red-hued room that balances modernity with a touch of rustic charm. The food is simple and reassuringly familiar, so don't expect your socks rocked. A generous bowl of gnocchi gorgonzola cleverly walks the fine line between light and rich. But the chilli in blue swimmer crab and tomato fettuccine won't scare the horses. Crisp-skinned barra with crushed Jerusalem artichokes, asparagus and sauce vièrge struts its stuff, just as rare beef on sweet onion galette with anchovy butter mixes sweet and salty. In the mornings, the locals drop by before work for French toast, the house-made banana bread or a croque 'Simmone' with a fried egg.

Hours Breakfast Mon–Fri 7am–noon, Sat–Sun 8am–3pm; Lunch daily noon–5pm; Dinner daily 6–10pm
Bill E $15–$18 **M** $18–$28 **D** $10; 10% surcharge on public holidays
Cards AE BC MC V Eftpos
Wine Reasonable mix with some boutique interest; 15 by the glass; BYO (corkage $10 per bottle)
Chef Andy Logue
Owners Simmone Logue & Jeremy Brender
Seats 58; wheelchair access; outdoor seats
www.simmonelogue.com
And...drop in for a cake or pre-cooked dishes to take home and serve

Longrain

85 Commonwealth Street, Surry Hills
Tel 9280 2888   Map 3A

Thai

Score 16/20

Perennially hip, Longrain attracts everyone from fashionistas to foodies to this dark wood, plate glass, converted warehouse space. They come for the bloody Longrains (a rocket-fuelled bloody Mary), to be part of the cool gang and for an interesting take on modern Thai food. The downside is that you can't book for dinner, have to wait for a seat (spending more on cocktails than on dinner) and might have trouble hearing yourself think. But who cares, once you're squeezed onto the communal table, getting stuck into betel leaves with smoked trout, or hot and sour duck salad, eye-poppingly loaded with fresh coriander, chilli, mint and lime. Our caramelised pork hock was chewy, crunchy (perhaps just a smidgen too crunchy, as was the rice) and served with a power-packed five-spice-and-chilli vinegar. Whole fish in various guises are a speciality: the baby snapper may look like it's been swimming through the fire swamp, but delicate flesh is beautifully offset by thick red curry sauce, bolstered with both apple and pea eggplants along with baby corn.

Hours Lunch Mon–Fri noon–2.30pm; Dinner Mon–Sat 6–11pm
Bill E $4.50–$26 **M** $18–$48 **D** $8–$13.50
Cards AE BC DC MC V; bookings lunch only
Wine Comprehensive, high-end list, with many 'pinks'; 15 by the glass
Chef Martin Boetz
Owners Sam Christie, John Sample & Martin Boetz
Seats 96; private room, wheelchair access
www.longrain.com.au
And... Longrain sauces, music CDs and a cookbook are all available to buy

FISH & CHIPS

A Fish Called Coogee
229 Coogee Bay Road, Coogee
Tel 9664 7700
And also **A Fish Called Paddo**
239 Glenmore Road, Paddington
Tel 9326 9500
Pick from half a dozen marinated fish – perhaps Balinese snapper in sweet soy – to take home or cook on the coconut grill. There's lightly battered fish, plus Thai fish cakes, and chips which are cut daily.

Bottom of the Harbour
21 The Esplanade, Balmoral
Tel 9969 7911
There's a reason for the queue. The fish is restaurant quality, the oil is clean and smoking hot so there's not a hint of grease about the chips, and the beach is an idyllic location to ogle your battered bits.

Fish Face
132 Darlinghurst Road, Darlinghurst
Tel 9332 4803 (Takeaway 9332 4809)
One of Sydney's finest seafood chefs is doing yummy fish 'n' chips (and more) for takeaway from his fish cafe. Stephen Hodges serves the hand-cut chips in a paper cone.

Flying Fish and Chips
Lower Deck, Jones Bay Wharf, Shop 124, 19–21 Pirrama Road, Pyrmont
Tel 9571 6637
The flash fine diner has a cheaper takeaway, doing barramundi burgers, blue swimmer crab sandwiches and excellent battered fish. Grab a gaggle of potato scallops, dangle your legs over the wharf and make those inside dream of trading places.

Mohr Fish
202 Devonshire Street, Surry Hills
Tel 9318 1326
A tiny white-tiled corner cafe that's relentlessly popular, as much for the fish and prawn dumplings as the fillets, with a choice of toppings, plus potatoes done one of three ways. Grab takeaway if you don't feel like waiting at the pub next door.

Ocean Foods
154 Lyons Road, Drummoyne
Tel 9181 4336
The clue to the quality at this part fresh seafood store, part takeaway lies in the chef's whites on the staff and the lack of manky deep-fryer smells. Get wild barramundi in the finest batter, a crumbed fish burger or some dory fresh from the grill with fat chips.

Peter's Fish Market
Shop 4, Waterfront Arcade, Sydney Fish Markets, Blackwattle Bay
Tel 9552 2555
You'd hope to find some good fish and chips at Australia's best seafood market. Peter's does a whole lot of deep-fried, grilled and crumbed options for everybody to take down to the water's edge and eat within cooee of Sydney's shrinking fishing fleet.

Roger Fish Cafe Grill
6/2A Waters Road, Neutral Bay
Tel 9953 6242
Butcher's paper-topped tables; around a dozen fish (grilled or beer battered); oysters; whitebait; steamed mussels; chunky golden fish cakes; good, cheap wines. The $8 battered dory takeaway will have you hooked.

Sea Cow
110D Boundary Street, Paddington
Tel 9332 2458
Tables spills onto the footpath as Moby (of course) grooves away from this funky, laidback corner fisho. Savour oysters shucked to order and smart entrées, then deftly cooked fish, such as chargrilled tuna with tamarind–chilli jam, on a silver platter.

The One that Got Away
163 Bondi Road, Bondi
Tel 9389 4227
Perch on a stool in the aquatically lurid room, or take teriyaki-marinated tuna, sushi or sashimi down to the beach. Yam chips make a change, along with salt 'n' pepper prawns. They'll poach, steam or grill fish and serve it with rice for a healthy treat.

city + suburbs

Lotus

22 Challis Avenue, Potts Point
Tel 9326 9000   Map 2

Contemporary

Score 15/20

Since taking over the stoves in early 2004, Genevieve Copland has ensured that Lotus remains a perennial favourite. The small, square, designer space, with its Florence Broadhurst wallpaper and feature blackboard menu, is inevitably packed. Our one complaint might be the sleek white tables rammed too close together for comfort or privacy, but we've no such laments for the food. Butterflied sardines are crumbed and pan-fried to a crisp counterpoint for the tender, oily fish within. Scallop lasagne is a masterpiece of simplicity: a sweet, basil-laced tomato sugo caressing silken folds of pasta, dotted with five perfect, just-beyond-translucent scallops. The crisp skin of a chargrilled spatchcock carries a hint of chilli heat, contrasting beautifully with the succulent flesh. The tang of a creamy yoghurt sorbet offsets the sweetness of berries floating in a delectable berry 'soup'. Exemplary service echoes the quality of the food, but it's paired with an easy informality – a perfect fit for the über-hip atmosphere that Lotus does so well.

Hours Dinner Tues–Thurs 6–10.30pm, Fri–Sat 6–11pm
Bill E $16–$19 **M** $26–$29 **D** $12; 10% surcharge on public holidays
Cards AE BC DC MC V Bookings essential
Wine A well-selected, medium-sized list ensures perfect matches to the food; 10 by the glass
Chef Genevieve Copland
Owner The Hemmes family
Seats 50; wheelchair access; outdoor seats
www.merivale.com/lotus
And...allow time for a pre-dinner cocktail in the groovy back bar with the young, thin and beautiful

Lucio's

47 Windsor Street, Paddington
Tel 9380 5996   Map 4B

Italian (Northern)

Score 16/20

After more than two decades, Lucio's still exudes the energy and passion of its Italian origins. Add the enthusiastic charm of Lucio Galletto, good northern Italian-inspired food and seamless service, and it's no wonder its popularity never wanes. Appreciative regulars include the art luminaries whose extraordinary works adorn the walls, pollies, media moguls, the infamous and the Eastern Suburbs set. The food can be as dazzling as the surrounds, such as buffalo mozzarella, prosciutto and marinated grilled figs, which simply sparkle on the tastebuds. The menu changes seasonally, with plenty of enticing daily specials. Involtini of herbed salmon is a faultless execution of delicate flavours and texture that's also eye-catching when perfectly centred on a brilliant spring-pea risotto. The reason pasta is so popular is obvious in a generous bowl of farfalle with zucchini flowers, tomatoes, capers, bread and chilli that's honest tucker for the soul. The impressive wine list includes some wonderful stickies to accompany the celebrated tiramisu.

Hours Lunch Mon–Sat 12.30–3pm; Dinner Mon–Sat 6.30–11pm
Bill E $26–$29.50 **M** $36.50–$39.50 **D** $16
Cards AE BC DC MC V
Wine Expertly selected Italian and local range including an impressive cellar selection; 17 by the glass
Chef Timothy Fisher
Owners Lucio & Sally Galletto
Seats 75; private room
www.lucios.com.au
And...arrive early to enjoy the local galleries before dining surrounded by more legendary artworks

city + suburbs   L

Lunch

The Quadrangle, 5/100 Edinburgh Road, Castlecrag
Tel 9958 8441   Map 7

Contemporary

Score 13/20

There was a time, after Annie Parmentier left Lunch, when some of the magic waned. But now we're eager to get back in the paved courtyard at Castlecrag for a dose of newcomer Ben Peterson's feel-good fare, even if it isn't lunchtime. Yep, the plastic-sided, tent-like space is heated in the cooler months so you can duck in for brekkie or dinner in relative comfort. An ever-changing, cheerful menu of things you'll recognise and want to eat is written on the big whiteboards. The fish of the day could be marlin, topped with glassy-centred scallops and lashings of herb butter on tomato rice. There could be a caramelised onion and blue cheese tart or star anise-flavoured duck breast with bok choi and quince. Lamb rack may be roasted and served with hummus, the veal is pale and milk fed, pairing effortlessly with black olive butter and cavolo nero. Desserts, such as banana strudel, are sweet enough to have you coming back for dinner.

Hours Breakfast daily 8.30–11am; Lunch daily noon–3pm; Dinner Thurs–Sat 6–9pm
Bill E $14.50–$16.50 **M** $19.50–$25 **D** $9–$11; 10% surcharge on public holidays
Cards BC MC V Eftpos
Wine Licence pending; BYO (corkage $1.50 pp)
Chef Ben Peterson
Owners George Ng & Sally Schofield
Seats 85; wheelchair access; outdoor seats
And…bring a cardie for those cooler days as there's always a draft

L'unico

79 Elliott Street, Balmain
Tel 9810 5466   Map 5B

Modern Italian

Score 13/20

There's a colosseum's worth of Italian style packed into this elegant Victorian terrace, the name of which aptly translates as 'unique'. Its warm contemporary interior blends with original features, while stairs lead up to the kitchen and more dining space, down to the bar and outside to the garden courtyard. The mood is totally Italian, with wonderful green olives generously placed on white-cloth'd tables and polished floor staff who never miss a beat. And while it's bustling, L'unico is comfortable enough to chatter. Nominally Italian dishes are entwined with some stand-out modern fare such as slow-cooked pork belly, partnered with scallops and cauliflower purée. Tender involtini of veal, provolone and sage comes roasted and resting on radicchio salad. Freshly made pasta can come as entrées or mains. The gnocchi, with wild mushrooms, tomato and butter broth, plus a rocket, pear and parmesan salad both deliver delight to the palate. A sweet lasagne of pineapple and white chocolate with black Sambuca gelato keeps the unique reputation alive.

Hours Lunch Wed–Fri & Sun noon–3pm; Dinner Wed–Mon 6–10pm
Bill E $16–$22 **M** $26–$30 **D** $12–15; dégustation menu $90 pp
Cards AE BC DC MC V
Wine Premium selection of Australian and Italian labels; 18 by the glass; BYO Sun–Fri (corkage $5 pp)
Chef Chris Cossey
Owners Joseph & Jennifer Santoro
Seats 120; private rooms; outdoor seats
www.lunico.com.au
And…enquire about the Italian dining experience with suggested wines – ideal for groups

city + suburbs

Machiavelli
123 Clarence Street, Sydney
Tel 9299 3748   Map 1

Italian

Score 12/20

There's no subtle regional style in the food at this legendary terracotta-tiled basement home of the political power lunch. But there's definitely a sense of nostalgia as old-style Italian waiters in bowties deliver gracious service and morsels from the centrepiece antipasto table adorned with hanging garlic and salami. At lunch the place buzzes with current and ex-pollies (check how well they've aged by their portrait on the wall), and rich-list contenders enjoying old-style Aussie–Italian. The signature calamari fritte is good enough to not want to share, but veal pizzaiola was drowned in tomato sauce with indistinguishable chilli and garlic, even if the chips are good and creamed spinach is great comfort food. Grilled john dory is simple, fresh and delicious with a generous side salad. A waiter makes zabaglione at the table with sweet sherry, eggs, sugar and good old-fashioned elbow grease. While the food and value can be as mixed as backbench solidarity, you come here for the fun of it and the old-school experience.

Hours Lunch Mon–Fri noon–2.30pm; Dinner Mon–Fri 6–9.30pm
Bill E $16–$39 **M** $16–$39 **D** $14–$32
Cards AE BC DC MC V
Wine Expensive Italian & Oz list; 15 by the glass
Chefs Caterina Tarchi, Laurent Cambon & Giovanna Toppi
Owners Giovanna Toppi & Caterina Tarchi
Seats 230
www.machiavelli.com.au
And...see the huge photos of politicians adorning the walls, especially our beloved PM in his days as Treasurer

Macleay Street Bistro
73A Macleay Street, Potts Point
Tel 9358 4891   Map 2

Contemporary

Score 13/20

This petite Potts Point stalwart offers just about everything you'd ever want in a local bistro. Sure, the butcher's paper-topped tables are tiny and you'll probably bump elbows with the adjacent diner, and the din can get a bit much when it's packed, but it's always open, well-priced and vibrantly abuzz, with chirpy, efficient service. The simple, tile-floored white-walled room is a series of nooks and crannies with mirrors to make it look larger. The menu is mainly familiar bistro faves, plus blackboard specials that also seem rusted on, such as a (perhaps too) vinegary gazpacho with prawns and spiced avocado; or earthy barramundi on cauliflower purée, topped with shredded zucchini, currants and pine nuts. There's satisfying assurance in gently chargrilled octopus flecked with Persian fetta, oregano and piperade. Baked risotto has the crunch of deep-fried zucchini and a dollop of melting goat's cheese, but we really wanted stirred-in creaminess. The theatre of a crunchy-toffee-topped lemon curd brûlée in a martini glass sends you off with a smile.

Hours Dinner daily 6–11pm
Bill E $15–$15.50 **M** $22.50–$31.50 **D** $12.50
Cards AE BC DC MC V
Wine BYO (corkage $2.50 pp)
Chef Ben Fitton
Owner Carole Becka
Seats 50; outdoor seats
And...it's only closed Christmas day and Good Friday

We prefer

All it takes.

You are invited to join, for free!

my restaurant club

earn rewards
every time you dine

Enjoy a more rewarding dining experience with many of Australia's leading restaurants in My Restaurant Club. You can start earning Reward Points right now and use them to cover all or part of your restaurant bill!†

To activate your attached card now go online at www.myrestaurantclub.com.au or call the My Restaurant Club Service Centre on 1300 787 188.

Earn Rewards every time you dine

We prefer VISA
All it takes.

- Earn Rewards every time you dine at a participating restaurant nationwide
- You will earn Reward points to the value of 5% of your bill
- Use these points to cover all or part of your restaurant bill at any time
- Use any form of payment – we prefer VISA
- Membership is free

Start earning right away
- Your My Restaurant Club card is attached. You can start earning Reward points right now
- Simply register online at www.myrestaurantclub.com.au or call the My Restaurant Club Service Centre on 1300 787 188

Welcome to My Restaurant Club, and bon appétit!

A selection of the hundreds of My Restaurant Club member restaurants

NSW
Al Porto
Alio
Arcardi Restaurant & Lounge Bar
Arena
Arun Thai
Astral
Bilson's
Bistro CBD
Cadmus
Cafe B & C
Confucius Chinese Restaurant
Cruise
Darcy's
Deco at the Civic
Devonshire Thai
Dish Pizza & Gelato
Emperor's Garden
Forty One
Inside Out Restaurant
Jazushi
Kuali
Lotus
Malabar Indian Restaurant
Manly Bay Seafood Restaurant
Oh! Calcutta!
Pello Restaurant
Produce Café and Catering Provision
Puntino Trattoria

Pyrmonts
Qmin
Reflections on the Promenade
Restaurant Atelier
Rock Salt Restaurant
Royal Bar & Grill
Santorini on Oxford
Summit Restaurant
The Table Guesthouse
Waterfront Restaurant
Wolfies Grill

QLD
Bryce's Dining & Wine Bar
Bulimba Bean Café & Restaurant
Domani's Cafe Restaurant Bar
Glassworks Wine Bar Bistro
Harley Street Brasserie
Harvey's
Mariosarti Ristorante Italiano
Melange
Oberoi's Taj
Omeros Bros Seafood Restaurant
Reflections on the Promenade
Ruffino's
Sage Cafe Restaurant
Thai Mali
Vue Restaurant & Bar
Zak's Bistro & Bar
Zinc Port Douglas

VIC
Aya Japanese Restaurant
Bottega
Di Palma's Restaurant Bar (Kew East and Hawthorn)
Eurasia
Finz Seafood Restaurant
Le Gourmet
Saucier Restaurant
Shalimar Indian Restaurant
Watson & Di Palma's Restaurant Bar
Windows On The Bay

WA
C Restaurant In the Sky
Chanterelle At Jessica's
Friends Restaurant
Jetty's Restaurant
Roxby Thai Cafe Restaurant
Sensations en Ardross
Shun Fung On The River
Sunsets Cafe Bistro
The Cross Cafe Restaurant Bar
The Fishy Affair
The Gala Restaurant

TAS
La Carafe

Restaurant listing current as at time of production.
†Please refer to www.myrestaurantclub.com.au for full program Terms and Conditions.

city + suburbs M

Mahjong Room

312 Crown Street, Surry Hills
Tel 9361 3985   Map 2

Chinese

Score 13/20

Entering this lively Chinese-style diner just off Oxford Street is like entering the set of *In the Mood for Love*, that romantic, colour-drenched Hong Kong flick. The room is filled with Chinois style: red lanterns (er, lamps, actually) abound and there's an atmospheric narrow alley-style area where pairs of diners can eat at solid stone tables. Entrée choices are strong on dim sum-style items, such as the siu mai chicken and prawn, or poached blue swimmer crab dumplings – the latter seemed a tad short on crab. Salmon wontons also lacked any discernible salmon. Crisp san-dong chicken, served with a light ginger sauce, is a tender treat; black pepper scotch fillet with mushroom and red onion is a crowd-pleaser. The more adventurous are kept happy by sweet vinegar pork belly ribs or roast duck with Chinese mushrooms and snowpeas. And while there are no mahjong games, this is an easy-going, reliable place with commendably friendly and efficient service, especially during quieter moments in the early or late evening.

Hours Dinner Mon–Sat 6pm–10.30pm
Bill E $9–$22 **M** $14.50–$28 **D** $9–$12
Cards AE BC MC V
Wine Short, but surprisingly international (French, Spanish and Germans); 8 by the glass; BYO (corkage $3 pp)
Chef Billy To
Owners Erika Chan & William Hui
Seats 50; private rooms
www.mahjongroom.com.au
And...warning, warning: no espresso coffee, just plunger

Malabar

332 Pacific Highway, Crows Nest
Tel 9906 7343   Map 5A
Also at 6/274 Victoria Street, Darlinghurst
Tel 9332 1755   Map 2

South Indian

Score 12/20

Lord Vishnu might be a little miffed to discover Malabar offering a beef vindaloo rather than a real Goan pork version, but then we suspect Malabar's dharma is a little askew, especially when the menu says that 'vindaloo' means vinegar and potato, when it really means vinegar and garlic. And while the newer Darlo sibling bustles along, despite a clunky and somewhat clichéd décor with Raj-era photo-murals (where's Lakshmi when you need her?), the two-storey Crows Nest version offers a refreshingly spare interior. No matter which deity you pray to, the Malabar version of that South Indian staple, dosa (rice and lentil crêpes) are heaven sent: golden, crunchy and deliciously filled with prawns, minced lamb or potato. The rest of the fare has a strong emphasis on protein, but it's competently handled – from a genuinely Goan prawn balchau to a hearty northern lamb shank rogan josh. And the thalis, large plates with a variety of dishes, shouldn't be missed if you're visiting on weekdays.

Hours Lunch Sun–Fri noon–2.30pm; Dinner daily 5.30–10.30pm
Bill E $5–$13 **M** $11–$19 **D** $3–$5
Cards AE BC DC MC V
Wine Functional Oz list; 10 by the glass; BYO (corkage $1 pp)
Chef Pandian Palani
Owner Wilson Varghese
Seats 165; private rooms
www.malabarcuisine.com.au
And...you need only two to have a banquet

city + suburbs

The Malaya

39 Lime Street, King Street Wharf, Sydney
Tel 9279 1170   Map 1

Malaysian

Score 13/20

This well-oiled 30-year-old institution (though in a newer location) offers slick service and unimpeded views across the Darling Harbour expanse. The large and bustling room with a galley-long bar has young Turks mixing cocktails at one end and older Asian chefs working the woks at the other. At lunch, it's packed with businessmen washing down the Malay spices with Tiger beers, and by night, with tourists and celebratory revellers at large tables. The huge menu ventures through Malaysia and beyond. A generous, above-average sang choi bau fills crisp lettuce cups with a deliciously moist and spicy blend of water chestnuts, pork and shallots. However, popiah – thin pastry skins filled with chicken, prawns and shallots – tasted lifeless. Chilli snake beans are invigorated by succulent prawns with the delicious addition of shredded Chinese mushrooms. A deep coconut marinade of a traditional chicken rendang delivers complex flavours, with lemongrass and chilli adding fresh texture. And the Malaya's signature laksa is a worthy old standby if you want to try the original, and one of the best.

Hours Lunch daily noon–3pm; Dinner daily 6pm–late
Bill E $9–$19 **M** $17–$26; 10% surcharge on Sundays, 15% on public holidays
Cards AE BC DC MC V; bookings essential
Wine Solid boutique list; 15 by the glass
Chef Mustapa Jaffar
Owners Lance & Givie Wong
Seats 300; private room; wheelchair access; outdoor seats
www.themalaya.com.au
And...remember to book, because it's very popular

Mamma Barone

1/341 Rocky Point Road, Sans Souci
Tel 9529 0600   Map 8

Italian (Southern)

Score 13/20

You'll discover this modern and comfortable restaurant along an unpromising stretch of suburban road, but it's worth the stop for honest Neapolitan cooking, with strong, unrestrained flavours that really satisfy. Neonata (traditional whitebait fritters) are thick and perfectly fried, the moist interior exploding with briny lushness to the bite. Good pizza has a crisp, thin base; the Napoletana topped with a bold and salty mix of sun-dried tomatoes, capers, olives and anchovies. Spaghetti bolognese made with beef, veal, pork and chicken livers was a little unbalanced, with an assertive tomato flavour and too much meat for the pasta. The misto di mare is brimming with fresh seafood – mussels, vongole, prawns, calamari and scallops – in a good supporting broth of tomato and white wine. Even the salads are worth a mention, especially the crisp radicchio e rucola (rocket) with a restrained balsamic dressing. Desserts change daily, but thankfully always include an Italian classic like strawberries with zabaglione.

Hours Dinner Tues–Sat 6–10pm
Bill E $13.80–$21.80 **M** $23.80–$36.80 **D** $10.80–$12.80
Cards AE BC MC V; bookings essential
Wine Good, smallish list; some notable Australians and some Italians; 6 by the glass; BYO (corkage $2 pp)
Chef/owner Riccardo Roberti
Seats 55
And...parking behind the restaurant

city + suburbs

Manly Phoenix

Shop 22–23 Manly Wharf, East Esplanade, Manly
Tel 1300 883 892/9977 2988   Map 7

Chinese (Cantonese)

Score 12/20

Few restaurants have a better location, looking across to the city skyline from Manly Wharf. But maybe the clientele is a warning that this Phoenix no longer measures up to its siblings in Castle Hill and the city, for the room is alarmingly devoid of Chinese faces. Service is slick and attentive and the menu, while largely traditional, has a contemporary bent. On our visit, steamed scallops with soy, ginger and shallot were beautifully just-cooked but dominated by shards of shallot. Incredibly tender chunks of beef fillet had a pleasant kick from wasabi but arrived on shredded cabbage and carrot, surrounded by Pringles (yes, chips!) and sliced strawberries (we kid you not). Better was the lamb pancake, with tiny strips of succulent, sweet lamb. Imperial pork ribs turned out to be one huge rib, and tender enough if swimming beneath a tomato-dominated sauce with preserved plum. Lovers of authenticity may prefer Buddhism favour: a golden orb of beancurd encasing myriad vegetables including baby corn, mushrooms and bok choi.

Hours Mon–Sat 11am–10.15pm; Sun 10am–10pm
Bill E $6.60–$16.80 **M** $16.80–$29.80; live seafood at market prices; 10% surcharge on Sundays & public holidays
Cards AE BC DC MC V Eftpos; bookings essential
Wine Varied list with some good choices; 12 by the glass; BYO (corkage $6 per bottle, sparkling $8)
Chefs Bill Su & Sum Tang (Yum Cha)
Owners Anita Fung, Alice Lee & Raymond Yuen
Seats 150; private rooms; wheelchair access
www.phoenixrestaurants.com.au
And…yum cha is popular at lunchtime

Manly Wharf Hotel

Manly Wharf, East Esplanade, Manly
Tel 9977 1266   Map 7

Contemporary

Score 12/20

No need to worry about getting a view here – poised on the water beside the ferry terminal, you can see the Harbour from every table. On hot days, relax with a beer on the wooden outdoor decking; in winter retreat to the sleek Iain Halliday interior – full-length windows, open kitchen, clean lines – decorated in shades of grey sky and sand. You may have to use sign language with the friendly and helpful staff when noise levels rise on busy nights. And while the restaurant began with promise, such relentless popularity seems to have taken a toll on consistency. Fresh figs stuffed with blue cheese and prosciutto are a tangy combo of sweet and salty, but crisp duck with scallops and Asian herbs was slightly dry and stringy. Grilled snapper with nutty pumpkin, baby spinach and confit tomato is satisfying comfort food, but seafood risotto managed to be both claggy and undercooked at the same time. All is forgiven with a wonderful chocolate fondant swimming in rich sauce, butterscotch swirls and creamy vanilla ice-cream.

Hours Lunch Mon–Fri noon–3pm, Sat noon–4pm, Sun noon–4.30pm; Dinner Mon–Sat 6–10pm
Bill E $12–$22 **M** $24–$34 **D** $12–$14; 10% surcharge on Sundays & public holidays
Cards AE BC DC MC V Eftpos
Wine Reasonable Australian list; 17 by the glass
Chef Daniel Woodbridge
Owner Ben May
Seats 170; private room; wheelchair access; outdoor seats
www.manlywharfhotel.com.au
And…don't forget you can just have a beer at one of the four bars

city + suburbs

Manna

Cnr West & Station streets, Petersham
Tel **9568 4644**   Map 8

Contemporary
Score 14/20

The neighbourhood larrikin on the corner is growing up, with a cheerful nature and relaxed regulars intact. The wooden chairs are as eclectic as ever but now bottom-friendly, the floor is red tiled, and the colourful walls now have noise reduction panels. For once you get exactly what's on a menu: well-executed bistro-style dishes that not only please vego, carnivore and fish fancier alike but exceed expectations. Mushroom soup is dark, grainy, forest-floor earthy, brightened by a slurp of white truffle oil. You'll wish you'd ordered a main-course serve of the sweetbreads sautéed in butter with garlic and wild mushrooms, nubbins of snails adding a savoury touch. Pan-fried veal escalopes come with an aubergine fritter and a soupçon of white wine cream that doesn't overwhelm, the dish sparked by anchovy, caper and parsley sauce. Specials really are special – such as figs with a balsamic reduction and fruity raspberry sorbet. And service, as ever, is very well, um, manna'd.

Hours Lunch Sun noon–2.30pm; Dinner Tues–Sun from 6pm
Bill E $14.50–$17 **M** $21.50–$26.50 **D** $12.50–$13
Cards AE BC MC V
Wine Lovingly chosen, quality over quantity, with wide price range; 11 by the glass; BYO (corkage $5 per bottle)
Chef Matthew Lightowler
Owners Matthew Lightowler & Nina Alidenes
Seats 65; private room; wheelchair access
www.mannarestaurant.citysearch.com.au
And...bless the silent sommelier: there's a description of every wine on the list

Manta

The Wharf, 6 Cowper Wharf Road, Woolloomooloo
Tel **9332 3822**   Map 2

Italian/Seafood
Score 15/20

Where Manta Ray once stood, now you'll find Manta. At first glance, the shortened title is the only obvious change since last year. Okay, so the space has been remodelled slightly, with a blond colour scheme and some candle-style lighting inside, but the only things that matter are the chairs that dot the outside of the Finger Wharf – and their city views. The best change is that, with new chef Steve Manfredi at helm, the food has taken a turn for the better. No longer a lucky dip, now it's all good, and occasionally great, such as the yabby tails with tagliatelle and sesame seeds. Oysters are from the best suppliers, opened to order, and the seafood is as fresh as possible. It could be blue-eye with fresh Umbrian black truffles and farro, or potato with olive oil-braised tuna and tomato. Expect more from Manfredi once he finds his feet, but with Coast the next restaurant in the team's sights (it has the same owners), changes may be slow in coming.

Hours Lunch daily noon–3pm; Dinner daily from 6pm
Bill E $17–$28 **M** $19–$38 **D** $15; 10% surcharge on Sundays & public holidays
Cards AE BC DC MC V
Wine A real cracker of a list, with plenty of internationals; 18 by the glass
Chefs Stefano Manfredi & Alex Smith
Owners Tim Connell & Michael McCann
Seats 160; wheelchair access; outdoor seats
www.mantarestaurant.com.au
And...the menu is updated daily

city + suburbs

Marigold Citymark★

Levels 4 & 5, 683 George Street, Haymarket
Tel 9281 3388   Map 3A

Chinese (Cantonese)
Score 14/20

Favourite Yum Cha

Closer to the Capitol Theatre than the hubbub of Chinatown, Marigold continues to dish up all the old Cantonese favourites, a good variety of specials and fresh seafood from the tank. There's a well-represented Chinese diaspora that clearly feels at home, while proficient floor staff dash and dart from water tank to table to kitchen and back again. It's all a little frenetic, but fun, and works ideally for a group keen to give the lazy Susan a spin or tackle a renowned yum cha trolley at midday. Rice paper prawn rolls are plump and fresh while the crab and sweetcorn soup is as good as you'll find this side of Hong Kong. A duet of live cod, with stir-fried fillets, steamed head and belly, isn't for everyone (those who appreciate it certainly will). Crisp duck is a flavour feast that will please all palates. Golden, lightly battered salmon and eggplant with black beans and garlic is more-ish and well balanced with Buddha's crisp mixed vegetables.

Hours Lunch daily 10am–3pm; Dinner daily 5.30–11pm
Bill E $4.80–$15.80 **M** $14–$52 **D** $4–$8; $2 pp surcharge on public holidays
Cards AE BC DC MC V
Wine Typical range to accompany the fare; few by the glass
Chef Hon Hung Lai
Owner Nedosu Pty Ltd
Seats 800; private rooms
www.marigold.com.au
And...this popular yum cha palace also offers good-value banquet menus

Marque

4–5/355 Crown Street, Surry Hills
Tel 9332 2225   Map 3B

French
Score 19/20

This elegant room is a quietly sophisticated backdrop to quietly sophisticated food. Mark Best experiments with the art of surprising your mouth and your mind but never loses sight of his classic techniques or clientele. You can play safe with a millefeuille of Hervey Bay scallops, potato and olive 'truffles'. Then there's the unexpected: lobster broth, a fusion of bouillon and froth, atop a soft-centred ox-heart tomato, bathed in references to bouillabaisse and seafood chowders. Almond jelly with crab and almond gazpacho is a triumph that startles with echoes of sweetcorn. Muscovy duck with 'liquorice' (dried black olive and star anise) riffs like a powerhouse pinot noir. Roast venison with carrot confit and bitter chocolate plays sweet and piquant with the mellow meat. Goat's cheese marshmallow with lychees and coffee jellies is a fancy that will tickle yours. The wine list is exemplary and so too sommelier Nick Hildebrandt. It's all so extraordinary that you can't wait to tell someone. Luckily, the dedicated floor staff happily lend their ears.

Hours Dinner Mon–Sat 6.30–10.30pm
Bill E $24–$27 **M** $39–$44 **D** $18
Cards AE BC DC MC V Eftpos
Wine Pages of famous and lesser-known Australian and imported wines, spirits and fortifieds; 24 by the glass; BYO (corkage $12 per bottle)
Chef Mark Best
Owners Mark & Valerie Best
Seats 50; private room
www.marquerestaurant.com.au
And...there's an excellent selection of half bottles

city + suburbs

Maya Da Dhaba

431 Cleveland Street, Surry Hills
Tel 8399 3785 Map 3B

Indian

Score 13/20

The detailed menu descriptions imply that Maya Da Dhaba takes its food seriously; indeed, fail to take note and you may end up just as the tandoori chicken is described: impaled. And while the furniture is Gothic-heavy and décor a little preschool Raj, the flavours are well versed in the subcontinent's ancient ways, showcasing a cross-section of India's many cuisines. A mixed Dhaba platter proffers succulent fish tikka from the tandoor. The samosa is a door-stopper and almost a meal on its own. Mains come out in copper balti dishes, with plenty of sauce to mop up with excellent naan. A seriously heady goat curry bathes in luxurious gravy studded with cardamom pods, and the chicken curry is also moist and tender. However, the vegie dishes let down their carnivore peers. Punjabi eggplant was undercooked and paneer saag (homemade cheese in spinach purée) lacked the silkiness we'd hoped for. Yet with service that's friendly, cheeky and professional in equal amounts, it's a meal fit for a rajah.

Hours Lunch daily noon–3pm;
Dinner daily 5.30–11pm
Bill E $4.50–$14.90 **M** $7.90–$14.90
D $2.50–$5.50; banquet menu $27.90 pp
Cards AE BC DC MC V Eftpos
Wine BYO (corkage $2 pp)
Chefs Sumit Kumar, Lucky Singh & A. Bhandari
Owner Ajay Raj
Seats 100
www.mayamasala.com.au

And…you can always take home sweets from Maya's sister sweet shop opposite

MCA Cafe

140 George Street, The Rocks
Tel 9241 4253 Map 1

Contemporary

Score 14/20

Like real estate-mad Sydneysiders say, it's all about location. Book an outdoor table and enjoy one of the world's best views: Circular Quay. The art deco main room is pretty good, too, with high ceilings and a feeling of space and luxury. Bestowed with such physical advantages, it's good to find food worthy of the surrounds thanks to new chef Jason Faulconbridge. A huge slab of seared tuna with ponzu sauce is hardly delicate, but superb quality makes it hugely satisfying. An entrée of warm duck confit salad is so generous that it could be a main. Swordfish with harissa is a perfect balance of two strong flavours, but the eye fillet with herbed galette and jus, while well crafted, was let down by fairly flavourless beef. Desserts include a big selection of cakes. The service can be erratic – failing to acknowledge (let alone seat) waiting diners and sometimes forgetting entire orders. Just smile, forgive and admire that view.

Hours Breakfast Sat–Sun 10am–noon;
Lunch daily noon–3pm
Bill E $16–$19 **M** $25–$30 **D** $5–$12;
10% surcharge on Sundays & public holidays
Cards AE BC DC MC V
Wine Good list with some unusual gems;
8 by the glass
Chef Jason Faulconbridge
Owners Charles Wilkins & Richard Brown
Seats 100; wheelchair access; outdoor seats
www.culinaryedge.com.au

And…what a location, what a view!

city + suburbs Ⓜ

Mere Catherine

166 Victoria Street, Potts Point
Tel 9358 2000   Map 2

French (Provincial)

Score 13/20

Okay, so you may think we've made a mistake with the number of seats: 16. Yep, at most, 16 people can eat at this tiny hole in Victoria Street, tucked between backpacker joints and terrace houses. But that's just the way boldly moustachioed Swiss-born Gérard Humair likes it. He wants the numbers low so he can dish up his old-school French provincial tucker with just a single waiter. As the sound of piano accordion fills the air, you lean over the patterned tablecloth, smell the dried flowers and sup on the best and most famous clichés from the 1960s. There's chateaubriand, of course, and snails, and chicken liver and pork pâté with a fanned cornichon. Half a roast chicken with tarragon sauce is moist; the flour-thickened sauces a bit claggy, but profiteroles perfectly creamy. And yep, we may have been generous with the score, but there's something so gloriously retro about the place that we'd rather celebrate it than put it down just for fashion's sake.

Hours Dinner daily from 6pm
Bill E $9.90–$15.50 **M** $20.80–$44.90 **D** $10.90
Cards None; bookings essential
Wine Really tiny and ever changing; 2 by the glass; BYO (corkage $3 per bottle)
Chef/owner Gérard Humair
Seats 16
And…when they say 'No Children Allowed', sadly, they mean it

Mezzaluna

123 Victoria Street, Potts Point
Tel 9357 1988   Map 2

Italian (Northern)   ♈

Score 14/20

When the moon hits your eye like a big pizza pie…go to this modern Italian institution – sleek chic inside, Tuscan terracotta outside – with one of Sydney's best views. Soak up the sight of St Mary's cathedral backlit by every skyscraper in town and savour a perfectly textured crab and scallop soufflé or wonderful fresh figs with goat's cheese and prosciutto lifted by explosions of fresh pomegranate. Staff are solicitous and happy to explain everything: from how the outdoor heaters work to the loo's whereabouts. Sweet Western Australian scampi simply baked in their own juices are marvellously fresh and clean, if a little on the small side, but beef eye fillet with herb butter is generously sized, properly aged and filled with rich, aromatic flavours. Desserts shimmer like the skyline: the tiramisu, lemon soufflé, and prune brûlée are all melt-in-the-mouth good. A holy trinity of chocolate options – pudding, parfait and gelato – will stop the most determined addict in their tracks. It's not quite amore, but certainly comes close.

Hours Lunch Fri noon–3pm; Dinner Mon–Sat 6–11pm
Bill E $22.50–$25 **M** $32.50–$43 **D** $16–$22
Cards AE BC DC MC V
Wine Well-presented list of Italians and Australians; 17 by the glass
Chef Joe Camilleri
Owners Norma, Beppi & Marc Polese
Seats 120; outdoor seats
www.mezzaluna.com.au
And…try to book a table outside: it's quieter, and it feels like Italy

city + suburbs

Milsons

17 Willoughby Street, Kirribilli
Tel 9955 7075   Map 5A

Contemporary

Score 15/20

Yep, it's still here. More than a decade since it opened, the iconic Kirribilli eatery continues to woo. Wide timber floorboards, three long windows at the street end and the multitude of angles that make up the room/the vestibule/the kitchen are now etched in stone as Milsons' style. The food, too, feels very up to date. How about a rabbit terrine with madeira jelly, perhaps? Or a sensational hapuka fillet, cooked so expertly that it glistens within, topped with an excellent tomato salsa and resting on white beans. Lamb shanks stripped from the bone are bound together and laid on garlic mash and artichokes. Of the trio of restaurants run by Paul Sarlas, Milsons truly has a touch of magic. There's a wine list that implores you to decadence, the waiters are always cheery (except for one grumpy old man on our visit), and the food rarely misses a beat. Passionfruit bombe Alaska, for instance, is the perfect modern interpretation of yesteryear, flamed at the table, just like the good ol' days.

Hours Lunch Mon–Fri noon–3pm; Dinner Mon–Sat 6–10pm
Bill E $22–$28 **M** $32–$39 **D** $12–$16
Cards AE BC DC MC V
Wine Well-crafted, Aussie boutique label-driven list; 13 by the glass; BYO except Sat (corkage $7 pp)
Chef Lee Kwiez
Owners Paul Sarlas & Richard Nicholl
Seats 90; private rooms
www.milsonsrestaurant.com.au
And...best to book ahead; this place is very popular

Miltons

25 Bligh Street, Sydney
Tel 9232 0007   Map 1

Mediterranean

Score 14/20

A hushed, understated elegance pervades this basement restaurant as you descend the stairs and leave behind the daily rush of the CBD. The place has the aura of a five-star hotel dining room: big dining room chairs and sexy leather banquettes, complete with an upstairs bar. It's an expensive fit-out that works. The service is well mannered and attentive, while behind a white wall the chef discreetly tends the stove. The menu spans several cultures, with imaginative entrées that include classic calf's liver with caramelised onion; risotto with asparagus and porcini; and pan-fried sardines with herb crust. Homemade fettuccine with crisp, salty prosciutto, poached egg, sage and parmesan is hearty but refined. Roast spatchcock wrapped in vine leaves is perfectly moist and a stuffing of spring vegetables heightens the taste, with smoked paprika and sage as a finishing touch. Peaches baked in Samos muscat, with coffee-infused savoiardi with a lush mascarpone cream, are a highlight.

Hours Lunch Mon–Fri noon–3pm; Dinner Tues–Sat 6pm–late
Bill E $18–$22 **M** $29–$34 **D** $15
Cards AE BC DC MC V
Wine More-than-adequate list; 12 by the glass
Chef Costa Skamnidis
Owners Aneza Skamnidis-Ulmer & Costa Skamnidis
Seats 160; private rooms; wheelchair access
www.miltons.com.au
And...on weekdays enjoy a quick lunch for just $28

city + suburbs Ⓜ

Minh

506 Marrickville Road, Dulwich Hill
Tel 9560 0465   Map 8

Vietnamese   Score 12/20

Every day, all day, this Vietnamese stayer (now 21 years old) serves up lashings of fresh, lively and spicy flavours. Downstairs is café spartan – tiled floor, bare timber tables – spilling onto the footpath, and upstairs the carpeted room softens the din as Vietnamese songs waft over the hubbub. The large, appealing menu runs from soothing pho to curries and noodle dishes in pork, beef, chicken or seafood combinations, awash with beansprouts and mint. Pick over lush bo la lot – grilled, betel leaf-wrapped minced beef; or a refreshing green papaya salad laced with prawns, chilli and peanut. Alas the prawns in all dishes were watery and bland, and passionate flavours went missing on occasion. The theatre of campfire venison – spice-redolent slices cooked at the table – to wrap in DIY rice paper rolls is fun. Among many fine vego choices, the Buddha plate is a pleasing mix of stir-fried vegies and tofu sprinkled with peanuts. Washed down with Vietnamese beer, and costing so few dong, it's a great deal.

Hours Daily 11am–11pm
Bill E $4.80–$9.90 **M** $8.90–$17.90
D $1.50–$4.80
Cards AE BC DC MC V Eftpos
Wine Small list, usual suspects; 3 by the glass; BYO (corkage $1 pp)
Chef Thuy Truong
Owners Thuy & Tam Truong
Seats 180; private rooms; wheelchair access; outdoor seats
And…they also do discount takeway

Mino

521 Military Road, Mosman
Tel 9960 3351   Map 7

Japanese   Score 14/20

In the past, Sydney's traditional kaiseki restaurants have been formal and expensive. Here's a simply furnished shopfront gem that breaks with tradition by offering two excellent-value kaiseki banquets – the 'Mino' and the 'Goshu' – with understated but friendly service. Think of a dégustation and you've understood kaiseki, a blend of seasonality, harmony and artistry. The appetisers might include a sweet prawn delicately wrapped in tofu with a miso dressing or superbly tender tataki of wagyu beef. Then it's squeaky fresh, thickly cut sashimi of ocean trout and tuna. Amidst the grilled entrées, a Japanese vinegar marinade disappointingly muffled the fine flavour of soft-shell crab. The star dish is a steaming sukiyaki hotpot swirling with the yolk of an egg and served with pungent, but not irascible, Japanese pickles. We loved the unctuous, smoky eel kabayaki on rice, too. At the end, chef Nakoji's artistic chestnut pudding, green tea chocolate and black sesame dessert dégustation is cooling and welcome. And if you must, you can still go à la carte.

Hours Dinner Tues–Sun 6–10pm
Bill E $14–$18 **M** $22 **D** $8; kaiseki banquet Tues–Thurs & Sun $38 or $55 pp, Fri–Sat $55
Cards AE BC MC V; bookings essential
Wine Very small list (go the Shochu-on-the-rocks or sake option); an insulting 1 by the glass; BYO (corkage $2 pp)
Chef/owner Takaaki Nakoji
Seats 40
And…take a pre-dinner cocktail at the buzzy bar and lounge over the road

city + suburbs

Mint

62 Bridge Street, Sydney
Tel 9240 1210   Map 1

Contemporary

Score 14/20

Mint is as slick and contemporary as its home, the InterContinental Hotel, is grand and historic. It bristles with Zeitgeist: a hip bar, lounge and trendy dining spot, with drinks, food and service to match. Here is food to share, with clean and distinct flavours, as dramatically presented as the décor. Perspex columns divide dining area from lounge, and there's a mint-green colour scheme. Try the myriad pleasures on a tasting plate: huge green olives on crisp spaghetti skewers, Kervella goat's cheese-filled zucchini flowers with caper dressing, or scallop with diced tomato. Vegetarians will adore the mushroom duxelle atop toasted brioche. Pomegranate-glazed duck in onion crêpes is deserving of its growing reputation. Cleverly presented desserts include a seductive buttermilk pannacotta, caramelised Turkish delight and figs; or brûlée with syrupy strawberries, chocolate mousse and caramel ice-cream. You may not find anything to really get your teeth into, but James Viles is a young chef to watch and Seenie Kahukura works the floor like a ballroom dancer.

Hours Lunch Mon–Fri noon–3pm; Dinner Mon–Sat 6–10.30pm
Bill Dishes are designed to share $9–$25; 2-course lunch $35 pp
Cards AE BC DC MC V
Wine Varied list with plenty of interest; 23 by the glass
Chef James Viles
Owner Mulpha Pty Ltd
Seats 70; private room; outdoor seats
www.mintbaranddining.com.au
And...the secluded bar at the back has an appealing menu and screens showing action on the Harbour

Mohr & Mohr

204 Devonshire Street, Surry Hills
Tel 8399 0887   Map 3B

European

Score 12/20

Hans Mohr's companion restaurant to his adjacent famous fish-'n'-chip joint is a plain square room, with white tiles, pale walls and wooden tables arranged with Germanic precision. The staff compensate for the slightly clinical exterior, smiling and shouting (it can get noisy, but they've since tried to mitigate this) and keeping the varied clientele happy. The menu is designed to cater for every taste, although there's a strong German tavern influence in many hearty dishes. Gravlax is moist and firm, although the accompanying potato cake was a little too fast-food. A slab of duck terrine offers densely packed flavour. Salmon with chives and crunchy potatoes is reliably good, and two enormous lamb shanks with broad beans, mash and cherry tomatoes will sate even the most ravenous beast. Summer berry pudding with mascarpone is a balance of tart sweetness to make your eyes water. But be warned – Hans obviously believes that good things come in big servings. There's always mohr where that came from.

Hours Lunch Mon–Fri noon–3pm; Dinner daily 6–10pm
Bill E $8.50–$14.50 **M** $18–$24 **D** $8.50–$10.50
Cards AE BC MC V Eftpos
Wine Small and familiar; 7 by the glass; BYO (corkage $5 per bottle)
Chef/owner Hans Mohr
Seats 60; outdoor seats
www.mohrandmohr.com.au
And...there are tables outside and a children's menu on request

city + suburbs

Mohr Fish

202 Devonshire Street, Surry Hills
Tel 9318 1326   Map 3B

Seafood

Score 12/20

The Shakespeare Hotel next door is busy most nights. You can bet many drinkers are simply waiting for a head to poke in with glad tidings – that they've scored one of four small tables, or a bar stool at the stainless-steel bench, at Mohr Fish. This tiny, white-tiled corner shop is looking a little weary but the shoals keep lining up. It's a simple formula: a handful of seafood entrées, then fish with a topping – avocado salsa, eggplant, or asparagus and hollandaise (or mango salsa? No thanks!) – salad and potato (chips, gratin or mash). Fish cakes with chilli and coriander are old-fashioned pleasure; fish and prawn dumplings are lusciously silken with chilli, garlic, coriander and soy. But not all is as vibrant and clean as you'd hope. Garlic prawns with aïoli were lost in a thick suit of armour-like batter. And some mains lacked a deft hand – fish oily from cooking, salads overdressed. Still, the lemon curd tart is a fine finish.

Hours Daily 10am–10pm
Bill E $10.50–$14.50 **M** $16–$22 **D** $7
Cards None; no bookings
Wine BYO (no corkage)
Chef/owner Hans Mohr
Seats 30
www.mohrandmohr.com.au
And...grab a takeaway if you can't wait

MoS Cafe

37 Phillip Street (cnr Bridge Street), Sydney
Tel 9241 3636   Map 1

Contemporary

Score 13/20

Come nightfall, the suits who fill the tables by day have all but vanished, but a lineup of brown paper bags filled with takeaway orders – soon to be delivered to surrounding office blocks – suggests they haven't gone home just yet. If anything could make you linger in the city after dark it's Grant Gordon's menu and this sleek room, hidden behind cool, thick sandstone beneath the Museum of Sydney. More tables fill a portico and the courtyard outside, around which the city rises toward the sky. At dinner, a selection of dips, labna and Turkish bread, plus salt-and-pepper squid, teamed with a couple of glasses of wine, should put a bad day at the office nicely behind you. Then there's bistro-style pizzazz: hiramasa kingfish with eggplant moussaka; beer-battered fish with shoestring fries; or chargrilled beef fillet with sautéed scallops, broccolini and anchovy butter. Service is attentive, friendly and knowledgeable, but we wish they weren't so keen to start stacking chairs while we're still eating.

Hours Mon–Fri 7am–9pm; Sat–Sun 8am–4pm
Bill E $13–$19.50 **M** $22–$34 **D** $2–$12.50; 15% surcharge on Sundays & public holidays
Cards AE BC DC MC V
Wine A smart, enticing selection; 21 by the glass
Chef Grant Gordon
Owners Paul Lockrey & Ramy Shelhot
Seats 160; wheelchair access; outdoor seats
www.moscafe.com.au
And...the breakfasts are good, too

city + suburbs

mu shu

108 Campbell Parade, Bondi Beach
Tel 9130 5400   Map 9

Modern Asian

Score 14/20

The daybeds are as big as an opium den; the bar is as long as a stroll along Shanghai's Bund; and the kitchen is so open you can see every twitch of every chef's muscle. To match the moody lighting and the Bond-hai décor, the menu is an arresting voyage from northern China to southern Thailand with favours erring on the sweet side. Oysters wrapped in bean skin, stuffed with prawn and water chestnuts, then fried, are a juicy explosion. Honey and soy-glazed quail is richly stuffed with sticky rice and paired with sweet red cabbage. Roast jewfish fillet is topped with tender calamari and a sweet hoisin dressing that's strangely similar to the five-spice sauce on the beautifully cooked crisp pork belly with wok-fried egg. And while expensive cocktails sound fascinating they didn't live up to their promise. Most disappointingly, we found floor attitudes ranged from pirouetting to pouting, forgetful or too busy feeding themselves. There are some redeeming moments (thanks for a great wine suggestion!) but such great food deserves better support.

Hours Lunch Fri–Sun noon–3pm; Dinner daily 6pm–midnight
Bill E $12–$25 **M** $21–$40 **D** $15; 10% surcharge on Sundays & public holidays
Cards AE BC DC MC V
Wine Good mix of interesting imports, local boutique wines and nice stickies; 16 by the glass
Chef Jo Ward
Owners Joanna and Maurice Arbib
Seats 178; private room; wheelchair access; outdoor seats
www.mushu.com.au
And...the yum cha (Sunday only) and tea selection are a good bet

Nelsons Brasserie

Lord Nelson Brewery Hotel,
1st floor, 19 Kent Street, The Rocks
Tel 9251 4044   Map 1

Contemporary

Score 13/20

You can argue about which is Sydney's oldest pub, but there's no question this is the city's oldest existing brasserie. The handsome, heritage hulk, circa 1831, has an in-house master brewer to keep the place hopping and a good restaurant upstairs. The menu is concise, from fish and properly charred steaks to osso buco, duck confit and kangaroo; the last a poignant link to the convicts' neat adze marks on the sandstone walls. Portions are substantial and spicing is confidently assertive in a well-balanced seafood broth and in four Momo (Tibetan rice-flour dumplings) with casings nicely elastic around dense minced turkey filling. And if the skordalia mash bolstering a fine fillet of barramundi could use more garlic, you can't go wrong with a white chocolate crème brûlée hiding a layer of raspberry coulis. Service is charming in this cleanly decorated room. And with summer sun glancing off burnished wood, or winter fire crackling in the grate, it's hard not to stop for a fresh-brewed pint on the way out.

Hours Lunch Wed–Fri noon–3pm; Dinner Tues–Sat 6–10pm
Bill E $14–$17 **M** $24–$29 **D** $12.50
Cards AE BC DC MC V Eftpos
Wine All-Australian, with magnums, museum and vintage releases; 9 by the glass
Chef Lama Ang-Tendi
Owners Blair R. Hayden & Partners
Seats 80
And...look out for regular wine or beer dinners, with expert hosts.

city + suburbs (N)

Neptune Palace

Level 1, Gateway Building,
Cnr Pitt & Alfred streets, Circular Quay
Tel 9241 3338 Map 1

Malaysian/Chinese

Score 14/20

At first glance, you could make the mistake of categorising Neptune Palace as standard-issue Malaysian. This popular business lunch venue rises well above the ordinary with the finesse of its dishes, despite a less-than-cutting-edge interior design that brings together turquoise blue carpet and wallpaper, dark wood panelling and framed historical photographs. A room full of businessmen (and the odd businesswoman) will easily find something to, ahem, suit, with a numbered menu that runs to 151, covering Chinese stalwarts as well as traditional Malaysian offerings. The fresh, clean flavours of enormous scallops with ginger and shallot elevate the dish to memorable status. 'Grandma Tofu' is a comforting, almost soupy dish of silken tofu, minced chicken and vegetables with a nice chilli kick; and beef rendang has a clarity of flavour rarely seen in that most common of dishes. With good, professional service, it is easy to see why, even early in the week, this upstairs dining room is full.

Hours Lunch daily noon–3pm;
Dinner daily 5–10.30pm
Bill E $9.80–$26.80 **M** $18.80–$45
D $6.80–$8.80; live seafood at market prices
Cards AE BC DC MC V
Wine Long and impressive list, from $35 labels to Hill of Grace and Chateau d'Yquem; 10 by the glass
Chef Lam Kim Fai
Owners Derek Lim & Lee Ngann Ly
Seats 200; private room
And...you get a Harbour Bridge view from some tables

Nilgiri's

81–83 Christie Street, St Leonards
Tel 9966 0636 Map 5A

Indian (Regional)

Score 14/20

When Ajoy Joshi is not serving in the restaurant, he's providing all-day snacks in the tiffin room, preparing ready-cooked meals to take home, masterminding a function, giving cooking classes or hosting a chef's table. It's always with his eye on the quality and integrity of authentic Indian flavours, with a different region celebrated each month. Favourites remain, such as mini masala dosa: thin, crisp rice and fermented lentil pancakes scrolled around carefully spiced potatoes with a superb fresh coconut chutney; and there are fascinating dishes from lesser-known regional cuisines. Spicing is deft. Bengal-style eggplant is marinated with pepper and tamarind, then batter-fried and served with seasoned yoghurt. Stand-out dishes include baby okra in tamarind, tempered with black mustard and fresh curry leaves; and the goat stew, slow-cooked with potatoes cumin and turmeric. Joshi's kulfi is better than most (that wouldn't be hard); date and honey are an appealing combination dotted with rose petals. The upstairs setting, too, rises to the occasion, though it retains some of its Japanese sensibility from a former incarnation.

Hours Lunch Sun–Fri noon–3pm;
Dinner daily 6–10pm
Bill E $14–$16 **M** $18–$26 **D** $9–$10
Cards AE BC DC MC V
Wine Good, diverse list appropriate to food style; 11 by the glass; BYO (corkage $6 per bottle)
Chef Ajoy Joshi
Owners Ajoy & Meera Joshi
Seats 175; private rooms
www.nilgiris.com.au
And... Sundays are family days with a $25 ($15 for the under-12s) regional buffet

city + suburbs

Northbridge Bistro

Northbridge Hotel, 57 Strathallen Avenue, Northbridge
Tel 9958 5228   Map 7

Modern Bistro

Score 14/20

Gotta love this city. When a talented young bloke like John Evans (ex CBD) heads across the bridge to bring his deft touch to a reasonably characterless, hard-floored pub bistro, you know that things are looking good for the future. With partner Sonia Greig beaming as she works the floor, it's the perfect local. Yes, they do have pork belly. And duck. And there's expertly cooked, full-flavoured sirloin with red wine and tarragon butter, or mussels steamed open with white wine and saffron. Sure, the tables could be bigger, the lights dimmed, the chairs more comfortable. But you come here for salt-and-pepper squid with a biting, crunchy salad or the intelligent cheese platter. Greig doubles as dessert chef, her fine-shelled, warm chocolate tart a lesson in simple harmony. We're thinking about cloning Evans and Greig to spread decent pub grub across the state, but failing that we'll be happy to dine here every week.

Hours Lunch Tues–Fri noon–3pm; Dinner Tues–Sat 6–10pm

Bill E $13–$14 **M** $15–$24 **D** $12–$14

Cards AE BC DC MC V Eftpos

Wine An above-average pub list that suits the food; 11 by the glass

Chefs/owners John Evans & Sonia Greig

Seats 65; wheelchair access; outdoor seats

And...the courtyard is pretty special when the weather's right

Ocean King House

247 Prices Highway, Kogarah
Tel 9587 3511   Map 8

Chinese (Cantonese)

Score 13/20

In a charming, old two-storey house, with a decidedly 'suburban Chinese' ambience, you'll find some remarkably good Cantonese food, especially the live seafood from the tanks that line the entrance. There's crab (the Singapore chilli mud crab, with a choice of male or sweeter female with roe, has just the right bite), abalone (the hotpot shabu shabu looks wonderful), lobster, fish, prawns and pipis. Plump oysters are steamed to just warm them through, with a dressing of shallots, ginger, soy and sesame oil; grilled eel is slightly smoky, oily and delicious; and green beans come with a scattering of soft sweet pork mince and XO sauce. Despite the eye for detail in some things, service staff can't always explain dishes and specials can have very loose translations: 'free range chicken' turns out to be an excellent platter of cold-cut chicken, jellyfish and boiled peanuts with a bitey relish of minced garlic and shallots. Don't be afraid to ask questions, and take your lead from what's on the large tables of Chinese families.

Hours Lunch Mon–Fri 11am–3pm, Sat–Sun 10am–3pm; Dinner Sun–Thurs 5.30–10.30pm, Fri–Sat 5.30–11pm

Bill E $4.20–$13.80 **M** $12.80–$26.80 **D** $4–$7; seafood at market prices; $2 pp surcharge on public holidays

Cards AE BC DC MC V Eftpos

Wine Dated and limited list, with a couple of good wines at good prices and cold Tsingtao beer; BYO (corkage $6 per bottle)

Chef Albert Chan

Owners Albert & Eleanor Chan

Seats 280; private room

www.oceankinghouse.com.au

And...there's excellent yum cha seven days

city + suburbs

Ocean Room

Ground Level, Overseas Passenger Terminal, The Rocks
Tel 8273 1277   Map 1

Modern Asian/Seafood

Score 13/20

'Interactive style dining' sounds like a new mobile phone feature, but it's actually the promise of this swellegant room, where Raita Noda challenges palates, giving shimmering seafood unexpected twists. An eight-page menu holds plenty of intrigue, but too many fruit 'n' sea pairings detract from the star: the seafood, including the otherwise excellent roasted lobster salad with pomegranate and vanilla-clove-infused oil. A spectacular fried flounder salad arrives in the basket of its own skeleton, but the crisp flesh was lost in a mustard oil-dressed jungle of rocket, leeks, garlic and almonds. Salt-and-pepper tofu with eggplant and chilli is addictive, and anything from the tank, kept simple and sexy, is smooth sailing, especially a bowl of wok-fried chilli yabbies. With striking opium poppy-shaped feature lights dangling from the 10-metre-high ceilings in the gently lit room, the edible 'aquarium' wall and Opera House views, there's a lot to like, especially when eager staff make sure you feel special.

Hours Lunch Tues–Fri noon–3pm; Dinner Mon–Sat 6–11pm
Bill E $7–$24 **M** $23–$48 **D** $17; seafood at market prices; 10% surcharge on Sundays & public holidays
Cards AE BC DC MC V
Wine Wonderful list with more depth than breadth; 11 by the glass
Chef Raita Noda
Owners Mark Miller & Tonci Farac
Seats 200; private room; wheelchair access; outdoor seats
www.oceanroomsydney.com
And...check out the white-tipped reef shark swimming in the top tank

Oh Calcutta

251 Victoria Street, Darlinghurst
Tel 9360 3650   Map 2

Indian

Score 14/20

The sanguine Basil Daniell is still at it. The effusive greeting, humouring diners with repartee, intricate dish explanations, effortlessly working the floor, suggesting half serves, flirting with the girls, pouring Taj Mahal lager for the boys, making it a night to remember. All these years later and he remains the showman in a showroom that retains enough Bollywood glamour to impress with a sense of occasion. The Mogul carpet upstairs is worn, but downstairs designer Iain Halliday's Moorish interior is as modern as ever, complementing a thoroughly contemporary take on the food of the Indian subcontinent spiced nicely with caraway seeds, cinnamon quills and star anise. There has been the odd letdown – fried whitebait too gritty, a duck curry too salty – but mostly it's rich tastes and textures of utter delight. The northern Pakistani steamed lamb dumplings are mandatory, and the baked kingfish with green mango and shredded coconut is highly recommended. Good news: BYO is back. Basil sure knows how to keep you happy.

Hours Dinner Mon–Sat 6–11pm
Bill E $10.90–$14.90 **M** $18.90–$27.90 **D** $8.90–$12.90
Cards AE BC MC V
Wine Fashionably boutique with a few foreign drops; 8 by the glass; BYO (corkage $5 pp)
Chef/owner Basil Daniell
Seats 60; private room; outdoor seats
www.ohcalcutta.com.au
And...for a dégustation of Pakistani, Afghani, Sri Lankan and Indian flavours, try the $44.90 pp tasting menu

good food guide   99

city + suburbs

Oliveto

Brays Bay Reserve,
443 Concord Road, Rhodes
Tel 8765 0006   Map 6

Italian

Score 13/20

Its heritage may come via some of the Grappa team, but this flash park-side diner has it all over its sibling in the looks department. A sheer screen behind the entry has an image of an Italian vineyard, there are huge look-at-me windows to gaze out of, and a wood-fired oven greets you on arrival. Much comes from the oven – plenty of pizza, breads and the occasional Grappa-esque dish, such as the prawns with verjuice. The hard floor and boisterous crowd give the room a party feel. Dishes can be as humble as pork and fennel sausages, wood-roasted with grapes, with a handful of rocket cast on top. Veal cutlets may be grilled; roasted spatchcock served with pancetta; and asparagus-and-veal-filled arancini (deep-fried rice balls) are correctly unctuous and crunchy at the same time. Not everything does the space justice. A fluff and bubble of lacklustre strawberry crème didn't benefit from balsamic-dressed white-centred strawberries, but thankfully the mood easily makes up for any slips.

Hours Lunch Tues–Fri & Sun noon–3pm; Dinner Tues–Sun 6–10.30pm
Bill E $18–$24 **M** $22–$29.50 **D** $10.50–$16.50; pizze $12.50–$22
Cards AE BC DC MC V Eftpos
Wine Handsome selection of popular but good names; 13 by the glass; BYO (corkage $4.50 pp)
Chef Ricky Keeley
Owners Antonio & Charlie Colosi, Alessandro & Carmen Milozzi
Seats 140; wheelchair access; outdoor seats
And...best to drive; getting a taxi can be tiresome

Omega

161 King Street, Sydney
Tel 9223 0242   Map 1

Modern Greek

Score 16/20

If Stanley Kubrick had met Florence Broadhurst their boudoir might have looked something like this. Sydney's best-known Greek chef has chosen Werner Panton-inspired retro-space age modular PVC chairs, Japanese-style printed screens, and a sparkling plexiglass 'lighting wall' feature for his surreal, subterranean restaurant at basement level on King Street. Conistis's food is never less than exciting and sometimes it can be a revelation. This year he continues his dazzling BASE-jumping kitchen act, with a slew of new dishes such as a brilliant confit tomato with truffled lobster pilafi and roast garlic purée; and a richly satisfying twice-cooked sumac duck, spanakopita and grilled fig, served in a pomegranate caramel sauce. At lunchtime the conservative CBD crowd orders and re-orders old favourites such as the signature moussaka of eggplant and scallops; Milos-style rabbit pie; and the voluptuous, irresistible, raspberry, rosewater and mastic ice-cream. A new team of efficient, professional floor staff, all genuine fans of their boss, can guide you in more thrill-seeking directions – just ask.

Hours Lunch Mon–Fri noon–2.30pm; Dinner Mon–Sat 6–late
Bill E $22–$28 **M** $32–$38 **D** $17
Cards AE BC DC MC V; bookings essential
Wine Intelligent, wide-ranging list; some excellent-value Languedoc wine; 15 by the glass
Chef/owner Peter Conistis
Seats 110; private room
www.omegarestaurant.com.au
And...throw a party in the funky functions room

> " The more you know Champagne, the more you'll love Bollinger. "

CHAMPAGNE
BOLLINGER
MAISON FONDÉE EN 1829

city + suburbs

Onde

346 Liverpool Street, Darlinghurst
Tel 9331 8749 Map 2

French

Score 14/20

A queue says a lot and there is nearly always one at this Darlinghurst stalwart. Laif Etournaud began serving his brand of classic bistro fare here nearly a decade ago, and the flavours remain as true and comforting as ever. The small, simple room, with a floor-to-ceiling window to Liverpool Street, has a cute little bar and an open kitchen. It's all very groovy to match the Darlinghurst crowd – from a table of waiters from another top restaurant to designer-clad families with kids. The casual theme follows through to the blackboard menu that includes staples like pork, rabbit and duck terrine with pickled cherries; grilled T-bone with red wine butter; and duck confit with walnuts, caramelised apple and mesclun. Roasted beetroot with gruyère, baby beans and mayonnaise tasted a touch sharp, but gnocchi with tender shredded rabbit, green olives and bacon is as comforting as it is satisfying: a study in balance and technique. The service might seem a tad rushed at times, but that's only because Onde is so very popular.

Hours Dinner Mon–Thurs 5.30–11pm, Fri–Sat 5.30–11.30pm, Sun 5.30–10pm
Bill E $13–$16 **M** $17–$26 **D** $9
Cards AE BC DC MC V; no bookings
Wine Well-chosen, modestly priced list; 35 by the glass
Chef Laif Etournaud
Owners Laif Etournaud, Simone Lai & Michael à Campo
Seats 38
And...get there early or prepare to wait

Oscillate Wildly

275 Australia Street, Newtown
Tel 9517 4700 Map 8

Contemporary

Score 13/20

The white interior – a shopfront looking out onto Newtown Courthouse – is a nice blend of style and suburbs with a chandelier looking like a ball of spun sugar hanging from a pressed-metal ceiling. Fans of the 1980s indie band The Smiths will recognise the name as an old instrumental in homage to Oscar Wilde. We're grateful that this charming man, Ross Godfrey, didn't choose The Smiths' 'Meat is Murder', because chef Guillermo Viscara has a wonderful way with protein. The menu changes fortnightly, but you might get lamb's tongue beautifully poached with star anise; or roast duck layered with homemade marjoram pasta, leek and water chestnuts. Prawns may be lemon-cured, ceviche style, in a salad with house-smoked chillies adding a little heat. The spicing may be a little heavy-handed, but it's tempered by judicious cooking. You only have to tuck into desserts (please, please, please let me get what I want...), such as the warm apricot pudding with cardamom crème fraîche, to know why this place is so packed, so often.

Hours Dinner Tues–Sat 6–10pm
Bill E $14 **M** $22–$24 **D** $10; 3 courses for $43
Cards AE BC MC V Eftpos
Wine BYO (corkage $3 pp)
Chef Guillermo Viscarra
Owner Ross Godfrey
Seats 30
And...the owner works the floor – and he is very good at it, too

good food guide

city + suburbs

Osso

19 Lawson Street, Penrith
Tel 4722 6102   Map 11

Contemporary

Score 12/20

With a make-over that pays homage to Sydney's minimalist peccadillo of chrome/glass/dark wood, Osso makes the most of its meagre location – think back-street Penrith – with simple, spanking-fresh, mod Oz–Italian fare. Table menus hint at a tapas bent to enjoy with an ambitious cocktail list. The specials also keep it uncomplicated, perhaps proffering fat curlicues of salt-and-pepper squid that are spot-on for bite and salty crunch. Spaghetti with prawns, chilli and fragrant olive oil is a down-to-earth delight, while a seafood cassoulet delivers a bowl brimming with fish, mussels, vongole and prawns, topped with lightly fried scampi, with large discs of crusty, rustic bread to ensure the pungent garlic and tomato broth is not wasted. On our visit the bright, young, shy service was seen, occasionally heard but near impossible to pin down. Best to come with time to spare on a busy night when the jacaranda tree winks with fairy lights and the bar fills this uncluttered canvas with personality.

Hours Lunch Mon–Fri noon–3pm; Dinner Mon–Sat from 6pm
Bill E $14–$19 **M** $27–$32 **D** $9–$14
Cards AE BC MC V Eftpos; bookings essential
Wine Great cocktails; concise, moderately priced, mainly Oz list; 5 by the glass
Chef Steven Keaton
Owners Clayton Jude & Anthony & Norman Italiano
Seats 110; wheelchair access; outdoor seats
www.osso.com.au
And…watch out for special fixed-price deals like 'Hot Gossip' Mother's Day lunches

Osteria dei Poeti

73 Glebe Point Road, Glebe
Tel 9571 8955   Map 5B

Italian

Score 13/20

From the carriage-style lamps on the façade through to the timber-furnished room, this osteria lives up to its name, translating as something like 'tavern of the poets'. There's something marvellous about a simple space where paper placemats dot the tables, poetry is in the air and chef Aurelio Spagnuolo dishes up the true tastes of the old country. Pick at the excellent goat's cheese-stuffed fried green olives and dip into a menu that strides Europe's boot. There could be house-made cannelloni filled with ricotta and radicchio, dotted with walnuts and topped with melted smoked scamorza (cheese). The melanzane positano pairs finely sliced eggplant with fresh mozzarella and a superb tomato sauce. Crostini crudely smeared with chicken liver are made lively by the addition of capers. Noise levels can soar as chirpy waiters deliver humungous bowls of calabrese burrida: a tomato-based fish stew laced with mushrooms. Dessert is as comforting as a hug from nonna – perhaps affogato, or ricotta-and-chocolate-filled cannoli siciliani.

Hours Dinner Mon–Sat from 5.30pm
Bill E $10.50–$19.50 **M** $16.50–$28 **D** $8.50
Cards BC MC V
Wine Brief but well constructed, some Italians; 9 by the glass; BYO (corkage $5 per bottle)
Chef Aurelio Spagnuolo
Owners Stefano Arlenghi & Aurelio Spagnuolo
Seats 60; outdoor seats
And…poetry evenings and ancient Roman banquet evenings from time to time

city + suburbs

Otto

Area 8, 6 Cowper Wharf Road, Woolloomooloo
Tel 9368 7488   Map 2

Modern Italian
Score 15/20

From the day it opened, Otto seemed destined for iconic status as a 'Sydney institution'. This is a high-octane, swish dining experience at any time of the day. Indoors or out on the marina you enjoy an intimate relationship with the Harbour and a moody city skyline. Tanned middle-aged gigolos and women whose wrists drip with bling mingle with flirty, pretty young PR things; water-taxi men wait like gondoliers for clients who are martyrs to a dozen Port Stephens oysters and a magnum of Bollinger. It's the city's moneyed class preening, but it feels strangely democratic and open to all comers. Chef James Kidman's smart–casual Mediterranean menu aims for the heart of southern Italy with dishes such as beautifully simple capesante (deep-sea scallops, pencil leeks, verbena and a subtle vanilla oil); delicate zucchini flowers filled with salt cod; fresh egg taglierini with vongole; and a soulful rabbit stew. The mature floor is rarely inattentive. It ain't cheap, but you get plenty of bang for your buck.

Hours Lunch daily noon–3pm; Dinner Mon–Sat 6pm–late, Sun 6–8.30pm
Bill E $18–$27 **M** $24–$37 **D** $16–$17; 10% surcharge on Sundays & public holidays
Cards AE BC DC MC V Eftpos
Wine Pricey list, strong in French, Italian and boutique Oz; 19 by the glass
Chef James Kidman
Owner Otto Ristorante Italiano P/L
Seats 120; private rooms, outdoor seats
www.otto.net.au
And...children are treated with respect, in true Italian style

Out of Africa

43–45 East Esplanade, Manly
Tel 9977 0055   Map 7

Moroccan/North African
Score 13/20

The ornaments may be from all around Africa and the zebra-striped banquettes have definitely strayed a bit far from home, but the food in this large room – French doors flung open to a covered terrace and harbour breezes – is distinctly Moroccan. That fragrant fusion of Africa and Europe – olive oil and tomatoes, preserved lemon, cumin, coriander leaves and sweet paprika, oranges and dates, couscous and chickpeas, almonds and saffron – can be found in various Moorish combinations. Four pan-fried sardine fillets have a fine reduced tomato sauce. Zaluk (akin to ratatouille), a slew of roasted and sautéed vegetables, is piled on warm bread. Pork cutlet is marinated in honey and orange-blossom water, cinnamon and dates, and oven roasted. A claypot tagine is lifted to reveal tender, steaming lamb chunks and vegetables, underpinned by a mound of light, couldn't-be-fluffier couscous. There's even Hassan M'Souli's own Moroccan chocolate cake, preferably washed down with a few glasses of sweet mint tea served ceremoniously from a large silver teapot.

Hours Lunch Thurs–Sun from noon; Dinner daily 6–10.30pm
Bill E $11.50–$17.50 **M** $19.50–$29.50 **D** $8.50–$12.90; 10% surcharge on public holidays
Cards AE BC DC MC V
Wine An interesting range of varietals, chosen to complement the food; 10 by the glass; BYO (corkage $5 per bottle)
Chef/owner Hassan M'Souli
Seats 120; outdoor seats
www.outofafrica.com.au
And...you can buy the cookbook on the way out

city + suburbs

Paddington Inn

338 Oxford Street, Paddington
Tel 9380 5913 Map 4B

Contemporary
Score 13/20

It's a landmark pub – always bustling, bordering on boisterous with an eclectic crowd out for a good time – with a popular front bar providing a perfect view of Oxford Street's passing procession. In the sleek back section, plush booths line the wall and scattered tables create an inviting dining area. Ordering at the counter is no hardship with efficient staff and an open kitchen to see the top-notch bistro fare being dished up by Matt Hilford. Carrying your own cutlery and drinks, however, doesn't suit everyone. There's barely time to tap your foot to the up-tempo music (which, thankfully, drowns out the raucous front bar) before a perfectly seared barramundi fillet lands on crisp polenta, simply adorned with roma tomatoes and balsamic vinaigrette. Succulent chicken breast with tiny lentils, pancetta and roasted red onion is all good. Regulars contentedly tuck into beer-battered fish 'n' chips, or the Italian pork and veal sausages with roast garlic mash. It's real, no-nonsense pub food that shines.

Hours Lunch Mon–Fri noon–3pm, Sat noon–4pm; Dinner Mon–Thurs 6–10pm, Fri–Sat 6–9pm, Sun 1–9pm

Bill E $4–$16 **M** $11–$20 **D** $8

Cards AE BC DC MC V Eftpos; no bookings

Wine Plenty of worthy choices that change with the menu; 17 by the glass; impressive cocktails

Chef Matt Hilford

Owner Solotel Pty Ltd

Seats 100; private rooms; wheelchair access

www.paddingtoninn.com.au

And... book one of the two mini-themed rooms for a special soiree

Palace Chinese

Level 1, Piccadilly Tower,
133 Castlereagh Street, Sydney
Tel 9283 6288 Map 1

Chinese (Cantonese)
Score 13/20

'Palace' is right – it's a palatial restaurant on the first floor of Piccadilly Arcade, which looks more like an opulent oriental hotel lobby than an arcade, full of marble and bustling waiters. Unlike so many other Cantonese restaurants, the waiters have excellent English and fine manners, and the wine list has real depth. All the Cantonese favourites are here, including a good selection of live seafood – we recommend it simply steamed with a side serve of XO sauce. Soft-shell crab (imported fresh from Vietnam) is deep-fried, but be warned that the interior remains so moist that it can explode over your shirt. Crocodile is a revelation, delivering a resolute and appetising flavour somewhere between chicken and fish. Kangaroo fillet is served with secret '3A' sauce (a mix of chilli and Chinese black vinegar). Even the special fried rice is, ahem, special. If indifferent service, noise, uncomfortable seating and weirdly described menus keep you out of other Chinese restaurants, this could be the palace for you.

Hours Lunch daily 11am–3pm; Dinner daily 5–10.30pm

Bill E $7.80–$23.80 **M** $16.80–$42 **D** $5.80; live seafood at market prices; $2 pp surcharge on public holidays

Cards AE BC DC MC V

Wine Great list of Oz and NZ; 11 by the glass

Chefs Lee Ming & Ma Song

Owner Lee Ngann Ly

Seats 280; private rooms; wheelchair access; outdoor seats

www.palacechinese.com.au

And... get the Piccadilly subsidised parking voucher at $7

city + suburbs (P)

Palisade Dining Room

35 Bettington Street, Millers Point
Tel 9251 7225   Map 1

Contemporary

Score 14/20

Wonderfully unrenovated pubs often lose their charm when food beckons and the bar menu comes out. Not so at Palisade, for up a rickety wooden staircase is a restaurant where Brian Sudek and Matthew Quinn have been serving impressive food for a decade. Ad agency suits and office workers fill the light and airy dining room for lunch, glimpsing the historic terraces and Harbour Bridge through big original wooden windows. Paper-on-cloth-covered tables, honey-coloured floorboards and bright canvases add to the relaxed feel, and the appealing menu cajoles you into eating far more than you need. No one's complaining when a memorable dish of perfectly opaque scallops, with a mound of good garlicky eggplant and tomato with deep-fried capers, arrives. Snapper with peas and carrots, cooked in a white wine stock, with creamy aïoli is simply excellent; so too moist Thirlmere chicken breast with hazelnut and sage dressing and crisp bacon. It's superior food at surprisingly good prices, with a view to match, all housed in a 1916 building. Charm indeed.

Hours Lunch Tues–Fri noon–3pm; Dinner Tues–Sat 6–10pm
Bill E $16–$19 **M** $23–$31 **D** $13
Cards AE BC DC MC V Eftpos
Wine What it lacks in choice it makes up for in interest; 12 by the glass
Chefs Brian Sudek & Matthew Quinn
Owner Palisade Properties Pty Ltd
Seats 60; private room
www.palisadehotel.com
And…book a table in the corner room for the best view

Paua

555 Crown Street, Surry Hills
Tel 9319 2976   Map 3B

Modern Mediterranean

Score 14/20

With its crimson ceiling, white walls showcasing contemporary oils, lantern candles and mix of sleek moulded chairs and bentwood originals, Paua has a cosy sophistication. Andrew Saxon and Alice Hyde have created a menu of original dishes with influences from all shores of the Med. Tender quail blanketed in vine leaves nestle on a bulgar pilaf with pine nuts, currants and saffron in a harmonious blend of textures and flavours; a quenelle of creamy labna provides the perfect finishing touch. Less successful was the calamari with harissa and bastourma – the seafood all but lost amidst an all-pervading, unrelenting chilli hit. Saffron-roasted spatchcock on a Catalan 'stew' of eggplant, zucchini and herbs is comforting and much more cohesive. Bistecchia – somewhat sweet, biscuity Jewish–Italian pastries filled with pumpkin and amaretti – contrast well with an earthy mushroom ragù. Rosewater pannacotta rates perfection on any wobble-o-meter, the flower water adding a subtle but distinctive touch, with a peach poached to almost jammy consistency the perfect accompaniment.

Hours Dinner Tues–Sat 6.30–10.30pm
Bill E $14–$16 **M** $22–$27 **D** $9–$13.50
Cards BC MC V Eftpos
Wine Brief list, with mainly Antipodean whites and Spanish and French reds; 7 by the glass; BYO (corkage $6 per bottle)
Chefs/owners Andrew Saxon & Alice Hyde
Seats 30
www.paua.com.au
And…last Sunday night of each month is either cassoulet (March–September) or bouillabaisse (October–February)

city + suburbs (P)

Pavilion on the Park

1 Art Gallery Road, The Domain, Sydney
Tel 9232 1322   Map 1

Modern European
Score 14/20

Sit on the elegant terrace and watch the world go by: everyone from personal trainers to apoplectic joggers will eventually appear before you on the grassy slopes of the Domain. And you'll have plenty of time to watch the workouts – service is both unequivocally charming and almost unbelievably slow. Fortunately, the food from a small and refined menu is more than worth the wait, with every dish a thing of beauty. Warmed goat's cheese is surrounded by baby beetroot and sprigs of greenery and herbs; scallop and crab squid-ink cannelloni with braised witlof is a symphony of subtle colours. Wild mushroom and asparagus risotto with champagne and truffle oil is nutty and creamy, with a wonderfully earthy depth of flavour, while the very buttery duck and foie gras pie reveals this rich, smoky bird at close to its best. As if this isn't enough, the lemongrass and star anise sorbet with pineapple semifreddo is heaven on a stick – or at least in a martini glass. Frankly, who cares about personal fitness anyway?

Hours Cafe, daily 9am–4.30pm; Restaurant, lunch Sun–Fri noon–3.30pm
Bill E $18–$22 **M** $28–$36 **D** $14–$15; 10% surcharge on weekends & public holidays
Cards AE BC DC MC V
Wine Wonderful 6-page list courtesy of sommelier Guy Valliant with overseas options; 18 by the glass
Chef Christian Poulsen
Owners Maralyn & Keir Preedy
Seats 180; wheelchair access; outdoor seats
www.pavilion.com.au
And...check out an exhibition: the Art Gallery of New South Wales is right across the road

Pazzo

583 Crown Street, Surry Hills
Tel 9319 4387   Map 3B

Italian
Score 12/20

This is the type of low key, reassuring restaurant everyone should be able to call their local. Walls of deep claret and mosaic tiles exude warmth, as do the candle-lit tables, while the service is friendly, assured and apologetic when so busy that there are inevitable delays. It's unpretentious food, big on flavour and doled out in generous, effortless style. Loyal customers keep coming back for the excellent value and for house specialities like 'mama's ravioli' of potato, pecorino, pine nuts and mint. However, in the convivial atmosphere of controlled chaos, there were some disappointments: beautifully moist chicken breast was let down by an overpowering sweet and sour eggplant and an inedible deep-fried hash brown. Stick to tried and true staples like the fork-tender calamari, gently spiced with chilli and salt; or crumbed veal – rustic classics that showcase the talents of the Umbrian chef and Sicilian host, while the dessert 'antipasto' (or is that 'dopopasto'?) knocks sweet-tooths back into rehab.

Hours Dinner Mon–Sat 6–10pm
Bill E $14–$15.50 **M** $23.50–$25 **D** $9.50–$11.50
Cards AE BC DC MC V
Wine BYO (corkage $2.50 per bottle)
Chef Bruno Mazzoni
Owner Raffaele Faro
Seats 90; private room; outdoor seats
And...watch out for regional dinners ($60 pp)

city + suburbs

Pello

71–73 Stanley Street, East Sydney
Tel 9360 4640 Map 2

Modern European

Score 16/20

Thomas Johns's food is a joy to behold, whether it's a tiny tarte Tatin of golden beetroot topped with goat's curd on an entrée tasting plate; or paper-thin discs of potato inlaid with a single parsley sprig atop perfectly cooked kingfish. The former Aria chef is also generous, from an amuse bouche of beef broth with a Balmain bug dumpling to a gratis pre-dessert of apricot compote with banana foam. Pello is what dining in Sydney so often isn't: prices are reasonable for the quality on display, floor staff are friendly and knowledgeable, basics like bread and chips are exemplary, and the wine list is impressive. There is whimsy too, in an elevated pineapple vacherin, sandwiched between two rounds of meringue to resemble a mini airport control tower. The room itself remains stylish and comfortable, with tea lights, white-cloth'd tables and timber windows that open onto the busy street. The whole package is one to savour and celebrate.

Hours Lunch Mon–Fri noon–3pm; Dinner Mon–Sat 6–10pm
Bill E $17–$18 **M** $27–$28 **D** $15–16; cheaper at lunch; dinner dégustation menu $70 pp
Cards AE BC DC MC V
Wine Wide-ranging, well-priced list; 13 by the glass; BYO Mon–Thurs (corkage $8 per bottle)
Chef/owner Thomas Johns
Seats 80; outdoor seats
www.pello.com.au
And...parking can be a nightmare, but you can walk from town or it's a very short cab ride

Perama ★

88 Audley Street, Petersham
Tel 9569 7534 Map 8

Modern Greek

Score 14/20

Favourite Mediterranean

Don't even think of not ordering the signature dish of crisp kataifi pastry with bastourma, warm ricotta and figs – it's too good to miss. This airy white room, reminiscent of a contemporary Greek taverna, is always abuzz, so it matters not if you sit upstairs or down, by the open window or on the street. Thankfully, other dishes come in two sizes so you can sample as much as possible of David Tsirekas's individual, appealing modern Greek food. Seafood saganaki is sensational: pilaf soaked with seafood tomato sauce groaning with chunky prawns, calamari, fish and mussels, finished with melted kasseri (cheese). Lamb is a must – perhaps the perennial slow-baked, cooked to melt-in-the-mouth tenderness with herbs and lemon. Nothing tired or oily here: flavours are clean and fresh, each dish distinct from the next, and service is personable, helpful and informed. There's an impressive specials list, so finish with what's in season, perhaps perfectly poached peach halves and very good olive oil ice-cream studded with dried figs.

Hours Lunch Sun 11.30am–3pm; Dinner Tues–Sat 6–10.30pm
Bill E $14.50–$16.50 **M** $16.50–$26 **D** $2.50–$11
Cards BC MC V; bookings essential
Wine Small but continually improving list with many good Greek wines; 12 by the glass; BYO (corkage $2.50 pp)
Chefs/owners Harry Tamvakeras & David Tsirekas
Seats 100; private room; outdoor seats
www.perama.com.au
And...try the fabulous banquet menu for only $45

city + suburbs

Phamish

354 Liverpool Street (cnr Boundary Street), Darlinghurst
Tel 9357 2688 Map 2

Vietnamese

Score 12/20

When four previously, er, phamished people leave, um, phulphilled for less than $100, it's no surprise that for most of the evening the, ah, phootpath outside is phull (sorry) of hopeful diners, patiently waiting. This snappy Vietnamese cafe is lively, crowded, a touch chaotic and always fun, delivering lively, herbaceous flavours. After scoring a tightly packed, small table with snazzy vermilion stools, choose from dishes on red magnetic strips above the kitchen (they're pulled off when sold out), order at the counter and pay up-front. Beef la lot, betel-leaf-wrapped cigars of spicy mince with a tamarind hit, are addictive, along with crisp prawn-and-duck-stuffed pancakes. But the real disappointment was that the home-town (if it's Ho Chi Minh) hero, soft-shell crab, was rendered listless, the addition of chilli, lemongrass and shallots unable to overcome a turbid batter. The duck and banana blossom salad is always fragrant bliss; and bo loc lac, wok-seared eye-fillet beef cubes, with red onion, watercress, soy, and salt 'n' pepper–lime dipping sauce delightfully lush.

Hours Dinner Tues–Sun 6–9.30pm
Bill E $8–$12 **M** $13.50–$18.50
Cards BC MC V Eftpos; no bookings
Wine BYO (corkage $1 pp)
Chef Van Pham
Owners Van Pham & John Burrow
Seats 40; outdoor seats
And...bring an extra bottle to help pass the time

Pier ★

594 New South Head Road, Rose Bay
Tel 9327 6561 Map 9

Seafood

Score 17/20

Favourite Seafood

Dining over the water with the beautiful people is a stunning experience, thanks to Greg Doyle's assured cooking. Pier is a temple to the exquisite beauty of truly fine fish, and Doyle's fervent passion for quality seafood sparkles like the sunlit view across Rose Bay. The menu explains the origins of every day's offerings and an equally passionate waiter will recite the specials. Start with some of Sydney's most luscious oysters, or crab lasagne full of delicate flesh with a white wine and herb sauce of subtle complexity. Pastrami of king salmon is remarkable, the finely textured flesh having layers of spice overtones thanks to two days of curing. Vongole are cooked in a Mediterranean-style saffron and tomato broth. Crisp-skinned john dory on a bed of scallop and herb risotto lets its sweetly fragrant flavour star. There's a token wagyu beef if you really, really must. For dessert, soufflé is superbly crafted, with rich strawberry ice-cream and syrup. With polished service and a clean, fresh room, Pier remains deeply pleasurable and stylish.

Hours Lunch daily noon–3pm; Dinner Mon–Sat 6–10pm, Sun 6–9pm
Bill E $30–$34 **M** $39–$42 **D** $18–$20; $7 pp surcharge on Sundays, $9.50 on public holidays
Cards AE BC DC MC V
Wine A list of great depth with hard-to-find Australian vintages and a comprehensive offering from the old world; 15 by the glass
Chefs Greg Doyle & Grant King
Owners Greg & Jenny Doyle
Seats 120; private room; outdoor seats
www.pierrestaurant.com.au
And...moonlight over the Harbour waves makes a romantic backdrop

city + suburbs

Pilu at Freshwater★

On the beach, Moore Road, Harbord
Tel 9938 3331   Map 7

Italian (Sardinian)

Score 16/20

Best New Restaurant

Sydney's surf-battered northern beaches might not be the first place you'd expect to find a true taste of Sardinia. But that's precisely what awaits at Giovanni Pilu's eponymous restaurant, in an airy, neutral-toned, heritage-listed beach house overlooking the cliff-framed ocean. Since moving from Mosman's Cala Luna in late 2004, Pilu has upped the ante on his regional Italian cucina. A salad of bottarga (dried mullet roe), fennel and celery heart is a symphony of salty and aniseed flavours. Piccolo fritto misto features an ethereally light batter on prawns, squid, zucchini flowers and wafer-thin vegetables. Oven-roasted suckling pig presented on a wooden platter is fall-apart tender, with crackling that redefines the term. Simplicity and freshness reign in handmade pasta with a sugo of crisp-to-the-bite vegetables and daubs of melting buffalo mozzarella – and culurzones (parcels of potato, mint and pecorino). Service borders on irreverent, adding to the experience. This could be Sardinia's Costa Smeralda, were it not for that surf.

Hours Lunch Wed–Sun noon–3pm; Dinner Tues–Sat 6–10pm
Bill E $17–$23 **M** $24–$36 **D** $14–$15; 10% surcharge on Sundays & public holidays
Cards AE BC DC MC V Eftpos
Wine Fabulous list of Italians including all styles and regions; 27 by the glass
Chef Giovanni Pilu
Owners Giovanni Pilu & Marilyn Annecchini
Seats 110; private rooms; wheelchair access; outdoor seats
www.piluatfreshwater.com.au
And...try pannacotta with abbamele, a slow-cooked mix of honeycomb, honey and pollen

Pink Peppercorn

122 Oxford Street, Darlinghurst
Tel 9360 9922   Map 2

Modern Laotian

Score 13/20

You might hope that this long, narrow room, with polished dark wood interior and images of Laotian monks, could be a haven of peace away from the Oxford Street mayhem of police sirens, thumping nightclub sounds and the constant traffic of people and vehicles. But on a busy Saturday night, the mayhem has come inside and it's packed. Friendly staff apologised for the extremely long delays, but there simply aren't enough of them to cope. Thankfully, such refined and original food is usually worth the wait. For starters, prawn and chicken in a fragrant lemongrass curry sauce with spicy crackers made for dipping. Steamed salmon is moist and lush, kaffir lime leaf adding its aromatic tang, while sticky rice and baby spinach make perfect accompaniments. A spicy green papaya salad with chargrilled salmon is zesty, exciting and fresh. For dessert, the lime sorbet is also a delight although hardly necessary after the complex yet subtle flavours of previous pleasures.

Hours Dinner daily 6pm–late
Bill E $10.50 **M** $16–$21.50 **D** $10.50; 10% surcharge on public holidays
Cards AE BC MC V Eftpos
Wine Short, predictable list; 11 by the glass; BYO (corkage $3 pp)
Chef Anouvong Kaseum
Owners Peter Barker & Anouvong Kaseum
Seats 55; outdoor seats
And...don't try to drive unless you come early in the week

good food guide

city + suburbs

Pool Caffe

94 Marine Parade, Maroubra
Tel 9314 0364 Map 9

Contemporary

Score 13/20

Perched on the rise of Marine Parade, with Maroubra beach a short stroll away, the Pool Caffe is a bit of a hidden treasure: it does better breakfasts than most, plus great lunches and dinners. The interior is white and cheerful, the floors are wooden and the windows wide, letting in the sky and sea. Service is good-natured, if at times a trifle haphazard, and food can take a while but is worth the wait. Great classic burgers and pasta are on offer for beach-goers, as well as more sophisticated fare: try the fresh seafood tapas of squid, prawns, octopus and barramundi, simply grilled and served with salsa verde; or a sweet thick fillet of mahi mahi. Angelhair pasta with delicate blue swimmer crab and shellfish oil is subtly laced with chilli; chicken risotto is wonderfully textured, with chunks of breast meat muscling through the fennel and leek. Tempt yourself with poached figs, chocolate brownies, or sticky date pudding with date and Drambuie ice-cream.

Hours Mon–Tues 8am–3pm, Wed–Sat 8am–10pm, Sun 8am–5pm

Bill E $13 **M** $22–$24 **D** $8.50; 10% surcharge on weekends & public holidays – daytime only

Cards AE BC MC V Eftpos; no bookings for breakfast or weekend lunch

Wine 10 Aussie options; 8 by the glass; BYO (corkage $2.50 pp)

Chef Andrew Damianos

Owner Louis Ajaka

Seats 90; private room; outdoor seats

And... Maroubra baths are just across the road: or take in the stunning cliff-side views from the rocks

Post Seafood Brasserie

Lower Ground Floor, GPO, 1 Martin Place, Sydney
Tel 9229 7744 Map 1

Seafood

Score 14/20

Set under the wonderfully restored sandstone GPO, tucked away on one side of Martin Place, Post continues to impress in its smart, calm, understated way. Suits take other suits out for lunch, perching on the long banquettes and whispering about the boss over stiff white linen, usually with a glass of something terrific in hand. While some areas of the GPO have changed, Post stays true to its brief, a New York-inspired brasserie where the colour scheme is muted browns, the service swift and pleasant, and the food top-notch. Seafood is the theme these days: the menu boasts that all the fish is iki-jimi (brain-spiked) for quality. For a land-based entrée, the Thirlmere chicken-liver parfait is seriously rich. Saltwater barramundi is ringed with oyster broth and given tang with lemon zest. Just-seared blue fin tuna is surrounded by chopped herbs. And while the tiramisu was a splodgy mess, spiced with a little rum and a lot of coffee, the wine cellar makes it hard to return to work.

Hours Lunch Mon–Fri noon–3pm; Dinner Mon–Sat 6–10pm

Bill E $12.50–$19.50 **M** $23.50–$33 **D** $14.50

Cards AE BC DC MC V Eftpos

Wine Clever, white-dominated list, with good eye to price and food-friendly styles; 21 by the glass

Chef Iwao Yamanishi

Owner Peter Petroulas

Seats 140; wheelchair access

www.gposydney.com

And...they're very swift at lunch

city + suburbs

Prasit's Northside

77 Mount Street, North Sydney
Tel 9957 2271   Map 5A

Thai

Score 13/20

Thai food lovers are not short on choices across Sydney, yet the popularity of Prasit's continues because it delivers some of the freshest, most innovative Thai. The North Sydney lunch crowd are by far the most regular supporters. Watch them roll up for crisp whitebait on betel leaves or tuck into legendary Prasit's rolls of crabmeat and pork, wrapped in tofu skin with a splash of plum sauce. It's well positioned: one floor up with a light, spacious room and wraparound terrace above the clutter of the North Sydney canyons. The bustle of workers below is replaced in the evening by a quieter, less frenetic pace. Barbecue king prawn salad with pomegranate, okra and garlic dressing is delicious with a full-on chilli hit; while grilled squid, stuffed with a spiced mix of rice, chicken and water chestnut, is a more delicate feast of flavours. There's still plenty of adventure on the menu, with spicy stir-fries and curries delivering a step above most suburban Thais.

Hours Lunch Mon–Fri noon–3pm; Dinner Tues–Sat 6–10pm
Bill E $12.50–$13.50 **M** $21.50–$25.50 **D** $7.50–$8.50
Cards AE BC DC MC V
Wine Concise, well-chosen and well-priced list; 10 by the glass
Chef Supachai Kongkham
Owner Eric Sudardja
Seats 140; private room; wheelchair access; outdoor seats
And...try their new outlet at 191 Darling Street, Balmain, tel 9555 5693

Prime

Lower Ground Floor, GPO, 1 Martin Place, Sydney
Tel 9229 7777   Map 1

Steakhouse

Score 14/20

They're big on provenance, whether it's a 400-gram rib-eye (dry-aged, yearling, 80–100 days grain-fed, angus–hereford cross, from New England) or muscovy duck (Thirlmere free-range, corn-fed, from the Southern Tablelands). The only thing you don't know about the protein on your plate is the colour of the farmer's gumboots. Peopled by money marketeers, Prime is a dimly lit carnivore cavern, with plush leather banquettes lining the historic basement's sandstone walls. There's variety: zucchini Tatin (disks of wafer-thin zucchini atop crisp buttery pastry) and millefeuille of crab (surprisingly bland despite its cumin and coriander mayonnaise); local line-caught blue-eye; Far North Queensland wild barramundi. But Prime's raison d'être is steak: sirloin, rib-eye, T-bone; dry-aged for four weeks for tenderness and flavour; served with a choice of sauces and creamy mash or gratin potatoes. There's a separate wagyu menu. A superbly juicy fillet (marbling score 6) from Darling Downs, Queensland, is so tender that a wave of a knife cuts it. At $75 it would want to.

Hours Lunch Mon–Fri noon–3pm; Dinner Mon–Sat 6–10pm
Bill E $17–$33 **M** $28–$44 **D** $14–$19
Cards AE BC DC MC V Eftpos
Wine Encyclopaedic, expensive list of 450, including good French; 14 by the glass
Chef Iwao Yamanishi
Owner Peter Petroulas
Seats 86; private room; wheelchair access
www.gposydney.com
And...wagyu chateaubriand is $165 for two

city + suburbs

Qmin

207B Pacific Highway, St Leonards
Tel 9966 5557   Map 5A

Indian

Score 14/20

When affable Anil Ashokan moved from Pyrmont's Kokum, his menu also shifted to span the whole Indian subcontinent. Goan specialities such as pastelao, a spicy meat pie whose crust crowns beef, sausage, pork and root vegies, survive in a dinner menu that now reads like an Indian cuisine primer. If, at times, execution fails to match expectations, it's mainly because he's aiming high, widely and handsomely to begin with. A tender goat curry with garlic, chilli and tomatoes is rich and aromatic, but lamb slow-cooked in almond milk was less so. Lunch includes thalis, those enticing stainless-steel platters with bread (something of a speciality here) and dosa – the large rice and lentil pancake – ringed with small pots of meat or vegetarian dishes. Tucked away behind an office block and painted in clean, stylish colours, with upholstered chairs and (sensible) butcher's-paper-over-crisp-linen tablecloths, Qmin is considered a local haven – especially for that marvellous pot of chickpeas and cashews with crisp spinach fritters.

Hours Breakfast Mon–Fri 8–11am; Brunch Sun 11.30am–2.30pm; Lunch Mon–Fri noon–3pm; Dinner Mon–Sat 6–10pm
Bill E $11–$15 **M** $17–$24 **D** $9–$10
Cards AE BC DC MC V Eftpos
Wine 27 listed, well chosen, fairly priced; 26 by the glass (not the Taittinger); BYO (corkage $7 per bottle)
Chef/owner Anil Ashokan
Seats 80; wheelchair access; outdoor seats
And...there's a terrace with tables for smokers

Quadrant

Quay Grand Sydney, Level 2, 61–69 Macquarie Street, East Circular Quay
Tel 9256 4044   Map 1

Contemporary

Score 12/20

This elegant space has pristine views looking straight across Circular Quay to the impressive-looking MCA building. Ferries bob at the docks while tourists and city workers hustle and bustle on the promenade below. There's much to like about the location, and the service is efficient and obliging. The interior is a bit of a clash, with wild 80s-style carpet jarring against clean minimal lines. And since it's part of a hotel chain, it's no surprise there's a hotel feel, while the international menu tries to please all-comers, including bush tucker for the tourists. A starter of seared tuna and grilled king prawn is simple and fresh, with miso and lime dressing a delightful enhancement. Simply cooked chicken breast is cleverly paired with celeriac purée and a salty of pancetta. Kangaroo loin on a bed of native-spiced kumera lacked tenderness and the rosella sauce simply didn't work. A side of chips is generous and crisp. And a bread-and-butter terrine with butterscotch sauce certainly hits the spot.

Hours Lunch Tues–Fri noon–3pm; Dinner Tues–Sat 5.30–10pm
Bill E $18–$22 **M** $32–$39 **D** $16
Cards AE BC DC MC V
Wine Respectable Australian list; 6 by the glass
Chef Jonathan Bruel
Owner Mirvac Hotels Corporation
Seats 55; wheelchair access
And...try the lunch special of $59 for 2 courses and wine

city + suburbs ®

Quay

Upper Level, Overseas Passenger Terminal, West Circular Quay, The Rocks
Tel 9251 5600 Map 1

Contemporary

Score 18/20

It takes a brave chef to drop an iconic dish (pork belly and scallops) after five years, but Peter Gilmore is master of his waterfront domain. Soon every other restaurant will be trying to imitate his pressed suckling porker. Their challenge is to create succulent flesh with a golden, crunchy top, pairing it with prunes, black pudding and cauliflower cream with a bold confidence that's simultaneously playful. Gilmore loves a dance of textures: tender quail ravioli, squeaky shaved abalone and celery heart purée are adrift in exquisite quail consommé; and crisp-skinned Murray cod is paired with barely cooked, potato-stuffed squid, samphire and green taro with a whiff of browned butter. The elegant, shiny room (despite a lurid carpet giving ageing hippies flashbacks) is a stage for the city's harbourside glory. A stunningly beautiful millefeuille with rose-scented cream, topped by caramelised raspberries and rose petals, is equally breathtaking. Service is deferentially restrained and prices creep towards international levels – but, what the hell, this is a world-class restaurant.

Hours Lunch Tues–Fri noon–2.30pm; Dinner daily 6–10pm
Bill E $33–$38 **M** $38–$48 **D** $20; 10% surcharge on public holidays
Cards AE BC DC MC V
Wine Long, wide and lovely, with good Europeans, at a premium; 10 by the glass
Chef Peter Gilmore
Owner Leon Fink
Seats 220; private rooms; wheelchair access
www.quay.com.au
And...there's more view to enjoy dining by daylight

Ravesi's

118 Campbell Parade, Bondi Beach
Tel 9365 4422 Map 9

Contemporary

Score 13/20

The suntanned, sunglassed, salt-stained, groovy and glam gather upstairs at this breezy dining room. You can watch the passing street life out on the verandah, overlooking Bondi beach, or you can settle on the white beehive chairs at polished-concrete tables in the airy, kirk-like dining room with its whitewashed walls and arched windows. The simple bistro menu concentrates on doing the familiar well, with a mix of Asian and Mediterranean flavours delivered by laidback, amiable service. A rustic and earthy chorizo and chickpea soup is a shallow pool studded with chunky vegetables. Yabby tail salad with jerusalem artichokes, bacon and celeriac dressing is crunchy, light and refreshing. Chargrilled sirloin with chips, roasted mushrooms and a red wine sauce was workmanlike. But black bean sauce didn't make a happy union with chargrilled tuna steak; and buttermilk pudding was a little too stiff with gelatine, accompanied by pickled cherries and shortbread. Kick back, enjoy the view, order another glass of wine and there's not a lot to complain about.

Hours Lunch Mon–Fri noon–3pm, Sat–Sun noon–4pm; Dinner Mon–Sat 6–10pm
Bill E $12–$18.50 **M** $26–$31 **D** $14–$17; 5% surcharge on weekends & public holidays
Cards AE BC MC V
Wine Moderate list of popular names at reasonable prices; 19 by the glass
Chef Darren Elms
Owners Geoff Vaughan, John Douglass & Malcolm Norburn
Seats 120; wheelchair access; outdoor seats
www.ravesis.com.au
And...the downstairs bar is a good watering hole

city + suburbs

Red Chilli

Shop 3, 51–53 Dixon Street (enter from Little Hay Street), Haymarket
Tel 9211 8122 Map 3A

Chinese (Sichuan)

Score 13/20

Dixon Street is littered with restaurant spruikers vying for business with an enthusiasm that seems inversely proportional to the quality of food they're likely to offer. So it's a joy to discover, with no fanfare, a place serving outstanding Chinese provincial fare out of the line of sight. This brightly lit, mod-minimal Chinese canvas on the first floor also extends to a second floor dedicated to the 'hotpot'. As the saying goes, 'Eat in China, taste in Sichuan', because the food really sings on the specialist menu. Service is sweet, friendly and very attentive, although skip the suggested kung pao (fiery deep-fried chicken dice, perfect with beer) and opt for the enormous and soul-satisfying mapo tofu (silky beancurd with spicy pork mince). Braised duck with konjak (a gelatinous root vegetable) drifts in a luxuriously duck-heavy broth, heady with chilli. Barramundi with pickled vegetables is another huge bowl of broth, cut with the tang of vinegar. We rarely see authentic Chinese eateries champion a province other than Canton. Red Chilli is a worthy competitor.

Hours Lunch daily 11.30am–3pm; Dinner daily 5–11pm
Bill E $3.20–$9.80 **M** $9.80–$28 **D** $3.20–$6; $2 pp surcharge on public holidays
Cards AE BC DC MC V Eftpos
Wine Limited range of cheap hits; house wine by the glass; BYO (corkage $2 pp)
Chef Yaoxiao Zhou
Owners Jian Chen, David Zhang & Teresa Dai
Seats 200
www.redchillirestaurant.com.au
And...the $8.80 lunch special with soup is a steal

Red Jujube

41 Shelley Street, Sydney
Tel 9279 0338 Map 1

Northern Chinese

Score 12/20

What at first glance seems to be an oriental furniture store is actually a northern Chinese diner. The chairs look like they're from Beijing and the room is dotted with mahogany tables and carved screens, but the menu is where it's all happening. They try hard to push the envelope beyond the Cantonese clichés that dominate most Sino–Sydney restaurants, looking at the sweetness of Shanghai, the pungency of Beijing and the sparkle of Shandong. Start with cold dishes, such as sliced lotus root in sweetened vinegar; or the beef strips marinated in black tea. Dip into the intriguing Nanjing salty duck, and make sure you have the so-called pot-sticker, or boiled, dumplings – we love the pork and cabbage version. The shallot pancakes are sublime; butterfish is smoked with tea; boiled noodles get a dose of Beijing-style soy paste and pork mince; and there's jellyfish with shredded chicken and sea cucumber if you're feeling homesick. Oh, and if you really are that homesick, the furniture actually is for sale.

Hours Lunch Mon–Sat noon–3pm; Dinner Mon–Sat 6–9pm
Bill E $7.80–$14.80 **M** $9.60–$28.80 **D** $3.80–$5.80
Cards AE BC DC MC V Eftpos
Wine Pretty decent if predictable list; a generous 13 by the glass; BYO (corkage $4 per bottle)
Chef Bruce Han
Owner Terry Huang
Seats 58; private room
And...take a walk down to the Harbour pre- or post-meal as you can't see it from the restaurant

city + suburbs　R

Red Lantern

545 Crown Street, Surry Hills
Tel 9698 4355　Map 3B

Southern Vietnamese

Score 14/20

Vietnamese has yet to become Sydney's new Thai, but more restaurants like the stylish Red Lantern will only advance the cause. This old terrace with polished floors, red walls and antique cabinets has a touch of faded Saigon glory. Words like crisp, caramelised, flaming, poached and slow-cooked leap off the menu while friendly staff are quick to offer explanations. They're mindful that what's actually being caramelised – perhaps pork leg and whole eggs with chilli, shallots and red pepper – might be a stretch for some. The menu includes salads, noodles and 'at the table' DIY ricepaper dishes like wok-fried salt-and-pepper blue swimmer crab. A special of pipis with chilli, fish sauce and holy basil is similarly hands-on and just as memorable. Crisp-skinned corn-fed chicken cooked in master stock is served with a more-ish tomato-infused rice but is better suited to lunch, while the prawn and pork dumplings with egg noodles in broth is great comfort food at any time.

Hours Lunch Tues–Fri 12.30–3pm; Dinner Tues–Sun 6.30–10.30pm
Bill E $9–$14 **M** $15–$19.50 **D** $10–$12; 10% surcharge on Sundays & public holidays
Cards AE MC V; bookings essential
Wine Well-chosen, reasonably priced list; 26 by the glass
Chefs Luke Nguyen & Mark Jensen
Owner Luke Nguyen
Seats 50; outdoor seats
www.redlantern.com.au
And...try the city's best banana fritters with vanilla ice-cream

Relish at Balmain Bug

55 Darling Street, Balmain
Tel 9810 5510　Map 5B

Contemporary

Score 14/20

This endearing 150-year-old Balmain institution, with its black-and-white chequered marble floor and aged sandstone walls adorned by Norman Lindsay and Elizabeth Durack art, has been home to Relish for over four years. Kelly Garske greets everyone like an old friend (although sitting by the front windows makes you feel like a store display), while husband Michael cooks an elaborate mod-Oz menu favouring Asia. Sea-sweet bug tail ravioli drift in a hot, sour, fragrant Thai broth. Wickedly crisp, sticky pork belly is earthed by lentils, refreshed with gremolata, then given a (perhaps too) sweet edge from pomegranate syrup. Beautiful lamb rack with onion and quince jam has a clever 'charlotte' companion – short pastry filled with succulent shredded lamb. Regulars love twice-cooked duck on Asian greens, with crisp water chestnut dumplings and chilli caramel. Rose-scented pav with rhubarb compote and rosewater fairy floss is a Turkish delight sugar hit. A slightly sweet tooth dominates the palate, but there's a generosity of spirit in Relish that's hard to resist.

Hours Dinner Tues–Sat 6.30–9.30pm
Bill E $17–$21.50 **M** $30–$32 **D** $14.50–$15
Cards AE BC DC MC V Eftpos; bookings essential
Wine BYO (corkage $3 pp)
Chef Michael Garske
Owners Kelly & Michael Garske
Seats 65; private rooms
www.balmainbug.com.au
And...there's a decent bottleshop, 60 Darling Street, directly opposite

R city + suburbs

Rengaya

73 Miller Street, North Sydney
Tel 9929 6290   Map 5A

Japanese

Score 13/20

This is not a place for those still wedded to the idea that a restaurant is a place where other people cook your food. No, it's all make your own here in this little oasis of wooden beams and paper screens among the concrete brutalism of North Sydney. There's a little circular barbecue at the centre of every table – which means that the gorgeous, heavily marbled wagyu is at the mercy of amateur cooks. If you do decide to leave it to the pros, the results can be mixed. Just by looking at the tempura prawns we could tell that something had gone awry – the batter was far too yellow, far too thick and a little too greasy. The tonkatsu (pork cutlets crumbed and fried), on the other hand, turn out to be beautifully moist and succulent. We do, however, wonder why they were served with a mysterious side dish of salad and pasta. If you're doing the cooking, there could be tongue, liver and other more familiar body parts that you decide just how to cook.

Hours Lunch Tues–Fri noon–2.30pm; Dinner daily 6–9.30pm (closed 2nd & 4th Monday of each month)
Bill E $8–$13.80 **M** $14.80–$33.80 **D** $7.80–$9.80; 10% surcharge over Christmas and New Year holidays
Cards AE BC MC V
Wine Short, uneventful list; 5 by the glass
Chef Yoshihiro Akiba
Owner Yoshiro Inoue
Seats 84; private rooms; outdoor seats
www.yakiniku.com.au

And...if you're frightened of burning the meat but you still want to cook your own, try the shabu shabu hotpot

Republic Dining

Republic Hotel, cnr Pitt & Bridge streets, Sydney
Tel 9252 6522   Map 1

European

Unscored

We love lunching four floors up at the financial end of town. The Republic's dining room is one long rectangle, with gorgeous timber windows, a banquette facing them, plus a bar and peephole to the kitchen helping to break up the space. While former MG Garage chef Jeremy Strode hit the pans, it was better than ever. Mostly the crowd is blokey, as red wine slurping gourmands take time out from the office to get their lips around superb house-cured smoked salmon, and stunning celeriac and potato soup with a drizzle of Worcestershire sauce. Like most restaurants this year, Republic is serving corned beef; in this case wagyu poached so long that it melts like butter on the tongue, the flavours going on longer than an ASIC investigation. Roast spatchcock has perfectly crisp skin, a delectable bread sauce and the most exquisite spring onions as a fitting counterpoint. The steak is invariably good, and there's a tart of the day, perhaps a decadently dark Tatin, to fuel the next deal. As we go to press, however, Strode steps out of the kitchen so we must leave this year's entry unscored.

Hours Lunch Mon–Fri noon–4pm
Bill E $18 **M** $28–$33 **D** $12
Cards AE BC DC MC V
Wine Excellent list for the bistro-style food; 18 by the glass
Chef Chris Coolahan
Owner Patrick Ryan
Seats 80; wheelchair access
www.republichotel.com

And...take the lift unless you want four floors of exercise

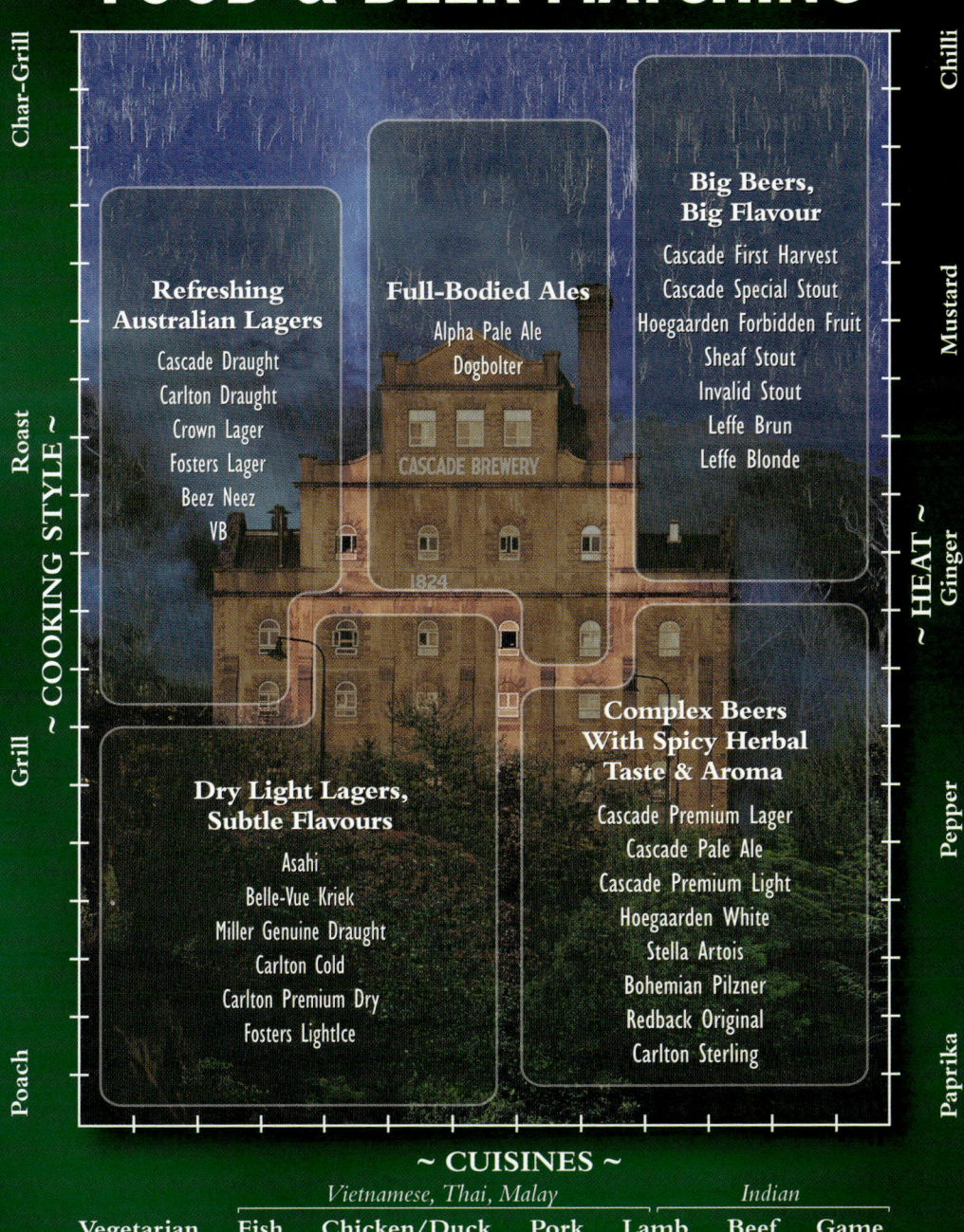

Ingredients: grass, air, water

RETAIL PROCESSOR 2001RP
AUSTRALIAN CERTIFIED ORGANIC

www.**sam the butcher**.com.au

ORGANIC MEAT SUPPLY

naremburn   sans souci   bondi   beecroft

Restaurant Atelier

22 Glebe Point Road, Glebe
Tel 9566 2112   Map 5B

Modern European

Score 15/20

Wow. We've always been fans, even when Atelier was in a dog-ugly site in Newtown. But now, with the talented duo of Darren and Bernadette Templeman having moved to a lovely old cottage in Glebe, it's even better. Sure, Bernadette still effortlessly graces the room, and yes, there is a courtyard for milder months. But the real improvement is in the finely honed, Brit–French style of the menu. Templeman's food is seriously good; a wondrously smooth and nutty amuse bouche of butternut pumpkin soup with pumpkin seed oil is a gentle start. Later, there's a complimentary and seriously sexy pre-dessert of vanilla and citrus peel pannacotta with strawberry granita. And in between are outstanding dishes, such as tomato tarte Tatin with goat's cheese, which blow your tastebuds away. Lamb with eggplant and zucchini compote pairs with an intriguing pastilla (a bit like a strudel) in which the richness of lamb blends magnificently with the sweetness of sultanas, almonds and hints of cinnamon.

Hours Dinner Tues–Sat from 6pm
Bill E $15–$20 **M** $27–$28.50 **D** $10–$12
Cards BC MC V Eftpos
Wine Compact and well-priced list; 10 by the glass; BYO (corkage $5 per bottle)
Chef Darren Templeman
Owners Darren & Bernadette Templeman
Seats 77; private room; wheelchair access; outdoor seats
www.restaurantatelier.com.au
And... from Tuesday to Thursday a starter and main are only $39.50

Restaurant Balzac

141 Belmore Road, Randwick
Tel 9399 9660   Map 9

French/British

Score 16/20

In Paris, they call it le fooding – a mix of food and feeling. Such Franglais could apply to this rollicking room where the vigour of the waiters under Lela Radojkovic's warm gaze, the charm of the sandstone walls, and the stage-quality lighting seem to energise the customers. Everyone seems determined to have fun. The food – modern but not demanding, hearty and gamy yet whimsical in places – is integral to this package, thanks to the competent, classical French technique of Matthew Kemp who achieves much without emptying your wallet. There's a moist and meaty galantine of duck with figs and walnuts; and a carpaccio of seared venison – OK it's a culinary contradiction – with celeriac and apple salad. Roast lamb loin is topped with pickled lamb tongues; and braised veal shin with savoy cabbage is as rustic as a country cottage. There's magic, though less these days than we're used to in the kitchen. While an ambitious assiette of pear and prune is interesting, it's still no match for Australia's best bread-and-butter pud.

Hours Lunch Fri noon–2.30pm; Dinner Tues–Thurs 6–10.30pm, Fri–Sat from 5.30pm
Bill E $20 **M** $30 **D** $16
Cards AE BC DC MC V
Wine Small and well-formed list, with French and German appearances; 15 by the glass; BYO Tues–Thurs only (corkage $12 per bottle)
Chef Matthew Kemp
Owners Matthew Kemp & Lela Radojkovic
Seats 120; private room; wheelchair access
And... book ahead for the popular Sunday dégustation nights

Ristorante Riva

379 Liverpool Street, Darlinghurst
Tel 9380 5318   Map 2

Italian (Northern)

Score 15/20

Do we go to be cosseted by Eugenio Riva's deft casalinga cooking or by Beverley Wood's reassuringly warm service? Well, both, because this brilliant symbiosis makes a whole greater than the sum of some very fine parts. The long, narrow, smart room of dark timber floors and washed-brick walls adorned with vibrant abstract art is a haven from Darlo's hubbub, even if it can generate its own din when packed. The northern Italian menu knows it doesn't have to try too hard to impress, from ebullient chilli-marinated mackerel fillets, arranged in compass points, topped with finely sliced radish and fennel; to house-made flour and polenta angelhair pasta with vivaciously sweet crab and chilli. Sliced eye fillet on broccolini has the salt kick of a parsley and anchovy dressing; Tuscan-style pigeon has just enough gaminess for a mix of spinach, pine nuts and sultanas with a game jus. Rice ice-cream with tart amarene cherries is a textural revelation. A great grappa selection helps that increasingly contented feeling wash over you.

Hours Lunch Fri 12.30–3pm;
Dinner Mon–Sat 6.30–10.30pm
Bill E $21–$24 **M** $33–$36.50 **D** $13.50
Cards AE BC DC MC V
Wine Smart, concise list of Oz and Italian; 12 by the glass
Chef Eugenio Riva
Owners Eugenio Riva & Beverley Wood
Seats 47
And...four wonderful daily specials

Rocket

Shop P1, 1–5 Railway Street, Chatswood
Tel 9411 8233   Map 7

Contemporary

Score 13/20

In an area best known for Chinese restaurants, Rocket is an oasis of mod-Oz charm. Encased in glass, with a shiny and contemporary fit-out, it is smart to look at, as is its longish menu of crowd-pleasing dishes. Service is, if it's possible, over eager. Josef Schacher's food manages to be enticing but not too predictable, so it can be hard to choose between dishes such as white rabbit pie with bush tomato chutney; and a trio of prawns on a powerfully sweet and tangy mango chilli salsa with watercress and palm sugar dressing. It's no easier at mains, where the (perhaps too) gutsy flavours of lamb rump with eggplant, hummus and fried haloumi compete with elegant combinations such as Thai-spiced boned baby barramundi with gai lan, preserved lemon and pine nuts. Sometimes it felt as if dishes weren't quite hitting the peaks they aimed for, but there is certainly plenty of cosy comfort in a rhubarb and custard tart with pistachio ice-cream.

Hours Lunch Mon–Fri noon–3pm;
Dinner Tues–Sat 6–10pm
Bill E $18 **M** $29.50 **D** $14
Cards AE BC DC MC V Eftpos
Wine Very well-priced, well-chosen four-pager; many in the $30–$40 bracket; 10 by the glass; BYO (corkage $7 per bottle)
Chef Josef Schacher
Owners Peter Fletcher & Josef Schacher
Seats 80; wheelchair access; outdoor seats
www.rocketrestaurant.com.au
And...free parking under the building from 6pm

Rockpool

107 George Street, The Rocks
Tel 9252 1888   Map 1

Contemporary

Score 16/20

Sleek, modern and comfortable, Rockpool keeps evolving. Like the room – all aquamarine carpet and stainless steel Alessi uplights – entrées are daring, combining unlikely and seemingly incongruous flavours in gastronomic brinkmanship. Poached lobster, just cooked through, comes with pork salad dressed with 20-year-old balsamic vinegar; snow crab matches wits with caramelised pork belly and peppered tofu; the freshest prawns relax on hand-cut Chinese-style noodles dressed with prawn oil. Mains didn't quite reach the same high notes, and sweeter flavours abound. The nuances in rare anchovy-spiked tuna wrapped in prosciutto and dressed with red wine sauce are finely balanced, but john dory was lost under a murtabak pastry with curry sauce. Chinese roast pigeon has a French twist in that it comes medium–rare, but did tea-smoked duck really need a sugary hit of both pineapple and caramel? An apple mousse and jelly competes for attention with an excellent calvados and the date tart remains simply sublime. While we have found the food standards have slipped a little, service remains polished and as professional as ever.

Hours Dinner Tues–Sat 6–11pm
Bill E $32–$43 **M** $54–$70 **D** $23; dégustation menu $160 pp
Cards AE BC DC MC V
Wine Great list with the best of Australia and Europe; 17 by the glass
Chefs Neil Perry, Khan Danis & Catherine Adams
Owners Neil Perry & Trish Richards
Seats 120; private room
www.rockpool.com
And...explore the special Anders Josephson cellared wine selection

Royal Bar & Grill

Level 2, Royal Hotel, 237 Glenmore Road, Paddington
Tel 9331 5055   Map 4B

Contemporary

Score 13/20

After 15 years spent cooking at this landmark pub, Keith O'Leary has a good notion of what people want: honest flavours in prop forward-sized portions, served with Paddo poise. Sure you can have a caesar salad – why not after a couple of schooners downstairs or a cocktail in the legendary Elephant bar? But why not try deftly handled lamb brains, soft and yielding under their crumbed coat; although perhaps not octopus salad that was charred and chewy. Four large slices of high-quality lamb's liver, properly grilled, loll in a robust red wine reduction; steaks come cooked as ordered; roast Barossa chicken is delicate and moist; and there's always plenty of seafood among the specials. Dessert faves include flourless chocolate cake and a jolly sticky date pudding. Waiters cope admirably as numbers swell amid the burnished brass and well-buffed browns of this venerable old space, hoisting its Royal bosom over a corner at Fiveways. This is the sort of place that gives pub grub a good name.

Hours Sat noon–10pm, Sun noon–9pm; Lunch Mon–Fri noon–3pm; Dinner Mon–Fri 6–10pm
Bill E $8.50–$17.50 **M** $17.50–$27.50 **D** $8.50–$9.50; 10% surcharge on public holidays
Cards AE BC DC MC V Eftpos
Wine A who's who of your favourite drops at friendly prices; 21 by the glass
Chef Keith O'Leary
Owner Foodsmith Pty Ltd
Seats 100; private rooms; outdoor seats
And...couples should ask for a balcony table

PENNY PINCHING
(when the cost counts)

An Restaurant
27 Greenfield Parade, Bankstown
Tel 9796 7826
It's fast food Vietnamese style as this giant barn bustles with people hunched over big steaming bowls of pho (soup). A quick refuelling at communal tables and you're shopping again only $10 lighter.

Emma's on Liberty
59 Liberty Street, Enmore
Tel 9550 3458
Gee it's loud. And really crowded. And a nightmare to get in. But persevere, because Emma Sofy's Lebanese food is bargain-priced and you'll never leave hungry after blowing around $20 a head.

Jimbaran
129 Avoca Street, Randwick
Tel 9398 8555
Amazing Indonesian food on plastic-covered tables. Lunch may offer pempek – light as a feather fish cakes – while at night it's all deep, dark beef rendang, lush prawns tossed with salty egg, or sweet fried chook. You'll fork out very little for quite a lot.

Nove
Area 9, 6 Cowper Wharf Road, Woolloomooloo
Tel 9368 7599
While the glitterati are swanking away at this trattoria's adjacent sibling, Otto, tuck into good crisp pizza, pasta and regional Italian dishes, with chilled-yet-smart service and the same million-dollar city views – all for much less.

Oscillate Wildly
275 Australia Street, Newtown
Tel 9517 4700
Hardly oscillating, and certainly not wildly, is a modest, bargain-priced bistro where lamb tongue may be poached with star anise. Three courses for $43 is a bargain.

Pompei
126 Roscoe Street, Bondi Beach
Tel 9365 1233
What George Pompei doesn't know about pizza isn't worth knowing. Slowly risen dough, superb minimalist toppings and the best hand-crafted gelato in Sydney are yours for a fraction of most restaurant meals.

Restaurant Atelier
22 Glebe Point Road, Glebe
Tel 9566 2112
Hatted Atelier is always darned cheap for the level of classical technique and produce. Midweek, get an entrée and a main for $39.50. Tomato tarte Tatin is superb, kaffir-scented beef cheeks even better.

Spice I Am
90 Wentworth Avenue, Sydney
Tel 9280 0928
Sydney's most authentic Thai food comes at a price – about $10–$15 a head for superbly aromatic curries, herbaceous salads and the fieriest larb. Get the order written in Thai for the real double-burn chilli effect.

WildEast Dreams
102 Norton Street, Leichhardt
Tel 9560 4131
The quirky mod-Asian joint in the heart of predominantly Latino Norton Street is doing great things with prawns, with squid and with mains starting at a really decent $15 (and you usually share dishes). There's live piano some nights, too.

Woodland's
Shop 4–5, 55–67 George Street, Parramatta
Tel 9633 3838
Also at 238 George Street, Liverpool
Tel 9734 9949
A thali plate for under $20. Whopping great, crisp, golden-brown dosa (pancakes) and lashings of southern Indian vegetarian dishes. For lunch there's a $10 buffet. The spice is right, so come on down.

R city + suburbs

RQ

294 Crown Street, Darlinghurst
Tel 9360 8688   Map 2

Vietnamese/Thai

Score 14/20

There's black sticky rice, then there's the black sticky rice at Rice Quarter (aka RQ): sweetness and saltiness nicely balanced, bite just right, a splodge of coconut cream, and, happily, an unexpected lacing of juicy lychee strips. When an Asian restaurant gets dessert this right it's confirmation of the preceding excellence of an interesting and inviting menu that spans two nations. Gold band snapper revels in the glorious tangle of flavours in a cumin-and-Sichuan-pepper crust, along with the zip of chilli and murky blachan in the kang kong (water spinach). Dinky pork ribs are sweet and sticky while lamb rissoles threaded on sugar cane sticks are nicely tender. Warm, professional service adds an extra dimension, from the way bowls are swiftly removed after every course to replacing the rice bucket when they deem it has sat there too long. The two-storey modern space is sparsely white, with a few green leaves for garnish, and regulars pile in intent on 'Sydney's best Thai-style spicy beef salad'.

Hours Dinner daily 6.30pm–late
Bill E $14 **M** $19.50 **D** $9; 10% surcharge on Sundays & public holidays
Cards AE BC DC MC V Eftpos
Wine Cleverly constructed at two price levels; 8 by the glass; BYO Sun–Thurs (corkage $3.50 pp)
Chef Nhut Huynh
Owners Nhut Huynh & Jeremy McNamara
Seats 88; private room
And...did we mention the rosewater ice-cream?

Sailors Thai Restaurant

Lower Level, 106 George Street, The Rocks
Tel 9251 2466   Map 1

Thai

Score 14/20

This landmark Sydney restaurant helped redefine the city's attitudes and approach to Thai cuisine. But the long absence of British-based super-chef David Thompson has seen the lemongrass zing dissipate. You'd hope that prices almost double those of a suburban Siam eatery would result in food to match, but sadly it's not always the case. Amidst a predominantly seafood menu, stir-fried beef with cumin and onions was somewhat dry and lacked the distinctive flavours we've become used to; while a thick sauce made it hard to distinguish the meat in a muslim duck curry. Thankfully, there are plenty of highlights: grilled Western Australian sardines with a perfect sweet, fresh sauce; a wonderfully pungent mix of spicy Kangaroo Island chicken, pomelo with mint and coriander salad. Service is generally efficient, and the room boasts a lovely mix of sandstone history and slick modernity, with glimpses, for a few, of West Circular Quay. Leave room for that rarest of Asian treats: great desserts like the intriguing black ash pudding or smoked coconut ice-cream and pineapple sorbet.

Hours Lunch Mon–Fri noon–2.30pm; Dinner Mon–Sat 6–10pm
Bill E $18–$29 **M** $26–$35 **D** $10–$12; tasting menu $70 pp; minimum food charge $35 pp
Cards AE BC DC MC V
Wine Smallish but classy Australasian list; 10 by the glass
Chef Ty Bellingham
Owners Peter Bowyer & David Thompson
Seats 80; outdoor seats
And...the gravel just down the stairs from the entrance is great for boules

city + suburbs (S)

Sailors Thai Canteen

Street Level, 106 George Street, The Rocks
Tel 9251 2466   Map 1

Thai

Score 14/20

Diners are often shocked at the casual nature of the Canteen. Yep, it's just one very long zinc table that is stained from years of green curry, pad thai and sauvignon blanc. And yes, that is the fully open kitchen, raised up on the left-hand side. And yes, those waiters could smile more as they pick up plates fresh from the wok and deliver them to hungry folk who've found this place in The Rocks' historic converted Sailors Home. But one mouthful of the food and you'll be hooked. It's heady with lime, spiked with chilli, decadently herbaceous and invariably fresh. The curries are always made from scratch: perhaps a light version drizzled over fried prawns with crisp rice-flour-battered herbs. Whole snapper may be deep-fried, and the salads are lively and interesting. If you're after some privacy, try to get one of the tiny tables out on the deck; and if you'd like the food hotter, just ask for a dish of chillies to light your fire.

Hours Mon–Sat noon–10pm
Bill E/M $12–$23.50 **D** $6–$10
Cards AE BC DC MC V; no bookings
Wine Spice-friendly list and good beers; 15 by the glass
Chef Pacharin Jantrakool
Owners Peter Bowyer & David Thompson
Seats 54; outdoor seats
And…sole diners can ask for half portions to try more dishes

Sails on Lavender Bay

2 Henry Lawson Avenue, McMahons Point
Tel 9955 5998   Map 5A

Contemporary

Score 13/20

'How's everything, guys?' That's a big question, mid-meal, among the birthday celebrations and more furtive gatherings. The view is grand: a watermelon sunset bathes the Bridge, ferries to and fro, Luna Park twinkles, and across the water there's a certain opera house. Pinch yourself. Yet the interior of this McMahons Point wharf site sets no design high-water marks, feeling very 80s condominium. Tables are undressed in that casual Sydney style, the crockery old hat, and service – although with good intent – was unassured. Brett Deverall's (ex-Mezzaluna) cookery has hits and the odd miss: most plates packed with flavours and an inventive use of ingredients, like oysters with a white tomato and champagne sorbet. Chargrilled squid tops a parcel of Lebanese couscous with hot chilli jam wrapped in shaved cucumber. But baked snapper with green mango salad and shaved coconut was overwhelmed by coriander pesto. Poached veal fillet with full-flavoured morel mushrooms deserves our compliments. And everything's just fine, thanks, over a rhubarb and spiced cherry tarte Tatin.

Hours Lunch Tues–Fri from noon; Dinner Mon–Sat from 6pm
Bill E $18–$25 **M** $29–$36 **D** $15
Cards AE BC DC MC V Eftpos; bookings essential
Wine Fulfilling list of mostly Oz labels, most from South Australia; 14 by the glass
Chef Brett Deverall
Owner Derek Taylor
Seats 80; wheelchair access
www.sailslavenderbay.com
And…the last ferry to the Quay departs about ten minutes after midnight

city + suburbs

Sakana-Ya

336 Pacific Highway, Crows Nest
Tel 9438 1468   Map 5A

Japanese/Seafood

Score 14/20

There are few places in Sydney where you can get seafood so good, at the right price. Little is spent on the décor at this unassuming bolthole, but the largely Japanese clientele flock anyway for the extensive, ever-changing array of top-quality fish. Consult the paper specials sheet for whatever is best that day, and have it raw as sashimi or cooked in a variety of enticing ways: grilled, salted, fried, in teriyaki, or in nimono (delicately simmered in a sweet sake and soy sauce). You won't be disappointed whichever way you go, although the nimono dishes – in which the fish is butter-soft – really stand out. So too does the raw tuna salad with a sesame dressing, lemon and leafy greens. Sides like cold spinach with sesame, or deep-fried eggplant covered in rich, caramelised miso paste, prove a perfect foil to the simple goodness of the fish, and even the miso is better than average. Service, naturally, is ultra-polite.

Hours Lunch Mon–Fri noon–2.30pm; Dinner daily 6–10pm
Bill E $5–$25 **M** $12–$36 **D** $5–$7; banquets $33–$75
Cards AE BC DC MC V
Wine An uninspiring list – opt for the beers or sake; BYO (corkage $5.50 per bottle)
Chef Nobuaki Matsuzawa
Owner Yasushi Yasuoka
Seats 75; private room
And...banquet menus available too

Sanders

D'Albora Marina, Cabarita Park, Cabarita Road, Cabarita
Tel 9736 2468   Map 6

Seafood

Score 14/20

Despite its humble origins as a kiosk on a marina, Sanders is nothing less than a delightful restaurant these days. There are gorgeous views over Putney and Gladesville (sometimes through the plastic fold-down walls), the waiters are formally dressed, and they put down carpet in the cooler months to stop the breeze coming up from below decks. Mark Ferraro's food ravages the sea, and the globe, for inspiration. On a mostly seafood menu you might find crabmeat-stuffed zucchini flowers; and barbecued king prawns with roasted pepper mayonnaise and fresh lime. Even his land-based options work well, as seen in succulent slices of Dutton Park duck breast with walnut and fig paste. Tiles of scored, grilled squid are drizzled with lively salsa verde, beside cherry tomatoes, green olive and chorizo. The gold band snapper with saffron mayo and white asparagus is superb. Desserts didn't quite push our boat out, with the chocolate pudding not as good as the summer berry pud, but those water views are the sweetest treat.

Hours Breakfast Sun 8–11am; Lunch daily noon–3pm; Dinner Mon–Sat 6–9.30pm
Bill E $20–$24 **M** $29–$37 **D** $15; 10% surcharge on Sundays & public holidays
Cards AE BC DC MC V
Wine Wise, small list; mid-range prices; 8 by the glass
Chef Mark Ferraro
Owner Matthew Filson
Seats 80; wheelchair access; outdoor seats
www.sandersrestaurant.com.au
And...access by water taxi, plus private boat berths available

city + suburbs (S)

Sapporo

94 Willoughby Road, Crows Nest
Tel 9436 3435   Map 5A

Japanese

Score 13/20

You could easily walk past this ordinary shopfront, yet within its confines is a dining gem that attracts sushi and sashimi connoisseurs. They beam as the chef's freshly selected specials – a work of art – hit the hard-topped table. It makes up for the uninspiring décor and harsh lighting, which camouflages even more surprises, especially for sushi-scoffing sports fans. There are framed celebrity rugby jerseys and an invitation to enjoy Super 12, or Sumo live from Japan or some other sporting frenzy, viewed on the mega-screen in the outside dining area. A menu with photographs can't do justice to delicate prawn dumplings with pork mince, or crisp whitebait tempura, matched well with spinach and sesame sauce. Grazing on smaller dishes is a wise way to savour flavours such as succulent grilled pork belly slices with black pepper; or grilled eel on rice. Traditionalists will appreciate the succulent teriyaki chicken. Service requires patience, as the language of the food is predominant both among diners and on the floor.

Hours Lunch Tues–Fri noon–3pm;
Dinner Tues–Sun from 6pm
Bill E $28.50–$30.50 **M** $41.50–$45.50
D $17.50–$20
Cards AE BC DC MC V
Wine Reliable, well-priced list including plenty of sake and beer choices; BYO (corkage $5.50 per bottle)
Chefs Shintaro Kosugi & Nao Mizoi
Owners Nobuo Ishikawa & Shuichiro Sugisaki
Seats 100
And...perfect for Sumo-sized appetites

Sea Oracle

12 Fitzroy Street, Kirribilli
Tel 9956 7992   Map 5A

Chinese

Score 12/20

The aroma of warm oriental spice wafts down the stairs of this old terrace house as you climb up to the small modern room set with double linen and enlarged by well-placed mirrors. Tables on the enclosed balcony are more casual but are still set with generous linen napkins. The menu lists the usual lemon chicken and Mongolian lamb beside some less common, Sichuan-influenced dishes, such as superb fried green beans with dried pork mince and dried red chillies; and squeaky, just-cooked prawns on a sizzling platter, also with dried red chillies. XO scallops are thick and meaty, served on the half-shell with ginger, onion and a good dash of cognac; and 'dry lamb stick' is delicious strips of lamb wrapped in slightly thick Chinese pancakes. Service is friendly, especially from owner David Shen, who pokes his head through the window to the balcony to check how things are going. Special Chinese ice-creams flavoured with black sesame, lychee and sticky rice are quite icy and may be an acquired taste.

Hours Lunch daily noon–3pm;
Dinner daily 6pm–late
Bill E $6–10.90 **M** $13.90–$28.90 **D** $6–$9.50;
yum cha $5–$6 per dish
Cards AE BC DC MC V Eftpos
Wine Reasonable list with good service; 8 good ones by the glass; BYO (corkage $4 pp)
Chef David Shen
Owners David & Cathryn Shen
Seats 90; outdoor seats
And...yum cha served noon–3pm every day

city + suburbs

Sea Treasure

46 Willoughby Road, Crows Nest
Tel 9906 6388   Map 5A

Chinese/Cantonese

Score 14/20

Sea Treasure is an institution that just keeps on keeping on. Ordering is like putting together a puzzle: perhaps something to start from the small items on one little menu, interesting Cantonese dishes from the laminated one, or king crab and all manner of seafood scooped from the large tanks and cooked in different ways with any of six sauces. You'll need to assert yourself to ask for help because service is perfunctory or rapid-fire, rather than attentive and personable, as waiters weave between the crowded tables, live fish choices held up in plastic bags for approval. Parrotfish, de-boned at the table, flaking perfectly, is beautifully steamed and delicately flavoured with the classic combination of ginger, shallots and soy. Pigeon, poached in master stock then deep-fried to a mahogany lacquer colour, is rich, soft and gamy, with spiced salt and black vinegar for dipping. Beancurd is deep-fried to a crisp exterior and fall-apart interior. Décor is pastel rather than glitzy, but then the food is the hero.

Hours Lunch Mon–Fri 11am–3pm, Sat–Sun 10am–3pm; Dinner daily 5.30–11pm
Bill E $5.50–$19.80 **M** $13.80–$32.80 **D** $5–$13; live seafood at market prices; $2.50 pp surcharge on public holidays
Cards AE BC DC MC V
Wine Reasonable selection; some aged choices; a shameful 2 by the glass; BYO (corkage $4 pp)
Chef Yui Wah Lau & King Tong Lau
Owner King Tong Lau
Seats 280; private rooms; wheelchair access
And...yum cha continues to pack 'em in, with great value seven days a week

Sean's Panaroma

270 Campbell Parade, Bondi Beach
Tel 9365 4924   Map 9

Contemporary

Score 16/20

In another life, Sean Moran could well be Epicurus ... or your mother – his cookery and good-heartedness fulfilling senses with simple pleasures of food and drink. But Mum never had upturned sea urchin lamps glowing henna on the table or oyster shell salt cellars, and the kitchen table never overlooked lifesavers rowing flush into Bondi breakers. And surely Epicurus never roasted a plump Barossa free-range chook so golden or served it with a parsnip purée so sweet? Talk about thrilling us slowly with lightly floured, deep-fried and delightfully crunchy Clarence River school prawns; silky aubergine baked with buffalo mozzarella; pan-fried veal on sweet potato mash; and raspberry jelly and peach leaf ice-cream for pud. It's a room of whimsy and wonderment (lit by a conch shell) with a panelled blackboard menu. It's reassuring in a city of fizz and instant gratification that such a throwback to old-fashioned aesthetics, and the Sunday roast, endures in safe hands. Smell the vase of roses and share this small, casually unassuming room with best friends and lovers.

Hours Lunch Sat–Sun noon–2.30pm; Dinner Wed–Sat 6–9.30pm
Bill E $18–$25 **M** $21–$42 **D** $15–$16; $7 pp surcharge on Sundays & public holidays
Cards BC MC V; bookings essential
Wine Crafted boutique list with new drops from France, Italy, New Zealand; up to 30 by the glass; BYO (corkage $8 per bottle)
Chefs Sean Moran & Alex Kearns
Owners Sean Moran & Michael Robertson
Seats 74; outdoor seats
www.seanspanaroma.com.au
And...they sell jars of homemade peach marmalade and spiced grape and apple jam

city + suburbs (S)

SeLAh

12 Loftus Street, Circular Quay
Tel 9247 0097   Map 1

Contemporary

Score 13/20

It's a curious yet busy location, in a bus-lined street leading up from the Quay's ferry terminals. Join the hoards venturing into the simple square space with colourful art, sit at a laminate table and watch the chefs cooking in the open kitchen. Smoked goat's cheese is barely touched by the fumes, wrapped in vine leaves and cleverly matched with diced apple and black olives, as well as (curiously) battered green beans. Javier Carmona's dishes are bold to the eye and even livelier in the mouth. Pork spare ribs are braised, finely shredded and muddled into a watercress salad with black and white sesame with discs of red radish and slivers of cucumber. The rigatoni with chunks of buttery-soft braised beef cheeks and a lemony gremolata is superb, though Cajun-tasting eight-spiced flathead probably didn't need both its red wine sauce and a pipi and kipfler salad. Dessert offers the usual suspects: pannacotta, a citrus tart and a baked soft-centred chocolate pudding. Changes to the space are afoot as we go to press but we expect Carmona's menu to remain on song.

Hours Lunch Mon–Fri noon–3pm; Dinner Mon–Sat 5.30–9.30pm
Bill E $14 **M** $16 **D** $10
Cards AE BC DC MC V Eftpos
Chef Javier Carmona
Owner Sam Pask
Wine Brief accessible list, all from below the equator; 15 by the glass
Seats 60
www.selah.com.au
And...you can forgive paper serviettes when they offer such excellent coffee

Seri Nonya

561 Kingsway, Miranda
Tel 9525 0036   Map 8

Malaysian

Score 13/20

Don't be deceived by appearances – this single-room, plate-glass, busy-road shopfront conceals a restaurant focussed on genuine care and expertise. Chef/owner Alvin Tan has mastered the complex, labour-intensive art of nonya – an intensely flavoured, occasionally explosive mix of Chinese and Malay, with accents of Indo and Thai – while his wife Jessica runs the floor with quiet grace. Delicate patties of mashed potato, chicken, carrot, chilli and fresh herbs are spiked with a fantastic dipping sauce. Kueh pie tee (top hat) is a nonya speciality of hand-crafted crisp pastry cups packed with vegetables, prawns and beancurd and served, endearingly, in cardboard egg cartons. Excellent sambal prawns are lifted by lime leaves and spiked with tamarind; creamy curry chicken is soothed by coconut. Spinach, okra and eggplant are all served with blachan: power-packed dried prawn and chilli paste. There's a small selection of straight Chinese and Thai dishes; the Sichuan beef is sizzling and tender. For dessert, try the tapioca pudding with palm sugar syrup and coconut: accomplished, unprepossessing and very good – like Seri Nonya itself.

Hours Lunch Wed–Sun 12.30–2.30pm; Dinner Tues–Sun 5.30–10pm
Bill E $6–$9 **M** $10.50–$29.50 **D** $4–$5.50; $2 pp surcharge on public holidays
Cards AE BC DC MC V Eftpos
Wine BYO (corkage $1 pp)
Chef Alvin Tan
Owners Alvin & Jessica Tan
Seats 55
And...the whole menu is available as takeaway

city + suburbs

Sevardi Cucina Italiana

12–14 Hannah Street, Beecroft
Tel 9980 1150   Map 6

Italian

Score 13/20

There's a sense of occasion in this sweet little room. It's in the intimacy, soft lighting, dark hardwood floors and white double-linen tabletops. A feature wall displays artfully hung black-and-white photos by Roberto Sevardi (b. 1865): sensitive impressions from his home town of Reggio nell' Emilia in Italy's north. Charismatic restaurateur Antonio Abassi is from the south, born in Napoli and cooking traditional recipes handed down by his mother. So expect plenty of rich napolitana sauces – the tastes of tomato, garlic, oregano, chilli and cream – on a fillet of baked blue-eye or with calamari piccanti, served on a polenta cake, proving that the cuisines from both ends of Italy's long leg can meet congruously in the middle. The menu is simple and filled with steadfast flavour: pumpkin ravioli, or knock-out eye fillet wrapped in pancetta and pan-fried with porcini mushrooms in a white wine and cream sauce. Yes, it's wickedly rich, but isn't this the kind of comfort cookery that makes dining out such a memorable experience? Especially when it climaxes with tiramisu.

Hours Dinner daily 5.30–10pm
Bill E $17–$28 **M** $28–$33 **D** $9–$15; 10% surcharge on public holidays
Cards AE BC DC MC V Eftpos; bookings essential
Wine BYO (corkage $3 pp)
Chef/owner Antonio Abassi
Seats 70; private room; wheelchair access
www.sevardicucina.com.au
And...there's an upstairs private function room that seats about 45

Shanghai Yangzhou House

177 Forest Road, Hurstville
Tel 9580 9188   Map 8

Chinese (Shanghainese)

Score 14/20

You have to love a place that lists on its menu 'the number 1 dish of the world'. OK, that may be a touch excessive, but there is a lot to like at this very basic shopfront. Don't be put off by the bains-maries of cold dishes by the front door. Many people like ducks' tongues and pigs' ears, and those who don't will find plenty of other appealing dishes on the very diverse menu. Travel around China with the excellent savoury northern-style dumplings, followed by the caramelised sweetness of dark and steaming Sichuan-style eggplant hotpot with pork. Step sideways again with the superb Singapore-style chilli mud crab, covered in a sauce that finely balances heat and the sweetness of the sea. Or try the barramundi, first shown to you in a bucket, still flapping, then reappearing covered in a sweet but astringent ginger and black vinegar sauce. Even vegetable dishes like soybeans with Chinese cabbage and fresh bamboo have more spark than usual. It may not be number one, but it's pretty damn good.

Hours Lunch daily 11am–3.30pm; Dinner daily 5.30–10pm
Bill E $3.80–$13.80 **M** $7.80–$19.80 **D** $3.80–$12.80; $1.50 pp surcharge on public holidays
Cards None
Wine BYO (no corkage)
Chefs Tony Jiang & Jin Sheng Feng
Owners Tony Jiang & Dianna Yan
Seats 75
And...service is surprisingly friendly too

city + suburbs (S)

Shun Tak

57 Macquarie Street, Parramatta
Tel 9635 8128 Map 6

Chinese (Cantonese)

Score 14/20

Sunday yum cha is a very civilised and very satisfying affair inside this bright and light corner restaurant. It's deservedly popular, but the biggest queue is of trolleys banking up on approach to tables. The trolley with the crunchy things kept reappearing when all we really wanted was the steamed things, but patience is eventually rewarded. If you see the fried eggplant, grab it; ditto the garlic and lemon pipis, pork buns, prawn dumplings, whitebait, or fried chicken wings – 'better than KFC', the waiter declared. A golden phoenix and golden dragon keep an eye on proceedings from a red feature wall. It all runs smoothly, as first families, then bamboo baskets, fill the tables. The Singapore chilli crab, from the à la carte menu, remains one of Sydney's best. The crab is weighed and brought to the table, before re-emerging as a red and glossy thing of beauty ready to be wrestled with, the sweet and hot tomato sauce begging to be mopped up with fine fried buns – so order an extra serve.

Hours Lunch & yum cha daily 10am–3pm; Dinner daily 5pm–midnight
Bill E $4.80–$14.80 **M** $12–$27.50 **D** $3.20–$7.80; $2 pp surcharge on public holidays
Cards AE BC MC V (card minimum $35)
Wine A good selection at a decent price
Chef/owner Chi Fung Lee
Seats 200; private room
And...the kitchen remains open until midnight

Silver Spring

Level 1, 477 Pitt Street (cnr Hay Street), Haymarket
Tel 9211 2232 Map 3A

Chinese (Cantonese)

Score 13/20

A trolley with steamed flounder wheels past – the fish's succulent flesh dressed with ginger and shallots and bathed in sweetened soy sauce. Children play with digital cameras while fathers dish out Peking duck. Welcome to a seafood utopia: an upstairs Cantonese banquet hall with a full catch, much of it swimming in fish tanks in the foyer, all sold by the kilo, presented at the table for approval, still flapping in a plastic bag. Yup, it's fresh. As is the room: after twelve years of dutiful service it has at last had a make-over, enlivened for lunch sittings of yum cha or the rituals of dinner. The menu embraces the southern provinces – the 'rice bowl' of China – with no real surprises but no letdowns either. It's elaborate banquet cookery – braised scallops with crab roe, honey king prawns, fried whitebait with salt and pepper, barbequed suckling pig – with the trinity of ginger, spring onions and garlic. The old food that fattened the courts of great dynasties is now savoured here at the top of shopping centre escalators.

Hours Lunch Mon–Sun 10am–3pm; Dinner daily 5.30–11pm
Bill E $5–$10 **M** $12–$40 **D** $5–$10; $2 per adult, $1 per child surcharge on public holidays
Cards AE DC MC V
Wine Usual suspects of Oz chardonnays; 8 by the glass; plus Tsing Tao beer and West Coast Cooler (a fad best forgotten); BYO (corkage $10 per bottle)
Chef Ng Chi To
Owners Henry Tang, Ellis Choy & Albert Cheung
Seats 500; private rooms
And...yes, of course they do banquets and wedding feasts (with a karaoke system available)

city + suburbs

Sky Phoenix

Level 3, Skygarden, 77 Castlereagh Street, Sydney
Tel 1300 883 892 or 9223 8822   Map 1

Chinese (Cantonese)

Score 13/20

Sky Phoenix consists of a main dining room with soaring ceiling studded with star-like lights, and a modern black and grey colour scheme with plenty of light from the large atrium windows, as well as tables spread – more food-court-style – around the escalators outside. Yum cha at lunch covers the usual range of steamed dumplings and buns as well as barbecued meats from their own BBQ stall. Dinner is à la carte, with some live seafood offerings. Scallops with XO sauce are plump and fresh in a rich, oily chilli sauce; and prawns and vegetables in thin, crisp beancurd skin is fresh and light; while Peking duck was thick and chewy and the accompanying sang choi bau a little bland. Deep-fried beancurd with spicy salt is crisp, with a firm texture and little spice. The boneless, crisp Shandong chicken, however, is a sophisticated sweet and sour, with deliciously lacquered skin, succulent flesh and plenty of pineapple pieces – it's salty, sweet and sour, and very hard to leave alone.

Hours Lunch daily 11am–3pm; Dinner daily 5.30–10.30pm, closed public holidays
Bill E $5.80–$13.80 **M** $14.80–$26.80 **D** $4.80–$12.80; live seafood at market prices; 10% surcharge on public holidays
Cards AE BC DC MC V Eftpos
Wine Short, well-priced commercial wine list, with some excitement in the premium list; 6 by the glass; BYO (corkage $10 per bottle)
Chefs Tom Leung & Keung Chau (yum cha)
Owners Alice Lee & Anita Fung
Seats 300; private rooms; wheelchair access
www.phoenixrestaurants.com.au
And...on weekdays yum cha starts really rolling around midday when the city workers pack in

Sosumi

Lower Ground Floor, GPO, 1 Martin Place, Sydney
Tel 9229 7700   Map 1

Japanese

Score 13/20

Here's one train system that can safely claim genuine efficiency and reliability. More or less a Sydney landmark within a city landmark, this sleek, modern, stainless-steel 'kaiten zushi' (revolving sushi) system looks both imposing and inviting viewed from the ground level of the cavernous GPO complex. Once seated at the long bench you'll soon discover that the passing parade of morsels is among this city's best. One of the real tests of a decent sushi train is in the volume of clientele: the more ravenous the customers, the fresher the offerings. Sosumi, at least at lunchtime, easily passes this test and as everyone chugs in and out no one has to wait too long for a seat. Expect the standard sushi and sashimi train offerings, plus a somewhat try-hard selection of California-style rolls. The colour of the plate tells you how much you're spending. Supplement it with inexpensive, good à la carte offerings: cone-shaped tempura prawn (or the tad pricier lobster) hand rolls, and, by night, the small range of tempura and soup dishes.

Hours Lunch Mon–Fri 11.30am–3pm; Dinner Tues–Wed 6–9pm, Thurs–Fri 6–10pm
Bill Sushi plates $4.50–$6.50; Hand rolls $6.50–$11.90
Cards AE BC DC MC V Eftpos; no bookings
Wine Tiny list of four by the glass; stick to beer or sake (or Japanese lemonade called 'lamune')
Chefs Edy Rivai Ismail & Toshio Higashio
Owner Peter Petroulas
Seats 47; wheelchair access
www.gposydney.com
And...check out the illuminating 'History of Sushi' on the back of the menu

city + suburbs (S)

Spice I Am ★

90 Wentworth Avenue, Sydney
Tel 9280 0928   Map 3A

Thai
Score 14/20

Favourite Asian

OK: get in, sit down, shut up and hold on. This is the scariest, most thrilling restaurant ride you'll find in this city: nowhere else takes you to such dizzying heights with lemongrass, kaffir lime and chilli. No other Sydney restaurant spices food like Spice I Am, and very few boast this many Thai expats. Ask for your order to be written in Thai, then be prepared to taste the real food of old Siam. The fish cakes are a brilliant tangle of crisp fried whitebait dressed with a hot, sweet chilli sauce and coriander. Pork satay is excellent; a red curry of chicken may contain its liver. Rice vermicelli is funky from being fermented, the top heavy with a complex peanut paste. Tom klong, roasted fish soup, is eye-poppingly sour. On the downside, it's a pretty ugly space – just a kitchen with chairs really; the staff can struggle with English; and there's often a queue to get in. Rest assured the food is always worth the wait.

Hours Lunch Tues–Sun 11am–4pm; Dinner Tues–Sun 6–10pm
Bill E $4.50–$10.90 **M** $6.90–$20 **D** $6.50
Cards None; no bookings
Wine BYO (no corkage)
Chef Sujet Saenkham
Owners Padet Nagsalab & Sujet Saenkham
Seats 45; outdoor seats
And…a young coconut drink is the perfect fire retardant

Strangers with Candy

96 Kepos Street (cnr Phillip Street), East Redfern
Tel 9698 6000   Map 3B

Contemporary
Score 14/20

The food at this euphemistically named eatery is as colourful and eclectic as the rambling corner terrace it occupies at the 'Greek end' of Redfern. The cosy front room is all timber and banquettes; the rear courtyard's teak tables and sleek wooden chairs mix it with peeling paint, rattling hot water pipes and a corrugated plastic roof that leaks when it's wet. Enthusiastic and genuinely warm service combines with Veronica Stute's deft touch with strong flavours and striking combinations to exceed expectations. A free-form blue cheese soufflé's fluffy centre hides chunks of creamy Shadows of Blue, beautifully matched with a fine dice of pickled pear and a heady, smoky eggplant. Benchmark duck confit slips from the bone to meet sweet and sour notes from sautéed apple and ginger. Bouillabaisse is cooked and served en papillote: chunks of gold band snapper, prawns, scallops and mussels poached in a complex broth, a creamy rouille adding further depth. Crowd-pleasing desserts run the full gamut of temptation, including a simply sublime lime mascarpone shortcake.

Hours Breakfast & Lunch Sat–Sun 9.30am–3.30pm; Dinner Wed–Sat 6pm–9.30pm
Bill E $12.50–$14.50 **M** $18.50–$26.50 **D** $8.50–$12.50
Cards No cards
Wine BYO (corkage $2.50 pp)
Chef Veronica Stute
Owners Justin Wells & Veronica Stute
Seats 40; private rooms; wheelchair access; outdoor seats
www.strangerswithcandy.com.au
And…breakfast and lunch are deservedly popular on weekends

s city + suburbs

Sugaroom

Shop 2, 1 Harris Street, Pyrmont
Tel 9571 5055 Map 5B

Contemporary
Score 14/20

The former CSR site at the watery end of Harris Street is now the aptly titled Sugaroom, where sweet waiters work a dulcet room delivering dishes that occasionally err on the sugary side. Part bar, part restaurant with tables spilling outside, the smart fit-out (with a touch of warehouse grunt) has a ringside seat to the working Harbour. It's also home to the talents of ex Pello chef Greg Anderson, whose menu is a familiar-sounding list of hiramasa kingfish (carpaccio, perhaps?), wagyu, hand-cut chips, and buffalo mozzarella and tomato salad. Okay, so the tomato salad didn't need onion jam; and a perfectly chargrilled pork chop could have done without the so-called 'white balsamic' (sugared white vinegar) because the roasted jerusalem artichokes are marvellous enough. Fabulous, soft, delicately flavoured chicken galantine has a sweet mustard dressing; rich duck-liver parfait is matched deftly with caramelised fig; and immaculately textured crab and roasted fennel risotto delights. Fine banana crêpes with chocolate sorbet are also right on the money.

Hours Lunch Tues–Sun from noon; Dinner Mon–Sat from 6pm
Bill E $12 **M** $23 **D** $10; 10% surcharge on Sundays & public holidays
Cards AE BC DC MC V Eftpos
Wine Nicely constructed if modest list; an admirable 14 by the glass; BYO (corkage $6 per bottle)
Chef Greg Anderson
Owners Greg Anderson & Patricia Nunes
Seats 90; wheelchair access; outdoor seats
www.sugaroom.com.au
And...parking's tricky around the clock, but they're good at getting cabs

Summerland

457 Chapel Road, Bankstown
Tel 9708 5107 Map 6

Lebanese
Score 12/20

The ornate archway over the entrance to the parking area suggests that this may once have been a Chinese restaurant. The big, bright room with large, linen-topped tables and generous paper serviettes could be set to serve any type of food, but the rugs, plates and giant coffee pots decorating the walls spell out Middle Eastern, and the cooking of Ali Sayed says Lebanese very clearly. A banquet is the best option for variety: the table quickly covered with dishes of pickles, hummus, baba ghanoush and creamy labna; an array of salads, including excellent fattoush (salad topped with crisp fried Lebanese bread); light, crisp felafel; tiny, moist kibbeh; sausages, vegetables, super-fresh kibbeh naye (raw minced lamb with spices) and, when available, the more unusual asbi naye (thin strips of raw liver). Chicken kebabs with garlic sauce, lamb cubes and minced lamb are the main course for those who haven't already over-indulged. While the Lebanese coffee and small baklava weren't a highlight, there's plenty of sunshine in dining at Summerland.

Hours Mon–Sat noon–10.30pm; Sun 11am–9pm
Bill E $5–$10 **M** $10–$18 **D** $5–$8
Cards AE BC MC V Eftpos
Wine Short, predictable list, 10 by the glass; BYO (corkage $3 pp)
Chefs Ali, Fouad & Taysear Sayed
Owner Ali Sayed
Seats 150; wheelchair access
And...delicious, puffed-up Lebanese bread arrives at the table fresh from the oven

Cafés

Baia San Marco	9283 3434
Blackbird Café	9283 7385
CMC	9283 3393
Nick's 103	9267 4404

Restaurants

Chinta Ria	9264 3211
Coast	9267 6700
I'm Angus Steakhouse	9264 5822
Nick's	9264 1212

Take Away

Bayside Grill	9264 1022
Health Tree	9264 9755
Tandoori Connection	9283 6400

Bars

Home Bar	9266 0600
Pontoon Bar	9267 7099
The Terrace Bar	
Wallaby Bar	9267 4118

Nightclub

Home	9266 0600

Function Centres

Dockside	9261 3777
L'Aqua	8267 0300

COCKLE BAY WHARF
at Darling Park

www.cocklebaywharf.com

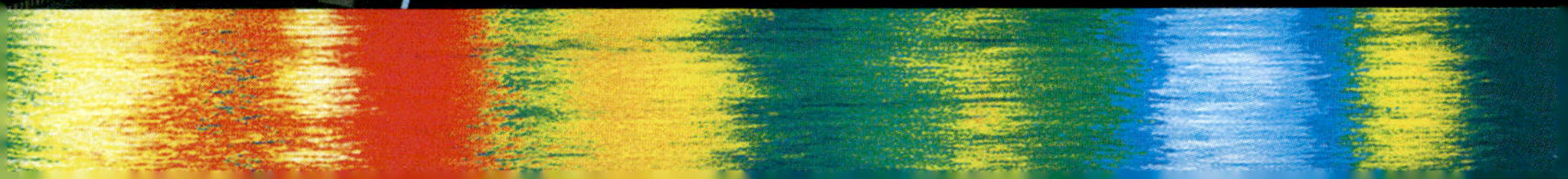

VILLA MARIA
ESTATE
NEW ZEALAND

*New Zealand's
Most Awarded Wines*

city + suburbs

Summit

Level 47, Australia Square,
264 George Street, Sydney
Tel 9247 9777   Map 1

Contemporary

Score 13/20

It can be unsettling when you haven't had a drink and the room is already spinning. Welcome to the original revolving restaurant: a 105-minute, 360-degree, 47-floors-up tour of the city. Since 1968, others have eclipsed the Summit, literally and metaphorically, but it still wins with spin. The doughnut room has a Jane Fonda-era retro-chic; wire chairs, red carpets and a groovy lounge bar. An ambitiously flavoured international menu, under globetrotting chef Michael Moore, suits the sightseeing crowd, delivering architectural splendour. Not everything gels: prawn tapas features fried chilli beans, a spicy rice coating, and palm sugar and lime chilli jam. Thankfully, quail breast confit beside a tart of Kervella goat's cheese, fig and walnuts, with pomegranate molasses, has elegant sophistication. Chargrilled wagyu rump and mushrooms, topped with polenta onion rings, felt a little too RSL bistro but pepper-crusted snapper with brandade, tomato sugo and fried anchovies is richly satisfying. Enthusiastic service isn't always deft, but who's worried when the world glides by over a decent Aussie cheese selection.

Hours Lunch Mon–Fri & Sun noon–3pm; Dinner daily 6–10.30pm
Bill E $18–$25 **M** $35–$43 **D** $16–$18; 15% surcharge on public holidays
Cards AE BC DC MC V
Wine Suitably Australian showcase; 16 by the glass
Chefs Michael Moore & Jess Ong
Owner AADC Restaurants
Seats 60; wheelchair access
www.summitrestaurant.com.au
And...$10 happy hour cocktails in the Orbit lounge, Monday to Thursday, 5–6.45pm

sushi e

Level 4, Establishment Hotel,
252 George Street, Sydney
Tel 9240 3041   Map 1

Modern Japanese

Score 15/20

Dining at sushi e is a wonderful combination of great food and great theatre. Perched on blond wood stools around a white marble sushi counter, the cool and beautiful enjoy the support act of observing each other and the main performance of three chefs (only one of whom is Japanese), intently and deftly scooping rice from large stainless-steel rice cookers. They're busy skinning and slicing glistening fish and positioning garnishes with fine chopsticks to create some of the best traditional and innovative Japanese flavours in town. Sashimi snapper dressed with sesame, lime and white soy; sushi of salmon roe wrapped in shiso leaf and nori; minced grilled eel in cucumber; and oily just-seared salmon are all explosive mouthfuls of exquisite flavours and textures. For something more modern, Shaun Presland's take on ceviche – citrus-marinated tuna, baby coriander, jalapeños and teardrop tomatoes – is inspired. Mains of tempura bug tail or grain-fed beef tataki fill any gaps left after sushi rolls featuring exciting combinations like scallop tempura with chilli-infused tobikko.

Hours Lunch Tues–Fri noon–2.30pm; Dinner Tues–Thurs 6–10.30pm, Fri 6.30–10.30pm, Sat 7–10.30pm
Bill E $10.50–$18.50 **M** $25.50–$39
Cards AE BC DC MC V; bookings essential
Wine Superb, concise, mostly local list; 12 by the glass; good sake selection; extensive list of spirits
Chef Shaun Presland
Owner The Hemmes family
Seats 32; wheelchair access
www.merivale.com
And...you can wander down to est. for dessert after dinner

city + suburbs

Swordfish

Level 2, South Sydney Junior Leagues Club, 558A Anzac Parade, Kingsford
Tel 9344 4404 Map 9

Italian/Seafood

Score 13/20

Even before you sit down, Swordfish has a few challenges to overcome. You have to register your name and address at the front desk before ascending (unless you take the lift) to the sound of tinkling pokies. But that's where any concerns cease. You're in the safest hands with the fratelli Cipri: their seamless, courteous service is among the best in Sydney. The Italian menu (strong on seafood, as the name indicates, with up to half a dozen fish dishes on the daily specials list) has something for everyone. There are well-handled entrées, such as de-boned, juicy quail, splayed and wrapped with pancetta, oven-roasted and served with a well-matched, unmistakeably Italian radicchio and cannellini bean salad. Spaghetti with prawns, mussels, garlic, tomato and chilli shows off the seafood. Hearty, football-sized veal meatballs with napoletana sauce, sliced in half, reveal a generous pea, smoked ham and mozzarella stuffing. Grilled baby octopus with mixed herbs and extra virgin olive oil passes the tenderness test with flair. Swordfish is a crowd-pleaser – and we're pleased.

Hours Lunch Tues–Fri & Sun noon–3pm; Dinner Tues–Sun 6–10pm
Bill E $14.50–$17.50 **M** $20.50–$27.50 **D** $8–$11
Cards AE DC MC V
Wine Good range of Australasians and Italians; 12 by the glass
Chef Carmelo Cipri
Owners Joe, Carmelo & Anthony Cipri
Seats 250; private rooms; wheelchair access; outdoor seats
And…if you want to avoid the pokies, take the foyer lift to level 2

Szechuan Garden

Shop 1, 599 Pacific Highway, St Leonards
Tel 9438 2568 Map 5A

Chinese (Sichuan)

Score 13/20

Sichuanese food is a powerful combination of chilli and Sichuan peppercorns. The latter has a dominating hot taste and actually numbs the mouth to prepare you for even more chilli, leading to an explosion of unique flavours. Sadly, Western palates seldom appreciate that epiphany. Chef Mark Deng has banished the peppercorns from the kitchen saying his locals can't stand them, but what's left is a cuisine still strong on flavour – mostly chilli – and a loyal following addicted to pure heat. To go with the modern feel of a new location there are 'new dishes': chilli mud crab, calamari cooked in wine with chilli, and spicy scallops with honey peas. Of course it's still hard to pass up old favourites like barramundi with chilli bean paste; the spicy Hunan classic General Tso chicken (sans Sichuan peppercorns – sigh); and a very hot wok chicken. Newer dishes are more sophisticated, with several layers of flavours, but they still have the chilli punch that gave the restaurant a cult following.

Hours Lunch Mon–Fri noon–3pm; Dinner daily Sun 6pm–late
Bill E $6–$12.90 **M** $11.90–$29.90 **D** $6–$6.80; $3 pp surcharge on public holidays
Cards AE BC DC MC V
Wine Good list; 4 by the glass; BYO (corkage $3 pp)
Chef/owner Mark N Deng
Seats 160; wheelchair access; outdoor seats
And…no MSG added here

city + suburbs (T)

Tables

1047 Pacific Highway, Pymble
Tel 9983 1047   Map 7

Contemporary
Score 14/20

As popular as ever, this modern restaurant brings Big City style to the North. Start with small 'on arrival' plates, which might include crisp deep-fried zucchini flowers and a smoky eggplant dip with real depth of flavour, plus good pizza-oven bread. The menu circumnavigates the globe. Tuna tataki with wakame salad shows real Japanese simplicity. Linguini arrives with mussels and chorizo; chermoula-coated lamb has more than a hint of the Middle East; fresh prawns are seared and come with a fried wonton and micro-cress salad dressed with lime, chilli and ginger; pepper-encrusted beef fillet, topped with morel and onion jam, shows French flair. The cooking couldn't be called minimalist, with lots of flavours on the plate. Seared scallops served on apple and onion tart, plus black pudding, champagne vinegar and beurre blanc, still manages to find perfect balance. For dessert there's a textbook-perfect orange brûlée. Service is friendly and efficient, and some evenings are more like a big, happy party in this bright and shiny room.

Hours Lunch Mon–Fri noon–2.30pm; Dinner Mon–Sat 6–9.30pm
Bill E $18.90–$19.20 **M** $28.90–$30.50 **D** $14.80
Cards AE BC DC MC V
Wine Medium in size, but well balanced; 19 by the glass; BYO (corkage $3.30 pp)
Chef Kim de Laive
Owners Kim de Laive & Dan Brukarz
Seats 98; private room
www.tablesrestaurant.com
And... $49.70 fixed price menu 7–9pm

Tabou ★

527 Crown Street, Surry Hills
Tel 9319 5682   Map 3B

French
Score 14/20

Favourite Bistro

Paris has never been so close. Just enter through timber-and-glass doors into Tabou's bistro interior complete with stained glass, tiled floors, butcher's-paper-over-pristine-white-damask-cloth'd tables, wooden chairs and daily specials written on mirrors. Service is quietly assured and friendly, and the food, while classic in discipline, is anything but old fashioned. Two zucchini flowers, full of scampi and crab, in a light, crisp batter, are crossed in simple but dramatic presentation. Mussels are plump, simply stuffed with herb butter and breadcrumbs. Cotriade, a traditional fish stew, is full of sea flavours, plus cream, leeks and sorrel. Thin crisp slices of pan-fried calf's liver are soft and pink inside, the richness cut with raspberry vinaigrette and radish and watercress salad. A delicate dessert comprising three discs of orange and buttermilk roulade with poached rhubarb, slices of strawberry and candied pine nuts proves that less is more. The coffee is really good, which is more than you can say for Paris.

Hours Lunch Mon–Fri noon–2.30pm; Dinner Sat from 6pm, Sun–Fri 6.30pm–late
Bill E $16–$19 **M** $25–$32 **D** $10–$14
Cards AE BC DC MC V
Wine Thoughtful French and Australasian list including reserve; 9 by the glass; BYO except Fri & Sat nights (corkage $8 per bottle)
Chef Jacob Brown
Owner Rod McPherson
Seats 80; private room
And... the inexpensive regional prix fixe lunch menu changes monthly

T city + suburbs

Tan Viet

2–3/100 John Street, Cabramatta
Tel 9727 6853   Map 6

Vietnamese

Score 12/20

There are oodles of noodles at this brightly coloured, very basic eating house with a menu divided into thin egg noodles, flat white rice noodles, thick Hokkien-style 'drop' noodles, plus rice and crusty white bread rolls. Most toppings are offered with a range of bases, though some matches are a natural – like the hot, sour, thin, red goat curry with the bread roll for mopping up all the delicious sauce. The Hainan chicken is a delicate dish of steamed chicken, ideal with the rice noodles floating in a clear broth and a handful of fresh herbs; while the roast duck in a soup rich with warm spices is slurp material with the thin firm egg noodles. Criskin chicken (with very crisp skin) appears on almost every table, and the multicoloured sweets – refreshing, creamy combinations of shaved ice with green noodles, golden peanuts, red beans and fruit – are a must. By late morning on weekends diners can be queued outside the door, but tables turn over fast, so no one waits too long.

Hours Daily 9am–7pm
Bill M $9–$9.50 **D** $3
Cards None; no bookings
Wine BYO (no corkage)
Chef/owner Hung Kiem Lam
Seats 90
And...you can wander through the food markets before or after lunch

the tearoom

Level 3, Market Street end of Queen Victoria Building, 455 George Street, Sydney
Tel 9269 0774   Map 1

Australian

Score 14/20

Victoria's secret is hidden in a spacious, soaring, beautifully proportioned room with chocolate-brown carpet and comfortable, colour-matched seats. Shoppers, tourists and informed business lunchers find their way up for cuisine that, too, has seen a lift in finesse and flair. Consider a pot of leek soup, with a subtle edge of red onion, carefully poured around a soft-boiled egg sitting atop a slice of ham. Risotto has a fine base of vegetable stock with tomato water, zucchini flowers folded through and topped with diced tomato. Moist, pan-fried barramundi is schooled with pearl barley, grilled cuttlefish, coconut and ginger. Roast lamb rump and cured lamb fillet gambol with couscous, pistachio and garlic chives. None of it is typical tearoom fare, though other tables opt for triple tiers of finger sandwiches, small pies and cakes. Dessert might be a nectarine, blueberry and pistachio bombe, or the nostalgic delight of two warm, crumbly scones with a fine, gooey strawberry conserve and clotted cream if you can't stay for low (early afternoon) tea.

Hours Lunch daily noon–3pm; morning & afternoon tea daily from 11am
Bill E $14–$16 **M** $23–$25 **D** $9–$13; 10% surcharge on weekends & public holidays
Cards AE BC DC MC V
Wine Stylish, well-composed list; 13 half bottles; 19 by the glass
Chefs Mark Holmes & Robert Crichton
Owner Manuel Spinola
Seats 160; wheelchair access
www.thetearoom.com.au
And...20 high-quality leaf teas, including white Silverleaf

city + suburbs T

Temasek

Shop 2–4 Roxy Arcade,
71 George Street, Parramatta
Tel 9633 9926 & 9687 5495   Map 6

Nonya/Malaysian

Score 14/20

Close your eyes and you could almost be in a hawker's hut in Malaysia. A very big one, to be sure, with the occasional Australian voice hollering through the noisy crowd. But apart from that, Temasek is pretty much the real deal, from the wipe-clean tablecloths and the plastic serving plates to the fiery nonya cuisine (with some Singaporean and Chinese additions). Around for 14 years, its favourites include the widely loved and chilli-heavy laksa, and Singapore chilli crab – although it requires a day's notice. If you haven't planned ahead, beef rendang is outstanding: impossibly tender meat swimming in a luxurious sauce of coconut milk, lemongrass and chilli. Sambal prawns were less enticing – the pale-orange sauce had a slightly bitter edge – but nasi goreng (fried rice) is authentically rich with the sweet and smoky appeal of sugary kecap manis. For the full street-food experience, save a little room for the sweet chendol drink of green jelly, red beans, palm sugar and coconut milk.

Hours Lunch Tues–Sun 11.30am–2.30pm; Dinner Tues–Sun 5.30–9.30pm
Bill E $4–$15.50 **M** $9.50–$22.80 **D** $3.80; seafood at market prices; $1.50 pp surcharge on public holidays
Cards AE BC DC MC V Eftpos (card minimum $20)
Wine BYO (corkage $1.50 pp)
Chef/owner Susan Wong
Seats 170; private room; wheelchair access; outdoor seats
And...banquets are available for groups of five or more

Temple

165 Wycombe Road, Neutral Bay
Tel 9904 0688   Map 5A

Modern Asian

Score 13/20

If you're picturing a tranquil place for meditation, forget it. Temple is always busy, loud and lots of fun. Popular with the polo-shirt-and-deck-loafers set, in some ways this small dining room with its dark-wood interior, Chinese calligraphy and open kitchen is the North Shore's answer to Billy Kwong, although the menu casts a wider net over South-East Asia to take in Malaysian, Vietnamese and Thai classics. Crisped egg noodles with a choice of prawns or beef is pure comfort food and we love the sang choi bau of non-greasy duck wrapped in cool, firm iceberg lettuce. Fabulously fresh Singaporean soft-shell chilli crab was let down by an ingratiatingly sweet chilli sauce; and crisp-skin chicken in citrus, tamarind and plum sauce seemed too polite. Despite a slightly wayward hand in the kitchen with the coconut cream, grilled barramundi dressed with ginger and shallot kept us very content. Portions are generous and service is delivered with a beatific smile.

Hours Dinner Tues–Sat 6pm–late, Sun from 5.30pm
Bill E $10–$14 **M** $15–$24 **D** $8–$10
Cards AE BC DC MC V Eftpos
Wine Small, sensible commercial list; 5 by the glass; BYO wine only (corkage $3 pp)
Chef Hien Van Tran
Owner Amy Tran
Seats 60
And...don't forget to look for the blackboard specials list

city + suburbs

Tetsuya's

529 Kent Street, Sydney
Tel 9267 2900   Map 3A

Japanese/French

Score 19/20

Great artists have a leitmotif that they spend a lifetime exploring. For Tetsuya Wakuda it might be his konbu-sprinkled ocean trout confit and unpasteurised roe. With every visit, it changes subtly, perhaps draped over matchsticks of fennel and daikon. In a nation addicted to the shock of the new, Tetsuya offers a steady-handed lesson in nuance, marrying French technique and Japanese flavours for the inspired crescendo of a 12-course, seafood-strong dégustation. Be surprised by the fragrantly sweet harmony in cold, creamy sweetcorn soup with basil ice-cream; trevally tartare with a pink peppercorn crunch and preserved lemon tang; sublime lobster and crab raviolo on scallop terrine, fragrant with kaffir lime, basil and tomato, scattered with tobikko. Veal with wasabi butter is a melting pas de deux; grilled wagyu has a lime jus kick. Walnut praline counterpoints blue cheese ice-cream with pear and sauterne jelly. It's all a work of art, from cosseting service to the elegant Japanese rooms adorned with contemporary art, and such breathtaking brushstrokes on the plate.

Hours Lunch Sat from noon; Dinner Tues–Sat from 6.30pm
Bill Set dégustation menu $175 pp
Cards AE BC DC MC V; bookings essential
Wine Fascinating, long and luscious list, with a great sommelier to guide you; 17 by the glass; BYO (corkage $18 per bottle)
Chef/owner Tetsuya Wakuda
Seats 90; private rooms
www.tetsuyas.com
And…if you really want something different, simply ask

Thanh Binh

111 King Street, Newtown
Tel 9557 1175   Map 8
Also at 52a John Street, Cabramatta
Tel 9727 9729   Map 6
33 Arthur Street, Cabramatta
Tel 9724 9633   Map 6

Vietnamese

Score 13/20

Dining choices are abundant deep in the heart of Newtown, including this popular offshoot of Angie Hong's Cabramatta institution. The menu is daunting, with 74 choices, plus the 'special wishes' menu of dazzling daily specials. Waiters whiz around the spacious room instilling a feeling of efficient service that even then doesn't quite match the pace. Flavour-filled food is the focus with no tricks, just good, fresh Vietnamese favourites that keep us coming back. A myriad of ricepaper rolls provides the perfect start and it's worth rolling up your sleeves to try the roll-your-own variety. Then there's super-fresh steamed rice noodles with salad greens, or tempting choices like lemongrass beef in wild betel leaves. Sweet-potato-and-prawn fritters are lightly battered and served as straws, perfect for dunking in bean dipping sauce. Twice-cooked duck leg falls apart on egg noodles, baby bok choi, shiitake mushrooms and pickled green papaya. Add amazing seafood and vegetarian choices, and it's no surprise that those in the know return.

Hours Sat–Sun noon–11pm; Dinner Tues–Fri 5–11pm
Bill E $7–$15 **M** $15–$30 **D** $5
Cards AE BC DC MC V Eftpos
Wine Short, average wine list; 5 by the glass; BYO (corkage $2.50 pp)
Chef/owner Angie Hong
Seats 130
www.thanhbinh.citysearch.com.au
And…the Cabramatta menu has 250 choices!

city + suburbs

Three Clicks West

127 Booth Street, Annandale
Tel 9660 6652   Map 5B

Modern European
Score 14/20

In this converted Federation shopfront with its wide wooden floorboards, cosy booths and mood lighting, Chris Woodyard has created a smart, inviting local that is the envy of most inner-city precincts. While we've had the recent impression that the service can be inconsistent, for the most part it's professional, guiding you through an intriguing menu of some startling combinations. Steamed blue swimmer crab parcel wrapped in savoy cabbage in a refined tomato consommé is a stand-out. Squid 'two ways' comes confit with citrus salad or Sichuan pepper and cumin-spiced with candied ginger. Assiette of pork is technically clever, aesthetically beautiful and, with the addition of a Scotch egg, tinged with playfulness; however, like patches of the menu, we found it tried a little too hard. Desserts are a strength, especially crisp crêpes filled with caramel mousse, green apple sorbet and toffee apples. Resident professionals obviously love the relaxed sophistication – on busy nights the air is filled with their bonhomie, perfectly complementing the general feel-good factor.

Hours Dinner Mon–Sat 6.30pm–late
Bill E $15–$16 **M** $27–$28 **D** $14–$16; tasting menu $75 pp
Cards AE BC MC V; bookings essential
Wine Fantastic and fascinating European and local selection; 13 by the glass; BYO Mon–Wed, 6 bottles limit (corkage $8 per bottle)
Chef/owner Chris Woodyard
Seats 60; private room
www.threeclickswest.com.au
And...keep an eye out for themed monthly dégustation nights

Three Weeds

197 Evans Street, Rozelle
Tel 9818 2788   Map 5B

Modern European
Score 15/20

All hail the revamped Rose, Shamrock and Thistle, and not just for the comfy couches in the bar, those hard, tall tables to pound fists on during political debates, and a wine list that puts most pubs to shame. Three cheers for the dining room – if not for the space with a ceiling that slopes down to the back and camel-coloured carpet, then for Lucinda Newton, who runs the floor with pep and a smile. And three big pats on the back to Darrell Felstead for his sumptuous redefinition of pub grub. A joyous scallop lasagne using squid ink pasta may be joined on the modern European menu by rabbit terrine. Scotch fillet may be dressed with bordelaise sauce; roasted quail breast with a tortellini of confit leg; or slices of pink pot-roasted lamb rump given a garnish of ravioli filled with shredded lamb's tongue and braised shank on eggplant purée. In season, the apricot tarte Tatin is stunning, with the simplest, satiny vanilla-bean ice-cream you've ever had.

Hours Lunch Fri noon–2pm; Dinner Tues–Sat 6.30–10pm
Bill E $14–$18 **M** $24–$28 **D** $13
Cards AE BC MC V; bookings essential
Wine Mostly boutiques at very fair prices; 14 by the glass
Chef Darrell Felstead
Owners Todd & Diane Salter
Seats 80; wheelchair access
And...there's bar food if you don't feel like leaving your pub stool

city + suburbs

The Tilbury Hotel

12–18 Nicholson Street, Woolloomooloo
Tel 9368 1041   Map 2

Modern Italian

Score 13/20

Tan is the new black at the Tilbury. It's everywhere in the modernist interior of this made-over 1920s hotel: nut-brown polished floorboards, caramel leather banquette, and tawny suede hotpants on the (bottle) blonde at the next table. Our friendly waiter says no, his shirt is actually 'mustard'. Regardless, the colour is essential Sydney in a jazzed-up bistro with a new head chef, Craig McFarland (ex Aqua Luna, Bistro Moncur), who continues the kitchen's tradition of tested Italian cookery: pine mushroom risotto, pheasant sausage with warm lentils, marinated goat's cheese. It's the new food of old Mother Italy, such as deliciously rich, fatty, pull-apart tender pork shoulder; or the lamb breast coated in dijon mustard, crumbed, cooked and served under a trinity of cutlets. But be warned: good as the food is, on weekends the Ab Fab crowd flocks in, the doof-doof beats crank up, and it's like dining at a nightclub during Fashion Week. And the eye candy distracts even the hardened from a double chocolate tart.

Hours Breakfast Sun 10am–noon; Lunch Tues–Sun noon–3pm; Dinner Tues–Sat 6–10pm
Bill E $16–$19.50 **M** $25.50–$29.50 **D** $10.50–$13.50
Cards AE BC MC V Eftpos
Wine Impressive list of mostly South Oz and Victorian labels with a few Italian varietals; high-priced; 16 by the glass
Chef Craig McFarland
Owner Mac Whitehouse
Seats 70; wheelchair access; outdoor seats
www.tilburyhotel.com.au
And...the pub is a good meeting place for pre- or post-dining drinks

Tran's

523 Military Road, Mosman
Tel 9969 9275   Map 7

Vietnamese

Score 13/20

Tran's, more so than most neighbourly kitchens, has its unashamed fans, from the celebrities cited on the menu to the locals practically queuing up at the door on any given weeknight. So booking is strongly recommended for this charming lantern-filled room overlooking traffic and historic Boronia House. Lanna Tran has played with the flavours of her mother country with joyous results for a decade. Chargrilled pork belly strips atop a bed of soft rice noodles epitomises her style – the dish buoyant with Vietnamese and perilla mints, sorrel, lemongrass, chilli, pickling onions, roast eschalots and peanuts – all at once light, nutty, smoky and delicious. Then there's beaut duck, roasted, de-boned, crisp-skinned and served with pan-fried gai choi and with ginger and plum dipping sauce for a dash of French colonial flavour. Regardless of the odd Chinese spice, this is the contemporary cuisine of South Vietnam. Makes you want to travel, if not to Saigon then (sigh) Spit Junction will do just fine.

Hours Dinner Tues–Sun from 6pm
Bill E $7.50–$14 **M** $17–$28 **D** $8–$11; tasting menu $60 pp
Cards AE BC DC MC V Eftpos
Wine BYO (corkage $2 pp)
Chef/owner Lanna Tran
Seats 80; private room
www.transrestaurant.com.au
And...framed black-and-white photographs of French Indo–China are quite mesmerising, though renovations are planned

city + suburbs

Tsukasa

200 Crown Street, East Sydney
Tel 9361 3818   Map 2

Japanese

Score 13/20

Guests always receive a traditional warm and hearty Japanese basement-restaurant greeting when they arrive at this minor East Sydney institution. Once inside, perched preferably on the blond timber stools at the buzzy sushi bar, such goodwill is easily reciprocated. Outside of Tsukasa's swankier counterparts, this is one of our favourite Sydney sushi beats. It's not flash but you can rely on the fish to be smackingly fresh and the sushi fashioned with considerable skill by the chefs behind the counter. Combine sushi and sashimi with a range of the wonderful appetisers we recommend over the more (yawn) predictable teriyaki and tempura choices. Always refreshing are niku tataki (thin-sliced raw beef with a special sauce); and grilled salmon, served on the bone, the glistening pink flesh easily picked off with chopsticks. We never go past the skewered chicken meat balls, dipped in a sweet sauce with a dab of English mustard on the plate. You leave content with the price as well as the flavours.

Hours Lunch Tues–Fri noon–2pm; Dinner Tues–Sat 6–10pm, Sun & public holidays 6–9pm
Bill E $5–$10 **M** $15–$28 **D** $4.50; sushi $1.70–$4
Cards AE BC MC V
Wine Small list; 3 by the glass; stick to Japanese beer or sake; BYO (corkage $2 pp)
Chefs Masayuki Takegawa & Shinsuke Toda
Owner Manabu Masuda
Seats 75
And...at last! Snazzy, easier-to-read menus

Two Chefs on Stanley

115–117 Riley Street, East Sydney
Tel 9331 1559   Map 2

Mediterranean

Score 13/20

Gotta love the location, gotta love the building: those large windows open on a summer night to the more charming end of Stanley Street; the interior walls are white but not clinical, softened by intelligent, sensitive lighting. This is a calm, collected and centred place to eat. The food is centred, too: not orgasmic but balanced. An entrée of king prawns, for example, arrives beautifully cooked, married with chorizo in a salad. Balance is perhaps a bit more of a challenge for a grilled beef medallion on potato fondant, which turns out be to a large lump of meat loaded onto a large lump of spud – a bit too architectural for us, although the porcini butter is superb. On the upside, the oysters are freshly shucked, the scallop-and-pea risotto has a light hint of vermouth, and the desserts are spot-on. It's always a good time to enjoy old favourites such as summer berry pudding and just-perfect crème caramel.

Hours Lunch Mon–Fri noon–3pm; Dinner Mon–Sat 6–10pm
Bill E $16.50–$18 **M** $24–$29 **D** $10.50
Cards AE BC DC MC V Eftpos
Wine Short, Australian list with lots of familiar names; 10 by the glass; BYO (corkage $4 pp)
Chef Wesley Valenton
Owner Marvin Taouk
Seats 80; private room; outdoor seats
www.twochefsonstanley.com.au
And...a private dining room with a very affordable menu

city + suburbs

Uchi Lounge

15 Brisbane Street, Surry Hills
Tel 9261 3524   Map 2

Modern Japanese

Score 13/20

A jaunty youngster at the downstairs bar sips a lychee sake cocktail wearing a black T-shirt that says 'Nothing ever happened'. Upstairs, a cool-cat waiter in a tight-fitting Astro Boy top serves chrysanthemum sushi and delicious grilled eggplant with miso and parmesan to 20-somethings with straight-cut fringes, flirting with boys keen on the seared beef sashimi. This way-cool, back-street warehouse space still wows diners with its retro-kitsch interior and contemporary take on tempura and sashimi. The dishes of Tokyo-born chef Takashi Ohuchi are creative – adding artichokes and balsamic honey or basil miso sauce to established Japanese ingredients – if sometimes a bit too much like a manga comic. Vibrant, futuristic, post-modern even, but a little is lost in translation. A visual feast certainly, though it's hoped the whims of fashion don't detract from the essentials of eating – after all, this was once home to Sydney's rag trade. Tradition brings substance, such as kingfish sashimi with shallot, umeboshi and tamari dressing, where delicacy and flavour entwine harmoniously.

Hours Dinner Mon–Sat 6.30–11pm
Bill E $5.50–$12.50 **M** $13.50–$18.50 **D** $9.50; 10% surcharge for groups larger than 8
Cards AE MC V Eftpos; no bookings on Fri & Sat
Wine Brief but well-priced list; 6 by the glass; Japanese beers and sake; BYO (corkage $2.50 pp)
Chefs Takashi Ohuchi & Alex Lee
Owner Takashi Ohuchi
Seats 50
And…believe it or not, after all these years they now take bookings Mon–Thurs, and they may open for lunch

Vatel

374 Lyons Road, Russell Lea
Tel 9712 4024   Map 5B

Modern French

Score 13/20

Set on a prominent corner location on busy Lyons Road, Vatel has the goods in the looks department: all bistro aesthetics and clean lines. And with a chef who's ex Quay and more recently from that fabulous city bistro Republic Dining, there's plenty of promise to Philippe Pinson's menu. The French-born chef uses the world as his muse, perhaps for a basil risotto or a salad of king prawns with avocado and aïoli. A house-made boudin was a little dark, filled with chicken meat, on good sautéed mushrooms. The coulibiac of house-smoked salmon is shrouded in golden brown filo, rather than the expected brioche, with indulgent flavours thanks to a creamy white wine and leek sauce. In a sign of pure talent, the fish retains its exquisite rare blush. Alas, a mixed grill of seafood had few highlights, because charred prawns and a stodgy risotto let down otherwise decent blue-eye, garlicky mussels and a Sydney rock oyster. There's compensation enough in a dessert of profiteroles with almond milk ice-cream.

Hours Dinner Mon–Sat 6–10pm
Bill E $13.50–$18 **M** $19.50–$26.50 **D** $8.50–$10.50
Cards AE BC MC V Eftpos
Wine Tiny list, suburban prices, but all fine wines; 8 by the glass; BYO (corkage $2.50 pp)
Chef/owner Philippe Pinson
Seats 40
www.vatelrestaurant.com.au
And…good cheeses to have with the last of your wine

city + suburbs (V)

Vera Cruz

314 Military Road, Cremorne
Tel 9904 5818 Map 5A

Mexican

Score 14/20

There is not a nacho to be seen at Vera Cruz, or a sombrero, or anything even remotely resembling a small Mexican mouse. Instead there's a long white room, modernist white tables, and fluorescent pink crosses glowing softly on the walls. The menu is similarly spare and stylish: joining the classic empanada, tostada, tortilla and fajita favourites are seasonally adjusted variations, like sweet cuttlefish with smoky chipotle (dried, smoked jalapeño chilli), or delicate ceviche of fish with avocado, coriander, tomato and lime. Enchiladas with creamy chicken and salsa verde are substantial and full of subtle, well-balanced herbaceous hints. Mexican meatballs are a powerful combination of finely ground pork and lamb amidst a profusion of capers, green olives, raisins and rice. Informed, interested staff tempt you to a dessert – perhaps ice-cream with chilli, honeycomb, et al.; or chocolate and almond slice with crème fraîche and Kahlua sauce – but it does get noisy, so be ready with your ear trumpet on busy nights. You may have to resort to the Mexican wave.

Hours Dinner Mon–Sat 6pm–late
Bill E $14.50 **M** $25.50 **D** $11; $3.50 pp surcharge on public holidays
Cards AE BC MC V
Wine Good list, reasonably priced; 20 by the glass; 24 tequilas, plus Mexican and Aussie beers; BYO (corkage $3.50 pp)
Chef Joel Ollier
Owner Annette Zubani
Seats 70; private room; wheelchair access
And...most dishes are available as takeaway

Viet Nouveau

19 Falcon Street, Crows Nest
Tel 9966 0999 Map 5A

Vietnamese

Score 12/20

Now in a simple shopfront room just off the restaurant row of Crows Nest, Viet Nouveau has been introducing Vietnamese flavours to the lower northside for many years. Linda Wong's 'nouveau' style keeps heady fish and fiery chilli sauces well away, leaning towards the gentler and more sophisticated French style, while remaining essentially Asian at heart. Duck breast salad features lean and flavoursome meat with a hint of pungent Vietnamese greens. Stuffed, crisp-fried pancakes are a wonderful contrast of gentle pork, coriander and other herb flavours and textures. Fish cakes have delicate and subtle flavour, but the steamed whiting was just a little bland, needing more old-fashioned Vietnamese punch from fish sauce. Considering Viet Nouveau's well-deserved popularity, we'd like to see the team introduce to its happy regulars some more of those full-flavoured Vietnamese dishes we love. That said, the gentle style of French-meets-Asian cooking is well suited to wine, so don't be afraid to bring a fine vintage to this friendly BYO.

Hours Dinner Tues–Sat 6.30pm–late
Bill E $11.90–$13.90 **M** $17.90–$19.90 **D** $7.90
Cards AE BC MC V Eftpos
Wine BYO (corkage $1.50 pp)
Chef Linda Wong
Owner Ben Wong
Seats 90; private rooms
And...they do takeaway

city + suburbs

Wasavie

8 Heeley Street, Paddington
Tel 9380 8838   Map 4B

Japanese

Score 14/20

Eating with the eyes is well rewarded at this small shaft-like room with its large communal table inset with wine coolers. Good Japanese doesn't get much better value than this. Order edamame and pod the pale little green soybeans from their salty exterior while you try not to order everything in sight. From your wooden seating cube, watch the dexterous chef up the far end prepare your sushi and sashimi. It glistens with freshness and sings in your mouth. Beef tataki (seared rare beef) is a geometric triumph, smoky and tender as expected. In a pork-belly-mad city, the butakakuni is surely some of the richest, fattest and most melt-in-the-mouth: three thick slices in a dark, rich soy-based sauce finished with hot English mustard. Don't overlook the creative salads, nor Wasavie's rare understanding of dessert: perhaps one of the famous glass desserts or a banana and ginger tarte Tatin served with green tea ice-cream. Wasavie (wasabi) may be hot, but so is this restaurant.

Hours Lunch Thurs–Sun noon–3pm; Dinner Tues–Sun 6–10pm
Bill E $4–$14 **M** $15–$25 **D** $5–$10
Cards AE BC DC MC V Eftpos; no bookings for dinner
Wine BYO (corkage $3 pp)
Chef Ryoichi Shiratsugu
Owner Saqura Investment & Consulting
Seats 30; outdoor seats
www.wasavie.com

And... for amazing value at lunch try the bento box set for $25 or special lunch set for $16

Watermark

2A The Esplanade, Balmoral Beach
Tel 9968 3433   Map 7

Contemporary

Score 13/20

Life doesn't come much better than this. Cormorants dot the wharf, kids are pegged out on the jetty tugging aimlessly on fishing lines, and the sparkle of Middle Harbour is simply breathtaking. And while there have been changes in the ownership at this Balmoral stalwart, the pale suede chairs remain comfy, the well-trodden wide timber floorboards are still in place and the food is still worthy of the location. Crisp ravioli are packed with mushrooms and stacked with haloumi on a warm red capsicum sauce. Crisp-skinned saltwater barramundi with snowpeas and a riesling and lemon butter sauce didn't need red grapes as well. Okay, so the salt-and-pepper squid was only a notch above bistro fare and they did use chipped glassware and lose our side order, but the mash is complimentary, the view stunning and the service quietly proud. If they forget to tell you the Chandon Cuvée Riche is a sweet sparkling, save it until you're downing the dark chocolate and meringue tart with an excellent organic raisin terrine.

Hours Breakfast daily 8–10.30am; Lunch Mon–Fri noon–3pm, Sat–Sun 12.30–3.30pm; Dinner daily 6.30–10pm
Bill E $17–$26 **M** $25–$42 **D** $17–$17.50
Cards AE BC DC MC V Eftpos; bookings essential
Wine Insightful list with good aged riesling and semillon; 16 by the glass
Chefs Ringo Au & Harnady Susantio
Owner Peter Miric
Seats 95; outdoor seats
www.watermarkrestaurant.com.au

And... they're very comfortable coping with kids midweek, and there's a separate children's menu

city + suburbs (W)

Welcome Hotel

91 Evans Street, Rozelle
Tel 9810 1323 Map 5B

Contemporary
                                Score 14/20

'My name is Cindy and I'm your waitress tonight. You're welcome!' Thankfully the Welcome avoids clichéd US chain-style service for a relaxed, down-played Irish theme and warm staff who don't feel the need to say 'You're welcome.' While the knockabout vibe of the pub remains, the restaurant creeps ever so slowly up-market as the years roll by. No counter queuing necessary at this pub dining room – just take a seat in the small dining room or head for the inviting pub courtyard. Chef Finola Healy has earned a rabid following for her Ireland-meets-mod-Oz fare. Her menu ranges widely, perhaps pork belly with scallop tortellini and snowpeas; or a cracking crab cake with lobster and mango. You may find it hard to see much of the old country in a rump of lamb with a spring roll and balsamic jus, but the Irish mash is superb. For afters, the lemon tart is nearly as good as her darkly attractive apple tarte Tatin.

Hours Lunch daily noon–3pm;
Dinner daily 6–10pm
Bill E $13.50–$17 **M** $23–$29 **D** $12.50–$16
Cards AE BC DC MC V Eftpos;
bookings essential
Wine Good pub list of mostly local wines;
10 by the glass; plenty of whiskies, to be sure
Chef Finola Healy
Owner Damian Silk
Seats 200; outdoor seats
www.thewelcomehotel.com
And... pop into the bar for a well-drawn pint of Guinness

Wet Paint Cafe

50 Macpherson Street, Waverley
Tel 9369 4634 Map 9

Contemporary
                                Score 13/20

This is a well-priced and welcoming neighbourhood eatery that anyone would be happy to have in their neck of the woods. Candle-lit tables and corrugated-iron touches enhance a comfortable and relaxed interior that's corner-store-meets-share-accommodation chic. The service puts you at ease even if the menu alarms in its geographical diversity – chicken comes grilled, Moroccan, and Louisiana-stuffed. Stick to simpler fare to be rewarded. Seafood chowder is a comforting entrée, though leek and blue swimmer crab filo parcels failed to excite, leaving us ruing a decision not to opt for steamed black mussels with tomato and Pernod. Southern US and North African side trips aside, mains are straightforward enough – a barbecue lamb rump with a green peppercorn sauce, scotch fillet with a balsamic reduction, and chargrilled salmon fillet – with a couple of vegetarian options for good measure. The dessert list is brief: a tart, a torte and a curiously chilly crème brûlée.

Hours Dinner Tues–Sat 6–10pm
Bill E $6–$14.50 **M** $17–$24.50 **D** $9
Cards BC MC V Eftpos; bookings essential
Wine Cheap and cheerful; 9 by the glass;
BYO (corkage $3 pp)
Chef/owner Scott Luland
Seats 40; wheelchair access
And... a cheese platter where you least expect one

city + suburbs

The Wharf

End of Pier 4, Hickson Road, Walsh Bay
Tel 9250 1761   Map 1

Contemporary

Score 14/20

The Wharf could so easily be a show-off restaurant, sitting right on the water with a killer view of the Bridge and Luna Park. But instead it has an unpretentious, casual feel and food that's interesting enough to take your eye off the scenery. Tim Pak Poy (ex Claude's) is now back in the kitchen with Aaron Ross, turning out clever dishes such as potted sand crab with a cottage cheese dressing and trout roe, and some unusually salty crispbread. There is a wonderfully alluring play of flavours in a main of wagyu scotch fillet with caramelised onion, asparagus and mizuna; and five-spice roast chicken is saturated with taste, deftly paired with mayonnaise. Verve and originality continue into dessert, with the strong and clear taste of berries matched with a soft take on meringue. There is always a lot to love about The Wharf: the luscious wooden floorboards, the sweeping space, and the calming effect of the water.

Hours Lunch Mon–Sat noon–3pm; Dinner Mon–Sat 6–11pm; Pre-theatre Mon–Sat 6–8pm
Bill E $18.50 **M** $26.50–$32 **D** $12.50; 10% surcharge on Sundays & public holidays
Cards AE BC DC MC V
Wine Wide-ranging and interesting list, with a smaller reserve list; 25 by the glass
Chefs/owners Aaron Ross & Tim Pak Poy
Seats 200; private rooms; wheelchair access; outdoor seats
www.thewharfrestaurant.com.au
And...arrive after 8pm to avoid the theatre crowd

Whiteblue

53 Cross Street, Double Bay
Tel 9327 4015   Map 4A

Greek

Score 13/20

Whiteblue rises well above any daggy Greek décor clichés. The interior of this modern taverna is smart and simple Santorini-esque – white walls, white-cloth'd tables, and a swirly blue glowing bar running across the back. On Friday and Saturday they like to party, with live bouzouki music, DJs, dancing and an early demise for a few plates as the night wears on, but there's also plenty on the menu to enjoy. Dips are excellent – superbly creamy taramasalata and a very spicy tyrokafteri (fetta with dry ricotta) – and difficult to resist, even though you'll want to leave room for chunky bastourma and prawns in wonderfully light filo pastry. Among the mains, lamb leg baked in paper with garlic and rosemary can be a bit heavy on the spicing, but skewered souvlakia are delicious with their parsley salad and tzatziki. Include Greek salad – lightly dressed and with a huge chunk of fetta – and you might well need a bit of Zorba-style dancing to work it off.

Hours Dinner Tues–Fri 5–10pm, Sat 6–10pm
Bill E $8.50–$18 **M** $16.50–$28.50 **D** $4–$10.50; 10% surcharge on public holidays
Cards AE BC DC MC V Eftpos
Wine Relatively brief, Antipodean–Hellenic; some familiar local labels, some less so; 12 by the glass
Chef Chris Georgakopoulos
Owners Con Magias, Peter Gallanos, Kon Daris & Alex Macris
Seats 180; outdoor seats
www.whiteblue.com.au
And...the terrace outside is a great place to finish off with a Greek coffee and a Metaxa brandy

city + suburbs Ⓦ

Whitewater

35 South Steyne, Manly
Tel 9977 0322   Map 7

Contemporary
Score 14/20

The man with the Midas touch, Michael McCann, who designed two of last year's hottest new restaurants – Flying Fish and mu shu – offers another designer industrial space. This time, the theme's white on white: white ceiling, floor, leather chairs and bar stools, and large white plates on white paper over white linen cloths. Opening onto Manly Beach, it's inhabited by surfwear-clad locals and casual waiters in jeans and blue-and-white-striped shirts. Chef Dean Keddell brings his take on Peking duck across from mu shu, but sadly some entrées lacked punch, including a prawn cocktail with horseradish tomato mayo that we felt needed salt, sourness or a trace of horseradish heat to lift it. No concerns, however, with the mains, where flavours are bold and beautiful. Crisp-skinned Thirlmere chicken breast is coated in mouth-tingling Sichuan salt. Tofu is served two ways: meltingly soft with eggplant, and crisp with coconut, accompanied by a deliciously fresh Asian slaw. Desserts also shine, making the 'indulgent plate' selection of four desserts a great option.

Hours Breakfast Sat–Sun 8.30–11.30am; Lunch daily noon–3pm; Dinner daily 6.30pm–late
Bill E $16–$24 **M** $28–$35 **D** $12–$14; 3-course banquet $68; 10% surcharge on Sundays & public holidays
Cards AE BC DC MC V Eftpos
Wine Comprehensive with a good range of styles and prices; 15 by the glass; smart selection of digestives and single malts
Chef Dean Keddell
Owner Allan Simpson
Seats 120; wheelchair access; outdoor seats
And…a good selection of loose-leaf teas and excellent coffee round out the experience

WildEast Dreams

102 Norton Street, Leichhardt
Tel 9560 4131   Map 5B

Modern Asian
Score 13/20

Some restaurants are inseparable from their owners' personalities. The grand piano, elegant South-East Asian artifacts, hip architectural magazines, spooky paintings – at WildEast Dreams you could be in the tasteful apartment of a young Singaporean urban professional. But this is Mediterranean Leichhardt, so Albert Wong's eclectic oriental dining room and tropical courtyard is a quirky experience. That's quirky in a very good way if you sample the excellent nasi goreng with its deep, spicy flavours enhanced by anchovies; a truly Indonesian cha-cha chicken (ayam goreng); and superb Chinese 'black marbles' (warm sesame dumplings in ginger broth). Not so inspiring were deep-fried 'kung fu tofu' filled with shaoxing wine and black vinegar – too sweet, too messy – nor the metallic-tasting 'Chinese sleeping bags' (prawns in pastry) which we'd be happy to leave snoring. Still, Wong's menu message of 'I believe in cooking to bring you happiness and conviviality' is one we're totally in sympathy with. The young staff are friendly and enthusiastic if occasionally too dippy for comfort.

Hours Dinner Tues–Sun 6–10pm
Bill E $8–$12 **M** $15–25 **D** $6–$10; 10% surcharge on public holidays
Cards AE BC MC V Eftpos
Wine Commercial but thoughtful Oz list; 6 by the glass; BYO (corkage $5.50 per bottle)
Chefs Prakarn Prasitwuttisak & Albert Wong
Owner Albert Wong
Seats 100; private rooms; outdoor seats
www.wildeastdreams.com
And…after dinner enjoy a gelato and coffee along Norton Street

city + suburbs

Wildfire

Ground Level, Overseas Passenger Terminal, The Rocks
Tel 8273 1222   Map 1

Mediterranean

Score 12/20

Wildfire promises so much and for Big Night Out aesthetics it delivers in spades. However, the food is often underwhelming and the niggling question remains: why try to be all things to all people when half the menu would suffice? This might be just one of the challenges for US-based chef Mark Miller but, gauging by the customers, perhaps grandiose ostentation *is* the point. With its Circular Quay views, it feels like being in the cavernous engine room of a runaway showboat. Over open flames, chefs fence with metre-long skewers of churrasco (Brazilian-inspired marinated barbecue meats), waiters babble, the crustacean bar glows ice-blue and the wine wall conjures up images of a side-show alley. Wok-fried chilli–salt Moreton Bay bugs are a lip-smacking delight. Sadly, salted pork belly with tamale arrived cold, while juicy churrasco roasted rack of lamb was barely lukewarm. The dessert platter has sensational lemon meringue and blueberry crème brûlée. Wildfire ain't cheap and its value is questionable, but, by George, it can be a good night out.

Hours Lunch Mon–Fri noon–3pm; Dinner Sun–Thurs 6–11pm, Fri–Sat 6pm–midnight
Bill E $24–$29 **M** $36–$54 **D** $17; 10% surcharge on Sundays & public holidays
Cards AE BC DC MC V
Wine An encyclopaedic tome with super-knowledgeable sommeliers; 15 by the glass
Chef David Griffiths
Owners Mark Miller & Tonci Farac
Seats 350; private room; wheelchair access; outdoor seats
www.wildfiresydney.com
And…the churrasco at $59 per head, (whole tables only), is an 'all you can eat' bargain

Wine Banq

Basement, 53 Martin Place, Sydney
Tel 9222 1919   Map 1

French Provincial

Score 14/20

Yep, it's still here. Despite a slight change in spelling (from Banc to Banq), and a change of owner in late 2004, this sexy subterranean diner still looks the same as it did in 1998. From those glass-fronted wine racks behind the jade-green banquettes to the glow-in-the-dark bar and comfy padded chairs, it's all as it was. The hard-topped tables, low roof and grand piano remain, too. And while the wine list itself is shorter than in years gone by, there's plenty of allure to be found in the bottom of a glass of Alsatian pinot gris, Tasmanian chardonnay or French cabernet. There's even more allure in Sean Ford's no-nonsense menu. The mussels steamed open with white wine and parsley are seriously fantastic. Snags are from AC Butchery and the accompanying mash is full of butter superior. Mostly a hangout for the young in-loves and hoping to be in-loves, this place will seduce aficionados of civilised wine bars of any age with its mood and food, particularly fragrant quince millefeuille with a luscious scoop of lightened mascarpone.

Hours Lunch Mon–Fri noon–3pm; Dinner Mon–Sat 6pm–late
Bill E $12–$16 **M** $21–$28 **D** $13–$14.50
Cards AE BC DC MC V Eftpos
Wine Long, lovely list; 20 by the glass
Chef Sean Ford
Owner Sean Jones
Seats 77
www.winebanq.com.au
And…live music Friday and Saturday nights, and often during the week

city + suburbs

Woodland's

Shops 4 & 5, 55–67 George Street, Parramatta
Tel 9633 3838 Map 6
Also at 238 George Street, Liverpool
Tel 9734 9949 Map 6

South Indian Vegetarian

Score 12/20

It's always a good rule of thumb that if an Indian is full of subcontinental families it's the real deal. While Woodland's – a plain, tile-floored shopfront with turmeric-coloured walls and bhangra on the sound system – won't win any downunder décor or atmosphere awards, wonderfully spiced vegetarian dishes for very few rupees are a good reason to swing by Parramatta's CBD. Service is Raj-era polite and happy to steer you in the right direction with very generous portions. To start, there's plenty of deep-fried fun, from addictive samosa to masala vada (herby deep-fried ground lentils), or a mound of lightly battered, chilli- and garlic-spiced matchstick vegies. Follow with crisp, golden-brown, satellite dish-sized dosa (lentil and rice pancakes), like that perennial fave masala dosa, filled with fragrant potato and onion. The thali plate is a bargain: two curries, perhaps a spicy tomato and chickpea, and a vegetable korma; a lentil soup; poori and many more vibrant flavours in the condiments. Washed down with a lassi, it'll keep Ganesh smiling.

Hours Lunch Mon–Fri 11.30am–2.30pm, Sat–Sun 11.30am–3pm; Dinner daily 6–9.30pm
Bill E $5–$8 **M** $7–$15 **D** $6–$8
Cards BC MC V Eftpos
Wine BYO (corkage $1 pp)
Chefs Natarajan Narayanan; Jastin Santiago (Liverpool)
Owner Jai Prakash Margasahayam
Seats 50 (80 Liverpool); wheelchair access
And...the Liverpool version is bigger and busier

XO

490 Crown Street, Surry Hills
Tel 9360 7007 Map 3B

Asian

Score 14/20

Pork belly is not sexy. Unless, of course, it's roasted crisp, glazed with sweet Sichuan sauce, top-dressed with toasted sesame seeds and served as a centrepiece at Neil Perry's latest Asian incarnation. After some teething troubles in this new space (vale MG Garage, sob...), the menu has been abridged and standards lifted. So four seasons later, with Surry Hills the new Potts Point, XO again hits the spot with its buzz, immediacy, sense of occasion, and seductive lighting making us all look and feel glamorous. The service is as silken as the tofu paired with steamed scallops, and as refreshing as a salad of salted sea trout, strips of green pawpaw and a rally of mints, coriander and Thai basil. Perry knows that in a city where anything new is instantly lustworthy it takes more than a few party tricks to stay in the spotlight. It's good to see XO now set a more assured course.

Hours Lunch Wed–Fri noon–2.30pm; Dinner Tues–Sat 6–10pm
Bill E $12–$27 **M** $19–$39 **D** $8–$12
Cards AE BC DC MC V
Wine Eloquent and extensive, plenty of French drops and big-occasion bottles; 17 by the glass
Chefs Neil Perry & David Young
Owners Neil Perry, Trish Richards & Ian Pagent
Seats 110; private room
www.neilperrychef.com
And...you have the orange blossom martini from the Asian cocktail list and I'll have a Japanese beer

good food guide

city + suburbs

Yellow Bistro

57–59 Macleay Street, Potts Point
Tel 9357 3400   Map 2

Contemporary

Score 14/20

This stylish eatery and food store glows at the chic end of Macleay Street. A warm, low-key ambience draws the neighbourhood into this intimate dining room just like a gathering at a friend's home. It's an understated space beautifully lifted by a vibrant pink padded wall and an extraordinary chandelier overhead. For brunch, lunch and dinner passionate, enthusiastic floor staff deliver good coffee and George Sinclair's smartly rustic fare. The genuine flavours of potato gnocchi with just the right blend of tomato, marjoram, zucchini flowers and ricotta are worth relishing. Roast lamb rump, resting on superb soft white polenta, melts in the mouth with a marinated eggplant, red onion, pomegranate and balsamic salad. Boldly flavoured chicken tagine combines prunes, saffron, almonds, preserved lemon, couscous and chilli jam with meat so tender it almost cries. Dessert is mandatory, with pastry pin-up Lorraine Godsmark dishing up sublime delicacies, including that legendary date tart. Her apricot flan or the croque madame are great starts to the day.

Hours Breakfast Mon–Fri 8–11am; Brunch Sat–Sun 8am–3pm; Lunch (summer) Mon–Fri 11am–3pm; Dinner Tues–Sat 6–10.30pm, Fri–Sat (winter) 6–10.30pm
Bill E $15.50–$16.50 **M** $23.50–$31.50 **D** $14–$16; 15% surcharge weekends & public holidays
Cards AE BC MC V Eftpos
Wine Well-priced, short but appealing list; 11 by the glass
Chefs/owners George Sinclair & Lorraine Godsmark
Seats 50; wheelchair access; outdoor seats
And… be lured into the foodie's paradise next door for extra take-home supplies

Ying's

270 Pacific Highway, Crows Nest
Tel 9966 9181   Map 5A

Chinese/Seafood

Score 14/20

Chinoiserie gives way to orange walls and yellow screens, space around tables, low noise levels, carpet and glass walls at Ying's. The food is authentic Cantonese, cooked with finesse and judicious balancing of flavours. The ebullient Ying Tam and his loyal waiters help you through a menu of old favourites – yes, there is lemon chicken and sweet-and-sour pork – and bubbling tanks of seafood (check the day's prices before diving in). In-the-know families and Hong Kong expats turn to the 'Home Style Cooking' section. Don't be scared: it's not all wobbly bits. There's delicacy in a plate of improbably white steamed beancurd with a minced fish stuffing. Whole barramundi, steamed and flash fried, contrasts soft flesh and crisp skin, with a scattering of black beans, translucent shards of bitter gourd and sweetly piquant preserved mustard greens. Green beans are garnished with pork mince and pungent shreds of olive. To finish, a fond nod to the old suburban Chinese: dry ice billows from under the fresh fruit platter.

Hours Lunch & yum cha daily 11am–3pm; Dinner daily 6–11pm
Bill E $6–$29.50 **M** $14.50–$38.80 **D** $4.50–$8.80; seafood at market prices; $3.50 pp surcharge on public holidays (children over 10 years $2 pp)
Cards AE BC DC MC V
Wine Long list of good names; 7 by the glass; BYO (corkage $5 pp)
Chef Ken Yau
Owner Ying's Seafood Restaurant Pty Ltd
Seats 120; private rooms
And… there's yum cha, plus small servings of dishes from the à la carte menu

city + suburbs

Yoshii

115 Harrington Street, The Rocks
Tel 9247 2566   Map 1

Japanese

Score 17/20

Food as performance art never tasted this good. Sit at the sushi counter, eyes irresistibly drawn to the flicking of Ryuichi Yoshii's knife as he transforms cucumber into a single, fine but very long strip to scroll around fresh ginger and eel; or creates sushi in Japanese decorative styles of wildlife, which border on twee but taste sublime. Or sit more formally in the quiet dining room – all muted dark tones and subdued lighting – and try one of the two set menus acknowledging the kaiseki tradition of numerous small courses: venison tataki in appealingly smoky jelly of soy and bonito; translucent seared tuna slices reminiscent of a Mondrian painting, with splashes of parsley oil, sherry vinegar and dijon. Each dish arrives on beautiful tableware, perhaps Mitsuo Shoji ceramics or a black bento box – all the better to display slices of rare-roasted duck breast or tofu with abalone. Service is as precise as the dessert of mascarpone quenelles covered in black sesame and crushed soybean. Never was restraint so dynamic.

Hours Lunch Tues–Fri noon–3pm; Dinner Mon–Sat 6–9.30pm
Bill Lunch from $40; Dinner set menus $90–$120
Cards AE BC DC MC V; bookings essential
Wine Extensive, well-thought-out list; 16 by the glass
Chef Ryuichi Yoshii
Owner Saqura Investment & Consulting
Seats 40; private room
www.yoshii.com.au
And... Japanese beer and sake heaven (and no children allowed)

Zaaffran

Level 2, 345 Harbourside Shopping Centre, Darling Harbour
Tel 9211 8900   Map 5B

Indian

Score 13/20

Zaaffran, Hindi for saffron, is a waterfront room for big-night curries and the tandoor. And while recent renovations have jettisoned the glittering beads on the mirrored wall, it's still a visual feast: city lights shimmer like a chandelier across the water, a black-haired woman in a persimmon-coloured sari glistens with gold jewellery. Chef Vikrant Kapoor impresses with his famed chicken biryani, baked in a pastry case and lifted with minted yoghurt. Southern dishes from Madras are even better: try tiger prawns in sweet coconut cream and tomato broth, simmered with garam masala, coriander, fennel, pepper and tamarind. A similar curry accompanies stand-out barramundi fillets, the richness of the dish soothed in part by English spinach and spoonfuls of basmati rice steamed with saffron. A Kingfisher beer also does the trick. It all makes for a night to savour, redolent with the colours of the subcontinent – crimsons, pinks, yellows, burnt oranges – dazzling us with some of the best Indian dishes in the big city.

Hours Lunch daily noon–2.30pm; Dinner Sun–Thurs 6–9.30pm, Fri–Sat 6–10.15pm
Bill E $9.50–$16 **M** $15.50–$26.50 **D** $6.90–$8.50; $3.50 pp surcharge on public holidays
Cards AE BC DC MC V
Wine A mature list of well-chosen, spice-friendly drops; 9 by the glass
Chef Vikrant Kapoor
Owners Freddie Zulfiqar, Rush Dossa & Vikrant Kapoor
Seats 220; outdoor area; private room
www.zaaffran.com.au
And...if you drink beer, try a cleansing Kingfisher

city + suburbs

Zenith on Booth

37 Booth Street, Annandale
Tel 9660 6600 Map 5B

Italian

Score 14/20

Like Liza Minnelli and Martin Amis, chef Mario Percuoco has had to journey out from the shadow of a famous parent (Armando at Buon Ricordo). To do that, your passport must be stamped with passion and Mario has it in spades, even if it doesn't always translate on the plate. The neutral, contemporary fit-out in the upstairs dining room and on the balcony overlooking Booth Street serves as a minimalist canvas for the broad, often idiosyncratic brush strokes he applies to Neapolitan classics. Seared King Island beef carpaccio is presented quite formally as a tower layered with fine shavings of radish on a superb tarragon mayonnaise. Cleverly made eggplant roulade bound with ricotta and smoked mozzarella pulses with the flavours of the sun: basil, vine-ripened tomatoes, pine nuts. In a town where cafe crimes abound, Percuoco shows pasta real love and respect. His brilliant penne with house-made pork sausage and black truffle will change your attitude too. Service is friendly and unflappable.

Hours Lunch Sat noon–2.30pm; Dinner Tues–Sat 6.30–10.30pm
Bill E $16–$21 **M** $25–$31.50 **D** $14
Cards AE BC MC V Eftpos
Wine Very smart domestic and Italian selection assembled by sommelier Stuart Sanders; 25 by the glass; BYO Tues–Thurs (corkage $8 per bottle)
Chef Mario Percuoco
Owner Jim Koutsogeorgis
Seats 60; wheelchair access; outdoor seats
www.zenithonbooth.com.au
And...on a warm night try for a table on the balcony

Zinc

77 Macleay Street, Potts Point
Tel 9358 6777 Map 2

Contemporary

Score 13/20

When the sun dips, this busy cafe morphs into a slick neighbourhood bistro. Lights are dimmed, candles flicker and moulded plastic chairs replace the sugar shakers and white stools. Instead of buffed Potts Pointers, by night it's tables for one, two or more – diners who find the homely cooking more appealing than queuing at the supermarket next door. Italian-inspired dishes still have universal appeal, such as salt-and-pepper calamari on a bed of chilli-laced cannellini beans, the former somewhat heavily battered, the latter a perfect mix of earthiness and peppery heat. Wild mushroom risotto is generous with fungi – including pine mushrooms – and beautifully flavoured, although its pilaf-like texture lacked true risotto creaminess. On first reading, pappardelle with chicken ragù would trouble Italophile purists; one taste, however, of the delightfully light, tomatoey sugo and all fears are allayed. Yoghurt pannacotta is a modern take on an Italian classic – the vanilla-bean-studded custard quite stiff but soft, passionfruit syrup echoing the yoghurt tang.

Hours Breakfast daily 7am–noon; Lunch daily noon–3pm; Dinner Tues–Sat from 6.30pm
Bill E $6.50–$14 **M** $19–$25 **D** $8–$12; 10% surcharge on weekends & public holidays
Cards AE BC MC V Eftpos; no bookings
Wine Small, succinct list nicely matched to the food; 10 by the glass; BYO ($10 per bottle)
Chefs Peter Fisher & Christopher Richardson
Owners Peter Hurren & Nigel Nickless
Seats 85; outdoor seats
And...the weekly-changing set menu ($25 for three courses) is great value

CAFES

cafes

NORTH

Bacino Bar
18 The Strand, Dee Why
Tel 9982 1988
Also at Shop 7, 1a The Corso, Manly
Tel 9977 8889
From their own coffee blend, for sale at the street-front cafe just a frisbee's throw from Dee Why beach, to Manly's two-level space facing the wharf, it's all Italian *passione*. Good gelati and decent sarnies, plus Italian-style scrambled eggs, and coffees with an indulgent crema.

Swell
Shop 3, 74 Old Barrenjoey Road, Avalon
Tel 9918 5678
The windows fold back, the thin, tanned and gorgeous perch on the bench seats, and the sticky sweets are heaven. Try date porridge with banana or a baked egg with creamed spinach. After superb coffee, plan an attack on the beach.

Sea la vie
Shop 4, 3–6 The Strand, Dee Why
Tel 9984 8644
Find a pew under the outside brollies and watch the surf just a little way off and across the street. You can buy ingredients to make your own *cucina* from the deli, but the coffee is better than most places this close to the surf.

Don Adan Coffee House
Shop 2/5 Spit Road, Mosman
Tel 9968 2828
A moody little space where the Lower North Shore's most serious of caffeine addicts come to find the meaning of life in the bottom of their cup, or in the centre of their bagel.

Awaba
67 The Esplanade, Balmoral Beach
Tel 9969 2104
The mirror-lined, bleached-white interior is filled with well-dressed, well-tanned patrons tucking in to buttermilk flapjacks with berries; fig, prosciutto, rocket and goat's curd salad for lunch; or flathead fish 'n' chips by night. It's above your average cafe, but so are the prices.

Maisy's Cafe
1/164 Military Road, Neutral Bay
Tel 9908 4030
The look is utilitarian, but this all-day and all-night hang out has the goods. Twenty-four hours a day they dish up hearty food and, more importantly, excellent coffee. Maisy's doesn't need to be so reliable, but we're thankful it is.

Primavera Espresso Bar
Shop 3, Little Spring Street, North Sydney
Tel 9955 2492
A recent demolition reveals this gem in a narrow laneway. The cosy bar brings back memories of Naples, an omelette with pancetta, tomato and mushrooms has memories of the Mezzogiorno (south), or try an Italian beef burger with bocconcini, pesto and marinated vegetables. The coffee is as seriously good as the welcome.

Cibo
71 Walker Street, North Sydney
Tel 9922 2293
A traditional trattoria, with petite cloth'd tables and walled menu, you'll find it packed to the rafters with the suited set for both *prima colazione* (brekkie) and *pranzo* (lunch). Drop by for linguine with prawns, chilli, garlic and fresh tomato or a tramezzino with grilled chicken fillet and avocado salsa accompanied by chilled prosecco. *Salute*!

Oven
89 Parraween Street, Cremorne
Tel 9908 3536
It's little more than a narrow room with one black wall, tucked between a rollerdoor and a driveway. An equally small menu may have googy eggs with toast; minestrone; or cute cakes with old-fashioned fluted pink paper or passionfruit shortbread with excellent coffee.

Atomic Espresso
148 Wycombe Road, Neutral Bay
Tel 9953 0666
All hail the return of cafe genius Richard Simec (think Swell, in Avalon, and Ecabar, in Darlinghurst). At this functional, narrow space, with a bold orange floor and a mirror along one wall, they bake their own pastries and make arguably the area's best coffee.

AND ALSO (SEE RESTAURANT SECTION)... **THE CHELSEA TEA HOUSE** 48 Old Barrenjoey Road, Avalon • **BATHERS' PAVILION CAFE** 4 The Esplanade, Balmoral Beach • **CREDO** 504 Miller Street, Cammeray

cafes

SOUTH

Allpress Espresso
58 Epsom Road, Rosebery
Tel 9662 8288
You can see the roaster and the beans through the glass wall behind the counter, so you know the coffee's fresh. The company also bakes Brasserie bread, so get something starchy (e.g. a panino) to fill you up and a demitasse of something strong and dark to see you through.

A Little on the Side
Cnr Boundary Street & Ivy Lane, Darlington
Tel 9698 7767
Last year's hot newcomer is growing old (in cafe terms, a year is a long time) gracefully. They still have excellent omelettes, wonderful pancakes and more substantial meals; the courtyard is still a calm oasis midweek; and the Grinder's coffee continues to seep into our soul.

The Art Lounge Cafe
275 Arden Street, Coogee
Tel 9665 2500
Some may come to check out the art on the walls. Some come to lounge around on the sofas, pretending to be interested. But everybody comes here for the superb cakes and even better coffee.

Campos Coffee
193 Missenden Road, Newtown
Tel 9516 3361
A lot of people left, miffed by the drink-or-leave rules, but thankfully it seems a little less hectic now. Have a Belgian chocolate fuss or white chocolate nougat with some of the country's best artisan-roasted coffee or keep drinking lattes all day just to keep your seat.

Wall
80 Campbell Street, Surry Hills
Tel 9280 1980
Groovy Melbourne style comes to the inner East. The bar opens to the street for takeaway, and the raw concrete finish is inlaid with found objects. Nestle into the sunken pit or one of the private nooks, sip a Genovese coffee and munch on a pide or kransky sausage and relish.

Di Lorenzo Caffe
85 Boundary Street, Darlinghurst
Tel 9326 9388
This tiny street corner space behind St Vincent's Hospital keeps the medicos going, thanks to its own brand of roast coffee, a simple menu of Italian staples – including arancini, calzone and pasta – simple breakfasts, plus sweet treats from Pasticceria Papa.

Single Origin Roasters
60–64 Reservoir Street, Surry Hills
Tel 9211 0665
From the muscly timber tables and bench seats to the stone-fronted bench, it's all about modern coffee drinking. Watch the roaster at work, let them regale you with stories of their magical milk (Country Valley organic) and just be in awe of the tiniest, darkest, creamiest ristretto.

Bourke Street Bakery Cafe
633 Bourke Street, Surry Hills
Tel 9699 1011
Lamb and harissa sausage rolls. Beef cheek pie. Wicked tarts, tempting pastries, and great sourdough breads suspended in the windows of this tiny corner cafe. Pull up a street-side seat and watch inner-city life stroll by.

The Book Kitchen
255 Devonshire Street, Surry Hills
Tel 9310 1003
Browse the food books to buy over a Single Origin coffee in this warehouse-like space. The food is mostly organic: house-made baked beans and pork hock, hand-cut chips, and dinner (Thurs–Sat) as delicious as roasted veal marrow or cassoulet. Closed Tuesdays.

Toby's Estate Coffee & Tea
32–36 City Road, Chippendale
Tel 9211 1459
Also at 129 Cathedral Street, Woolloomooloo
Tel 9358 1196
Also at 81 Macleay Street, Potts Point
Tel 8356 9264
This burgeoning empire now boasts its largest 'branch' in Chippendale, where stellar coffee shares the limelight with over 40 varieties of tea and good snacks – from quiche to cinnamon scrolls.

AND ALSO (SEE RESTAURANT SECTION)...**POOL CAFFE 94 Marine Parade, Maroubra • BILLS 359 Crown Street, Surry Hills • DANKS STREET DEPOT 2 Danks Street, Waterloo • IL BARETTO 496 Bourke Street, Surry Hills • CAFE MINT 579 Crown Street, Surry Hills**

cafes

EAST

Gertrude & Alice
40 Hall Street, Bondi Beach
Tel 9130 5155
A bookshop that isn't just a cafe by name too. Try Moroccan-spiced chickpeas, chicken and sweetcorn soup, excellent coffee, and the books that satisfy any hunger between the ears.

Le Petit Crème
118 Darlinghurst Road, Darlinghurst
Tel 9361 4738
We're big fans of a rustic French cafe with big bowls of milky coffee and spunky girls who look like they've come from the Sorbonne. But the croque boum boum (monsieur with added tomato) is the reason we come back.

Uliveto
33 Bayswater Road, Kings Cross
Tel 9357 7331
Walter Rosin's got the Midas touch. Sure, his latest cafe has a copper-clad façade, but the mood is pure gold. From the brolly-covered tables to designer sandwiches, Belle Fleur chocolates and warm service, it's all good.

Heeley Street Espresso
Heeley Street, Fiveways, Paddington
Tel 9361 3575
Okay, so you feel like you should be parking or washing the car, but the urban grittiness is the perfect outdoor hangout. Grab a bench seat for pancakes, Turkish, or the perfect example of its namesake, the suitably short short black.

Flat White
98 Holdsworth Street, Woollahra
Tel 9328 9922
This wedge, on a corner opposite a pub, is known partly for its panini but mostly for its espresso and every other coffee combo, thanks to a team who understands that the words flat and white don't mean weak.

Swell
Shop 3, 465 Bronte Road, Bronte
Tel 9386 5001
A 'brekkie wrap' – scrambled egg, parmesan, avocado and tomato – and milky Karmee coffee are perfect after a dip. Settle at a communal bench facing the sea for salt-and-pepper squid or crab and corn fritters.

Crave Deli Cafe
98e Bellevue Road, Bellevue Hill
Tel 9327 1670
The best part of hanging out on Bellevue Road is stopping at a small stretch of shops that's home to this pocket-sized deli and cafe as well as the funky homewares store of the same name (one door up). Good cheat's food to take home; great cakes and biscuits to eat in.

Ten Buck Alley
1/185a Bourke Street, Darlinghurst
Tel 9356 3000
Named in tribute to the price of sole-trader ladies in the adjacent lane, this postage stamp-sized kitchen has Di Lorenzo coffee and a short, smart menu, from chorizo frittata for brekkie to pasta.

Fideli
29 Albion Street, Waverley
Tel 9369 4369
Find a place at the communal table while your companion orders at the glass counter. Expect feel-good food such as the legendary chicken pie, pizza, or a sweet biscuit to keep the kids happy while you catch up on the goss.

Zuppa Uno
166 Riley Street, Darlinghurst
Tel 9331 7163
With its polished-concrete floors and aubergine-painted front, there's not much to this hideaway. But there's a BLT with lots of bacon, and soups galore such as duck and white bean, and hearty minestrone, served with excellent rolls.

Nest
165 Victoria Street, Potts Point
Tel 8356 9505
What it lacks in size Nest makes up for in taste – in both the décor and food: fabulous eggs, more-ish muffins, and papaya with lime. Try doorstopper sandwiches (roast chicken with herb mayo) and sensational homemade pies.

AND ALSO (SEE RESTAURANT SECTION)... **BILLS** 433 Liverpool Street, Darlinghurst • **FRATELLI PARADISO** 12–16 Challis Avenue, Potts Point • **DOV** 252 Forbes Street, cnr Burton Street, Darlinghurst • **CAFÉ SEL ET POIVRE** 263 Victoria Street, Darlinghurst • **BLUE ORANGE** 49 Hall Street, Bondi Beach • **YELLOW BISTRO** 57–59 Macleay Street, Potts Point • **ZINC** 77 Macleay Street, Potts Point

cafes

WEST

Bertoni Casalinga ★
281 Darling Street, Balmain
Tel 9818 5845

Favourite Cafe

Simply the best cafe in Balmain, it's run by Italian descendants with the emphasis on fresh flavours, short coffees and the most amazing Italian pastries bought in from the experts.

Espresso Galleria
84 Ramsay Street, Haberfield
Tel 9798 2112

From the Greek pastries to the excellent pide, a lot is squeezed into this tiny corridor of a cafe. Emanuel Patniotis does great things with several blends of coffee, and Dimitra's kourambiethes (nut biscuits) are superb.

Hopscotch
61 Annandale Street (cnr Reserve Street), Annandale
Tel 9560 2698

The best tables on the footpath. But careful where you park the pram or the dog as it's narrow and council are strict. What everybody comes for are the green eggs and ham; the specials, such as Asian-style noodles or omelettes; and to let the kids play with the toys inside.

La Deliziosa
141 Great North Road, Five Dock
Tel 9712 0240

Okay, so it's famous as a pastry shop. No wonder, as the sfogliatelle – Neapolitan conical-shaped wonders – are as good as in the old country, and the biscotti marvellous. But you can sit and enjoy a cuppa with your focaccia or a brioche with your house-made gelato.

Concrete
224 Harris Street, Pyrmont
Tel 9518 9523

While the neighbourhood has toned up and spunked up, Concrete has always had the goods. And that's just the staff. From the concrete sunflowers on the walls to the pancakes and great breakfasts, this corner cafe always feels like the perfect place to be.

Sideways Cafe
37 Constitution Road, Dulwich Hill
Tel 9560 1425

From its hillside location, look out over the houses at (wow!) a horizon, sit at a window-side bench and order, say, roasted pumpkin risotto or penne with chorizo, from the open kitchen. The cakes are invariably good.

The Coffee Emporium
Shop T231, The Grand Market Centro, Bankstown
Tel 9709 6560

It may not be the usual place you'd expect an Italian staple – a shopping mall. But roaster John Ayoub is happy sourcing, roasting and extracting his brilliant Nonno blend coffee, and selling everything anybody interested in coffee could want.

Envy Fine Foods
109 Smith Street, Summer Hill
Tel 9797 1668

Everybody loves lingering in the back courtyard of this iconic cafe tucked away from the madding crowds. The breakfasts are good, the coffee is strong and the mood is perfect for bringing the kids. There's plenty of space for a pram, too.

Washhouse
711 Darling Street, Rozelle
Tel 9810 0040

Yep, it is next door to a laundry, so you can wash your smalls while you sup on arancini or salad. There's a good art gallery, which you pass through at the front, and a fabulous pebble-floored courtyard out the back. The coffee is pretty good, too.

XXII
Cnr Union and Pyrmont streets, Pyrmont
Tel 9552 3093

The menu may look a little like a bills franchise (ricotta pancakes with honeycomb butter, sweetcorn fritters with bacon) but the location is pleasant on a relatively quiet street, the staff are cheery, and the courtyard is cosy and the Karmee coffee right on the money.

cafes

CITY

La Renaissance Pâtisserie Française
47 Argyle Street, The Rocks
Tel 9241 4878
Yes, the staff do speak with French accents, the croissants are superb, and the back courtyard is simply the best haven from the tourist madness of The Rocks. But the pies are as good as from an Aussie bakehouse and coffee takes its lead from Italy, both being all the better for it.

Apartment
155 Macquarie Street, Sydney
Tel 9241 1488
Sure, it looks a bit like a fishbowl, all full-length glass windows and a corner location, but this apartment is the perfect pit stop for a decent brew. The sandwiches are excellent, the braziers and soups warming.

Misto
127 Kent Street, Sydney
Tel 9251 9669
In most other parts of Sydney, this would look like a restaurant. Northern CBD workers duck into the bistro for decent pasta and salads, a quick after-work meal or some of the best coffee within cooee.

GG espresso
175 Pitt Street, Sydney
Tel 9221 1644
One of the many caffeine-obsessed GG's (from founder George Gregan's initials). They all do little besides Turkish stomach fillers and the occasional little cake. Pitt Street's has one of the best short blacks in the city.

Bar Coluzzi
322 Victoria Street, Darlinghurst
Tel 9380 5420
Here the cognescenti grapple with politics and philosophy while perched on tiny stools. Bar Coluzzi dishes up seriously good coffee and we hope they also continue to do so for decades to come.

Fire Station Cafe
465 Pitt Street, Sydney
Tel 9211 2348
Run by a couple of blokes with a passion for what comes from the group handle (i.e. the thing the coffee comes out of), Sydney's former fire station has the goods. Sit outside for your wrap, Turkish or soup, but remember the best things come from the espresso machine.

Lindt Concept Store and Cafe
53 Martin Place (cnr Phillip Street), City
Tel 8257 1600
Sure, you've come for a smoked salmon and goat's cheese club sandwich at the elegant former Banc restaurant site. But you might as well have a hot or iced chocolate (dark or milk), pour chocolate over the waffles, try the chocolate tart and take some chocolates home. Coffee's good – better have a mocha.

Caffe Corto
10 Barrack Street, Sydney
Tel 9279 0070
From the designer outdoor chairs to the switched-on staff, there's a touch of the Milanese about Corto. The pizzette are thick, the salads large, and there's a juliet balcony inside where you wouldn't be surprised to find a suitably thin opera singer (if it wasn't for the fact that it's just access to some very high cupboards).

Lido Bar
98 Clarence Street, Sydney
Tel 9262 2402
How good it is to find Western Australian scampi, or crab in a delicate risotto, at a virtual hole in the wall in Clarence Street? Mussels are threaded through spaghetti and there's a good wine list to fuel you through the afternoon, plus a great mood thanks to buoyant staff.

AND ALSO (SEE RESTAURANT SECTION)...**BAMBINI TRUST** Ground Floor, 185 Elizabeth Street, Sydney • **BOND CAFE** 111 Phillip Street, Sydney • **CAFE SYDNEY** Level 5, Customs House, 31 Alfred Street, Circular Quay • **MOS** 37 Phillip Street (cnr Bridge Street), Sydney • **THE TEAROOM** Level 3, North End, Queen Victoria Building, 455 George Street, Sydney

BARS
BY BONNIE MALKIN

bars

Bayswater Brasserie
32 Bayswater Road, Kings Cross
Tel 9357 2177
Walking into this Kings Cross institution is like strolling straight into a Parisian bistro: white-tiled floor, dark wooden fittings and a long, deep bar stacked with every worthy liquor under the sun. If you're after a stiff drink well made, you're in the right place. With bartender Naren Young doing the honours, you're in safe hands.

Blu Horizon Bar
36th Floor, Shangri-La Hotel, 176 Cumberland Street, The Rocks
Tel 9250 6000
The former Horizons has had a revamp and now boasts a much healthier cocktail list and an even more sophisticated look. Best of all for non-smokers, you've been allocated those coveted Circular Quay views, with nicotine addicts hustled away around the still picturesque side.

The Bourbon
24 Darlinghurst Road, Kings Cross
Tel 9358 1144
Despite its relatively recent transformation – dropping the Beefsteak to become simply The Bourbon – this Kings Cross stalwart maintains its trashy mantle. Now there are leather booths, mod-Oz fittings and lightshades that defy design rules; but it's still, essentially, a rather large, rather rowdy pub. For a big night that bleeds seamlessly into a big morning, this is the place to be.

Bridge Bar ★
Level 10, 2 Macquarie Street, East Circular Quay
Tel 9252 6800

Favourite Bar

Known far and wide for its jaw-dropping view of the Bridge and the Harbour, this swanky, sky-high drinking hole is *the* place to take virgin visitors. Bridge Bar is also the best cure for Sydney malaise because, when you're feeling a little jaded about life in the Emerald City, nothing beats a sunset drink over the sparkling water.

The Civic
388 Pitt Street (cnr Goulburn Street), Sydney
Tel 8080 7040
Part late-night music venue, part bawdy city pub, part trendy cocktail bar, the Civic is many things to many people – and plays all its roles well. This corner hotel prides itself on its past, maintaining the feel of the glory days. So, whether you're there for the music, the food or the atmosphere, a night at the Civic is always guaranteed to be good.

Cruise Bar
Level 2, Overseas Passenger Terminal, West Circular Quay
Tel 9251 1188
Cruise is everything you'd expect from a big, harbourside bar smack bang in the big city. It's large, it's loud and it's often packed with suits getting drunk as quickly as they can. The location is spectacular, perched on the very lip of the Quay, so close you can smell the salt and see through the portholes when a liner docks at the terminal.

The Eastern
500 Oxford Street, Bondi Junction
Tel 9387 7828
With four floors of drinks, food and fashionable people to choose from, it's hard not to find something to like at this newie. Pub it, head upstairs for a more intimate setting, or try the top-floor restaurant. As sparkly and alluring as the mega-mall it butts up against, The Eastern is a haven for tired shoppers, pre-club party people and anyone out for a bit of fun. But be warned: they often charge for entry.

Firefly Winebar
17 Hickson Road, Dawes Point
Tel 9241 2031
Tucked away in one of the multi-million dollar developments that bump up against the Wharf Theatre, this is one blink-and-you'll-miss-it bar. Firefly is tiny; it amounts to no more than a couple of rather fancy poufs (we mean ottomans, dear) on the pavement. It also boasts an extensive wine list and rather lovely view of very expensive boats and very expensive apartments. Perfect, too, for a pre-theatre sundowner.

Hemmesphere
Level 4, 252 George Street, Sydney
Tel 9240 3040
More than a hint of exclusivity hangs over this city favourite, famed for its slow service, snooty staff and pretentious patrons. If you're dead set on spending the night here, you might want to try to put your name on the door. Once you're

in, however, it's all high times, tall drinks and, more often than not, late nights. But only visit when you're feeling very self-assured.

Hugo's Lounge
Level 1, 33 Bayswater Road, Kings Cross
Tel 9357 4411
Nothing much changes in this Kings Cross haunt. The patrons are still beautiful, the drinks are still pricey and the staff are still fantastically frosty. Hugo's has a dedicated following who like dressing up, queuing up and, eventually, air kissing in the bar. If you can't stand the wait, visit on a weeknight when you'll be assured a good table, attentive service and easy passage from footpath to bar.

Icebergs Dining Room & Bar
1 Notts Avenue, Bondi Beach
Tel 9365 9000
Despite the trendy publicity, this cliff-top haunt is a surprisingly friendly, unpretentious place. Yes, it's kind of fancy and the drinks list contains some scary-sounding cocktails, but the staff are helpful and the vibe is welcoming. And then there's the view. If you're sick of the city skyline and fancy a night staring out to sea, there's no better place to sit down, chill out and soak up the Bondi breeze.

bars

Industrie – South of France
107 Pitt Street, Sydney
Tel 9221 8001
This French-tinged bar had been looking a little lacklustre until management came up with the idea of the dark and enticing Emerald Room in early 2005. Now, the Pitt Street pied-à-terre is back on its feet again, benefiting from the seasoned and steady hands of former Longrain and Flying Fish mixmaster Christof Brandon.

jimmy liks
188 Victoria Street, Potts Point
Tel 8354 1400
Some call it fashionably snooty, some call it simply stuck up, but either way this skinny slice of a bar is still a hit. Attached to the mod-Asian restaurant of the same name, its self-reliance can be attributed to an outstanding, adventurous cocktail list that does marvellous things with Asian ingredients rarely seen elsewhere in the city.

The Loft
King Street Wharf, Level 1, 3 Lime Street, Sydney
Tel 9299 4770
No one had heard of King Street Wharf before The Loft opened. The barren stretch of land sandwiched between uncool Cockle Bay and dead East Darling Harbour was more daggy than to-die-for before this über-exclusive über-bar opened (think twice about jeans on a Saturday night). If you can get past the door, it's worth it as much for the water views as for the expensive cocktails.

Longrain
85 Commonwealth Street, Surry Hills
Tel 9280 2888
Long lauded as Sydney's home of the stick drink (think the potent caipiriñha and its cousin, the refreshing caipiroska) Longrain isn't resting on its laurels. The converted warehouse space is always immaculate, the bar staff are always friendly and the drinks are always impeccable. Take a foray into the Thai-flavoured bar menu, especially for tea-smoked trout on betel leaf.

Lotus
22 Challis Avenue, Potts Point
Tel 9326 9000
The maxim 'good things come in small packages' never rang more true than when settling down to a Stiletto Martini at Lotus. Perching on a pouf in this cocktail-lounge-cum-walk-in-wardrobe tucked away behind a sliding door at the back of the restaurant is always a pleasure. It's small, it's sweet, it's sexy and the drinks list is very special.

Mars Lounge
16 Wentworth Avenue, Surry Hills
Tel 9267 6440
If you can fight your way past the sometimes-picky door patrol, a night at Mars Lounge is excellent value. The bar has been known to pack a few too many people in, so you're doing well to stake out a seat and a table on a weekend night. Expect excellent service, good (and sometimes live) music and a young crowd at this Surry Hills fixture.

Middle Bar
Level 1, Kinsela's, 383 Bourke Street, Taylor Square, Darlinghurst
Tel 9331 6200
Believe it or not, this Taylor Square trooper is still delivering the goods. After more than a decade of serving drinks to the delirious and the debauched, Middle Bar pumps out cracking caipiriñhas and mouth-watering mojitos. Busy, bustling, crazy and crammed full of Darlo darlings, late at night it's still the place to be.

mu shu
108 Campbell Parade, Bondi Beach
Tel 9130 5400
Post surf, head to the mod Asian-themed bar, complete with day beds, live lobster tanks and the very lovely cucumber and lychee martini. The staff are friendly and the wine list is restaurant standard (hence the restaurant). Once you're in, you'll find leaving very, very hard.

Opera Bar
Lower Level Concourse, Sydney Opera House, Sydney
Tel 9247 1666
If you want to impress an out-of-towner (and not just for the harbourside prices), be they from Newcastle or New York, the Opera Bar beckons. It has everything: from a very laidback vibe (live music on Sundays) to stunning views of the House, the Bridge and the Harbour. At its best in summer, when you can take a table outside, this is the place to catch the sunset and listen to the water lapping at the walls.

bars

Ruby Rabbit
231 Oxford Street, Darlinghurst
Tel 9326 0044

As the green crystal floors, *Clockwork Orange*-esque furniture and Florence Broadhurst wallpaper suggest, this bar is hip and wants you to know it. The drinks are fashionably expensive, the staff are aloof and the chairs are uncomfortable – in other words it's perfect for the super-cool crowd. They're doing something right, even if we're not always sure what it is.

Sapphire Suite
2 Kellett Street, Kings Cross
Tel 9331 0058

It might look like a souped-up version of any other bar in the Cross, but the Suite is actually breaking ground. Look past the (three!) glitter balls, make your way to the bar and find clued-up bartenders and some very lovely drinks. Our pick is the sapphire martini, an unlikely but successful mix of lavender vodka, apple and lychee juice. And if you're in danger of staying too long, don't worry: they also do breakfast.

Soho Bar & Lounge
171 Victoria Street, Potts Point
Tel 9358 6511

The compulsory stop on any decent Potts Point bar crawl is still going strong. Be it for a cosy start-of-the-night drink or a boozy nightcap, Soho has the goods. Suck on a beer, pout over a cocktail, sip on a flute of champagne and you won't be disappointed. What's more, Soho stocks the holy grail of the bar-hopper: free snacks, including olives, cheese and cornichons.

Statement Lounge Bar
49 Market Street, Sydney
Tel 9373 6758

Tucked away down two flights of stairs under the State Theatre is Sydney's answer to the New York lounge bar. All muted beige banquettes, low lighting and jazzy music, Statement is perfect for that intimate after-work or casual first-date drink. Dark and secluded, the best bit is that it doesn't have mobile phone reception, so you can't be disturbed.

The Tilbury Hotel
12–18 Nicholson Street, Woolloomooloo
Tel 9368 1041

Taking its lead from London's gastro pubs, the Tilbury – a light, bright and spacious pub-cum-bar – is so popular that it's hard to get through the door on Friday nights. The formula is simple: downstairs for dining and upstairs for drinking, a concept every customer grasps with almost reckless abandon. On busy nights it can be a long wait for a drink, but grin and bear it – there's a long line of thirsty punters behind you.

Vanilla Room
153 Norton Street, Leichhardt
Tel 9569 9411

The inner west isn't known for cocktail bars, but here's one that's worth a visit. It's small, so don't bring the whole gang, but if you're after a cosy night for two, then it should suit you to a tee. And if all that vanilla gives you a sweet tooth, you're in luck: the bar is within spitting distance of Leichhardt's gelato hangout, Bar Italia.

The Victoria Room
Level 1, 235 Victoria Street, Darlinghurst
Tel 9357 4488

It's old world gentleman's club meets Cuban cocktail house. There's always something to look at: the mesmerising orange glow from the giant lightshades, slowly turning ceiling fans or boxer-quick bartenders. Catering for the young and the restless at night, it also does a roaring trade in Sunday-afternoon high tea, when it transforms into a place to take granny. If scones aren't her thing, the cocktail list is spectacular.

Water Bar
W Hotel, Cowper Wharf Road, Woolloomooloo
Tel 9331 9000

Can't afford a night at the plush and palatial W Hotel? Then act like you can and sidle up to the Water Bar, smack in the middle of the hotel's vast atrium. You'll be treated like a star, even if the closest you've been to Nicole is *BMX Bandits*. More importantly, bar manager Natalie Stamos knows her stuff, which makes Water Bar as good a choice for cocktail lovers as it is for wannabes.

PROVEDORES
WITH HELEN GREENWOOD

Food Stores 166

Delis 168

Butchers 169

Greengrocers 170

Bakers 171

Fish 172

Farmers' Markets 172

Wine Stores by Huon Hooke 173

VPQMeat

More than 85% of Sydney's 'Hat' Restaurants can't be wrong

Your search for a great butcher is over

Enjoy restaurant quality meat at home, with brilliant produce and easy online ordering

http://www.vicsmeat.com.au

Meat this good should be impossible to find

Australia's Number 1 Meat Company 10 Merchant Street Mascot NSW 2020 Australia
P: 02 9317 6900 F: 02 9667 3048 W: www.vicsmeat.com.au E: info@vicsmeat.com.au

First Class Restaurants & Modern Kitchens

choose wine storage cabinets by

Transtherm & Vintec

Six Transtherm Reserve multi-temp cabinets, in situ at Forty One Restaurant, Chifley Tower, Sydney

Cabinets available for storing, serving and ageing. 40 bottles - 3,900 bottle capacity

VINTEC 190SGE
Single-zone / multi-zone

Transtherm Australia
210 Crown Street Darlinghurst NSW 2010
Tel: 02 9360 3199 or **1800 666 778**
Fax: 02 9360 2411
email: sales@transtherm.com.au
New Zealand Agent | Toll Free: 0800 550020
www.transtherm.com.au | www.vintec.com.au

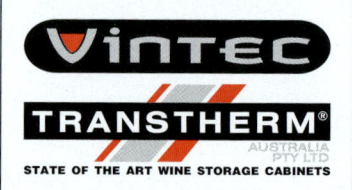

STATE OF THE ART WINE STORAGE CABINETS

provedores

FOOD STORES

Best Value Supermarket
Shop 32, Old Town Centre Plaza, Bankstown
Tel 9708 2288
Wide aisles, fruit and veg out the front, Chinese olives and pickles down the middle, and the complete array of groceries everywhere else in this neat store. Love the funky biscuit tins.

David Jones Foodhall
Westfield, 500 Oxford Street, Bondi Junction
Tel 9619 1111
65–77 Market Street, City
Tel 9266 5544
Revamped to look like the epitome of cool, this ode to eating remains the benchmark food store. As well as everything for everyday eating and the dinner party, it looks brilliant at Easter and Christmas.

Deli Cucina
Shop 18, Eastpoint Food Fair,
235 New South Head Road, Edgecliff
Tel 9328 0399
Shop 38, 52 President Avenue, Caringbah
Tel 9531 0377
This up-market food store with an eye for the organic, the gourmet and the taste-tempting has been so successful that it has opened a sister, complete with cafe, at Caringbah.

De'lish
340 Pacific Highway, Lindfield
Tel 9416 5916
A full-on deli with excellent cheese and smallgoods. Good cakes (try the orange syrup) and restaurant-quality prepared meals raise this smart shop into the food store stakes.

The Essential Ingredient
4–6 Australia Street, Camperdown
Tel 9550 5477
A warehouse of equipment, speciality food products (their own brand is very good), books and tableware. Don't expect great service but go for the new imports and the serious sales.

Food Stuff Mona Vale
9/11 Bungan Street (off Akuna Lane), Mona Vale
Tel 9999 3033
With its marshmallows from France, paella dishes from Spain and the most beautiful yellow polenta, this fine food emporium has impeccable knowledge and cooking classes.

Good Luck Supermarket
12/90 The Crescent, Homebush West
Tel 9746 2636
A large, airy warehouse space filled with all the usual products, but most of the fresh produce (note the sugar cane) comes directly from the growers, and the selection of 'chois' (leafy vegetables) would be hard to beat.

The Health Emporium
263–265 Bondi Road, Bondi
Tel 9365 6008
More proof that gourmet can be good for you. Organic fruit and vegetables, plus a coffee and juice bar, good breads, and specialities like Japanese cooking ingredients and a range of gourmet salts.

Herbies Spices
745 Darling Street, Rozelle
Tel 9555 6035
This is spice central: the best and only place in town to get the spices and herbs for every cuisine. Five grades and kinds of peppercorns, exotic spice blends, all sourced directly. Try mail order if you're out of town.

Hurstville Asian Supermarket
127 Forest Road, Hurstville
Tel 9580 3650
A well-lit and ordered stockist of everything pan-Asian from the fresh (greens and noodles) to the frozen (myriad buns, balls, dim sum and dumplings). Check out the tubs of pickled green mustard.

jones the grocer
68 Moncur Street, Woollahra
Tel 9362 1222
Cookbooks and communal tables for a light lunch and a latte, an impressive cheese room and loads of gourmet products, from chocolates and charcuterie to rices and tarts that will liven up any meal. And a coffee haven.

Lamonica IGA
155 Ramsay Street, Haberfield
Tel 9798 4105
A bright Italian supermarket. The deli has wedges of cheese and metres of smallgoods, the shelves groan with sauces, pasta and coffee, while the butchery does capretto (baby goat) and veal in season.

provedores

Macro Wholefoods
13–19 Willoughby Road, Crow's Nest
Tel 9004 1240
31–37 Oxford Street, Bondi Junction
Tel 9389 7611
A healthy pulse beating at the heart of Sydney's gourmet scene. These amazing organics emporia carry an impressive selection of yoghurts and breads, and serve up a chic cafe.

Norton Street Grocer
Norton Plaza, 51 Norton Street, Leichhardt
Tel 9572 7511
Shop 1027, Westfield, 500 Oxford Street, Bondi Junction
Tel 9386 5800
Is it a great greengrocer or a fine food store? The smallgoods and cheeses are beautifully judged and handled, the Italian products are so tempting – oh, and the fruit and veg are pretty good, too.

Oriental and Continental Foods
43 Carlotta Street, Artarmon
Tel 9906 8990
Primarily Middle Eastern but with a touch of Greek, Armenian and Turkish, this glass and concrete warehouse has a good selection of rices, olive oil, pulses, wheels of cheeses and exotics.

Orion Continental Foods
327 Penshurst Street, Willoughby
Tel 9417 5493
From barley to burghul and bulk pulses and grains, this is another shop where you'll find everything for every kind of Middle Eastern recipe and then some products you've never heard of. Friendly staff.

Provedore Pelagio
235 Victoria Street, Darlinghurst
Tel 9360 1011
A rustic-looking, groovy store with a huge array of quality produce, from pasta and organic meat to artisan breads and a tempting deli counter. It comes at a price. Come Christmas, the floor is piled high with treats. Good coffee is served too.

Randwick Oriental Supermarket
57–63 Belmore Road, Randwick
Tel 9398 2192
Thai, Indonesian, Japanese, Chinese and Korean ingredients in bright, revamped surroundings. The fresh greens are exceptional and we love the gourmet Asian ice-creams. There's a Western section, too.

Simon Johnson Purveyor of Quality Foods
Shop 6, 100 Edinburgh Road, Castlecrag
Tel 9967 9411
181 Harris Street, Pyrmont
Tel 9552 2522
55 Queen Street, Woollahra
Tel 9328 6888
Each store has the signature fromagerie: a serious offering of fragrant farmhouse cheeses from across the globe. There is also a superb selection of oils and chocolates, vinegars and teas, and those little extras that elevate home cooking. Ask them anything – staff knowledge is exceptional, and there's always an interesting cooking class coming up.

Tokyo Mart
Shop 27, Northbridge Plaza,
83–113 Sailors Bay Road, Northbridge
Tel 9958 6860
Mysterious and miraculous Japanese delicacies. Aisles full of noodles and shoyu (Japanese soy sauce), seaweed and bowls and pots, takeaway sashimi and sushi made on the spot, and those sweeties.

provedores

DELIS

Arena's L'Antipasto Deli
908 Military Road, Mosman
Tel 9969 9905
Ah, the smell of polpettone (meatballs), the sticks of homemade grissini, the fine Sicilian olive oils. Mainly Italian yes, but also lots of the Sydney specialities you'd expect.

Blackwattle Deli
Shop 8a, Sydney Fish Market, Bank Street, Pyrmont
Tel 9552 3591
Choice, choice and more choice. It's almost overwhelming here. Cheeses, Australian olive oils, butters, imported biscuits and a good supply of every kitchen basic.

Con's Beecroft Village Delicatessen
Shop 4, 5 Wongala Crescent, Beecroft
Tel 9484 7618
This tiny shop is crammed with cheese, smallgoods and gourmet lines, plus the bonus of lots of their own cooking, from antipasto through casseroles and quiches to pies and tarts.

Cyril's Delicatessen
181 Hay Street, Haymarket
Tel 9211 0994
Piroshki. Smoked trout. Kaiserfleisch. Corn-fed ducks. Spanish quince paste. The art of good living, modern meets mittel-European style, comes together in this institution. A must visit.

Four Olives Deli
4–8 Darley Road, Manly
Tel 9977 4611
Very Italian, mostly Australian in this bright, snazzy interior with products from Umbria to the Riverina and a cafe where you can sample the risotto and lasagne made by the in-house chef.

Lamia Foods
278 Marrickville Road, Marrickville
Tel 9560 2440
Greek at heart but meeting the Sydney challenge with Italian, Lebanese and, good heavens, Estonian products. Fetta, bacalao, broad beans, you get the drift.

Morgan's Fine Foods
Shop 9, 9 Bungan Street, Mona Vale
Tel 9997 4431
A dozen different olives, good charcuterie, a splendid cheese board and excellent takeaway dishes. The wall of confectionery is mouth-watering.

Queen Street Deli
142 Queen Street, Woollahra
Tel 9328 7121
It's hard to believe how much is packed in to this tiny store. Look up and you'll see products literally on the rafters. The new, the seasonal and the essential are always in stock.

Raineri's Continental Delicatessen
97 Great North Road, Five Dock
Tel 9713 6886
Italian down to its soap powder. Ham cut perfectly, Vecchiet salami, good antipasto ingredients, olives and a wall of dried pasta – not to mention the old ladies in black – make this deli a shopping experience.

Russki's Deli
131 Bondi Road, Bondi
Tel 9387 6313
Local Russians come here for dried fish and the famous pashka (moulded cheese dessert), but there are also other traditional European deli offerings from charcuterie to dips and dry goods.

provedores

BUTCHERS

AC Butchery
174 Marion Street, Leichhardt
Tel 9569 8687
Shop 15 Norton Plaza, 51 Norton Street, Leichhardt
Tel 9550 9030
22 Plumer Road, Rose Bay
Tel 9363 4971
Shop 9, 19 World Square Centre,
George Street, Sydney
Tel 9264 1414
Four locations for famous Italian smallgoods (prosciutto, pancetta, bresaola), sausages, organic meats, goat and game. The veal and pork mince cannot be bettered; true believers visit the Marion Street original.

Emperor's Garden Meat Market
211 Thomas Street, Haymarket
Tel 9281 2206
The selection of pork cuts beggars belief but there is also a good selection of lamb, less beef, and an amazing range of game, farmed and wild. Soup balls and tofu are in the fridge.

Hummerston's Gourmet Meats
225 Burns Bay Road, Lane Cove West
Tel 9427 1983
Big on value-added if you can't be bothered thinking about cooking too much – the butterflied marinated boneless chickens and seasoned lamb fly out the door – and prepared cuts, with smoked smallgoods and sausages.

Iseli Butcher
Shop T235, Centro Bankstown Shopping Centre,
Frederick Street, Bankstown
Tel 9709 5342
People travel from the northern beaches to bag their traditional cuts of pork from this Swiss–German–middle-European butcher. A full range of salame, sausages and smoked goods.

Penny's Quality Butcher
Shop 2, 18 Bungan Street, Mona Vale
Tel 9997 1581
880 Military Road, Mosman
Tel 9969 3372
Quaintly and thoughtfully decorated, with aged beef, an impressive range of game and prepared cuts that will make you never want to marinate again. Service is cheery if lacking in product knowledge.

Pino's Dolce Vita and Fine Foods
45 President Avenue, Kogarah
Tel 9587 4818
The shop has been enlarged and enhanced and has changed its name, but salame are still an art form. The same goes for the prosciutto, the sausages and every pork product from this classy Italian butcher. But now you can also get fresh pasta, biscotti, and cheeses – and sit down in the cafe.

Sam the Butcher
129 Bondi Road, Bondi
Tel 9389 1420
371 Rocky Point Road, Sans Souci
Tel 9583 1144
3–5 Wongala Crescent, Beecroft
Tel 9484 7138
296 Willoughby Road, Naremburn
Tel 9437 1090
Organic meat shops that will tempt the most hardened vegetarian. Great range of sausages (gourmet and organic), charcuterie (organic prosciutto and duck confit, for instance), organic beef, lamb, pork and poultry. Check out the nifty on-line shop, too.

Terry Wright Gourmet Meats
32 Clovelly Road, Randwick
Tel 9398 1038
Restaurant-quality meat from all over Australia, featuring White Rocks veal from Western Australia, Flinders Island lamb from Tasmania and Barossa chickens from South Australia. Wagyu beef is a speciality and there are top-quality condiments, trout and charcuterie.

TJ's Quality Meats
319 Darling Street, Balmain
Tel 9810 2911
Highly organic and highly principled, this conscientious butcher has Kangaroo Island chickens, Bangalow pork and biodynamic lamb. Oh, and good snags, too.

provedores

GREENGROCERS

Antico's Northbridge Fruit World
Shop 24, Northbridge Plaza,
83–113 Sailors Bay Road, Northbridge
Tel 9958 4725
Fresh sugar cane and horseradish. Pandan leaves and kaffir limes. This place stocks the ultimate range in fresh chillies – more than a dozen varieties.

Emile's Fruit & Vegetables
321 Darling Street, Balmain
Tel 9810 2759
Eccentric and excellent. Liberally festooned with chillies and garlic, with everything you'd want for a basic or a grand meal either on display or out the back – that's where the great tomatoes are.

FJ Galluzzo & Sons
187 Glebe Point Road, Glebe
Tel 9660 2114
Looks entrenched and it is. But it also stocks much more than your average greengrocer, offering Italian favourites, including wild mushrooms, ox-heart tomatoes in season and designer figs.

Frank's Fruit Market
94 Ramsay Street, Haberfield
Tel 9798 6388
Tomatoes are the speciality here, along with broccolini, baby artichokes, excellent melanzane and turnip tops. Very Italian, very family and very quick to offer advice and a recipe or two.

Fratelli Fresh
7 Danks Street, Waterloo
Tel 1300 552 119
Wholesale meets retail as this restaurant supplier crates up first-quality fruit and vegies to the public at remarkable prices. There are also fabulous Italian cheeses, imported pasta, olive oils and other Italian goodies and a cafe upstairs (see Café Sopra in main section).

Fruit Ezy
Shop L7G, Chatswood Chase, 345 Victoria Avenue, Chatswood
Tel 9411 5367
Modern, brilliant lighting and fine fruit and veg in wide aisles, with consistently good quality and the odd surprise now and then.

Martelli's Fruit Market
Shop 28, Cherrybrook Shopping Village, Shepherds Drive, Cherrybrook
Tel 9481 0444
101 Carlingford Road, West Epping
Tel 9868 2531
Both stores, one in a 1970s architect-designed barn in Epping, the other in the revamped Cherrybrook Shopping Centre, have amazingly good produce at amazingly reasonable prices. You'll find every exotic and new product – and the house-made soups are a bonus.

Parisi's
15 Dover Road, Rose Bay
Tel 9371 0870
One of the originals and still a good operation in its long hangar space, with the pick of seasonal fruit, the latest new products and good mark-downs.

Pontip
16 Campbell Street, Haymarket
Tel 9211 2208
If this amazing specialist in Thai and Asian fruit and vegetables were in New York or Paris, it would be a sensation. And it is here, too. Pandan leaves or banana blossoms anyone?

Ripe Grocer
8 Bungan Street, Mona Vale
Tel 9999 6899
Quite simply, a gem of a store. The best-looking shop and produce in the area and a very strong contender for the best in Sydney. Unbelievably friendly and helpful.

provedores

BAKERS

Abla Pastry
48 Railway Parade, Granville
Tel 9637 8092
Just to confuse matters, there is also Abla at Merrylands and Dulwich Hill. All are good but Granville is grand with mountains of syrupy pastry and the excellent za'atar croissant.

Bowan Island
183 Victoria Road, Drummoyne
Tel 9181 3524
Sourdough is the mother culture here, literally. But you'll also find Turkish bread, Italian style, yeast-free, rolls and muffins. Widely distributed, and deservedly so.

Brasserie Bread
1737 Botany Road, Botany
Tel 9666 6845
Sourdough batard, organic rye, olive and rosemary, ciabatta, sour cherry, walnut and fig are just some of the wonderful breads on offer. Go Thurs–Sat for the caramelised garlic bread.

Haberfield Bakery
153 Ramsay Street, Haberfield
Tel 9797 7715
Italians and spongy bread lovers swear by their crusty ciabatta and crunchy pane di casa, the gentle focaccia and the excellent panini. They also do pasta and roast coffee. Bella.

Infinity Sourdough
225 Victoria Street, Darlinghurst
Tel 9380 4320
The sourdough of choice for many of Sydney's top restaurants. This small outlet offers speciality breads, great pastries, raisin and walnut buns, shortbreads and divine seasonal fruit jams.

La Gerbe d'Or
255 Glenmore Road, Paddington
Tel 9331 1070
Three of our favourite French words describe this tiny Paddo institution: *pâtisserie*, *boulangerie*, *traiteur*. Wonderful for traditional country breads and now with a bistro menu, coffee and tables.

Pasticceria Papa
145 Ramsay Street, Haberfield
Tel 9798 6894
It's always a toss up between this and Sulfaro as the maestro of Italian pasticce but we plump for the babas, the sensational panzarotti and that dolce vita feeling of Roma in the caffe.

Sonoma
215A Glebe Point Road, Glebe
Tel 9660 2116
Spelt is the hot loaf in this bakery and cafe. The extensive range, sold throughout Sydney, includes fruit spelt, olive bread, walnut and raisin, soy and linseed, and country white, an organic sourdough. The addictive granola is still toasted in a wood-fired oven.

Victoire
285 Darling Street, Balmain
Tel 9818 5529
For many, the benchmark baguette, croissant, sourdough and fougasse. The tartes are terrific, and the walnut bread beckons nuts – sorry, fans – from far and wide.

Wellington Cake Shop
157 Bondi Road, Bondi
Tel 9389 4555
For kugelhopf and ponchkes (jam-filled doughntus), poppyseed cake and cheesecake, this little slice of Jewish Hungarian can't be bettered. There's house-made ice-cream, too.

provedores

FISH

Christie's Seafoods
Shop 1, Market Arcade, Sydney Fish Market,
Bank Street, Pyrmont
Tel 9552 3333
The oyster kings of the market with a fabulous cook-to-order cafe and pristine crustaceans. The mud crab often never makes it out the door, just into a sizzling wok.

Claudio's Quality Seafoods
Shop 29, Sydney Fish Market, Bank Street, Pyrmont
Tel 9660 5188
It's hard to pick among all the offerings at the market, but this retailer consistently wins the awards, with a personality all its own and stand-out seafood.

Demcos
Unit 34, 566 Gardeners Road, Alexandria
Tel 9700 9000
It may look like takeaway at the front but out the back is the serious business. Ring a day ahead and you can score amazing sea scallops, sweet crabmeat and everything else that Sydney's top restaurants put on their menus.

Haymarket Seafoods
1st floor, Market City, 9–13 Hay Street, Haymarket
Tel 9211 7858
Among the discount clothes is this vibrant spick-and-span shop. The clientele is mainly Asian, so it's big on whole fish and tanks of live silver and jade perch, but they will happily fillet for you.

Peter Michaels Seafood at Cronulla
47 The Kingsway, Cronulla
Tel 9544 0033
Prawns are a speciality here but everything is market-fresh, every morning. The selection is good and whole fish sell as well as fillets.

Sydney Fish Market
Bank Street, Pyrmont
Tel 9660 1611
Seven days 7.30am–4pm
Energy, atmosphere and your choice of the best that the ocean has to offer. Browse among half a dozen fine fishmongers, then shop at the deli (*see* Blackwattle Deli), greengrocer, little homewares shop and, of course, the bottleshop.

FARMERS' MARKETS

Farmers' Market
The Entertainment Quarter, Lang Road, Moore Park
Tel 9383 4163
Wed & Sat 10am–4pm
Among the gift stalls and the manufactured goodies, this friendly market is still a great way to get to growers of herbs and vegetables, artisan bread and farm-fresh eggs – and avoid those supermarket aisles.

Good Living Growers Market
Pyrmont Bay Park (opp Star City Casino)
Tel 9282 3603
First Sat of the month (except Jan) 7–11am
A fete of food with a waterside location and not a craft stall in sight. You can fill your basket with restaurant buzz names such as Mandagery Creek venison, Mandalong lamb, Willowbrae cheese, Jannei goat's cheese, Eumundi smokehouse smallgoods and more.

Northside Produce Market
Civic Park, 200 Miller Street, (between McLaren and Ridge streets), North Sydney
Tel: 9922 2299
Third Sat of the month, 8am–noon
A village market that winds its way through a park. It makes no claim to be a farmers' market that sells only produce direct from the farm, but much of what is on offer is locally made and grown.

Sydney Fresh Food Market
D Shed, Sydney Markets, 250–318 Parramatta Road, Flemington,
Tel 9325 6200
Sat 6am–2pm
You need to experience the abundance and bustle of this huge growers' market once in your life. Local market gardeners bring just-pulled produce and wholesalers come in to sell off surplus, too.

provedores

WINE STORES
WITH HUON HOOKE

Annandale Cellars
119 Johnston Street, Annandale
Tel 9660 1947
Walk into this reborn shop and you sense that the proprietors are dedicated and enthusiastic. Their special passion is for pinot noir, and New Zealand is strongly represented.

Best Cellars
91 Crown Street, East Sydney
Tel 9361 3733
A small but expertly staffed shop, where good advice and passion are always on hand. New Zealand wines are a speciality, with a huge annual Kiwi tasting.

Dan Murphy's
350–360 Liverpool Road, South Strathfield
Tel 1300 723 388
An impressively vast, smart-looking shop, groaning with the weight of a massive range of wine, including some remarkably good-value exclusive imports such as Zonin (Italy), Dopff au Moulin (Alsace) and Carpineto (Tuscany). Staffing isn't a strong point.

Five Way Cellars
4 Heeley Street, Paddington
Tel 9360 4242
A tiny, terrace-house shop stuffed to the ceiling with exciting, cutting-edge wines from far and wide. They sell what they like best, and their enthusiasm will infect you. Boutique wines from the cooler climes and Italian imports are specialities.

George's Fine Wines
37 Willoughby Road, Crows Nest
Tel 9438 1352
Together with Jim's Cellars (formerly George's Liquor Nest, at 95 Willoughby Road, Tel 9437 6688), the Georges family have sewn up good grog retailing in this street. This shop is more up-market; Jim's has the bigger range.

Kemeny's
137–147 Bondi Road, Bondi
Tel 13 88 81
Combines a large range with great prices in a big bustling store. Excellent newsletter, and their many deals are well publicised in advertising. Some interesting, quirky imports, including South Africa and Alsace.

North Sydney Cellars
Shop 4, 105 Miller Street, North Sydney
Tel 9954 0090
Helpful advice from keen, young staff. Small but attractive shop with an active tastings calendar and a well-designed price list/newsletter.

Palm Beach Wine Co.
1109 Barrenjoey Road, Palm Beach
Tel 9974 4304
Great range of French wines; a very personal selection of local Australian and imported, especially obscure but exciting, small-output wines. Gourmet foodstuffs, too.

Ultimo Wine Centre
99 Jones Street, Ultimo
Tel 9211 2380.
A treasure trove of wine! Imports are the speciality, from the famous to the downright obscure, many of which they bring in themselves. Large floor area is covered in cut-cases and shelves. A visit here is an absorbing experience. Good advice is plentiful.

Vintage Cellars Double Bay
396 New South Head Road, Double Bay
Tel 9327 1333
The flagship store in the VC group, staffed by knowledgeable pros who are passionate about fine wine. Imports are a speciality, with lots of French and Italian and the locals can drink a different champagne every day of the month. See also the VC stores in Mosman and Leichhardt.

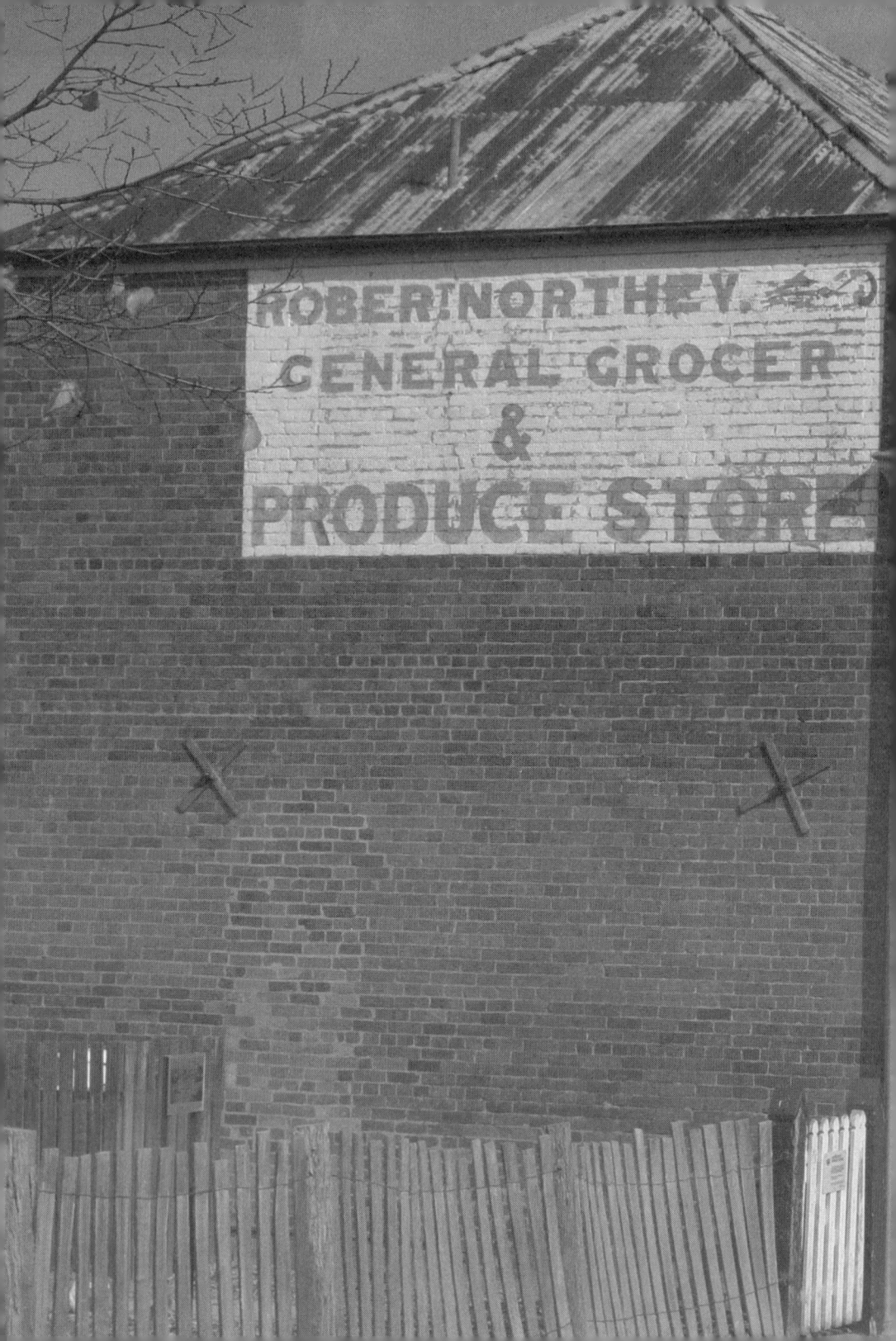

REGIONAL

Blue Mountains 176

Canberra & Snow Regions 184

Hunter Valley 199

Central Coast & Newcastle 208

South Coast 218

Southern Highlands 229

North Coast 236

The West 248

regional

BLUE MOUNTAINS

JAMES MAYSON, SALLY WEBB & SIMON THOMSEN

A food lover's destination just 90 minutes from the city, the Mountains enjoy perfectly cool conditions for stone fruit, pears and apples, while a warm welcome is afforded by the crackling log fires. They're a busy mob up here – poke your head around and you'll find an artisan bakery and fantastic delis and cafes packed with local preserves and homemade jams and serving up old-school Devonshire teas. As a gateway to the vast agricultural lands beyond, the Mountains act like a weather vane for seasonal produce, so when you do head back to the Big Smoke, remember to fill the boot with the bounty of the orchards from a trip down the Bells Line of Road. While the surge of Sydney hordes, tour buses and Sunday-afternoon traffic jams continues to swell, there's still a slower pace enveloping the mountains like ethereal morning mist. The freedom to 'take the time' is mirrored in the cooking – slow braises, fall-apart roasts and succulent game are the perfect accompaniment to bristling evenings. Keep an eye out for forest mushrooms around autumn, local berries, cider vinegar and fresh apple juice, walnuts, chestnuts and sensational sourdough.

But food's not the only attraction for three million visitors annually. Savour the stunning vistas and gorgeous bushwalks, the plethora of galleries, the antique and bric-a-brac emporiums, vintage bookshops and a rich saga of indigenous history and culture (Tel 4787 8877 for details). If Ye Olde Worlde is ye thing, stop by the art deco edifices of Katoomba's legendary Paragon Café (Tel 4782 2928) for handcrafted chocolates; clink glasses of bubbly to toast the unrivalled views of the Megalong Valley at the Hydro Majestic (Tel 4788 1002); or step into the time warp of high tea at the Carrington Hotel (Tel 4782 1111).

The Blackheath Festival (see *Provedores*) is a celebration of the region's produce, while those who can't wait for Christmas head to the hills for a mid-winter Yuletide. Whenever you come, there's still plenty of space to enjoy and reflect on in this World Heritage gem.

Ashcrofts

18 Govetts Leap Road, Blackheath
Tel 4787 8297   Map 11

Contemporary

Score 14/20

This unassuming shopfront eatery in the heart of the Blackheath strip eschews designer trends, with its clunky metal chairs and somewhat dated fabrics. Corinne Evatt's menu, however, is anything but dated, featuring a strong understanding of seasonal produce and flavours, and inspired dishes with a few surprises. Crisp filo encases Milawa black ash goat's cheese in a rich and flavoursome strudel accompanied by a smoky capsicum coulis. Deep-fried silken tofu cubes are encrusted with za'atar, then dressed with 'firestorm' oil (infused with a concoction of peppers and chilli), and served with both a green garlic aïoli and a piquant sweet chilli and pickled ginger sauce. Comfort food goes up-market with sublimely tender slices of pickled pork on creamy mash, a delicate mustard sauce (made from the pickling juices) completing the dish. Desserts are hearty 'get hiking' fare. Try the not-too-sweet baked vanilla bean custard topped with a 'fascinator' of spun sugar; it's a delicately balanced crowd pleaser and a flamboyant finale.

Hours Lunch Sun noon–2.30pm; Dinner Wed–Sun 6–9pm
Bill E $15–$24 **M** $29–$34 **D** $12–$15
Cards AE BC DC MC V Eftpos; bookings essential
Wine Short, well-selected list spanning popular Oz/NZ styles and regions; 7 by the glass; BYO (corkage $4 pp)
Chef Corinne Evatt
Owners Mary-Jane Craig & Corinne Evatt
Seats 44
www.ashcrofts.com
And...pick the eminent Aussies in Graham McCarter's fabulous photographs

Blue Mountains

Collits Inn ★

Hartley Vale Road, Hartley Vale
Tel 6355 2072   Map 11

French

Score 16/20

Best Regional Restaurant

The rich history of this restored 1823 staging inn at the mountain foothills seeps from every pore of the whitewashed walls. It'd be nice if the present could reach back into the past to let former convict Pierce Collits know his creation has turned out just fine. Sitting at an old timber table on the rug-strewn heavy floorboards, he'd thrill to the earthy sophistication of Laurent Deslandes' provincial French cooking. The trio of pork is a time-worn lesson in classic technique, from cheek that yields softly on the tongue to pressed head and lush, pastry-wrapped hock. Cured trout and potato tart, with horseradish cream and parmesan, is both frisky and grounded. Juicy Mt Tomah chook is heady with North African spices in a vegetable broth. Succulent blue-eye lolls across a clever United Nations of plump gnocchi, shiitake, English spinach and herby provençale sauce. Blueberries in a seductively spicy red wine syrup with ice-cream; or pear and chocolate charlotte with Poire William sorbet only adds to the delight.

Hours Lunch Fri–Sun noon–3pm; Dinner Thurs–Sun 6–10pm

Bill 2 courses $60 pp; 3 courses $70 pp; 10% surcharge on public holidays

Cards AE BC MC V Eftpos

Wine Short, smart mix of boutique; 6 by the glass; BYO Thurs–Fri (corkage $8.50 per bottle)

Chef Laurent Deslandes

Owners Laurent Deslandes & Cyrillia van der Merwe

Seats 44; private rooms; wheelchair access; outdoor seats

www.collitsinn.com.au

And...stay in the historic old rooms and go for a walk to the old graveyard

Darley's

Lilianfels Resort & Spa, Lilianfels Avenue, Katoomba
Tel 4780 1200   Map 11

Contemporary

Score 15/20

Governor Darley would be impressed. His former summer residence, built in 1889, is now the Lilianfels-owned, heritage-listed home to former Milsons chef Hugh Whitehouse – and all the better for it. The grand old rooms retain their former glory and the deck is now enclosed and heated, making it perfect for all-year-round Sunday lunches with a view. Darley would love the comfortable blend of provincial food and city sophistication on the plate. It could be pork hock and barley soup, with croutons spooned in at the table. It could be the most amazing pot-roasted pheasant with parsnip purée and wild mushrooms. Whitehouse's quail tortellini should be a lesson in perfect pasta making for all his try-hard city counterparts. The citrus tart is a suitably runny curd finish. Amiable staff know their stuff, so quiz them on the excellent cheese board and the (smaller than it was, but...) well-selected wine list. Then have a port and toast the guv'nor.

Hours Lunch Sun noon–2.30pm; Dinner Tues–Sat 6.30–9.15pm

Bill 2/3 courses $68/$88 pp; 6-course tasting menu $120 pp; 10% surcharge on public holidays

Cards AE BC DC MC V Eftpos; bookings essential

Wine Wise, wide-ranging and perfect for the food; 13 by the glass

Chef Hugh Whitehouse

Owner Orient-Express

Seats 80; private rooms

www.lilianfels.com.au

And...they have a separate vegetarian menu if you ask

regional

Dry Dock
54 Waratah Street, Katoomba
Tel 4782 7902   Map 11

Seafood

Score 12/20

This tiny mountain legend is a study in simplicity and dedication. Randi Svensen, a descendant of Sydney's Halvorsen boat-building family, has brine for blood – and plenty of petrol in her tank, travelling 1000 kilometres weekly in daily trips to the Sydney fish markets for spanking fresh fish to enjoy for a fraction of the price you'd pay closer to the sea. Whimsy, luck and generosity might see whole mud crab with dill mayo for $35 on the daily menu. The small blue room is a sailor's cabin of oceanic paraphernalia. The menu is DIY: for entrée, make a platter with as many Sydney rock oysters, grilled Tassie scallops covered in a crab mornay (perhaps not), BBQ prawns and fat, satisfying prawn and chicken spring rolls as fancy incites. Then choose from a handful of fish: perhaps silver dory, griddle-cooked, with lemon butter, accompanied by boiled new potatoes or great big fat fries. There's even steak and house-made pasta if you really, honestly must – but why deprive Randi of tomorrow's seaside adventure?

Hours Dinner Mon–Sat from 5.30pm
Bill E $13–$17 **M** $19–$27.50 **D** $12.95
Cards AE BC MC V
Wine Well-priced but limited list; 7 by the glass; BYO (corkage $2 pp)
Chef James Rickards
Owners James Rickards & Randi Svensen
Seats 20
And...there's an $18.50 special if you arrive before 6.30pm

Lochiel House
1259 Bells Line of Road, Kurrajong Heights
Tel 4567 7754   Map 11

Contemporary

Score 15/20

This 1825 homestead is an original pioneer port of call for fit and fine lodging. Little has altered, although the winds of change have delivered a revolution in flavours to this character-laced, wonky wooden building with its floorboards worn shiny. By day, relax with an additional (and affordable) chalkboard menu in the sun-soaked courtyard surrounded by a well-tended garden that invites contemplation under the dappled light of a jacaranda. By night, wax romantic by the log fires. House-made potato bread arrives with truffle and porcini butter. A mixed entrée plate has incredible mousse-like duck liver pâté, a terrine of roasted capsicum, eggplant and goat's cheese, and juicy chargrilled quail crowned with guava sauce and fresh herbs. Son-in-law eggs are deep-fried, yolk-soft wonders among a fresh herb and peanut salad. Mains introduce clever twists to time-honoured classics: Chinese red-roast pigeon with peaches and barley, and 'humble' chicken and leek pie in feather-light pastry with seeded mustard asparagus.

Hours Lunch Thurs–Fri 11am–3pm, Sat 10am–3pm, Sun 10am–4pm; Dinner Thurs–Sat 6–9pm
Bill E $16.50 **M** $28–$35 **D** $11.50; 12% surcharge on public holidays
Cards BC MC V Eftpos
Wine Well-crafted, wide-ranging Aussie list with several European highlights; 10 by the glass; BYO (corkage $4 pp)
Chefs/owners Monique Maul & Anthony Milroy
Seats 40; private room; wheelchair access; outdoor seats
And...don't miss the chocolate lava pudding with orange curd ice-cream

Blue Mountains

Mes Amis

The Old Church, Cnr Waratah & Lurline Streets, Katoomba
Tel 4782 1558   Map 11

French
Score 14/20

In a converted corner church, chef Stephane Stanisic is preaching a passionate doctrine of contemporary French fare, utilising quality produce with (mostly) outstanding results. Service from partner Effie is unhurried and professional, smoothing over the occasional extended hiatus between courses. As befits its former use, the cavernous, candle-lit space, with its towering wood-panelled ceiling, is suitable for quiet reflection and perhaps just a few hushed prayers of thanks as the food arrives. A year down the track, Stanisic is back on song: these are clever, thought-provoking flavours that remain sympathetic to the ingredients. Scallop ravioli with prawns, in a remarkable tarragon broth, has intense crustacean flavour. Crisp-skinned deep-sea bass with kipfler potatoes, in vanilla and Earl Grey broth, is delicate and mouth-watering. Prosciutto-wrapped crépinette of lamb with goat's cheese is earthy and rustic, served with a mound of ratatouille and perhaps a somewhat superfluous parmesan–almond tuile. Plum tart with chocolate hazelnut shortcrust and vanilla bean ice-cream is sure to convert the tired and the hungry.

Hours Dinner Wed–Sun from 6pm
Bill E $15.50–$17.50 **M** $23.50–$29.50 **D** $12.50–$15; dégustation $85 pp; 10% surcharge on Sundays and public holidays
Cards AE BC MC V
Wine Concise, quality mix; a page for high rollers; 13 by the glass; BYO (corkage $4.50 pp)
Chef Stephane Stanisic
Owners Stephane & Effie Stanisic
Seats 60; wheelchair access
www.mesamis.com.au
And...dégustation including foie gras for $85 pp

Restaurant Como

134 Great Western Highway (access via carpark on Hope Street), Blaxland
Tel 4739 8555   Map 11

Contemporary
Score 13/20

What a joy to discover, in a backstreet mall, a fresh young team putting out inventive food with equal amounts of passion and enthusiasm. Prodigal Blaxland couple Grant Farrant and Rachel McNabb have returned to open a simple fine diner with sparkling fervour. A seafood tasting plate offers bouncy-fresh prawns with rocket aïoli, Danish fetta, olives, roast capsicum, Cajun-dusted calamari (alas slightly limp) and a stand-out snapper and fennel sausage. Roast duck, atop duck-and-pork sausage, with cauliflower mash and asparagus, is well executed despite a slightly oversweet reduction. Moist snapper fillet arrives with herb-crusted kipfler potatoes and a subtle orange beurre blanc, while stuffed chicken breast with shiitake mushrooms on a vanilla risotto with demi-glace is likewise well balanced. Don't come for the décor – suburban shopping-mall-basement make-over with painted besser bricks and one of the most extraordinary clocks hanging above the faux-Federation stained glass door – but do come for sensational desserts, such as rosewater meringue with mango ice-cream.

Hours Lunch Thurs–Sat 11.30am–2pm; Dinner Wed–Sat 5.30pm–late
Bill E $14–$18 **M** $22–$30 **D** $10–$14; 10% surcharge on public holidays
Cards BC MC V Eftpos
Wine Budget-friendly list with tasting notes; 15 by the glass; BYO (corkage $5 per bottle)
Chef Grant Farrant
Owners Grant Farrant & Rachel McNabb
Seats 45
And...the menu changes monthly

regional

The Rooster
48 Merriwa Street, Katoomba
Tel 4782 1206   Map 11

European

Score 11/20

The Rooster manages that fine balance between twee and the antique pleasures of a French auberge. The lovingly restored, time-locked terrace, with its pressed-metal ceilings, art deco chandeliers, antique furniture, dried flowers and earth-and-sun-coloured walls harks from a less hurried era. The Gallic menu also veers to the classic, though not every lesson is well taught. Spot-on French onion soup gratin has a golden bubbling elephant skin of gruyère. But red onion tarte Tatin, with goat's cheese and olives, was too astringent with white balsamic. A similar fate befell a warm mussel salad (just five bivalves seemed a little stingy) with weary kipfler potatoes. Rabbit ragoût is big on flavour; seafood cassoulet is a pleasant and lighter variation; while tender veal cutlet with potato gratin and broad beans was workmanlike. Baked figs with almond cream soothes the senses, just as the gorgeous view down Jamison Valley refreshes the soul and the chatty service makes you feel at home.

Hours Dinner daily 6–10pm
Bill 2 courses $54 pp; 3 courses $68 pp
Cards AE BC DC MC V Eftpos
Wine Francophile heaven; some heavy-hitting domestic; 10 by the glass; BYO (corkage $6 pp)
Chefs Stefan & Michael Hagbeck
Owner Michael Hagbeck
Seats 95; private rooms
And…there's even a serious Lebanese red on the list

Silk's Brasserie
128 The Mall, Leura
Tel 4784 2534   Map 11

Contemporary   ♀

Score 14/20

Whoever designed the elegant interior of Silk's had a penchant for 19th-century French painting. Put a buxom *femme* behind the impressive mirrored bar, and you've got a modern version of Manet's *Bar at the Folies-Bergère*. The soaring walls of this century-old greengrocer are paint-marbled in shades of ochre and rust, with chequerboard flooring and huge vases filled with dried bamboo. There's a lot to love here: from excellent and genuinely warm service to David Waddington's home-baked tarragon and honey bread. He's been rattling the pans at Silk's for the best part of a decade, using strong technique and turning out consistently good food. A mushroom tartlet filled with an earthy button mushroom duxelle is finished off with a 'ragoût' of forest fungi – morels, chanterelles and occasionally locally gathered pines. Beautifully tender lamb loin is topped with a creamy herb mousseline. While veal and mushroom ravioli lacked finesse – plump pasta parcels swamped by an overabundance of puttanesca sauce – desserts do justice to the mountain air, with the right balance of wickedness and sophistication, as an orange and almond pudding with cardamom sauce and crème fraîche attests.

Hours Lunch daily from noon; Dinner daily from 6pm
Bill E $18–$21 **M** $26–$33 **D** $15
Cards AE BC DC MC V
Wine Interesting, extensive list with a focus on wines of the Central West; 12 by the glass
Chef David Waddington
Owner Stewart Robinson
Seats 60; wheelchair access
www.silksleura.com
And…it's a rewarding lunch after a morning's hike

Bondi Junction • Broadway • Castle Hill • Charlestown • Edgecliff

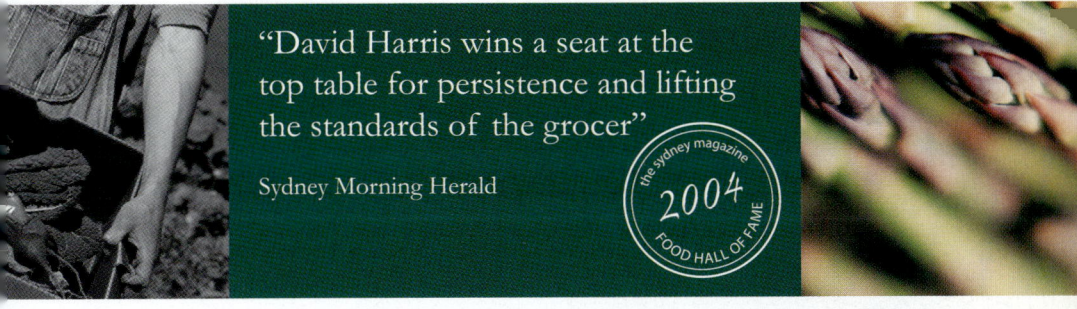

"David Harris wins a seat at the top table for persistence and lifting the standards of the grocer"

Sydney Morning Herald

the sydney magazine
2004
FOOD HALL OF FAME

Erina • Merrylands • Mosman • North Strathfield • Orange • Parramatta

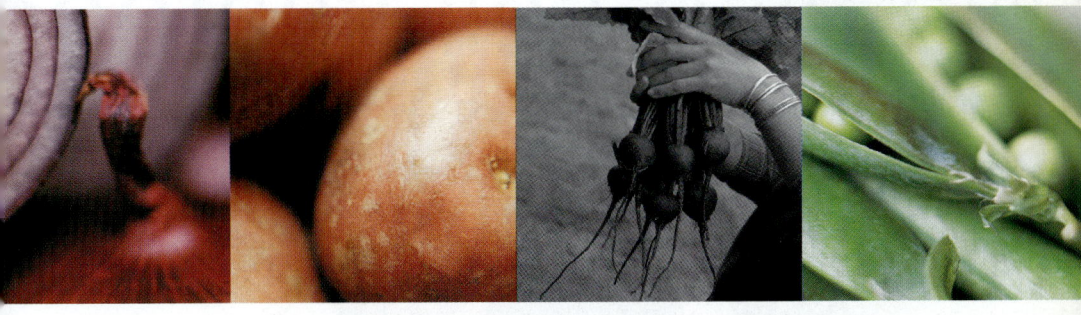

Pennant Hills • Penrith (Opening late 05) • Rhodes • St Ives • Willoughby

HARRIS FARM
MARKETS

All About Ingredients

Sydney's Premier Fresh Food Retailer
www.harrisfarm.com.au
Enquiries: 02 9746 2055

1) Chinese Noodle Soup Thin egg noodles, oriental mixed vegetables and bok choy, with shredded chicken.

2) Prawn and Bean noodles, bamboo shoots, p a coconut milk sauce.

3) Thai Basil Chicken thigh fillets with peppercorns fresh basil and chillies in a cocon

4) Cantonese Chicken Chow Cantonese dish made with Long Life noodles.

5) Lamb and Green Beans Stir-fried lamb with shredded green beans and a Hoi Sin sauce.

6) Shredded Beef Stir-fry with Crunchy Noodles Rump steak, celery, carrots and bamboo shoots with fried noodles.

7) Chilli Beef Beef strips with chopped red and green capsicum, and tomato in a Black Bean Sauce

Noodle Salad Thinly sliced coriander, basil and noodles with a fish sauce dressing.

9) Barbequed Pork Ribs with Hoi Sin Sauce Chang's version of a Chinese favourite.

10) Thai Style Prawn and Fish Curry A green curry with shredded ginger using soy, fish and sweet chilli sauce.

11) Thai Fish Cakes with Water Chestnuts Served with a Sweet Chilli Sauce.

12) Steamed Salmon Fillets with Asparagus Served with shredded ginger and black bean vinaigrette.

13) Fried Rice A traditional version with soy sauce.

14) Singapore Noodles Bean Sprouts, shredded chicken, prawns and curry powder, and rice vermicelli noodles.

For authentic Asian recipe ideas, visit our web site:
www.changs.com

CHANG'S
For authentic Asian cooking.

What's on Chang's menu tonight?

We also sell seafood

With so much great produce available it would be easy to forget!

Sydney Fish Market really is a one stop shop for all your cooking needs. With an onsite deli, bakery, fruit and veg, bottle shop, sushi bar and gift shop, the range of quality produce available is amazing. (Don't forget, we have a fantastic selection of seafood too!)

Sydney Fish Market, Bank Street, Pyrmont, Sydney NSW 2009
Call us **02 9004 1100** or visit **www.sydneyfishmarket.com.au**

Blue Mountains

Solitary
90 Cliff Drive, Leura Falls
Tel 4782 1164 Map 11

Contemporary
Score 15/20

Indeed the restaurant stands alone, sentinel-like, jealously guarding its view – as you will too if you grab one of the front tables during the day. At night, the coffee-coloured rooms, with mustard-painted floorboards in one room and chocolate-coloured carpet in another, give warmth to this charming Blue Mountains classic. The service too must be polished because you hardly notice it's there, although it's always at hand to answer a question or pre-empt a request. Bangalow sweet pork with creamy tuna mayonnaise and shaved parmesan is an interesting take on vitello tonnato. Snapper tartare with Clarence River prawns virtually jumps off the plate with freshness – but alarmingly an orange–wasabi glaze was so jarringly bitter it ruined the dish. Mains such as roast lamb rump with sweet potato and salsa verde boast simple, beautifully clean flavours, as does the chermoula-crusted barramundi with hummus and crème fraîche. Grunt and sophistication meet in angus fillet, asparagus, glazed eschalot, tomato and a seriously lip-smacking reduction.

Hours Lunch Sat–Sun noon–3pm; Dinner Wed–Sun from 6.30pm

Bill E $15.50–$21.50 **M** $25.50–$35.50 **D** $13; tasting menu 5/6 courses $79/$90 pp; 15% surcharge on public holidays

Cards AE BC DC MC V Eftpos

Wine Sensational list, matched to dishes; good stickies; 12 by the glass

Chef John Cross

Owners Georgia Shepherd & John Cross

Seats 65; private room

www.solitary.com.au

And... the 1913 kiosk was originally built for visitors to the Leura Cascades picnic grounds (back then the Leura Baths)

Solitary Kiosk
90 Cliff Drive, Leura Falls
Tel 4782 1164 Map 11

Contemporary
Score 13/20

Perhaps it's the mountain air or the superlative view over the Jamison Valley, but somehow Vittoria coffee tastes even better at Solitary Kiosk. There's no finer mountain place to linger over a latte. When the weather's favourable, rest your derrière on the French faux-rattan chairs outside, looking over a small landscaped garden to the magnificent view beyond. When it's colder, tuck yourself inside at a small wooden table, or even in the restaurant proper. Breakfast on feather-light ricotta hotcakes with sublime orange curd, or eggs 'en cocotte' (steamed, with piperade or mushroom jus). For lunch, enjoy a benchmark steak sarnie lifted by caramelised onions and a lively tomato relish; or a Vietnamese-style salad, with coconut-milk-poached chicken and glass noodles, beansprouts and cashews – a gorgeous combination of flavours and textures. There are scones any time of the day, indulgent ice-cream sundaes for greedy grown-ups (using Callebaut choccie), plus wicked cakes and pastries. It's simple fare, superbly executed, in one of the state's all-time amazing locations.

Hours Mon–Fri 10am–4pm; Sat–Sun & public holidays 9am–4pm

Bill Breakfast $3.50–$10.90; Lunch $8.80–$16.50; 15% surcharge on public holidays

Cards AE BC MC V Eftpos; no bookings

Wine Abbreviated version of the restaurant list; 12 by the glass

Chef John Cross

Owners Georgia Shepherd & John Cross

Seats 35; outdoor seats

www.solitary.com.au

And... plan to walk there and back from Leura or Katoomba to work up an appetite

regional

Vulcans
33 Govetts Leap Road, Blackheath
Tel 4787 6899   Map 11

Wood-fired

♛♛

Score 16/20

Many accolades have been thrust upon Phillip Searle and his Blackheath beacon of fine food, but the truth is that visiting Vulcans is a lesson in the simple splendour of a great meal. The décor may be glorified cafe – rustic, rust-coloured walls and polished-concrete floors – but the devil is in the detail. A visit to the loo, behind the 100-year-old wood-fired oven, reveals a separate kitchen where Searle sweats over the spice combinations that create the enigmas in dishes that seemingly change little over the years. The short seasonal menu is subtly whittled and honed to perfection to maintain the awe. Swoon over the signature glazed duck sausage with pickled beetroot; or fragrant spicy Thai-style broth with feather-light smoked salmon dumplings. Asian-scented pot roasts remain a specialty; as does tuna with burnt butter, mustard seeds, curry leaf and caramelised-lime dressing. The venerated chequerboard ice-cream still wows converted and virgins alike. Most restaurants follow a style; Vulcans has always created its own. Be warned and enjoy it while you can: as we go to press, the restaurant is up for sale.

Hours Lunch Fri–Sun noon–2.30pm; Dinner Fri–Sun 6–9.30pm
Bill E $19.50 **M** $32 **D** $13–$18
Cards AE BC DC MC V
Wine BYO (corkage $4 pp)
Chef Phillip Searle
Owners Phillip Searle & Barry Ross
Seats 38; outdoor seats
And...incredibly efficient service; such a finely honed team is a pure joy to watch

And also...

The Backyard Deli-Cafe
128 Main Street, Lithgow
Tel 6351 3300
The Collits Inn team runs this hard-to-find Aladdin's cave of all things gourmet. Come for a heart-starting Vittoria coffee, a gourmet hot dog or warm duck confit salad. The larder is stocked with local cheeses and preserves and the freezer with cassoulet and ice-creams.

Cafe Razz
150 Macquarie Road, Springwood
Tel 4751 7500
This is a spunky new cafe with a colourful fit-out, with an enormous outside deck. They roast their own coffee, satiate the all-day breakfast crowd, and pump out light lunches and fresh juices. At night it's tagine time.

The Elephant Bean
159 Katoomba Street, Katoomba
Tel 4782 4620
Still packing 'em in despite the increase in competition. There's always a bowl of hearty soup, vegie burgers, muffins, and fine coffee.

Fresh Espresso and Food Bar
Shop 5/181 Katoomba Street, Katoomba
Tel 4782 3602
Open for all-day breakfast and lunch with specialities of ricotta hotcakes with banana and homemade butterscotch sauce, fresh juices and homemade pies. They also roast their own coffee, which you can buy to take home.

Megalong Valley Tea Rooms
Megalong Valley Road, Megalong Valley
Tel 4787 9181
Rainforest-shrouded Megalong Road (10 km from Blackheath) descends to this rural idyll. Pink-hued tearooms offer eggs 'from the farm', organic porridge, old-fashioned milkshakes and feather-light scones. Coffee isn't a strong point.

Stockmarket Cafe
179 Leura Mall, Leura
Tel 4784 3121
Start the day with great coffee, or hot chocolate, and bacon and eggs, at this hole-in-the-wall former bakery. The welcome can be as brisk as the mountain air, but soothing soups and gourmet sarnies hit the spot.

Blue Mountains

Provedores

Bakehouse on Wentworth
105 Wentworth Street, Blackheath
Tel 4787 7255
208 Leura Mall, Leura
Tel 4784 3588
225 Macquarie Road, Springwood
Tel 4751 5788
At the flagship Blackheath shop, there are outside tables to enjoy a malty Segafredo coffee and scrummy pastries. Take away organic, stoneground sourdough breads, including French yeasted, olive and rosemary, and Middle Eastern fruit loaf. Other temptations include raspberry frangipane tarts, chocolate mudcake and fabulous pies.

Bilpin Springs Orchard
2550 Bells Line Road, Bilpin
Tel 4567 1294
Ring ahead – their answering machine will let you know what's current for picking. There are apples from mid-February to June; citrus, cherries and berries in spring; and a range of stone fruit over summer. Don't forget to grab some of their excellent apple juice or cider vinegar.

Blackheath Butchery
10 Govetts Leap Road, Blackheath
Tel 4787 8759
Good-quality, well-priced meat fills the tiled window – ideal for a self-catering stay – backed by enthusiastic butchers. Choose from fifteen types of preservative- and gluten-free sausages, with real gut skins, to spice up any barbie: beef with garlic, thyme and native pepper or our favourite – the Blackheath bratwurst

Blackheath Continental Deli
32 Govetts Leap Road, Blackheath
Tel 4787 8984
A top spot to stock the larder at the weekend getaway, from Pastabilities pasta to cheeses, smallgoods, boutique olive oils and local produce, including Collits Inn preserves, plus a good range of coeliac-friendly goodies. Grab a quick Belaroma coffee and gourmet sarnie.

Food and Wine with Altitude Fair
www.blackheathfestival.com
Usually held in the first weekend in May when autumnal colours abound. Contributors from Orange to the Hunter converge, with over 40 stalls, growers' markets and live music.

Hominy Bakery
185 Katoomba Street, Katoomba
Tel 4782 9816
The sourdough starter here has been going for 16 years – that's a lot of flavour passed on in every loaf. Traditional cakes, slices and pies complement the fantastic crusty loaves that come plain or flavoured with potato, pumpkin, fruit or walnuts.

Leura Cellars
169 Leura Mall, Leura
Tel 4784 1122
You can always get a good boutique drop upstairs, but a trip downstairs to the cellar is where the fun really begins, revealing a string of back vintages of great Aussie marques plus some Euro-treasures. There's also a great choice of specialist beers and malt whiskies.

Leura Gourmet
159 Leura Mall, Leura
Tel 4784 1438
A cornucopia of condiments and deli items, some local (like Blue Mountains Food Co passion butter or Whisk and Pin biscuits and mueslis) and others from further afield (French vinegars and mustards, Tetsuya's truffle butter, and Maggie Beer goodies). Stop for a fresh juice or coffee or a light lunch or snack in the cafe.

Logan Brae Orchard
Shipley Road, Blackheath
Tel 4787 8440
Drop by the shed, have a chat to the laconic Graham, and grab a box of crisp apples from the 10 varieties grown in a season between January and August. Graham also makes the best apple juice, his missus makes a cracker apple jelly, and a mate supplies the honey. In summer, you might score a tray of stone fruit.

Mountain Blue Seafood
208 Katoomba Street, Katoomba
Tel 4782 5522
The owners rise at 3am three days a week to bring back the best from the Sydney fish market auctions. On display there are over a dozen varieties of fillets, while a deli section provides fresh sandwiches and seafood soup, marinated sardines, homemade smoked ocean trout and mackerel pâtés.

regional

CANBERRA + SNOW REGIONS

CATRIONA JACKSON & DUGALD JELLIE

Peer under the political fog blanketing the ACT for around a third of every year and you'll find a cosmopolitan country town, which punches significantly above its weight when it comes to eating and drinking out (thank you taxpayers). You just need to know where to go.

A big day out touring the great national institutions, especially the War Memorial and Parliament House, should be punctuated by a bite in one of the growing number of outdoor eateries. Eating 'out' is one of the national capital's great pleasures, made possible by the year-round clear, sunny weather, with serious heaters deployed in winter to cut the chill.

This year's hot item is the assiette – a fancy name for a plate of duck, pork, oysters or whatever, often done four ways – and as long as you order it for more than one it's not a bad fad. Conservatism at the top end is lessening (we mean gastronomically, not politically) as restaurants mature into their own styles. However, there is still much over-finessing – everything comes stuffed, reduced and/or smothered in an essential essence. Thankfully some establishments remain nobly immune, including Artespresso, Waters Edge and Ottoman Cuisine (see entries).

Local produce, including great stone fruit and cherries, smoked trout, strawberries and terrific apples, jams and jellies straight from the orchard (Pialligo), are increasingly available at local markets (see *Provedores*).

The cocktail and wine bar scene is on the up, with newcomers the Julep Lounge (upstairs in Manuka) and Benchmark (Civic) adding to the established favourite, Hippo (Civic). Grab a brace of pies and tarts from Canberra's best bakery, Silo (see entry), and you'll be well equipped to head out of town for a day's tour of the surrounding hills and vineyards.

Further afield the snowfields offer sunny beer gardens at the base of the mountains with snow flurries in the peaks (even out of season in Thredbo), and an impressive concentration of fine diners designed for an alpine appetite.

Abell's Kopi Tiam
Shop 7, Furneaux Street, Manuka
Tel 6239 4199 Map 10

Malaysian/Modern Asian
Score 12/20

Abell's Kopi Tiam was one of the first places in fashionable Manuka to offer medium-priced, casual dining with a touch of panache – an approach that has won them a loyal following. It's a casual eatery – all bold colours and modest chairs – filled by a wok-load of journalists, politicians and the last few not in the city's main game. Staff are forever enthusiastic, if not always expert, as they squeeze between closely packed tables. Big flavour is the name of the game here and, in most cases, Malaysian dishes are the best bet. Fall-apart beef rendang, 20-chilli lamb (not as inedibly hot as it sounds) and Bali chicken are among the best offerings. Anything in a hotpot is reliable, including the menu staple, teochow (chiu chow) slow-cooked pork. The succulent, oversized duck ricepaper rolls reappear on the specials board by popular demand and make a good lunch. Desserts are a pleasant surprise for few ringgit: try the slippery, cool sago pudding coated in coconut milk and dark palm sugar syrup for a study in contrasts.

Hours Lunch Tues–Sun 11.30am–2.30pm; Dinner Tues–Sat 5.30–10pm, Sun 5.30–9pm
Bill E $3.20–$9.90 **M** $9.50–$24.90 **D** $6.90–$7.90
Cards AE BC DC MC V Eftpos; bookings essential
Wine Small, well-priced list; about 20 by the glass; BYO (corkage $5 per bottle)
Chef Abell Ong
Owners Lorna Sim & Abell Ong
Seats 75; outdoor seats
And...kids love Abell's; it bustles and the coconut pancakes are bright green!

Canberra & Snow Regions

Anise
Melbourne Building, 20 West Row, Canberra City
Tel 6257 0700   Map 10

Contemporary

Score 13/20

Aniseed, despite the restaurant's name, is absent from a menu filled with stout flavours and choice regional ingredients. Perch on the long banquette to enjoy the best view of the crowd and the seductive room swathed in oyster-mushroom browns. Rabbit and prune terrine with dijon is desirously rustic. A silken entrée allows seared scallops to gather around a sweet cauliflower purée. But despite the high points – and there are many in a restaurant championing local produce and wines – there are some kitchen quibbles when the prices charged could be considered a touch uppity for a city that values authenticity and simple pleasures. Pepper-crusted lamb rump would have been better served by something more than a cold zucchini and mint salad. And while a kangaroo fillet is tender and delicate, there was no excitement in its smoky eggplant salad. Yet as the seasons change so does the menu, and with them Anise will always be offering something to entice.

Hours Lunch Tues–Fri noon–2.30pm; Dinner Tues–Fri 6.30–10.30pm, Sat 6–10.30pm

Bill E $15.50–$18 **M** $26.50–$28 **D** $13.50–$15.50

Cards AE BC DC MC V

Wine Impressively long, with 18 Canberra district wines at the forefront; 18 by the glass; BYO (corkage $7 per bottle)

Chefs Jeff Piper & Nick Carter

Owners Aspa & Nick Carter, Justin Kavanagh & Jeff Piper

Seats 55; private room; wheelchair access

www.bestrestaurants.com.au/anise

And...they have quarterly Canberra region wine dinners to pit a Lake George pinot noir against a Murrumbateman merlot

Artespresso
31 Giles Street, Kingston
Tel 6295 8055   Map 10

Contemporary

Score 15/20

Artespresso is the kind of place you could take anyone for an excellent dinner, lunch or breakfast – from elderly grandparents to foodie mates in town for the weekend. The menu is very impressive, mixing beautifully executed crowd-pleasers with more adventurous dishes. The vitello tonnato, cold veal fillet with yellow fin tuna mayonnaise, is a delicately balanced version of a classic with the added crunch of minute croutons. Thai salad of pork, calamari and green papaya makes a lovely starter or light lunch. Rabbit pie, with peas and mash, is rightly popular with the business crowd, as are the excellent chargrilled lamb cutlets set off by a parsley, fennel and goat's cheese salad. Staff are efficient and well informed, and the hard-lined space is pleasant, if nowhere near as spectacular as the food. It can get noisy inside, but there are a number of little outside pockets, with big heaters for those bristling Canberra nights. Desserts are divine, especially the mango sorbet and shortbread.

Hours Breakfast & Brunch Sat–Sun 9am–2.30pm; Lunch Tues–Fri noon–2.30pm; Dinner Tues–Sat 6–10pm

Bill E $14–$16 **M** $24.50–$28 **D** $13

Cards AE BC DC MC V Eftpos

Wine A good but not enormous list, with decent cellar options; 17 by the glass; BYO (corkage $6.50 per bottle)

Chef Dean Sammut

Owners Nik Gravias, Dean Sammut & Jo Taylor

Seats 120; private room; outdoor seats

www.artespresso.com.au

And...you can drop by for just a coffee or a glass of wine

regional

Aubergine
18A Barker Street, Griffith
Tel 6260 8666   Map 10

European   ♁
Score 14/20

Despite the shift in focus for chef James Mussillon to his new city venture Courgette, Aubergine still possesses considerable class. Less formal than its newer city cousin, the caramel-toned, comfortable split-level space boasts a lovely balcony overlooking the park. The relaxed ambience is well supported by super-comfortable chairs and floor-to-ceiling windows, plus efficient and friendly staff. Emphasis is on fish and seafood, and – like the diners – the food is often rich and saucy. Game terrine arrives as a gutsy slab, bordered by piquant chopped cornichons, sweet port and sauterne jelly. Spatchcock is boned (apart from sweet little drumsticks) and crisp-skinned, sensationally juicy and with a wonderful truffled stuffing, while green pea purée and a pad of potato play solid supporting roles to the highly flavoured meat. That menu staple Aubergine mixed fish is topped with a stunning king prawn, while aïoli and pesto sauce add light punctuation. First-rate technique shows in the crème brûlée deftly matched with lychee and mango.

Hours Lunch Mon–Fri noon–3pm;
Dinner daily 6–10pm

Bill E $17.50 **M** $28.50 **D** $14;
dégustation menu from $80 pp

Cards AE BC DC MC V Eftpos

Wine Terrific and extensive list; 14 by the glass; BYO (corkage $9 per bottle)

Chefs Jason Rodwell & James Mussillon

Owner James Mussillon

Seats 80; private room; wheelchair access; outdoor seats

www.auberginerestaurant.com

And...nice touches such as grapefruit sorbet, petit fours, and a savoury as you peruse the menu

Benchmark Wine Bar
65 Northbourne Avenue, Canberra City
Tel 6262 6522   Map 10

European/French   ♁
Score 13/20

Benchmark helps to fill a yawning gap in Canberra's drinking/dining scene. This seriously good wine bar has around 100 slurps by the glass on a global and very well organised list. Well-dressed public servants and businesspeople have made Benchmark their own after work; they cluster at nondescript high-backed chairs and bare tables in the corner diner for a fine drop from a *War and Peace* list that runs for 73 pages (including explanations of old world regions and styles). Thankfully, food is anything but an afterthought. Laurent Rospars turns out terrific, French-inspired dishes from a very compact menu with frequently changing specials. A scallop, eggplant and mushroom salad is a fresh and exciting starter, while his provincial veal and potato casserole is singular and hugely satisfying. The chocolate fondant and meringue-stacked sandwich is decadently rich. Service is mostly well informed, with plenty of wine advice available when you need it, especially to accompany a good selection of French and Australian cheeses.

Hours Lunch Mon–Fri 11am–late;
Dinner daily 5pm–late

Bill E $16.50 **M** $26.50 **D** $13.50;
10% surcharge on public holidays

Cards AE BC DC MC V Eftpos

Wine A huge global list; around 100 by the glass

Chef Laurent Rospars

Owner Tasso Rovolis

Seats 110; wheelchair access; outdoor seats

And...the $15.50 express lunch – main course and a glass of wine – is a sensational deal

Canberra & Snow Regions

The Chairman & Yip
108 Bunda Street, Civic
Tel 6248 7109   Map 10

Modern Asian
Score 14/20

After all these years, all the palm sugar and chilli oil, table talk and king prawns, hot dates and hotpots, the Chairman remains as lustrous as ever. And the aesthetic – candle-lit tables glowing red, soft lighting, a silvery metallic wall and drapery that gives a sense of theatrical occasion – stays ageless and not without whimsy, much like tofu and aubergine tossed in a yellow bean sauce. Yes, the plates are still hand-painted and the menu's still rather quirky (but we like it), pasted as it is in the front pages of an *Art Asia Pacific* quarterly journal. The beef and scallop hotpot is a heart-warming dish, piquant with pepper and lifted with lime leaves. Slow-roasted duck breast and the Portuguese (Macao) spiced chicken are easy to love. It's still an enchanting night out, with a bubble of revelry and exotic illusion that's well worth dressing up for and keeps everyone returning with deservedly high expectations.

Hours Lunch Mon–Fri noon–2.30pm; Dinner Mon–Sat 5.30–10.30pm
Bill E $12.50–$18.50 **M** $24.50–$29.50 **D** $11.50–$14.50
Cards AE BC DC MC V
Wine Crafted list, much of it stored artfully in pigeon holes; 10 by the glass; BYO (corkage $6.50 per bottle)
Chef William Suen
Owner Josiah Li
Seats 150; private room
And… make sure you see the seafood specials

Courgette
54 Marcus Clarke Street, Canberra City
Tel 6247 4042   Map 10

Contemporary
Score 14/20

Courgette has large shoes to fill on two fronts. Firstly, it's the sister restaurant to the well-known and loved Aubergine and secondly it sits on the former site of one of Canberra's legendary fine diners, Fringe Benefits. However, in both cases, it more than meets expectations. This is a seriously luxurious restaurant: the food is rich and artfully presented, while the furnishings are plush and sensationally comfortable. Staff members flit efficiently between the various levels and offer mostly well informed advice on the food and extensive wine list. The whole joint reeks of class – and James Mussillon's cooking is no exception. Spice-crusted tuna with pickled ginger, soy and mustard seed dressing is an inspired must-have: ruby-red inside, with the contrast of the crust and tender flesh providing real excitement in the mouth. John dory with chips and lemon beurre blanc is a lovely dish of simple, beautifully combined elements. Calf's liver with mash, caramelised carrot and balsamic onion is sticky perfection. Desserts are terrific, including a velvety Cointreau pannacotta with macerated berries.

Hours Lunch Mon–Fri noon–3pm; Dinner Mon–Sat 6–10pm
Bill E $17.50 **M** $28.50 **D** $14; dégustation menu from $80 pp
Cards AE BC DC MC V Eftpos
Wine Large, high-quality list from around the globe; BYO (corkage $9 per bottle)
Chef/owner James Mussillon
Seats 110; private rooms; wheelchair access; outdoor seats
www.courgette.com.au
And… the wonderful walk-in cellar makes an excellent private room

regional

Crackenback Cottage

Alpine Way, Thredbo Valley
Tel 6456 2198   Map 11

Contemporary

Score 14/20

About 20 minutes from the main ski field at Thredbo, Crackenback's most desirable cottage is all exposed beams, heritage-style crockery and seriously good food with a modern twist. Fresh oysters with watermelon and a hint of chilli could have done with a little more fire, but boy, the ocean isn't that handy, and they worked nonetheless. Tomato and basil soup is just that: uncluttered, vibrant flavours that have you slurping the last mouthful and wiping the bowl with bread. A ploughman's platter showcases local produce, like Hobbitt's Farm cheeses, smoked trout pâté and various other regional specialities. Monaro lamb pie is a generous bowl of tender lamb in flavoursome gravy, topped with a cascade of fresh peas under a thatch of puff pastry. Crackenback's service matches the surrounds – friendly but not suffocating, with the bonus of plenty of local knowledge.
A giant wooden maze, lovely old toys and a dedicated children's menu make the place very welcoming for kids (and their parents might have fun too).

Hours Winter & school holidays, Lunch daily 10am–5pm, Dinner Wed–Mon 6–10pm; Other times, Lunch Thurs–Sun 10am–5pm, Dinner Fri–Sun 6–10pm

Bill E $10–$18 **M** $22.50–$29 **D** $10

Cards AE BC DC MC V Eftpos

Wine A well-selected list; 9–12 by the glass; good list of classic and modern cocktails

Chef Greg Harmer

Owners Tania & Rob Ward

Seats 110; private room; outdoor seats

www.crackenback.com

And...jams and relishes, as well as the terrific coconut ice, are on sale in the upstairs gift store

Credo

Diggings Terrace, Thredbo
Tel 6457 6844   Map 11

Contemporary

Score 13/20

With its garnish of fairy lights and a chalet-like room filled with timber tables and cane chairs, Credo makes the most of its mountain location. Looking straight over the spectacular Thredbo River and ski fields, it combines generous flavours with good old-fashioned hospitality. You need to spend the day exercising, because in many cases the entrées are the size of mini-mains. A terrific, juicy, dukkah-dusted quail with scallop (as in seafood) mash and snowpeas is perhaps overly generous, but the whole scallops in the mash seemed a trifle odd. A 'scaloppine' of slightly tough veal rolled around smoked trout didn't work too well, flavours crashing at the first mogul. Velvety smooth seafood chowder is a stand-out, bursting with a beautiful essence of ocean and dotted with local smoked trout. The seduction continues with beef fillet cooked to perfection and teamed with an intense reduction and a mini snowy mountain of mash. A zesty lemon tart makes a refreshing end to the meal.

Hours Dinner from 6.30pm (daily in winter, reduced nights at other times)

Bill E $11.50–$18.50 **M** $27.50–$31.50 **D** $12.50

Cards AE BC DC MC V Eftpos

Wine Terrific list with a range of vintages; alas, only 2 pretty average wines by the glass.

Chef Paul Antone

Owners Ron & Noni Plewes

Seats 94; outdoor seats

www.credo.com.au

And...the head chef comes and goes depending on the season

Dijon

Melbourne Building, 24 West Row,
Canberra City
Tel 6230 6009 Map 10

Contemporary

Score 14/20

Since its move to the city, Dijon has played its part in turning the wonderfully columned West Row into one of Canberra's best eating strips – and has gone from strength to strength in the process. It's an elegant and welcoming space with comfortable chairs and clean lines. The staff are well versed, ready to explain and inform or step back, depending on your demands. Tiny, crunchy ricepaper rolls are a lovely, cleansing and complimentary start to the meal. Oysters, done three ways, are spectacular to look at and eat: some wrapped in ricepaper, others in little spoons, and the best in shot glasses with sake. Tuna tartare is a luxurious adventure with the added crunch of seaweed salad. Grain-fed eye fillet is meltingly tender, surrounded by exquisite baby carrots and with a breezy little kick courtesy of the sea urchin and soy butter. And on a chilly Canberra night, it's hard to resist the apple and rhubarb tart.

Hours Lunch Mon–Fri noon–3pm; Dinner daily 5.30–9.30pm

Bill E $16.50–$18.50 **M** $25.50–$29.50 **D** $14–$24

Cards AE BC DC MC V Eftpos

Wine A very good list; 17 by the glass; BYO (corkage $9 per bottle)

Chef/owner John Balkwell

Seats 120; private room; wheelchair access; outdoor seats

www.dijon.com.au

And...the eight-course dégustation with wine is a bargain ($135 pp)

Fekerte's

74/2 Cape Street, Dickson
Tel 6262 5799 Map 10

Ethiopian

Score 13/20

Fekerte Tesfaye is already well known to the regulars at Kingston's Sunday market for her fresh and unusual Ethiopian curries. Finally she has spread her wings to open a neat, spacious and contemporary restaurant to showcase the chilli-spiced flavours of her African homeland, backed by friendly and enthusiastic service. Terrific samosas are a world away from the Indian variety, and a warm and hearty broad bean dip with crisp bread defies expectations. Key wat (spicy beef curry) has real punch, cut by sharp, homemade Ethiopian cottage cheese. There are lighter dishes, like zilzil alicha, a kind of Ethiopian Irish stew, the lamb flavoured with ginger and jalapeño chilli. Vegetarian dishes are deeply satisfying, like adenguare, a kidney bean curry. You can try a traditional platter, which teams a handful of mains with salad and side dishes and savoury, pancake-style bread for mopping up; or simply put yourself in Fekerte's capable hands using recommended combinations that provide a terrific guide to what goes with what.

Hours Lunch Tues–Fri noon–2pm; Dinner Tues–Sun 6–10pm

Bill E $3.80–$7.90 **M** $15.90–$19.90 **D** $6; lunch banquet $19.90, dinner $25.90–$29.90

Cards AE BC DC MC V

Wine Small, workman-like list; 8 by the glass; BYO (corkage $4.50 per bottle)

Chef Fekerte Tesfaye

Owners Fekerte Tesfaye & Sendaba Gerba

Seats 100; outdoor seats; wheelchair access

And...you can still try the food at the Old Bus Depot market on Sundays

regional

the ginger room
Old Parliament House (entry via Queen Victoria Terrace at rear), Parkes
Tel 6270 8262 Map 10

Contemporary

Score 14/20

There's something slightly humbling about dining in a venerable institution (even if humility isn't normally associated with the previous inhabitants). Janet Jeffs and her team have got the atmosphere just right in the former private dining room of Old Parliament House. It's been modernised with class, making the most of the view to the building's modern sibling. Service is polished, efficient and friendly. Chairs are deep and comfortable, lighting is seductive and the food usually spot on. The menu is concisely written and pulls together a mix of French and Vietnamese influences. On our visit, seven of eight starters featured seafood: sweet Spring Bay scallops among the best, nestled in the shell with the perfumed zing of kaffir lime, shallots and lemongrass. Duck breast is nicely cut by an earthy beetroot and orange jelly. Warm baked figs with a cone of cool vanilla bavarois topped by Persian fairy floss makes for a spectacular dessert. The cheese platter is a delight: perfectly matured and presented at the table for you to choose.

Hours Dinner Tues–Sat 6pm–late
Bill 2/3 courses $45/$55 pp; 'secret vegetarian menu' 2/3 courses $39/$49 pp
Cards AE BC DC MC V Eftpos
Wine Excellent list (and cellar list) with skilled advice; about 18 by the glass
Chef Janet Jeffs
Owners Janet Jeffs & Maryanne Ellem
Seats 80; private room; wheelchair access
www.gingercatering.com.au
And...visit the National Portrait Gallery while you're there

Grazing
The Royal Hotel, cnr Cork and Harp Streets, Gundaroo
Tel 6236 8777 Map 10

Contemporary

Score 13/20

In the sheep-country plains by the Yass River is a one-pub town called Gundaroo. And what a pub it has – the 1865 Royal Hotel, with thick stone walls, high-pitched rusted tin roof and iceberg roses by the verandah, and serving boutique cheeses with an impressive local wine list and the knowledge to explain it. Chef Jodie Johnson (ex-Lynwood Café) has helped put the place on the map, boosting civic pride with an adventurous menu, including honey-glazed, smoked duck breast, that has weekend gourmands navigating back roads to see what the fuss is about. But after the justifiable first-year fanfare a little sparkle has been lost, its promise only partly quelled by dishes that could well be stripped back. So while farm dam yabby cannelloni is deliciously subtle, it's the tender beef and Guinness pie or a crown roast of Cootamundra goat that make the trip worthwhile. More servings, please, of rustic contemporary cooking and the homespun charm and we'll keep turning happily off the highway.

Hours Breakfast Sat–Sun 9–11.30am; Lunch Fri–Sun noon–3pm; Dinner Thurs–Sun 6pm–late
Bill E $9.50–$16 **M** $19–$30 **D** $11
Cards AE BC DC MC V Eftpos; bookings essential
Wine Nicely parochial list of local wines and Braidwood beers; most by the glass
Chef Jodie Johnson
Owners Mark & Jennie Mooney
Seats 200; private rooms; outdoor seats
www.grazing.com.au
And...they have their own coffee blend plus speciality teas and tisanes if you just want to have a cuppa by the fire

Canberra & Snow Regions

The Lobby

King George Terrace, opposite Old Parliament House, Parkes
Tel 6273 1563   Map 10

Contemporary

Score 13/20

Half the press gallery was lunching at The Lobby the day Gough was sacked. Laurie Oakes is said to have run(!) to get to the steps of the then Parliament House to hear the proclamation. Thirty years later, this Canberra institution opposite the rose garden has a new lease of life under chef Christian Hauberg, and the floor shares his fresh, relaxed yet well-versed approach. With floor-to-ceiling windows surrounded by a fern garden, the overall feeling is of feasting in an intimate, secretive forest. A tart of scallops, nashi pear and gorgonzola sorbet is an exciting exercise in contrasts – hot, cold, sweet and savoury. Pan-fried soft-shell crab in bouillabaisse didn't work as well – the crab's sweetness was a little lost in the soup's competing flavours. However, a lovely, crisped piece of kingfish sits on a bed of terrific watercress and rhubarb risotto and tastes as sprightly as it sounds. Warm Valrhona chocolate tart with vanilla bean ice-cream is dark, sinful, bitter and delicious.

Hours Lunch Tues–Fri noon–2.30pm; Dinner Tues–Sat from 6.30pm
Bill E $15–$18.50 **M** $28–$36 **D** $14–$16; 2/3/4 course lunches $39/$49/$59
Cards AE BC DC MC V Eftpos
Wine Comprehensive list, with emphasis on Aussie boutiques; 10 by the glass
Chef Christian Hauberg
Owners Christian Hauberg & Bruce Gibbs
Seats 60; wheelchair access; outdoor seats
www.thelobby.com.au
And... The Lobby can cater for a function at the Carillon

Lynwood Cafe

1 Murray Street, Collector
Tel 4848 0200   Map 11

Contemporary

Score 14/20

There is romance in the pastoral idyll. It's at a circa-1830s charm-filled stone cottage (and erstwhile bakery) by a creek, in a one-horse town (pop. 150) south of Goulburn. And it's sitting (on the world's most uncomfortable chairs) in sunshine in the walled garden, among peach and walnut trees, drinking pinot and eating plump pork, sage, veal and thyme bangers with buttery mash and onion marmalade. Congratulate yourself. For being here, with bone-handled Sheffield knife in hand, and having the good fortune to enjoy rustic provincial cookery: rich duck liver pâté, beef and stout pie, a crisp and salty-skinned duck confit, succulent chook breast. Antique egg baskets and enamel pitchers, pots and colanders hang in the jam room. A tractor clatters over a timber bridge. Herbs are picked from local kitchen gardens. And the chocolate mousse cake with poached plums beats CWA all-comers. This is the good life, bristling with the seasonal splendour of country living.

Hours Thurs–Sun 10am–1pm; Dinner Fri–Sat from 6pm
Bill E $9.50–$12.50 **M** $17.50–$26.50 **D** $11–$16; 10% surcharge on Sundays & public holidays
Cards AE BC MC V Eftpos
Wine Straightforward and simple list; 11 wines, 6 beers, all by the glass; BYO (corkage $2.50 pp)
Chef Warrick Brook
Owners Alan & Robbie Howard
Seats 50; private rooms; wheelchair access; outdoor seats
www.lynwoodcafe.com.au
And...nobody leaves without at least one jar of their homemade fig jam (or cumquat marmalade, or tomato mango chutney, or beetroot relish, or...)

regional

Mezzalira

Melbourne Building, cnr London Circuit and West Row, Canberra City
Tel 6230 0025   Map 10

Modern Italian

Score 13/20

With unusually high ceilings, curved, banquette-lined booths and outdoor tables, this Italian diner is infected with a breezy feel. The same can be said of the Trimboli family's *cucina rustica* – it's fresh, vibrant and well made, never cloying or fiddly. You can eat very simply or take advantage of fancier fare. At lunch the place is crowded with lawyers and judges from the nearby courts. The restaurant's hub (and heart) is the wood-fired oven tended by Pasquale Trimboli. A serve of his beautiful thin focaccia is a great way to start. Real pizza, with thin crust and minimal, high-quality toppings, or a simple bowl of beautiful tomato soup, are terrific staples. Fish and seafood are also a speciality, with a frequently changing blackboard menu. Slow-braised lamb shoulder is heaven, and so too the Roman-style roast pork. Pumpkin-stuffed tortellini are textbook perfection: sweet, light and set off by nothing more than burnt butter. Sambuca brûlée with almond biscotti, or a classy tiramisu, are suitably sweet endings.

Hours Lunch Mon–Fri noon–2.30pm; Dinner Mon–Sat 6–10pm (and Sun on long weekends)
Bill E $14–$18.50 **M** $22–$34.50 **D** $12
Cards AE BC DC MC V
Wine Substantial list of Oz, NZ, Italian and French; 14 by the glass; BYO (corkage $7 per bottle)
Chefs Bruce Chapman & Pasquale Trimboli
Owner The Trimboli family
Seats 100; private rooms; wheelchair access; outdoor seats
www.mezzalira.com.au
And...the dégustation with matching wine is terrific

milk and honey

Ground Floor, Center Cinema Building, 29 Garema Place, Civic
Tel 6247 7722   Map 10

Contemporary

Score 13/20

Canberra's city centre has long been thirsting for a smart, youthful food and drink joint and this fits the bill nicely. Hipster-wearing 20-somethings sip on grand cocktails, while their parents tuck into duck and prawn salad with a glass of sauv blanc. It's a split-level space, with tables spilling out onto the footpath (and no doubt visitors from the bong shop opposite drop by asking for Tim Tams). Service is efficient, if not always super-attentive and the food is inventive. Little plates are a good way to begin: fried haloumi with green and cannellini beans and aïoli; or an antipasto of olives, fetta and Turkish peasant salad. A generous risotto, stacked with good-quality seafood, is redolent with saffron and herbs. Steak can't come much more traditionally than on decent mash with spinach and creamy peppercorn sauce. Duck confit was less successful, the decadent meat a little overwhelmed by a marmalade glaze. The brekkie menu is rightly popular, especially because of the wildly seductive coconut pancakes with grilled banana.

Hours Mon–Fri 7.30am–10pm; Sat 8am–10pm; Sun 9am–3pm
Bill E $12.90–$17 **M** $13.90–$25 **D** $6.90–$11.90; 10% surcharge on public holidays
Cards AE BC DC MC V Eftpos
Wine Terrific-value list; Australian and New Zealand; 23 by the glass.
Chefs Simon Collett & Malcolm Hatch
Owners Miriana Cavic, Jamie Thomson & Simon Collett
Seats 90; wheelchair access; outdoor seats
www.milkandhoney.net.au
And...great juices are a highlight to start the day

Ottoman Cuisine

9 Broughton Street (cnr Blackall Street), Barton
Tel 6273 6111 Map 10

Turkish

Score 15/20

Over 12 years, the Ottoman has built a reputation for excellent food while broadening our understanding of the potential of contemporary Turkish cuisine. Inside this opulent, freestanding faux-art-deco conservatory you can still take the familiar route to Istanbul with the best dips, pide and kebabs you've ever tasted – but that's only the tip of the crescent moon. The menu is huge, so a mix of starters served one after another to share is a good plan. Let intelligent, knowledgeable staff guide you, or simply surrender to the joys of a banquet. Chef Serif Kaya reserves his greatest passions for seafood, especially the acclaimed salmon dolma: a tender coil of vine-leaf-wrapped fish, prawns and cray, gently battered and fried. For the adventurous, there's excellent offal. Lamb's brains are sensational – incredibly tender and perfectly shielded inside a whisper-light coating of crisp batter – while lamb's liver is a gutsy, textural treat. Kaya is planning to open a new venture in Sydney in late 2005, while keeping Ottoman going. We hope this standard remains.

Hours Lunch Tues–Fri noon–3pm; Dinner Tues–Sat 6–10pm
Bill E $16–$21 **M** $24–$29 **D** $12
Cards AE BC DC MC V; bookings essential
Wine A large, accessible and well-selected list; mostly Australian; 11 by the glass
Chef Serif Kaya
Owners Serif & Gulbahar Kaya
Seats 200; private rooms; wheelchair access
And... the restaurant might sell, so ring and check

Rama's

Shop 6, Pearce Shopping Centre, cnr McFarland & Hodgson Crescents, Pearce
Tel 6286 1964 Map 10

Fijian–Indian

Score 13/20

Rama's is the pride of Woden Valley – the first of Canberra's satellite towns. This terrifically welcoming local curry house sits in a shopping precinct in suburban Pearce and packs them in just about every night. It succeeds because the food is honest, satisfying and at times intriguing, while the hostess, Mini Gaundar, wears hospitality like a vibrantly woven shawl. The brightly painted, modern-looking restaurant also offers exceptional value. Vegetable pakoras may have lacked va-va-voom, but they're satisfying nonetheless. Fijian pork in a tangy capsicum and coriander gravy, with real kick and freshness, is fork-tender, fall-apart meat. Excellent side dishes of dahl, curried beans and tomato round out the meal nicely, but don't forget to order a roti to scoop up all those wonderful sauces. If the heat gets too much, a mango lassi is not too sweet and cools things down. To finish, gulab jamun – those terrific little dumplings in sugar syrup – will satiate the sweetest tooth.

Hours Dinner Tues–Sun from 6pm
Bill E $6–$9 **M** $14–$18 **D** $5–$6.50
Cards AE BC DC MC V Eftpos; bookings essential
Wine BYO (no corkage)
Chefs Daya & Parsu Ram
Owners Mini Gaundar, Milton Smith, Daya & Parsu Ram
Seats 60; outdoor seats (summer only)
And... there's takeaway if you're feeling antisocial

regional

Sante

Shop 4, Squatters Run, Mowamba Mall, Thredbo
Tel 6457 6083 Map 11

Contemporary

Score 13/20

After a hard day's hiking or sliding through Thredbo's spectacular mountains, Sante is a very welcoming prospect. All warm and nooky inside, with Turkish kilims on bench seats, it readily makes you feel comfortable. Friendly, if slightly stretched staff know just enough about the menu and wine list to help you through. Tasting platters are available for all three courses and range the globe. Wafer-thin slices of premium raw beef carpaccio work well with horseradish and parmesan shavings; salt-and-pepper squid is fresh and feisty; but a fine-grained duck liver pâté was a little lacklustre and overly sweet with brioche and red-onion jam. And nondescript prawns on Asian noodles seemed a little uninspiring. Joy returns in the nursery fodder of a smooth and decadent fondue of Belgian chocolate – understandably popular after the ice-cool slopes – that comes with fruit and marshmallows for dipping. And the dessert platter is a sight to see: great sorbet and bright green midori and lime cheesecake.

Hours Dinner Tues–Sat from 6pm
Bill E $9.50–$15 **M** $19.50–$26.50 **D** $10.50–$21.50
Cards AE BC MC V Eftpos; bookings essential in winter
Wine Decent list of favourites, at a pretty hefty mark-up; 8–16 by the glass
Chef Corey Wheatley
Owners Suzanne Robb & Nigel Stevens
Seats 80; wheelchair access; outdoor seats
And…roasted duck leg with potato cakes and apricot is a post-ski refueller's favourite

Silo Bakery

36 Giles Street, Kingston
Tel 6260 6060 Map 10

European   ♀

Score 13/20

Silo could be simply described as Canberra's best bakery – if it weren't for the splendid cheese room, those luscious, irresistible pastries and the serious sit-down menu with wines to match. Scientist and chef couple Graham Hudson and Leanne Gray deliver consistently evocative food – to the point where they can even serve a convincing chicken caesar roll – in this long, thin, slick, loud and always hectic room. While the service isn't always all it could be, the food more than makes up for it; from a gutsy Spanish-style piperade omelette for breakfast to a thin-crust pizza – perhaps mushroom with salsa di noci and blue cheese – followed by one of those legendary tarts (make mine vanilla brûlée). Classics include the sweet, chunky Toulouse sausages with Clyde River oysters, or beef bruschetta – thin slices of beef and tiny fresh vegies – with wonderful juice soaking down into the great bread. A damned fine coffee simply seals the deal.

Hours Breakfast Tues–Sat 7am–noon; Lunch Tues–Fri 11.30am–3.30pm, Sat noon–3.30pm
Bill E $4–$11.50 **M** $13–$19 **D** $3.50–$11.50
Cards AE BC DC MC V Eftpos; bookings essential
Wine Really clever, multinational list; 8 by the glass
Chefs Sean McConnell & Leanne Gray
Owners Leanne Gray & Graham Hudson
Seats 49; wheelchair access; outdoor seats
www.silobakery.com.au
And…things sell out quickly on Saturdays, so get in early

Tasuke

122 Alinga Street, Civic
Tel 6257 9711   Map 10

Japanese

Score 13/20

Disguised by an unassuming front window full of workaday sandwiches and giant Anzac biscuits, Tasuke is a hidden gem. This tiny hole-in-the-wall diner is festooned with paper flags advertising specials and menu staples, so take your time and relax on the pine benches that run along the wall. Chef Yuji Takeda works away in his minuscule kitchen, producing the national capital's best Japanese, including a shiny array of mixed sashimi on rice, bowls of clear-as-day udon, and a terrific bento box. Smaller treats include sensational fish cakes with burdock, and deep-fried oysters with an unctuous dipping sauce. The tempura is classically super-crisp and light. Sushi and sashimi are flappingly fresh and beautifully presented, and the hotpots and noodles are reassuringly comforting. While service is friendly and functional, the prices are very wallet-friendly for the quality.

Hours Lunch Mon–Sat noon–3pm; Dinner Mon–Thurs & Sat 6–9pm, Fri 6–10pm

Bill E $5–$10 **M** $13–$29 **D** $4–$6; Fri–Sat minimum $20 pp

Cards BC MC V Eftpos

Wine BYO (corkage $3 pp)

Chef/owner Yuji Takeda

Seats 56; outdoor seats

And... for the buffs there are edamame (boiled, salted soybeans) and natto (fermented soybean) rolls

Waters Edge

Commonwealth Place, 40 Parkes Place, Canberra
Tel 6273 5066   Map 10

Modern European

Score 16/20

Overlooking Lake Burley Griffin and surrounded by the national capital's grand public buildings, the ultra-smart Waters Edge, with its decadent white leather chairs, continues to set the standard for Canberra's fine diners. New chef Pablo Tordesillas Garcia (ex Otto) maintains the European tradition, while incorporating his own mod-Med touches. Beautifully balanced sweetbreads and cuttlefish contrasts taste and texture, and also finds symphony in a sherry reduction. Sautéed yabbies with wild mushrooms, scallops and thyme offers defined flavours intuitively combined. Pheasant is a stand-out: gently yielding flesh, minuscule chicken livers, lardons and, in an inspired touch, brussels sprout leaves. This is balanced, often spectacular food, using nothing more or less than needed. Witness the kingfish, enriched with smoked eel, sweetened with grapes and mellowed with white bean purée. Highly assured and informed service completes the picture. Bitter chocolate pud with star anise is the black opal of desserts – mysterious and bursting with flavour.

Hours Lunch Tues–Fri noon–2.30pm, Sun noon–2.30pm; Dinner Tues–Sun from 6.30pm

Bill E $16–$22 **M** $26–$35 **D** $14–$16

Cards AE BC DC MC V Eftpos; bookings essential

Wine A long, exciting list; 16 by the glass; BYO by arrangement (corkage $10 per bottle)

Chef Pablo Tordesillas Garcia

Owner Fiona Wright

Seats 75; private room; wheelchair access; outdoor seats

www.watersedgecanberra.com.au

And... a limited choice menu for groups at $60 pp

regional

And also...

Altitude 1380
Shop 4, Upper concourse, Thredbo Alpine Village
Tel 6457 6190
Steaming coffee, mountainous breakfasts, snacks, light lunches and a more serious dinner menu in winter keep this casual eatery buzzing.

Cork Street Gallery Cafe
Cork Street, Gundaroo
Tel 6236 8217
Located in the old police station and stables, this cafe has an enormous menu of pizza as well as cakes, biscuits and decent coffee.

Le Julep Lounge
Level One, 8 Franklin Street, Manuka
Tel 6239 5060
This discreet upstairs hideaway (formerly A Foreign Affair) is a serious cocktail bar/restaurant with real spunk. The 60-odd-long cocktail list makes for great reading and even better drinking. There are good cocktail nibbles while the menu proper features a modern Italian slant.

Lambert Vineyards
810 Norton Road, Wamboin
Tel 6238 3866
This modern winery/cafe/restaurant overlooks the vines and surrounding hills outside Bungendore. A tasting lounge and terrace make great weekend nooks for enjoying the modern bistro food, including wood-fired pizza, a serious cheese plate, and antipasto featuring the chef's own cured and smoked meats and seafood.

Lott Street Food Store Bakery & Cafe
178–180 Sharp Street, Cooma
Tel 6452 1414
This bright, colourful cafe boasts cranking fresh juices, gourmet rolls packed with fresh ingredients and a compact menu that features plenty of local produce as well as great Belaroma coffee, cakes and jams to take away.

Tak Kee Roast Inn
10 Woolley Street, Dickson
Tel 6257 4939
Whole roast ducks and chickens hang next to sides of crisp-skin pork at Canberra's best Chinese BBQ joint. Take away or eat in for lightning fast service and great value.

Provedores

Blue Seas
5–7 Leeton Street, Fyshwick
Tel 6239 7111
Seafood supplier to Canberra's top restaurants, with an exceptional variety available to the rest of us. Produce is sourced from all over Australia according to season, as well as trans-Tasman, including the highly prized New Zealand snapper.

Bruno's Truffels
Southlands House, Mawson
Tel 6286 6377
Great rye bread, custard-filled pastries and terrific pasties are a bonus at Canberra's finest chocolatier. Tip your head back to allow the liqueur to run down the back of your throat, as you bite into the gorgeous chocolate apricots or any number of naughty chocoholic treats.

Capital Region Farmers' Market
Exhibition Park in Canberra (EPIC), Kuringai Building, access via Federal Highway and Wells Station Road
Tel 6230 2481
Every Sat 8–11am
Superb cheeses, excellent breads and pretty much everything that baas, clucks, swims or is edible is for sale at the showgrounds at the northern edge of Canberra.

Croissant D'Or
33 East Row, Canberra City
Tel 6247 0853
Get re-acquainted with real chocolate éclairs at this seriously good patisserie. The baguettes are terrific, as are the cakes, croissants and crème brûlée.

Fyshwick Fresh Foods Market
Cnr Dalby and Mildura Streets, Fyshwick
Tel 6295 0606
A great European deli, the best selection of organic potatoes and excellent local stone fruit are highlights, along with budget meats, fruit and veg, and health foods.

100% of people who receive a fortune cookie read the message!

Fortunate®

home of the gourmet fortune cookie

Introducing Fortunate's Gourmet Fortune Cookies
where the messages are better and the taste is too!

CORPORATE
Promotions & launches
direct mailers

RETAIL & HOSPITALITY
Cafes and restaurants
functions & catering

PRIVATE
Weddings, parties, gifts
with a cup of coffee

Individual gourmet base flavours

Chocolate — Citrus — Cinnamon
Pineapple — Ginger — Vanilla

www.fortunate.com.au

Fortunate Biscuits - Fortunate Biscuits is a division of Fortunate Things Pty Limited ABN 97 107 711 544
Phone (02) 9652 0519 - Fax (02) 9652 0217
Email sales@fortunatebiscuits.com

7 days for only $6.50 a week - SAVE MORE THAN 33%

A subscription to *The Sydney Morning Herald* and *The Sun-Herald* means you'll be a step ahead before you've even taken a step outside. Enjoy FREE home delivery, in-depth coverage of news, sport and business, plus entertaining lift-outs such as Good Living and Sunday Life. All for only $6.50 a week.*

Call 9282 3886 or visit www.smh.com.au/delivery

The Sydney Morning Herald | The Sun-Herald

Terms and conditions: Offer is valid in NSW and the ACT where normal home delivery exists and is valid until December 31, 2005. Price is GST-inclusive. *Payment is direct debited every four weeks from your credit card or bank account and continues unless otherwise advised.

Griffith Butcher & Bakery
10 Barker Street, Griffith
Tel 6295 9781
Gathering organic produce from all over the region, Richard Odell runs the best butcher in Canberra, with superb meat that costs what it is worth. A bakery has now been added on, with decent bread and sweet treats.

Hobbitt Farm
Barry Way, South Jinabyne
Tel 6457 8171
Hobbitt boss Mike Corbett has worked hard to popularise his terrific white mould, ash chèvre and fresh curd quark – the proof be in the eating. Ask nicely and Mike might even give you a nibble of his favourite matured cheese.

Le Petit Fourneau Patisserie
Shop 9, Chapman Shops, Perry Drive, Chapman
Tel 6288 7714
From glossy tarts and quiches to sensational almond croissants and Paris Brest, Le Petit Fourneau is the real thing. And they make birthday and special occasion cakes to order.

Nimmitabel Butchery
225 Sharp Street, Cooma
Tel 6452 7800
Skinless 'lamb stick' snags are Eddie Hope's latest sensation, bringing the number of sausage varieties he sells to 27. Housemade smallgoods, including prosciutto and brawn make a great grab on the way to the snowfields.

Old Bus Depot Markets
27 Wentworth Avenue, Kingston
Tel 6239 5306/6292 8391
Every Sun, 10am–4pm
A growing presence from local producers makes this a great place to shop and eat. Best bets are local smoked trout, organic fruit and veg, full-flavoured strawberries and stalls selling fantastic pre-prepared food from Laos, Ethiopia, Japan, France and Spain.

Poachers Pantry
Marakei, Nanima Road, via Hall
Tel 6230 2487
Tasting rooms for the more than 20 smallgoods, including kangaroo prosciutto, smoked duck breast and Wily Trout wines, are open all week at the Pantry, while the farmhouse turns into a buzzy cafe, using the Poachers' products, Fri–Sun and some public holidays.

Red Hill Butcher Shop
16 Duyfken Place, Red Hill
Tel 6295 6854
Great raw ingredients and a terrific ready-to-eat range make this butcher stand out. Choose from beef or salmon, roasted or smoked to order, as well as homemade sausage rolls, meatloaf and lasagne to take away.

Tutto Continental
Shops 1–2, off 142–152 Mawson Place, Mawson
Tel 6286 8800
A great wedge of Italian parmesan, huge jars of Sicilian anchovies, pasta-making machines and real mozzarella are just some of the delights at Canberra's best continental supermarket. The great cooking advice comes free.

regional

Canberra Wines
BY HUON HOOKE

The Canberra region is a small but very exciting one, with 38 producers, 18 of which are open for visits. Most of these are in the Murrumbateman area of the Yass Valley, where Helm grows fine riesling, Clonakilla grows its revolutionary shiraz viognier – which influenced the entire nation – as well as an outstanding pure viognier, and Kyeema produces solid reds from shiraz and cabernet.

The other sub-regions are Hall, Lake George and Bungendore. The last is where Lark Hill makes super-fine whites from chardonnay and riesling and subtle reds from pinot noir, all in the region's highest vineyard at 860 metres.

Altitudes vary, with the result that lower-lying vineyards (around 500 metres) can happily ripen shiraz. The only big company in the region is Hardys, which spent $12 million building the ambitious Kamberra Wine Centre fronting Northbourne Avenue at Lyneham, with a big, modern winery and a snappy, commercial tasting/sales facility.

Brindabella Hills
156 Woodgrove Close, via Hall
Tel 6230 2583
In a beautiful location, high above the Murrumbidgee River at Hall, Roger and Fay Harris produce variable but often excellent wines, especially the steely riesling, the buttery chardonnay and elegant spicy shiraz. Cabernet can be stylish but hovers on the herbal border. Well worth the drive.

Clonakilla
Crisps Lane, Murrumbateman
Tel 6227 5877
Clonakilla vies with Lark Hill for honours as top dog of the region. Powerful yet elegant, intensely spicy shiraz viognier is simply great and defies the odds by being so almost every year. So commanding is this wine it's easy to overlook the cabernet blend, the riesling, the semillon–sauvignon blanc, the dry white viognier, and the Hilltops shiraz, which are often superb.

Helm
Butt's Road, Murrumbateman
Tel 6227 5953
Run by the irrepressible, white-handlebar-moustached Ken Helm, this is a source of very good riesling and gewürztraminer, although the reds are variable and can be rather herbal.

Kamberra
Cnr Northbourne Avenue & Flemington Road, Lyneham
Tel 6262 2333
Hardys is the only major company with a presence in the region, but what a presence! Their impressive complex is on the main road at Lyneham, with modern tasting facilities and a 2000-tonne capacity winery, which dwarfs all others. The vineyards are at Holt. There are two ranges: the premium Kamberra wines and the $15 Meeting Place line, which is cheap for Canberra, although some are multi-region blends.

Lark Hill
521 Bungendore Road, Bungendore
Tel 6238 1393
The highest altitude in the district (860 metres) results in ultra-delicate, refined wines that in some ways set a benchmark for Australian cool-climate wine. The riesling can be quite Germanic, the chardonnay is one of the most subtle yet enchanting in the country, and the bubbly is also worthy. Pinot noir is very good at the delicate end of the spectrum; rich shiraz and merlot are sourced from warmer, lower sites.

Madew Wines
'Westering', Federal Highway, Lake George
Tel 4848 0165
Madew is a tourism-orientated winery sited on the main highway, overlooking Lake George. With a fine restaurant, an active program of concerts and a mature, well-sited vineyard, the wines can also delight. Best are whites: riesling and pinot gris, especially the Belle reserve selection.

Others to visit: Gallagher, Pankhurst, Mount Majura, Jeir Creek, Wimbaliri.

HUNTER VALLEY

JAMES MAYSON & CATHERINE KEENAN

Australia's oldest wine region is something of a tourist Mecca for the still-burgeoning wine industry. There's a lot of wineries putting truckloads of money into extravagant altars to their craft – 'cellar door' doesn't quite do justice to the architectural extravagance – yet very little of that money seems directed towards creating seriously focussed restaurants. After all, in most parts of the world great food and sensational wine are inseparable bedfellows. We yearn to see the Hunter put its mouth where the money is.

Local produce continues to shine, thanks in part to excellent olive growers, like Pukara Estate, producing table olives and quality virgin oils to mix with the latest craze – caramelised 'balsamic' vinegar. Add exquisite cow's and goat's milk cheeses, Morpeth's amazing sourdough, fantastic preserves and chutneys (see *Provedores*) and, of course, the wines. Our suggestion is to head away from the madding crowds to the quieter back hills and some well-established boutique wineries (see *Wines*).

There's plenty to do in between quaff stops, from ballooning to golfing; or, alternatively, make your form of transport the focus. Wine tours can be done by a range of means, from limos to horse-drawn carriages, although too-happy, meandering cyclists are literally becoming a bit of a hit-and-miss adventure.

There are festivals and concerts year round, although, on the third weekend in May, it's hard to go past the Lovedale Long Lunch (www.lovedalelonglunch.com.au) whereby visitors dine their way around eight wineries over the weekend. The Harvest Festival runs for a month from late February with the occasional big-name music act, while historic Morpeth pays homage to food's burning issues with its Fiery Food Festival in April.

Amanda's on the Edge

1039 Windsor's Edge Vineyard,
McDonalds Road, Pokolbin
Tel 4998 7900   Map 12

Contemporary

Score 12/20

Along a suitably countrified dirt road sits this recreated Federation homestead with two dining areas of terracotta tiles and corrugated iron features. Choose a window seat or dine on the terrace to enjoy the rural views over the family's Windsor's Edge vineyards. Tables are graced with bottles of olive oil and balsamic – a generous introduction to soak up the $1 bread rolls. Service is young, friendly and generally efficient under the watchful eye of Amanda North, while chef Karl Avis whips up clever, simple concoctions, such as roast field mushrooms topped with labna, the crunch of fried breadcrumbs and a sticky balsamic reduction. Sri Lankan chicken curry is redolent with cloves, but regrettably the accompanying rice was clumpy and the chutney hardly piquant enough to cut the flavours. Slow-cooked lamb loin is fall-apart tender, arriving on a moist hill of barley, although the pot-roasted parsnips and carrots were a little underdone. Desserts are tried-and-true crowd-pleasers such as sticky date pudding.

Hours Lunch Fri–Mon noon–3pm; Dinner daily 6.30–9pm

Bill E $15.50–$17.50 **M** $26.50–$32 **D** $12.50–$14.50; 10% surcharge on Sundays & public holidays

Cards AE BC DC MC V Eftpos; bookings essential

Wine Reasonably priced locals; 7 by the glass; BYO (corkage $4 pp)

Chef Karl Avis

Owner Amanda North

Seats 80; private rooms; wheelchair access; outdoor seats

www.amandas.com.au

And... stay in the cottages on the estate

regional

Beltree @ Margan

266 Hermitage Road, Pokolbin
Tel 6574 7216   Map 12

Mediterranean

Score 13/20

In an area where the natural beauty is sometimes marred by unsympathetic buildings, this unassuming cafe uses simplicity to great effect. On a clear day, wooden and old iron tables and chairs are strewn lazily across the rear deck, the surrounding gums standing tall and beautiful. If the weather's less inviting, sit inside where the open kitchen adds to the happy hum. The food is designed for long, lingering lunches. The Mediterranean-inspired dishes are meant to be shared, so bring along some friends (and a designated driver). Zucchini flowers stuffed with four Italian cheeses are crisp and inviting. Yet, sadly, whitebait fritters tasted slightly blander than we expected of such spiky, arresting-looking morsels. Chunky chipolatas work well with prosciutto, sage and the inspired addition of lots of sweet cooked grapes. Service can be a little on the haphazard side, but it's well meaning. And, especially if you're washing it all down with Andrew Margan's wines, who's in a rush anyway?

Hours Lunch daily 10am–5pm
Bill Shared plates $16–$24; **D** $6–$9; 10% surcharge on Sundays & public holidays
Cards BC MC V Eftpos
Wine All Margan wines; 14 by the glass; BYO (corkage $5 per bottle)
Chef Mark Delandro
Owners Andrew & Lisa Margan
Seats 52; wheelchair access; outdoor seats
And…pop next door before your meal to taste the wines served at lunch

The Cellar

Hunter Valley Gardens Village, Broke Road, Pokolbin
Tel 4998 7584   Map 12

Contemporary

Score 13/20

Reminiscent of an après-ski lodge – enormous fireplace, textures of stone and dark-wood beams – The Cellar seems at odds with the rest of the gaudy Hunter Valley Gardens complex. Service is bright and enthusiastic, rarely missing a beat. Dishes are as busy as the local tour buses: flavours jostling and colliding but mostly to good effect. Pan-fried Yamba prawns on a crumbed lemon risotto cake come balanced on figs with a moat of saffron aïoli. A herculean slab of perfectly cooked jewfish sways on potato flavoured with thyme and fetta, surrounded by salsa verde, topped with tomato and caper salsa (saffron aïoli joins the party unannounced). Linguini with a robust melange of all things Mediterranean – olive tapenade, artichoke, roast pumpkin, semi-dried and fresh tomato, capers, roast capsicum – seems more than its 'light meal' menu description, but why complain when portions and service remain on the gregarious side of generous?

Hours Lunch Mon–Sat noon–3pm; Dinner Mon–Fri 6.30–9pm, Sat 6–9pm
Bill E $19 **M** $32 **D** $14; $3 pp surcharge on weekends & public holidays
Cards AE BC DC MC V Eftpos
Wine Enjoyable, mostly Hunter list, great back vintages; 14 by the glass; BYO Mon–Fri (corkage $6 per bottle)
Chefs Mark Hosie & Andy Wright
Owners Mark & Jacqui Hosie, Andy & Janet Wright
Seats 120; private room; wheelchair access; outdoor seats
www.the-cellar-restaurant.com.au
And…mid-week bargain set lunch and dinner: two courses $34; three courses $44

Hunter Valley

Esca Bimbadgen
790 McDonalds Road, Pokolbin
Tel 4998 4666   Map 12

Contemporary
Score 13/20

Up the winding driveway, towards the signature belltower, there's a sense of expectation as you enter the restaurant, passing huge steel vats holding the latest vintages from Bimbadgen Estate. Take your seat in this modern, airy, glass-sided space, with views across the vines to the Shark's golf course resort, interspersed with a few bright splashes of colour thanks to creeping bougainvillea. Chef Bradley Teale's European, Asian or North African-accented dishes are matched to a Bimbadgen drop and aim to please the tourist lunch crowd, while smiling staff will happily explain the wines. The verdelho goes particularly well with an elegant yet crowd-pleasing dish such as coils of calamari atop a lychee and coriander salad with roasted peanuts and chilli jam. Altogether different, and almost as successful, is pan-fried veal loin fillets with figs, kipfler potatoes, sorrel and lemon–caper mayonnaise. It's edged out, though, by a terrific, tender ocean trout fillet on soba noodles, cucumber and mizuna, with a ginger relish and sesame–soy dressing.

Hours Lunch daily noon–3pm
Bill E $19.50–$21.50 **M** $31.50–$32.50 **D** $12; 10% surcharge on public holidays
Cards AE BC DC MC V Eftpos
Wine Winery drops, other Hunter varieties and some internationals; 15 by the glass
Chef Bradley Teale
Owner Mulpha Pty Ltd
Seats 120; private room; wheelchair access; outdoor seats
www.bimbadgen.com.au
And... the tasting room is downstairs if anything takes your fancy

Mojo's on Wilderness
84 Wilderness Road, Lovedale
Tel 4930 7244   Map 12

Contemporary
Score 13/20

Sitting on the back patio as the sun washes over the green fields, you almost feel as if you're at a friend's house. Service is as warm as the colours adorning the walls of this brightly painted cottage, with its oversized fireplace and glass doors leading to the patio and beyond. Happily, the food is as vibrant as the surrounds, drawing effortlessly on European, Asian and North African influences. Although there are bold flavours in grilled sardines on slow-roasted tomato sauce, with gremolata crème fraîche and a parmesan crisp, they are blended with real finesse. Ditto the lamb rump with harissa-scented chickpeas, roast pumpkin and spinach, which really shows up the skills of husband-and-wife team, Ros and Adam Baldwin. Less imaginative but equally well executed is a tandoori chicken salad with minted yoghurt. Desserts are especially tempting, and the raspberry jelly in the passionfruit and meringue trifle is better than anything you had as a kid – passionfruit curd turns it into trifle heaven.

Hours Brunch Sun from 10am; Lunch Sun from noon; Dinner daily from 6.30pm
Bill Lunch **E** $17 **M** $18–$28 **D** $13; Dinner 2/3 courses $48/$60
Cards AE BC DC MC V Eftpos
Wine Great two-pager including many rarely seen boutique local wines; 10 by the glass
Chefs/owners Ros & Adam Baldwin
Seats 50; wheelchair access; outdoor seats
www.mojos.net.au
And... try it for dinner to sample the full breadth of the menu

regional

No. 13 Cafe
13 Belmore Road, Lorn
Tel 4933 5213 Map 12

Contemporary

Score 13/20

Tell someone you've found a great cafe in Lorn and they'll immediately ask what you were doing on the Great Ocean Road. No, we mean the village just near Maitland, where, down a lane behind a beautician, there's a warm and welcoming little slice of Tuscan-style cafe. By day, it's decent coffee in the cobbled courtyard, plus solid breakfasts, including the ubiquitous corn fritters and ricotta hotcakes. Lunch might be braised beef cheeks or a salmon niçoise-style salad. Inside at night, by candlelight, local art decorates the whitewashed walls beneath exposed timber beams. Brett Niven keeps everyone happy offering around a dozen hearty dishes in both entrée and main sizes, such as snapper with an open lasagne of roasted tomato, spinach, mascarpone and preserved lemon. Quail with roasted fig and pine nut salad perhaps didn't need the honey yoghurt dressing, but osso buco with a tangy gremolata is wonderfully comforting. The chocolate bliss – a brownie, ice-cream and biscotti – is appropriately decadent; and youthful, fresh-faced service also raises a smile.

Hours Wed–Fri 10am–9pm; Sat 9am–9pm; Sun 9am–3.30pm
Bill Dinner **E/M** $16–$27 **D** $10.50–$12.50, less at breakfast and lunch; 10% surcharge on public holidays
Cards AE BC MC V Eftpos
Wine BYO (corkage $2 pp)
Chef Brett Niven
Owners Brett & Nancy Niven
Seats 54; wheelchair access; outdoor seats
www.no13cafe.com.au
And...vegies are complimentary with main-sized meals

The Old George & Dragon
48 Melbourne Street, East Maitland
Tel 4933 7272 Map 12

Anglo–French

Score 14/20

For more than 22 years Jenny and Ian Morphy have bestowed upon Maitland its one true refuge of tranquil hedonism. To be sure the Old George is not a place of wild adventure but a more hearty, assured and generous spirit of hospitality would be hard to find. Originally built in the 1830s as a travellers' inn, the building remains true to its intentions (you can stay in the guesthouse next door). Rich wallpaper, lavish settings, prints of hunting hounds and pioneer ships battling high seas all help to embellish a Victorian-era feel that flows through the Anglo–French menu. Seared scallops loll in a rich, velvety pea purée with sautéed leeks. Scampi are au gratin in a creamy truffle-scented sea of velouté. Tender veal medallions relax in a forest of sautéed pine mushrooms. Thankfully, the now legendary rhubarb and apple crumble escapes the truffle shavings, as does the exceptional vanilla ice-cream. All in all, an untold indulgence awaits all ye who this way come.

Hours Dinner Wed–Sat 6.30–10pm
Bill 2/3 courses $56/$68; $2 pp surcharge on Saturdays, $5 pp on public holidays
Cards AE BC DC MC V Eftpos
Wine Exceptional list including large 'classics' section; plenty of half bottles, several by the glass
Chef Ian Morphy
Owners Ian & Jenny Morphy
Seats 55; private rooms
www.oldgeorgeanddragon.com.au
And...allow Jenny to steer you through the tome of wines

Hunter Valley

quince
109 Susan Street, Scone
Tel 6545 2286   Map 12

Contemporary
Score 13/20

This quaint 100-year-old cottage, lovingly restored with polished floorboards, pale hues on wood-panelled walls and rustic furniture, seems torn from the pages of *Country Style* magazine. The modest restaurant, nestled opposite a peaceful patch of grass and gums, delivers far more than taste and style. Service is warm and obliging. Lunch can be as simple as a gourmet open sandwich or choose from the homemade, tapas-style menu: white bean and garlic dip, olive tapenade, gently spiced yellow lentil dahl or tomato chilli jam. Chargrilled chorizo and to-die-for duck and pistachio sausages are from Sydney's AC Butchery. Confit spatchcock risotto with sugar snap peas, garlic chunks and parmesan is a lesson in simplicity and depth, the al dente rice flavoured with a light stock enriched with cream. There's bliss in the first spoonful of an earthy and wholesome mushroom and lentil soup, garnished with parsley, plus Bacco sourdough. Dinner heralds more substantial fare such as a tantalising beef fillet with blue cheese soft polenta and caramelised onions.

Hours Brunch Sun 10am–noon; Lunch Thurs–Sat 11am–3pm, Sun noon–3pm; Dinner Thurs–Sat 6pm–late

Bill E $9.50–$14 **M** $16–$29 **D** $9–$9.50; 10% surcharge on public holidays

Cards BC MC V Eftpos

Wine Short, local centric; some New Zealand and Western Australian varieties; 6 by the glass

Chefs Jason & Nicole Larsen

Owners Jason Larsen & Anjela Hjorring

Seats 100; wheelchair access; outdoor seats

And... visit the Wine Centre next door for some Upper Hunter tastings

Roberts at Peppertree
Halls Road, Pokolbin
Tel 4998 7330   Map 12

European
Score 14/20

Some Hunter places feel contrived, but not Roberts. You enter through the lived-in-looking 1876 slab hut and make your way to the barn-sized dining room, where candlelight, flowers and country antiques lend real warmth and grace. Since opening the restaurant in 1991, Algerian-born Robert Molines has carved out an impressive reputation for traditional European fare. After some recent wavering, it's great to see this Hunter institution back on song. A charcuterie plate of salami, house-made pâté and terrine clearly shows why. A pitch-perfect rendition of another classic dish – figs wrapped in prosciutto with gorgonzola – is just as classy. The ever-changing menu can lean towards the hearty, but the quality of produce and skilled preparation bring a light touch to two triangles of butter-soft lamb that combine magnificently with the sweet smokiness of a red capsicum sauce. Steak lovers will be enraptured by the richness of grain-fed sirloin with sautéed mushrooms, braised baby leeks, red wine sauce and béarnaise. There's absolutely nothing contrived about that.

Hours Lunch daily noon–4pm; Dinner daily from 7pm

Bill E $17–$25 **M** $38–$42 **D** $13–$15; $5 pp surcharge on weekends & public holidays

Cards AE BC DC MC V

Wine Deeply interesting and wide-ranging list; 17 by the glass

Chefs Robert Molines & Daniel Hunt

Owners Robert & Sally Molines

Seats 110; private rooms; wheelchair access; outdoor seats

www.robertsrestaurant.com

And... try the very good Peppertree wines

good food guide

regional

Shakey Tables

1476 Wine Country Drive, North Rothbury
Tel 4938 1744   Map 12

Contemporary   ♀
Score 13/20

'Quirky' Tables would seem a more apt name for this restaurant festooned by chef Paula Rengger's idiosyncratic art, décor and food. It's a country lodge in so much as it's a log cabin, but that's where the similarity ends. Knives sit on edge at rustic, chunky tables, surrounded by lolly-coloured dining chairs. A Gothic candelabra weeps puddles of wax onto the floor. Naïve, colourful paintings of the staff gaze out over the diners. There are few light touches on a menu where heavily worked dishes at times detracts from excellent produce. A terrine of smoked and tartare salmon with crème fraîche and kipfler potatoes is a densely packed triangle surrounded by dots of roe – aesthetically beautiful yet onerous. Bacon-wrapped de-boned pigeon, stuffed with prunes and black sausage, and balancing on cabbage rolls surrounded by red wine jus was rare and flavoursome yet tough. Apple charlotte partnered an undercooked rhubarb crumble, with knockout homemade ice-cream. Service, particularly from wine aficionado Simon, smooths over the wait between courses.

Hours Lunch Sun noon–3pm; Dinner daily from 6.30pm

Bill E $20 **M** $34 **D** $16; 10% surcharge on public holidays

Cards AE BC DC MC V Eftpos; bookings essential

Wine Great showcase of Hunter marques, with bottle age, plus great bubblies; 10 by the glass

Chef Paula Rengger

Owners Paula & Simon Rengger

Seats 60; wheelchair access; outdoor seats

www.shakeytables.com.au

And…rooms in the log cabins are good value

The Table

3 Water Street, Greta
Tel 4938 7799   Map 12

European Provincial
Score 14/20

You don't 'buy' dinner at The Table. True, by the end of your stay, you'll cross your host's palm with barely sufficient silver, but what your money does secure is a truly unique experience. To completely surrender to all that's on offer, stay the night. With rough white-plaster walls, dark-wood beams, black wrought iron, rustic country furniture and a sun-drenched courtyard blooming with olive trees and wisteria, you could be in an Andalusian hacienda or a Tuscan farmhouse…albeit an hour west of Newcastle. There's no menu, just the imaginative whim of Malcolm Martin conjuring local produce into country European comfort food. Home-baked bread with duck liver pâté and local marinated olives puts you in the mood before a textbook vichyssoise. Then it's paella brimming with roast quail, prawns, mussels, fish and sausage, uplifted with 'North African spices'. Figs poached in cognac, with fresh mango, complete the seduction. It's not rocket science – just a charming, intuitive host who infuses the relaxed ambience with genuine warmth and the personal touch.

Hours Dinner daily 7–9pm

Bill 3 course set menu with hors d'oeuvres and coffee $60

Cards AE BC MC V; bookings essential

Wine BYO (no corkage!)

Chef/owner Malcolm Martin

Seats 30; private room; outdoor seats

www.thetable.com.au

And…the sumptuous brekkie is a great start to the day

Hunter Valley

Terroir

1 Broke Road, Pokolbin
Tel 4990 0711   Map 12

Contemporary

Score 13/20

The landmark Hungerford Hill Winery – you can't miss what appears to be a giant flying saucer (apparently an architect's attempt at a wine barrel with the lid half off) perched right in the middle of the tourist wine trail – is blessed with an open, airy ambience, overlooking some of the prettiest vineyards in the valley. Chef Darren Ho's talent has an inventive and humorous edge that, for the most part, works brilliantly in a wide-ranging menu, matched to suggested wines by the glass or bottle. Plump, enormous and barely seared scallops lounge in a laksa-style sauce with crisp noodles and carrot ribbons. Chinese pork sausage is sliced, fried and served with a sweet Asian sauce. Tender lamb, smoked with French oak shavings, enjoys a blueberry vinaigrette. Butter-soft angus beef comes with Paris mash, beetroot relish and roasted bone marrow. Service is assured, if a little dry. The novelty returns with banana split 'revisited' – pan-fried bananas on a cumin almond tuile.

Hours Lunch daily noon–3pm; Dinner Wed–Sat 6.30–9.30pm
Bill E $16.50–$19.90 **M** $28.90–$35.50 **D** $12.50–$14.90; 6-course dégustation menu $85 pp, minimum 2 people; $3 pp surcharge on weekends & public holidays
Cards AE BC DC MC V Eftpos
Wine A great showcase of French, Italian, US, Hunter and Hungerford; 22 by the glass
Chef Darren Ho
Owner James Kirby
Seats 200; private room; wheelchair access; outdoor seats
www.hungerfordhill.com.au/terroirrestaurant
And… the cafe does simpler nibbles, coffee and cakes

And also…

Bliss Coffee Roasters
Shop 2, Hunter Valley Gardens Shopping Village, Broke Road, Pokolbin
Tel 4998 6700
Lynn Couchman-Frame learnt all about the addictive bean while growing up amongst coffee plantations in Papua New Guinea (her father was the original owner of Campos Coffee in Newtown, where she learnt to roast). She now runs this minimalist cafe, roasting her own beans to produce a mellow-malty brew, served with cakes and biscuits.

Henri's Brasserie
85 John Street, Singleton
Tel 6571 3566
An ambitious menu attempts to fuse French, Asian and Mediterranean flavours in this stylishly renovated terrace. Seared scallops are sublime, paired with powerfully flavoursome pork and peanut relish; corn-and-yabbie soup with basil oil has a blast of chilli; and snapper with buttered leaks and roast capsicum peperonata is assured. Then there's classic country fare such as apple pie or steamed date pudding.

Kerv Espresso Bar
108 Liverpool Street, Scone
Tel 6545 3111
This über-groovy cafe just off the New England Highway doubles as a homewares store and gallery. Decent coffee, takeaway gourmet dinners and light, fresh, flavoursome lunches, such as dukkah-crusted chicken tenderloin on grilled eggplant salad with hummus, are waking up the neighbourhood.

Oishii
Tempus Two Winery, Cnr Broke & McDonalds roads, Pokolbin
Tel 4998 7051
You can't miss this grey, hulking, post-modern winery, which looks as if it may have landed from another galaxy. Fortunately, Lisa McGuigan's Tempus Two wines inside are more tasteful. And, offering some respite from the Hunter's mostly Eurocentric menus are Oishii's pan-Asian dishes: sushi, satay, tom yum goong, green curry or teriyaki. It's best on a good day, on the verandah looking down over the crisply mown lawns, especially since the service can be scatty and the wait quite sobering.

regional

Provedores

Australian Regional Food Store & Cafe
The Small Winemakers Centre, McDonalds Road, Pokolbin
Tel 4998 6800
If you're visiting hoping to sample hard-to-come-by wines, this is a good place to start. Taste a few from small winemakers, then head to the shop to try some of the area's other fine produce, such as Morpeth Sourdough, Hunter Valley Cheeses and Pukara Estate olive oil. Jams, chutneys, pastas and other gourmet items from around Australia are also available. Sample them in the adjoining cafe.

Binnorie Dairy
Cnr Hermitage Road & Mistletoe Lane, Pokolbin
Tel 4998 6660
Don't miss the duetto: a combination of gorgonzola and mascarpone that's heaven for blue cheese fans. Simon Gough makes many other cheeses from both cow's and goat's milks. You can also visit his small shop in the Tuscany Wine Resort to try the fetta, labna, fromage frais and mascarpone, and grab jams and chutneys to go with them.

The Hunter Olive Centre
Pokolbin Estate Vineyard, McDonalds Road, Pokolbin
Tel 4998 7524
A fantastic place to sample the best of the Hunter's regional produce. There are several olive oils for tasting, along with marinated olives, spice blends for dipping, preserves, pastes, tapenades, jams and honey.

Hunter Valley Cheese Co.
McGuigan Wine Complex, McDonalds Road, Pokolbin
Tel 4998 7744
Monty Python would bless this place and you can too – watching the cheese makers or viewing the ripening rooms. Just don't forget to taste the swoon-worthy washed-rind cheeses to match those dusky local reds.

Morpeth Sourdough
148 Swan Street, Morpeth
Tel 4934 4148
In a quintessentially historic town, Stephen Arnott – yes of Arnott's family fame – bakes only sourdough, so that no yeast spores can escape to 'infect' his starter. This beautifully restored bakery, where his great grandfather first plied the trade back in 1862, produces a range of dense, flavoursome loaves, including a remarkable fruit and nut and a traditional German rye from a recipe dating back centuries.

Sandalyn Wilderness Estate
162 Wilderness Road, Rothbury
Tel 4930 7611
The people walking around with aprons on and flour in their hair have just finished doing one of the popular pasta-making classes. If you haven't got time, stop by for comprehensive and generous olive oil tastings (Sandalyn also runs olive oil appreciation classes) and pick up some excellent olives, locally made biscuits and the knockout Wilderness Grove caramelised balsamic vinegar. Oh, and sample the wines, of course.

Tea Lovers & Coffee for Others
Heritage Mall, 346 High Street, Maitland
Tel 4934 1816
137 Swan Street, Morpeth
Tel 4934 6616
The original owners have sold their Morpeth shop; however, both premises continue to stack the shelves with decorative tins full of various brews – black, green and herbal. Take away or enjoy on site with a light snack or local cakes and biscuits.

Tinklers Family Wines and Farm Produce
Pokolbin Mountains Road, Pokolbin
Tel 4998 7435
From November through March, there's an abundance of stone fruit and grapes; while from April to October, it's mainly citrus and avocados. You can still picnic under the 120-year-old pepper trees after grabbing some of their chutneys, honey and jams – including the ever-popular apricot and pumpkin.

Hunter Valley

Hunter Valley wines
BY HUON HOOKE

The Hunter Valley, just inland from Newcastle, is Australia's oldest continuing major wine region, established in 1825. Quite by coincidence, it also produces some of Australia's most distinctive regional wines. While struggling against the 'old hat' syndrome of the trendy wine business, the Hunter is also devaluing its own currency to some extent, as many wineries now import grapes to make varietals with which the Hunter cannot naturally compete, such as sauvignon blanc, pinot noir and cabernet. Meanwhile, it continues to make Australia's and possibly the world's finest and most age-worthy dry white semillon, and one of our most individualistic shiraz styles. Verdelho is its modestly priced, crowd-pleasing soft white, and chardonnay can occasionally hit the heights.

The Hunter has evolved in the last 20 years into a massive tourist destination, with golf threatening to take over from wine as the key attraction. But a lot of effort and money have also been poured into smart cellar doors and wineries, none smarter than Tempus Two or offering a more beautiful view than Audrey Wilkinson.

Indeed, there are 127 cellar doors and many excellent places to stay. Nowhere else is the wine tourist so well catered for.

Boutique Wine Centre
Broke Road, Pokolbin
Tel 4998 7474
Taste the wines of some elite and rare small makers including Glenguin, Meerea Park and Chateau Pato.

Brokenwood
McDonalds Road, Pokolbin
Tel 4998 7559
Graveyard is arguably the Hunter's greatest shiraz. The semillon (including the lovely, mature ILR bottling) is consistently superb, but you'll find wines from many other regions among Brokenwood's high-quality offerings, such as Beechworth pinot noir and viognier, Orange chardonnay and McLaren Vale shiraz.

McWilliam's Mount Pleasant
Marrowbone Road, Pokolbin
Tel 4998 7505
Hunter wine doesn't come more traditional or regionally typical. Semillon is the stand-out, plus, from the best years, succulently smooth shiraz from the oldest vines in the region. Lovedale semillon is simply great, while benchmark Elizabeth is an affordable intro to a classic style.

Small Winemakers Centre
McDonalds Road, Pokolbin
Tel 4998 7668
A one-stop showcase for a clutch of boutique wines, including Keith Tulloch, Andrew Thomas, Little's Olivine, Macquariedale and Verona. Cafe lunches, too.

Tower Estate
Cnr Broke & Halls Roads, Pokolbin
Tel 4998 7989
The rendered walls of Len Evans's Tuscan-style boutique enclose a purist project focussed on quality: small lots of 1000 cases maximum, including Coonawarra cabernet, Clare riesling, Adelaide Hills sauvignon blanc, as well as the Hunter classics. If quality is your target, don't miss this.

Tyrrell's
Broke Road, Pokolbin
Tel 4993 7000
The Hunter's finest combination of semillon, chardonnay and shiraz. With most of the region's best semillon vineyards in their holdings, Tyrrell's make a specialty of this crisp flinty dry white, with seven different bottlings, some of them released wonderfully mature.

Others to visit: Capercaillie, Allandale, Lake's Folly, Lindemans, Hungerford Hill, Kulkunbulla, Margan, Petersons, Pothana, Rothvale, Scarborough, Pepper Tree, De Iuliis, Rothbury Estate.

regional

CENTRAL COAST + NEWCASTLE

JAMES MAYSON, LYNNE MULLINS & AMANDA HOOTON

The Central Coast spans a rare symphony of beaches, mountains, national parks and great waterways. Sadly, the landscape continues to be whittled away by the Colorbond sprawl, but the good news is that after years of languishing as a dining backwater there's a palpable lift in standards. Brian Lizotte has moved his eponymous restaurant (see entry) inland and opened the fun Yum Yum Eatery (see entry) in Hardy's Bay, while talented chef Brad Dawson has lifted the standards at that prime piece of Terrigal waterfront, the Reef (see entry).

When travelling around, look out for the endangered (yet dangerously addictive) Sydney rock oyster, freshly shucked from a variety of riverfront barns. An abundance of seafood provedores, their produce often direct from the trawlers, can be found in just about every waterfront settlement (see *Provedores*).

In Newcastle, a spectacular redevelopment of the harbour foreshore known as the Honeysuckle 'Boardwalk' precinct retains some of the city's industrial heritage in a cluster of new buildings that surpasses the efforts around Sydney's Darling Harbour.

This growth spurt has helped stir the pot in Newcastle's eating precincts. Darby Street was looking a little tired; however, street improvements have begun and there's genuine heart and soul among its character-ridden collection of Boho cafes – especially the student haunt Goldberg's Coffee House (Tel 4929 3122) the rustic Three Monkeys (Tel 4926 3779), and the great coffee of Grind (Tel 4929 4710). Thankfully, Peter and Therese Bryant, the duo behind sorely missed hat-winner Scott Street Restaurant return with a new digs in Bolton Street (see *Stop Press*) as the Guide goes to print. Leading the way currently is Zest (see entry), in Nelson Bay.

The Brewery

The Boardwalk, Unit E2,
1 Honeysuckle Drive, Newcastle
Tel 4929 5792 Map 12

Contemporary

Score 13/20

Part of the flotilla of new establishments on the redeveloped Boardwalk facing Newcastle's workaday harbour, the Brewery is a fantastic spot by day to watch nautical comings and goings or, at night, to observe the human traffic of all things Novocastrian young and totally sick (which is, apparently, a good thing). The restaurant has separated from its gruff, pubby big brother further down the strip and opened as a sophisticated, sleek space, spilling out under umbrellas towards the harbour. Glistening fresh oysters come with a vodka, lime and chilli dipping sauce. Linguini with crab, chilli, tomato and parmesan is light and refreshing. Just-rare-in-the-centre salmon fillet in a roast shellfish bisque is simple enough to allow the quality of produce to shine through. Service is attentive and friendly, although – perhaps like some of the dishes on the menu – in need of firmer direction. To finish, passionfruit crème brûlée with macadamia white chocolate shortbread is solid, but serious dessert lovers will go for the chocolate plate, which includes chocolate tart, ice-cream and mousse.

Hours Lunch daily noon–3pm; Dinner Mon–Sat 6–9pm
Bill E $15–$18 **M** $28–$32 **D** $9.50–$15
Cards AE BC DC MC V Eftpos; bookings essential
Wine Decent list of locals plus a page for the connoisseur; 18 by the glass
Chefs Elizabeth Box & Anthony Kocon
Owners Elizabeth Box, Ian & Marnee Burford
Seats 126; wheelchair access; outdoor seats
And…the fantastic chilli corn bread with chilli coriander butter remains

Cafe Supply

Cnr Watt and King Streets, Newcastle
Tel 4929 2222   Map 12

Contemporary

Score 13/20

This minimalist renovation of an old corner bank – polished-concrete floors, black laminate tables, white seats – is a stunning transformation of subtle contrasts. Banquette seating breaks up the space while a cornucopia of colourful throw cushions, an enormous blond-wood communal table, the wide staircase with wrought-iron banister and wine cellar underneath, and mixed-textile wall hangings all help set the sassy, funky mood. And a menu filled with clever twists seems to say 'we know what we're doing' (courtesy of the original owners of Darby Street's Longbench). Bruschetta appears as a bowl of salsa with pressed toast; Peking duck and glass noodle salad is a jumble of fragrant mixed herbs, crunchy greens and lime dressing; pork with braised fennel and apple is a door-stopping one-inch-thick cutlet with a cumin-dusted, sweet and sour glaze, given added support by nut-crumbed cauliflower 'fritti'. Service, like the atmosphere, is young, friendly and switched on. Bitter choc tart with vanilla cream and shiraz coulis is a wickedly rich finale.

Hours Breakfast daily 8am–3pm, Lunch daily 11am–11pm; Dinner Tues–Sat until 10.30pm
Bill E $6.90–$17 **M** $19–$32 **D** $9; 10% surcharge on Sundays & public holidays
Cards AE BC DC MC V Eftpos; no bookings
Wine Decent mid-priced list of Oz/NZ varieties; 23 by the glass; BYO (corkage $5 per bottle)
Chefs/owners Georgina Chiragakis & Matthew Bilton
Seats 85; wheelchair access; outdoor seats
And…excellent breakfasts, including a vanilla risotto with fruit compote

Dekk

3–5 Kurrawyba Avenue, Terrigal
Tel 4385 3100   Map 11

Contemporary

Score 12/20

Just a stone's throw from the beach, Terrigal's hippest hot spot has a cocktail 'dekk' upstairs, a modern, open-plan restaurant downstairs and a young spunky vibe shaking all over. Earthy red and tan colours abound on vibrant feature walls lit with retro light shades. When the weather allows, enormous sliding doors open the room to the elements, inviting alfresco dining. With-it staff swing their narrow hips between the tables – such boundless enthusiasm makes light work of explaining an enormous menu. Former Ravesi's chef Aaron Stewart has compiled a menu to appeal to just about everyone. A scallop and pea risotto boasts gorgeous buttery bisque flavours, while duck salad with figs, goat's cheese and rocket is crammed into a filo pastry shell. Pick from a trio of steaks and your choice of accompaniments – perhaps mash and mushrooms. Desserts might include a light, tangy option of balsamic strawberries, although it's no surprise that everyone seems to hoe into the decadent signature dish: a taste of chocolate.

Hours Lunch daily noon–3pm; Dinner daily from 6pm
Bill E $15–$22 **M** $22–$34 **D** $12; 10% surcharge on Sundays & public holidays
Cards AE BC DC MC V Eftpos
Wine Solid Aussie list of affordables; 7 by the glass
Chef Aaron Stewart
Owners Mark Lambert & Daryl Peat
Seats 200; private rooms; wheelchair access (ground floor only); outdoor seats
www.dekk.com.au
And…a special lunch menu including a glass of wine for $15

regional

Emma's a la Carte
120 Beaumont Street, Hamilton
Tel 4969 6905   Map 12

Contemporary

Score 12/20

The recycled shopfront may be a little uninspiring but it's Emma Hill's food that keeps the regulars coming back for more. It's a small restaurant yet the sole waiter, Glen, is committed and knowledgeable and skips from one table to the next keeping everyone happy. You may recognise the snapper pie – served in a cute little pot with crusty golden pastry, tender fish fillets enhanced with a smidgen of white truffle oil – as Hill is a graduate of Sydney's bel mondo and Boathouse restaurants. Meltingly soft mussels, steamed in garlic and white wine, are complemented by a fragrant pea and saffron risotto, but the goat's cheese tart could be lifted with a little more asparagus and piquant cheese. Perfectly seared barramundi fillet on a creamy cauliflower purée, topped with super-fresh micro salad leaves, is a great follow up. If that's not enough to make your mouth water, the ice-cream plate of tartufo, tutti frutti and ice-cream spike is pure indulgence.

Hours Dinner Wed–Sat 6–11pm
Bill E $15–$18 **M** $26–$32 **D** $12–15
Cards AE BC DC MC V Eftpos
Wine BYO (corkage $3 pp)
Chef/owner Emma Hill
Seats 40; wheelchair access
And... dégustation once a month on Wednesdays

Engine Room
The Boardwalk, 1 Honeysuckle Drive, Newcastle
Tel 4926 4200   Map 12

Contemporary

Score 13/20

This is one of the jewels in the new Honeysuckle precinct, one of the sleekest casual dining spots in Newcastle and reminiscent of the finger wharf at Sydney's Woolloomooloo. The vista is a perfect palette of a working industrial port with burly tugs dwarfed by massive iron cargo ships. The slick fit-out, with its bright interior, cosy banquettes and engaging view, has made the Engine Room one of the places to dine, thanks to polished food served by the stylish and attentive red-shirted staff. Roasted tomato and saffron goat's curd tart is piled high and balanced nicely with wild rocket and a sticky balsamic essence. Prawn linguini is perfectly al dente with tomato confit and tossed with chilli, garlic and baby capers – combining magic Italian flavours. But the highlight is the world's best wood-fired apple tart with gorgeous caramel notes, that's only if you can pass up the superb lemon and lime tart with double cream and candied orange.

Hours Daily 7am–late
Bill E $16–20 **M** $24–28 **D** $4.50–10; pizze $17–$20
Cards AE BC DC MC V Eftpos; bookings essential
Wine Good selection from the Hunter, Barossa and Clare; 14 by the glass
Chef Scott Dudgeon
Owner Mark Prince (MAP Projects P/L)
Seats 118; wheelchair access; outdoor seats
And... pizze and tapas also feature on the menu

Central Coast & Newcastle

Feast

Shop 3, 85 Avoca Drive, Avoca Beach
Tel 4381 0707   Map 11

Modern French

Score 14/20

Perched on the end of the beach, this charming restaurant is even closer to the sparkling blue Pacific than the surf club. The foyer is adorned with pictorial memoirs of Chouvin's early career in France, notably the diminutive Chouvin dwarfed by Paul Bocuse. Opt for a table on the balcony if the day is fine and glance upon one of the Central Coast's finest beaches. Inside, soft pastel walls, linen cloths and quality tableware create a relaxing ambience. Service is polished and professional to complement Chouvin's French 'Cuisine of the Sun' and it's great to see a return to form with cleaner, true flavours. The dégustation menus are a highlight, but make sure you try a piquant tart of goat's cheese with crisp buttery pastry, which sits well with a tomato confit and rocket salad. Steamed barramundi is fresh, moist and more-ish, accompanied by summer vegetables and a light creamy sauce. Luscious nougat with red fruit coulis satisfies the sweet tooth and the complimentary petit fours are as cute as they come.

Hours Breakfast Sun 8.30–11.30am; Lunch daily from noon; Dinner daily from 6.30pm
Bill E $18.50–$25 **M** $26–$34 **D** $14; 2-course lunch $35
Cards AE BC DC MC V
Wines Well-considered list of Australian and French wines; 13 by the glass
Chef André Chouvin
Owners André & Tracey Chouvin
Seats 110; wheelchair access; outdoor seats
www.feast.com.au
And...there's a $68 five-course vegetarian dégustation menu

Flair

1/488 The Entrance Road, Erina Heights
Tel 4365 2777   Map 11

Contemporary

Score 14/20

Former TV chef Lawry Gordon has performed a small suburban miracle. He has transformed an uninspiring location in a row of neighbourhood shops into a restaurant where everything – from the complimentary semillon and mango shooter to the elaborately worded menu – speaks of a genuine interest in fine food. The interior is city-smart, with white walls and dramatic textile art; staff are as carefully trained as silver-screen actors. The real star of the show, however, is the food. King prawns and scallops in Thai lime sauce are beautifully fresh and delicate. Slow-roasted rabbit leg in prosciutto, on oxtail ravioli, is a knockout, filled with dark, smoky flavours. Among the mains, chargrilled lamb marinated in mustard and chilli flakes is melt-in-the-mouth tender, and the snapper, perfectly pan-fried, is sweet and clean. Desserts such as lychee pannacotta with scrumptious baby pear, toffee banana and lime crème brûlée, or chocolate pithivier with honey ice-cream, are prepared with care, imagination and, dare we say it, true flair.

Hours Lunch Wed–Fri noon–2.30pm; Dinner Tues–Sat from 6pm
Bill E $13–$22 **M** $27–$35 **D** $14; $1.50 pp surcharge on Saturdays, $4.50 pp on public holidays
Cards AE BC MC V Eftpos
Wine Neat, thoughtful list; surprisingly reasonably priced; 8 by the glass; BYO (corkage $3.50 pp)
Chefs Lawry Gordon & Robert Wells
Owners Lawry & Wendy Gordon
Seats 50; wheelchair access; outdoor seats
And...look out for the special four-course dinner deal with wine

regional

Letterbox
4 Ash Street, Terrigal
Tel 4385 4222   Map 11

Contemporary

Score 12/20

Terrigal's former post office is almost a century old, but its current lease on life owes as much to its high ceilings, polished floorboards and air of tranquil history as it does to food. The genuinely friendly service would make the postmaster proud, as would the clarity of a top-of-the-bistro-pops menu: vegetarian and gluten-free dishes are clearly marked. But not everything is worth writing home about. Begin with the bruschetta with tomato, basil and organic goat's cheese, then excellent salt-and-pepper squid: tender, spicy, and very more-ish. Alas, peeled tiger prawns failed to mesh with an avocado and cocktail sauce, and gristly beef rib-eye, smothered in blue cheese, let down wonderful caramelised onions and a flavoursome sauce. Oven-baked blue-eye was overwhelmed by its garlic and anchovy crust and spaghettini puttanesca base. Thankfully, plump homemade ravioli with roast pumpkin, spinach and ricotta is more successful. A white chocolate and rose petal pannacotta will satiate the sweet tooth.

Hours Lunch Tues–Sun noon–3pm; Dinner Tues–Sat from 6pm
Bill E $15–$19 **M** $25–$35 **D** $13; 10% surcharge on Sundays & public holidays
Cards AE BC DC MC V Eftpos
Wine Good selection; 9 by the glass; BYO (corkage $5 per bottle)
Chefs Karl Kard & Shayne Bedford
Owners Nicole & Karl Kard
Seats 124; private room; outdoor seats
www.letterboxrest.com.au

And... there's a conservatory, and a special lunch deal for summer

Lime
52 Glebe Road, The Junction, Newcastle
Tel 4969 2060   Map 12

Contemporary

Score 13/20

Right at The Junction's eponymous meeting point, you'll find the thoroughly mod Lime cafe. Sharp and zesty, the interior is expansive, modern and breezy with feature walls finished in – you guessed it – lime. Service on our visit was shy, friendly and on its P-plates, but the aromas wafting from the open kitchen tease the senses and keep you coming back throughout the day. For breakfast, the corn fritters, bacon with aged balsamic, rocket and tomato combo is handsome and a great start; or try eggs Benedict (weekends only). For lunch, perfectly crisp and golden salt-and-pepper calamari is topped with a green papaya and Asian herb salad given the salty, chilli zing of nam jim. Oven-baked salmon is beautifully moist, nestled on a tomato salsa, drizzled with herb pesto and accompanied by blissful roasted potatoes. We love the gorgeous, refreshingly sweet fruit sorbet terrine, with berry compote to balance the flavours. A superb, silky-smooth crème brûlée, accented with lemongrass with a paper-thin wafer, also vies for our affections.

Hours Breakfast daily 7–11.30am; Lunch 11.30am–3.30pm; Dinner 6–9.30pm
Bill E $14.90–$17.50 **M** $25.90–$31.90 **D** $10.50–$11.90; 10% surcharge on public holidays
Cards AE BC DC MC V Eftpos
Wine Limited list includes most varietals; 23 by the glass; BYO Mon–Thurs (corkage $5 per bottle)
Chef Lesley Taylor
Owners Jenny & Garth Ashford
Seats 120; private room; wheelchair access; outdoor seats

And... alfresco dining is also available on the pavement under the shadows of the war memorial

Central Coast & Newcastle

Lizotte's
Lot 3, Avoca Drive, Kincumber
Tel 4368 2017   Map 11

Contemporary

Score 13/20

In mid-2005, chef Brian Lizotte's cheerful restaurant relocated to smarter digs (that also house an art gallery) in a palm-fringed contemporary space of high-backed white leather chairs at dark-timber tables. The alfresco verandah overlooks a gully of tall eucalypts and there's a bar filled with signed concert posters, plus a small stage for live music. The menu works just as hard to please all-comers, showing a strong bush food influence amidst a mix of bistro dishes – perhaps 'Mum's roast' (turkey and cranberry) – that often have a sweetish tinge. You might start with local Brisbane Water oysters: plain rather than the syrupy 'Waggy' dressing; then try BBQ-spiced whitebait with a lime–onion marmalade; and two finger-licking blue swimmer crabs with bok choi and a sweet chilli sauce. Four cumin-dusted long-ribbed lamb cutlets are draped across a (perhaps too) oily jumble of snowpeas, capsicum and kumera. With genuinely warm nothing's-too-much-trouble service, and a tangy rhubarb crumble to finish, Lizotte's has made a move in the right direction.

Hours Lunch daily noon–3pm; Dinner Sun–Thurs 6–9pm, Fri–Sat 6–10pm
Bill E $7–$14.50 **M** $15–$26.50 **D** $9.50–$13
Cards AE BC DC MC V Eftpos
Wine Modest, good-value range of popular names; 5 by the glass
Chefs Jon Juanengo & Brian Lizotte
Owners Brian & Jo Lizotte
Seats 110; wheelchair access
www.lizottes.com.au

And...regular dinner & live music nights from the likes of Lizotte sibling Diesel, plus Vince Jones, Barnsey and Jenny Morris

Longbench on Darby
161 Darby Street, Cooks Hill, Newcastle
Tel 4927 8888   Map 12

Contemporary

Score 12/20

Among the long throng of eateries lining both sides of Darby Street, Longbench, with its wall-hugging banquette, is one of the most popular at all times of the day. You can't book, so grab a footpath table or one just inside near the open bi-fold windows if you enjoy people watching – although the downside is the cruising hot-rodders testing magnified exhaust systems. If you prefer a quieter retreat, the two-tiered courtyard behind the kitchen caters for a mixed suburban crowd in a relaxed leafy setting. Service would benefit from an injection of enthusiasm and finesse, but this is a very casual diner open from breakfast (which is popular) until late, with menu specials after 6pm. Barbecued duck comes with soba noodles and scallops – an unusual combination – served in a cute box with disposable chopsticks. Lamb cutlets were sadly overcooked but piled generously on lemon-spiked kipfler potatoes with a sweet capsicum sauce. The Belle cheese plate with dried fig salami and lavosh is from the local boutique cheese factory.

Hours Daily 7am–10pm
Bill E $8.90–$16.90 **M** $21–$31 **D** $3.50–$7.90; 10% surcharge on Sundays & public holidays
Cards AE BC DC MC V Eftpos; no bookings
Wine A well-constructed sample of mid-priced Oz favourites, 13 by the glass; BYO (corkage $2.50 pp)
Chef Lisa Ryan
Owner Nathan Bilton
Seats 95; outdoor seats

And...the best food is served at dinner time

regional

Merretts

Peppers Anchorage Resort, Corlette Point Road, Corlette
Tel 4984 2555   Map 12

Contemporary

Score 12/20

The nautical atmosphere of the adjacent marina overflows into this bright airy restaurant, open from breakfast till late evening. Sit outdoors and covet the seaplanes or be mesmerised by the wall-to-wall cruisers and fishing boats returning from an afternoon off the coast. Inside, the mood in the conservatory-style dining room is that of a resort attachment and is let down by dated chairs and napery. Initially the service is promising – a warm welcome and a polite 'I've got your bread in the oven for you' – but unfortunately failed to stay the distance. A twice-baked King Island Endeavour Blue soufflé is light as a feather and complemented by steamed asparagus and truffle essence dressing. Pan-roasted lamb rack with crisp ricotta and basil-filled tempura zucchini flowers is scrumptious and sits high on a pile of soft polenta that's ideal for mopping up the rich jus. And for a fitting finale, juicy macerated cherries accompany luscious white chocolate shards in the succulent 'Cherry Ripe' semifreddo.

Hours Daily 7am–9pm
Bill E $15 **M** $35 **D** $15
Cards AE BC DC MC V Eftpos
Wine A pricey selection of New Zealand, French and newer Oz regions
Chef Jean-Marc Pollet
Owner Peppers Anchorage Port Stephens
Seats 170; private rooms; wheelchair access; outdoor seats
www.peppers.com.au
And... you can stay the night at this manicured resort

The Reef

The Haven Beach, Terrigal
Tel 4385 3222   Map 11

Contemporary

Score 14/20

Perched at the southern corner of Terrigal's seaside arc, this clubhouse-like edifice has the area's most sought-after view: north along the golden crescent of sand. By day the airy atmosphere, blond floors and nautical colours perfectly match the setting. By night it feels in need of a softer mood to complement the menu's fine dining aspirations. Brad Dawson takes control from the nearby (and now closed) Haven. Given time to settle, his well-crafted style will fire up the stunning location. A terrine of john dory is outstanding – a fragrant, soufflé-like slice topped with shaved fennel and seared scampi tails. Crisp-skinned barramundi with sensational, moist and gelatinous flesh sits on robust little lentils redolent with cinnamon, star anise and fennel. Lamb rack is relaxed and pink with a mash-and-leek crumble. Raspberry soufflé has the bittersweet berries combined with goat's cheese ice-cream (disappointingly vanilla on our visit) and roast fig. Service is friendly, efficient – if a little stilted – and proud of the fine selection of imported beers.

Hours Lunch daily noon–2.30pm; Dinner Mon–Sat 6–10pm
Bill E $15–$24 **M** $23–$35 **D** $12; $2.50 pp surcharge on weekends & public holidays
Cards AE BC DC MC V Eftpos
Wine Solid selection of Oz favourites; 11 by the glass; great beers
Chef Brad Dawson
Owner Neil Gay
Seats 120; private room; wheelchair access
www.reefrestaurant.com.au
And... the Dive-Inn cafe underneath is even closer to the sand with a low-key cafe menu

Yum Yum Eatery

60 Araluen Drive, Hardy's Bay
Tel 4360 2999   Map 11

Modern Asian

Score 12/20

Pan-Asian fusion may be a dirty word to purists but this shiny new cafe – an addition to the Lizotte empire – manages to pull it off with light-hearted charm. Perched across the road from glistening Hardy's Bay, you can choose from tables on the pavement or go up a few steps to the restaurant proper, where the doors are flung open for patrons to enjoy the view and the breeze. It's a snazzy little space with dark-wood furniture, blood-red highlights and sweet, enthusiastic staff. Weekend breakfasts are already popular, while the lunch and dinner menu reaches far and wide for inspiration – complimentary chilli-salt prawn 'feet' are a crisp, novel idea that only hint at the variety on offer. A sweet bonito broth with soba noodles, fresh soybeans and grilled salmon is well executed, but it's the cast-iron-pot-baked Vietnamese fish – redolent with shards of ginger and fresh herbs, and cut with the tang of green tomatoes – that marks this as a spot with ambition and talent way above any regulation cafe.

Hours Breakfast & Lunch daily from 9am; Dinner Wed–Sun from 6pm
Bill E $13.50–$28 **M** $25–$31 **D** $11–$12; 10% surcharge on Sundays & public holidays
Cards BC MC V Eftpos
Wine Cocktails and sake are backed by a small, dependable list; 4 by the glass; BYO (corkage $5 per bottle)
Chef Matthew Webber
Owners Brian & Jo Lizotte
Seats 50; wheelchair access; outdoor seats
www.lizottes.com.au
And...lunchtime specials include a free Nudie juice or glass of wine

Zest

16 Stockton Street, Nelson Bay
Tel 4984 2211   Map 12

European

Score 14/20

At the back of a long, narrow room with teal-green walls and rather odd, forgettable décor, chef Glenn Thompson creates dishes with such passion, care and attention to detail that it can take your breath away. Seared scallops with pork belly tortellini and a soy beurre blanc propels Sydney's most abused pairing to new, stratospheric heights. Saffron linguini with squid, chilli rocket and tomato is all balance and finesse. Butter-soft wagyu beef with the dreamiest mash imaginable is so all-consuming that it will dispense with cursory conversation. Suckling pig comes as moist slices and minced in cabbage rolls, with the cutest poached pears, crackling and jus. It's a dish designed to show off technique and the flavours are exquisite to boot. While service and atmosphere are a little sombre, the only real disappointment was an undercooked peach tarte Tatin, although the accompanying orange and olive oil ice-cream restores the faith. Zest is truly something to celebrate – a culinary oasis in a desolate landscape.

Hours Dinner Tues–Sat from 6.30pm
Bill 2 courses $50 pp; 3 courses $60 pp; **D** $12; 10% surcharge on Sundays & public holidays
Cards AE BC MC V Eftpos
Wine Reasonably priced list of mainly locals with a few stars; 14 by the glass
Chef Glenn Thompson
Owners Glenn & Jennifer Thompson
Seats 70; outdoor seats
www.zestrestaurant.net.au
And...watching the open kitchen is a good way to pick up cooking tips

regional

And also...

Aloi Thai
Shop 2, 50 Beaumont Street, Hamilton
Tel 4969 1434
133 Darby Street, Cooks Hill
Tel 4929 3610
The large menu at both places ensures plenty of choice, with some dishes more authentic than others. Hamilton offers a noodle express menu and it's always good for a takeaway.

Bean and Leaf Cafe
52 Cleary Street, Hamilton, Newcastle
Tel 4969 7100
Fresh and natural says it all. We love the way there's no deep-fryer and on the 'Young Set' menu no nuggets or chips. Try buttermilk pancakes for breakfast, washed down by one of the many smoothies and juices. Later it's scotch fillet with steamed vegies and fluffy mash.

Bodyfuel
1/9 Williams Court, Gosford
Tel 4323 6669
This sleek cafe serves the best white chocolate and strawberry muffins. Have one with a truly good coffee, or pick from an enticing menu that includes Vietnamese duck rolls and Thai beef salad.

Caffe Jam
Shop 4, 103 Victoria Street, East Gosford
Tel 4324 8708
If only all cafe–delis were this good! An outstanding selection of pre-made goodies sit teasing customers who just came for good coffee and wicked homemade cakes. Choose from over two dozen specials, such as ocean trout, black-eyed bean, green bean and potato salad; or baked spanakopita with roasted tomatoes.

Estabar
61 Shortland Esplanade, Newcastle
Tel 4927 1222
For excellent coffee, a stylish breakfast or a snack visit this groovy cafe so close to the surf that you can almost dangle your toes in it. Little lemon polenta cakes are so yummy you can't stop at one. Warm ham croissants and spinach and fetta pastries hit the spot. And there are 20 gelati to choose from.

Harry's Cafe de Wheels
Wharf Road, Newcastle
Just in case you're missing your pie and peas, Harry's Cafe de Wheels is now on Wharf Road and identical to the Woolloomooloo original!

Pearls on the Beach
1 Tourmaline Avenue, Pearl Beach
Tel 4342 4400
You can almost taste the brine from this majestic weatherboard restaurant with panoramic views over golden stretches of sand. There's no holding back on punchy flavours in grilled tandoori tiger prawns, red lentil dahl, raita, pappadams and chilli chutney; and sumac lamb loin with eggplant fritters, baba ghanoush and pomegranate molasses jus.

Scratchleys on the Wharf
200 Wharf Road, Newcastle
Tel 4929 1111
You can't get much closer to the harbour than on it. On a good day the louvres go up and tables hang over the water. The prawn and oyster platter is popular and the chef's pick of the day is a sure bet, especially when it's chargrilled swordfish in a spicy pepper crust.

Silo Lounge Bar
18/1 Honeysuckle Drive, The Boardwalk, Newcastle
Tel 4926 2828
This super-sexy, stylish lounge is 'so hot right now'! Newcastle's slinky set sizzles within the dark, moody interior, which opens onto the brand-new Honeysuckle development. Cocktails and nibbles appear as epicurean accessories.

Three Bean Espresso Bar
103 Tudor Street, Hamilton, Newcastle
Tel 4961 2020
The thoroughly slick fit-out, with black vinyl bench seats, white moulded chairs and a communal high table, is matched by Three Bean's own range of preserves for sale, along with local honey and Morpeth sourdough. There are top brekkie treats, like baked white beans on sourdough with crisped speck and poached egg, while lunch heralds seafood chowder.

Central Coast & Newcastle

Provedores

Bb Cc Wicked Chocolates
27 King Street, Newcastle
Tel 4929 2735
This complete chocoholics cafe melts down Belgian chocolate to create a vast array of everything sinful – from caramel slices, cakes and tortes to choc-coated pieces of ginger, orange peel, etc., sold by the gram.

Caesar's Coffee & Fine Food
222 The Entrance Road, Erina
Tel 4365 1988
Behind the red brick lies a cornucopia: teas, pasta, cheese, chocolate, olive oil, ready-made meals, homemade sauces and snail shells. Treat yourself to a takeaway coffee, ground daily by owner Franckin himself.

Commercial Fisherman's Co-op Ltd
97 Hannell Street, Wickham
Tel 4965 4221
Fish so fresh the gills are still pumping. Check out the Asian corner for fresh ray flaps, Thai fish cakes, luderick and pepper cod – and don't leave without a dozen local Corie Island Sydney rock oysters. Mangrove Jack's seafood restaurant is on the upper level.

Darby Street Gourmet Deli
Shop 6, 115 Darby Street, Cooks Hill, Newcastle
Tel 4926 2115
Next to a car park, there's an outside deck to enjoy freshly made pasta, sarnies, salads, gelati and sweets. Or choose from the plentiful deli selection and make up your own hamper.

Euro Patisserie
68 Orchardtown Road, New Lambton, Newcastle
Tel 4957 7188
From the outside it looks like an ordinary cake shop, but step inside and you could be in Paris! Pastry chef Steven Bampton creates spectacular tortes and gateaux as well as quiches, pies and tarts. Stay and enjoy a coffee, and refuel with a pumpkin-bread sandwich.

Giovanni's Deli Cafe
72 Beaumont Street, Hamilton, Newcastle
Tel 4961 1093
A Beaumont Street stalwart, this is a great place for a street-side, rib-sticking coffee, or hop inside for Italian specialty smallgoods and cheeses.

Growers Best
Carpark, Markettown Shopping Centre, Cnr Parry & steel Streets, Newcastle West
Tel 4929 2211
You know you're at Frank Frasca's greengrocer when Italian music blares out onto the street. It's crammed with fresh produce and other goodies: mango and passionfruit yoghurt or sheep's milk cheeses. Mountains of amaretti suggest Frank's still Calabrian at heart.

Honeysuckle Markets
Honeysuckle Railway Workshop Buildings, Merewether Street, Newcastle
Tel 4927 5366
Every Sun, 9am–3pm
Local produce dominates the former railyards with growers selling everything from Redgate ducks to Asian groceries. The Produce Cafe, open most days, does heavenly asparagus on poached eggs with lemon myrtle aïoli while the freshest fruit salad comes with piquant Hastings organic yoghurt.

Pina Deli Cafe
48 Lindsay Street, Hamilton
Tel 4961 5224
Hospitable owner Maria loves to chat about all things Italian, particularly her huge range of pecorino and mozzarella. This deli is packed with interesting things, but don't leave without some smoked beef prepared by the German butcher in Taree – ask Maria for a family recipe.

R & R Sellers Quality Meats
41 Mitchell Street, Stockton
Tel 4928 1506
Rodney Sellers and team continue to put out a range of sausages, from pork, apple and sage to a fresh chilli (choose a heat ratio between 5 and 10). The meat is sourced from around Scone to produce kransky, frankfurts and knackwursts, as well as ham, speck and bacon.

The Snapper Spot
104B The Esplanade, Terrigal
Tel 4384 3780
Fresh fish up one end, takeaway down the other, this unprepossessing shop has drawn converts for the past 21 years. Tuggerah Bay prawns and local mullet feature, while owners Edgar and Pam Felton set off at 3am to get the rest at the Sydney and North Coast markets.

regional

SOUTH COAST

CATRIONA JACKSON, JESSICA HOUGH, CAROLINE BAUM & BRUCE ELDER

The South Coast's rich pastures combine with its turquoise coastline to provide an ever-increasing supply of quality produce. Growers' markets are mushrooming all along the coast, showcasing a diversity of fresh produce: stone fruit, berries, fresh vegetables and herbs, olives, Nelligen organic honey, smoked meats and fish, grapes and award-winning wines, goat's and fetta cheeses from Dromedary Hills, wood-fired sourdough breads, fresh local seafood and Clyde River oysters, all direct from the producers. Savvy growers are linking up with local chefs to support their region.

Around every corner is another spectacular stretch of pristine coast that provides a magic beachfront picnic spot to savour treats such as Jim Wild Oysters from Nowra Bridge washed down with a drop from Coolangatta Estate Winery. Or deep down south in whale-watching territory, Eden's Wheelhouse (Tel 6496 3392) dishes up the freshest straight-from-the-trawler seafood, on the water's edge.

Sea-changers have been settling in for years. And why not? The beaches win awards for everything from being the cleanest to inspiring the best community spirit. The extra houses may blight previously pristine landscapes, but new blood means new chefs and food producers, which in turn swells the optimism of South Coast foodies (along with their waistlines).

Check out local treats – such as wood-fired sourdoughs and myriad house-made condiments at Berry Sourdough Bakery (or pick up other's loaves at Moruya's Saturday market), cheeses at Central Tilba and Bega cheese factories, and condiments from the popular Tathra Beach Pickle Factory, which recently opened a beach shopfront of its own.

Of course the other exciting development is the emergence of the Shoalhaven wine region. Most wineries are still very much a boutique concern, but these days a good cellar door isn't too difficult to find.

With its laidback attitude, improving standards and beautiful vistas, is there a better place to scoff and quaff than the South Coast?

Bannisters

Bannisters Point Lodge, 191 Mitchell Parade, Mollymook
Tel 4454 1933   Map 11

Contemporary

Score 14/20

Perched above the headland at Mollymook, this elegant retreat is one of the South Coast's prettiest places to eat. The modern refurbishment is cool and coastal, with mirrors ensuring an ocean view from every table, and there's a lovely outdoor terrace to enjoy the salty air. Friendly staff keep things running relatively smoothly, and an emphasis on the freshest seafood and local ingredients given a modern twist make Bannisters a welcome exception to the local rule. Tuna tartare is full of clean, luxurious sea-fresh flavours. Chilli lobster on corn cakes is gorgeously meaty, with subtle chilli overtones, but slightly stodgy corn cakes didn't do it justice. Southern Thai seafood curry is packed full of great in-season seafood, including pippies, but was somewhat overwhelmed by the zesty and plentiful sauce. A traditional Aussie trifle is elevated to special by giant, juicy cherries and great custard, layered in a huge brandy balloon; and the pavlova roulade full of berries and cream is as joyous as a southern sunrise.

Hours Breakfast daily 7.30–11am; Brunch Sat–Sun 11am–2pm; Dinner Tues–Sun 6.30–10pm
Bill E $17–$22 **M** $32–$37 **D** $14; 10% surcharge on Sundays & public holidays
Cards AE BC MC V Eftpos
Wine Interesting, broad mix of boutique and marque; 7 by the glass
Chef Andrew Phelan
Owner Conbrae Pty Ltd
Seats 80; private room; outdoor seats
www.bannisterspointlodge.com.au
And...the pizza and cocktail bar is open daily

Berry Wood-fired Sourdough Bakery

23 Prince Alfred Street, Berry
Tel 4464 1617 Map 11

Contemporary

Score 13/20

First up, ignore the score. This marvellous wood-fired sourdough bakery in a Berry side street may not tally like Tetsuya's, but these days it's far more than just a place to buy sensational bread. The cafe has thrilled us on frequent visits, fuelled us on trips up and down the coast, and proven (boom-tish!) itself over and over again. Score a table on the front deck to indulge in a truly great extra-virgin-olive-oil-laden bruschetta with stunning, sun-kissed red tomato. If it's bleak, the white, hard-walled vaulted bakery space is the perfect haven for a thick, garlicky bourride: a heady soup filled with potato and white-fleshed fish chunks. A breakfast omelette may contain goat's cheese and red onion; and baked eggplant is layered with grilled haloumi. The mostly organic produce is for sale, and the croissants are nothing short of sublime. If you can't fit in the brioche with caramelised pear at the time, then be sure to take home a gorgeous fruit tart to savour later.

Hours Breakfast & Lunch Wed–Sun 8am–3pm (coffee and cake 8am–5pm; Sun 8am–4.30pm)
Bill E/M $8.50–$16.90 **D** $7–$8
Cards BC MC V Eftpos
Wine BYO (corkage $4 per bottle)
Chef Warwick Noble
Owners Jelle & Joost Hilkemeijer
Seats 36; outdoor seats; wheelchair access
And...they provide a water bowl outside for your best friend

Caveau

122–124 Keira Street, Wollongong
Tel 4226 4855 Map 11

Modern French

Score 14/20

Locals have been slow to adopt Wollongong's newest fine-dining experience, and while the French moniker may intimidate some, it only hints at the style and standards you can expect. Previously sous chef at Banc, Peter Sheppard's technical mastery and classical repertoire of elaborate and labour-intensive dishes proves he's used to impressing a sophisticated clientele. A complimentary demitasse cup of fragrant cauliflower soup is a winning touch. Behind wooden venetians, the softly lit, pastel room is more informal than the menu suggests, while service is polished, not pretentious. Start with an excellent charcuterie plate or an earthy mix of polenta and wild mushrooms. Duck confit, studded with sweetcorn, wrapped in a herbed pancake and topped with a small dollop of foie gras, was perhaps over-ambitious; more successful is gutsy gnocchi sautéed with autumn vegetables, full of earthy flavours. Sinfully rich gratin dauphinois is creamy and golden. The pièce de résistance is the signature puff pastry cupola of a perfectly executed pithivier, oozing a molten lava flow of dark chocolate.

Hours Dinner Tues–Sat from 6pm
Bill 2 courses $46; 3 courses $58; 4 courses $69
Cards BC MC V Eftpos
Wine Small but good French selection; 8 by the glass; BYO Wednesday only (no corkage)
Chef Peter Sheppard
Owners Peter & Nicola Sheppard
Seats 50; private rooms
www.caveau.com.au
And...there's a more elaborate monthly dégustation menu and regular cooking classes

regional

Donna's Cantina
56 Market Street, Merimbula
Tel 6495 1085   Map 11

Contemporary

Score 14/20

It's important to take both your sense of humour and your appetite to Cantina, where the hip, cool mood combines well with top-shelf tucker. There's a pirate look-alike roaming the floor with a dry sense of humour that fits like a glove in these laidback surrounds. The style is fun with an interior that never leaves you short of discovery – an eclectic array of Mexico meets Merimbula! The blackboard menu will have you salivating. Share a few tapas delicacies while contemplating succulent pork spare ribs; a generous platter of beetroot, capsicum, hummus, olive and pesto dips; chargrilled Moroccan vegetables with coriander chutney on couscous; or some of the best Thai fish cakes around. It's all about fresh, local produce served simply and with culinary care. Mains are equally exciting and the chermoula-crusted rock ling combines superbly with a tangy roast pumpkin and green bean salad. Enjoy sweet tapas from the dessert cabinet (which constantly catches your eye), even if it's just a slab of luscious pistachio nougat or Turkish delight.

Hours Lunch Mon–Sat noon–2.30pm; Dinner Mon–Sat 6–8.30pm; all-day tapas Mon–Sat
Bill E $10.50–$14.50 **M** $19.50–$26.50 **D** $9
Cards AE BC MC V Eftpos
Wine Small, smart, thoughtful list; 10 by the glass
Chef Julian Marshall
Owners Donna Shannon, Denis Lees & John Crosby
Seats 68; outdoor seats
And...relax in the bar and watch Merimbula's passing parade

55 on Collins
55 Collins Street, Kiama
Tel 4232 2811   Map 11

Contemporary

Score 14/20

When Simon Everett moved his restaurant, esse, from Kiama to Shellharbour it was hard to imagine that his assistant, Jason Hughes, who took over this site, would surpass his boss in the excitement and innovation stakes, but it has happened. With his partner Christobel Forster as both decorator and a friendly front-of-house presence, Hughes has kept the menu simple, retained a few old favourites and added some elegance and subtlety. The restaurant received a facelift with Forster's original artworks (all for sale) gracing the walls, but it's the food that has captured the attention of discriminating patrons. Enjoy an outstanding mixed tapas of frittata, warm olives, capsicum and fetta tostitos, salt and chilli prawns, and warm anchovy and zucchini salad. Tuna tartare with rocket and grilled sourdough is an equally tempting alternative. A risotto of salmon, green peas and prawn is feather-light; and whole barramundi with lemon, thyme, baby capers, potato and rocket is a perfect match of flavours and textures.

Hours Daily 9am–4pm; Dinner Mon–Tues, Thurs–Sat from 6pm
Bill E $10.50–$16.50 **M** $21.60–$27.50 **D** $9.50; 10% surcharge on Sundays & public holidays
Cards AE BC MC V Eftpos
Wine Small, discriminating, modestly priced selection; 10 by the glass; BYO (corkage $5 per bottle)
Chef Jason Hughes
Owners Christobel Forster & Jason Hughes
Seats 65; wheelchair access; outdoor seats
And...the blackboard desserts are always exceptional

South Coast

Frati

6/345 Lawrence Hargrave Drive, Thirroul
Tel 4268 3404   Map 11

Italian

Score 13/20

Step through the small glass front of Frati, along the mirrored corridor and into the elegant dining room. Walls are adorned with a mix of Italian art and even the ceiling has a neon-highlighted Sistine Chapel effect. The welcome is warm and friendly, quickly followed up with complimentary bread and olive oil. The menu might seem like traditional Italian, but it's the respect with which chef Giuseppe Iacovelli cooks that makes this cafe-cum-trattoria special. Fresh, yielding gnocchi is interlaced with lightly fried pumpkin and enlivened with walnut butter. Tender salsa-verde-crusted bream fillets rest on a light bed of mashed potato with shallots. Veal zucca – thin fillets with pumpkin and pine nuts in a prosciutto sauce – demonstrate a deft hand. Frati is just a stroll away from the train station, so during the day it's a perfect stop for a relaxing coffee in the leafy courtyard, while at night everyone has the opportunity to have a few drinks with dinner.

Hours Restaurant: Lunch Tues–Sun 11.30am–3pm; Dinner Tues–Sat 6pm–late; Cafe Tues–Sat 8am–3pm, Sun 10am–4pm; Dinner Tues–Sat 5.30pm–late

Bill E $10.50–$18.50 **M** $19–$29 **D** $8.50–$9.90

Cards AE BC DC MC V

Wine Well-priced list; 3 (house wine) by the glass; BYO (corkage $2.50 pp)

Chef/owner Giuseppe Mario Iacovelli

Seats 80; outdoor seats

www.frati.com.au

And…finally! Pasta for coeliacs: a great gluten-free menu

The Gunyah

Paperbark Camp, 571 Woollamia Road, Huskisson
Tel 4441 7299   Map 11

Contemporary

Score 12/20

Fancy dinner with the possums, possum? The Gunyah is an airy, softly lit room of natural timbers, nestled high up in the treetops where curious marsupials wander past the balcony tables, pausing to consider the meals. It's part of an eco-friendly luxury resort, but you don't have to 'rough it' in the posh tents to enjoy the bush tucker-tinged food – macadamia pesto, seared kangaroo fillet with bush tomato chutney – by the camp…er…log fire. Fabulous local seafood includes creamy Greenwell Point oysters, even if they were disappointingly over-crumbed, but thankfully salmon works beautifully with a slightly bitter eggplant jam. John dory salad is intuitively balanced: chunks of pan-fried fillet on a salad with Bulgarian fetta, roasted parsnip, kalamata olives and semi-dried tomatoes. Vegetarian wildlife will enjoy the delightful diversion of 'gnoccicelli' – Japanese pumpkin, ricotta and garlic tart with the texture of gnocchi. To finish, the lemon myrtle and ironbark honey pannacotta is sure to have you warbling like the magpies.

Hours Dinner daily 6–9pm

Bill E $15–$17 **M** $26–$29 **D** $15; 10% surcharge on Sundays

Cards AE BC MC V Eftpos; bookings essential

Wine Single page of reasonably priced, diverse options; 6 by the glass; BYO Sun–Thurs (corkage $5 per bottle)

Chef Gary Fishwick

Owners Irena & Jeremy Hutchings

Seats 40; wheelchair access; outdoor seats

www.paperbarkcamp.com.au

And…dig deep, spend the night at Paperbark Camp and work up an appetite by taking out a canoe before dinner

regional

Lorenzo's Diner
119 Keira Street, Wollongong
Tel 4229 5633   Map 11

Contemporary
Score 14/20

While the revheads cruise the strip, this colourful ristorante is a haven from the Gong's rumbling hubbub. It's a spartan yet warmly stylish room, with a bare stone floor, curving red wall and a large, vibrant painting of espresso cups by co-owner Rebecca Wilford. There's a strong passion for spices in a modern Italian menu that also borrows from Asia and Africa, and chef Lorenzo Pagnan may well be found acting as ebullient host, explaining the dishes in intimate detail. A Tuscan pasta al forno with béchamel, breadcrumbs and a hint of duck is straight from an Arezzo osteria. Rice-stuffed calamari has a smartly Asian twist in a rich pool of master stock with shiitake and bok choi. Alas, chargrilled quail marinated in Algerian spices were dry beside a tight tumble of eggplant, zucchini and capsicum, but grilled kingfish is wonderfully aromatic on a hearty bed of chermoula-scented tomato, potato, chickpeas and rice. The toasted almond flakes, which crunch atop a richly, perfectly bitter tiramisu, is a satisfying sublime counterpoint.

Hours Lunch Fri only noon–2.30pm; Dinner Tues–Sat 6–9pm
Bill E $19–$23 **M** $29–$33 **D** $13–$15
Cards AE BC DC MC V
Wine Small, smart boutique list; 6 by the glass; BYO (corkage $6 per bottle, groups excluded)
Chefs Lorenzo Pagnan & Jeff Crawford
Owners Lorenzo Pagnan & Rebecca Wilford
Seats 50
And…chef's selection of four courses for $71

Michael's Trattoria
Shop 1, 50 Crown Street, Wollongong
Tel 4225 9542   Map 11

Italian
Score 13/20

Located in a simple, unpretentious room at the eating end of Crown Street, Michael's has long been a mainstay of Wollongong, earning a reputation for being the place to take those you'd like to quietly impress. The formal white tablecloths topped with functional sheets of paper are a good metaphor for the mix of people who eat here. The sign says 'classic cucina' but the traditionalists might struggle to find it on occasion. Duck leg salad – sweet meat, bitter walnut and balsamic apple – isn't exactly from mamma's kitchen, but we don't mind. Seared scallops are meltingly fresh and delicate, topped with old-style sauce vierge. If you're seeking a classic, then veal scaloppine is cooked tenderly in white wine and lifted by the tangy addition of taleggio cheese. Service is excellent: efficient, attentive and friendly without being over-familiar or intrusive. Leave room for the pannacotta – although richly flavoured with vanilla, it is a wondrously light and flavoursome finish.

Hours Lunch Tues–Fri noon–3pm; Dinner Tues–Sat 6–9pm
Bill E $16.90–$18 **M** $24.50–$32.50; **D** $12.50–$14.50
Cards AE BC MC V
Wine BYO (corkage $2 pp)
Chef Michael Ciot
Owners Michael Ciot & Jennifer Rowles
Seats 60; outdoor seats
And…be guided by the seasonal produce on offer

South Coast

ploys at tuross
2 Trafalgar Road, Tuross Head
Tel 4473 6203   Map 11

Contemporary

Score 14/20

This South Coast dining gem is incredibly popular and can present a challenge when it comes to securing a booking, particularly during holiday season, but it's a top-notch reward for perseverance. Enthusiastic owners Barbara and Guenther Ploy transformed this corner store into a stylish, contemporary space that offers elegant indoor dining and polished service, with a more relaxed feel on the vast deck. Enjoy water glimpses and a grand old Moreton Bay fig tree through the expanse of glass. A creamy gorgonzola pannacotta, with a stack of walnut toast and warm pear, confirms they know their stuff. Fresh mahi mahi wrapped in spring onion ricepaper, served with Asian greens and a light touch of ginger beurre blanc, reveals a delicate balance of flavours. Supremely tender prime beef fillet rests perfectly on parmesan mash, mushroom ragoût and crisp onion rings. Desserts are heavenly – especially the mini pav with vanilla bean custard and sauterne-glazed peach, washed down with a top Manfredi espresso.

Hours Lunch Sun only from noon; Dinner Wed–Sat from 6.30pm, Wed–Sun during holiday periods
Bill E $11–$17.50 **M** $18–$28 **D** $10
Cards BC MC V Eftpos
Wine BYO (corkage $2 pp)
Chef Luke Asplin
Owners Barbara & Guenther Ploy
Seats 50; wheelchair access; outdoor seats
And...excellent house-made ice-cream and pizze for family holidaymakers

The River
16B Church Street, Moruya
Tel 4474 5505   Map 11

Contemporary

Score 14/20

From the gorgeous location, perched above the majestic Moruya River, to the building – a mostly recycled-timber and slate indoors-meets-outdoors space designed by co-owner and architect turned part-time restaurateur Stuart Whitelaw – it's all good. Since chef Reuben Poole took up the pans in late 2004 following stints in the UK, the food has really hit its straps. Sitting at the locally made tables on ladder-back chairs, you can savour humble simplicity in an excellent local black-skin pork quesadilla loaded with potato wedges and capsicum salsa. You might prefer the elegance of pecan-crusted goat's cheese with rocket, pear and beetroot. Guinea fowl may come with roasted garlic and cherry tomatoes. Poached tamarillo with mascarpone and biscotti is superb; custard apple is reinvented in a brûlée-style cream. With the majority of the wines available by the glass, and a great-value, simpler lunchtime menu, we couldn't be happier to be led up The River.

Hours Lunch Wed–Sun noon–3pm; Dinner Wed–Sun from 6pm
Bill E $10–$15 **M** $18–$29 **D** $10.50; 10% surcharge on public holidays
Cards BC MC V Eftpos; bookings essential in peak season
Wine Bargain priced one-pager of some depth; 12 plus by the glass; BYO (corkage $6.50 per bottle)
Chef Reuben Poole
Owners Stuart & Christine Whitelaw
Seats 55; wheelchair access; outdoor seats
www.therivermoruya.com.au
And...laidback live music on a Sunday afternoon

regional

The Silos

B640 Princes Highway, Jaspers Brush
via Berry
Tel 4448 6160   Map 11

Contemporary

Score 13/20

Silos has plenty of Aussie-style country refinement between its rustic brick and rough-hewn timber floors and exposed beams. The lively atmosphere can become quiet and cosy just as quickly, but either way, it's fun. While the food could be construed as hearty, there's a level of sophistication that raises it above country charm. Seared bug tails on baby lettuce with potatoes tossed in aïoli is a decent way to start. A delicate, savoury saffron custard tart, brushed with tomato jam, topped by oven-roasted cherry tomatoes and served with a side of sweetly roasted vegetables is simply inspired. Tender lamb fillets with dahl and minted yoghurt will warm your insides better than a log fire. Potato, walnut and parmesan gnocchi with sautéed mushrooms, white wine, gorgonzola, cream, baby spinach and pesto sauce is a heart-stoppingly rich and satisfying dish. Finish on crème brûlée with toasted tortilla – an unusual but perfect complement to the firm texture of the custard.

Hours Lunch Wed–Sun noon–3pm;
Dinner Wed–Sun 6–10pm
Bill E $17–$25 **M** $26–$33 **D** $11
Cards AE BC DC MC V Eftpos
Wine Great range and variety, well matched to food; 16 by the glass; BYO (corkage $5 per bottle, $10 Sat night)
Chef Robert Salmon
Owners Andrew & Alenka Knevitt
Seats 80; private room; outdoor seats
And...the locals are regulars for the $25 lunch special (not available Sun and public holidays)

Wheelhouse

Main Wharf, 253 Imlay Street, Eden
Tel 6496 3392   Map 11

Seafood

Score 12/20

There's nothing better than spending the day touring a coastal town as breathtaking as Eden, then discovering a great place for a good fish meal while the sun sinks below the horizon. The Wheelhouse's décor is a tidal wave of seagoing bric-a-brac, creating a kind of comfy fisherman's-den feel. It overlooks Eden's hardworking wharf and is run by a fishing family, so it's no surprise to find local seafood as the backbone of the menu. There's a nod to the modern (oysters Japanese-style, chilli bugs and crab) but most of the offerings are well-known favourites. Seafood platters, unlike many others, only feature produce in season. Seafood chowder tastes as it should: creamy, sweet with the flavour of the sea, and studded with all things fishy. Flathead fillets in homemade, nutty breadcrumbs (or any of four other ways) come with quality chips and salad. A plentiful bowl of Balmain bugs is full of juicy meat. Wheelhouse is that rare beast: a good coastal seafood restaurant. Take advantage of it.

Hours Lunch daily from noon;
Dinner daily from 6pm (Reduced hours in winter)
Bill E $14–$18 **M** $25–$35 **D** $8.50;
10% surcharge on public holidays
Cards AE BC DC MC V Eftpos
Wine Medium-sized, medium-value list of big-name Oz and a few from New Zealand; 4 by the glass
Chefs Kerrie Kelly & Lynn Slater
Owner Kerrie Kelly
Seats 100; outdoor seats
And...plenty to make the kids happy

South Coast

Zanzibar Cafe

Cnr Main & Market Streets, Merimbula
Tel 6495 3636   Map 11

Contemporary

Score 14/20

Perched atop a corner in one of the far South Coast's prettiest spots, Zanzibar is the simple yet sophisticated eatery you hope to find in every Australian beach town. Well-known Canberra restaurateur Alby Sedaitis seized the reins in the summer of 2004, imbuing the place with a relaxed, friendly professionalism and some great food to boot. Plump oysters, from up the road in Broadwater, are sweet enough to be enhanced, but not obliterated, by a feisty Thai nam jim sauce, enlivened with fresh coriander and chilli. A mussel broth is subtle and refreshing, with bobbing slivers of fish, prawns and mussels all vying for attention. Excellent homemade fettuccine tossed with juicy prawns and glistening fish in a zesty tomato and chilli sauce was let down by rubbery mussels. However perfectly cooked, crisp-skinned kingfish is well teamed with crunchy discs of potato, shaved fennel and white bean salad. To finish, a meringue and cold caramelised banana stack with cream is a terrific way to satiate the child in us all.

Hours Lunch Tues–Sat 11am–2pm; Dinner Tues–Sat 6–9pm
Bill E $10–$16 **M** $18–$26 **D** $10
Cards BC MC V Eftpos
Wine Concise, carefully selected, food-friendly list; 8 by the glass
Chefs Brett Sedaitis & Rowena Love
Owners Pam and Alby Sedaitis
Seats 42; wheelchair access; outdoor seats
And...enjoy a sun-drenched lunch at one of the outdoor tables

And also...

Air Raid Tavern
73 Vulcan Street, Moruya
Tel 4474 2074
Quite simply the best coffee for hundreds of kilometres up and down the coast. The slices and cakes (we love the citrus almond version) are breathtaking (made by the boss's wife), and there are outdoor tables at which to sit and enjoy an amazing apricot flan.

Crooked River Winery
11 Willow Vale Road, Gerringong
Tel 4234 0975
From the road it looks like any other winery. Once you reach the top of the driveway, however, you'll be drinking in the sweeping view of the bright green rolling hills. The open-plan, bright, airy cellar-door-cum-restaurant is perfectly situated to trap afternoon sun. Sample the small but impressive lunch menu while tasting the cellar-door priced wines, or just drop in for a quick quaff.

Diggies Beach Cafe
1 Cliff Road, North Wollongong
Tel 4226 2688
Breathe the refreshing sea breeze while overlooking the beach from the glassed-in alfresco area or take in a surf carnival from indoors – either way Diggies is a great place to watch the brown and the beautiful go by. It keeps it simple with quality salads, pastas and burgers for lunch and dinner. Eggs Benedict from the all-day breakfast menu is a must.

Fireworks Cafe
40 Moore Street, Austinmer
Tel 4268 1139
Scotty uses local free-range eggs to make generous omelettes with Middle Eastern spices, capsicum and Turkish bread for a hearty brekkie. At night, the menu roams the world with a fragrant tagine, robust cassoulet and gutsy Italian meatballs. On Friday nights live music can drown out conversation, but it all comes from a very primitive kitchen at very reasonable prices. Open Thursday to Sunday.

regional

Fresh at the Bay
64 Owen Street, Huskisson
Tel 4441 5245
One of a trio of good cafes lining the village's caffeine strip, this corner spot has a big indoor area and a few outdoor tables at which to enjoy the excellent banana bread, great muffins and wonderful Genovese coffee.

Hyams Beach General Store & Jervis Blue Cafe
78 Cyrus Street, Hyams Beach
Tel 4443 3874
We're not sure about the beach's claim to the whitest sand in the world but we sure do love the excellent lamb burger tasting of the Middle East, the vegetarian chickpea version and the foodstore-meets-cafe vibe. What's more, it's such a short walk to the beach to check out that sand.

Jervis Bay Kiosk
2/66 Owen Street, Huskisson
Tel 4441 5464
With its cute moulded chairs spilling out under the windows onto the street, this is the smartest cafe in the stretch. The staff are cheerful, the coffee is Grinders and they do an excellent BLT.

Merimbula Aquarium & Wharf Cafe
Lake Street, Merimbula
Tel 6495 4446
One of the best views on the South Coast and a simple coastal menu with a bit of flair at lunch and dinner make this a lovely rest stop after a day at the beach. It's on top of the Merimbula Aquarium, so ponder the sharks and wonder who's hungriest.

Mylan
198 Keira Street, Wollongong
Tel 4228 1588
A spotless modern interior makes this a welcome change from the more down-at-heel cheap eateries dominating the main eat street. Hearty laksa, with just the right amount of heat rather than fire, make a perfect slurpy lunch, as does a generous Vietnamese dumpling soup. At night, it's a good range of stir-fries, noodle and rice dishes, all served swiftly and with a smile.

Saltwater
On the Harbour, Bermagui
Tel 6493 4328
It's no surprise that this stylish, perfectly positioned boatshed dishes up fabulous, fresh local seafood simply and expertly prepared. By day, there's a constant stream lining up with the seagulls for top takeaway. By night, it's more sophisticated: dining under the stars on the day's finest catch.

Seagrass Brasserie
13 Currambene Street, Huskisson
Tel 4441 6124
There's a lot to like about this softly lit, white-linen-graced cafe. Linguini may come with king prawns, and the pork and fennel sausages with sweet onion relish are superb. A fried terrine, though, had muddled flavours, while the waiters can seem just as sunstruck as the holiday crowd.

Seahaven Cafe
19 Riverleigh Avenue, Gerroa
Tel 4234 3796
Looking like a beach shack painted battleship grey, Seahaven has a lovely aspect across from a park and a gorgeous long beach. It also has things such as smoked salmon handrolls, a Sri Lankan lamb curry and decent coffee.

Twenty three at Berry
85 Queen Street, Berry
Tel 4464 2323
Berry's main street is busting with cafes so Twenty-three (so named for the number of teas available) can be difficult to pick out, but persist. It's simple and cosy, while on sunny afternoons a perfectly brewed cuppa in the garden can't be beaten. For lunch, it's hearty, stylish cafe fare; for dinner, mod Oz with an Asian twist.

Willow Cafe
Princes Highway, Mogo
Tel 4474 5445
This bright, bubbling cafe has plenty of outdoor seating under an enormous willow tree or indoors within primary-coloured walls. It's kid-friendly and serves decent coffee, simple breakfasts, open grills, soups, salads, pastas and desserts.

South Coast

Provedores

ABC Cheese Factory
37 Bate Street, Central Tilba
Tel 4473 7387
There are 19 varieties, although the vintage cheddar and 'trilogy' – a layered cheese – are the most popular. Situated in the historic 19th-century factory, it's open for daily tastings.

Bay Marlin Seafoods
Shop 17, Bridge Plaza, Clyde Street, Bateman's Bay
Tel 4472 3244
The area's best fish and seafood shop has a great range of seafood, much of it local and all very fresh. Handy cooking advice comes readily from the friendly proprietors.

Bermagui Coolo Cream Gelati
1/6 Bunga Street, Bermagui
Tel 6493 3555
The converted vets has gone up-market with pavement seating, great coffee and biscotti – just what you'd expect from charming Italian owners Alberto and Francesca. It's popular, with summertime queues waiting patiently for scrumptious flavours: pear, rhubarb, liquorice, fig, and – an Aussie nod – pavlova.

Braidwood Bakery
99 Wallace Street, Braidwood
Tel 4842 2541
Great French sourdough and impressively long opening hours make this country bakery a must stop on the way to the coast. It also does terrific, pies, pastries, tarts and, occasionally, a little local fruit and veg. The wholemeal cob is legendary.

The Educated Palate
87 Crown Street, Wollongong
Tel 4225 0100
Situated in an historic building, this spunky new deli has an unusual selection of marinades, oils, chutneys and relishes. Try fetta-stuffed peppers, beetroot dip and pre-prepared gourmet pasta. There's also a spotless lunch counter out the back offering antipasti, salads and sandwiches.

Hayden's Pies
166 Princess Highway, Ulladulla
Tel 4455 7798
Chef Hayden Bridges opened this pie shop for a quieter life – and has been flat out ever since. The ever-changing selection can include smoked chicken with leek and gruyère, salmon with prawn and creamy leek, and the more traditional chunky steak. But everyone takes home the apple and rhubarb pie.

Kiama Produce Market
Black Beach, Kiama
Tel 0438 387 387
8am–1pm 4th Sat of the month
Walking the Kiama promenade is pleasant enough, but when it's lined with the best Illawarra produce it's magic. Sweet strawberries (dipped in chocolate on request), robust breads, antipasti, cheeses and even flowers.

Leisure Coast Fruit Market and Deli
75 Princes Highway, Fairy Meadow
Tel 4285 1211
It all seems bigger, fresher and shinier than anywhere else – from pomegranates to fresh borlotti beans. The deli boasts real pasta flour and some fun food adventures.

Nut and Deli Hut
102 Kembla Street, Wollongong
Tel 4226 2269
This deli is a foodie Mecca so it's not uncommon to chat with someone who has travelled two hours for the Persian figs. Staff will readily interpret the more mysterious items (even doing out the odd taste test). The smell of roasting nuts often greets you, but hunt down the much lauded home-blended cereals.

The Olive Farm
1106 Princess Highway (cnr Peterson Road), Falls Creek
Tel 4447 8791
The turn-off is on the right, 12 km south of Nowra. Stop for stunning olive oil, excellent artichokes and anything else the Italian-descent owners Maria and Bruno Morabito have grown themselves.

good food guide

regional

Pasta Fina
63 Crown Street, Wollongong
Tel 4228 1021
Flaminio's gold medal-winning dried pasta spans 24 varieties, from fettucine to fidelini (angelhair), pappardelle and small soup shapes. There's also frozen lasagne and minestrone.

Steve's Quality Meats
252 Cowper Street, Warrawong
Tel 4274 2013
The occasional pig's head in the window might send the sensitive scurrying, but they breed 'em tough south of the Gong. Grab familiar cuts, and more exotic game. There are no labels, so ask; cooking advice is happily proffered.

Supply
1/54 Owen Street, Huskisson
Tel 4441 5815
Thank goodness for all the goodness: fruit and vegetables laid out in baskets, great risotto rice and other staples plus the pleasure of Toby's Estate coffee. Supply does cooked breakfasts too, if the goodness becomes too much.

Suzanne's
15 Princes Highway, Mogo
Tel 4474 3238
Suzanne McDonald's one-stop shop has a fabulous range of organic goodies – nuts, oils, honey, confectionery, condiments galore – top-notch sourdough (don't leave without a loaf of the almond-studded version). Plus there's a cafe.

Pickle Factory + Plus
Shop 2, 37 Andy Poole Drive, Tathra
Tel 6494 4232
Suzy Hacker's beachfront food store sells fabulous condiments alongside fresh local organic produce, deli delights and gourmet kitchenware. Pick up local cheeses, sourdough, confectionery, fresh pastas and smoked fish. Browse the cookbook library over a coffee.

Zweefers Divine Cakes
43–45 Princes Highway, Fairy Meadow
Tel 4285 4155
Arguably the best European-style patisserie in the Illawarra, partnered with fantastic fresh coffee. Outstanding lemon and dark chocolate tart, and apple and rhubarb crumble – cakes are all freshly baked on the premises.

Shoalhaven Coast Wines
BY HUON HOOKE

Centred on the coastal resort towns of Nowra, Berry, Gerringong, Wandandian and Shoalhaven Heads, this small but growing wine region now has 11 registered producers, all of whom offer cellar door sales. The total vineyard area is just 52 hectares but it has received a major boost from two recent arrivals: Crooked River (14 hectares) and Kladis Estate (10 hectares).

The Shoalhaven enjoys the advantage of a steady flow of tourists but viticulturally there are some major disadvantages – chiefly, the high coastal rainfall (at least before climate change came along!). The high humidity is the reason chambourcin is a favoured grape, not only here but also up and down the New South Wales coast, simply because it has an almost supernatural resistance to downy mildew. It's a French hybrid which makes a brilliantly purple-coloured wine with high acidity and distinctive smoky, meaty flavours.

Other favoured grape varieties are chardonnay, semillon, verdelho, cabernet sauvignon and merlot, while botrytis-affected sweet whites can excel and should be a natural in the region.

The two outstanding producers have their wines made by established wineries in the Hunter Valley: Coolangatta Estate by Tyrrell's and Cambewarra by Tamburlaine. Coolangatta's semillons and chardonnays are high-class and have won trophies at major wine competitions. This historic property is a resort with accommodation, restaurant and catering facilities for functions and conferences.

Wineries: Coolangatta Estate, Cambewarra Estate. See also: Bundewallah Estate, Crooked River, The Silos, Jasper Valley Wines, Kladis Estate.

SOUTHERN HIGHLANDS

ROSEMARY STANTON

The Southern Highlands boasts fresh country air; wonderful spring and autumn gardens; dozens of antique and second-hand furniture stores; and a winery trail thrown in for good measure. And if you know where to look, there's also some great food – which we believe would be even better if it moved away from gargantuan portions with too many flavours towards simpler, more refined and intuitive combinations.

Dominated by Bowral, the area is dotted with country lanes and small charming villages. Bring your bike or hire one from Bundanoon and unwind as you cycle through Sutton Forest or the tiny village of Exeter. Other delights include canoeing in picturesque Kangaroo Valley or bushwalking in Morton National Park (Fitzroy Falls is a good place to start).

Bowral's tulip festival is famous, but you can also wander through glorious open gardens and visit some great nurseries, including the charming Bundanoon Village Nursery (for unusual herbs) and Quindalup on the road between Bowral and the Illawarra Highway.

For indoor pursuits, browse around Antiquariat's Fine Books in Bowral for rare books and prints (Tel 4861 2199); visit Abbey's Bookhouse for a great selection of second-hand books (Tel 4861 4533); or travel a little further to Berkelouw's Book Barn and Cafe on the Hume Highway, with over 250 000 second-hand books, including 40 000 rare volumes in their antiquarian department (Tel 4877 1370). Berrima also has The Art of Bookbinding, a fascinating business that restores precious old books (Tel 4877 1705).

Dr Charles Throsby planted vines in the area in the 1820s. There are now 60-odd vineyards contributing to a bourgeoning wine industry (see *Wine*).

Berry farms are dotted throughout the Highlands at Fitzroy Falls, Sutton Forest and Alpine, so keep an eye out for farm-gate stalls and in particular the area's highly prized berries and stone fruit.

Bistro Mont

250 Bong Bong Street, Bowral
Tel 4862 2677   Map 11

Contemporary

Score 13/20

It always feels like a party at Mont, as laughter resounds off mostly hard surfaces. You enter from the – by comparison – quiet end of Bong Bong Street, through the glass display frontage to a long rectangular room with gorgeous wide floorboards and paper over the timber tables (huh?). A buoyant floor team carrying plates seriously laden with food flits from birthday party to out-of-towners. It isn't for the faint hearted – if anything, it seems quantity has far overtaken quality. A seriously huge cassoulet had bland duck maryland and chunks of pork and looked perfect under its breadcrumb crust but lacked any serious punch. Pesto replaced tartare (we can tell, you know) in the blue-eye that could've seen less of the wood-fired oven. Thankfully, pumpkin tortellini are pleasant with their burnt sage-butter sauce, even if we didn't need the garnish of tomatoes and spinach. For pud, a fine apple and treacle tart is just the trick to ward off those cold Highland nights.

Hours Lunch Tues–Fri & Sun noon–2.30pm; Dinner Tues–Sun 5.30–9pm
Bill E $12.50–$16.50 **M** $24–$28 **D** $9–$11.50
Cards AE BC MC V Eftpos
Wine Pleasant, far-ranging Aussie list, a touch of local content; 12 by the glass; BYO (corkage $2 pp)
Chefs Mark Chance & Jeff Morris
Owners Mark Chance & Ranee Monaghan
Seats 90; wheelchair access
And…they're great with kids

regional

Centennial Vineyards
'Woodside', Centennial Road, Bowral
Tel 4861 8701   Map 11

Contemporary
                                    Score 12/20

It's perfect for a medieval banquet: the vaulted ceiling, flagstone-sized pavers, enormous fireplace, and those majestic timber beams wouldn't be out of place in a King Arthur epic. And while the portions in this part of the world would suit a knight fresh from jousting, the menu is more modern. Smoked cod and potato soup is fabulous, even if it doesn't benefit from anonymous oil on top. Beef and merlot pot pie (just the top is pastry, thanks for the honesty) is delectably dark, the cabbage and bacon mash to one side rib-stickingly good. Braised lamb shanks are a gallant 21st-century carnivore's dream, all gelatinous and fall-apart goodness, with parsnip mash and plenty of peas. Apple, quince and rhubarb crumble arrived with one-third of the dish a muesli-style crumble over stewed, fragrant fruit. There were niggles: rancid olive oil and below par ice-cream – but really it's all about location. The front porch's sound system makes you think an orchestra is playing on yonder hill.

Hours Daily 10am–5pm; Dinner Thurs–Fri 6–9pm
Bill E $14.50–$19.50 **M** $22.50–$32 **D** $13; less at lunch
Cards AE BC MC V
Wine All their own stuff by the bottle; sadly just a miserable 4 by the glass
Chef Luke Croston
Owners Robin & Mandy Murray
Seats 120; private room; wheelchair access; outdoor seats
www.centennial.net.au
And...morning and afternoon tea are just as pleasant

Eschalot
Links House, 17 Links Road, Bowral
Tel 4861 6177   Map 11

Contemporary   ♇
                                    Score 14/20

Part of the boutique Links House hotel, Eschalot evokes a comfortable, casual elegance. Relax with a quiet drink in the lounge before moving to the gracious front dining room or a larger, refurnished room towards the back. A complimentary tiny chorizo and chickpea fritter topped with avocado, seared scallop and a dab of crème fraîche whets the appetite. Crab, coriander and lime stuffed squid sits in a puddle of delicate saffron essence. A tangle of mushrooms (from a local disused railway tunnel) teams with strips of fresh lemon pasta, braised capsicums, charred asparagus and basil butter. For mains, succulent duck leg confit with a generous splodge of roasted fig and eschalot pickle takes some beating, but there's strong competition from grilled kingfish atop a fragrant pilaf, partnered by smoked eggplant yoghurt, spicy lentils and tomato chutney. Servings are generous and satisfying but the wickedly rich, oozy-centred chocolate and hazelnut pudding with double cream is definitely for sharing.

Hours Breakfast Mon–Fri from 8am, Sat–Sun from 8.30am; Brunch Sun 10.30am–2.30pm; Dinner Tues–Sat from 6pm
Bill E $12–16 **M** $28–34 **D** $12; 5% surcharge on Sundays & public holidays
Cards AE BC DC MC V Eftpos
Wine Excellent list; 16 quality wines by the glass; BYO Tues–Thurs (corkage $10 per bottle)
Chef Tony Capps
Owners Richard Kemp & Tony Capps
Seats 90; private room; wheelchair access; outdoor seats
www.linkshouse.com.au
And...enjoy some golf, stay the night and ask yourself why you don't move to the Highlands

Southern Highlands

Fitzroy Inn

26 Ferguson Crescent, Mittagong
Tel 4872 3457   Map 11

Contemporary

Score 14/20

Built of convict-hewn sandstone in the 1830s and once used to house prisoners travelling between Sydney and Goulburn, this historic landmark has been restored to provide two modern dining rooms, a comfortable lounge and delightful accommodation for travellers. The produce from the herb and vegetable gardens is prominent in the fresh, confident dishes that avoid any pretence, while the competent and friendly service is reassuring. Gai Lovell's delicate touch is displayed in her homemade pasta accompanied by fresh crabmeat, and we also love the lightness of the potato gnocchi served simply with garden-fresh pesto. Vegetarians will be delighted with a delicate pastry encasing colourful grilled vegetables and topped with semi-soft goat's cheese. For mains, a slow roasted, de-boned spatchcock with a lime–chilli dressing rests on a bed of sautéed vegetables; while a succulent chunk of perfectly cooked mahi mahi is accompanied by a zesty celeriac salad. Finish with a light mango mousse served with fresh mango and a small jug of Galliano.

Hours Lunch Thurs–Sun noon–2.30pm; Dinner Wed–Sat 6–10pm
Bill E $16–$22 **M** $28–$34 **D** $12
Cards AE BC DC MC V Eftpos
Wine Reasonably priced; some local wines; 10 by the glass
Chefs Gai Lovell & Stefan Simmonds
Owners Cosmo & Maria Aloi, Paul & Gai Lovell
Seats 80; private rooms; wheelchair access; outdoor seats
www.fitzroyinn.com.au
And...enjoy a tour of the old prisoner cells (now the ultimate wine cellar)

Hordern's

Milton Park Country House Hotel, Horderns Road, Bowral
Tel 4861 1522   Map 11

Modern European   ♀

Score 14/20

Set in the grounds of one of Australia's most elegant country gardens, this gracious estate is worth a visit for its glorious trees alone. The dining room exudes a slightly formal air but three small tables in the bay window area are just right for a romantic occasion. An excellent, somewhat expensive wine list could do with some matching glassware. A 'local' goat's curd – surprisingly, the waitress said the chef wouldn't disclose his 'secret source' – on toasted walnut bread served with apple, rocket and pumpkin seed salad is a fine entrée. Scallops marinated in vodka and lime tasted of neither, but the abundant flavour of the accompanying fresh gazpacho dressing partly compensates. A rare kangaroo fillet with a generous dollop of spiced onion jam is succulently tender, and crisp-skinned ocean trout is set off by a restrained chilli saffron oil and a flavoursome cauliflower purée. Cinnamon and honey roasted pear with walnut ice-cream on toasted brioche is an ideal finish.

Hours Breakfast daily 7.30–10am; Lunch daily noon–2pm; Dinner daily 6–9pm
Bill E $12–$18 **M** $24–$32 **D** $12–$15; 10% surcharge on Sundays & public holidays
Cards AE BC DC MC V Eftpos
Wine Extensive if pricey list; 10 by the glass
Chefs Peter van Kryssen & Christopher Teale
Owners John & Marlene Dobler
Seats 110; private room; wheelchair access
www.milton-park.com.au
And...wander around the wonderful gardens and marvel at Australia's oldest weeping beech trees

regional

The Journeyman
Old Hume Highway, Berrima
Tel 4877 1911   Map 11

Contemporary
Score 14/20

The Journeyman is set below Berrima's main street, with a grapevine-covered outdoor area (ideal for lunch) and slightly austere-looking dining room. The corner stove protects you from any frosty Highlands' weather, while warm, knowledgeable service matches solid food with excellent wines. A complimentary crisp toast topped with smoked eggplant whets the appetite. Starters include a delicate stack of pork belly confit, seared scallops, blue swimmer crab and kumera with white balsamic vinaigrette. Or choose a fine crêpe of roast jerusalem artichoke, tomato and mushroom, with a dollop of salsa verde. For mains, succulent confit of lamb shoulder with carrot purée, caramelised eschalot and braised witlof is a winter evening's delight. Vegetarians will love ras-el-hanout-spiced potato, pine nuts, leeks and eschalots, wrapped in filo, and topped with slow-roasted tomatoes and spinach purée. For dessert, there's lemon curd, soft meringue and poached rhubarb, but it's outshone by five spice and plum ripple ice-cream that's indulgent and not too sweet. Homemade chocolate sends you off smiling sweetly.

Hours Lunch Wed–Sat 11.30am–3pm; Dinner Wed–Sat 5.30pm–9pm; Sunday 11.30am–8pm
Bill E $16–$18 **M** $25–$30 **D** $12; 10% surcharge on public holidays
Cards AE BC MC V Eftpos
Wine Well-chosen, with excellent vintage list; 16 by the glass; BYO (excluding Sat pm) (corkage $3.50 pp)
Chef/owner Tim Pratt
Seats 60; outdoor seats
www.highlandsnsw.com.au/journeyman
And…take the kids for the special two-course lunch (and great ice-creams)

Katers
Peppers Manor House, Kater Road, Sutton Forest
Tel 4868 2355   Map 11

Contemporary
Score 14/20

Another wonderful Highlands country house hotel, Katers has gorgeous gardens and a dining room that is dignified but not stuffy. Service matches the convivial atmosphere, and the food, thankfully, emphasises quality over quantity. A terrine of goat's cheese and roma tomato, sitting prettily on crisp melba toast with roasted kalamata olives and tiny dabs of rich pesto, tastes as good as it looks. A delicate-sized serving of Sichuan spice-crusted lamb fillets with pear chutney, on a tiny crisp blue cheese tart, tempts the tastebuds without ruining the appetite for the main courses. Succulent aged beef fillet revels in a pinot reduction and is well complemented by delicate potato gnocchi, Swiss brown mushrooms and snowpeas. The chef's artistry is also apparent in crisp-skinned barramundi fillet dabbed with celeriac remoulade and accompanied by a slender potato stack and rolled spinach. There's room for dessert (there's always room), so try the rich hazelnut and espresso semifreddo and almond praline, served with magical, lighter-than-air, Persian fairy floss.

Hours Daily 7am–9pm
Bill E $16 **M** $35 **D** $16; 10% surcharge on public holidays
Cards AE BC DC MC V Eftpos
Wine Expensive, dependable list; 14 by the glass
Chef Ian Shankly
Owner Peppers Leisure Ltd
Seats 120; private rooms; wheelchair access; outdoor seats
www.peppers.com.au
And…you can work up an appetite on the excellent golf course

Southern Highlands

That Noodle Place
279 Bong Bong Street, Bowral
Tel 4861 6930   Map 11

Modern Asian

Score 13/20

The two small rooms of this bright, breezy casual place attract kid-toting regulars who happily push the tiny tables together and allow the Asian-inspired dishes to teach the young ones the delights of real food. Noodle dishes, laksa, steamed dumplings and curries are all reliably good, but order from the specials list for something different. Tempura – stuffed zucchini flowers, asparagus and prawns – is light and luscious, while fresh figs sit simply and well with spiced ricotta and slivers of BBQ Singapore pork. Salt-and-pepper squid with snake bean and roasted capsicum salad comes as a lip-smacking entrée or main. Mermaid tresses (flash-fried Asian greens with seared scallops and prawns) will tempt reluctant vegetable eaters (of any age). Spicy spatchcock with snake beans is served with dahl dotted with toasted almonds – a bit out of left field, perhaps, but a delicious triumph. Finish with a refreshing gin and tonic sorbet with fresh lychees and berries, or join the kids enjoying a coconut, mango or melon popsicle.

Hours Lunch Fri–Sun noon–2.30pm; Dinner Tues–Sun 5.30–9pm
Bill E $3–$14.50 **M** $17.50–$25.50 **D** $10.50; 10% surcharge on public holidays
Cards AE BC DC MC V Eftpos
Wine Small, dependable list; 22 by the glass; good Asian beers; BYO (corkage $2 pp)
Chef Sharon Cox
Owner Pamela Charity
Seats 75; private room; wheelchair access
And...enjoy the relaxed, slightly zany and definitely local atmosphere

Willowvale Mill
Mill Road, Laggan
Tel 4837 3319   Map 11

Contemporary

Score 13/20

Willowvale really is unique. It has no wine list and no menu and is slightly chaotic, but it works wonderfully. You drive in between the plum, pear, apple, nut and olive trees to the stone mill. Lavender and herbs grow amid the stone flagging and there's usually a few ducks or chooks waddling around. Inside the heavy-beamed casual dining room, with its huge fireplace, there are no frills, but camaraderie builds as guests dodge children and help themselves to the groaning buffet. For starters, there are Takako's sushi, local olives and nuts, handmade salami, a whole pecorino and sourdough bread. Then Graham's soup (chicken, potato and leek) and pasta, often featuring smoky, Trunkey Creek bacon from 'up the road'. The main buffet might include Barossa chicken, venison rump with elderberry jelly, rare-roasted beef, vegetable platters, beans and delicious spuds. Desserts feature tarts with apples, grapes or marinated pears from the garden and perhaps a huge bowl of local raspberries and cream. It's real and delightfully unpretentious.

Hours Lunch Sun, Dinner Fri–Sun at 7pm, or by appointment
Bill $50 pp set menu
Cards AE BC DC MC V Eftpos; bookings essential
Wine Selection varies, but is always good; ask about prices; 2 by the glass
Chefs/owners Graham & Takako Liney
Seats 150; private rooms; outdoor seats
And...share a glass of wine with a host who has a love of spuds and everything that grows 'up the road'

regional

And also...

Cafe Bella
151 Main Road, Kangaroo Valley
Tel 4465 1660
This cafe in a beautiful valley epitomises what's good about country life – friendly service and generous serves at reasonable prices. Come for breakfast or lunch (the mezze plate is excellent), or enjoy dinner on weekends with dishes such as crisp, pan-fried dory on spinach risotto.

Cafe Fraîche
2/9 Old Hume Highway, Berrima
Tel 4877 1342
The décor is simple but it's a genuine place with good food and excellent coffee. Start the day over ricotta pancakes with fresh fruit, yoghurt and nuts or Bircher muesli. Drop in for cake, or lunch on hearty soups or a delightful platter of toasted breads with tapenade, and chunks of free-range roasted chicken.

Coffee Culture
Shop 6, Empire Cinema Complex, Bong Bong Street, Bowral
Tel 4862 2400
A perfect example of why you need to look for good food. Tucked down behind the Bowral Cinema, this is a great place for fine coffee, breakfast or lunch. They do dinner Fri and Sat.

Le Bijoux
Shop 2, Wingecarribee Street, Bowral
Tel 4861 1173
A gracious air is created by friendly service as well as old-style cut-crystal water pitchers, bone china and silver tea service. Breakfast on local mushrooms with goat's cheese or a perfect herby omelette, or relax over a simple lunch that may include a caramelised onion and goat's cheese tart.

McVitty Grove
Wombeyan Caves Road, Mittagong
Tel 4878 5044
Overlooking a sweeping rural view to the Blue Mountains, enjoy the local produce platter with olive tapenade, trout mousse and venison sausages, or tuck into a chicken and bacon pie with mash. Taste the wines (pinot gris and pinot noir) and take home olive oil, preserves and condiments.

Provedores

The Cheese Store at Bowral
Shop 6B, Corbett Plaza, Wingecarribee Street, Bowral
Tel 4862 3749
An excellent deli stocking a good range of cheeses and local products. In summer, pop in for berries from Alyssa and Jonathon Hatcher's Alpine berry farm, including English gooseberries and dewberries (a cross between a blackberry and a raspberry), and take home a bottle of mulberry vinegar, delicious jams or delicious real berry syrup.

Gumnut Patisserie
Shop 7, Grand Arcade, Bong Bong Street, Bowral
Tel 4862 2819
Also Post Office Corner, Berrima
Tel 4877 2177
Try the award-winning pies, pastries or croissants, or indulge in one of the delectable fruit tarts or special order birthday cakes. If you're into healthier fare, you can also pick up a loaf of sourdough bread – the best in Bowral.

jones the grocer
294 Bong Bong Street, Bowral
Tel 4862 2203
A mini version of Woollahra's jones the grocer, where you can find superb coffee, a range of cheeses, fresh pasta and some pre-prepared meals, as well as a wide range of oils, preserves and other goodies.

Mauger's Meat
21 Hoddle Street, Burrawang
Tel 4886 4327
An old-fashioned butchery that satisfies yearnings for the quality of yesteryear. The art of making excellent sausages, smoking hams and ageing steaks has been passed down through three generations of Maugers. Long may they and their devotion to their craft continue to delight! They also grow much of the beef they sell.

Southern Highlands

Montrose Berry Farm
Cnr Exeter Road and Ormond Street, Sutton Forest
Tel 4868 1544

It's an idyllic setting with an 1861 homestead surrounded by gardens, which include all manner of berries and asparagus (from October to December). You can pick your own berries (November to April), or choose from the fine range of jams and sauces on offer. They also sell frozen berries.

The Old Goulburn Brewery
23–31 Bungonia Road, Goulburn
Tel 4821 6071

Designed by Francis Greenway, the Goulburn brewery opened in 1836 (then closed in the 1920s and reopened in the 1980s) and claims to be Australia's oldest brewery. Take a tour and enjoy the top-fermented, preservative-free Goulburn Gold (a light ale), Goulburn Black (a mild stout), or GB Fine Sparkling Ale, made from local barley and hops. You can even stay in the restored brewer's cottage.

The Pig N Whistle Cafe
The Old Cheese Factory, Hoddle Street, Robertson
Tel 4885 1300

The visitors who flocked to Robertson after the town was the setting for *Babe* have petered out and the town has reverted to its quaint old self. The ghosts of the local cheese makers would at least appreciate that the old cheese factory now houses a pleasant cafe and an adjoining shop that stocks a variety of cheeses, plus local olive oil and other foods, including berries.

Southern Highlands Wine
BY HUON HOOKE

This is one of the state's newest wine regions and is rapidly becoming a winery tourism destination. With about 110 hectares of vines and 13 wine producers, nine of them catering to visitors, this region – based on Bowral and Mittagong – is potentially exciting.

Within an hour of Sydney, but cooler thanks to a high, inland location, it's well suited to cooler climate varieties such as chardonnay, sauvignon blanc, riesling and even pinot noir. The wet, semi-coastal climate coupled with deep, fertile soils can create vigour problems for grapevines, with the consequence that grapes – especially the late-ripening varieties – can struggle to achieve full ripeness. When they do, varietal flavours can be intense and sharply defined, the wines delicate and refreshing. While new players find their feet viticulturally, some of their wines are being made from grapes trucked in from other regions, such as Orange.

There are winery restaurants, including Centennial Vineyards (Bowral) and Southern Highland Wines (Sutton Forest). These two are easily the region's biggest vineyards, with 40 and 31 planted hectares respectively. Centennial's Woodside Chardonnay, Mundrakoona's Artemis Pinot Noir and SHW's Golden Vale Botrytis Sauvignon Blanc are impressive.

Wineries: Centennial Vineyards, Southern Highland Wines, Mundrakoona Estate (Mittagong), Joadja/Blue Metal (Berrima). See also McVitty Grove, Greenbrier Park and Kells Creek (all Mittagong), and Eling Forest Winery (Sutton Forest).

regional

NORTH COAST

BELINDA JEFFERY & JAMES MAYSON

It used to be a long, hot drive from Sydney before reaching Byron Bay and a restaurant worthy of a stop. Thankfully the long stretch of stunning coastline from Tea Gardens to the Tweed is now dotted with restaurants, cafes and provedores worthy of a detour. In fact, the joy of travelling north is all about the journey – taking the time to explore some of the backwaters and by-ways of Port Macquarie, Bellingen, Yamba and Bangalow.

As the coastal plains give way to the hinterland of the Great Dividing Range, the sub-tropical climate and the rich soil offer a paradise for farmers – and plenty use little else to create magical organic produce. There's an extraordinary diversity: milk, cheese, bananas, avocados, mangoes, native finger limes, exotics like dragon fruit, turmeric, lychees, persimmons and jackfruit, plus Asian greens and the famed Bangalow sweet pork. Further inland, the grazing country produces great beef: Casino claims the title of beef capital of Australia.

Quality restaurants have long appreciated this abundance, intuitively working with and developing a burgeoning interest in native bush foods. And there's plenty to celebrate, with Casino's Beef Week in May (www.casinobeefweek.com.au), Lismore's Northern Rivers Herb Festival in August (www.herbfestival.org) and Tuncurry's Bounty of the Sea Festival (www.midnorthcoastbridge.com.au/bounty).

Have a chat with the locals, who'll give you the good oil on top tucker, including great seafood – especially Wallis Lake oysters and Yamba (aka eastern king) prawns, and live muddies in Ballina. Then there's yabbies, Aabenraa beef, Knockrow Ridge and Zventfelds coffees, Capparis goat's cheese, Madura tea, Hastings Valley dairy products, and a variety of bush foods.

Add some breathtaking national parks to explore, pristine rivers and estuaries to dip your toes in and, of course, the endless stretch of stunning beaches, and if it wasn't for the rapidly rising real estate prices, you'd be moving north.

Bang Thai

2/39 Byron Street, Bangalow
Tel 6687 2000   Map 12

Modern Thai

Score 14/20

When a country town restaurant is packed on a cold, wet Tuesday night, you know it's doing something right. As soon as you step into this lively Thai, the appeal is obvious: the greeting is bright and chirpy; the cheerful space with its silvery ceiling, Sanskrit motif and bright red accents is welcoming; and the chefs in their open kitchen exude an air of quiet confidence. When the first zingy Thai flavours of betel leaf wraps explode in our mouths we understand why the joint is jumping – this is *seriously* good food. There's delicate salt-and-pepper tofu given a vivid jolt from a rich tamarind caramel; and although organic duck in a red curry with longans was a little chewy, flavours are deep and complex. A slew of mushrooms stir-fried with tempe, Thai eggplant, basil and chilli is a glorious combination. To finish, we scrape up every last morsel of a subtly perfumed sencha quince 'crème brûlée' while a serene painting of Buddha looks on, just as equally satisfied.

Hours Dinner daily 5.30–9pm
Bill E $7.50–$15 **M** $14.50–$30 **D** $10–$12; 10% surcharge on Sundays
Cards AE BC DC MC V Eftpos
Wine Small, Thai-friendly, well-priced list of mainly Aussie wines; 13 by the glass; BYO Sun–Tues (corkage $2.50 pp)
Chefs Graeme Stockdale & Sam Hughes
Owners Georgina & Jonathan Allison
Seats 55; wheelchair access; outdoor seats
And…the produce is generally free-range, hormone and antibiotic free, non-GM and, where possible, organic

North Coast

Boomerang
5/2 Fletcher Street, Byron Bay
Tel 6685 5264   Map 12

French/Japanese
Score 15/20

Light floods this sleek, casually elegant room, pouring through windows and doors flung open to catch the sea breeze, bouncing off highly polished glasses and reflecting from smoky glass panels. A slim, suede-covered banquette runs the length of the windows and smartly laid tables set the scene for Marc Romanella's intelligent, sometimes edgy cooking. You build your own dégustation menu from a choice of 20 or so 'tasting' dishes – the personable staff well versed if you need a helping hand. Braised stuffed pork hock is rich and deeply flavoursome, made even more unctuous by a nugget of foie gras and beautifully balanced by the crisp tartness of apple. Tender lobster is all briny sweetness, its honey and kaffir lime sauce acting as a delicate counterpoint. Occasionally dishes don't quite work – the wasabi crème glacée that partnered a lusty piece of crisp beef was a little too sweet – but misses are rare and, on the whole, this is fusion cooking done with great finesse by a gifted chef.

Hours Lunch Thurs–Sun from noon; Dinner daily from 6.30pm
Bill 2 courses $40 pp; 3 courses $58 pp; 4 courses $75 pp; 5 courses $90 pp; 10% surcharge on Sundays, 15% on public holidays
Cards AE BC MC V Eftpos
Wine Wide-roaming and interesting global list; 24 by the glass
Chef Marc Romanella
Owners Marc & Paul Romanella
Seats 55; private room; wheelchair access; outdoor seats
www.bestrestaurants.com.au/boomerang
And...there's a very comfortable bar for a pre-dinner drink

Ça Marche
Cassegrain Winery,
764 Fernbank Creek Road, Port Macquarie
Tel 6582 8320   Map 12

Contemporary
Score 13/20

Pull off the Pacific Highway just outside Port Macquarie for a well-earned break, a tasting tipple and some light, lip-smacking fare at Cassegrain's manicured winery. Perch on the sundeck with wide umbrellas and rustic benches overlooking the vines and the incongruous landscaping alchemy of roses and Aussie bushland, or withdraw to the groovy polished-concrete interior. New chef Eric Robinson has taken little time to install a menu designed to complement the restaurant's raison d'être – the wines. Hence half the menu is a pricey $10 tapas-style: excellent homemade bread with various tapenades, white bean purée or knockout confit garlic prawns. But a rocket and parmesan salad at $17.50 leaves (no pun intended) a bitter taste. Mains frequently look to Asia for inspiration, such as zealously spiced turmeric and sesame-crusted squid with a gorgeous salmon fish cake. Thankfully, porcini and gorgonzola tart is bang-on for earthy flavours, lifted with tangy walnuts and a balsamic-dressed rocket and pear salad.

Hours Lunch daily noon–3pm; Dinner Fri 6–9pm
Bill E $10–$22 **M** $26–$32 **D** $12;
10% surcharge on Sundays & public holidays
Cards BC MC V Eftpos
Wine Cassegrain, of course; 14 by the glass
Chef Eric Robinson
Owners Micheal Kelly & Julia Hickey
Seats 140; private room; wheelchair access; outdoor seats
www.camarche.com.au
And...try some of their unusual wines such as biodynamic chambourcin or durif

regional

Castalia

Shop 1, 15 Clarence Street, Yamba
Tel 6646 1155 Map 12

Contemporary

Score 14/20

This former 1920s general store is now a bright, breezy restaurant with a dining spot to match your mood and the time of day. Join locals for breakfast on the footpath deck; cosy into the old-style booths in the colourful gallery shopfront for lunch, or soak up sparkling river views from the more formal dining area out the back. Whirring overhead fans, potted plants and dado rails all add to a rustic feel, while the food showcases local produce with a refined modern touch. The bite of gorgonzola and crisp prosciutto are perfect salty counterpoints to soft and sweet roasted figs. Crisp-skin duck is sensational – crunchy skin lacquered to deep mahogany, and fork-tender flavourful meat. An unusual combination of smoked quail, offset by the bittersweet tang of cumquats and silken leeks, is remarkably good – the only jarring note was overly salty haloumi strips. Our cheerful waiter rightly recommended the caramelised peach tart; it's light and luscious, as is an accompanying rosella-glazed vanilla bean bavarois.

Hours Breakfast Sat 8–11.30am; Lunch Fri–Sat 11.30am–2.30pm; Dinner Mon–Sat 6pm–late (daily during school holidays)
Bill E $10.90–$23.50 **M** $24.90–$31.50 **D** $9.50–$11.50; 15% surcharge on public holidays
Cards AE BC DC MC V
Wine Mid-sized, well-priced list, mainly smaller wineries; 12 by the glass; BYO (corkage $2.50 pp)
Chef Andrew Causley
Owners Margaret Matthews & Gregory Gray-Matthews
Seats 142; private rooms; wheelchair access; outdoor seats
And...try their fab, ultra-modern take on a traditional seafood platter

dish

Cnr Jonson & Marvel Streets, Byron Bay
Tel 6685 7320 Map 12

Modern European

Score 15/20

The fact that, seven years on, dish is better than ever is testament to its owners' continued hands-on involvement and the inspired cooking of Luke Southwood and his team. The airy space remains – the long façade open to the comings and goings on the pavement outside, while inside rough-hewn beams contrast with white stucco walls and smartly set tables. Whether you rock up in jeans and a T-shirt or dressed to the nines, the welcome is always warm from the knowledgeable and refreshingly down-to-earth but nonetheless proud staff.
A simple dish of white asparagus and poached egg is lifted to new heights by silken garlic, apple and cauliflower purée, tangy tomato vinaigrette and the surprise crunch of roasted macadamias. Ditto a juicy chunk of macadamia-smoked gold band snapper, its delicate smoked salmon sauce and tart sorrel hollandaise giving just the right lift. Desserts are a must, with a tropical trio of pretty-as-a-picture mango tart, piña colada sorbet and earthy saffron syrup a stand-out.

Hours Dinner daily 6pm–midnight
Bill E $17.90–$22 **M** $26–$35 **D** $13–$14; 10% surcharge on Sundays, 15% on public holidays
Cards AE BC MC V Eftpos; bookings essential in peak season
Wine A well-chosen, wide-ranging list; 20 by the glass; plus an interesting selection of beers and cocktails
Chef Luke Southwood
Owners Ben & Belinda Kirkwood
Seats 60; wheelchair access
And...if you're after something lighter check out the excellent bar menu

Fins

Beach Hotel, Cnr Jonson & Bay Streets, Byron Bay
Tel 6685 5029 Map 12

Seafood

Score 16/20

It's like taking a refreshing dip in the ocean (only a stone's throw away) when you step from the lively buzz of the Beach Hotel into this oasis of calm, with its tropical Asian plantation-house feel. Mood lighting gives a warm intimate glow to the honey-coloured timber of the curved ceiling and slatted screens. Describing Steven Snow's highly personal, exuberant cooking – it's as if his briny produce hails from a secret ocean – is a challenge to any vocabulary of superlatives. Brunswick River prawns are luscious and meaty, their accompanying beetroot and pinot noir risotto adding an earthy note, along with a vivid saffron mayonnaise. Fleshy jewfish fillet paddles in a beautifully balanced sweet, sour and salty tamarind sauce, with Asian mushrooms adding length and depth of flavour. The signature cataplana – a Portuguese-style bouillabaisse flavoured with saffron and star anise – only gets better. For dessert, a sophisticated combination of fragrant pear parfait, warm pastry-wrapped brie and intense pinot noir syrup is outstanding.

Hours Dinner daily from 6.30pm
Bill E $13.90–$23.90 **M** $28.90–$38.90 **D** $15; 15% surcharge on public holidays
Cards AE BC MC V
Wine Extensive, well-researched list with limited-release and aged wines; 18 by the glass
Chefs Steven Snow & Phil Woolaston
Owner Steven Snow
Seats 90; wheelchair access; outdoor seats
And... very knowledgeable staff are infectiously enthusiastic about the food and wine

Georgie's at the Gallery

Grafton Regional Gallery, 158 Fitzroy Street, Grafton
Tel 6642 6996 Map 12

Contemporary

Score 13/20

Built in the late 1800s, one of Grafton's finest examples of colonial architecture houses the Regional Art Gallery – and Georgie's restaurant/cafe to boot. For those who like their art up close grab an inside table. Alternatively, outside, under the umbrella of a golden rain tree and surrounded by a courtyard of fairy lights, the peaceful ambience of Georgie's is soothing. For starters, a jumble of Iluka calamari dusted in five spice comes tossed with parsley, tomato, rocket and an overload of red onion. Occasionally, fewer flavours would allow star ingredients to shine, such as the spanking fresh crabmeat partnered with saffron aïoli, mint, peach, semi-dried tomatoes, avocado, baby spinach, all served on fetta and zucchini fritters (phew!). Beautifully moist deep-sea perch was a little overwhelmed by a super-rich red curry. Lamb fillet rolled in cumin is full of juicy, honest flavour. There's a divine selection of homemade ice-creams you can even take home; and buttery, ginger-spiked nectarine and peach upside-down cake tastes even better than it sounds.

Hours Tues–Sun 10am–4pm; Dinner Tues–Sat from 6pm
Bill E $12.50–$15.50 **M** $15.50–$25.90 **D** $2.50–$9; 10% surcharge on Sundays, 15% on public holidays
Cards AE BC MC V Eftpos
Wine Smallish, appealing list; 12 by the glass
Chefs Mark Hackett & Geoff Platt
Owners Mark & Judy Hackett
Seats 80; private rooms; wheelchair access; outdoor seats
And... the cafe does a pared-down menu for lunch

regional

Milk and Honey
Shop 5, 59A Station Street, Mullumbimby
Tel 6684 1422 Map 12

Wood-fired pizza

Score 12/20

Ten minutes from Byron Bay, just far enough off the highway to escape the homogenising developers, you'll discover this charming village with a little secret the locals want all for themselves. In a box-shaped room with polished-concrete floors, dark-wood furniture, a splash of art and a couple of outside tables is some of the best pizza you'll find within coo-ee of Naples. An antipasto plate arrives brimming with smoky garlic eggplant purée, roast beets, beans, bocconcini, tomato, fetta, roast capsicum and prosciutto. Out of a roaring wood-fired oven come crisp, thin bases topped with a sprinkling of defined, well-married flavours – field mushrooms with parsley, garlic and parmesan; chorizo with olives, anchovies and chilli; pumpkin with ricotta and pesto. To finish, a lemon curd tart with fresh passionfruit puts a zing back on the palate and sends the locals back to the hills, whispering about their good fortune.

Hours Dinner Mon–Sat from 5pm
Bill E $4.50–$12.80 **M** $12.80–$19.80 **D** $6.50
Cards BC MC V Eftpos
Wine BYO (no corkage)
Chef/owner Chris Pellen
Seats 60; wheelchair access; outdoor seats
And...takeaway available

No. 2 Oak Street
2 Oak Street, Bellingen
Tel 6655 9000 Map 12

Contemporary

Score 15/20

Host Toni Urquhart treats guests like old friends, welcoming them with jovial sincerity into the homely, 1912 weatherboard cottage with polished floorboards, pastel walls and soft lighting. Husband Ray shows similar compassion on the pans, cajoling the most out of top-notch ingredients by imparting just a gentle twist of his obvious talents. A 'pot' of bread arrives with an intense lip-smacking oven-dried tomato salsa. Mushroom ravioli with reggiano and thyme is simple and classy, while whole chargrilled squid with a zippy Thai-style dressing does justice to its title of 'signature dish'. More complex, yet sympathetically spiced, is an enormous slab of jewfish beautifully married to a coriander and tamarind-soused curry sauce. Rack of lamb is classic comfort food – flavour-packed and deliriously moist, paddling in a pool of excellent jus. An espresso parfait with chocolate sauce and walnut praline is wicked fun – a bit like the host who seems to genuinely enjoy the warm, fuzzy buzz that her personality provokes as she flits between tables.

Hours Dinner Tues–Sat 6.30pm–late
Bill E $14–$18 **M** $28–$32 **D** $12; 10% surcharge on Sundays & public holidays
Cards AE BC MC V; bookings essential
Wine Great Oz/NZ selection (Toni's passion); 20 by the glass; BYO (corkage $4 per bottle)
Chef Ray Urquhart
Owners Toni & Ray Urquhart
Seats 45; wheelchair access; outdoor seats
www.bellingen.com/no2oakst
And...complimentary vegies or salad with main courses

North Coast

Olivo
34 Jonson Street, Byron Bay
Tel 6685 7950   Map 12

Contemporary

Score 13/20

Locals and visitors happily return time and again to this narrow sliver of a restaurant smack bang on bustling Jonson Street. Simple and stylish, with subtle lighting, exposed brick walls and comfortable (true!) banquettes and chairs, it emanates laidback Byron charm, although there's nothing too chilled about the well-priced food or the genuinely warm and child-friendly service. Shang Bradley's cooking takes you on a round-the-world adventure. Pork belly layered with roasted figs cuts like butter and melts in your mouth. Spanish mackerel sashimi is as fresh and briny as an ocean breeze – as are its accompanying salmon cake and crunchy tempura prawn. The mackerel hits the mark in a heady main course, this time perfectly chargrilled with saffron-scented chickpeas. The only slight disappointment was a red curry of duck and fresh lychees with too much coconut milk overwhelming the spices. But that doesn't stop a silky smooth chocolate semi freddo, topped with espresso mousse, slipping down a treat.

Hours Dinner daily 6pm–late
Bill E $12–$15 **M** $24–$28 **D** $10–$12; 15% surcharge on public holidays
Wine Interesting, well-priced list from smaller producers; 8 by the glass; BYO (corkage $3 pp)
Chef Shang Bradley
Owner James Lancaster
Seats 50; wheelchair access
www.olivo.com.au
And... try the innovative vegetarian dishes

Paupiettes
56 Ballina Street, Lismore
Tel 6621 6135   Map 12

Contemporary

Score 14/20

Serendipity is a wonderful thing: who would think that, tucked away in Lismore's commercial strip, a neat-as-a-pin country town restaurant would be turning out seriously sensuous food? If David Forster was cooking in a capital city, food lovers would flock to his door; they still do, albeit from further afield, for his beguiling mix of classic and contemporary dishes. The restaurant itself is plain and comfortable, with timber-panelled walls and white-cloth'd tables; the welcome warm, from David's wife, Shirley, who runs the floor and fields questions about the blackboard menu. Duck lovers are in seventh heaven with David's succulent duck confit, the richness cut by hints of winter tarragon, juniper and pepper, served with a compote of potatoes, bacon and Chinese cabbage that's outstanding. A mellow, roasted garlic aïoli and ratatouille-like red-braised vegetables add just the right notes of smoothness and sharpness to simply cooked lamb fillets. By dessert, you'll feel like a happy kid again with a feather-light rendition of banana fritters and luscious honeycomb ice-cream.

Hours Dinner Tues–Sat 6.30–9.30pm
Bill E $11–$22 **M** $23–$26 **D** $8–$12
Cards AE BC DC MC V Eftpos
Wine Small reasonably priced list; 4 by the glass; BYO (corkage $3.50 per bottle)
Chef David Forster
Owners David and Shirley Forster
Seats 50
And... a rarity these days but all meals are served with a bowl of complimentary vegetables

regional

Poinciana
55 Station Street, Mullumbimby
Tel 6684 4036   Map 12

Contemporary/Tapas

Score 13/20

By day, a steady stream of colourful locals flow through this rustic, laidback cafe to enjoy breakfast (they have the freshest free-range eggs, homemade jams and buckwheat crêpes), great coffee and simple lunches (the tofu burger with caramelised onion on Turkish is excellent), beneath the lovely old poinciana trees. Come evening, a welcoming glow and eclectic music spill from the intimate tapas-bar-cum-restaurant with its quirky retro feel from plush velvet banquettes, whimsical 1950s lamps and overhead fans. Sit under the stars and feast on a series of small dishes, ranging from tender baby octopus bathed in a mellow red wine sauce to crisp saganaki, the sizzling haloumi golden and crunchy outside and properly gooey within – a squirt of lemon the only accompaniment needed. Thin slices of subtly spiced chargrilled lamb with chermoula are fork-tender and well paired with deceivingly simple steamed sesame eggplant that's long on flavour. A surprisingly delicate house-made Pernod and rosemary ice-cream is an inspired combination – and conclusion.

Hours Breakfast daily 8am–noon; Lunch daily noon–3pm; Dinner summer Tues–Sat 5pm–late, winter Thurs–Sat 5pm–late
Bill E $4.50–$12.50 **M** $9–$18 **D** $3–$12; 10% surcharge on Sundays & public holidays
Cards BC MC V Eftpos
Wine Moderate list, plus decent selection of beers and cocktails; 12 by the glass
Chef Adam Dalton
Owner Matt Lane
Seats 70; private room; wheelchair access; outdoor seats
And...they're very child-friendly here, with a kids' menu and big sandpit (yay!)

Portabellos
Shop 6, 124 Horton Street, Port Macquarie
Tel 6584 1171   Map 12

Contemporary

Score 12/20

This Port's stalwart has fresh new owners; however, the familiar menu remains, along with the enthusiastic and ever-friendly service. In a nondescript corner setting on the main shopping strip, Portabellos creates unfussed, flavoursome dishes for the masses. While noise can get intimidating among all the hard surfaces, there are outside tables and an equally refreshing BYO policy. Potato and goat's cheese dumplings with an orange and tomato relish is a minor revelation – the whole being greater than the sum of its parts. Scallops with a fennel and roast corn salad delivers a subtle ensemble in which the seafood failed to shine. Roast pepper-rubbed salmon fillet is cooked to perfection atop steamed potatoes, capers, olives and shallots – a simple production honouring the produce. Rump steak with café de Paris butter, potato gratin, wilted spinach and cabernet jus is red-blooded delight. But a fridge-cold, weary apple and frangipani tart disappointed. However, excellent coffee any time of day returns our confidence that this is Port's most reliable cafe.

Hours Breakfast & Lunch Tues–Sat 8am–3pm; Dinner Wed–Sat 6.30–9.30pm
Bill E $9.90–$14 **M** $21–$25 **D** $7.95
Cards AE BC MC V Eftpos
Wine BYO (no corkage)
Chef Anthony Hudson
Owners Chandra & Maureen Chandramohan
Seats 41; wheelchair access; outdoor seats
And...they serve some of the best-value breakfasts in town

North Coast

Rae's on Watego's

8 Marine Parade, Watego's Beach, Byron Bay
Tel 6685 5366   Map 12

Modern Asian
Score 13/20

It's not just weary seafarers who trust the beam of Byron lighthouse to deliver them safely to their destination; that same beacon guides expectant diners to a warm welcome in the luxurious surroundings of Rae's. The setting is magical: by day, the crystal-clear waters of Watego's Beach beckon; by night, couples settle into the canopied Moorish-style restaurant with its romantic lighting and seductive alcoves. Those cushioned surrounds and attentive staff plying you with exotic food and wines are clearly designed for patrons who like the finer things. The trouble is that the setting and especially the prices lead to high expectations. Not everything delivered the desired finesse – a tough, chewy smoked trout spring roll didn't do justice to tender sea scallops and tingly papaya salad; nor an intensely sweet turmeric caramel to hauntingly spiced cardamom cake. There are luscious moments, like spicy, melt-in-the-mouth massaman duck, offset by honey-sweet dates; and sweet snapper paired with deep, rich black bean sauce and plump betel mousse dumpling. Another Cristal '83 sweetie? Oh, why not.

Hours Lunch & Dinner daily noon–late
Bill E $24–$30 **M** $38–$45 **D** $18–$20; dégustation menu from $150 pp; 15% surcharge on public holidays
Cards AE BC MC V; bookings essential
Wine Considered list of interesting Australians and, of course, champagne; 13 by the glass
Chef Kylie Day
Owner Vincent Rae
Seats 60; outdoor seats
www.raes.com.au
And... Rae's, for most, is definitely a big night (or lunchtime) out

Utopia

13 Byron Street, Bangalow
Tel 6687 2088   Map 12

Contemporary
Score 13/20

There's something delightfully incongruous about this stylish cafe situated in the quaint village of Bangalow. Nothing quite prepares you for the contemporary, light-flooded, airy space, with its shimmer of chain dividers, coffee-coloured floor and chairs, and café au lait banquettes. At night, mood lighting makes the room sparkle, while Michael Delaurence's fresh, simply cooked dishes are delivered by cheerful, friendly and enthusiastic staff. You could happily eat your way through the day, starting with a breakfast of brilliant ruby-red rhubarb lifted by the tang of fresh ginger. Come lunchtime it's the antipasto platter (which includes a shot glass of lively red pepper soup and cheesy arancini). For dinner, juicy chunks of yellow fin tuna, permeated with bay leaf, lemon and the slightly bitter sharpness of artichoke, are right on the mark. So too the buttery pastry and luscious lemon filling of a seriously good lemon tart. Occasionally dishes have one too many elements, but overall the flavours are clear and true.

Hours Tues–Sun 8.30am–4.30pm; Dinner Fri–Sat 6–11pm
Bill E $13–$16.50 **M** $24.50–$26.50 **D** $9–$10; 10% surcharge on Sundays & public holidays
Cards BC MC V Eftpos
Wine Small, mid-range selection to match their menu; 6 by the glass; BYO (corkage $2 pp)
Chef Michael Delaurence
Owners Ross Skinner & Michael Delaurence
Seats 70; wheelchair access
And... Saturday's farmers' market takes place behind the cafe

regional

And also...

Ate – the Art of Food
33 Byron Street, Bangalow
Tel 6687 2555
This unusual cafe-cum-gourmet takeaway is licensed. Shannon Debreceny whips up light hotcakes with berries and vanilla yoghurt, and sautéed field mushrooms on ciabatta. Later on he shows classical training in Bangalow sweet pork with roasted apples and parsnips, and chicken liver terrine with sourdough and truffle salad. There's a takeaway menu (crisp pork belly and braised lamb shanks). Or book for a dégustation dinner in the private dining room.

Basilico
Cnr Club Lane and Molesworth Street, Lismore
Tel 6622 6100
A lovingly restored old bank is well suited to Peeter Pruul's careful seafood dishes and the regularly changing art. It feels like a classy old hotel dining room, yet the cooking is anything but traditional. Delicate spring rolls burst with mahi mahi, sand crab, noodles and seaweed; baked calamari is stuffed with lemony risotto and served with basil cream sauce; and an Asian-style seafood broth is chock-a-block with local shellfish.

Cafe Wunderbar
2 Fletcher Street, Byron Bay
Tel 6685 5909
Europe comes to Byron in this tiny cafe-cum-konditorei. Go early morning to snaffle one of the few window seats, along with a slice of still-warm plum tart, or spicy linzer torte, plus a really good coffee, while you watch Ursula and Andrea fill the cabinet with their lovingly made European cakes, pastries and pies.

Fatbellykat – Shared Food
26–28 Tweed Street, Brunswick Heads
Tel 6685 1100
A contemporary taverna serving authentic Greek (the chef's family hails from Rhodes) with clean, fresh flavours. Choose local oysters with walnut and anchovy with parmesan crumbs, or with horseradish cream and salmon roe. Crab and prawn dolmades are 'gin soaked', while the bean soup is a true, robust fasolada. Kataifi is a deep bowl of ethereal shredded pastry, with toasted macadamias and almonds, cinnamon cream and mastic-thickened custard.

Fresca
Bangalow Hotel, 1 Byron Street, Bangalow
Tel 6687 1711
There are few better places to sit on a balmy evening than the broad balcony of the palm-fringed Bangalow Hotel. Its popular bistro offers food a cut well above usual pub grub, with dishes such as tender chilli sesame squid and slow-braised duck. There are also plenty of familiar favourites, including very good burgers and steaks, and a kids' menu. Staff are country-friendly and serves are very generous.

Fresh
28 Hickory Street, Dorrigo
Tel 6657 2356
This really is a step back in time – the effervescent Liz and Lynne run their countrified cafe/antique/homewares shop with warm smiles and a mountain of country baking. Great coffee and a variety of teas are just the thing to ease down one of their amazing homemade cakes, muffins, friands and more.

Harvest Cafe
18 Old Pacific Highway, Newrybar
Tel 6687 2644
A haven for highway travellers, Harvest is also a popular spot with locals – and it's easy to see why. This lovely old cottage is transformed into a stylish, airy cafe of wide verandahs beckoning for a long lunch or brunch. The coffee is good, the breakfasts are innovative – the jalapeño yoghurt served with tender corn fritters, roast tomatoes and a properly gooey poached egg gets the thumbs up – and there's a modern lunch menu featuring local produce.

Lodge 241 Gallery Cafe
117–121 Hyde Street, Bellingen
Tel 6655 2470
Situated in the landmark old Masonic Lodge, this fantastic weatherboard cafe, with huge pine communal table inside and verandah out, has prime location at the end of Hyde Street, overlooking Bellingen Valley – *the* place for brekkie with decent coffee, slabs of toast and that intoxicating, sun-drenched aspect. A specials board for lunch ensures that some people just stay the whole day.

North Coast

Melba's Verandah
Cnr Fischer Street & Pacific Highway, Broadwater
Tel 6682 8099
It's hard to believe this lovely turn-of-the-century house with its peaceful gardens and wide verandah is smack-bang on the Pacific Highway. Generous breakfasts include eggs Benedict and homemade baked beans. Lunch features country soups (pea and ham, or oxtail) and prawn frittata with seared scallops and garlic greens. Morning and afternoon teas revert to tradition with fantastic scones and a sensational sour cream and golden syrup cake.

Misty's
33 Hickory Street, Dorrigo
Tel 6657 2855
A quaint cottage with leadlight windows situated just down from the historic Dorrigo bakery, doing simple brasserie fare such as Dorrigo-peppered duck 'boobies' (breast – maybe its brassiere food?) and seafood bisque. If there's too much wine imbibed, there's a cute little room behind the kitchen to stay the night.

Fishmongers Takeaway
Shop 1, Bay Lane, Byron Bay
Tel 6680 8080
It's standing room only at this neat little shop tucked away behind Byron's iconic Beach Hotel, and it's not hard to see why. If you can get past the exceptional fish and chips, there are many more aquatic treats – excellent grilled fish, octopus and salads – all just a hop-skip-and-a-splash from beautiful Main Beach.

The Parkside Cafe
97 River Street, Woodburn
Tel 6682 2493
It's not often we feature a truckies' stop, but this quintessential Aussie cafe is too good not to. Neat as a pin and open 24/7 the menu reads like a roll-call of classic caff faves: brilliant chips, proper burgers, huge fried breakfasts – the mega is a mountain of eggs, sausages, bacon and doorstop-thick toast, enough to stop two hungry people. And that's not to mention the ten different pies and homemade sausage rolls. Best of all, it's served up with great humour and lashings of hospitality.

perenti
69 Church Street, Gloucester
Tel 6558 9219
This classy, modern cafe with a ruby-red interior does simple breakfasts and lunches using local produce where possible. Great quiches and soups, and plenty of interesting homemade preserves, such as onion and rosemary jam or dark whisky confiture, sell from well-stocked shelves.

Pogel's Wood Cafe
Lot 1, Federal Drive, Federal
Tel 6688 4121
It always feels like a wonderful piece of serendipity to find this quaint cafe tucked away in Byron's beautiful hinterland. Enjoy good coffee with a piece of cake, settle in for a long lunch or join the mainly local crowd at night for generous servings of mod-Oz food, including dishes like lamb fillet in olive and herb damper or crisp-skin ocean trout with African spicing.

The Rails Kitchen
The Railway Hotel, Jonson Street, Byron Bay
Tel 6680 9009
This enormous open beer barn, next to the sadly defunct railway station and featuring an old carriage of its own, is one of the best options for top-quality pub grub. Tuck into kransky bangers with onion jam or more adventurous dishes such as a potato and aubergine soup with caraway, then cavort to the live music.

Short Order Cafe
Shop 1, 10 Princess Street, Macksville
Tel 6568 4550
Cakes are house-made, including two gluten-free choices. The coffee is Espresso Di Manfredi. There's loads of organic produce, including tofu burgers with roast pumpkin and peanut sauce. Enjoy the sunny courtyard or grab the lot takeaway and walk down to the riverbank for the perfect picnic spot.

regional

Spinnakers
Ballina RSL Club, 240 River Street, Ballina
Tel 6686 2544
Good food sometimes turns up in the most unlikely places and this riverside restaurant in the bustling Ballina RSL Club is one. It's not your regular club food: gloriously plump, feather-light ravioli, chock-full of sweet lobster; succulent baby lamb cutlets with kumera mash; chocolate malt crème brûlée sandwiched with delicate honey hazelnut wafers. At times there is too much happening on the plate, but at these prices and with such courteous service, it's well worth a visit. Open Fri–Sat from 6pm.

Threeways
Malcolm's Corner, Cnr Wilson's Creek & Huonbrook roads, Huonbrook
Tel 6684 0255
Negotiate your way up the twists and turns of Wilson's Creek Road to this funky cafe to be rewarded with lovely views over the rainforest plus eclectic fare, ranging from Asian-style salads and noodles to a steak sandwich with mustard aïoli. Utterly satisfying thin-crusted pizze have simple toppings: anchovy and olive, Calabrese salami and roasted pepper.

Tillermans
77 Marine Drive, Tea Gardens
Tel 4997 0138
This rustic formal general store on the shores of the Myall River does great cafe fare by day, like a ploughman's lunch or Thai-style salt-and-pepper squid salad. At night, it's more formal and the food is more serious: bouillabaisse brimming with local seafood, lamb shanks with lentils, and an up-market bangers and mash. There's a little nook selling local jams and Simon Johnson provisions.

Zen Sushi
15 Woodlark Street, Lismore
Tel 6621 3141
A little slice of downtown Tokyo can be found in this country-town sushi bar, with its communal wooden tables, stools and the sushi chef's father dressed traditionally for a *konichiwa* and *arigato*. Grab a bowl of miso, and choose from around a dozen pre-made sushi at the counter – eel, salmon, burdock and unari – plus contemporary flavours such as tuna mayo.

Provedores

Barnett's Rainbow Reach Oyster Barn
551 Rainbow Reach Road, South West Rocks
Tel 6565 0050
For over 30 years this has been a great spot to stop by the Macleay River and buy freshly shucked or unopened Sydney rock oysters. Closed Sundays.

Bent on Food
22 Bent Street, Wingham
Tel 6557 0727
A cheap and cheerful cafe with excellent coffee, plus a deli specialising in local and organic produce. Next door, Duck Under the Table is a new cooking school with classes in cheese-making and Middle Eastern cuisine with guest chefs.

Coffs Harbour Fishermen's Co-op
69 Marina Drive, Coffs Harbour
Tel 6652 2811
Seafood straight off the trawlers, to take home or fried up in decent fish and chips. Grab some sushi and enjoy the view of the trawlers or the ocean from the breakwater.

Darrel's Gourmet Butchery
39 Church Street, Gloucester
Tel 6558 1009
Local breeders and herb growers contribute the contents for a great range of bangers at the Butchery, formerly the North Coast Sausage Kings. There are house-made smoked hams, rabbit and goat, and top beef and pork.

Dangerous Dan's Butchery
13 Princess Street, Macksville
Tel 6568 1036
Bruce Parker has taken over from the original 'Danger Man', adding to the list of wacky-sounding, sensational-tasting snags with the chunky, smoked Bushman's sausage with Dorrigo pepper. The Jolly Jumbuck (lamb, warrigal greens and native mint) and the Pork Witchetty (pork, dried apricots, macadamias, lemon myrtle and warrigal greens) remain.

North Coast

Farmers' Markets

Bangalow, Byron Street (behind the Bangalow Hotel), every Sat, 8–11 am
Banora Point, Club Banora, 1st & 3rd Sun of month, 7am–noon
Bellingen Organic, Bellingen Showground, 2nd & 4th Sat of month, 8am–1pm,
Byron Bay, Butler Street Reserve, every Thurs, 8–11am
Coffs Harbour, Streets Ahead, City Square, 2nd Thurs of month 4–7pm
Grafton, Market Square, 2nd Thurs of month, 7am–2pm
Great Lakes Produce Market, School of Arts Building, Little Street, Forster (next to Visitor Centre), 3rd Sat of month, 8am–noon.
Hastings, Wauchope Showground, 4th Sat of month, 8am–noon
Maclean, Maclean Showground, 2nd Sat of month, 8am–noon
Nabiac, Nabiac Showground, Nabiac Street, last Sat of month, 8am–noon
North Coast, Lismore Showground, every Sat, 8am–noon
Wingham, Wingham Showground, Gloucester Road, 1st Sat of month, 8–11am
Rainbow Region Organic, Lismore Showground, every Tues, 7am–10am

Fishy Fishy
Shop 3, 80–84 Ballina Street, Lennox Head
Tel 6687 5599
This friendly, family-run business is no run-of-the-mill fish takeaway. The seafood sparkles and they do all sorts of interesting ready-to-go dishes to slap on the barbie (chilli lime squid, Moroccan-style fish with couscous and eggplant relish, and a fabulous salmon escabeche). Or have it cooked to order, then dine across the road on the beach.

Green Garage
Cnr Tennyson & Browning streets, Byron Bay
Tel 6680 8577
This is a gourmet, mostly organic greengrocers and supermarket–deli that would make most city greenies weep. Great fruit and veg, loads of local produce – often available for tasting – macro-healthy treats, fresh flowers, worm farm workshops and, to keep that yin in balance, the dreaded durries.

Kombu Wholefoods
105 Hyde Street, Bellingen
Tel 6655 9299
From one of the original Macro workers, and based on the same concept, this new shop offers organic/macro/enviro-friendly choices. Great yoghurts, bread and gluten-free pasta.

Lick The Spoon
53 Hickory Street, Dorrigo
Tel 6657 1373
The ever-talkative Jo Sweeney runs this funky, modernist deli. She has her family's fruit wines; in the freezer she stocks take-home dinner packs, such as Thai green fish curry with eggplant; and on the shelves offers preserves, mueslis, olive oils, marinades and spice rubs.

L'Ultime
5 Lawson Street, Byron Bay
Tel 6685 5822
This tiny patisserie offers beautifully crafted traditional French baking: wonderfully chewy baguettes, buttery croissants, gorgeous fruit tarts, heavenly pastries, and handcrafted petit fours and chocolates.

Northern Rivers Seafood
Pacific Highway, West Ballina
Tel 6686 2187
This bustling market has some of the coast's best seafood. Crates are piled high with clear-eyed fish, octopus, prawns, local oysters and more, with live crays and crabs in the tank. They also knock up decent fish and chips.

Red Ginger Foodstore
2/111 Jonson Street, Byron Bay
Tel 6680 9779
You've gotta love a gorgeous little emporium that stocks a comprehensive range of Asian foodstuffs, including a fantastic selection of teas, fresh kimchee, black sticky rice with coconut cream and yum cha.

Wholly Smoked Organic Foods
Shop 7, 130 Jonson Street, Byron Bay
Tel 6685 6261
Nothing is too much trouble in this butchery where much of the meat is organic. The chicken and lamb are exceptional, and there's also smoked tuna, ostrich cabana and duck confit. House-made sausages are full of flavour.

regional

THE WEST

JAMES MAYSON, SIMON THOMSEN, SALLY WEBB & PHILLIP PUTNAM

Clichés abound out west – the sky really does seem bigger, the horizon far, the land wide and very, very brown. One in particular rings frighteningly true: we live on the driest inhabited continent on earth – and on the other side of the Great Divide, this daily burden is clocking up its fifth consecutive year of drought. In the face of such adversity, we can only admire the remarkable output of those with the good fortune and resolve to continue. For among the hardship, many strive towards organic and/or environmentally aware farming methods, producing remarkable outcomes.

What really changed the landscape and west over the years was the influx of migrants and irrigation. Around Wagga Wagga and Griffith, where the Murrumbidgee's 'Irrigation Way' brings life to the state's largest wine-growing region, the area's Italian heritage has ensured an abundance of grapes, wine, citrus and olives.

Young is famous for its cherries, stone fruit and olives. The Lithgow–Orange–Cowra–Mudgee circuit has gorgeous berries, figs, Bumbaldry rabbit, Mandagery Creek venison, Dutton Park ducks and fantastic cool-climate wines. Around Tamworth there's Bellata Gold pasta, Blue Stripe beef, Mandalong lamb and Arc-En-Ciel trout (see *Provedores*).

Festivals are the place where the disparate producers, provedores and restaurants come together to show off their wares. Orange has the annual FOOD (Food Of the Orange District) Week (www.orangefoodweek.com.au) in early April, showcasing local wine and food dinners, tastings, cooking classes and more. Taste of Tamworth is also in April, the Riverina's UnWINEd is held in Griffith over the June long weekend, the Mudgee Wine Festival in September, Dubbo's Macquarie Valley Food & Wine Festival also in September, the Cowra Wine and Food Festival in November, and the Young Cherry Festival in late November.

Blue Wren

433 Cassilis Road, Mudgee
Tel 6372 6205   Map 12

Contemporary

Score 13/20

On a sunny day, there can be few nicer ways to whittle away an afternoon than at a picnic table on the grass, enjoying the vineyard views while conducting a by-the-glass tasting of the efforts from this six-year-old winery. Inside the grey–blue corrugated iron barn, along with the tasting bench, there's a surprisingly elegant restaurant space for urbane yet earthy fare at white-linen-cloth'd tables. The menu can be as smart as succulent pork belly with lentils, broad beans and a tinge of sweet soy, or as smoothly refreshing as a warm potato salad with smoked trout and lemon mayonnaise. The 'Drover's Pie' – red wine-braised beef with mash – wasn't our idea of a long paddock favourite, the meat drier and less yielding than we'd hoped, but there's simple delight in a flavoursome local scotch fillet with red wine sauce, chips and salad. And the fig pudding is as good an excuse as any to try the Blue Wren white port.

Hours Lunch daily noon–4pm; Dinner Wed–Sat from 6.30pm

Bill E $10–$16.50 **M** $20–$29.50 **D** $8.50; 10% surcharge on Sundays & public holidays

Cards AE BC DC MC V Eftpos

Wine Seven house wines, all by the glass; BYO (corkage $7.50 per bottle)

Chefs Arnaud Theurillat & Ben Roth

Owners James & Diana Anderson

Seats 150; private room; wheelchair access; outdoor seats

www.bluewrenwines.com.au

And…there are changes in ownership as we go to press, so ring and check

The Crowded House
1 Ribbon Gang Lane, Bathurst
Tel 6334 2300   Map 11

Contemporary

Score 12/20

Assuming the banks remain in this thriving country town, look for the narrow lane between the Westpac and ANZ to discover this lovely cafe–restaurant. There's a leafy courtyard for daytime and a lunch of pasta, salad, pane di casa or house-made sausages. Inside the airy 1850s Gothic-style sandstock church school there's a casual feel, with slowly twirling fans, fireplaces, canvas deck chairs and lashings of cheerful evening bistro dishes to keep everyone happy. The 'mezze' platter is enough for two – a chock-a-block jumble of everything from lamb kofta to octopus, grilled vegies, braised chickpeas, goat's-cheese-smeared focaccia, olives and fetta. Duck terrine with beetroot relish is lush and assured. Crumbed pork chop with mash, preserved lemon and a parsley, onion and fetta salad was right in the comfort zone, but the lasagne had an over-zealous combination of eggplant, artichoke, zucchini, mushroom and ricotta and was let down by a poor tomato sauce. Thanks to friendly hospitality everyone leaves with a smile, feeling well sated.

Hours Lunch Tues–Sat 10am–3pm; Dinner Tues–Sat from 6pm
Bill E $9.50–$16.50 **M** $15.50–$28.50
D $9.50–$11.50
Cards AE BC DC MC V Eftpos
Wine Moderate list of some Mudgee and Orange, plus familiar Oz labels; 12 by the glass
Chefs Jason Saxby & Baden Mendez
Owners Colin & Nikki Barnett
Seats 190; private room; wheelchair access; outdoor seats
www.crowdedhousecafe.com.au
And...the evening cafe meals, such as kransky with kipfler potatoes, are all under $20

Eltons Brasserie
81–83 Market Street, Mudgee
Tel 6372 0772   Map 12

Contemporary

Score 13/20

The menu is decorated, if that's the word, with stickers: Withams Coffees and Teas; Sensational Hollandaise – a must try; Baked Daily – bread, cakes, etc. It's indicative of a cafe-cum-restaurant whose menu works so very hard to please. There are salads, sandwiches, an all-day breakfast and lunch specials. Sweet local figs grace a salad of warm, grilled prosciutto, kipfler potatoes and pistachios. Zucchini fritters stack up cleverly with smoked salmon and sour cream. Ceiling fans twirl behind the handsome old double shopfront, with polished wood floor, pressed-tin ceiling and blood-orange walls. In the evenings everything changes. A wood-fuelled courtyard oven fires up for pizze and mains. Eggplant is stuffed with couscous, walnuts, sultanas and roast pear. Lime-cured salmon comes with cucumber, horseradish and soy dressing. Roast pork fillet lolls in a sage and apple sauce. Though lunchtime service could do with a little firing up of its own, who can complain when a pot of vanilla tea with a wedge of bread-and-butter pudding is simple perfection?

Hours Mon 8am–5.30pm, Tues–Sat 8am–late, Sun 8am–4pm
Bill E $8.50–$13.50 **M** $17.50–$26.50
D $7.50–$10; pizze $14–$20.50;
10% surcharge on public holidays
Cards AE BC DC MC V Eftpos
Wine Interesting quality locals, including a barbera; 4 by the glass; BYO (corkage $2.50 pp)
Chef David Cox
Owners David & Anna Cox
Seats 60; private room; wheelchair access; outdoor seats
And...yes, the loo is called Elton's John

regional

Highland Heritage Estate
Mitchell Highway, Orange
Tel 6361 3054   Map 11

Contemporary

Score 13/20

Just a few clicks outside Orange, this picturesque winery offers views of swathes of healthy vines reclining down the hill. Lorikeets dot the grassy slopes between, a treat for those emerging from the cellar door in the converted train carriage after a tasting. The restaurant at this estate is a rustic function centre with bullock-solid wooden posts and floor-to-ceiling glass overlooking the vineyard. It's a very comfortable and serene ship, only the scuffed dance floor hinting at its other life hosting wedding receptions. Service is snappy and professional, bringing forward solid contemporary fare with few faults (or surprises). Flash-grilled prawns are full of flavour but were let down by a lacklustre corn tartlet. Veal loin on wilted spinach, with the resoundingly earthy note of a wild mushroom ragoût, is far more accomplished. Spatchcock marries beautifully with porcini and parmesan polenta. To finish, apple and hazelnut tart with calvados syrup is just the thing to partner the Estate's very own sticky.

Hours Lunch Fri–Sun noon–2.30pm; Dinner summer Thurs–Sat 6pm–late, winter Fri–Sat

Bill E $16–$17 **M** $29 **D** $13.50; 15% surcharge on public holidays

Cards AE BC MC V Eftpos

Wine The entire Estate range of 17 by the bottle and glass, plus well-priced Aussie competitors; BYO (corkage $8 per bottle)

Chef Keith Wilson

Owners Rex & Jacky D'Aquino

Seats 100; private rooms; wheelchair access; outdoor seats

And...don't forget to try the wines with a visit to the old train carriage

Jenkins Street Guesthouse
85 Jenkins Street, Nundle
Tel 6769 3239   Map 12

Contemporary

Score 13/20

Nundle is the quintessential Australian country town, with one huge difference. When Peter and Judy Howarth became disillusioned with the rural atrophy of local services, they tried 'commercial philanthropy', building a wool mill and restoring the main street to its glory days. That includes the former bank, now home to this inviting guesthouse and restaurant of wide, worn floorboards, an original fireplace and breakfast sundeck. Even the vault is reinvented as the kitchen. You can just dine here, but this is a destination in which to surrender all control in favour of pleasure and relaxation. The chalkboard menu is concise to reflect the best of the produce: perhaps duck breast with pickled ginger and soy reduction; or salt-and-pepper squid with tomato chilli jam. Mains feature local gems such as de-boned Arc-En-Ciel trout, stuffed with dill-flecked salsa verde; and the Howarth's own unctuous Blue Stripe beef rib-eye with buttery mash, wilted spinach and beetroot jus. To finish, pannacotta with warm berry compote is the final touch before retiring to the luxurious rooms.

Hours Lunch Tues–Sun noon–3pm; Dinner Thurs–Sat 6–10pm

Bill E $14–$16 **M** $24–$26 **D** $9; 10% surcharge on public holidays

Cards BC MC V Eftpos

Wine Modest list; 3 by the glass; BYO by arrangement only (corkage $5 per bottle)

Chefs David Cassells & Nick Cummins

Owner David Cassells

Seats 45; private room; outdoor seats

And...the kitchen will make up a picnic hamper to take on local walks

The West

Lolli Redini
48 Sale Street, Orange
Tel 6361 7748 Map 11

Contemporary
Score 15/20

The atypical streets of Orange harbour wide thoroughfares lined with enormous deciduous trees, which make any trip to this city of colour a seasonal treat. Increasingly, the stunning Federation houses are being turned into restaurants, cafes and homeware stores. Inside one such treasure is a frantically busy restaurant where chef Simonn Hawke has an obvious love affair with the seasons too – local produce stars with inventive twists in an essentially contemporary menu. Twice-cooked gruyère soufflé is wonderfully cheesy, its richness cut with a tiny shredded-spinach salad. Sea-sweet, roe-on scallops arrive with a zippy salad of coriander, mint, fried eschalots, cucumber and (unnecessary, play-it-safe) avocado. Homemade pappardelle is coated with a seductive rabbit and parmesan ragù; lovingly rested veal rack arrives on parmesan-flavoured truffled polenta with green beans and roasted tomato (although strangely, Indian kasundi). A wicked amaretto, praline and nougat parfait with fresh strawberries is a memorable finale. Service is exceptional – friendly, efficient and reassuring – showing a true understanding of the essence of hospitality.

Hours Brunch Sun 9am–1pm; Lunch Fri–Sat noon–2.30pm; Dinner Tues–Sat 6–9.30pm
Bill E $16–$19 **M** $27–$31 **D** $10–$16
Cards AE BC DC MC V Eftpos
Wine Concise, mainly local list; 4 by the 250ml carafe; BYO (corkage $6.50 per bottle)
Chef Simonn Hawke
Owners Fem, Courtney & Simonn Hawke
Seats 50; wheelchair access; outdoor seats
www.lolliredini.com.au
And...the restaurant always features fascinating art from mainly local talent

Michelin
72 Banna Avenue, Griffith
Tel 6964 9006 Map 11

Contemporary
Score 13/20

An up-market restaurant on a former service station site on the main thoroughfare seems quite out of place. That's until you realise it's the folly of the Nugan family, one of Australia's largest winemakers, who at least look at something stylish from their office opposite. With polished-concrete floors, shimmering walls and plush seats, the minimalist refinement feels somewhat forced; however, there are no such affectations from chef Antony Moore. Seared half-shell scallops are topped with tiny morsels of pea purée, goat's cheese and prosciutto. Hapuka fillet rests on a white bean cassoulet with a sharp aïoli. Slightly overcooked sumac-crusted lamb loin relaxes on a well-crafted combination of eggplant, roast tomato and goat's cheese, topped with green olive tapenade. Service is well versed in Nugan Estate's fine wines, which they like to push, perhaps too enthusiastically. To finish, rosewater brûlée misses the trademark crackle but, like all the dishes, is a flourish of great flavours.

Hours Brunch Sun from 10am; Lunch Tues–Sun noon–2.30pm; Dinner Tues–Sat from 6.30pm
Bill E $16–$19 **M** $26–$29 **D** $10–$12
Cards AE BC DC MC V Eftpos
Wine A great cross-section of their own vineyards; 10 by the glass
Chef Antony Moore
Owner Michelle C Nugan
Seats 80; private rooms; wheelchair access
And...the lunch menu is lighter

regional

Neila
5 Kendal Street, Cowra
Tel 6341 2188   Map 11

Contemporary
Score 15/20

Wow! Is this the future of regional dining? Take an Aussie chick born to Chinese parents, put her with an Aussie bloke born to Greek parents, then let them loose on a property to grow fabulous produce and to source the best of the Central West direct from growers. Let them bring it all together in a brilliant kitchen alchemy and whacko – welcome to Neila! The carpeted, rectangular room at the bottom of Cowra's main drag has a little aquamarine silk for highlights, some local art and timber tables, but nobody really notices. They bring their best wine to pair with carrot and fetta ravioli; a mound of sliced Mandagery Creek venison cured with Sichuan pepper tossed with red dates; or caramelised pork with mint and cashew salad. Anna Wong's food is worth driving to from any distance, be it the lean yet luxurious slow-cooked duck with shiitakes and turnip, or the seriously sensual black sesame crème caramel. With Jerry Mouzakis on the floor, you're in the very best country hands.

Hours Dinner Thurs–Sat 6.30pm–late
Bill E $15 **M** $29 **D** $12
Cards AE BC MC V; bookings essential
Wine BYO (corkage $2 pp)
Chef Anna Wong
Owners Jerry Mouzakis & Anna Wong
Seats 48; wheelchair access; outdoor seats
www.neila.com.au
And...they often cater to groups by appointment

Restaurant Legall
56 Keppel Street, Bathurst
Tel 6331 5800   Map 11

French
Score 14/20

It's akin to being invited around by gracious old friends to dine in their gracious old home: lights glowing, atmosphere warm and welcoming, each small room a dining alcove with original fireplace, flowers on the mantel and walls in soft tones of mustard and mandarin. The menu is a memory lane of classic French cuisine. The soup might be a hearty stand-your-spoon-up-in pistou – a stroll around the vegie stalls of a Niçoise market – with heady notes of basil, garlic and olive oil. Mushrooms scent a tender roasted chicken supreme; juniper enhances the rich venison pie under a golden pastry crust. Duck breast, roasted pink, sits well with soft slices of local quince. A melting beurre bosc pear is sliced, splayed and splashed with caramelised sugar, a smooth caramel ice-cream and accents of vanilla. The service can be (should be?) leisurely, in the French manner. We're lucky to have the Legalls in town, and best of all, you can invite yourself around to dinner.

Hours Dinner Tues–Sat 6.30–9.30pm
Bill E $13.50–$16.50 **M** $28.50–$29.50 **D** $11.50
Cards AE BC DC MC V
Wine Interesting and well-priced half local/half French; 7 by the glass; BYO (corkage $5 per bottle)
Chefs Philippe & Gwenael Legall
Owners Philippe, Gwenael & Angele Legall
Seats 45; private rooms; wheelchair access
And...heat-and-serve dishes (coq au vin, etc.) available vacuum-packed for dinner parties

The West

Restaurant Q
Girraween Shopping Centre,
Queen Elizabeth Drive, Armidale
Tel 6771 1038   Map 12

Contemporary
                                Score 12/20

With a change of ownership and chef, Restaurant Q is flat stick trying to iron out the hiccups that come with a relatively new team. We're hopeful that this oasis in a suburban shopping centre will return to its former glories. The interior is all clean lines, with pastel-coloured walls and gentle lighting softening the mood, while the natural textures of a parquetry floor and timber venetians help shield you from the outside reality. A 'fagot' (bundle) of asparagus with a Chinese spoon of hollandaise is eloquently simple, if a tad rich at this price ($17.50). More substantial mains include a beautifully moist poached chicken breast on chicken velouté circled by vegetables. Barramundi fillet was topped with a disappointingly flowery almond gratin, partly redeemed by pea and white truffle mash and a vegetable flan. Service ranges from sweetly naïve to professional and a tad too serious. Wickedly rich chocolate marquise with mint sorbet ends things on a high note.

Hours Lunch Thurs–Mon noon–2.30pm; Dinner Thurs–Mon from 6pm
Bill E $13–$23 **M** $19.50–$32 **D** $8.50–$13.50; 3-course dinner $45 pp; 10% surcharge on public holidays
Cards BC MC V Eftpos
Wine Dependable if predictable list; 14 by the glass; BYO (corkage $5 per bottle)
Chef David Pommier
Owners Charles Tesoriero & Richard See
Seats 96; private room; wheelchair access; outdoor seats
www.restaurantq.com.au
And…monthly wine tastings and dinners with local wineries

Rylstone Food Store
47 Louee Street, Rylstone
Tel 6379 0947   Map 12

Regional
                                Score 14/20

From the moment her broad, warm smile welcomes you like an old friend, you hope Kim Currie will invite you over regularly for comforting meals such as those savoured at this homely, converted 1925 general store. The spacious room, with cushioned bench seats at long tables, doubles as an art gallery that might feature linocuts by her kitchen companion Na Lam. Currie champions local produce, so on Friday nights (which are more easygoing than Saturdays) you might be served fresh local pistachios, and bread from her nearby venture, the Bridge View Inn Café & Bakery (see *And also...* at the end of this section), with the unexpectedly glorious Jamindama olive oil. Soon after, it's a platter of chilli-roasted olives, Mudgee fetta and AC Butchery salami (made from locally raised meat). Then it's time for an assured zucchini-flower risotto, flecked with leek, zucchini, and the floral saltiness of preserved lemon, with AC's chicken and rocket sausages. By the time you have the irresistible fig and almond tart with vanilla ice-cream, you may well be inspired to visit the village real estate agent.

Hours Dinner Fri–Sat from 6.30pm
Bill Set menu Friday $33 pp, Saturday $44 pp
Cards BC MC V Eftpos
Wine BYO (no corkage)
Chef/owner Kim Currie
Seats 60; wheelchair access
www.rylstonefoodstore.com.au
And…you can take home the store's own jams, pickles and preserves, plus local olive oils

regional

Selkirks
179 Anson Street, Orange
Tel 6361 1179   Map 11

Contemporary
Score 16/20

When a gas explosion destroyed the kitchen late in 2004, we worried that, after 43 years, Michael Manners had gone out with the wrong kind of bang. We now know his resilience is matched only by his talent, for the reborn Selkirks is better than ever. From chairs at roomy, damask-cloth'd tables, the elegant Federation-era home, repainted a sunny ochre, feels brighter. The menu too, seems lighter, while maintaining its earthy local focus – dishes anchored in history but reinvented with contemporary flair. The charcuterie platter's decadence – lush rabbit rillettes, pork terrine and potted ham – remains. Thin, cool corned veal slices with tuna mayonnaise and cauliflower purée are a snappy vitello tonnato make-over. Amidst usually deft, friendly service, Josephine Jagger's proudly local wine list cleverly pairs with every dish, like the Borrodell gewürztraminer for slow-roasted pork loin with spicy orange sauce. Satisfyingly pink venison fans around a saffron-scented pilaf studded with almond and date. Rosé wine jelly and lemon financier with nectarine (poached and as sorbet) is both clever and deeply pleasurable.

Hours Dinner Tues–Sat & long-weekend Sundays from 6.30pm
Bill E $20–$24 **M** $30–$33 **D** $13–$14
Cards AE BC DC MC V Eftpos
Wine A comprehensive tour of Orange wineries at good prices; 14 by the glass
Chef Michael Manners
Owners Michael Manners & Josephine Jagger
Seats 60; private room; wheelchair access
www.selkirks.com.au
And...tea buffs have 20 choices, which come with an egg-timer to keep an eye on the brew

Three Chefs
Townhouse International, 70 Morgan Street, Wagga Wagga
Tel 6921 5897   Map 11

Contemporary
Score 14/20

In a neutral space, designed and lit as a gallery and located on the ground floor of a nondescript motel, Three Chefs defies its surrounds. The food is anything but innocuous, with rustic local produce adding earthy cred to the rather stilted atmosphere. Service couldn't be more charming from a witty and wily Scotsman (wearing a clankingly loud tie), whose seductive explanations of the food will have you pondering everything on the menu. A mixed plate of entrées includes oysters with tomato and Spanish onion salsa, beautifully rare and tender beef with sweet potato and caramelised onion tart, and luxuriously rich oxtail ravioli lifted with enormous, spankingly fresh prawns and burnt sage butter. A main of 'Supreme Breast of Chicken' with parmesan, polenta, tomato confit, buttered asparagus and red wine reduction is pure comfort food. Less relaxed was an overdone pork cutlet with a too-dry mixed vegetable roesti, caramelised apples, green beans and jus. Faith returns with a knockout trifle; grapefruit jelly, stewed figs and double cream.

Hours Breakfast Mon–Sat 7–9am, Sun 8–10am; Lunch Mon–Fri noon–2pm; Dinner Mon–Sat 6–9.30pm
Bill E $8.50–$15.50 **M** $20.90–$27.90 **D** $10.50
Cards AE BC DC MC V Eftpos
Wine Decent list of across-the-board, affordable Aussies; 14 by the glass
Chef Karl Kelly
Owners Karl & Rebecca Kelly
Seats 180; private room; wheelchair access; outdoor seats
www.threechefs.com.au
And...the mixed dessert plate is a sensational finish – if you have the room

Three Snails

36 Darling Street, Dubbo
Tel 6884 9994 Map 12

Contemporary

Score 12/20

An industrial estate on the outskirts of Dubbo may not be everyone's ideal location, yet the outlook to the hills beyond affords the modern fit-out an overwhelming feeling of space. A large deck wraps around the air-conditioned restaurant where wood floors, masses of glass, and some seemingly out-of-place dance music abounds. Service is young and enthusiastic to perfectly match the lively, friendly vibe. The contemporary menu aims at enticing both local office workers for lunch and informal townsfolk in search of a casual dinner. An enticing tapas plate proffers corn fritters with sweet tomato relish, a slice of frittata, chilli pumpkin dip, a salmon and pesto tartlet, pickled spinach and local olives. Hefty mains include three lamb cutlets stacked atop enormous fried wedges of polenta, surrounded by olives, roast capsicum and artichokes, swimming in a light jus. The stand-out is the ballotine of chicken, stuffed with thyme and pork, on an earthly throne of mushroom and parmesan risotto – classy tucker for what is essentially an up-market cafe.

Hours Tues–Sat 11am–9pm
Bill E $8.50–$14.50 **M** $28.50 **D** $7; 10% surcharge on public holidays
Cards AE BC DC MC V Eftpos
Wine Concise local list; 9 by the glass
Chef/owner Stephen Neale
Seats 70; wheelchair access; outdoor seats
www.threesnails.com.au

And... watch out for special dinners such as the Men's Night – how to cook to impress the ladies!

Tonic

Cnr Pym & Victoria Streets, Millthorpe
Tel 6366 3811 Map 11

Contemporary

Score 14/20

There are plenty of reasons for a detour to historic Millthorpe, just south of the Bathurst–Orange highway, from turn-of-the-last-century architectural gems to an old-fashioned lolly shop. This former corner store has an airy bistro feel, with high ceilings, huge glass windows and a red banquette along the length of an exposed brick wall. Tony Worland's marriage of technique and local produce results in exciting but accessible food, from Jannei goat's curd in a creamy bavarois, topped with beetroot jelly, to a juicy Cowra lamb loin teamed with olives and braised eschalots. Sugar-smoked quail stacked on a potato tuile and topped with chilli jam is a delightful contrast of flavours and textures. Rabbit boudin (sausage) combines sweetly delicate meat with livers, herbs and garlic, and a delectable sauce with hints of star anise and cinnamon. While the pasta in duck tortellini was stodgy, we have no such complaints about crumbly shortcrust pastry on a lemon tart, matching the perfect balance of sweet and sour.

Hours Brunch Sat–Sun from 10am; Lunch Sat–Sun noon–3pm; Dinner Wed–Sat 6.30–10pm
Bill E $16 **M** $29 **D** $14
Cards AE BC DC MC V Eftpos; bookings essential
Wine Succinct, somewhat eclectic list; 14 by the glass; BYO (corkage $4 per bottle)
Chef Tony Worland
Owners Tony & Nicole Worland
Seats 70; wheelchair access

And... we love the pressed-metal sheeting surrounding the open kitchen

regional

And also...

Bridge View Inn Cafe & Bakery
28–30 Louee Street, Rylstone
Tel 6379 1807
This stately, two-storey, 1830s sandstone inn has a new lease on life thanks to local legend Kim Currie. It offers simple but extremely appealing tucker. By day, a smoked salmon roll on their own bread, crisp caesar salad, curried beef pie and cracker lasagne. At night, sushi, pizza, pasta and curries, AC Butchery steak and mash, all washed down with wines from a smart local wine list or Hopping Mad wheat beer. Great pastries and strong coffee revive drivers, or you can stay in the rooms upstairs and take home a sourdough from the lovely bakery.

Butcher Shop Cafe
49 Church Street, Mudgee
Tel 6372 7373
Yep, the walls are white-tiled because it was a butcher's. They roast their own coffee (and serve a decent one). There's a big communal table and hearty brekkies, including potted eggs prosciutto and rum-infused French toast. On weekends, the dinner menu might include spiced lamb with lentils.

Cactus Cafe & Gallery
33–35 Warne Street, Wellington
Tel 6845 4647
Formerly the Sacred Heart Infants School and re-designed in Spanish Mission style, this cafe/homewares/gift shop serves Illy coffee, and homemade frittatas and tortillas along with Mudgee wines and local produce.

Cafe Eataliano
251 Peel Street, Tamworth
Tel 6761 2993
Open daily from 5pm till late, specialising in crisp, wood-fired pizze, pasta and mod-Med dishes. The décor is a little Spartan but the food is spot-on. They also make their own knockout gelato and tiramisu.

Cafe Graze
21 Derby Street, Walcha
Tel 6777 2409
This ultra-chic cafe has a children's room at the back while grown-ups can enjoy sunning themselves on the front deck or inside by the fire. Allpress coffee, designer sarnies or butternut pumpkin, rosemary and blue cheese risotto are sure to appease any parental (hunger) pangs.

Cafe 2340
15b White Street, Tamworth
Tel 6766 9466
Pancakes with honeycomb butter, maple syrup and banana; eggs Benedict with salmon; and bruschetta with mushies, avocado and oven-roasted tomato make this a top spot for breakfast till noon.

The Commercial Hotel
Meridian Street, Walcha
Tel 6777 2551
It's a typical big barn-like space at the back of this classic country hotel, revamped to match the contemporary food. Come evening the menu includes roast duck, spinach, mushroom and pine nut risotto; and rack of suckling pork with roasted vegetables and apple cider sauce.

The Country Provedore
143 Boorowa Street, Young
Tel 6382 7255
Jack Stratford (ex Jonah's) discovered that the abundance of produce around Young provided the perfect excuse for this licensed cafe and provedore. The menu ranges from Vietnamese (Enviroganic) chicken to French omelette with blue swimmer crab, tomato and dill, and he also puts together a takeaway menu featuring beef tagine, plus lamb and barley casserole.

Dolce Dolce
449 Banna Avenue, Griffith
Tel 6962 1888
This family business used to run a hatted restaurant, so running a top-notch pasticceria/gelateria with true Italian coffee and feather-light, homemade gnocchi may be a step back for them – but a step up for Griffith locals searching for a little authenticity.

The West

La Colline Wines
Lake Canobolas Road, Nashdale
Tel 6365 3275
With its orchard and vineyard views and pretty kitchen garden, La Colline offers smart French fare. Brunch on potted baked eggs or rum-infused French toast. Weekdays, it's rabbit pot pies or moules marinière – with change from $20 – and on weekends it's beef with café de Paris butter.

L'Oasis
150 Yambil Street, Griffith
Tel 6964 5588
This chirpy yellow brasserie, with polished timber floors and a Bedouin feel from the wall carpets, delivers generous servings of crowd-pleasing bistro fare that's smarter than you'd suspect. From freshly shucked oysters to Moroccan-spiced quail and roasted pork with spiced pear.

Magpies Nest
Old Narrandera Road (cnr Pine Gully Road), Wagga Wagga
Tel 6933 1523
During lunch, Chris Whyte may just whip out and give you a brief rundown of his olive oil press or the story of their first release wine. Sit in the sunny courtyard with gorgeous rural vistas to enjoy his playful menu of local produce.

Maynely Lauries
343 Argent Street, Broken Hill
Tel 08 8087 2637
Cafe by day and restaurant Wed–Sat nights, the state's most westerly nosherie provides solid country comfort food such as Outback Duck (roast duck breast with sweet chilli and quandong sauce) and decent coffee.

Nabiha's Kitchen
Shop 10, Neslo Arcade, 117 Baylis Street, Wagga Wagga
Tel 6921 7813
Step down the nondescript arcade and find a pokey shop where the beaming Nabiha makes some of the best Lebanese food this side of Beirut. Soups, casseroles, kibbe and kebabs, herb and yoghurt bread, baklava and boormai are all freshly made. Take home a jar of labna.

Premium Coffee Roasters
34 Trail Street, Wagga Wagga
Tel 6921 4155
In a leafy backstreet, a transformed butcher's is now a thriving cafe that roasts its own beans. Food is limited to muffins, biscotti and friands, luncheon baguettes or, in winter, soup.

Squires Cottage
Country Comfort Motor Inn, 86 Barney Street, Armidale
Tel 6772 8511
Nestled against the nondescript motel, this charming, sympathetically restored 1885 homestead is a cut above, serving new-age bush food in the barramundi empanada or kangaroo millefeuille with lemon myrtle aïoli. Classicists will love slow-roasted venison with Cumberland sauce.

Zest BYO
168 Hoskins Street, Temora
Tel 6978 0332
In the middle of the broad main street sits a cute, contemporary restaurant offering mod-Oz flavours. On the last Sunday of each month there is a sumptuous brunch. Dinner Thurs–Sat includes sumac-coated squid with tomato coulis and grilled lemon, and free-range Bundawarrah pork with apple crust and balsamic.

Zieglers Cafe
52 Keppel Street, Bathurst
Tel 6332 1565
Regulars reserve tables for the scrambled eggs with onions and tomato; pear, basil and grape frappés; excellent coffee; and ranch eggs on a soft tortilla with chilli. For late risers the good vibes – and food – stretch through to dinner.

Zouch
26 Zouch Street, Young
Tel 6382 2775
Whether in the sunshine-drenched courtyard or inside the old Masonic Hall, this is a great place for a lazy brunch, extended lunch or casual dinner, washed down with the local Hilltop drops. Enjoy a warm salad of grilled pear and blue cheese; wondrously tender Moroccan lamb stew on couscous; and Dutton Park duck breast with stewed apricots.

regional

Provedores

Arc-En-Ciel Rainbow Trout
Malonga, Hanging Rock via Nundle
Tel 6769 3665
A 20-minute drive 'up the back of Nundle' will reward you with great regional views and, more importantly, with some gorgeous fresh or smoked trout, pâté and more.

Bacco's Bakeries
13 Mayne Street, Murrurundi
Tel 6546 6822
For 'fine Italian biscuits and breads', Luigi Papagni is the man (usually covered in flour at the counter). Taught by nonno in Puglia, he now creates the omnipresent 'Bacco Leaves': giant, salty, crisp, flatbreads. While there, stock up on his savoury and sweet biscuits.

Borenore Berry Farm
Watts Road, Borenore
Tel 6365 2296
David and Kate Dickson pick strawberries, raspberries, blackberries and blueberries from October to April. Drop by for a punnet or three, or catch them at the Orange and Bathurst farmers' markets. Open daily.

Broombee Organic Orchard & Vineyard
Castlereagh Highway, Apple Tree Flat
Tel 6373 1314
The farm gate, 15 km east of Mudgee, is open November to March, when the fruit is in season. They have organic stone fruit: peaches, apricots, nectarines, plums and cherries, and, later on, table grapes and olives.

CSU Cheese Factory
Charles Sturt University, McKeown Drive, Wagga Wagga
Tel 6933 2170
Food science students get hands-on lessons adding native flavours to mild cheddar. They also make fetta and ricotta. Take a tour on a Wed or any time to combine it with a tasting at the CSU wine cellar.

Farmers' Markets
Bathurst, Bathurst Showground, Mitchell Highway, 4th Sat of month, 7.30am–noon, Tel 6332 4447
Cowra, Cowra Showground Pavilion, 3rd Sat of month, 9am–noon, Tel 6342 9225
Dubbo, Visitor's Centre, Cnr Newell Highway & Macquarie Street, 1st Sat of month, 8am–noon, Tel 6885 4300
Mudgee, St Mary's Catholic Church grounds, 3rd Sat of month, 9am–noon, Tel 0407 837 739
Orange, Orange Showground, 2nd Sat of month, 8.30am–noon, Tel 1800 069 466
Tamworth, Peel Street, 3rd Sun of month 9am–1pm, Tel 6766 4810
Wagga Wagga, Civic Theatre, 2nd Sat of month, 8am–1pm, Tel 6926 9621

Green Gables Organic Produce
Woodlands Road, Kingsvale
Tel 6384 4263
The ideal time to visit is November to December for cherries and January to March for various other stone fruit. They also sell their own jams, sauces and dried prunes from the packing shed.

High Valley Wine & Cheese Co.
137 Cassilis Road, Mudgee
Tel 6372 1011
Former Cowra fetta 'big cheese' John Grant returns with a clever range of fresh, white-mould, hard and mixed-milk cheeses at this cellar door and cafe. Watch him in action, sample the wines, then try a cheese-slanted cafe meal, a steak sarnie, and decent coffee. Local produce is also for sale. Open daily.

Jannei Goat Dairy
8 View Street, Lidsdale
Tel 6355 1107
The 100 Saanen and Toggenberg goats on Neil and Janette Watson's organically inclined farm, 15 km west of Lithgow, all have names. So do the award-winning cheeses, from a cheddar chevre to the white-mould bent back, creamy buche blanc and noir (rolled in ash). Closed Sun.

The West

Junee Liquorice and Chocolate Factory
8–18 Lord Street, Junee
Tel 6924 3574
Just about every Riverina deli, cafe and corner shop worth its salt stocks this fantastic organic liquorice and chocolate. It's also known for Greengrove Organic – a stoneground flour from the restored 1920s flour mill.

La Piccola Grosseria
44A Banna Avenue, Griffith
Tel 6964 7266
The effervescent Salvatore Trimboli is living proof you can take a generation out of Italy but you can't take Italy out of the next generation. His modest deli is packed with authentic cheeses, salamis, olives, pasta, panettone and more.

M & J's Butchery
30 Moulder Street, Orange
Tel 6362 2037
Michael Borg is a traditional country butcher with smart ideas. His cuts even satisfy the high standards of Michael Manners at Selkirks. Take home-corned veal, Mandagery Creek venison, goat, granged chickens or a lamb pie.

Melrose Park Venison
Melrose Road, Mudgee
Tel 6373 1233
Drive up the dirt road in a beautiful valley 10 km from Mudgee, past the grazing fallow deer to the 1870s farmhouse. Michael and Anjo Tarte offer a taste of their sausages (including one by AC Butchery), smoked and cured meats (including prosciutto-style), plus cryovac-packed fresh cuts, from shoulders to shanks. Open Friday to Monday or by appointment.

Newtown Providores
62 Wingewarra Street, Dubbo
Tel 6882 0055
This gourmet deli offers coffee and antipasto platters, and champions local produce. There's a poppy seed dressing from Jandra Station, and sauces from the local (mainly) indigenous Brewarrina Central School, such as Yammagura Black Sauce – 'good with booglies' (freshwater crayfish).

Norland Fig Orchard
Bradley Road, Borenore
Tel 6365 2225/0423 495 352
Warren Bradley is the fourth generation to farm this land. The 740 fig trees are mainly black genoa, brown turkey and white Adriatic. From January to April, drop in for a tray. He also does a nice line in dried figs, ice-cream and jams.

Proven Artisan Breads & Pastries
26B Sale Street, Orange
Tel 6360 0722
Paul Wilderbeek's beef and shiraz, and chicken and chardonnay pies are a revelation, with a crisp base, flaky lid and lush filling. Then there are his breads – more than two baker's dozens, handmade, using organic flours, from sourdough to spelt – and scrumptious pastries and tarts. Closed Sun and Mon.

Quinty Cake & Bakehouse
42 Morgan Street (on Olympic Highway), Uranquinty
Tel 6922 9119
Owners Paul and the extra-chirpy Tania completely renovated this early 1900s roadside building, creating an enormous kitchen where they pump out stunning sourdoughs made with organic flour. They also make great pies, pastries and gelato.

Village Hot Bake Bakery Cafe
113 Darling Street, Dubbo
Tel 6884 5454
Three generations of bakers have delivered Dubbo its daily flour fix at this buzzy hub of things proven. The pies win prizes, the coffee is decent, and the place hums on weekends as locals fuel up with pizze, focacce and sarnies, warming up by the fireplace on cool mornings.

Yandilla Mustard Seed Oil
'Yandilla', Olympic Highway, Wallendbeen
Tel 6943 2516
Drop into this rural cafe to sample simple lunchtime dishes and salads incorporating the various mustard seed products. The cold-pressed nutty/buttery oil shines when used to pan-fry perch, or there's a more intense version perfect for curries or dressings. Open 10am–5pm daily.

regional

Western Wines
BY HUON HOOKE

West of the Great Dividing Range, the most important wine regions are the Riverina, Cowra, Orange, Mudgee and Hilltops. They are as diverse in styles as they are geographically.

ORANGE Its elevation (up to 1000 m), creates the coolest climate of the western regions. Most vineyards are on the lower slopes of volcanic Mount Canobolas. Predictably, the early-ripening varieties (chardonnay, sauvignon blanc, riesling, pinot noir) are best, although spicy elegant shiraz and fine-boned merlot and cabernet blends are remarkably good.

Bloodwood
4 Griffin Road, Orange
Tel 6362 5631
The highlight here is a minerally dry riesling, but chardonnay, occasional botrytis riesling and serious Champagne-style Chirac bubbly are worth making the appointment to visit.

Brangayne of Orange
49 Pinnacle Road, Orange
Tel 6365 3229
The Hoskins family, orchardists and opera buffs, diversified into grapes with impressive results, including a juicy cabernet blend called Tristan and a gently oaked chardonnay, Isolde. They also make aromatic sauvignon blanc and a fine perfumed pinot noir.

Burke & Hills Cellar Door
Lake Conobolas Road, Lake Conobolas
Tel 6365 3456
Doug Burke is a newcomer who is fast making up for lost time, with Burgundian winemaker Chris Derrez. Chardonnay is refined and complex, sauvignon blanc a pungent herbaceous style, and the Bordeaux blend, O'Hara, creditable.

Canobolas-Smith
Boree Lane (off Cargo Road), Lidster
Tel 6365 6113
Murray and Toni Smith run a small, homely winery producing wines of great character and interest. Stand-outs are an ultra-complex, mealy chardonnay and a power-packed cabernet blend called Alchemy.

Others to visit: Belgravia, Cumulus, Jarretts, Prince of Orange, Printhie, Templer's Mill.

MUDGEE makes no apology for being a specialist in red wine, the mainstays shiraz and cabernet sauvignon. One of NSW's oldest regions, it invites comparison with the nearby Hunter, but its continental inland climate produces firmer, more structured reds. Semillon and chardonnay are good, but so too is riesling.

Abercorn
Cassilis Road, Mudgee
Tel 1800 000 959
Having started in 1996, Abercorn is among the newer players. Tim Stevens makes concentrated reds from shiraz and cabernet which are a touch more oaky and robust than next-door neighbour Huntington's.

Huntington Estate
Cassilis Road, Mudgee
Tel 6373 3825
Bob Roberts is a sort of godfather to the region and, with his daughter Susie, makes timeless, statuesque reds which are seldom woody and age superbly. The Private Reserve reds are very special, as is the cellar-worthy dry semillon.

Poet's Corner
Craigmoor Road, Mudgee
Tel 6372 2208
Formerly named Montrose, the winery makes a reliable, good-value Black Shiraz as well as the high-quality Henry Lawson flagship range. Poet's Corner wines, however, aren't made from Mudgee grapes.

Others to visit: Peterson's Glen Esk, Robert Stein, Miramar, Thistle Hill, Lowe Family, Louee, Elliot Rocke, Blue Wren, Frog Rock, Simon Gilbert, Andrew Harris.

COWRA is not far from Orange but is substantially warmer because of its lower altitude. Good-value, easy-drinking wine is the order of the day. Dry whites, especially softly fruity but straightforward chardonnay, predominate. The original vineyard, Cowra Estate, makes a good cabernet merlot as well as chardonnay; its specialty is cabernet rosé. Windowrie's cellar door is a must-see, along with The Quarry Restaurant, which conducts tastings for Cowra Estate, Swinging Bridge and others.

The West

Mulyan
North Logan Road, Cowra
Tel 6342 1289
The wines are contract-made outside the district, but Mulyan has some of the region's best chardonnay and shiraz. Its well-priced second label is Bushranger's Bounty.

Windowrie Cellar Door
The Mill, 6 Vaux Street, Cowra
Tel: 6341 4141
Windowrie's modern winery, Cowra's biggest, is out of town among the vineyards, while the cellar door is a restored flour mill in town. Consistently decent quality and good value.

Others to visit: Falls Wines, Hamilton's Bluff, Wallington.

> **THE RIVERINA** makes the wine that everyone drinks but seldom makes headlines. The main game is inexpensive bottled and boxed wine, which has steadily improved with better viticulture and less heavy-handed irrigation. Excitement is added by wonderfully luscious, botrytis-affected dessert wines.

De Bortoli
De Bortoli Road, Bilbul
Tel 6966 0100
Noble One is arguably the best botrytis semillon – and also the first. You'll also find remarkably good drink-now table wines under the Deen De Bortoli and Sacred Hill labels.

Lillypilly Estate
Lillypilly Road, Leeton
Tel 6953 4069
Gentle giant Robert Fiumara makes the Riverina's widest and best array of botrytis wines, using five different grape varieties. All his wines are well made, none more widely appealing than the semi-sweet Tramillon (traminer–semillon).

McWilliam's
Jack McWilliam Road, Hanwood
Tel 6963 0001
This is the vast McWilliam family's nerve centre, where the wines range from top-notch Show Reserve fortifieds to bubbly and one of the greatest botrytis semillons. Their Hanwood range is a value-for-money beacon for the region and, indeed, the entire country.

Riverina Estate
700 Kidman Way, Griffith
Tel 6963 8300
Sam Trimboli turns out surprising, well-priced wines. There's a bewildering mass of brands, but shiraz, cabernet, merlot, chardonnay, semillon and verdelho have all impressed under the Warburn and Ballingal labels.

Westend Estate
1283 Brayne Road, Griffith
Tel 6964 1506
3 Bridges Reserve label is an excellent indicator of solid, hearty shiraz, cabernet sauvignon and durif. The cheaper Richland whites often punch above their weight, and Golden Mist is one of the region's most sumptuous botrytis semillons.

> **HILLTOPS** Formerly known as Young, after the nearby town, this small, stone fruit growing region discovered grapevines somewhat later. Its high altitude (upwards of 450 m), and gravelly soils are especially well suited to reds. Full-bodied cabernet, shiraz and merlot lead the way, while Brian Freeman is doing interesting things with Italian varieties corvina and rondinella. McWilliam's Barwang is the biggest and best-known vineyard, while Grove Estate produces fine reds and semillons.

Chalkers Crossing
387 Grenfell Road, Young
Tel 6382 6900
Award-winning French winemaker Celine Rousseau produces an array of wines ranging from very good to excellent, making this the area's outstanding winery. Look for Hilltops riesling, shiraz and cabernet; Tumbarumba chardonnay and pinot noir.

interstate

MELBOURNE

with Roslyn Grundy,
editor of *The Age Good Food Guide*

Flower Drum / CHINESE
17 Market Lane, Melbourne
Tel (03) 9662 3655
Eating at this landmark Chinese restaurant requires forward thinking. So book well ahead, then dream about delicate crab dumplings, Peking duck and steamed coral trout. Service borders on the psychic.

Cafe Di Stasio / PILGRIMAGE
31 Fitzroy Street, St Kilda
Tel (03) 9525 3999
There's always a frisson of excitement about this dimly lit room, a sense that at any moment the unexpected might happen. The Italian food is honest and from the heart, and the theatrical floor staff are adept at helping you splurge.

Taxi Dining Room / HOT
Transport Hotel, Federation Square, Melbourne
Tel (03) 9654 8808
Through slits in the steel-mesh skin you'll catch glimpses of Melbourne's best-known landmarks. There's plenty of action inside the soaring space, too. Taxi's tandem menu offers exacting sushi alongside edgy mod-Oz dishes such as roasted snapper fillet on a raft of snake beans, crowned with rice-crusted prawns.

Circa, The Prince / HOT
2 Acland Street, St Kilda
Tel (03) 9536 1122
Andrew McConnell has a way of taking half-forgotten ingredients such as sorrel, pearl barley or madeira and making you wonder why more chefs don't use them. His finely nuanced dishes are perfectly at home in this glamorous fabric-draped dining room.

mr wolf / HOT
9–15 Inkerman Street, St Kilda
Tel (03) 9534 0255
Sydneysiders will know Karen Martini from her stint at Icebergs. This is the place that brought her back to Melbourne (along with the Melbourne Wine Room, see entry opposite). Locals drop in for takeaways or stick around for artisan pizze, the daily 'wet dish' and something from the Italian-focused wine list.

Ladro / HOT
224 Gertrude Street, Fitzroy
Tel (03) 9415 7575
To call Ladro a pizzeria is to under-bake things just a little. Yes, they fire up pizze (sublime free-form things topped with stuff like artichoke spread, mozzarella, lemon and parsley), along with brilliant daily arrosto and pasta dishes. Plus there's flattering light and a pert wine list.

Mo Mo / PURE MELBOURNE
Basement, 115 Collins Street (enter from George Parade), Melbourne
Tel (03) 9650 0660
In this dusky den, Greg Malouf adds a pinch of stardust to ancient Middle Eastern recipes, resulting in dishes that are lighter, brighter and more riveting than the original. Malouf's mezze platter, perhaps featuring goat's cheese and honey puffs, is unmissable.

Cicciolina / PURE MELBOURNE
130 Acland Street, St Kilda
Tel (03) 9525 3333
Come early or be prepared to argue the pros and cons of Cicciolina's 'no bookings' policy in the moody back bar while you wait for a table. Once you're in, you can look forward to things like spaghettini with pippies, wine and garlic, or roasted pheasant breast with braised lentils and sauternes and juniper jus.

Botanical / FINE DINER
169 Domain Road, South Yarra
Tel (03) 9820 7888
A favourite watering hole for decades, the Bot is as hot as ever. Count the ways: bottle store, restaurant and bar. Paul Wilson cooks some of Melbourne's most exciting food, including sticky pork salad with green papaya and chilli caramel.

Becco / FINE DINER
11–25 Crossley Street, Melbourne
Tel (03) 9663 3000
Sharp service is the essence of Becco's success. The ever-present Simon Hartley and Richard Lodge ensure Italian-inspired dishes come out at the right pace, the wines are spot-on and everyone feels pampered. Head upstairs to Bellavista Social Club for late-night drinks.

interstate

Pearl / FINE DINER
631–633 Church Street, Richmond
Tel (03) 9421 4599
Some of Melbourne's best and brightest turn up in this monochrome dining room. An army of brown-shirts ferries red duck curry with its slew of accompaniments, and gold-strewn taro dumplings, to customers dressed, naturally, in Melbourne black.

Movida / SPANISH
1 Hosier Lane, Melbourne
Tel (03) 9663 3038
Gather the amigos for a whirlwind visit to Spain. This hard-to-find laneway bar has a long list of tapas that work well with a glass or three of sherry. Make your way to a blond-wood table for more substantial dishes, such as seafood paella.

Melbourne Supper Club / WINE BAR
Level 1, 161 Spring Street, Melbourne
Tel (03) 9654 6300
If making the trek up to this wood-panelled bar seems hard, wait until you're forced to choose from the wine list. It's as thick as an atlas and with a similarly worldly focus (France, Italy, Spain, even Greece). No need to rush your decision, though. It's open until 6am.

Melbourne Wine Room / WINE BAR
125 Fitzroy Street, St Kilda
Tel (03) 9525 5599
First impressions of the Melbourne Wine Room may be clouded by the smoke, noise and utilitarian fit-out. But you'll leave raving about the wine list brimming with Euro treasures, the robust Italianesque food from Karen Martini, and the room's remarkable energy.

Double Happiness / BAR
21 Liverpool Street, Melbourne
Tel (03) 9650 4488
The lack of signage can mean a long march to find this tiny Maoist-themed bar. You'll know it once you spy the bike in the entrance and the agit-prop posters inside. Ask the mixologist to fix you a Ho Ho La, with fresh lime, lychee vodka and apple juice, or just a sudsy Tsingtao beer.

Da Noi / BISTRO
95 Toorak Road, South Yarra
Tel (03) 9866 5975
Plonk yourself at this shabby-chic trattoria and ask Steven Salce to feed you. The five courses of genuinely rustic Italian food will depend as much on his whim as what's in the kitchen: antipasto, a salad and a pasta dish, followed, perhaps, by suckling pig or rabbit.

Balzari / BISTRO
130 Lygon Street, Carlton
Tel (03) 9639 9383
Defying Lygon Street trends, there's no tout outside Balzari. No need. The robust Mediterranean dishes, scintillating wine list and wise service are attractions enough. Long after you've left this rather stark terrazzo and timber bistro, you'll still be dreaming of pan-fried sardines and big pans of Spanish seafood stew.

Queen Victoria Market / MARKET
Cnr Elizabeth & Victoria streets, Melbourne
Tel (03) 9320 5822
Closed Mon & Wed
Forget trams and the Melbourne Cup. The garden state's greatest attraction is the largest open-air market in the southern hemisphere. Grab all the fixings for a picnic or for a serious cook-up. Also try **Prahran Market**, 163 Commercial Road, South Yarra, Tel (03) 8290 8220 (closed Mon & Wed).

Batch Espresso / CAFE
Shop 1, 320 Carlisle Street, Balaclava
Tel (03) 9530 3550
A corner of Carlisle Street that is forever Aotearoa, this happening wee cafe pulls more than just homesick Kiwis. There's a silver fern on every latte (master barista at work) plus bumper breakfasts, good NZ wines and, coming soon, relaxed dinners. Be sure to leave a tup.

Choix Crêperie Café / CAFE
Shop G22, 620 Collins Street, Melbourne
Tel (03) 9629 1883
It's 'lunch as theatre' at this chic-to-cheek crêperie. At centre stage there's the crêpiere folding discs of batter around fillings such as Swiss brown mushrooms, spinach and taleggio.

interstate

BRISBANE

Restaurant Rapide / BISTRO
Shop 1, 4 Martha Street, Camp Hill
Tel (07) 3843 5755
Brisbane's growing sophistication can be measured by the local alumni now flying solo. Paul McGivern's (ex e'cco) elegant, petite, suburban bistro serves contemporary European fare, from pan-fried sardines with fennel, blood orange and caper mayonnaise to Mandalong lamb with speck, roasted tomato and olive salsa.

E'cco / INSTITUTION
100 Boundary Street, Brisbane
Tel (07) 3831 8344
It's now a decade since Philip Johnson converted this century-old former tea warehouse into a slick bistro. The colourful, classically inclined menu remains a contemporary lesson in simplicity, such as roast rabbit with pappardelle, mushrooms and truffle.

Mecca Bah / HOT
Shop 19–21, 1000 Ann Street, Fortitude Valley
Tel (07) 3252 5299
Melbourne's Cath Claringbold replicates her similarly named Docklands diner in warmer climes. Chill on ottomans in the lounge, or enjoy lively Middle Eastern flavours – spicy tagines, wood-fired Turkish pizza and mezze – at brass tables. It's as sunshiney as the weather.

Restaurant II / INSTITUTION
2 Edward Street, Brisbane
Tel (07) 3210 0600
Dynamic duo David Pugh and Michael Conrad deliver generous pleasure in this split-level bar, casual diner and chic restaurant. Local produce propels solid Asian and Med flavours, such as a tartlet of scrambled eggs and crab. Wine buffs revel in the many gems.

Isis Brasserie / HOT
446 Brunswick Street, Fortitude Valley
Tel (07) 3852 1155
The epitome of the swanky rebirth of the Valley is found in this smart jazz-infused diner that's also a great place to watch the street life. A contemporary European menu lets you savour suckling pig with a surprising vanilla bean risotto. Enjoy a great list and the small bar.

Luxe / BAR
39 James Street, Fortitude Valley
Tel (07) 3854 0671
This is a too-cool-for-school, breezy bar-cum-brasserie designed for snacking over a drink or three while crowd watching. The striking interior matches fun tapas – pork short ribs, quail with olive paste – and satisfying mains. Infectious music and tempting cocktails to boot.

Circa / VIEW
483 Adelaide Street, Brisbane
Tel (07) 3832 4722
A groovy, boisterous, high-ceilinged, contemporary warehouse space featuring great wines and slick service. The French-influenced mod-Oz is as sassy as braised-beef-cheek croustade with swede fondant.

Cru Bar & Cellar / BAR
22 James Street, Fortitude Valley
Tel (07) 3252 2400
After market shopping, hipsters head for this funky, outdoorsy cafe/bar/restaurant to plonk on the chocolate leather lounges and watch the passing street life. By day, it's tapas and good cheeses. Evening is chirpy bistro; duck and venison sausage. It's also an excellent bottle-o.

The Gunshop Cafe / CAFE
53 Mollison Street, West End
Tel (07) 3844 2241
Yep, the century-old building, with its exposed red-brick walls and rear courtyard, was a gun shop. Now it goes off for weekend brunch with queues for potato fetta hash cakes, and orange, mint and lime granita. Beans means Brisbane roasters Merlo. And dinner fires both barrels.

Jan Power's Farmers' & Flowers Market / MARKET
Brisbane Powerhouse, Lamington Street, New Farm
2nd & 4th Sat of the month, 7am–noon
St Joseph's College, Kate Street, Indooroopilly
1st & 3rd Sun of the month, 7am–noon
A cockney fisho with amusing patter, artisan breads, Barambah organic milk and cheeses, game, meats, homemade lemonade, great breakfasts…all in a wonderful riverside location (or school grounds), with a sparkling hostess.

interstate

SOUTH AUSTRALIA

Art Gallery Restaurant / BISTRO
Art Gallery of South Australia, North Terrace, Adelaide
Tel (08) 8232 4366
Cath Kerry offers deceptively simple cafe fare. Her sense of culture permeates a menu influenced by the art. After a visual treat, drop by the glass-walled space for coffee and cake or the juvenile joys of gammon with bubble and squeak, and Eton mess.

Bridgewater Mill / INSTITUTION
Mount Barker Road, Bridgewater
Tel (08) 8339 9200
Modernity greets history in this picturesque 19th-century flour mill, which doubles as the Petaluma cellar door. The brilliant Le Tu Thai blends French technique with his Vietnamese ancestry and a love of bold, gamy flavours – like honey-glazed duck with shiitake custard.

barr-Vinum / HOT
8–10 Washington Street, Angaston
Tel (08) 8564 3688
Barossa wine legend Bob McLean hosts this 1840s cottage, with a superb wine cellar, but it's the earth-to-table emphasis and delicate balance of chef Sandor Palmai's food that draws you. Lunch is broad and breezy, like the Barossa chook with panzanella salad. Dinner includes prawns with harissa and white gazpacho.

Magill Estate / PURE ADELAIDE
78 Penfold Road, Magill
Tel (08) 8301 5551
This smart, glass-walled pavilion looks back across the vines to the city. Jerome Tremolet mixes Gallic technique with local flavours, such as Kangaroo Island marron. An all-encompassing Penfolds cellar list includes the '62 Bin 60A cab sav, Australia's best ever red.

The Grange / INSTITUTION
Hilton Adelaide, 233 Victoria Square, Adelaide
Tel (08) 8217 2000
Five-star hotel dining remains an extravagant, intelligent, whimsical and confronting flight of imagination thanks to the pioneer of mod-Oz, Cheong Liew. His tenth anniversary, eight-course 'harmony' dégustation includes the revelation of his brilliant signature 'four dances of the sea'.

Maggie Beer's Farm Shop / PURE SA
Pheasant Farm Road, Nuriootpa
Tel (08) 8562 4477
The original lakeside restaurant, which gave rise to a legend, is now a lunchtime cafe and provedore, selling wines, local produce and Maggie's ever-expanding range of products. Lunch begins with the famous pheasant pâté, then a handful of mains, and great cheeses.

Salopian Inn / WINE REGION
Cnr McMurtrie & Willunga Roads, McLaren Vale
Tel (08) 8323 8769
This marvellous 1851 stone inn has a three-room cellar to pair with a rustic, French and Italian-influenced menu showcasing local produce with contemporary panache. After local olives, there is chargrilled veal tongue with sweetbreads.

First / BAR
Hotel Richmond, 128 Rundle Mall, Adelaide
Tel (08) 8223 4044
The refurbished boutique hotel is very chic, with groovy chandeliers decorating a sophisticated, hip, first-floor bar-cum-lounge and adjacent restaurant for BL&D. An Italianesque mod-Oz menu offers basic bistro flavours.

Lucia's / CAFE
Shop 1–2, Western Mall, Central Market, Gouger Street, Adelaide
(08) 8231 2303
An Adelaide institution in the thick of the market hubbub, with snug tables and dark timber décor that hasn't changed since it opened in the 1960s. The late Lucia's daughters now carry on the tradition of serving bargain-priced rustic pasta, pizze, and the Friday night lasagne. Everyone drops in for coffee while shopping.

Adelaide Central Market / MARKET
Between Grote & Gouger streets, Adelaide
Tues 7am–5.30pm, Thurs 9am–5.30pm, Fri 7am–9pm, Sat 7am–3pm
A 135-year-old tradition, the 60-stall market is rich in history, characters and cultures. It's the way things used to be, from smallgoods to organic produce, cheeses, an Asian butcher, patisserie and good seafood. Also try **Barossa Farmers' Market**, Angaston. Every Sat 7.30–11.30am.

interstate

PERTH +

Balthazar / *BISTRO*
6 The Esplanade, Perth
Tel (08) 9421 1206
Gotta love a place that serves Lescure butter with baguette. By day, Balthazar is all bistro good looks: risotti, braises and excellent seafood. At night, the lights are so low it looks closed, as couples eye each other off in the tapas bar over the exceptional champagne list.

Matsuri / *JAPANESE*
Cnr Hay & Milligan streets, Perth
Tel (08) 9322 7737
You may have to line up with Japanophiles and expats at this fishbowl-like corner diner. The lights are bright and the décor is a bit on the shopping mall side, but do it for the best tempura and excellent sashimi. The ginger chicken will have you back in the queue again.

Star Anise / *PILGRIMAGE*
225 Onslow Road, Shenton Park
Tel (08) 9381 9811
Free-range pork, Hahndorf venison, Karridale organic lamb – the provenance of the produce is as important as the cooking at David Coomer's modestly sized bistro with its stately rooms. Liquorice ice-cream with slivers of meringue is powerfully restrained and beautiful to gaze at.

Duende / *TAPAS*
662 Newcastle Street, Leederville
Tel (08) 9228 0123
This casual diner has staff who know and love their wines, a tapas-bar mood and plenty of bold flavours. Dishes have a Middle Eastern feel, from the cauliflower fritters to the kofta, with the occasional diversion such as (far-eastern) duck pancakes, for good measure.

Little Creatures / *VIEW*
40 Mews Road, Fremantle
Tel (08) 9430 5555
You may think this is just a brewery, given that it won an award for best beer in the UK. Well, it is, but the deck of this converted warehouse offers great views over the Fremantle docklands. There's also lip-smacking drinking food – perhaps a wood-fired pizza – and fabulous beers while planning your America's Cup challenge.

Must Winebar / *BISTRO*
519 Beaufort Street, Highgate
Tel (08) 9328 8255
Perch at the bar for a cocktail, then slide into a wine list that makes Perth look as cosmopolitan as Melbourne. The up-market bistro food tries not to get in the way of your Dry River pinot, but when hapuka paired with fresh black truffles hits the table, you'll be overjoyed with both. Rotisserie-roasted Liberty chicken is a signature.

Eminem / *TURKISH*
224 Carr Place, Leederville
Tel (08) 9227 7407
What Ismail Tosun can't do with Turkish cuisine in this modern, tiny diner isn't worth doing. His mezze is a dégustation of bargain proportions: $45 for seemingly endless courses. Try tender lamb cooked en papillote perhaps, or simply the best baba ghanoush. Desserts, using dates, Iranian fairy floss and rosewater, are invariably amazing.

Fremantle Markets / *MARKET*
Cnr Henderson Street & South Terrace, Fremantle
Tel (08) 9335 2515
Fri 9am–9pm, Sat 9am–5pm, Sun 10am–5pm, Mon & public holidays 10am–5pm
This century-old market is a 200-stall cacophony of everything from fashion to craft and trinkets, but there's also good produce. Local seafood – especially fresh sardines and abalone – a banana bunch of greengrocers, herbs and spices, European-style breads, honey, plenty of nibbles, and a bar if you've worked up a thirst.

Albany Farmers' Market / *MARKET*
Aberdeen Street, Albany
Every Sat 8am–noon
Sure, it's a long drive from Perth, but you'll see how delicious the south-west region is: marron, venison, mussels and Albany oysters, free-range pork and chicken, exquisite Billawarra Dairy yoghurt, and top fruit and veg.

interstate

TASMANIA

Lebrina / PILGRIMAGE
155 New Town Road, New Town
Tel (03) 6228 7775
For many, this is Hobart's finest diner, in a National Trust-listed property, with an emphasis on Tassie produce from Highland cheeses to local venison, married with a European aesthetic and a wood-fired oven. House-made bread is a revelation, and anything Scott Minervini does with oxtail should also be on the national register.

sugo / CAFE
Shop 9, Salamanca Square, Hobart
Tel (03) 6224 5690
The walls are red, like the tomato-based sauce from which this chirpy cafe takes its name. The coffee is truly great, served by a friendly team you want to take home. Now that it's licensed you can sit in the courtyard, drinking wine, crunching on good pizze or a bowl of something wonderful in the soup department.

Stillwater / PILGRIMAGE
2 Bridge Road, Launceston
Tel (03) 6331 4153
A converted historic mill at the riverside in Launceston seems an ironic place for Tassie's most modern food. Inside it's all exposed beams and beaming staff while outside there's a dog bowl if you bring your best friend. Daytime cafe fare can disappoint, but at night the menu is astonishing – perhaps abalone with red miso and ginger pannacotta or a plateful of things from a rabbit.

The Source / WINERY
Moorilla Estate, 655 Main Road, Berriedale
Tel (03) 6277 9900
With Moorilla's hilltop restaurant being totally rebuilt in early 2005, there are now several reasons to drive to Hobart's northern fringe. They include vincotto-marinated roasted olives and riesling-pickled Bruny Island oysters. Nichols chicken may feature, while the elderflower semifreddo is awesome. Check out the antiquities museum but always pause long enough to pick up wine to take home.

Choux Shop / CAFE
4 Victoria Street, Hobart
Tel (03) 6231 0601
Chris Jackman's latest Hobart offering (remember the iconic Mit Zitrone?) is a Parisian-inspired patisserie with brass fittings and a please-all cafe vibe. As we go to press, however, plans are afoot to rename the place Ruby Chard, with a serious menu focussing on produce (including pheasant and guinea fowl) grown on Jackman's property nearby. If it goes ahead, Choux Shop will resurface at a new address.

Franklin Manor / OUT OF TOWN
The Esplanade, Strahan
Tel (03) 6471 7311
The century-old colonial house is now home to the talents of former Michelin-starred Meyjitte Boughenout and his superb, 1,000-strong wine list. Dishes hold less of his French accent these days, such as beef fillet with bucatini and tapenade, or the cured trout with teriyaki foam. The dégustation menu comes with Tassie wines, and local lobsters often feature. Stay overnight to make the most of the remote and spectacular location.

Restaurant Gondwana / BISTRO
22 Francis Street, Battery Point
Tel (03) 6224 9900
While many give lip service to Tassie produce, Gondwana's actions are proof of their commitment. The elegant corner building in historic Battery Point offers flavour at every turn. Doo-town venison arrives atop mushroom risotto with beetroot jam. Great Lakes wallaby leg is filled with madeira muscatels and figs, while Marrawah beef fillet is dressed with local pinot.

Salamanca Market / MARKET
Salamanca Place, Hobart
Tel (03) 6238 2843
Every Sat 8am–3pm
From the Hmong ethnic community's fantastic greens to gorgeous girls selling heirloom apples and excellent bread, everybody heads to this legendary waterfront market – as much to gossip, of course, as for the excellent produce.

interstate

QUEENSLAND RESORTS

Ristorante Fellini / VIEW
Level 1, Waterfront Marina Mirage, 74 Seaworld Drive, Main Beach
Tel (07) 5531 0300
Jewellery jangles and glistens as laughter ripples from the cocktail bar; others enjoy *la dolce vita* and soothing water views, pondering a sexy classic Italian menu and a luscious wine list, thanks to the generous hospitality of Percuoco siblings Tony and Carlo.

Berardo's / PILGRIMAGE
50 Hastings Street, Noosa Heads
Tel (07) 5447 5666
And **Berardo's on the Beach**
Shop 8/49 Hastings Street, Noosa Beach
Tel (07) 5448 0888
The cool white elegance of this tropically casual fine diner now boasts one-time Michelin-starred Bruno Loubet (ex Bruno's Table). Expect French technique with a lighter touch for the resort setting, an emphasis on local produce, and global classics, from tagine to cassoulet. On the beach it's French bistro fun and great breakfasts after a swim.

River House / HOT
301 Weyba Road, Noosaville
Tel (07) 5449 7441
After making his name locally at Berardo's, chef David Rayner flies solo in a sparkling white and glass-louvred room. A daily changing mod-Oz menu is clean and unfussed, from tuna sashimi with a ginger, lime and black sesame seed dressing to local lamb shanks on mash with braised mushrooms.

Sassi Cucina / PURE RESORT
4 Macrossan Street (cnr Wharf Street), Port Douglas
Tel (07) 4099 6100
It's Italian, with Asian touches, and a sushi bar next door in a beautiful and lushly tropical outdoor setting. Seafood shimmers, from carpaccio with virgin olive oil and a tear of soy to chilli mud crab with wine and garlic. House-made pasta, especially cannelloni, is addictive.

Reef House / VIEW
Sebel Reef House and Spa, 99 Williams Esplanade, Palm Cove
Tel (07) 4055 3633
Many come for this boutique resort's spa, but pleasure and paradise can also be found dining on the deck between the paperbarks and palms watching the ocean. Philip Mitchell's globe-trotting mod-Oz menu ranges from duck salad with raspberry vincotto to lamb rib-eye on chickpea pancake.

Alegria / SPANISH
56 Duke Street, Sunshine Beach
Tel (07) 5474 5533
The upstairs shopping-strip location isn't promising, but once the windows fold back and you sit with a glass of something from the eclectic wine list in your hand, and Glen Bowman's deftly spiced Spanish food in mind, you know you've hit a winner. The town itself is just shy of Noosa, but the locals want to keep this piece of Iberia to themselves. We won't tell if you don't.

Vanitas / FINE DINER
Palazzo Versace Hotel, 94 Seaworld Drive, Main Beach
Tel (07) 5509 8000
Yep, it's as opulent, as OTT and as full of pretension as you'd expect of the Versace owners. But Steve Szabo's reputation is about modern flavours, uncluttered plates and letting the produce speak. Join the white-shoe brigade discussing the merits of meursault over chablis from the extensive list, or whether the duck with cepe risotto is better than the lobster bisque. Everybody loves the warm lemon pud.

Noosa Farmers' Market / MARKET
AFL Ground, Weyba Road, Noosaville
2nd & 4th Sun of the month 7am–noon
More than 100 stalls showcase the Sunshine Coast, from Noosa red tomatoes to tropical fruits, goat's cheese and bush tucker sauces and preserves. Local chefs love shopping there.

INDEX

index

By Cuisine

African
Cafe Mint (Surry Hills) 30, 155
Out of Africa (Manly) 103

Asian/Modern Asian
Abell's Kopi Tiam (Canberra) 184
Banana Blossom (Cremorne) 13
The Chairman & Yip (Canberra) 187
China Doll (Woolloomooloo) 35
Fu Manchu (Darlinghurst) 58
Infusion@333 (Sydney) 69
jimmy liks (Potts Point) 70, 162
mu shu (Bondi Beach) 96, 162
Ocean Room (The Rocks) 99
Rae's on Watego's (Byron Bay) 243
Temple (Neutral Bay) 137
That Noodle Place (Bowral) 233
WildEast Dreams (Leichhardt) 121, 147
XO (Surry Hills) 149
Yum Yum Eatery (Hardys Bay) 215

Australian
the tearoom (Sydney) 136, 158

Belgian
Epoque (Cammeray) 50
Heritage (The Rocks) 50

Bistro
Bistro CBD (Sydney) 22
Bistro LuLu (Paddington) 23
Northbridge Bistro (Northbridge) 98

British
The Old George & Dragon (East Maitland) 202
Restaurant Balzac (Randwick) 117

Chinese/Modern Chinese
Avalon Chinese (Avalon) 11
Billy Kwong (Surry Hills) 20
Chequers (Chatswood) 33
Dragon Star Seafood (Haymarket) 46
East Chinese (Circular Quay) 46
Emperor's Garden BBQ (Haymarket) 49
Flavours of Peking (Castlecrag) 54
Fook Yuen (Chatswood) 55
Friendship Oriental Seafood (Beverly Hills) 58
Golden Century (Sydney) 60
Golden Kingdom (Kensington) 61
Hilltop Phoenix (Castle Hill) 64
Kam Fook Bondi Junction (Bondi Junction) 71
Kam Fook Chatswood (Chatswood) 72
Kensington Peking (Kensington) 72
Mahjong Room (Surry Hills) 85
Manly Phoenix (Manly) 87
Marigold Citymark (Haymarket) 89
Neptune Palace (Circular Quay) 97
Ocean King House (Kogarah) 98
Palace Chinese (Sydney) 104
Red Chilli (Haymarket) 114
Red Jujube (Sydney) 114
Sea Oracle (Kirribilli) 125
Sea Treasure (Crows Nest) 126
Shanghai Yangzhou House (Hurstville) 128
Shun Tak (Parramatta) 129
Silver Spring (Haymarket) 129
Sky Phoenix (Sydney) 130
Szechuan Garden (St Leonards) 134
Ying's (Crows Nest) 150

Contemporary
The Alley @ Cronulla (Cronulla) 5
Altitude (The Rocks) 6
Amanda's on the Edge (Pokolbin) 199
Anise (Canberra) 185
Aqua Dining (Milsons Point) 7
Arena (Moore Park) 8
Aria (East Circular Quay) 9
The Art Gallery Restaurant (Sydney) 9
Artespresso (Canberra) 185
Ashcrofts (Blackheath) 176
Bannisters (Mollymook) 218
Bayswater Brasserie (Kings Cross) 15, 160
bel mondo (The Rocks) 16
Bellevue Hotel Dining Room (Paddington) 17
Berowra Waters Inn (Berowra Waters) 18
Berry Wood-fired Sourdough Bakery (Berry) 219
bills (Darlinghurst) 19
bills surry hills (Surry Hills) 20, 155
Bilson's (Sydney) 21
Bistro 163 (Sydney) 21
Bistro Fax (Sydney) 22
Bistro Mont (Bowral) 229
Blue Orange (Bondi Beach) 25, 156
Blue Wren (Mudgee) 248
Botanic Gardens Restaurant (Sydney) 27
Brass Razoo (Willoughby) 27
The Brewery (Newcastle) 208
Brown Sugar Nights (Bondi) 28
Ça Marche (Port Macquarie) 237
Cafe Supply (Newcastle) 209
Cafe Sydney (Circular Quay) 31, 158
Castalia (Yamba) 238
Catalina Rose Bay (Rose Bay) 32
The Cellar (Pokolbin) 200
Centennial Vineyards (Bowral) 230
The Chelsea Tea House (Avalon) 33, 41, 154
CherriJam (Double Bay) 34
Clareville Kiosk (Clareville) 36
Coast (Sydney) 37
Cottage Point Inn (Cottage Point) 38
Courgette (Canberra) 187
Crackenback Cottage (Thredbo Valley) 188
Credo (Thredbo) 188
The Crowded House (Bathurst) 249
Danks Street Depot (Waterloo) 42, 155
Darley's (Katoomba) 177
Dekk (Terrigal) 209
Dijon (Canberra) 189
DISH (Newport) 43
Dome (Sydney) 44
Donna's Cantina (Merimbula) 220
DOV (Darlinghurst) 45, 156
Eat City (Sydney) 47
Eltons Brasserie (Mudgee) 249
Emma's a la Carte (Hamilton) 210
Engine Room (Newcastle) 210
Esca Bimbadgen (Pokolbin) 201
Eschalot (Bowral) 230
Essence (Sydney) 50
est. (Sydney) 51
Fare Nosh (Summer Hill) 51
55 on Collins (Kiama) 220
Fitzroy Inn (Mittagong) 231
Flair (Erina Heights) 211
Fuel Bistro (Sydney) 59
Georgie's at the Gallery (Grafton) 239
the ginger room (Canberra) 190
Grand National (Paddington) 61
Grazing (Gundaroo) 190
Guillaume at Bennelong (Bennelong Point) 63
The Gunyah (Huskisson) 221
harbourkitchen&bar (The Rocks) 63
Hickson Road Bistro (Walsh Bay) 64
Highland Heritage Estate (Orange) 250
Hugo's (Bondi Beach) 65
Hugo's Lounge (Kings Cross) 65, 161
Jaspers (Hunters Hill) 70
Jenkins Street Guesthouse (Nundle) 250
Jonah's (Palm Beach) 71
The Journeyman (Berrima) 232
Katers (Sutton Forest) 232
Les Trois Freres (Sylvania) 77
Letterbox (Terrigal) 212
Lime (Newcastle) 212
liquidity (Rozelle Bay) 77
Lizotte's (Kincumber) 213
The Lobby (Canberra) 191
Lochiel House (Kurrajong Heights) 178
Loco (Neutral Bay) 78
Lolli Redini (Orange) 251
Longbench on Darby (Newcastle) 213
Lorenzo's Diner (Wollongong) 222
Lotus (Potts Point) 82,162
Lunch (Castlecrag) 83
Lynwood Cafe (Collector) 191
Macleay Street Bistro (Potts Point) 41, 84
Manly Wharf Hotel (Manly) 87
Manna (Petersham) 41, 88
MCA Cafe (The Rocks) 90
Merretts (Corlette) 214
Michelin (Griffith) 251
milk and honey (Canberra) 192
Milsons (Kirribilli) 92
Mint (Sydney) 94
Mojo's on Wilderness (Lovedale) 201
MoS Cafe (Sydney) 95, 158
Neila (Cowra) 252
Nelsons Brasserie (The Rocks) 96
No. 2 Oak Street (Bellingen) 240

272 good food guide

index

No. 13 Cafe (Lorn) 202
Olivo (Byron Bay) 241
Oscillate Wildly
  (Newtown) 101, 121
Osso (Penrith) 102
Paddington Inn
  (Paddington) 104
Palisade Dining Room
  (Millers Point) 105
Paupiettes (Lismore) 241
ploys at tuross
  (Tuross Head) 223
Poinciana
  (Mullumbimby) 242
Pool Caffe
  (Maroubra) 110, 155
Portabellos
  (Port Macquarie) 242
Quadrant
  (East Circular Quay) 112
Quay (The Rocks) 113
quince (Scone) 203
Ravesi's (Bondi Beach) 113
The Reef (Terrigal) 214
Relish at Balmain Bug
  (Balmain) 41, 115
Restaurant Como
  (Blaxland) 179
Restaurant Q (Armidale) 253
The River (Moruya) 223
Rocket (Chatswood) 118
Rockpool (The Rocks) 119
Royal Bar & Grill
  (Paddington) 119
Sails on Lavender Bay
  (McMahons Point) 123
Sante (Thredbo) 194
Sean's Panorama
  (Bondi Beach) 126
Selkirks (Orange) 254
Shakey Tables
  (North Rothbury) 204
Silk's Brasserie (Leura) 180
The Silos (Jaspers Brush
  via Berry) 224
Solitary (Leura Falls) 181
Solitary Kiosk
  (Leura Falls) 181
Strangers with Candy
  (East Redfern) 41,
  131, 155
Sugaroom (Pyrmont) 132
Summit (Sydney) 133
Tables (Pymble) 135
Terroir (Pokolbin) 205
Three Chefs
  (Wagga Wagga) 254
Three Snails (Dubbo) 255
Tonic (Millthorpe) 255
Utopia (Bangalow) 243
Watermark
  (Balmoral Beach) 144
Welcome Hotel (Rozelle) 145
Wet Paint Cafe
  (Waverley) 145

The Wharf (Walsh Bay) 146
Whitewater (Manly) 147
Willowvale Mill (Laggan) 233
Yellow Bistro
  (Potts Point) 150, 156
Zanzibar Cafe
  (Merimbula) 225
Zinc (Potts Point) 152, 156

Ethiopian
Fekerte's (Canberra) 189

European/
Modern European
Alchemy 731 (Mosman) 3
Aubergine (Canberra) 186
Bambini Trust
  (Sydney) 13, 158
Benchmark Wine Bar
  (Canberra) 186
Bit Brasserie
  (Neutral Bay) 25
dish (Byron Bay) 238
Hordern's (Bowral) 231
Mohr & Mohr (Surry Hills) 94
Pavilion on the Park
  (Sydney) 106
Pello (East Sydney) 107
Republic Dining
  (Sydney) 116
Restaurant Atelier
  (Glebe) 117, 121
Robert's at Peppertree
  (Pokolbin) 203
The Rooster (Katoomba) 180
Silo Bakery (Canberra) 194
The Table (Greta) 204
Three Clicks West
  (Annandale) 139
Three Weeds (Rozelle) 139
Waters Edge (Canberra) 195
Zest (Nelson Bay) 215

Fijian
Rama's (Canberra) 193

French/French Bistro/
Modern French
Astral (Pyrmont) 11
Beach Road (Palm Beach) 16
Benchmark Wine Bar
  (Canberra) 186
Bilson's (Sydney) 21
Bistro CBD (Sydney) 22
Bistro LuLu (Paddington) 23
Bistro Moncur (Woollahra) 23
Boomerang (Byron Bay) 237
Café Sel et Poivre
  (Darlinghurst) 30, 156
Caveau (Wollongong) 219
Chez Pascal (Ramsgate) 34
Claude's (Woollahra) 36, 41
Cochin (Surry Hills) 38
Collits Inn (Hartley Vale) 177
Feast (Avoca Beach) 211

Forty One (Sydney) 56
Galileo (Millers Point) 59
Guillaume at Bennelong
  (Bennelong Point) 63
Industrie – South of France
  (Sydney) 69, 162
King 143 (Sydney) 73
La Goulue
  (Crows Nest) 41, 74
La Grande Bouffe
  (Rozelle) 75
La Grillade (Crows Nest) 75
Marque (Surry Hills) 89
Mere Catherine
  (Potts Point) 91
Mes Amis (Katoomba) 179
The Old George & Dragon
  (East Maitland) 202
Onde (Darlinghurst) 101
Restaurant Balzac
  (Randwick) 117
Restaurant Legall
  (Bathurst) 252
Tabou (Surry Hills) 135
Tetsuya's (Sydney) 138
Vatel (Russell Lea) 142
Wine Banq (Sydney) 148

Gelato
Pompei (Bondi Beach) 121

Greek/
Modern Greek
Omega (Sydney) 100
Perama (Petersham) 41, 107
Whiteblue
  (Double Bay) 146

Indian
Abhi's (North Strathfield) 2
Agni (Beverly Hills) 2
Aki's (Woolloomooloo) 3
All India Restaurant
  (Balmain) 5
Bukhara (Double Bay) 28
Darbar (Glebe) 42
Flavour of India Edgecliff
  (Edgecliff) 54
Indigo (Lindfield) 68
Malabar (Crows Nest;
  Darlinghurst) 85
Maya Da Dhaba
  (Surry Hills) 90
Nilgiri's (St Leonards) 97
Oh Calcutta (Darlinghurst) 99
Qmin (St Leonards) 112
Rama's (Canberra) 193
Woodland's (Liverpool;
  Parramatta) 121, 149
Zaaffran
  (Darling Harbour) 151

Indonesian
Jimbaran
  (Randwick) 121

Italian/
Modern Italian
Alio (Redfern East) 4
Amici (Cammeray) 6
Arte e Cucina
  (Double Bay) 10
Barolo (Oatley) 14
Bella Mia (Roseville) 17
Beppi's (East Sydney) 18
Bistro Moore
  (Paddington) 24
Bond Cafe (Sydney) 26, 158
Buon Ricordo
  (Paddington) 29
buzo (Woollahra) 29
Cafe Sopra (Waterloo) 31
Certo Ristorante (Sydney) 32
Credo (Cammeray) 39, 154
Cucina 105 (Liverpool) 39
Darcy's (Paddington) 43
Divino (East Sydney) 44
Ecco (Drummoyne) 47
Elio (Leichhardt) 48
Fiorenzoni (Chatswood) 52
Fratelli Paradiso
  (Potts Point) 56, 156
Frati (Thirroul) 221
Frattini (Leichhardt) 57
Grappa (Leichhardt) 62
Il Baretto (Surry Hills)
  66, 155
Il Perugino (Mosman) 67
Il Piave (Rozelle) 67
Il Tratto Ra Ro Pizzeria
  (Concord) 41, 68
La Locanda (Bronte) 41, 76
La Perla (Gladesville) 76
Logues (Elizabeth Bay) 79
Lucio's (Paddington) 82
L'unico (Balmain) 83
Machiavelli (Sydney) 84
Mamma Barone
  (Sans Souci) 86
Manta (Woolloomooloo) 88
Mezzalira (Canberra) 192
Mezzaluna (Potts Point) 91
Michael's Trattoria
  (Wollongong) 222
Nove (Woolloomooloo) 121
Oliveto (Rhodes) 100
Osteria dei Poeti (Glebe) 102
Otto (Woolloomooloo) 103
Pazzo (Surry Hills) 106
Pilu at Freshwater
  (Harbord) 109
Ristorante Riva
  (Darlinghurst) 118
Sevardi Cucina Italiana
  (Beecroft) 128
Swordfish (Kingsford) 134
The Tilbury Hotel
  (Woolloomooloo)
  140, 163
Zenith on Booth
  (Annandale) 152

good food guide 273

index

Japanese/Modern Japanese
Azuma (Sydney) 12
Boomerang (Byron Bay) 237
Galileo (Millers Point) 59
Mino (Mosman) 93
Rengaya (North Sydney) 116
Sakana-Ya (Crows Nest) 124
Sapporo (Crows Nest) 125
Sosumi (Sydney) 130
sushi e (Sydney) 133
Tasuke (Canberra) 195
Tetsuya's (Sydney) 138
Tsukasa (East Sydney) 141
Uchi Lounge (Surry Hills) 142
Wasavie (Paddington) 144
Yoshii (The Rocks) 151

Laotian
Pink Peppercorn (Darlinghurst) 109

Lebanese
Arabella (Newtown) 8
Emma's on Liberty (Enmore) 48, 121
Fifi's (Enmore) 52
Summerland (Bankstown) 132

Malaysian/Modern Malaysian
Abell's Kopi Tiam (Canberra) 184
Chinta Ria ... Temple of Love (Sydney) 35
Kuali (Lane Cove) 74
The Malaya (Sydney) 86
Neptune Palace (Circular Quay) 97
Seri Nonya (Miranda) 127
Temasek (Parramatta) 137

Mauritian
Bukhara (Double Bay) 28

Mediterranean/Modern Mediterranean
The Bathers' Pavilion Cafe (Balmoral) 14, 154
The Bathers' Pavilion Restaurant (Balmoral) 15
Beach Road (Palm Beach) 16
Beltree @ Margan (Pokolbin) 200
Bistro Stock (Balmain) 24
The Clock Hotel (Surry Hills) 37
Icebergs Dining Room & Bar (Bondi Beach) 66, 161
Local (Paddington) 78
Miltons (Sydney) 92
Paua (Surry Hills) 105

Two Chefs on Stanley (East Sydney) 141
Wildfire (The Rocks) 148

Mexican
Azteca's (Randwick) 12
Vera Cruz (Cremorne) 143

Moroccan
Alhambra (Manly) 4
Out of Africa (Manly) 103

Nonya
Seri Nonya (Miranda) 127
Temasek (Parramatta) 137

Pizza
Amici (Cammeray) 6
Milk and Honey (Mullumbimby) 240

Regional
Rylstone Food Store (Rylstone) 253

Seafood
Billingsgate Fish Bistro (Randwick) 19
The Boathouse on Blackwattle Bay (Glebe) 26
Bottom of the Harbour (Balmoral) 81
Dry Dock (Katoomba) 178
Emperor's Garden Seafood (Haymarket) 49
Fins (Byron Bay) 239
A Fish called Coogee (Coogee) 81
A Fish called Paddo (Paddington) 81
Fish Face (Darlinghurst) 53, 81
Flying Fish (Pyrmont) 55, 81
Fresh Ketch (Mosman) 57
Garfish (Crows Nest; Kirribilli) 60
Hugo's (Bondi Beach) 65, 161
Kingsleys Steak & Crabhouse (Woolloomooloo) 73
La Perla (Gladesville) 76
Manta (Woolloomooloo) 88
Mohr Fish (Surry Hills) 81, 95
Ocean Foods (Drummoyne) 81
Ocean Room (The Rocks) 99
The One that Got Away (Bondi) 81
Peter's Fish Market (Blackwattle Bay) 81
Pier (Rose Bay) 108
Post Seafood Brasserie (Sydney) 110

Roger Fish Cafe Grill (Neutral Bay) 81
Sakana-Ya (Crows Nest) 124
Sanders (Cabarita) 124
Sea Cow (Paddington) 81
Swordfish (Kingsford) 134
Wheelhouse (Eden) 224
Ying's (Crows Nest) 150

Spanish
Alhambra (Manly) 4
encasa (Sydney) 49

Steakhouse
Kingsleys Steak & Crabhouse (Woolloomooloo) 73
La Grillade (Crows Nest) 75
Prime (Sydney) 111

Tapas
Firefly Winebar (Walsh Bay) 53, 160
Poinciana (Mullumbimby) 242

Thai/Modern Thai
Arun Thai (Potts Point) 10
Bang Thai (Bangalow) 236
Longrain (Surry Hills) 79, 162
Prasit's Northside (North Sydney) 111
RQ (Darlinghurst) 122
Sailors Thai Canteen (The Rocks) 123
Sailors Thai Restaurant (The Rocks) 122
Spice I Am (Sydney) 121, 131

Turkish
Ottoman Cuisine (Canberra) 193

Vegetarian
Darley's (Katoomba) 177
Woodland's (Liverpool; Parramatta) 121, 149

Vietnamese
An Restaurant (Bankstown) 7, 121
Cochin (Surry Hills) 38
Green Bamboo (Panania) 62
Minh (Dulwich Hill) 93
Phamish (Darlinghurst) 108
Red Lantern (Surry Hills) 115
RQ (Darlinghurst) 122
Tan Viet (Cabramatta) 136
Thanh Binh (Cabramatta) 138
Thanh Binh (Newtown) 138
Tran's (Mosman) 140
Viet Nouveau (Crows Nest) 14

Wood-fired
Vulcans (Blackheath) 182

Wood-fired pizza
Milk and Honey (Mullumbimby) 240

Harbour Views
Altitude (The Rocks) 6
Aqua Dining (Milsons Point) 7
Aria (East Circular Quay) 9
The Art Gallery Restaurant (Sydney) 9
The Bathers' Pavilion Cafe (Balmoral) 14, 154
The Bathers' Pavilion Restaurant (Balmoral) 15
bel mondo (The Rocks) 16
Blu Horizon Bar (The Rocks) 160
The Boathouse on Blackwattle Bay (Glebe) 26
Bridge Bar (East Circular Quay) 160
Cafe Sydney (Circular Quay) 31, 158
Catalina Rose Bay (Rose Bay) 32
Chinta Ria ... Temple of Love (Sydney) 35
Coast (Sydney) 37
Cruise Bar (West Circular Quay) 160
East Chinese (Circular Quay) 46
Ecco (Drummoyne) 47
Essence (Sydney) 50
Firefly Winebar (Walsh Bay) 53, 160
Fresh Ketch (Mosman) 57
Guillaume at Bennelong (Bennelong Point) 63
harbourkitchen&bar (The Rocks) 63
Kingsleys Steak & Crabhouse (Woolloomooloo) 73
liquidity (Rozelle Bay) 77
The Loft (Sydney) 162
The Malaya (Sydney) 86
Manly Wharf Hotel (Manly) 87
Manta (Woolloomooloo) 88
MCA Cafe (The Rocks) 90
Ocean Room (The Rocks) 99
Opera Bar (Sydney) 162
Otto (Woolloomooloo) 103
Palisade Dining Room (Millers Point) 105

index

Peter's Fish Market (Blackwattle Bay) 81
Pier (Rose Bay) 108
Quadrant (East Circular Quay) 112
Quay (The Rocks) 113
Sailors Thai Canteen (The Rocks) 123
Sailors Thai Restaurant (The Rocks) 122
Sails on Lavender Bay (McMahons Point) 123
Watermark (Balmoral Beach) 144
The Wharf (Walsh Bay) 146
Wildfire (The Rocks) 148
Zaaffran (Darling Harbour) 151

Outdoor Eating

Abell's Kopi Tiam (Canberra) 184
Aki's (Woolloomooloo) 3
Alhambra (Manly) 4
All India Restaurant (Balmain) 5
The Alley @ Cronulla (Cronulla) 5
Amanda's on the Edge (Pokolbin) 199
Amici (Cammeray) 6
Aqua Dining (Milsons Point) 7
Arabella (Newtown) 8
Arena (Moore Park) 8
Arte e Cucina (Double Bay) 10
Artespresso (Canberra) 185
Aubergine (Canberra) 186
Bambini Trust (Sydney) 13, 158
Bang Thai (Bangalow) 236
Bannisters (Mollymook) 218
Barolo (Oatley) 14
Bayswater Brasserie (Kings Cross) 15, 160
Beach Road (Palm Beach) 16
bel mondo (The Rocks) 16
Bella Mia (Roseville) 17
Beltree @ Margan (Pokolbin) 200
Benchmark Wine Bar (Canberra) 186
Berry Wood-fired Sourdough Bakery (Berry) 219
bills surry hills (Surry Hills) 20, 155
Bistro 163 (Sydney) 21
Bistro LuLu (Paddington) 23

Bistro Moncur (Woollahra) 23
Bistro Stock (Balmain) 24
Bit Brasserie (Neutral Bay) 25
Blue Orange (Bondi Beach) 25, 156
Blue Wren (Mudgee) 248
Bond Cafe (Sydney) 26, 158
Boomerang (Byron Bay) 237
Botanic Gardens Restaurant (Sydney) 27
The Brewery (Newcastle) 208
Brown Sugar Nights (Bondi) 28
Ça Marche (Port Macquarie) 237
Cafe Mint (Surry Hills) 30, 155
Café Sel et Poivre (Darlinghurst) 30, 156
Cafe Supply (Newcastle) 209
Cafe Sydney (Circular Quay) 31, 158
Castalia (Yamba) 238
Catalina Rose Bay (Rose Bay) 32
The Cellar (Pokolbin) 200
Centennial Vineyards (Bowral) 230
The Chelsea Tea House (Avalon) 33, 41, 154
China Doll (Woolloomooloo) 35
Chinta Ria ... Temple of Love (Sydney) 35
The Clock Hotel (Surry Hills) 37
Coast (Sydney) 37
Cochin (Surry Hills) 38
Collits Inn (Hartley Vale) 177
Cottage Point Inn (Cottage Point) 38
Courgette (Canberra) 187
Crackenback Cottage (Thredbo Valley) 188
Credo (Cammeray) 39, 154
Credo (Thredbo) 188
The Crowded House (Bathurst) 249
Cucina 105 (Liverpool) 39
Danks Street Depot (Waterloo) 42, 155
Dekk (Terrigal) 209
Dijon (Canberra) 189
DISH (Newport) 43
Divino (East Sydney) 44
Donna's Cantina (Merimbula) 220
DOV (Darlinghurst) 45, 156
East Chinese (Circular Quay) 46
Ecco (Drummoyne) 47
Elio (Leichhardt) 48
Eltons Brasserie (Mudgee) 249
Engine Room (Newcastle) 210

Esca Bimbadgen (Pokolbin) 201
Eschalot (Bowral) 230
Essence (Sydney) 50
Feast (Avoca Beach) 211
Fekerte's (Canberra) 189
Fifi's (Enmore) 52
55 on Collins (Kiama) 220
Fins (Byron Bay) 239
Fiorenzoni (Chatswood) 52
Firefly Winebar (Walsh Bay) 160
Fish Face (Darlinghurst) 53, 81
Fitzroy Inn (Mittagong) 231
Flair (Erina Heights) 211
Fratelli Paradiso (Potts Point) 56, 156
Frati (Thirroul) 221
Fresh Ketch (Mosman) 57
Fuel Bistro (Sydney) 59
Garfish Crows Nest (Crows Nest) 60
Georgie's at the Gallery (Grafton) 239
Grappa (Leichhardt) 62
Grazing (Gundaroo) 190
Green Bamboo (Panania) 62
The Gunyah (Huskisson) 221
Hickson Road Bistro (Walsh Bay) 64
Highland Heritage Estate (Orange) 250
Hilltop Phoenix (Castle Hill) 64
Hugo's (Bondi Beach) 65
Il Baretto (Surry Hills) 66,155
Il Tratto Ra Ro Pizzeria (Concord) 41, 68
Industrie – South of France (Sydney) 69, 162
Jenkins Street Guesthouse (Nundle) 250
jimmy liks (Potts Point) 70, 162
The Journeyman (Berrima) 232
Katers (Sutton Forest) 232
Kingsleys Steak & Crabhouse (Woolloomooloo) 73
La Grande Bouffe (Rozelle) 75
La Grillade (Crows Nest) 75
La Locanda (Bronte) 41, 76
Letterbox (Terrigal) 212
Lime (Newcastle) 212
liquidity (Rozelle Bay) 77
Lizotte's (Kincumber) 213
The Lobby (Canberra) 191
Local (Paddington) 78
Lochiel House (Kurrajong Heights) 178
Loco (Neutral Bay) 78
Logues (Elizabeth Bay) 79
Lolli Redini (Orange) 251

Longbench on Darby (Newcastle) 213
Lotus (Potts Point) 82, 162
Lunch (Castlecrag) 83
L'unico (Balmain) 83
Lynwood Cafe (Collector) 191
Macleay Street Bistro (Potts Point) 41, 84
The Malaya (Sydney) 86
Manly Wharf Hotel (Manly) 87
Manta (Woolloomooloo) 88
MCA Cafe (The Rocks) 90
Merretts (Corlette) 214
Mezzalira (Canberra) 192
Mezzaluna (Potts Point) 91
Michael's Trattoria (Wollongong) 222
milk and honey (Canberra) 192
Milk and Honey (Mullumbimby) 240
Minh (Dulwich Hill) 93
Mint (Sydney) 94
Mohr & Mohr (Surry Hills) 94
Mojo's on Wilderness (Lovedale) 201
MoS Cafe (Sydney) 95, 158
mu shu (Bondi Beach) 96, 162
Neila (Cowra) 252
No. 2 Oak Street (Bellingen) 240
Northbridge Bistro (Northbridge) 98
Ocean Room (The Rocks) 99
Oh Calcutta (Darlinghurst) 99
Oliveto (Rhodes) 100
Osso (Penrith) 102
Osteria dei Poeti (Glebe) 102
Otto (Woolloomooloo) 103
Out of Africa (Manly) 103
Palace Chinese (Sydney) 104
Pavilion on the Park (Sydney) 106
Pazzo (Surry Hills) 106
Pello (East Sydney) 107
Perama (Petersham) 41, 107
Phamish (Darlinghurst) 108
Pier (Rose Bay) 108
Pilu at Freshwater (Harbord) 109
Pink Peppercorn (Darlinghurst) 109
ploys at tuross (Tuross Head) 223
Poinciana (Mullumbimby) 242
Pool Caffe (Maroubra) 110, 155
Portabellos (Port Macquarie) 242
Prasit's Northside (North Sydney) 111

good food guide 275

index

Qmin (St Leonards) 112
quince (Scone) 203
Rae's on Watego's
 (Byron Bay) 243
Rama's (Canberra) 193
Ravesi's (Bondi Beach) 113
Red Lantern (Surry Hills) 115
Rengaya (North Sydney) 116
Restaurant Atelier
 (Glebe) 117, 121
Restaurant Q (Armidale) 253
The River (Moruya) 223
Robert's at Peppertree
 (Pokolbin) 203
Rocket (Chatswood) 118
Royal Bar & Grill
 (Paddington) 119
Sailors Thai Canteen
 (The Rocks) 123
Sailors Thai Restaurant
 (The Rocks) 122
Sanders (Cabarita) 124
Sante (Thredbo) 194
Sea Oracle (Kirribilli) 125
Sean's Panaroma
 (Bondi Beach) 126
Shakey Tables (North
 Rothbury) 204
Silo Bakery (Canberra) 194
The Silos (Jaspers Brush
 via Berry) 224
Solitary Kiosk
 (Leura Falls) 181
Spice I Am (Sydney)
 121, 131
Strangers with Candy (East
 Redfern) 41, 131, 155
Sugaroom (Pyrmont) 132
Swordfish (Kingsford) 134
Szechuan Garden
 (St Leonards) 134
The Table (Greta) 204
Tasuke (Canberra) 195
Temasek (Parramatta) 137
Terroir (Pokolbin) 205
Three Chefs
 (Wagga Wagga) 254
Three Snails (Dubbo) 255
The Tilbury Hotel
 (Woolloomooloo) 140, 163
Two Chefs on Stanley
 (East Sydney) 141
Vulcans (Blackheath) 182
Wasavie (Paddington) 144
Watermark (Balmoral
 Beach) 144
Waters Edge (Canberra) 195
Welcome Hotel (Rozelle) 145
The Wharf (Walsh Bay) 146
Wheelhouse (Eden) 224
Whiteblue (Double Bay) 146
Whitewater (Manly) 147
WildEast Dreams (Leichhardt)
 121, 147
Wildfire (The Rocks) 148

Willowvale Mill (Laggan) 233
Yellow Bistro (Potts Point)
 150, 156
Yum Yum Eatery
 (Hardys Bay) 215
Zaaffran (Darling
 Harbour) 151
Zanzibar Cafe
 (Merimbula) 225
Zenith on Booth
 (Annandale) 152
Zest (Nelson Bay) 215
Zinc (Potts Point) 152, 156

Private Rooms

Abhi's (North Strathfield) 2
Alchemy 731 (Mosman) 3
Alio (Redfern East) 4
Altitude (The Rocks) 6
Amanda's on the Edge
 (Pokolbin) 199
Amici (Cammeray) 6
Anise (Canberra) 185
Arena (Moore Park) 8
Aria (East Circular Quay) 9
The Art Gallery Restaurant
 (Sydney) 9
Arte e Cucina
 (Double Bay) 10
Artespresso (Canberra) 185
Arun Thai (Potts Point) 10
Aubergine (Canberra) 186
Azuma (Sydney) 12
Bambini Trust
 (Sydney) 13, 158
Bannisters (Mollymook) 218
The Bathers' Pavilion
 Restaurant (Balmoral) 15
Bayswater Brasserie
 (Kings Cross) 15, 160
bel mondo (The Rocks) 16
Bella Mia (Roseville) 17
Bellevue Hotel Dining
 Room (Paddington) 17
Beppi's (East Sydney) 18
Bilson's (Sydney) 21
Bistro Moncur (Woollahra) 23
Bistro Moore (Paddington) 24
Bistro Stock (Balmain) 24
Bit Brasserie (Neutral Bay) 25
Blue Wren (Mudgee) 248
Boomerang (Byron Bay) 237
Botanic Gardens Restaurant
 (Sydney) 27
Buon Ricordo
 (Paddington) 29
Ça Marche (Port
 Macquarie) 237
Cafe Sydney (Circular
 Quay) 31, 158
Castalia (Yamba) 238
Caveau (Wollongong) 219

The Cellar (Pokolbin) 200
Centennial Vineyards
 (Bowral) 230
Certo Ristorante (Sydney) 32
The Chairman & Yip
 (Canberra) 187
Chequers (Chatswood) 33
CherriJam (Double Bay) 34
China Doll
 (Woolloomooloo) 35
Claude's (Woollahra) 36, 41
Coast (Sydney) 37
Collits Inn (Hartley Vale) 177
Courgette (Canberra) 187
Crackenback Cottage
 (Thredbo Valley) 188
Credo (Cammeray) 39, 154
The Crowded House
 (Bathurst) 249
Cucina 105 (Liverpool) 39
Darbar (Glebe) 42
Darcy's (Paddington) 43
Darley's (Katoomba) 177
Dekk (Terrigal) 209
Dijon (Canberra) 189
Divino (East Sydney) 44
Dragon Star Seafood
 (Haymarket) 46
Eat City (Sydney) 47
Ecco (Drummoyne) 47
Elio (Leichhardt) 48
Eltons Brasserie
 (Mudgee) 249
Esca Bimbadgen
 (Pokolbin) 201
Eschalot (Bowral) 230
Essence (Sydney) 50
est. (Sydney) 51
Fitzroy Inn (Mittagong) 231
Flavours of Peking
 (Castlecrag) 54
Flying Fish (Pyrmont) 55, 81
Fook Yuen (Chatswood) 55
Forty One (Sydney) 56
Fratelli Paradiso
 (Potts Point) 56, 156
Fu Manchu (Darlinghurst) 58
Galileo (Millers Point) 59
Georgie's at the Gallery
 (Grafton) 239
the ginger room
 (Canberra) 190
Golden Century (Sydney) 60
Golden Kingdom
 (Kensington) 61
Grazing (Gundaroo) 190
Guillaume at Bennelong
 (Bennelong Point) 63
harbourkitchen&bar
 (The Rocks) 63
Highland Heritage Estate
 (Orange) 250
Hilltop Phoenix
 (Castle Hill) 64
Hordern's (Bowral) 231

Hugo's Lounge
 (Kings Cross) 65, 161
Icebergs Dining Room & Bar
 (Bondi Beach) 66, 161
Il Perugino (Mosman) 67
Il Tratto Ra Ro Pizzeria
 (Concord) 41, 68
Industrie – South of France
 (Sydney) 69, 162
Jaspers (Hunters Hill) 70
Jenkins Street Guesthouse
 (Nundle) 250
Jonah's (Palm Beach) 71
Katers (Sutton Forest) 232
King 143 (Sydney) 73
Kingsleys Steak & Crabhouse
 (Woolloomooloo) 73
La Goulue (Crows Nest)
 41, 74
La Grillade (Crows Nest) 75
La Perla (Gladesville) 76
Letterbox (Terrigal) 212
Lime (Newcastle) 212
liquidity (Rozelle Bay) 77
Lochiel House (Kurrajong
 Heights) 178
Longrain (Surry Hills) 79, 162
Lucio's (Paddington) 82
L'unico (Balmain) 83
Lynwood Cafe (Collector) 191
Mahjong Room
 (Surry Hills) 85
Malabar (Crows Nest) 85
The Malaya (Sydney) 86
Manly Phoenix (Manly) 87
Manly Wharf Hotel
 (Manly) 87
Manna (Petersham) 41, 88
Marigold Citymark
 (Haymarket) 89
Marque (Surry Hills) 89
Merretts (Corlette) 214
Mezzalira (Canberra) 192
Michelin (Griffith) 251
Milsons (Kirribilli) 92
Miltons (Sydney) 92
Minh (Dulwich Hill) 93
Mint (Sydney) 94
mu shu (Bondi Beach)
 96, 162
Neptune Palace (Circular
 Quay) 97
Nilgiri's (St Leonards) 97
Ocean King House
 (Kogarah) 98
Ocean Room
 (The Rocks) 99
Oh Calcutta (Darlinghurst) 99
The Old George & Dragon
 (East Maitland) 202
Omega (Sydney) 100
Otto (Woolloomooloo) 103
Ottoman Cuisine
 (Canberra) 193
Palace Chinese
 (Sydney) 104

index

Palisade Dining Room (Millers Point) 105
Pazzo (Surry Hills) 106
Perama (Petersham) 41, 107
Pier (Rose Bay) 108
Pilu at Freshwater (Harbord) 109
Poinciana (Mullumbimby) 242
Pool Caffe (Maroubra) 110, 155
Prasit's Northside (North Sydney) 111
Prime (Sydney) 111
Quay (The Rocks) 113
Red Chilli (Haymarket) 114
Red Jujube (Sydney) 114
The Reef (Terrigal) 214
Relish at Balmain Bug (Balmain) 41, 115
Rengaya (North Sydney) 116
Restaurant Atelier (Glebe) 117, 121
Restaurant Balzac (Randwick) 117
Restaurant Legall (Bathurst) 252
Restaurant Q (Armidale) 253
Robert's at Peppertree (Pokolbin) 203
Rockpool (The Rocks) 119
The Rooster (Katoomba) 180
Royal Bar & Grill (Paddington) 119
RQ (Darlinghurst) 122
Sakana-Ya (Crows Nest) 124
Sea Treasure (Crows Nest) 126
Selkirks (Orange) 254
Sevardi Cucina Italiana (Beecroft) 128
Shun Tak (Parramatta) 129
The Silos (Jaspers Brush via Berry) 224
Silver Spring (Haymarket) 129
Sky Phoenix (Sydney) 130
Solitary (Leura Falls) 181
Strangers with Candy (East Redfern) 41, 131, 155
Swordfish (Kingsford) 134
The Table (Greta) 204
Tables (Pymble) 135
Tabou (Surry Hills) 135
Temasek (Parramatta) 137
Terroir (Pokolbin) 205
Tetsuya's (Sydney) 138
That Noodle Place (Bowral) 233
Three Chefs (Wagga Wagga) 254
Three Clicks West (Annandale) 139
Tran's (Mosman) 140
Two Chefs on Stanley (East Sydney) 141

Vera Cruz (Cremorne) 143
Viet Nouveau (Crows Nest) 143
Waters Edge (Canberra) 195
The Wharf (Walsh Bay) 146
WildEast Dreams (Leichhardt) 121, 147
Wildfire (The Rocks) 148
Willowvale Mill (Laggan) 233
XO (Surry Hills) 149
Ying's (Crows Nest) 150
Yoshii (The Rocks) 151
Zaaffran (Darling Harbour) 151

Wheelchair Access

Abhi's (North Strathfield) 2
Alhambra (Manly) 4
Alio (Redfern East) 4
All India Restaurant (Balmain) 5
Altitude (The Rocks) 6
Amanda's on the Edge (Pokolbin) 199
Amici (Cammeray) 6
An Restaurant (Bankstown) 7, 121
Anise (Canberra) 185
Arabella (Newtown) 8
Arena (Moore Park) 8
Aria (East Circular Quay) 9
The Art Gallery Restaurant (Sydney) 9
Astral (Pyrmont) 11
Aubergine (Canberra) 186
Azuma (Sydney) 12
Bambini Trust (Sydney) 13, 158
Bang Thai (Bangalow) 236
The Bathers' Pavilion Cafe (Balmoral) 14, 154
The Bathers' Pavilion Restaurant (Balmoral) 15
Beach Road (Palm Beach) 16
Beltree @ Margan (Pokolbin) 200
Benchmark Wine Bar (Canberra) 186
Berry Wood-fired Sourdough Bakery (Berry) 219
bills surry hills (Surry Hills) 20, 155
Bilson's (Sydney) 21
Bistro Fax (Sydney) 22
Bistro Mont (Bowral) 229
Bistro Stock (Balmain) 24
Bit Brasserie (Neutral Bay) 25
Blue Wren (Mudgee) 248

The Boathouse on Blackwattle Bay (Glebe) 26
Bond Cafe (Sydney) 26, 158
Boomerang (Byron Bay) 237
Botanic Gardens Restaurant (Sydney) 27
The Brewery (Newcastle) 208
Ça Marche (Port Macquarie) 237
Cafe Supply (Newcastle) 209
Cafe Sydney (Circular Quay) 31, 158
Castalia (Yamba) 238
The Cellar (Pokolbin) 200
Centennial Vineyards (Bowral) 230
Chequers (Chatswood) 33
Chinta Ria ... Temple of Love (Sydney) 35
Claude's (Woollahra) 36, 41
Coast (Sydney) 37
Cochin (Surry Hills) 38
Collits Inn (Hartley Vale) 177
Courgette (Canberra) 187
Credo (Cammeray) 39, 154
The Crowded House (Bathurst) 249
Cucina 105 (Liverpool) 39
Danks Street Depot (Waterloo) 42, 155
Darbar (Glebe) 42
Dekk (Terrigal) 209
Dijon (Canberra) 189
dish (Byron Bay) 238
DISH (Newport) 43
Dome (Sydney) 44
Dragon Star Seafood (Haymarket) 46
Ecco (Drummoyne) 47
Eltons Brasserie (Mudgee) 249
Emma's a la Carte (Hamilton) 210
Engine Room (Newcastle) 210
Esca Bimbadgen (Pokolbin) 201
Eschalot (Bowral) 230
Essence (Sydney) 50
est. (Sydney) 51
Fare Nosh (Summer Hill) 51
Feast (Avoca Beach) 211
Fekerte's (Canberra) 189
55 on Collins (Kiama) 220
Fins (Byron Bay) 239
Fiorenzoni (Chatswood) 52
Fitzroy Inn (Mittagong) 231
Flair (Erina Heights) 211
Flying Fish (Pyrmont) 55, 81
Forty One (Sydney) 56
Fratelli Paradiso (Potts Point) 56, 156
Friendship Oriental Seafood (Beverly Hills) 58

Fuel Bistro (Sydney) 59
Galileo (Millers Point) 59
Georgie's at the Gallery (Grafton) 239
the ginger room (Canberra) 190
Grappa (Leichhardt) 62
Green Bamboo (Panania) 62
The Gunyah (Huskisson) 221
harbourkitchen&bar (The Rocks) 63
Hickson Road Bistro (Walsh Bay) 64
Highland Heritage Estate (Orange) 250
Hilltop Phoenix (Castle Hill) 64
Hordern's (Bowral) 231
Hugo's Lounge (Kings Cross) 65, 161
Icebergs Dining Room & Bar (Bondi Beach) 66, 161
Il Baretto (Surry Hills) 66, 155
Industrie – South of France (Sydney) 69, 162
Infusion@333 (Sydney) 69
Jonah's (Palm Beach) 71
Kam Fook Bondi Junction (Bondi Junction) 71
Katers (Sutton Forest) 232
Kensington Peking (Kensington) 72
Kingsleys Steak & Crabhouse (Woolloomooloo) 73
La Grande Bouffe (Rozelle) 75
La Locanda (Bronte) 41, 76
La Perla (Gladesville) 76
Lime (Newcastle) 212
liquidity (Rozelle Bay) 77
Lizotte's (Kincumber) 213
The Lobby (Canberra) 191
Lochiel House (Kurrajong Heights) 178
Loco (Neutral Bay) 78
Logues (Elizabeth Bay) 79
Lolli Redini (Orange) 251
Longrain (Surry Hills) 79, 162
Lotus (Potts Point) 82, 162
Lunch (Castlecrag) 83
Lynwood Cafe (Collector) 191
The Malaya (Sydney) 86
Manly Phoenix (Manly) 87
Manly Wharf Hotel (Manly) 87
Manna (Petersham) 41, 88
Manta (Woolloomooloo) 88
MCA Cafe (The Rocks) 90
Merretts (Corlette) 214
Mes Amis (Katoomba) 179
Mezzalira (Canberra) 192
Michelin (Griffith) 251
milk and honey (Canberra) 192

good food guide 277

index

Milk and Honey (Mullumbimby) 240
Miltons (Sydney) 92
Minh (Dulwich Hill) 93
Mojo's on Wilderness (Lovedale) 201
MoS Cafe (Sydney) 95, 162
mu shu (Bondi Beach) 96, 162
Neila (Cowra) 252
No. 2 Oak Street (Bellingen) 240
Northbridge Bistro (Northbridge) 98
Ocean Room (The Rocks) 99
Oliveto (Rhodes) 100
Olivo (Byron Bay) 241
Osso (Penrith) 102
Ottoman Cuisine (Canberra) 193
Paddington Inn (Paddington) 104
Palace Chinese (Sydney) 104
Pavilion on the Park (Sydney) 106
Pilu at Freshwater (Harbord) 109
ploys at tuross (Tuross Head) 223
Poinciana (Mullumbimby) 242
Portabellos (Port Macquarie) 242
Post Seafood Brasserie (Sydney) 110
Prasit's Northside (North Sydney) 111
Prime (Sydney) 111
Qmin (St Leonards) 112
Quadrant (East Circular Quay) 112
Quay (The Rocks) 113
quince (Scone) 203
Ravesi's (Bondi Beach) 113
The Reef (Terrigal) 214
Republic Dining (Sydney) 116
Restaurant Atelier (Glebe) 117, 121
Restaurant Balzac (Randwick) 117
Restaurant Legall (Bathurst) 252
Restaurant Q (Armidale) 253
The River (Moruya) 223
Robert's at Peppertree (Pokolbin) 203
Rocket (Chatswood) 118
Rylstone Food Store (Rylstone) 253
Sails on Lavender Bay (McMahons Point) 123
Sanders (Cabarita) 124
Sante (Thredbo) 194
Sea Treasure (Crows Nest) 126
Selkirks (Orange) 254
Sevardi Cucina Italiana (Beecroft) 128
Shakey Tables (North Rothbury) 204
Silk's Brasserie (Leura) 180
Silo Bakery (Canberra) 194
Sky Phoenix (Sydney) 130
Sosumi (Sydney) 130
Strangers with Candy (East Redfern) 41, 131, 155
Sugaroom (Pyrmont) 132
Summerland (Bankstown) 132
Summit (Sydney) 133
sushi e (Sydney) 133
Swordfish (Kingsford) 134
Szechuan Garden (St Leonards) 134
the tearoom (Sydney) 136, 158
Temasek (Parramatta) 137
Terroir (Pokolbin) 205
That Noodle Place (Bowral) 233
Three Chefs (Wagga Wagga) 254
Three Snails (Dubbo) 255
Three Weeds (Rozelle) 139
The Tilbury Hotel (Woolloomooloo) 140, 163
Tonic (Millthorpe) 255
Utopia (Bangalow) 243
Vera Cruz (Cremorne) 143
Waters Edge (Canberra) 195
Wet Paint Cafe (Waverley) 145
The Wharf (Walsh Bay) 146
Whitewater (Manly) 147
Wildfire (The Rocks) 148
Woodland's (Liverpool; Parramatta) 121, 149
Yellow Bistro (Potts Point) 150, 156
Yum Yum Eatery (Hardys Bay) 215
Zanzibar Cafe (Merimbula) 225
Zenith on Booth (Annandale) 152

Yum Cha

Chequers (Chatswood) 33
Dragon Star Seafood (Haymarket) 46
Fook Yuen (Chatswood) 55
Kam Fook Bondi Junction (Bondi Junction) 71
Kam Fook Chatswood (Chatswood) 72
Marigold Citymark (Haymarket) 89
Shun Tak (Parramatta) 129
Sky Phoenix (Sydney) 130
Ying's (Crows Nest) 150

Provedores

ABC Cheese Factory (Central Tilba) 227
Abla Pastry (Granville) 171
AC Butchery (Leichhardt; Rose Bay; Sydney) 169
Adelaide Central Market (Adelaide) 267
Albany Farmers' Market (Albany) 268
Antico's Northbridge Fruit World (Northbridge) 170
Arc-En-Ciel Rainbow Trout (Hanging Rock via Nundle) 258
Arena's L'Antipasto Deli (Mosman) 168
Australian Regional Food Store & Cafe (Pokolbin) 206
Bacco's Bakeries (Murrurundi) 258
Bakehouse on Wentworth (Blackheath; Leura; Springwood) 183
Barnett's Rainbow Reach Oyster Barn (South West Rocks) 246
Barossa Farmers' Market (Angaston) 267
Bay Marlin Seafoods (Batemans Bay) 227
Bb Cc Wicked Chocolates (Newcastle) 217
Bent on Food (Wingham) 246
Bermagui Gelati Clinic (Bermagui) 227
Best Value Supermarket (Bankstown) 166
Bilpin Springs Orchard (Bilpin) 183
Binnorie Dairy (Pokolbin) 206
Blackheath Butchery (Blackheath) 183
Blackheath Continental Deli (Blackheath) 183
Blackwattle Deli (Pyrmont) 168
Blue Seas (Bowral) 196
Borenore Berry Farm (Borenore) 258
Bowan Island (Drummoyne) 171
Braidwood Bakery (Braidwood) 227
Brasserie Bread (Botany) 171
Broombee Organic Orchard & Vineyard (Apple Tree Flat) 258
Bruno's Truffles (Canberra) 196
Caesar's Coffee & Fine Food (Erina) 217
Capital Region Farmers' Market (Canberra) 196
The Cheese Store at Bowral (Bowral) 234
Christie's Seafoods (Pyrmont) 172
Claudio's Quality Seafoods (Pyrmont) 172
Coffs Harbour Fishermen's Co-op (Coffs Harbour) 246
Commercial Fisherman's Co-op Ltd (Wickham) 217
Con's Beecroft Village Delicatessen (Beecroft) 168
Croissant D'Or (Canberra) 196
CSU Cheese Factory (Wagga Wagga) 258
Cyril's Delicatessen (Haymarket) 168
Dangerous Dan's Butchery (Macksville) 246
Darby Street Gourmet Deli (Newcastle) 217
Darrel's Gourmet Butchery (Gloucester) 246
David Jones Foodhall (Bondi Junction; City) 166
De'lish (Lindfield) 166
Deli Cucina (Caringbah; Edgecliff) 166
Demcos (Alexandria) 172
The Educated Palate (Wollongong) 227
Emile's Fruit & Vegetables (Balmain) 170
Emperor's Garden Meat Market (Haymarket) 169
The Essential Ingredient (Camperdown) 166
Euro Patisserie (Newcastle) 217
Farmers' Market (Albany) 268
Farmers' Market (Angaston) 267
Farmers' Market (Canberra) 196
Farmers' Market (Moore Park) 172
Farmers' Market (Noosaville) 270

278 good food guide

index

Farmers' Markets (North Coast) 247
Farmers' Markets (The West) 258
Fishy Fishy (Lennox Head) 247
FJ Galluzzo (Glebe) 170
Food and Wine with Altitude Fair (Blackheath) 183
Food Stuff Mona Vale (Mona Vale) 166
Four Olives Deli (Manly) 168
Frank's Fruit Market (Haberfield) 170
Fratelli Fresh (Waterloo) 170
Fremantle Markets (Fremantle) 268
Fruit Ezy (Chatswood) 170
Fyshwick Fresh Foods Market (Canberra) 196
Giovanni's Deli Cafe (Newcastle) 217
Good Living Growers Market (Sydney) 172
Good Luck Supermarket (Homebush West) 166
Green Gables Organic Produce (Kingsvale) 258
Green Garage (Byron Bay) 247
Griffith Butcher & Bakery (Canberra) 197
Growers Best (Newcastle West) 217
Gumnut Patisserie (Berrimal; Bowral) 234
Haberfield Bakery (Haberfield) 171
Hayden's Pies (Ulladulla) 227
Haymarket Seafoods (Haymarket) 172
The Health Emporium (Bondi) 166
Herbies Spices (Rozelle) 166
High Valley Wine & Cheese Co. (Mudgee) 258
Hobbitt Farm (South Jindabyne) 197
Hominy Bakery (Katoomba) 183
Honeysuckle Markets (Newcastle) 217
Hummerston's Gourmet Meats (Lane Cove West) 169
The Hunter Olive Centre (Pokolbin) 206
Hunter Valley Cheese Co. (Pokolbin) 206
Hurstville Asian Supermarket (Hurstville) 166
Infinity Sourdough (Darlinghurst) 171
Iseli Butcher (Bankstown) 169

Jan Power's Farmers' & Flowers Market (Brisbane) 266
Jannei Goat Dairy (Lidsdale) 258
jones the grocer (Bowral) 234
jones the grocer (Woollahra) 166
Junee Liquorice and Chocolate Factory (Junee) 259
Kiama Produce Market (Kiama) 227
Kombu Wholefoods (Bellingen) 247
L'Ultime (Byron Bay) 247
La Gerbe d'Or (Paddington) 171
La Piccola Grosseria (Griffith) 259
Lamia Foods (Marrickville) 168
Lamonica IGA (Haberfield) 166
Le Petit Fourneau Patisserie (Canberra) 197
Leisure Coast Fruit Market and Deli (Fairy Meadow) 227
Leura Gourmet (Leura) 183
Lick The Spoon (Dorrigo) 247
Logan Brae Orchard (Blackheath) 183
M & J's Butchery (Orange) 259
Macro Wholefoods (Bondi Junction; Crows Nest) 167
Martelli's Fruit Market (Cherrybrook; West Epping) 166
Mauger's Meat (Burrawang) 234
Melrose Park Venison (Mudgee) 259
Montrose Berry Farm (Sutton Forest) 235
Morgan's Fine Foods (Mona Vale) 168
Morpeth Sourdough (Morpeth) 206
Mountain Blue Seafood (Katoomba) 183
Newtown Providores (Dubbo) 259
Nimmitabel Butchery (Cooma) 197
Noosa Farmers' Market (Noosaville) 270
Norland Fig Orchard (Borenore) 259
Northern Rivers Seafood (West Ballina) 247

Northside Produce Market (North Sydney) 172
Norton Street Grocer (Bondi Junction; Leichhardt) 167
Nut and Deli Hut (Wollongong) 227
Ocean Foods (Drummoyne) 81
Old Bus Depot Markets (Canberra) 197
The Old Goulburn Brewery (Goulburn) 235
The Olive Farm (Falls Creek) 227
Oriental and Continental Foods (Artarmon) 167
Orion Continental Foods (Willoughby) 167
Parisi's (Rose Bay) 170
Pasta Fina (Wollongong) 228
Pasticceria Papa (Haberfield) 171
Penny's Quality Butcher (Mona Vale; Mosman) 169
Peter Michaels Seafood at Cronulla (Cronulla) 172
Peter's Fish Market (Blackwattle Bay) 81
Pickle Factory + Plus (Tathra) 228
The Pig N Whistle Cafe (Robertson) 235
Pina Deli Cafe (Hamilton) 217
Pino's Dolce Vita and Fine Foods (Kogarah) 169
Poachers Pantry (Marakei via Hall) 197
Pontip (Haymarket) 170
Prahran Market (Melbourne) 265
Provedore Pelagio (Darlinghurst) 167
Proven Artisan Breads & Pastries (Orange) 259
Queen Street Deli (Woollahra) 168
Queen Victoria Market (Melbourne) 265
Quinty Cake & Bakehouse (Uranquinty) 259
R & R Sellers Quality Meats (Stockton) 217
Raineri's Continental Delicatessen (Five Dock) 168
Randwick Oriental Supermarket (Randwick) 167
Red Ginger Foodstore (Byron Bay) 247
Red Hill Butcher Shop (Red Hill) 197
Ripe Grocer (Mona Vale) 170
Russki's Deli (Bondi) 168

Salamanca Market (Hobart) 269
Sam the Butcher (Beecroft; Bondi; Naremburn; Sans Souci) 169
Sandalyn Wilderness Estate (Rothbury) 206
Simon Johnson Purveyor of Quality Foods (Castlecrag) 167
Simon Johnson Purveyor of Quality Foods (Pyrmont) 167
Simon Johnson Purveyor of Quality Foods (Woollahra) 167
The Snapper Spot (Terrigal) 217
Sonoma (Glebe) 171
Steve's Quality Meats (Warrawong) 228
Supply (Huskisson) 228
Suzanne's (Mogo) 228
Sydney Fish Market (Pyrmont) 172
Sydney Fresh Food Market (Flemington) 172
Tea Lovers & Coffee for Others (Maitland; Morpeth) 206
Terry Wright Gourmet Meats (Randwick) 169
Tinklers Family Wines and Farm Produce (Pokolbin) 206
TJ's Quality Meats (Balmain) 169
Tokyo Mart (Northbridge) 167
Tutto Continental (Canberra) 197
Victoire (Balmain) 171
Village Hot Bake Bakery Cafe (Dubbo) 259
Wellington Cake Shop (Bondi) 171
Wholly Smoked Organic Foods (Byron Bay) 247
Yandilla Mustard Seed Oil (Wallendbeen) 259
Zweefers Great Cakes (Fairy Meadow) 228

Wine Stores

Abercorn (Mudgee) 260
Annandale Cellars (Annandale) 173
Best Cellars (East Sydney) 173
Bloodwood (Orange) 260
Boutique Wine Centre (Pokolbin) 207

index

Brangayne of Orange (Orange) 260
Brindabella Hills (Hall) 198
Brokenwood (Pokolbin) 207
Burke & Hills Cellar Door (Lidster) 260
Canobolas-Smith (Lidster) 260
Chalkers Crossing (Young) 261
Clonakilla (Murrumbateman) 198
Dan Murphy's (Strathfield) 173
De Bortoli (Bilbul) 261
Five Way Cellars (Paddington) 173
George's Fine Wines (Crows Nest) 173
Helm (Murrumbateman) 198
Huntington Estate (Mudgee) 260
Kamberra (Lyneham) 198
Kemeny's (Bondi) 173
Lark Hill (Bungendore) 198
Leura Cellars (Leura) 183
Lillypilly Estate (Leeton) 261
McWilliam's (Hanwood) 261
McWilliam's Mount Pleasant (Pokolbin) 207
Madew Wines (Lake George) 198
Mulyan (Cowra) 261
North Sydney Cellars (North Sydney) 173
Palm Beach Wine Co. (Palm Beach) 173
Poet's Corner (Mudgee) 260
Riverina Estate (Griffith) 261
Small Winemakers Centre (Pokolbin) 207
Tower Estate (Pokolbin) 207
Tyrrell's (Pokolbin) 207
Ultimo Wine Centre (Ultimo) 173
Vintage Cellars Double Bay (Double Bay) 173
Westend Estate (Griffith) 261
Windowrie Cellar Door (Cowra) 261

Alphabetical

ABC Cheese Factory (Central Tilba) 227
Abell's Kopi Tiam (Canberra) 184
Abercorn (Mudgee) 260
Abhi's 2
Abla Pastry 171
AC Butchery 169
Adelaide Central Market (Adelaide) 167

Agni 2
Air Raid Tavern (Moruya) 225
Aki's 3
Albany Farmers' Market (Albany) 268
Alchemy 731 3
Alegria (Sunshine Beach) 270
Alhambra 4
Alio 4
All India Restaurant 5
The Alley @ Cronulla 5
Allpress Espresso 155
Aloi Thai (Cooks Hill; Hamilton) 216
Altitude 6
Altitude 1380 (Thredbo) 196
Amanda's on the Edge (Pokolbin) 199
Amici 6
An Restaurant 7, 121
Anise (Canberra) 185
Annandale Cellars 173
Antico's Northbridge Fruit World 170
Apartment 158
Aqua Dining 7
Arabella 8
Arc-En-Ciel Rainbow Trout (Hanging Rock via Nundle) 258
Arena 8
Arena's L'Antipasto Deli 168
Aria 9
The Art Gallery Restaurant 9
Art Gallery Restaurant (Adelaide) 267
The Art Lounge Cafe 155
Arte e Cucina 10
Artespresso (Canberra) 185
Arun Thai 10
Ashcrofts (Blackheath) 176
Astral 11
Ate – the Art of Food (Bangalow) 244
Aubergine (Canberra) 186
Australian Regional Food Store & Cafe (Pokolbin) 206
Avalon Chinese 11
Awaba 154
Azteca's 12
Azuma 12
Bacco's Bakeries (Murrurundi) 258
Bacino Bar 154
The Backyard Deli-Cafe (Lithgow) 182
Bakehouse on Wentworth (Blackheath; Leura; Springwood) 183
Balthazar (Perth) 268
Balzar (Melbourne) 265
Bambini Trust 13, 158
Banana Blossom 13

Bang Thai (Bangalow) 236
Bannisters (Mollymook) 218
Bar Coluzzi 158
Barnett's Rainbow Reach Oyster Barn (South West Rocks) 246
Barolo 14
Barossa Farmers' Market (Angaston) 267
barr-Vinum (Angaston) 267
Basilico (Lismore) 244
Batch Espresso (Melbourne) 265
The Bathers' Pavilion Cafe 14, 154
The Bathers' Pavilion Restaurant 15
Bay Marlin Seafoods (Batemans Bay) 227
The Bayswater Brasserie 15, 160
Bb Cc Wicked Chocolates (Newcastle) 217
Beach Road 16
Bean and Leaf Cafe (Newcastle) 216
Becco (Melbourne) 264
bel mondo 16
Bella Mia 17
Bellevue Hotel Dining Room 17
Beltree @ Margan (Pokolbin) 200
Benchmark Wine Bar (Canberra) 186
Bent on Food (Wingham) 246
Beppi's 18
Berardo's (Noosa Heads) 270
Berardo's on the Beach (Noosa Beach) 270
Bermagui Coolo Cream Gelati (Bermagui) 227
Berowra Waters Inn 18
Berry Wood-fired Sourdough Bakery (Berry) 219
Bertoni Casalinga 157
Best Cellars 173
Best Value Supermarket 166
Billingsgate Fish Bistro 19
bills 19
bills (Darlinghurst) 156
bills surry hills 20, 155
Billy Kwong 20
Bilpin Springs Orchard (Bilpin) 183
Bilson's 21
Binnorie Dairy (Pokolbin) 206
Bistro 163 21
Bistro CBD 22
Bistro Fax 22
Bistro LuLu 23
Bistro Moncur 23
Bistro Mont (Bowral) 229

Bistro Moore 24
Bistro Stock 24
Bit Brasserie 25
Blackheath Butchery (Blackheath) 183
Blackheath Continental Deli (Blackheath) 183
Blackwattle Deli 168
Bliss Coffee Roasters (Pokolbin) 205
Bloodwood (Orange) 260
Blu Horizon Bar 160
Blue Orange 25, 156
Blue Seas (Canberra) 196
Blue Wren (Mudgee) 248
The Boathouse on Blackwattle Bay 26
Bodyfuel (Gosford) 216
Bond Cafe 26, 158
The Book Kitchen 155
Boomerang (Byron Bay) 237
Borenore Berry Farm (Borenore) 258
Botanic Gardens Restaurant 27
Botanical (Melbourne) 264
Bottom of the Harbour 81
The Bourbon 160
Bourke Street Bakery Cafe (Surry Hills) 155
Boutique Wine Centre (Pokolbin) 207
Bowan Island 171
Braidwood Bakery (Braidwood) 227
Brangayne of Orange (Orange) 260
Brass Razoo 27
Brasserie Bread 171
The Brewery (Newcastle) 208
Bridge Bar 160
Bridge View Inn Cafe & Bakery (Rylstone) 256
Bridgewater Mill (Bridgewater) 267
Brindabella Hills (Hall) 198
Brokenwood (Pokolbin) 207
Broombee Organic Orchard & Vineyard (Apple Tree Flat) 258
Brown Sugar Nights 28
Bruno's Truffles (Canberra) 196
Bukhara 28
Buon Ricordo 29
Burke & Hills Cellar Door (Lidster) 260
Butcher Shop Cafe (Mudgee) 256
buzo 29
Ça Marche (Port Macquarie) 237
Cactus Cafe & Gallery (Wellington) 256

280 good food guide

index

Caesar's Coffee & Fine Food
 (Erina) 217
Cafe Bella
 (Kangaroo Valley) 234
Cafe Di Stasio
 (Melbourne) 264
Cafe Eataliano
 (Tamworth) 256
Cafe Fraîche (Berrima) 234
Cafe Graze (Walcha) 256
Cafe Mint 30, 155
Cafe Razz (Springwood) 182
Café Sel et Poivre 30, 156
Cafe Sopra 31
Cafe Supply (Newcastle) 209
Cafe Sydney 31, 158
Cafe 2340 (Tamworth) 256
Cafe Wunderbar
 (Byron Bay) 244
Caffe Corto 158
Caffe Jam
 (East Gosford) 216
Campos Coffee 155
Canobolas-Smith
 (Lidster) 260
Capital Region Farmers'
 Market (Canberra) 196
Castalia (Yamba) 238
Catalina Rose Bay 32
Caveau (Wollongong) 219
The Cellar (Pokolbin) 200
Centennial Vineyards
 (Bowral) 230
Certo Ristorante 32
The Chairman & Yip
 (Canberra) 187
Chalkers Crossing
 (Young) 261
The Cheese Store at Bowral
 (Bowral) 234
The Chelsea Tea House
 33, 41, 154
Chequers 33
CherriJam 34
Chez Pascal 34
China Doll 35
Chinta Ria ... Temple
 of Love 35
Choix Crêperie Café
 (Melbourne) 265
Choux Shop (Hobart) 269
Christie's Seafoods 172
Cibo 154
Cicciolina (Melbourne) 264
Circa (Brisbane) 266
Circa, The Prince
 (Melbourne) 264
The Civic 160
Clareville Kiosk 36
Claude's 36, 41
Claudio's Quality
 Seafoods 172
The Clock Hotel 37
Clonakilla
 (Murrumbateman) 198

Coast 37
Cochin 38
Coffee Culture (Bowral) 234
The Coffee Emporium 157
Coffs Harbour
 Fishermen's Co-op
 (Coffs Harbour) 246
Collits Inn (Hartley Vale) 177
Commercial Fisherman's
 Co-op Ltd (Wickham) 217
The Commercial Hotel
 (Walcha) 256
Con's Beecroft Village
 Delicatessen 168
Concrete 157
Cork Street Gallery Cafe
 (Gundaroo) 196
Cottage Point Inn 38
The Country Provedore
 (Young) 256
Courgette (Canberra) 187
Crackenback Cottage
 (Thredbo Valley) 188
Crave Deli Cafe 156
Credo 39, 154
Credo (Thredbo) 188
Croissant D'Or
 (Canberra) 196
Crooked River Winery
 (Gerringong) 225
The Crowded House
 (Bathurst) 249
Cru Bar & Cellar
 (Brisbane) 266
Cruise Bar 160
CSU Cheese Factory
 (Wagga Wagga) 258
Cucina 105 39
Cyril's Delicatessen 168
Da Noi (Melbourne) 265
Dan Murphy's 173
Dangerous Dan's Butchery
 (Macksville) 246
Danks Street Depot 42, 155
Darbar 42
Darby Street Gourmet
 Deli (Newcastle) 217
Darcy's 43
Darley's (Katoomba) 177
Darrel's Gourmet Butchery
 (Gloucester) 246
David Jones Foodhall 166
De Bortoli (Bilbul) 261
Dekk (Terrigal) 209
Deli Cucina 166
De'lish 166
Demcos 172
Di Lorenzo Caffe 155
Diggies Beach Cafe
 (North Wollongong) 225
Dijon (Canberra) 189
DISH 43
dish (Byron Bay) 238
Divino 44
Dolce Dolce (Griffith) 256

Dome 44
Don Adan Coffee House 154
Donna's Cantina
 (Merimbula) 220
Double Happiness
 (Melbourne) 265
DOV 45, 156
Dragon Star Seafood 46
Dry Dock (Katoomba) 178
Duende (Perth) 268
E'cco (Brisbane) 266
East Chinese 46
The Eastern 160
Eat City 47
Ecco 47
The Educated Palate
 (Wollongong) 227
The Elephant Bean
 (Katoomba) 182
Elio 48
Eltons Brasserie
 (Mudgee) 249
Emile's Fruit
 & Vegetables 170
Eminem (Perth) 268
Emma's a la Carte
 (Hamilton) 210
Emma's on Liberty 48, 121
Emperor's Garden BBQ 49
Emperor's Garden Meat
 Market 169
Emperor's Garden
 Seafood 49
encasa 49
Engine Room
 (Newcastle) 210
Envy Fine Foods 157
Epoque 50
Esca Bimbadgen
 (Pokolbin) 201
Eschalot (Bowral) 230
Espresso Galleria 157
Essence 50
The Essential Ingredient 166
est. 51
Estabar (Newcastle) 216
Euro Patisserie
 (Newcastle) 217
Fare Nosh 51
Farmers' Market
 (Moore Park) 172
Farmers' Markets
 (North Coast) 247
Farmers' Markets
 (The West) 258
Fatbellykat – Shared Food
 (Brunswick Heads) 244
Feast (Avoca Beach) 211
Fekerte's (Canberra) 189
Fideli 156
Fifi's 52
55 on Collins (Kiama) 220
Fins (Byron Bay) 239
Fiorenzoni 52
Fire Station Cafe 158
Firefly Winebar 53, 160

Fireworks Cafe
 (Austinmer) 225
First (Adelaide) 267
A Fish called Coogee 81
A Fish called Paddo 81
Fish Face 53, 81
Fishmongers Takeaway
 (Byron Bay) 245
Fishy Fishy
 (Lennox Head) 247
Fitzroy Inn (Mittagong) 231
Five Way Cellars 173
FJ Galluzzo & Sons 170
Flair (Erina Heights) 211
Flat White 156
Flavour of India Edgecliff 54
Flavours of Peking 54
Flower Drum
 (Melbourne) 264
Flying Fish 55, 81
Food and Wine with Altitude
 Fair (Blackheath) 183
Food Stuff Mona Vale 166
Fook Yuen 55
Forty One 56
Four Olives Deli 168
Frank's Fruit Market 170
Franklin Manor (Strahan) 269
Fratelli Fresh 170
Fratelli Paradiso 56, 156
Frati (Thirroul) 221
Frattini 57
Fremantle Markets
 (Fremantle) 268
Fresca (Bangalow) 244
Fresh (Dorrigo) 244
Fresh at the Bay
 (Huskisson) 226
Fresh Espresso and Food
 Bar (Katoomba) 182
Fresh Ketch 57
Friendship Oriental
 Seafood 58
Fruit Ezy 170
Fu Manchu 58
Fuel Bistro 59
Fyshwick Fresh Foods
 Market (Canberra) 196
Galileo 59
Garfish 60
George's Fine Wines 173
Georgie's at the Gallery
 (Grafton) 239
Gertrude & Alice 156
GG espresso 158
the ginger room
 (Canberra) 190
Giovanni's Deli Cafe
 (Newcastle) 217
Golden Century 60
Golden Kingdom 61
Good Living Growers
 Market 172
Good Luck
 Supermarket 166

good food guide 281

index

Grand National 61
The Grange (Adelaide) 267
Grappa 62
Grazing (Gundaroo) 190
Green Bamboo 62
Green Gables Organic Produce (Kingsvale) 258
Green Garage (Byron Bay) 247
Griffith Butcher & Bakery (Canberra) 197
Growers Best (Newcastle West) 217
Guillaume at Bennelong 63
Gumnut Patisserie (Berrimal; Bowral) 234
The Gunshop Cafe (Brisbane) 266
The Gunyah (Huskisson) 221
Haberfield Bakery 171
harbourkitchen&bar 63
Harry's Cafe de Wheels (Newcastle) 216
Harvest Cafe (Newrybar) 244
Hayden's Pies (Ulladulla) 227
Haymarket Seafoods 172
The Health Emporium 166
Heeley Street Espresso 156
Helm (Murrumbateman) 198
Hemmesphere 160
Henri's Brasserie (Singleton) 205
Herbies Spices 166
Heritage 50
Hickson Road Bistro 64
High Valley Wine & Cheese Co. (Mudgee) 258
Highland Heritage Estate (Orange) 250
Hilltop Phoenix 64
Hobbitt Farm (South Jindabyne) 197
Hominy Bakery (Katoomba) 183
Honeysuckle Markets (Newcastle) 217
Hopscotch 157
Hordern's (Bowral) 231
Hugo's 65
Hugo's Lounge 65, 161
Hummerston's Gourmet Meats 169
The Hunter Olive Centre (Pokolbin) 206
Hunter Valley Cheese Co. (Pokolbin) 206
Huntington Estate (Mudgee) 260
Hurstville Asian Supermarket 166
Hyams Beach General Store & Jervis Blue Cafe (Hyams Beach) 226
Icebergs Dining Room & Bar 66, 161

Il Baretto 66, 155
Il Perugino 67
Il Piave 67
Il Tratto Ra Ro Pizzeria 41, 68
Indigo 68
Industrie – South of France 69, 162
Infinity Sourdough 171
Infusion@333 69
Iseli Butcher 169
Isis Brasserie (Brisbane) 266
Jan Power's Farmers' & Flowers Market (Brisbane) 266
Jannei Goat Dairy (Lidsdale) 258
Jaspers 70
Jenkins Street Guesthouse (Nundle) 250
Jervis Bay Kiosk (Huskisson) 226
Jimbaran 121
jimmy liks 70, 162
Jonah's 71
jones the grocer (Bowral) 234
jones the grocer (Woollahra) 166
The Journeyman (Berrima) 232
Julep Lounge (Canberra) 196
Junee Liquorice and Chocolate Factory (Junee) 259
Kam Fook Bondi Junction 71
Kam Fook Chatswood 72
Kamberra (Lyneham) 198
Katers (Sutton Forest) 232
Kemeny's 173
Kensington Peking 72
Kerv Espresso Bar (Scone) 205
Kiama Produce Market (Kiama) 227
King 143 73
Kingsleys Steak & Crabhouse 73
Kombu Wholefoods (Bellingen) 247
Kuali 74
La Colline Wines (Nashdale) 257
La Deliziosa (Five Dock) 157
La Gerbe d'Or 171
La Goulue 41, 74
La Grande Bouffe 75
La Grillade 75
La Locanda 41, 76
La Perla 76
La Piccola Grosseria (Griffith) 259

La Renaissance Pâtisserie Française 158
Ladro (Melbourne) 264
Lambert Vineyards (Wamboin) 196
Lamia Foods 168
Lamonica IGA 166
Lark Hill (Bungendore) 198
Le Bijoux (Bowral) 234
Le Petit Crème 156
Le Petit Fourneau Patisserie (Canberra) 197
Lebrina (Hobart) 269
Leisure Coast Fruit Market and Deli (Fairy Meadow) 227
Les Trois Freres 77
Letterbox (Terrigal) 212
Leura Cellars (Leura) 183
Leura Gourmet (Leura) 183
Lick The Spoon (Dorrigo) 247
Lido Bar 158
Lillypilly Estate (Leeton) 261
Lime (Newcastle) 212
Lindt Concept Store and Cafe 158
liquidity 77
Little Creatures (Fremantle) 268
A Little on the Side 155
Lizotte's (Kincumber) 213
L'Oasis (Griffith) 257
The Lobby (Canberra) 191
Local 78
Lochiel House (Kurrajong Heights) 178
Loco 78
Lodge 241 Gallery Cafe (Bellingen) 244
The Loft 162
Logan Brae Orchard (Blackheath) 183
Logues 79
Lolli Redini (Orange) 251
Longbench on Darby (Newcastle) 213
Longrain 79, 162
Lorenzo's Diner (Wollongong) 222
Lott Street Food Store Bakery & Cafe (Cooma) 196
Lotus 82, 162
Lucia's (Adelaide) 267
Lucio's 82
L'Ultime (Byron Bay) 247
Lunch 83
L'unico 83
Luxe (Brisbane) 266
Lynwood Cafe (Collector) 191
M & J's Butchery (Orange) 259
Machiavelli 84

Macleay Street Bistro 41, 84
Macro Wholefoods 167
Madew Wines (Lake George) 198
Maggie Beer's Farm Shop (Nuriootpa) 267
Magill Estate (Magill) 267
Magpies Nest (Wagga Wagga) 257
Mahjong Room 85
Maisy's Cafe 154
Malabar 85
The Malaya 86
Mamma Barone 86
Manly Phoenix 87
Manly Wharf Hotel 87
Manna 41, 88
Manta 88
Marigold Citymark 89
Marque 89
Mars Lounge 162
Martelli's Fruit Market 170
Matsuri (Perth) 268
Mauger's Meat (Burrawang) 234
Maya Da Dhaba 90
Maynely Lauries (Broken Hill) 257
MCA Cafe 90
McVitty Grove (Mittagong) 234
McWilliam's (Hanwood) 261
McWilliam's Mount Pleasant (Pokolbin) 207
Mecca Bah (Brisbane) 266
Megalong Valley Tea Rooms (Megalong Valley) 182
Melba's Verandah (Broadwater) 245
Melbourne Supper Club (Melbourne) 265
Melbourne Wine Room (Melbourne) 265
Melrose Park Venison (Mudgee) 259
Mere Catherine 91
Merimbula Aquarium & Wharf Cafe (Merimbula) 226
Merretts (Corlette) 214
Mes Amis (Katoomba) 179
Mezzalira (Canberra) 192
Mezzaluna 91
Michael's Trattoria (Wollongong) 222
Michelin (Griffith) 251
Middle Bar 162
milk and honey (Canberra) 192
Milk and Honey (Mullumbimby) 240
Milsons 92
Miltons 92
Minh 93
Mino 93
Mint 94

282 good food guide

index

Misto 158
Misty's (Dorrigo) 245
Mo Mo (Melbourne) 264
Mohr & Mohr 94
Mohr Fish 81, 95
Mojo's on Wilderness
  (Lovedale) 201
Montrose Berry Farm
  (Sutton Forest) 235
Morgan's Fine Foods 168
Morpeth Sourdough
  (Morpeth) 206
MoS Cafe 95, 158
Mountain Blue Seafood
  (Katoomba) 183
Movida (Melbourne) 265
mr wolf (Melbourne) 264
mu shu 96, 162
Mulyan (Cowra) 261
Must Winebar (Perth) 268
Mylan (Wollongong) 226
Nabiha's Kitchen
  (Wagga Wagga) 257
Neila (Cowra) 252
Nelsons Brasserie 96
Neptune Palace 97
Nest 156
Newtown Providores
  (Dubbo) 259
Nilgiri's 97
Nimmitabel Butchery
  (Cooma) 197
No. 2 Oak Street
  (Bellingen) 240
No. 13 Cafe (Lorn) 202
Noosa Farmers' Market
  (Noosaville) 270
Norland Fig Orchard
  (Borenore) 259
North Sydney Cellars 173
Northbridge Bistro 98
Northern Rivers Seafood
  (West Ballina) 247
Northside Produce
  Market 172
Norton Street Grocer 167
Nove 121
Nut and Deli Hut
  (Wollongong) 227
Ocean Foods 81
Ocean King House 98
Ocean Room 99
Oh Calcutta 99
Oishii (Pokolbin) 205
Old Bus Depot Markets
  (Canberra) 197
The Old George & Dragon
  (East Maitland) 202
The Old Goulburn Brewery
  (Goulburn) 235
The Olive Farm
  (Falls Creek) 227
Oliveto 100
Olivo (Byron Bay) 241
Omega 100

Onde 101
The One that Got Away 81
Opera Bar 162
Oriental and Continental
  Foods 167
Orion Continental Foods 167
Oscillate Wildly 101, 121
Osso 102
Osteria dei Poeti 102
Otto 103
Ottoman Cuisine
  (Canberra) 193
Out of Africa 103
Oven 154
Paddington Inn 104
Palace Chinese 104
Palisade Dining Room 105
Palm Beach Wine Co. 173
Parisi's 170
The Parkside Cafe
  (Woodburn) 245
Pasta Fina (Wollongong) 228
Pasticceria Papa 171
Paua 105
Paupiettes (Lismore) 241
Pavilion on the Park 106
Pazzo 106
Pearl (Melbourne) 265
Pearls on the Beach
  (Pearl Beach) 216
Pello 107
Penny's Quality Butcher 169
Perama 41, 107
perenti (Gloucester) 245
Peter Michaels Seafood
  at Cronulla 172
Peter's Fish Market 81
Pharnish 108
Pickle Factory + Plus
  (Tathra) 228
Pier 108
The Pig N Whistle Cafe
  (Robertson) 235
Pilu at Freshwater 109
Pina Deli Cafe
  (Hamilton) 217
Pink Peppercorn 109
Pino's Dolce Vita and
  Fine Foods 169
ploys at tuross
  (Tuross Head) 223
Poachers Pantry (Marakei
  via Hall) 197
Poet's Corner (Mudgee) 260
Pogel's Wood Cafe
  (Federal) 245
Poinciana
  (Mullumbimby) 242
Pompei 121
Pontip 170
Pool Caffe 110, 155
Portabellos
  (Port Macquarie) 242
Post Seafood Brasserie 110
Prahran Market
  (Melbourne) 265

Prasit's Northside 111
Premium Coffee Roasters
  (Wagga Wagga) 257
Primavera Espresso Bar
  (North Sydney) 154
Prime 111
Provedore Pelagio 167
Proven Artisan Breads &
  Pastries (Orange) 259
Qmin 112
Quadrant 112
Quay 113
Queen Street Deli 168
Queen Victoria Market
  (Melbourne) 265
quince (Scone) 203
Quinty Cake & Bakehouse
  (Uranquinty) 259
R & R Sellers Quality Meats
  (Stockton) 217
Rae's on Watego's
  (Byron Bay) 243
The Rails Kitchen
  (Byron Bay) 245
Raineri's Continental
  Delicatessen 168
Rama's (Canberra) 193
Randwick Oriental
  Supermarket 167
Ravesi's 113
Red Chilli 114
Red Ginger Foodstore
  (Byron Bay) 247
Red Hill Butcher Shop
  (Red Hill) 197
Red Jujube 114
Red Lantern 115
The Reef (Terrigal) 214
Reef House (Palm Cove) 270
Relish at Balmain Bug
  41, 115
Rengaya 116
Republic Dining 116
Restaurant Atelier 117, 121
Restaurant Balzac 117
Restaurant Como
  (Blaxland) 179
Restaurant Gondwana
  (Hobart) 269
Restaurant II (Brisbane) 266
Restaurant Legall
  (Bathurst) 252
Restaurant Q (Armidale) 253
Restaurant Rapide
  (Brisbane) 266
Ripe Grocer 170
Ristorante Fellini
  (Main Beach) 270
Ristorante Riva 118
The River (Moruya) 223
River House (Noosaville) 270
Riverina Estate (Griffith) 261
Robert's at Peppertree
  (Pokolbin) 203
Rocket 118

Rockpool 119
Roger Fish Cafe Grill 81
The Rooster (Katoomba) 180
Royal Bar & Grill 119
RQ 122
Ruby Rabbit 163
Russki's Deli 168
Rylstone Food Store
  (Rylstone) 253
Sailors Thai Canteen 123
Sailors Thai Restaurant 122
Sails on Lavender Bay 123
Sakana-Ya 124
Salamanca Market
  (Hobart) 269
Salopian Inn
  (McLaren Vale) 267
Saltwater (Bermagui) 226
Sam the Butcher 169
Sandalyn Wilderness Estate
  (Rothbury) 206
Sanders 124
Sante (Thredbo) 194
Sapphire Suite 163
Sapporo 125
Sassi Cucina
  (Port Douglas) 270
Scratchleys on the Wharf
  (Newcastle) 216
Sea Cow 81
Sea la vie 154
Sea Oracle 125
Sea Treasure 126
Seagrass Brasserie
  (Huskisson) 226
Seahaven Cafe
  (Gerroa) 226
Sean's Panaroma 126
SeLAh 127
Selkirks (Orange) 254
Seri Nonya 127
Sevardi Cucina Italiana 128
Shakey Tables
  (North Rothbury) 204
Shanghai Yangzhou
  House 128
Short Order Cafe
  (Macksville) 245
Shun Tak 129
Sideways Cafe 157
Silk's Brasserie 180
Silo Bakery (Canberra) 194
Silo Lounge Bar
  (Newcastle) 216
The Silos (Jaspers Brush
  via Berry) 224
Silver Spring 129
Simon Johnson Purveyor
  of Quality Foods 167
Single Origin Roasters 155
Sky Phoenix 130
Small Winemakers Centre
  (Pokolbin) 207
The Snapper Spot
  (Terrigal) 217

good food guide 283

index

Soho Bar & Lounge 163
Solitary (Leura Falls) 181
Solitary Kiosk
  (Leura Falls) 181
Sonoma 171
Sosumi 130
The Source (Hobart) 269
Spice I Am 121, 131
Spinnakers (Ballina) 246
Squires Cottage
  (Armidale) 257
Star Anise (Perth) 268
Statement Lounge Bar 163
Steve's Quality Meats
  (Warrawong) 228
Stillwater (Launceston) 269
Stockmarket Cafe
  (Leura) 182
Strangers with Candy 41,
  131, 155
Sugaroom 132
sugo (Hobart) 269
Summerland 132
Summit 133
Supply (Huskisson) 228
sushi e 133
Suzanne's (Mogo) 228
Swell (Avalon) 154
Swell (Bronte) 156
Swordfish 134
Sydney Fish Market 172
Sydney Fresh Food
  Market 172
Szechuan Garden 134
The Table (Greta) 204
Tables 135
Tabou 135
Tak Kee Roast Inn
  (Canberra) 196
Tan Viet 136
Tasuke (Canberra) 195
Taxi Dining Room
  (Melbourne) 264
Tea Lovers & Coffee
  for Others (Maitland;
  Morpeth) 206
the tearoom 136, 158
Temasek 137
Temple 137
Ten Buck Alley 156
Terroir (Pokolbin) 205
Terry Wright Gourmet
  Meats 169
Tetsuya's 138
Thanh Binh 138
That Noodle Place
  (Bowral) 233
Three Bean Espresso Bar
  (Newcastle) 216
Three Chefs
  (Wagga Wagga) 254
Three Clicks West 139
Three Snails (Dubbo) 255
Three Weeds 139
Threeways (Huonbrook) 246

The Tilbury Hotel
  (Woolloomooloo) 140, 163
Tillermans (Tea Gardens) 246
Tinklers Family Wines
  and Farm Produce
  (Pokolbin) 206
TJ's Quality Meats 169
Toby's Estate Coffee
  & Tea 155
Tokyo Mart
  (Northbridge) 167
Tonic (Millthorpe) 255
Tower Estate (Pokolbin) 207
Tran's 140
Tsukasa 141
Tutto Continental
  (Canberra) 197
Twenty three at Berry
  (Berry) 226
Two Chefs on Stanley 141
Tyrrell's (Pokolbin) 207
Uchi Lounge 142
Ultimo Wine Centre 173
Utopia (Bangalow) 243
Vanilla Room 163
Vanitas (Main Beach) 270
Vatel 142
Vera Cruz 143
Victoire 171
The Victoria Room 163
Viet Nouveau 143
Village Hot Bake Bakery Cafe
  (Dubbo) 259
Vintage Cellars
  Double Bay 173
Vulcans (Blackheath) 182
Wall 155
Wasavie 144
Washhouse 157
Water Bar 163
Watermark 144
Waters Edge (Canberra) 195
Welcome Hotel 145
Wellington Cake Shop 171
Westend Estate (Griffith) 261
Wet Paint Cafe 145
The Wharf (Walsh Bay) 146
Wheelhouse (Eden) 224
Whiteblue 146
Whitewater 147
Wholly Smoked Organic
  Foods (Byron Bay) 247
WildEast Dreams 121, 147
Wildfire 148
Willow Cafe (Mogo) 226
Willowvale Mill (Laggan) 233
Windowrie Cellar Door
  (Cowra) 261
Wine Banq 148
Woodland's 121, 149
XO 149
XXII 157
Yandilla Mustard Seed Oil
  (Wallendbeen) 259

Yellow Bistro 150, 156
Ying's 150
Yoshii 151
Yum Yum Eatery
  (Hardys Bay) 215
Zaaffran 151
Zanzibar Cafe
  (Merimbula) 225
Zen Sushi (Lismore) 246
Zenith on Booth 152
Zest (Nelson Bay) 215
Zest BYO (Temora) 257
Zieglers Cafe (Bathurst) 257
Zinc 152, 156
Zouch (Young) 257
Zuppa Uno 156
Zweefers Great Cakes
  (Fairy Meadow) 228

maps

- main reviews   □ other recommendations

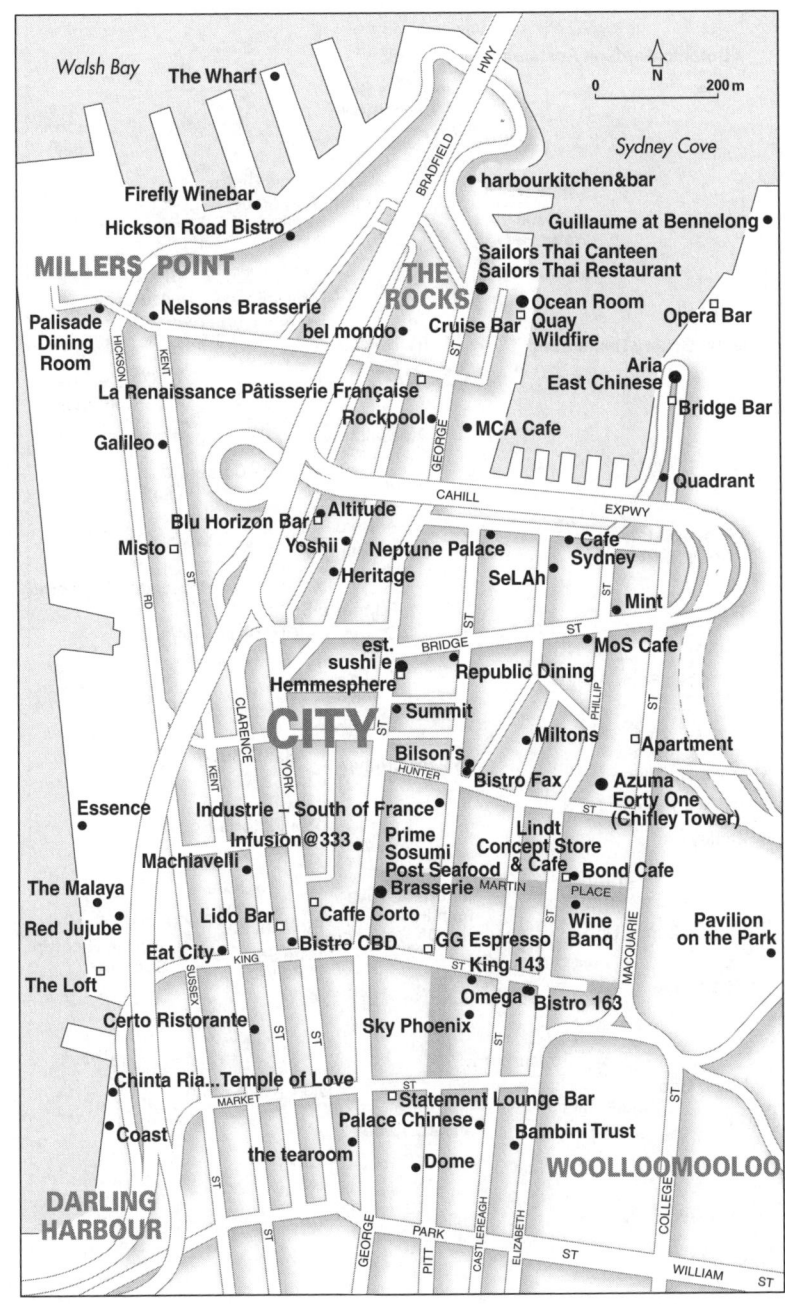

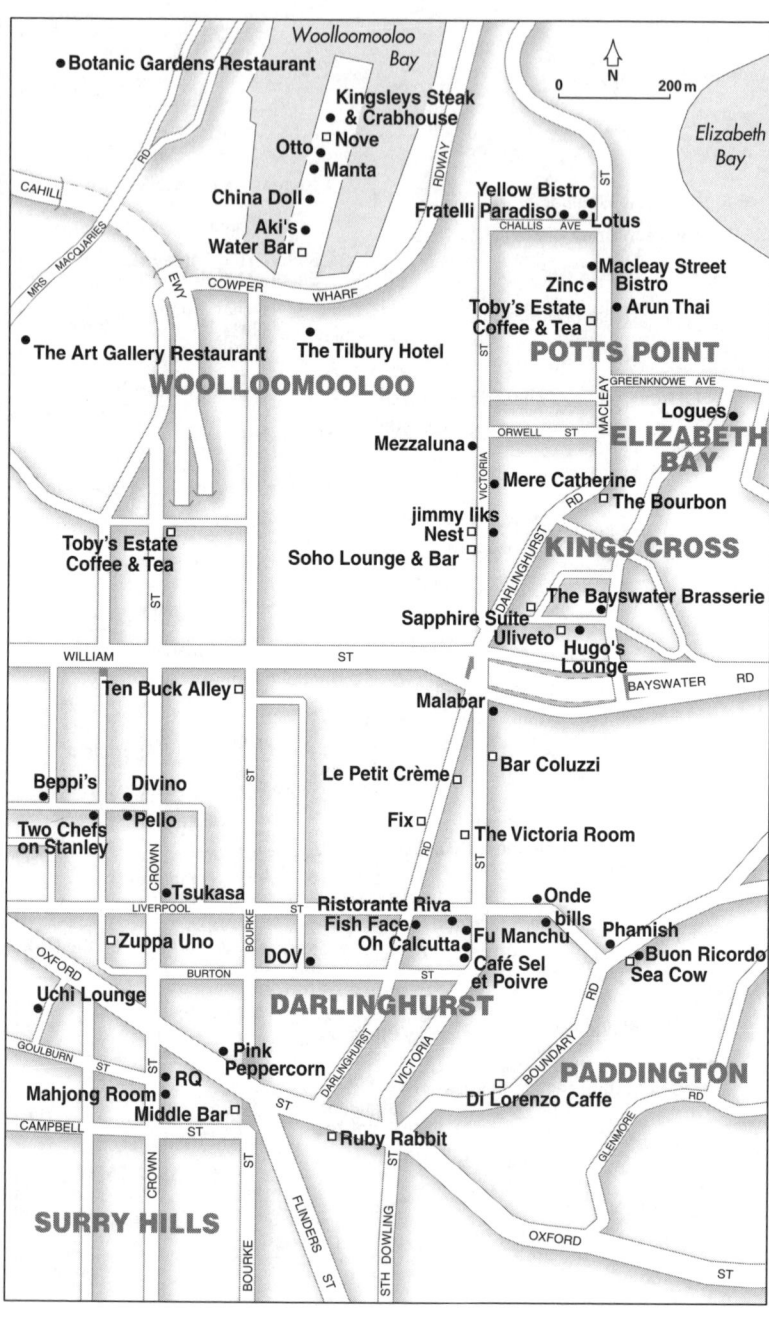

maps

- main reviews   □ other recommendations

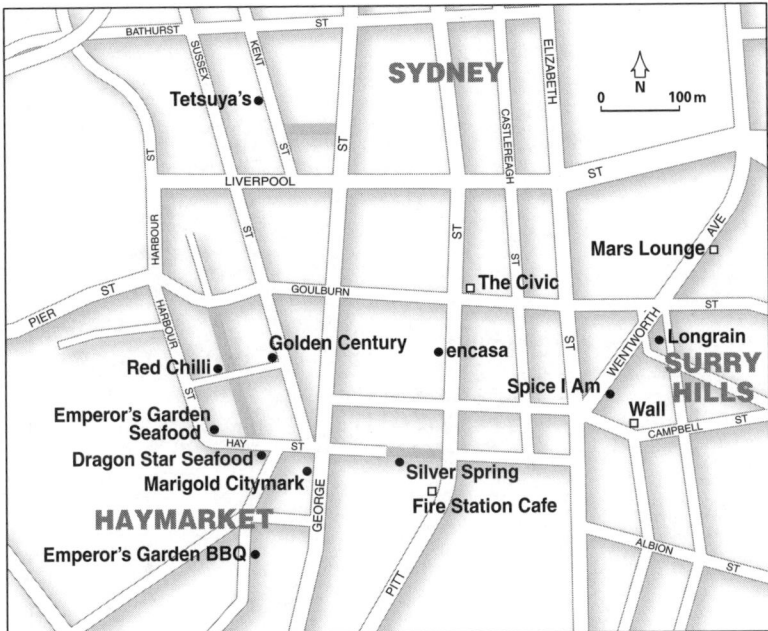

3A HAYMARKET

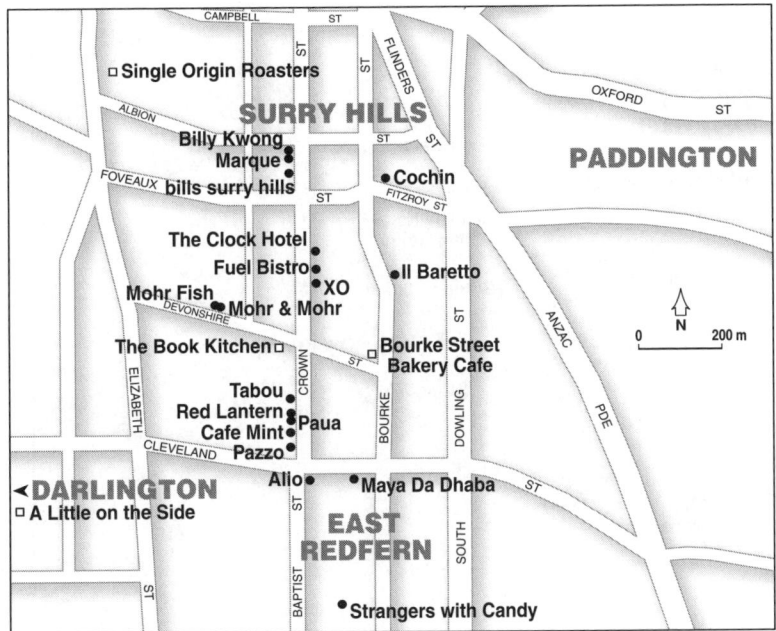

3B SURRY HILLS TO REDFERN

good food guide 287

maps

• main reviews   ▫ other recommendations

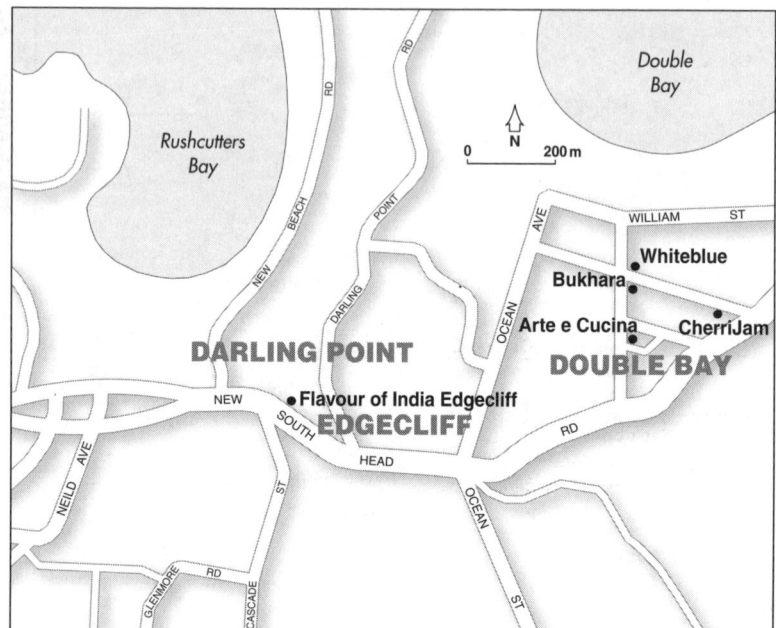

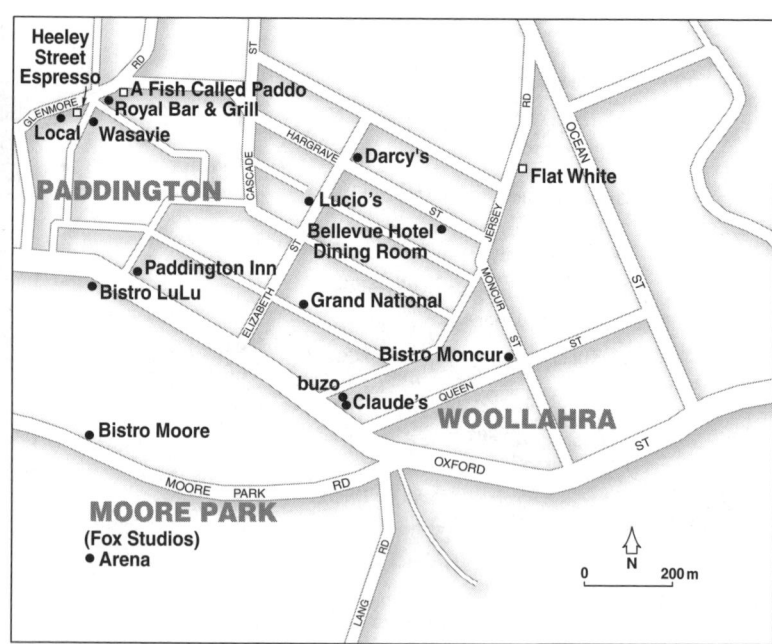

maps

• main reviews   □ other recommendations

5A ST LEONARDS TO MILSONS POINT

ST LEONARDS
- Credo
- Amici
- Epoque

CAMMERAY

CREMORNE
- Qmin
- Nilgiri's
- Szechuan Garden
- Garfish Crows Nest
- Sapporo
- La Grillade
- Oven
- Banana Blossom
- Sea Treasure
- Bit Brasserie
- Vera Cruz
- Sakana-Ya
- Roger Fish Cafe Grill
- Malabar
- Viet Nouveau
- Maisy's Cafe

CROWS NEST
- La Goulue
- Loco
- Ying's
- Atomic Espresso
- Temple

NEUTRAL BAY

0 500 m

- Primavera Espresso Bar
NORTH SYDNEY
- Prasit's Northside
- Cibo
- Rengaya

McMAHONS PT
MILSONS POINT
KIRRIBILLI
- Aqua Dining
- Milsons
- Garfish Kirribilli
- Sails on Lavender Bay
- Sea Oracle

5B DRUMMOYNE TO GLEBE

DRUMMOYNE

BALMAIN
- Relish at Balmain Bug
- All India Restaurant
- L'unico
- Bertoni Casalinga
- Ocean Foods
- Bistro Stock

RUSSELL LEA
- Vatel
- **ROZELLE**
- Il Piave
- Flying Fish
- Welcome Hotel
- Sugaroom
- Washhouse
- Astral
- La Grande Bouffe
- **PYRMONT** XXII
- Three Weeds
- Concrete
- Peter's Fish Market
- liquidity
- Zaaffran (Harbourside)
- The Boathouse on Blackwattle Bay

GLEBE
- Grappa
- Stephen Baker
- Three Clicks West
- Darbar
- Osteria dei Poeti
- Elio
- Zenith on Booth
- Restaurant Atelier
- Vanilla Room
- **ANNANDALE**
- Hopscotch
- Toby's Estate Coffee & Tea
- **LEICHHARDT**
- Frattini
- WildEast Dreams
- **CHIPPENDALE**

good food guide 289

maps

• main reviews   ▫ other recommendations

SYDNEY'S WEST

CASTLE HILL
• Hilltop Phoenix

BEECROFT
• Sevardi Cucina Italiana

PARRAMATTA
Woodland's
Shun Tak • • Temasek

RHODES
• Oliveto
Sanders
Il Tratto Ra Ro Pizzeria •

◀ **PENRITH**
Osso

CONCORD
• Abhi's

NORTH STRATHFIELD

CABRAMATTA
Thanh Binh • • Tan Viet

Summerland
An Restaurant • ▫ The Coffee Emporium

BANKSTOWN

BEVERLY HILLS
• Agni

• Woodland's
LIVERPOOL
• Cucina 105

Friendship Oriental Seafood •

PANANIA
•
Green Bamboo

N
0 ───── 5 km

290 good food guide

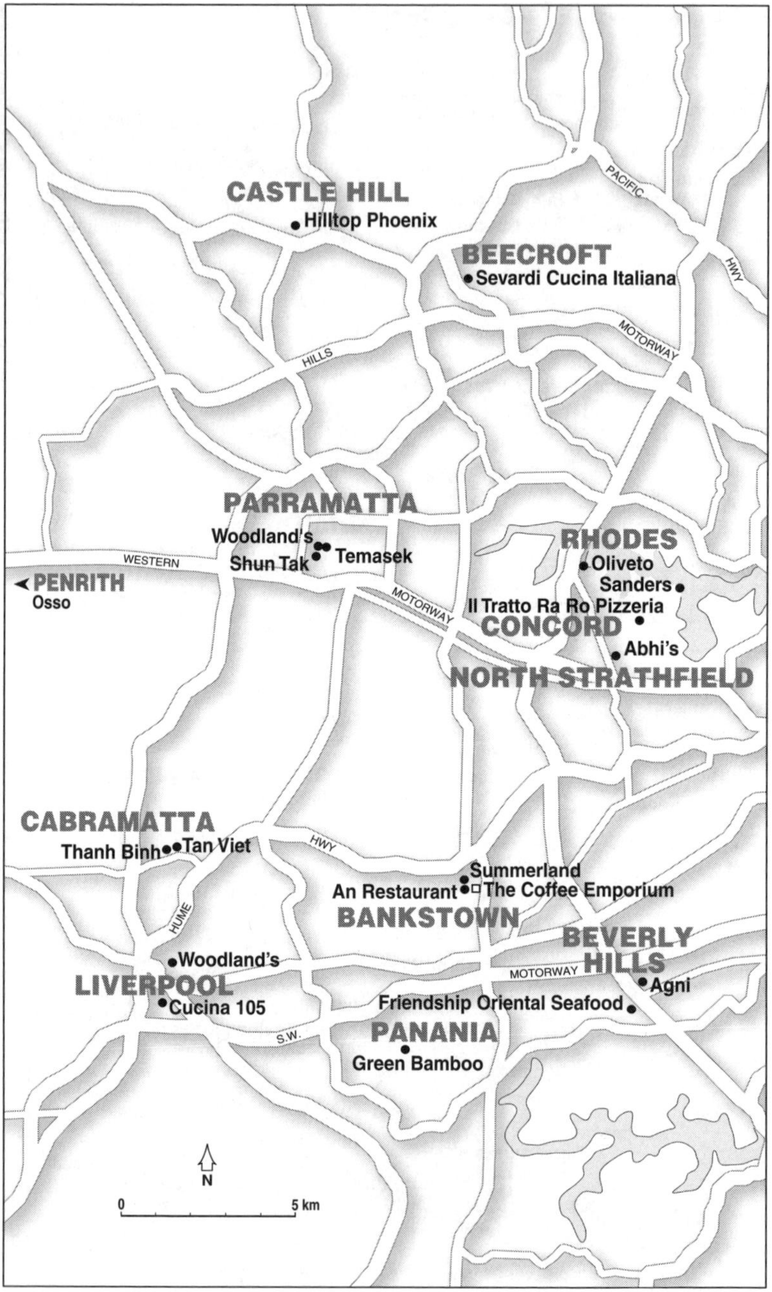

maps

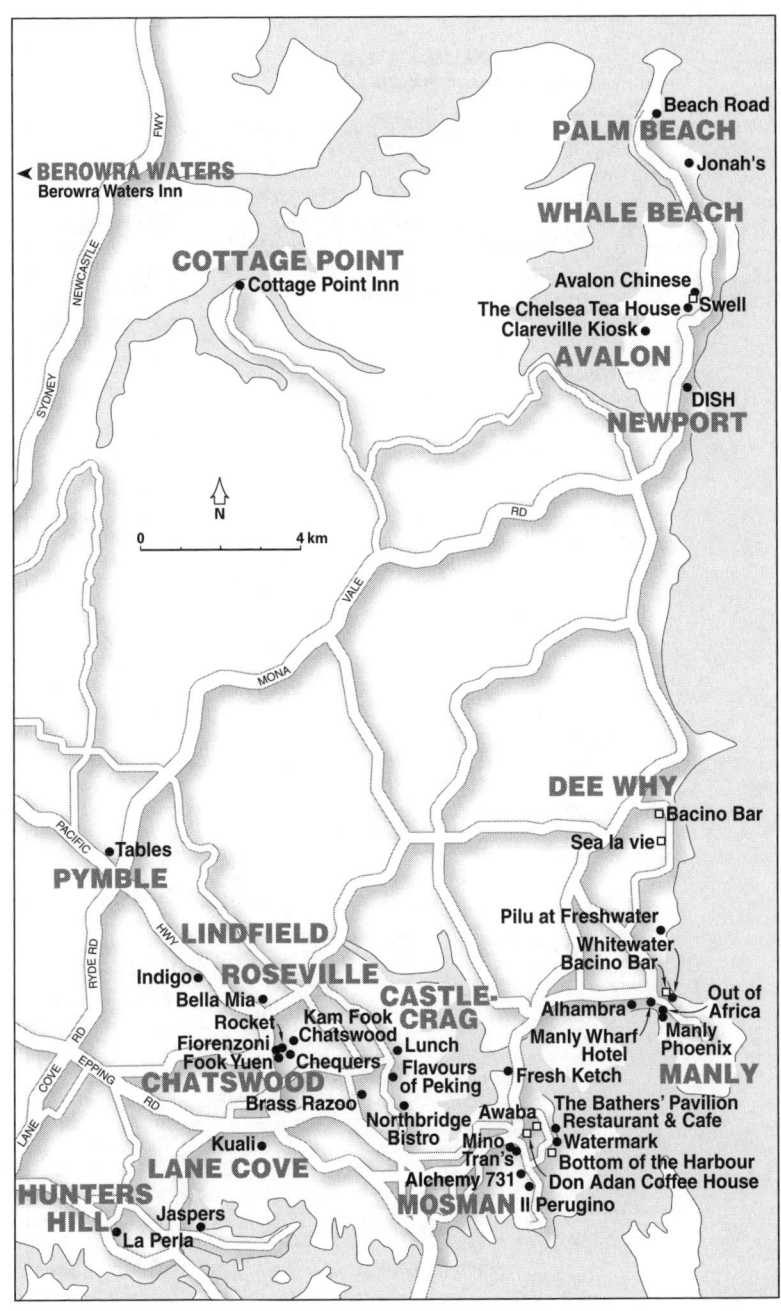

maps

• main reviews   ▫ other recommendations

SYDNEY'S SOUTH WEST

8

FIVE DOCK
La Deliziosa ▫ • Ecco

PARRAMATTA RD

HABERFIELD   Espresso Galleria ▫
PETERSHAM   **STANMORE**   **ENMORE**
Fare Nosh   Manna •   Oscillate   • Thanh Binh
Envy Fine Foods ▫ • Perama   Wildly • ▫ Campos Coffee
SUMMER HILL   Emma's on Liberty   Fifi's
Sideways Cafe •   • Arabella

LIVERPOOL RD   **NEWTOWN**

ASHFIELD   Minh •
                  DULWICH HILL

                                    MASCOT

                  S.W. MOTORWAY

KING GEORGES RD

                                          Botany Bay

                  HURSTVILLE
Shanghai Yangzhou House •
              Ocean King House • **KOGARAH**
                          RAMSGATE
                          • Chez Pascal

OATLEY   Mamma Barone •
Barolo •   **SANS SOUCI**

                  • Les Trois Freres
                  SYLVANIA

N   0 ——— 2 km

MIRANDA
Seri Nonya •   The Alley @ Cronulla
                 ▲ **CRONULLA**

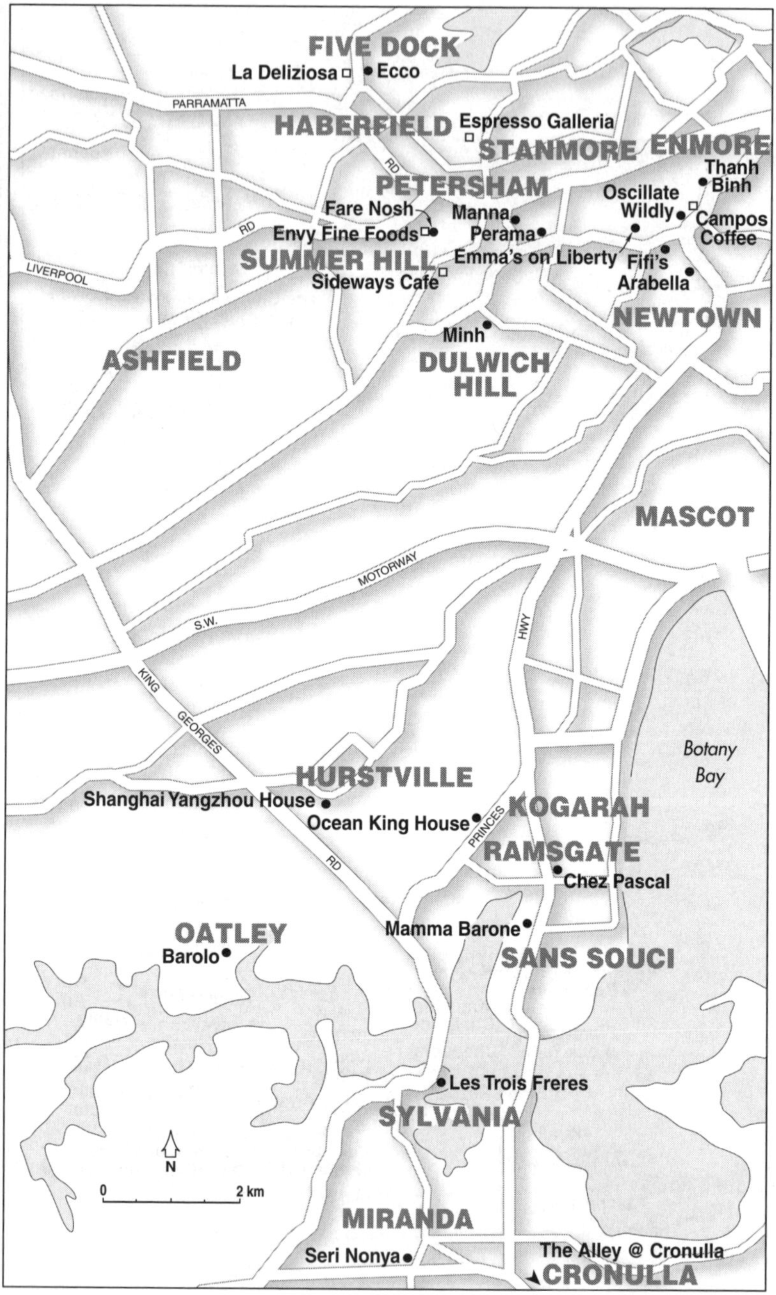

maps

• main reviews □ other recommendations

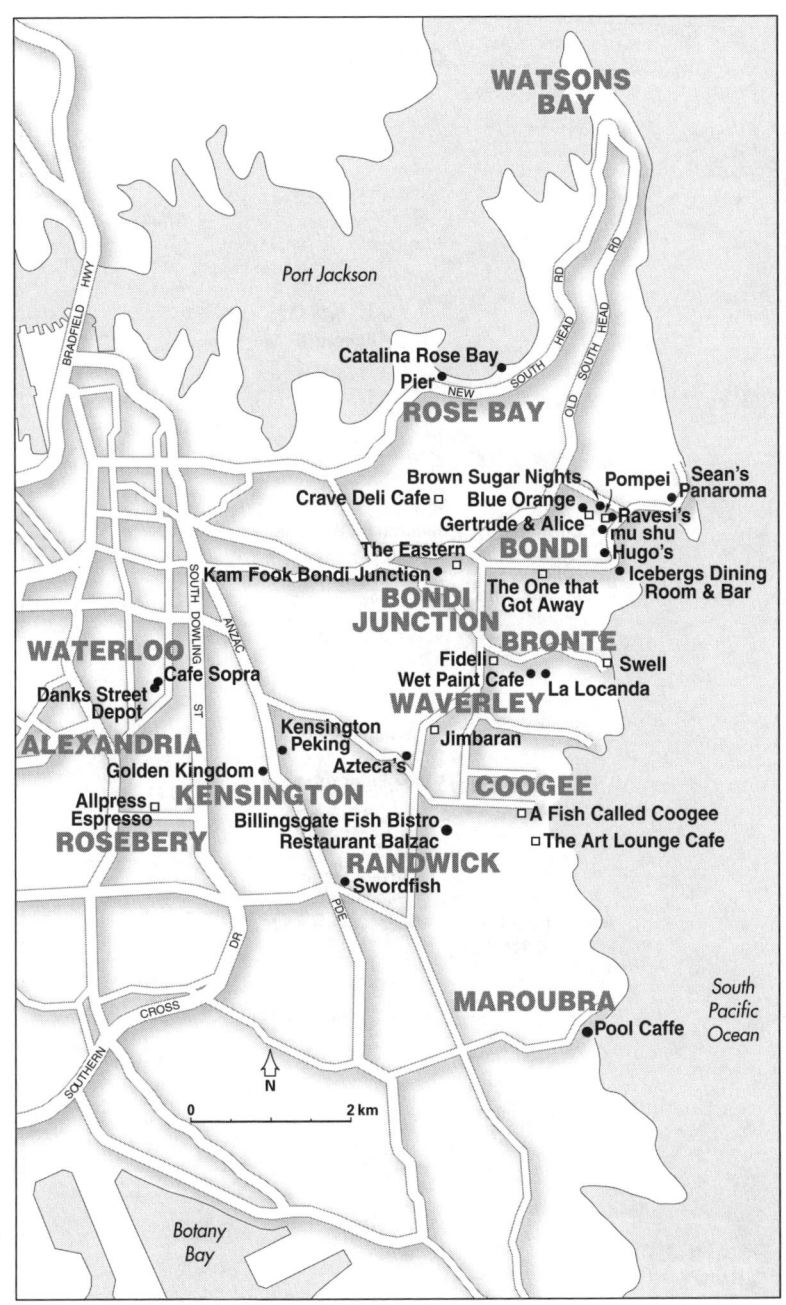

9 SYDNEY'S SOUTH EAST

good food guide 293

maps

10 CANBERRA

GUNDAROO
- Grazing

DICKSON
- Fekerte's

CITY / CIVIC
- Courgette
- Anise
- Dijon
- Mezzalira
- Benchmark Wine Bar
- milk & honey
- The Chairman & Yip
- Tasuke

PARKES
- Waters Edge
- The Lobby
- the ginger room

BARTON
- Ottoman Cuisine

KINGSTON
- Artespresso
- Silo Bakery

MANUKA
- Abell's Kopi Tiam

GRIFFITH
- Aubergine

PEARCE
- Rama's

0 1 km

294 good food guide

maps

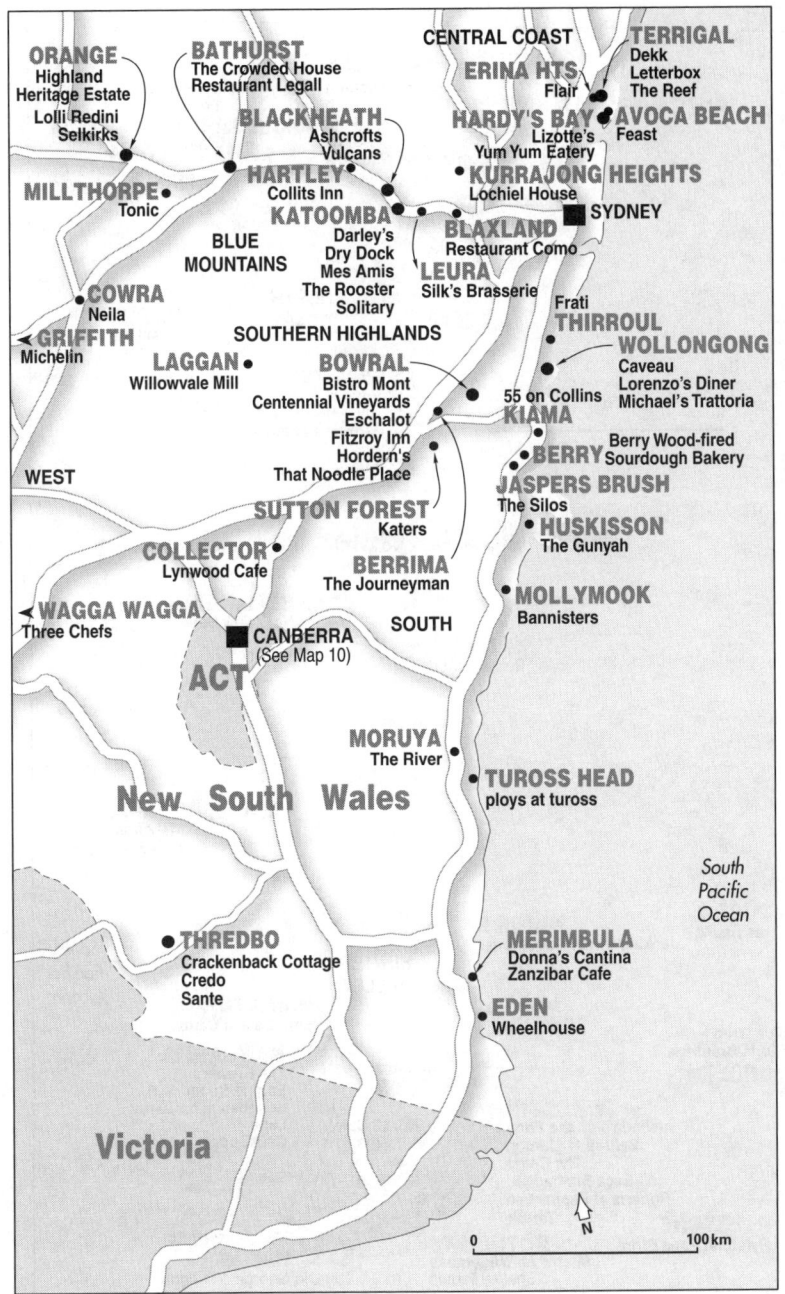

11 SOUTHERN NSW COUNTRY & COAST

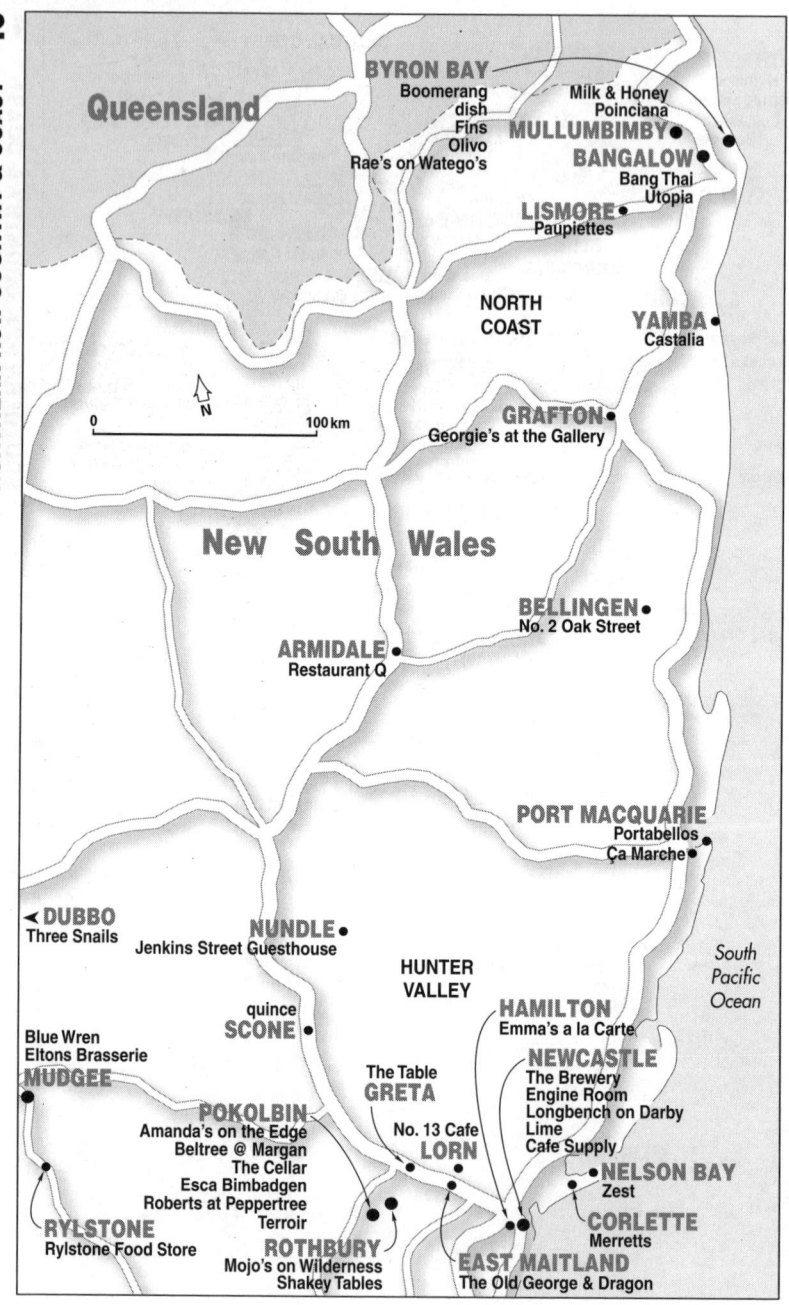